The Beginnings
of the Christian Religion

The Beginnings
of the
Christian Religion

*A Guide to the History and Literature of
Judaism and Christianity*

BY

MEREDITH F. ELLER, Ph.D.

PROFESSOR OF PHILOSOPHY AND RELIGION
CENTRAL COLLEGE, FAYETTE, MISSOURI

COLLEGE AND UNIVERSITY PRESS
New Haven, Connecticut

REPRINTED WITH PERMISSION OF BOOKMAN ASSOCIATES, INC.
BY COLLEGE AND UNIVERSITY PRESS, PAPERBACK DIVISION

MANUFACTURED IN THE UNITED STATES OF AMERICA BY
UNITED PRINTING SERVICES, INC.
NEW HAVEN, CONN.

FOREWORD

Eventually every teacher is impelled to write his own textbook. This is the product of one who has been able to do just that. This survey of the development of the Christian Religion, beginning with the origin of all Religion and moving through its Judaistic and Semitic backgrounds, is designed as a textbook in introductory courses in Biblical Literature, particularly at the college level. It is essentially the enlargement of an outline and a syllabus which have been in use in classroom situations for several years.

We owe so much to so many. No one is more aware of this truth than one who attempts to write a book. We wish to take this opportunity of expressing gratitude to parents who first awakened in the author a love of the Bible and religious matters; to teachers, fellow students, and friends, who have stimulated in him a love of learning, particularly of the culture of ancient times; to the authors of many books and research pamphlets, who have opened to him vast new worlds of information and inspiration; to college students who have listened and read with varying degrees of receptivity through the last eleven years; and to those, both known and unknown to us by name, who wrote of their deep search for spiritual reality and of their discovery of it in the sacred scriptures of Judaism and Christianity.

The author would like to give a special word of gratitude to the following, without whose help this project would have been impossible:

To the Board of Curators of Central College, Fayette, Mo., to President Ralph L. Woodward, and to Dean-emeritus Erastus P. Puckett, for the time to work on this project and the encouragement for bringing it to completion.

To his wife and children, for their patience and understanding in providing an atmosphere in which the work could the more easily be accomplished.

To the authors whose books were consulted and the publishers who granted permission to use quotations from them. Appropriate notations are made for each excerpt in the footnotes.

To Mr. Jacob Steinberg, managing editor of Bookman Associates, Inc., New York, N.Y., and to Mr. I. Frederick Doduck, president of United Printing Services, Inc., New Haven, Conn., for their wise counsel and wholehearted cooperation.

And beyond these, who can say? The author is grateful to all he has ever read, all with whom he has ever worked as colleagues in the ministry and in college teaching, all the words he has ever heard from teachers and preachers, and all the people he has ever met.

MEREDITH F. ELLER

TABLE OF CONTENTS

Part III. The Beginnings of Christianity

Part IV. Christianity in the Post-Apostolic Age

PART I

THE BEGINNINGS

OF

RELIGION

Chapter One

THE NATURE OF RELIGION

The beginning student of religion, just as the beginning student in any other field of study, may have a rather vague and unsatisfactory concept of what he is to investigate. Of all of the words in the English language which are most commonly misused, or misunderstood even when properly used, the word "religion" is among those most often mistreated.

Some would regard religion as being related to a denominational label; if asked "What is your religion?" they might reply: "I am a Baptist," or "I am an Episcopalian," or similarly for any one of the 256 denominations in America. Others might reply to the same question: "I don't know; I haven't any." And then there is the reply of the not-so-bright waitress; when asked "Have you got religion?" she answered: "It's not on the menu, but I'll go out in the kitchen and see." All of these are typical of the mistaken notions of religion current in our day. What's wrong with the third idea of religion is rather obvious. In answer to the first one, religion in its essence is something more than a matter of one's denominational or church affiliation; there are certainly characteristics regarded as religious which are common to all persons and groups, even non-Christian groups, which they would regard as religious. As to the second, every living person has some kind of religion; because a person does not happen to be a Two-Seed-in-the-Spirit Predestinarian Baptist does not mean that he is not religious in the broad sense of the word.

There is a tendency among some moderns to depreciate anything religious; those who do so are identifying religion with some form of religion which they regard as antiquated, ineffective, or unscientific. Religion properly understood cannot be separated from the life of man; and even if it could be taken from man's present

15

existence, it cannot be removed from his past. No study of the human race, or of the history of civilization, or of the growth of a custom, can fail to regard the testimony of religion. At every stage in the course of human development religion plays a vital part. Without a thorough and impartial study of religion many of the deepest springs of conduct and the controlling forces of human endeavor would be hidden to the investigator. Religion has been a part of human life for many thousands of years back beyond recorded history; in fact, religion is at least as old as man is. Also, some features of religion have been found among all human beings, whether they be the High Church Anglicans of Virginia or the aborigines of the Australian bush country.

What then is this ancient and universal factor of life which we call religion? The task of definition is not an easy one; unlike material objects, the definitions of which are fairly simple, religion is an abstract word representing a growing, dynamic thing difficult to classify at any one point in its development. Also, because religion is deeply personal and all-inclusive, there will be as many different definitions of religion as there are people interested in defining it. As we turn to authorities in the field of religion, we find a bewildering variety of contradictory definitions; to consider all of them would be the task of a lifetime.[1] We shall have to admit right at the start that there is no one definition of religion which is universally accepted; if we are looking for a complete and comprehensive definition we shall be disappointed, for religion covers a multitude of interests and activities. To say that religion is life perhaps oversimplifies the problem, but to say that religion is concerned with the whole of life helps us to understand the impossibility of defining it with any degree of certainty.

One authority in the field has summarized our task with startling clarity: "An approach to the goal (of finding a satisfactory descriptive definition of religion) may be made by defining the field of religion as including all the experiences that are generally recognized as belonging to the great historical movements which regard themselves as religious—such as Christianity, Judaism, Mohammedanism, Buddhism, Hinduism, Confucianism, and the like—together with the earliest experiences out of which these religions have grown and the movements now developing within them."[2] No wonder definitions of religion have been so widely divergent; every one of them has either correctly described certain aspects of religion or represented an honest evaluation of religion by the person making the definition.[3]

Failing in our task of formulating one comprehensive definition of religion, perhaps we will be more successful in arriving at a basis of identification so that we can separate what is religious from that which is not. What are the factors which must be included in any satisfactory definition of religion? What are the specific traits common to all forms of religion which help us to identify it? H. T. Houf suggests that there are three factors which practically always appear in any analysis of religion; these are: "(a) belief in a superhuman power (or powers) which may or may not be personified, (b) desire for certain values, material and spiritual, and (c) characteristic adjustments to the superhuman power for the purpose of securing these values."[4] All of these factors appear in the so-called great religions of the world, in the religion of primitive man, and to some extent in all definitions of religion by recent psychologists, sociologists, and historians of religion.

Perhaps it would be well to present some of the classic and more notable statements of the nature of religion. The Bible contains only one attempt to define religion;[5] evidently the writers of sacred literature were more interested in the experiences of religion than in any systematic attempt to describe what it was. Some, like the philosopher Hegel, reduced religion to a belief, an intellectual attitude; he said: "Thus religion is the Divine Spirit's knowledge of itself through the mediation of finite spirit."[6] Others have defined religion in terms of the emotions; one of the most famous of all definitions is that of Schleiermacher: "The essence of the religious emotions consists in the feeling of an absolute dependence"[7] upon the universe, or upon God. Still others have emphasized the volitional side of religion, finding religion's most characteristic expression in the fulfillment of moral obligation; Kant stands uppermost in this category with his declaration that "religion is (subjectively regarded) the recognition of all duties as divine commands."[8]

Another set of definitions divides on the question of the individual as contrasted with the social emphasis in religion. Following the former line of reasoning is this definition by William James: "Religion . . . shall mean for us the feelings, acts, and experiences of individual men in their solitude, as far as they apprehend themselves to stand in relation to whatever they may consider the divine."[9] A more recent definition is even more sharply individualistic: "Religion is the art and the theory of the internal life of man, so far as it depends on the man himself and on what is permanent in the nature of things . . . Religion is what the individual does with his own solitariness. . . . Thus religion is solitariness; and if you are never solitary, you are never religious."[10] The other side is presented by A. C. Watson, who defines religion as "a social attitude toward the nonhuman environment."[11]

There are those who define religion in terms of worship; others regard the conservation of values as most essential to religion; still others approach religion historically, psychologically, or sociologically. These all have their place, and each student of religion is ultimately faced with making a definition that will satisfy his interests. The definition which includes all the complex features of religion as successfully as any is this one of Brightman: "Religion is concern about experiences which are regarded as of supreme value; devotion toward a power or powers believed to originate, increase, and conserve these values; and some suitable expression of this concern and devotion, whether through symbolic rites or through other individual and social conduct."[12]

SUGGESTIONS FOR FURTHER STUDY

W. C. BOWER, *The Living Bible*, pp. 15-28.

E. S. BRIGHTMAN, *A Philosophy of Religion*, pp. 13-18.

E. DURKHEIM, *Elementary Forms of the Religious Life*, pp. 23-47.

V. FERM, *First Chapters in Religious Philosophy*, pp. 3-71.

JACK FINEGAN, *Youth Asks about Religion*, pp. 11-25.

H. T. HOUF, *What Religion Is and Does*, pp. 4-8.

E. D. SOPER, *The Religions of Mankind*, pp. 23-24.

H. N. WIEMAN and W. M. HORTON, *The Growth of Religion*, pp. xi-xiii.

Chapter Two

THE ORIGIN AND GROWTH
OF RELIGION

A. *The Historical Approach.*

Since religion is concerned with the whole of life and since it has been a part of human life even before recorded history, one might well raise the question of origin. What was the beginning of religion? Immediately we face a difference of opinion among authorities; while anthropologists generally agree that religion in some form or other is universal, they differ in their explanation of its origin. Some hold that the earliest religious conception was that of an "All-Father," a kind of father god who created the world and lives in the sky.[1] Magical elements in primitive religion are considered to be marks of degeneration from an originally purer form of religion rather than the first stages in religious evolution. Other authorities, however, are inclined to ascribe these tendencies toward monotheism to the influence of missionaries on the primitives or to point out that where such advanced beliefs do occur they are subordinated in practice to reliance upon lesser deities.

A very ancient theory of the origin of religion was stated by Lucretius (*ca.* 99-55 B.C.) and, in more recent times, by others,[2] to the effect that religion grew out of fear. Now we ought to recognize that the influence of fear in religion has been tremendous, and still is a powerful factor. But to make fear and fear alone the single ingredient in the complex process of religious development is to be guilty of oversimplification; other factors must also be considered. Even fear itself needs analysis; perhaps the impulse to self-preservation is more basic and accounts for much of the fear in primitive life.

The first theory of religious origins to be developed after a thorough study of the phenomena of primitive religion was that of E. B. Tylor in his book, *Primitive Culture* (first published in 1871).[3] It was his idea that early man attributed life to nature and the objects around him; he looked upon everything he saw as animated, as possessing a spirit like his own. Nature was alive and throbbing. This is called the "animistic" theory of the origin of religion; to Tylor, religion was the relationship man established with certain of the spirits of his animism and ancestor worship was its original form. However, later authorities, while agreeing that primitive man came finally to an animistic conclusion, feel that the finished animism of Tylor gives evidence of considerable development in early man. So we are driven to allow for a pre-animistic religion, or "animatism," thus leaving "animism" for the developed belief in spirits.

Sir J. G. Frazer, in his epoch-making work, *The Golden Bough*,[4] defined this preanimistic religion as a belief in the efficacy of magic. Religion arises, he maintains, when magic is seen to fail; it is an attempt to persuade the cosmic powers to be friendly to man and is based on the conclusion that magic is inadequate and that man's desires cannot wholly control the course of events. But, in spite of the fact that religion and magic are inextricably intertwined in the life of primitive man, it is impossible to say which came first; also, even in the most highly developed religions of today, remnants of magic continue.[5]

In 1912, Emile Durkheim published his monumental study of the problem of religious origins, *Elementary Forms of the Religious Life*,[6] in which he traced the origin of the totemic principle among the native tribes of Australia to a social source. To him, religion was not essentially a theory at all, but a practical social activity. Society becomes man's god; he worships the mysterious power of the group to which he belongs, that which protects him from forces over which he has no control. This theory has some merit; religion is social. However, there is more to religion than a highly developed social phenomenon; man persists in believing in something or some person beyond the level of his fellow human beings.

As a result of surveying these rival theories of the origin of religion (all of which have their merits and defects) one might well conclude that all attempts to trace the origins of religion to a single source are oversimplifications. Even the most primitive religion is complex. Soper wisely defines "that impulse from without to which the mind of primitive man responds" as "the total impress of nature, his environment, the outside world, the society of which he is a part, the unseen, mysterious world which surrounds him, on his primitive mind. The points of contact are without number, and through every one comes pouring in all kinds of stimuli. Most of these have no particular religious significance, but some affect him as so strange, so mysterious, so awesome that he trembles when he is in their presence. This sense of mystery and awe in the presence of what he conceives as higher powers coupled with a deep dissatisfaction with his condition, which urged him on to secure what he did not have—this must be the beginning of religion."[7]

Whatever its causes, religion actually arose and was differentiated from magic and superstition. Because of its humble beginnings, one might be led to say that religion is nonsense, but origin does not determine destiny. Modern chemistry had its origin in alchemy, and modern astronomy in astrology, but both grew into respectable disciplines. The Christian sacrament of the Lord's Supper may be traced back through the mystery cults to the early custom of eating the totemic animal, but that sacrament constitutes high moments of inspiration to the devout participant. Knowledge of primitive religion is necessary to an understanding of religion, but it must be supplemented by a study of the development of the primitive into the mature. Whatever its origin, religion grew up.

Like civilization itself, religion developed through certain stages. As man's needs became more complex, so the forms of his religious life became more extensive and refined. The religion of savage people was suited to their needs and was on the level of their advancement in culture and outlook on life. An intelligent people demand a religion suited to their outlook on life; if a religion is not able by reinterpretation or reformation to meet newer needs, then it is laid aside for other forms or for another religion. History is filled with examples of religions which deteriorated because they were unable or unwilling to grow with the advances in culture attained by their devotees.

Religion, as well as culture in general, goes through three stages of development; the tribal, the national, and the universal. In the tribal stage, the individual is of little consequence, and the group is everything. Material interests force themselves on the attention of the members of the clan so that there is little time for reflection and speculation. The laws are the customs of the tribe, and the members are united by the blood covenant. Piety is measured by loyalty to the tribe and obeying its mandates and those of the tribal deities. Primitive man never rises above his material wants and desires and his religion remains on that same low level. This was the level of the religion of the Semites before they moved into the fertile crescent and even after that until they became settled dwellers in Palestine.

The disappearance of the tribe and the rise of the nation produce a new set of needs which leads to another level in the growth of religion—the national. In the history of the Hebrew people, the nationalistic stage was reached with the accession of David to the kingship; under him, Jahweh became the god of the nation, with a capital city and the plan of a temple in which he could live. Among the Greeks, Zeus becomes the king of the gods, lording it over the subordinate deities. Among other peoples, the Egyptians, the Babylonians, the Assyrians, the Persians, the Indians, the Chinese, and the Romans, a national religion was developed in correspondence to their advance in civilization.

Out of the national developed the universal or prophetic stage of religion. Of the world's religions, only a few have burst the bonds of nationalism and sought to become international or universal; this is the highest form of religion and is represented in the world today by three great world faiths: Buddhism, Mohammedanism, and Christianity. This final stage began, in the Hebrew faith, during the five centuries from 750 B.C. on, under the guidance of prophets, universal in outlook, individualistic rather than nationalistic, ethical rather than ritualistic, and intellectual and mystical rather than formal.

The development of religion through these three stages does not present clear cleavages from one stage to the next. Remnants of tribal religion still persist in the nationalistic and even in the universal stages; vestiges of the particularism and exclusivism characteristic of the national stage persist into the universal. Even a casual observer of Christianity in many of its denominational forms can note that it is too often a universal religion in name only.[8]

B. *The Psychological Approach*

Because a study of history does not help us to determine with any degree of accuracy the origin of religion, many authorities in the field turn to the contributions of a psychological study of religious origins. Within recent years this approach has received increasing attention. Since psychology is a science, its chief method in the field of religion is observation; by studying the religion of present-day savages, such as the aborigines of Australia, one may see at first hand the characteristics of the animistic stage in the development of religion; by a thorough study of child psychology and an introspective analysis of one's own religious development, one may arrive at a clearer understanding of the genetic origins of religion and the factors which make its continued growth possible. If, as the so-called "recapitulation theory" assumes, the individual in his development goes through all the stages through which the race as a whole has gone, then a psychological study of religious behavior is a valuable supplement to the historical.

A few years ago, psychologists tended to speak of a "religious instinct," that religion begins with a sort of innate sense for religious matters. Now, however, the word "instinct" is tabu in scientific circles; instead, we may properly speak of basic, elemental drives of a religious nature. Man is incurably religious; religion is a part of his normal experience; it is something he possesses as soon as his life begins to be organized and he enters into relationship with his fellows and the nature surrounding him on all sides. That is not to say that all men will be or must be religious; but one must admit that it is easy for human beings to become so, there are natural tendencies, psychic roots of religion, which form a ready base for the development of religion in the individual.

The most elemental of these psychic roots is fear; just as primitive man is afraid of the unknown, so the infant very early shows fear in the presence of some stimuli, and this emotion abides throughout life. In many ways, fear is a self-preservative device, necessary at every stage of development; it does not become distinctively religious until it grows into awe and reverence. In the sense of awe, religion seems to begin; the person feels that there is something mysterious and powerful which he cannot explain; this awesome feeling easily passes over into reverence, which some regard to be the very essence of religion. As William Mc-Dougall has said:

> Suppose that the power that excites awe is also one that we have reason to regard as beneficent, one that, while capable of annihilating us in a moment, yet works for our good, sustains and protects us, one that evokes our gratitude. Awe then becomes compounded with gratitude and we experience the highly compound emotion of reverence. Reverence is the religious emotion *par excellence*; few merely human powers are capable of exciting reverence, this blend of wonder, fear, gratitude, and negative self-feeling.[9]

Another elemental tendency which contributes to religion is love in its several manifestations. The sex impulse is deep in human nature and necessary for the preservation of the race. Religion very early associated itself with the mysterious and the crucial in life, birth, and reproduction. Love is also revealed in tender emotion, a spontaneous feeling of sympathy for other persons, and a deep and disinterested reverence for personality, largely below the level of conscious experience. Consciously, love becomes the willing and rather consistent assumption of the attitude of good will toward mankind as such and toward individuals in particular. This is the very heart of some of the world's greatest religions, notably Christianity.[10]

Another basic tendency is usually called gregariousness. Though probably not an instinct, it is undeniably universal and leads men easily toward religion. In fact, religion is so much a social and group affair that some scholars have turned to the sociology of religion as the key to the whole phenomenon of religious behavior.[11] Organized religion in our time is rather largely a gregarious affair.

Curiosity is one of the elemental roots of religion in human nature. This is the same quality which leads scientists to discover new truth in the laboratory and explorers to cross uncharted seas. It leads the child to ask the perennial question "Why?" Unable to satisfy itself with the observable data of the sciences, this curiosity leads to philosophical speculation and further into religious explanations.

Two other strong tendencies are the opposite impulses of submissiveness and assertiveness. Self-preservation, the will to live, is achieved by either asserting the self vigorously or, failing that, submitting meekly and resignedly. In the presence of superlative power, beauty, goodness, or achievement, normal persons are submissive; in fact, all higher religion relies on this attitude of submission to the reality of a more than human order or power or being. The assertive tendency in religion has been equally important; all the founders of the great religions had it and the reformers who defied convention were filled with it. Religion may easily grow on both these qualities.

It seems plain that man will not soon outgrow these basic traits and deep needs. As in the past, so in the future, religion will continue to be a part of human life and culture.

To the same extent that a study of the psychology of religion has been helpful in determining the nature of the origin of religion, to that same extent such a discipline has been helpful in analyzing the development of religion. Without growth, religion declines; to the psychological observer of personal religious behaviour, growth is a religious imperative. At the various levels of physical growth, religion evidences those needs which must be met by changing emphases in accordance with the changing patterns of personality. From infancy to adulthood religion, to be effective, must grow toward an increasing integration of personality, a more effective coordination of interests, emotions, and purposes.

SUGGESTIONS FOR FURTHER STUDY

C. S. BRADEN, *Modern Tendencies in World Religions,* pp. 1-19.

E. S. BRIGHTMAN, *A Philosophy of Religion,* pp. 33-63.

E. DURKHEIM, *Elementary Forms of the Religious Life.*

H. T. HOUF, *What Religion Is and Does,* pp. 8-17.

P. E. JOHNSON, *Psychology of Religion,* pp. 13-32; 62-87.

G. F. MOORE, *The Birth and Growth of Religion,* pp. 1-20.

E. D. SOPER, *The Religions of Mankind,* pp. 35-54.

H. N. WIEMAN and W. M. HORTON, *The Growth of Religion,* pp. 7-21.

Chapter Three

THE RELIGION OF PRIMITIVE MAN:
ANIMISM

All the great religions of the world, including Christianity, have their roots in the past; they have passed through the various stages of development from the tribal up through the nationalistic in the direction of the universal. All of them had their dim beginnings in primitive religion and none of them can be fully understood without a knowledge of this early period of their development. To a greater or lesser degree among the various world faiths, vestiges of this early stage remain. Animists form a considerable part of the population of the world; no continent is without some representative of animistic culture and religion.

Wherever it has been found, animism has exhibited similar general characteristics. In the first place, it is traditional. The religion of primitive people is about what it was ages ago; it has been transmitted by word of mouth from generation to generation; there has been no written language, no literature, no history, and thus no possibility of any significant progress. The civilization of primitive man does not rise to higher levels until its acts can be recorded and passed on to later generations in more permanent forms.

Secondly, animism is natural. Primitive man is so occupied with material and physical needs that no other needs are felt. "Shelter and enough to eat, provision for his animals, protection against his enemies, the satisfaction of his primary impulses—these are about all he thinks about. His needs are simple and crude and can never be complex and refined so long as he continues to live this life. He is not awake to himself and the latent possibilities of his deeper nature. Spiritual attainment is denied him because he has never felt any aspiration after higher things."[1]

Then, the religion of primitive man is spontaneous. There are no founders, no crucial turning-points, no reformatory impulses; it is unconsciously a part of the life and culture of the tribe. The animist takes his religion for granted; it is as much of his normal life as eating, or sleeping, or going to battle against an enemy.

Also, the religious systems designated by the general term "animism" show some common features. In the first place, primitive man believes in a spirit world; the spirits are everywhere; nature is filled with a great company of spiritual beings not far away from man. They are the spirits of the visible objects around him and of the invisible forces of nature before which he cringes in abject terror. Whatever happens is caused by a spiritual agency; the animist's world is alive and throbbing with vitality. This aspect of his religion is sometimes called "dynamism." The spirit world is similar to the things primitive man sees; a spirit is a more or less thin, vapory substance, similar in nature to breath and often identified with blood.[2] The realm of the spirits was very real to primitive man, especially in his dreams; he noted that his body remained where it was while he slept, while his spirit traveled far and passed through strange and wonderful experiences. Death to him was like his dream world; in a dream, the spirit left the body only for a short while, whereas at death his spirit entered the dream world to live forever. This belief in a spirit world is summed up in the one word "Mana." A Melanesian word, it signifies primitive man's conception of a mysterious pervasive power in the universe, resident in every object and active in every event.[3]

Magic is very much a part of the religion of primitive man. He noticed very early that he could manipulate certain objects or forces and get from the world of spirits results which would be beneficial to him and avoid circumstances which would be harmful to him. Magic is the very endeavor through utterance of set words or the performance of set acts to control the spirits of the world and bend them to man's will. In the main, primitive man tried three methods to gain this control.

The first of these is fetishism. A fetish is a natural object which is reverenced, not for its own power, but because it is believed to be occupied by a spirit. Something about a particular object strikes primitive man as being out of the ordinary; perhaps it is a queer-shaped stone, a bright bead, a stick, parrots' feathers, a root, claw, seed, or bone, which attracts him. Or he may induce useful powers into an inanimate object; a gourd, a nut shell, or an antelope's horn may be filled with a mixture of ingredients prepared by the medicine man and thus become a useful instrument to help him secure what he wants. Fetishes are regarded as having a vague sort of personality, at least an active will; they are treated as objects of worship, have offerings made to them, and are addressed in prayer. If favorable issues do not result from this treatment, the owner passes to coaxing and cajoling, then proceeds to stern commands, scolding, and finally whipping or other chastisement. "If there is still no result, the conclusion is either that the spirit has left the fetish, in which case it is useless and another must be found to take its place, or that the spirit, still in the fetish, has been rendered impotent by some more powerful fetish or spirit-power in the neighborhood. In the latter case the magician must be visited and the fetish charged with more power, or substituted with another of adequate potency."[4]

Secondly, primitive man tried shamanism to establish control over the spirit-powers. This is the attempt to influence spirits by using a person presumed himself to be spirit-possessed. The shaman, medicine man, witch-doctor, exorcist, or sorcerer works himself up into a frenzy of spirit-possession and then is thought to control certain spirits, especially those of disease and death. These men, as they gradually come to be set apart from the normal life of the tribe, become the thinkers, the developers of the ritual, the collectors of the sacred traditions, the predecessors of priests and clergymen in more advanced religions.

Then, the people themselves, without the aid of fetish or shaman, sought either to prevent the spirit powers from doing harm to the individual or group or to make them serve private or group interests. Out of this have come various religious rites and customs, such as corn dances, fertility rituals, the offering up of human and animal sacrifices, the worship of the goddess of fertility, the worship of bulls and he-goats, etc.[5]

Still another feature of animism is tabu (from the Polynesian word "tapu," which means "sacred" or "prohibited"). It means a prohibition placed on contact with or use of certain things set aside as peculiarly sacred. The number and range of tabus is almost endless: there are tabus against coming into contact with rulers and chiefs, against having social relationships with strangers, against contact with other persons at certain times and under certain conditions, such as mourners, women, warriors, hunters, fishermen, murderers, newly born children, priests in worship ceremonies, etc. Articles also join the list of the things to be avoided: iron instruments, sharp weapons, blood, head and hair, cut hair and nails, spittle, certain foods (such as pork among the Hebrews). In fact, some authorities have maintained that almost anything and everything has at one time or another been tabu.[6] The idea of tabu seems best accounted for by the presence of "mana," the all-pervasive force which vitalizes and renders dangerous the things which possess it; the object or person believed to possess an especially large amount of "mana," which if released by contact will cause calamity, pain, ill-luck, or death, is tabu.

For the most part, worship in animism is based on fear of the innumerable invisible spirits which are around man. He tries to placate these powers by offering them in sacrifices things he himself needs or desires for his nourishment and comfort and pleasure. Thus, sacrifice was originally composed of food and drink, clothing, utensils, and even human beings. Since life was the most precious thing in the world, why not offer it to the gods in return for special favors?[7] Prayer is closely related to sacrifice; the earliest prayer may have been a call to the spirits to come and partake of the sacrifice. Prayer for primitive man seldom rises above his purely material needs and desires; often it was little more than an incantation in which the mere repetition of words was regarded as a means of bringing the desired end.

Primitive man took certain attitudes toward the dead. From prehistoric times there has been a persistent belief that the dead not only survive but have the same hungers and needs as in life. To conciliate the enemy and to please the friend, offerings have been made at the grave.[8]

Closely connected with the religion of primitive people and also partaking of the nature of magic was a practice known as totemism (from a word in the language of the Ojibway Indians meaning "group"). A totem is an animal, plant, or inanimate object held sacred by a group, clan, or tribe; it is that which separates the group from other groups. Sometimes the group is named after the totem, from which it is often thought to be descended. It becomes a form of social organization determining many features of the life of the tribe. As the ancestor of a group, the totem animal may even be worshiped; it must not be killed or mistreated. However, among some tribes the totem animal is killed on certain important occasions and eaten sacramentally by all who belong to that totem clan; by this the bond between the group and its totem is reestablished.

We cannot leave this brief survey of animism without pointing out that ultimately the animist turned in worship to some of the hundreds of spirits around him in preference to the others. Just which ones he worshiped first we do not know, but we do know that the ones to which he turned were those he regarded as having powers superior to his own. The worship of plants and trees is virtually universal among primitive peoples and is retained even among those of a more complex culture.[9] Deification of plants is a natural tribute to the mysterious growth-forces of nature. Stones were widely worshiped, particularly those of an unusual size, shape, or color.[10] Mountains, fire, winds, and waters were regarded as sacred, along with the sun, moon, stars, and the sky. Primitive man worshiped animals, full of life and movement and cunning: the majesty of the lion (Africa), the ferocity of the tiger (India), the wisdom of the elephant, the cunning of the fox, the mysteriousness of the snake led to an attitude akin to worship.[11] Then he turned to the worship of human beings: living men, such as chiefs and kings, emperors and saints; historical personages, legendary, mythical, or real ancestors. This led, at least among some primitive tribes, to a belief in a supreme being, a god over all, like Zeus was in the Greek pantheon, who had once been a great leader among men on earth and had then been transferred to the sky; this god, however, had little to do with man's everyday experiences; other and lesser spirits are much more active as determiners of destiny down on the earth.

SUGGESTIONS FOR FURTHER STUDY

E. Durkheim, *Elementary Forms of the Religious Life,* pp. 48-447.
J. G. Frazer, *The Golden Bough.*
G. F. Moore, *The Birth and Growth of Religion,* pp. 21-76.
J. B. Noss, *Man's Religions,* pp. 4-36.
E. D. Soper, *The Religions of Mankind,* pp. 55-90.

Chapter Four

THE RELIGION OF THE SEMITES

All the great religions of the world have developed through successive stages from the simple to the more complex, from humble beginnings in animism to complicated rituals and elaborate doctrines. Christianity exhibits the same development; it grew up out of Judaism; Judaism, in turn, developed from the religion of the Hebrews at the time of Moses, which may be designated as Jahwism; Jahwism had its roots in the primitive polytheism and animism of the Semitic nomads. Thus, in order to understand the religion of the Hebrews in its historical development it is necessary to have some knowledge of early Semitic religion.

The Hebrews were Semites, belonging perhaps to the northern branch of that race which had its home in the country lying to the north of the Arabian peninsula between the mountains of Iran and the Mediterranean Sea. The original home of all the Semites was the great Arabian peninsula itself. For many long centuries the Semites were nomads; later, they became agriculturists and, still later, city dwellers. Their religion follows the same pattern of development; yet there are remnants of nomadic animism in subsequent ages.

All the Semitic tribes shared the strong belief that trees, particularly evergreen trees, were special vehicles of spiritual energy. In his exhaustive study of Semitic religion, W. Robertson Smith found "no Canaanite high place was complete without its sacred tree standing beside the altar, . . . The local sanctuaries of the Hebrews . . . were altar-sanctuaries. But the altars were habitually set up 'under green trees,' . . ."[1] He continues:

> The general adoption of tree symbols at Canaanite sanctuaries must be connected with the fact that all Canaanite Baalim,

whatever their original character, were associated with naturally fertile spots (Baal's land), and were worshiped as the givers
of vegetable increase . . .[2]

. . . Prayers were addressed to them, particularly for help
in sickness, but doubtless also for fertile seasons and the like,
and they were hung with votive gifts, especially garments and
ornaments, perhaps also anointed with unguents as if they
had been real persons . . .[3]

. . . Oracles and omens from trees and at tree sanctuaries
are the commonest among all races, and are derived in very
various ways, either from observation of phenomena connected
with the trees themselves, and interpreted as manifestations of
divine life, or from ordinary processes of divination performed
in the presence of the sacred object.[4]

Semitic animists regarded water as being sacred in the same
degree they reverenced trees. This applied especially to living
(running) water, rivers, streams, and springs, and to a lesser degree
to lakes and the sea. Water was vitally necessary to the desert
nomad; the sources of it were considered dwelling-places of life-
giving deity. W. Robertson Smith points out that temples were
often erected near springs and rivers. He continues:

. . . The presence of living water in itself gave consecration to the place. The fountain or stream was not a mere
adjunct to the temple, but was itself one of the principal
sacra of the spot, to which special legends and a special ritual
were often attached, and to which the temple in many instances
owed its celebrity and even its name. This is particularly the
case with perennial streams and their sources, which in a
country like Palestine, where rain is confined to the winter
months, are not very numerous, and form striking features in
the topography of the region . . .[5]

Like sacred trees and sacred springs, sacred stones were a part
of the religion of the Semites in their early animistic stage. Stones,
no matter what their shape and appearance, were the first altars;
artificial pillars set up as symbols of deity and cairns of stones
chosen at random and set up by man's hand were regarded as
dwelling-places of the gods. Just why the animists used stones
in this way is a matter of conjecture; W. Robertson Smith thinks

it was just a matter of convenience for ritual purposes;[6] but other authorities feel that stones were erected for purposes of worship because they were the nearest approach to human forms.[7]

From time immemorial mountains have been considered the dwelling-places of deity; many of the "high places" used as sanctuaries by the later Canaanites and Hebrews were probably remnants of ancient animistic usages. Mount Sinai had been considered sacred from very ancient days by those who worshiped the moon god "Sin;" its volcanic nature would probably have been regarded by semi-cultured people as due to the spirit which lived there.

Totemism characterized the religion of the Semites on the animistic level. When they first became known to the historical investigator, there was only the fragmentary survival of totem ideas as special associations between certain kinds of animals on the one hand and certain tribes of religious communities and their gods on the other. In his *Kinship and Marriage in Early Arabia,* W. Robertson Smith found racial stocks named after plants and animals, the prevalence of the conception that the members of the tribe are sprung from the totem animal or plant, and the ascription to the totem of a sacred character.[8]

Closely associated with totemism is tabu. There were many tabus among the Semites, including the things which could not be touched because they were holy and those which could not be touched because they were unholy. The Greek writer Lucian (*ca.* 125-180 A.D.) says that pigeons and pigs could not be eaten among the ancient Syrians.[9]

Of the existence of ancestor worship among the Semites there is no doubt. This is the natural outcome of reverence for a totem-ancestor and of the feeling that a human ancestor could gradually become divine. Archaeological data all through the Near East suggest to some authorities a cult of the dead among all the ancient people who inhabited that area. Graves were considered sacred even down into Old Testament times.

In the belief of primitive Semites, the natural world was full of living beings of superhuman kind, the "jinn" or demons. They are not pure spirits; they are represented as being in the form of beasts or birds, usually hairy, and with mysterious powers of appearing and disappearing or of assuming human form. They frequent places far away from the usual habitats of man. Necromancy, the custom of communicating with the dead, was characteristic of the

Semites; there were mediums in Babylonian religion who were believed to have the faculty of receiving messages from the spirits of the departed. Semites believed that the spirits of the departed left their abode in the underworld and roamed about on the earth to the detriment of men; magicians were often employed to combat these activities. Another aspect of the most primitive elements of Semitic religion was magic. Closely related to the subjects of tabu, demonology, and necromancy, magical arts were employed by the Semites and their successors in Palestine. Ranging from rain-making to sorcery, magical practices persisted down into Bible times.

The chief items in the worship of the ancient Semites were prayer and simple sacrifices. As they emerged from animism, they began to direct their worship toward certain high gods. The chief of these gods for the Semitic nomad was the moon god, Sin. The sun was no friend of the nomad; in the daytime he sought refuge from its heat in the shade of some rock. But at night he moved his flocks and herds; thus the moon and the stars were regarded as beneficent spirits. Ur and Harran, both connected with the migrations of Abraham, were centers of moon worship; Sinai was evidently named after the cult of the moon. One of the festivals which grew to have particular prominence in the life of the Semites was the observance of the new moon, due to a desire to do honor to the god on his reappearance.

Another festival which probably goes back into the nomad period was the Sabbath. It probably has some connection with the festival of the new moon, for often in the Bible "new moons and Sabbaths" were grouped together.[10] Originally it was not a day of complete rest from labor, but for a change in the week's toil. Other nomadic festivals were sheep-shearing and Pesach; the latter was the predecessor of the Passover festival in later Judaism. Pesach was observed on the full moon of the month nearest the spring equinox (later the 14th day of the Jewish month Nisan); it was observed sometime between sunset and sunrise; either a sheep or a goat was sacrificed, and the blood was smeared on the outside of the dwelling-places of the worshipers, probably to ward off evil spirits.

Several institutions and customs, later developed in the Old Testament, have their roots in the religion of the Semites. One of these was the ban; anything under the ban was withdrawn from common use and devoted exclusively to a deity; this was used for destruction of material wealth and death for the conquered in battle. Another was the abstinence from food before or during a battle. A third was the rite of circumcision; many of the Semite tribes probably received this institution from Egyptian sources, for flint knives were used in the beginning; evidently it was originally a tribal mark to show that a youth was a full member of his social group and consecrated to the god of the tribe. Blood revenge characterized the Semites; under the basic idea of social solidarity, any wrong done to one member of a clan was done to all and all were bound to avenge it. Finally, the blood-covenant was a widely practiced desert rite based on the belief that the living element in an animal was its blood; two individuals or two groups could become one through a sprinkling or pouring of the blood of a sacrificial victim over both parties.

SUGGESTIONS FOR FURTHER STUDY

F. C. EISELEN, E. LEWIS, and D. G. DOWNEY, eds., *The Abingdon Bible Commentary,* pp. 165-166.

E. W. K. MOULD, *Essentials of Bible History,* pp. 116-130

J. B. NOSS, *Man's Religions,* pp. 475-479.

W. O. E. OESTERLEY and T. H. ROBINSON, *Hebrew Religion: Its Origin and Development,* pp. 3-102.

W. R. SMITH, *Lectures on the Religion of the Semites.*

E. D. SOPER, *The Religions of Mankind,* pp. 267-270.

PART II

HEBREW BACKGROUNDS
OF THE
CHRISTIAN RELIGION

Chapter Five

HEBREW BEGINNINGS IN PALESTINE

A. *The Old Testament World.*

The continent of Asia has often been called the cradle of the religions of mankind. That part of the continent of Asia which is nearest Africa—including Palestine and the Arabian Peninsula —has witnessed the birth of three of the world's great religions: Judaism, Mohammedanism, and Christianity. Palestine itself presents one of the miracles of the development of culture: how a strip of land so small,[1] mostly barren and rocky, could produce religious insights and institutions of such profound significance to the human race! But, in spite of its small size, Palestine was very strategically located between the two great oriental centers of civilization in the Nile basin and in the Tigris-Euphrates Valley. Since "the study of geography is basic to the study of the history and culture of any nation,"[2] the location of Palestine and the physical geography of the land help to explain its eventful history and the preoccupation of its people with religious matters. Palestine constitutes a "land-bridge" between Asia and Africa, connecting Egypt with Mesopotamia. Through this narrow strip of land between the Sea and the desert necessarily passed the caravans of commerce and the armies from the East and from the West. At most times in history Palestine has been a dependency, a buffer state, or a battleground.[3] Palestine was the first to feel the effects of the expansion of empires. The topography had its effect upon the characteristics of the people; the rugged isolation of the southern part made the people of Judah what they were; the openness of the northern highlands resulted in a more cosmopolitan people in that region; in the far north Mount Lebanon forced the Phoenicians to turn their attention toward becoming the maritime nomads of antiquity. The inhabitants of the land did not become great artists, but the nature of Palestine awakened in them a sense of religious dependence and influenced the development of their religious genius.

The Biblical world includes more than Palestine; it extends from Spain on the west to the Persian Gulf on the east, and from the Black and Caspian seas on the north to Nubia and the Gulf of Aden on the south. Actually, however, most of the events in the history of the Hebrew people occurred in a narrow strip of more or less fertile land designated appropriately as "the fertile crescent."[4] This is a crescent-shaped area beginning at the southeast corner of the Mediterranean Sea, stretching northward along the Mediterranean coast through Syria, thence northeastward to the headwaters of the Tigris and Euphrates rivers, and then southeastward to the head of the Persian Gulf. It is a kind of amphitheater, backed by the Zagros Mountains on the east, the Taurus Mountains on the north, and the Mediterranean Sea on the west. South of the crescent is the Arabian Desert, extending five hundred miles from Palestine in the west to Mesopotamia in the east. On the significance of the "fertile crescent" Mould writes:

Along the northern border of this desert (the Arabian) is a fringe of grasslands,

"the strip of herbage strown
That just divides the desert from the sown."

The grass is scanty, to be sure, for the winter rains are meager, and when these rains fail the grasslands furnish no pasturage for the flocks of the desert nomads. These nomads then push into the Fertile Crescent and come into conflict with others of their kind who have gone there before them. Throughout the centuries nomads have been thus drifting in from the sandy desert to the fertile lands. In the course of time they become established and give up the wandering life of the nomad for the settled life of the agriculturist. This drifting of nomads into the Crescent is, as a rule, gradual, but at times it becomes a wholesale migration. The history of the Fertile Crescent is the story of such migrations and the ensuing struggles for possession of the fertile lands, followed by the transformation of the nomads into settled agriculturists. This is precisely what we encounter in Old Testament history, which recounts the migrations of a Semitic nomad people called the Hebrews through the Fertile Crescent until they finally settle in Palestine, are there transformed into agriculturists and develop a culture of their own. The Hebrews were not, however, the first people to drift into Palestine. Indeed, as early as the third millennium B.C. Semites were drifting into that land. When, therefore, the Hebrews crowded into Palestine, they came into conflict with their Semitic predecessors there.[5]

Canaan, or Palestine, was located in the western horn of the fertile crescent. Its rugged terrain has evidently been due to the fact that all through geologic time the earth's surface in that region has been subject to violent volcanic activity and to vigorous shiftings of the earth's crust. In its physical features, Palestine has about all the variety the earth has to offer. "On the west is a coastal plain which varies in width from a few yards to fifteen miles, made up of swamps, rolling sand dunes, and rich, fertile soil. Back of this plain is a rugged mountain range, . . . On the east it descends into the Jordan Valley, which lies considerably below sea level, . . . On the east it is fringed by a highland plateau, somewhat higher than the western highlands and now generally known as Trans-Jordania, which extends back into the hinterland until it is lost in the Arabian Desert. Thus, within the space of a few miles one can visit fertile valleys, wild mountain gorges, depressions that are below sea level, or sandy steppes."[6]

The coastal plains along the shore of the Mediterranean Sea may be divided into the plain of Acre and Phoenicia in the north, the plain of Sharon in the central part, and the plain of Philistia in the southwest. Just to the east of the plain of Philistia is a region made up of low, rounded hills not over a few hundred feet high, called, in Bible times, the Shephelah. Between the coastal plains and the Jordan Valley is a range of mountains known as the Western Highlands; this begins in the north with the Highlands of Galilee, actually a continuation of the Lebanon Mountain range of Syria but with less rugged hills and many small picturesque valleys. Just to the south of Galilee lie the Plains of Esdraelon and Jezreel; the former, not much more than fifteen miles long and eight miles wide, is fertile enough to be the granary for the entire region and it has been, in history, the battle ground of the ages. These two plains form the most used pass across Palestine; trade routes found their way across its level expanse. Fortified cities like

Megiddo, Taanach, and Bethshean served as protecting fortresses for this important region. South of the plain of Esdraelon lies the Highlands of Samaria, a land of fruitful valleys, wooded hills, and numerous springs; it was a rugged plateau, yet fairly open to outside influences in every direction. South of Samaria is Judea, a broken plateau two or three thousand feet high, a land of rugged mountains and barren wilderness, more suitable to the shepherd than the farmer. To the South, the Judean highlands slope into a desert region known as the Negeb; sparsely settled and little cultivated, it has been from time immemorial the habitat of nomads. Running from north to south throughout the land, at a varying distance of forty to fifty miles inland from the Mediterranean Sea, is a deep fault in the earth's crust, known as the Great Rift, and comprising, for the most part, the valley of the Jordan River. Beginning in a group of springs fed by the snows on Mount Hermon, the Jordan flows down through Lake Huleh and the Sea of Galilee to the Dead Sea, a distance of about 135 miles and a descent of over 3000 feet. The Dead Sea is 1292 feet below sea level in one of the most torrid sections of the earth's surface. South of the Dead Sea the Jordan Valley continues through the semiarid Wadi Arabah until it emerges into the Gulf of Akabah. Trans-Jordania, the land east of the Jordan, was never under the complete suzerainty of Hebrew kings; varying in productivity, it is a land characterized by rugged plateaus with intersecting deep gorges.

Palestine lies in the subtropical zone, with a climate generally similar to that of southern California or southern Georgia. It is still in the zone of the westerly winds, which bring from the Mediterranean moisture in the winter and cooling breezes in the summer. However, when the wind comes from the east or southeast, Palestine suffers, for this desert wind ("sirocco") has no moisture. Only west of the mountainous backbone is the rainfall abundant; elsewhere it is uncertain. The rainy season begins toward the end of September and is heaviest in December, January, and February. Occasionally it is cold enough for snow. By March the rains become lighter; little falls after the end of April. The rains in March and April are known as the "latter rains";[7] they are slight in amount, but very important to agriculture. The average rainfall is between twenty and twenty-four inches, but both in ancient and modern times it frequently is less, resulting in times of famine.[8]

B. *The Hebrews Enter the Stage of History.*

Fossil human remains in Palestine indicate that the presence of man in Palestine goes back to 35000 or possibly even 50000 B.C. Throughout the Stone Age (ending *ca.* 5000 B.C.) caves and small huts were the chief dwelling places; in the Chalcolithic Period (*ca.* 4500-3000 B.C.) cultural advances were very pronounced, as men became food producers rather than mere food getters and lived more settled lives in villages.[9] The Early Bronze Age (*ca.* 3000-2000 B.C.) witnessed the coming into Palestine of the first wave of Semites, the linguistic precursors of the later Canaanites. Semites had found their way into the eastern end of the fertile crescent 2000 years earlier. In the Early Bronze Age, the non-Semitic Sumerians had established a civilization in Babylonia (*ca.* 2800-2360 B.C.), only to be supplanted by the Semitic Akkadians (*ca.* 2360-1960 B.C.). This was also one of the greatest periods in the history of Egypt with the third, fourth, fifth, and sixth dynasties comprising the Pyramid Age (*ca.* 2600-2150 B.C.). In Palestine, the religion of the early Bronze Age was much the same as that of the later Canaanites, as is shown by excavations of sanctuaries at Megiddo, Jericho, and Ai. Evidently the early Semitic invaders of Palestine found non-Semitic people there in advance of them; these people persisted in Palestine down to 2500 B.C.[10]

Other peoples found their way into the fertile crescent, both from the Arabian Desert to the South and from the mountainous Anatolian hinterland to the north. A Semitic race, the Amorites, infiltrated into Mesopotamia from the Syrian desert; after conquering the ancient cities of Ur and Larsa, they established the First Babylonian Empire, which lasted for ten generations. The greatest king of this dynasty was Hammurabi (*ca.* 1728-1676 B.C.), great lawgiver, author of a famous Code which influenced later Hebrew codes of law. Amorites found their way into Canaan, evidently securing the highlands while other Semites occupied the coastal plains.[11] The Hittites established a great empire in the central highlands of Asia Minor; they swept down into the fertile crescent, and some of them remained in Palestine.[12] Semitic nomads, the Hyksos, invaded Egypt *ca.* 1720 B.C. and established a powerful dynasty there which lasted until *ca.* 1550 B.C.; they were bedouins of the desert; their chief weapon was the bow. They ran an empire extending from the first cataract of the Nile to the Euphrates

River, including Palestine. It is possible that the Hebrew tribes went to Egypt as allies of the Hyksos invaders. A migration of Indo-Aryans into the upper Tigris-Euphrates Valley, combined with the older inhabitants of the region, known as Hurrians,[13] to make the powerful Mitannian Empire (*ca.* 1500-1370 B.C.); its capital was Nuzu, the excavation of which within recent years has yielded thousands of cuneiform tablets from the fifteenth century B.C., which give us a remarkably clear picture of life and customs in northern Mesopotamia at approximately the same time that Abraham migrated from Ur to Harran. Harran itself was a center of Hurrian cultural and religious influence. In the southern part of Mesopotamia, Kassites, Babylonians, Assyrians, Elamites, Medes, and Persians all established empires which rose and fell and made their mark upon conditions in Palestine. One of the most troublesome of all the competitors for Palestine was the group of "peoples of the sea" called the Philistines; they were non-Semites, perhaps the remnants of the Mycenaean civilization on the island of Crete, who were finally subdued by David. Other Semite groups settled parts of Palestine; the Phoenicians in the far north are noted for their alphabet; the Arameans came out of the Syrian Desert to found a civilization in the area surrounding Damascus.

As a result of this survey, it is very clear that the fertile crescent was a great melting pot of races and nations. Into this situation, as one of the great waves of Semite migration, the people later known as the Biblical Hebrews found their way. When did they first appear and what was their relationship to the people already mentioned?

The first appearance of the Hebrews in the Near East was in the form "Habiru," written thus in syllabic script in Babylonian literature. These people first appeared in the reign of Naram-Sin of the dynasty of Akkad (*ca.* 2287-2180 B.C.) in a Hittite account of the Habiru who stayed in the guardhouse, mercenary troops whom Naram-Sin used against the invading Hittites. They are also mentioned in inscriptions from the days of Rim-Sin, the ruler whom Hammurabi defeated for the mastery of Sumer; they also figure in tablets discovered at Nuzu. Among the Mitannians, the Habiru are often found entering voluntarily positions of slavery. The Dynasty of Larsa (*ca.* 1971-1960 B.C.), Hammurabi, the Kassites, and the Hittites all used these Habiru as mercenary troops; the Hittites brought them into northern Syria (*ca.* 1380 B.C.) when they were fighting Egypt for the mastery of Palestine. The word "Habiru" is an old Babylonian term which means "nomad," "bandit," or "mercenary." Its Hebrew equivalent is " 'ibri," which comes from a verb, " 'abar," meaning "to cross over." "The Habiri (Habiru) were crossers-over, or boundary-crossers; i.e., they were nomadic raiders or plunderers, who came from their desert haunts to pillage this or that country in the Fertile Crescent. . . ."[14]

The word "Habiru" (or " 'Apiru") appeared in Egyptian inscriptions as marauding raiders. In 1887 an Egyptian peasant woman accidentally discovered the archives of one of the kings of Egypt, Ikhnaton, at his capital city, Akhetaton; these consisted of letters written from his subordinates in Syria and Palestine and from kings in Babylonia, Assyria, Mitanni, and elsewhere. Some of these letters mention the Habiru as wandering marauders. In Jerusalem, Abdi-Hepa was governor, and he wrote repeatedly to Ikhnaton, pleading for Egyptian troops, stating that unless they were sent the entire country would be lost to Egypt. In one of them he says:

> As long as the king, my lord, lives
> I will say to the deputy of the king, my lord:
> "Why do you love
> The Habiru, and hate
> The regents?" But therefore
> Am I slandered before the king, my lord.
> Because I say: "The lands of the king,
> My lord, are lost," therefore
> Am I slandered to the king, my lord. . . .
> So let the king, the lord, care for his land. . . .
> Let the king turn his attention to the archers
> So that archers of the king,
> My lord, will go forth. No lands of the king remain.
> The Habiru plunder all lands of the king.[15]

Other letters continue to refer to the Habiru:

> Let the king care for his land.
> The land of the king will be lost. All of it

Will be taken from me; there is hostility to me. . . .
But now
The Habiru are taking
The cities of the king. . . .[16]

As to the exact origin of the Habiru, who were evidently the ancestors of the biblical Hebrews, there is difference of opinion. Perhaps the word "Habiru" was a general designation of any who crossed over a border and it was applied aptly to invading Israelites centuries later. "Whatever the discoveries of the future years may bring it seems safe to point out that of all foreigners, traders, raiders, or boundary-crossers who surged back and forth over that ancient land, one group established itself long enough in central Palestine to develop a national life, weave a traceable thread of continuous history, and lay down a deposit of literature that became one of the most important in the thinking of the world."[17]

The official history of the Hebrews begins when a tribe of Semitic bedouins settled in the neighborhood of Ur.[18] *Ca.* 2000 B.C., a group of them moved northward to Harran, under the leadership of a chieftain named Terah.[19] The causes which led to this migration were both economic and religious.[20] Ur of the Chaldees and the Aramean City of Harran were both noted for the worship of the moon god Sin. The economic cause would have been the age-old search of the nomad for better pastures for his flocks and herds.[21] Some of the tribes[22] still continued to move westward and southward. Some, known later as Arameans, settled down in the section known now as Syria, founding cities, of which the oldest and best known is Damascus. Others followed the lead of Abraham, a descendant of Terah, into Palestine proper. "For some generations the wanderings continued, sometimes to the West of the Jordan and sometimes to the east, and ranging from the region of Damascus (or even further east) to the borders of Egypt. Once we have an account of direct contact between Egypt and these pastoral nomads (Gen. 12:10-20) and several of the narratives describe the dealings of the Hebrew patriarchs with the settled inhabitants of Canaan (Gen. 20, 23, 26, 34, 38), while the stories of Jacob bring the ancestors of Israel into touch with both the Arameans to the northwest and the Edomites to the south (Gen. 28-33)."[23]

The first person in the Bible to bear the name "Hebrew" was Abraham; afterwards he was regarded as the father of the Hebrew people. The picture of Abraham is a correct portrait of a figure from the time of the Tell-el-Amarna tablets,[24] during the penetration of Palestine by the Habiru. Finegan sets the date for the migration of Abraham from Harran to Canaan at *ca.* 1935 B.C.[25] The stories of Isaac and Jacob in Genesis reveal the manners of life of nomadic tribes and their continual shifting about the western part of the fertile crescent; there is very little history in these stories, but they do describe the early life, customs, and religion of the Hebrew people. These tribes lived in or near the semi-arid Negeb anywhere from three to six centuries. Then, some of them, because of the pressure of a succession of famine years, migrated to the province of Goshen in the northeastern border of Egypt; they may have entered Egypt as allies of the Hyksos conquerors of Egypt (in power from *ca.* 1720 to *ca.* 1550 B.C.).[26] Into these facts of history the authors and compilers of the Book of Genesis wove the stories of Joseph.[27]

SUGGESTIONS FOR FURTHER STUDY

W. F. Albright, "The Biblical Period," in L. Finkelstein, ed., *The Jews: Their History, Culture, and Religion*, pp. 3-6.

A. E. Bailey, *Daily Life in Bible Times*, pp. 1-55.

A. E. Bailey, and C. F. Kent, *History of the Hebrew Commonwealth*, pp. 1-24.

G. A. Barton, *Archaeology and the Bible*, pp. 279-374.

G. A. Buttrick, ed., *The Interpreter's Bible*, I, pp. 175-176, 233-273.

F. C. Eiselen, E. Lewis, and D. G. Downey, eds., *The Abingdon Bible Commentary*, pp. 52-61.

J. Finegan, *Light from the Ancient Past*, pp. 9-105, 117-128, 164-167.

C. S. Knopf, *The Old Testament Speaks*, pp. 28-75.

E. W. K. Mould, *Essentials of Bible History*, pp. 3-42, 59-95.

J. B. Noss, *Man's Religions*, pp. 479-481.

Chapter Six

THE RELIGION OF THE HEBREWS
BEFORE MOSES

Hebrew religion developed out of the animistic religion of the Semites;[1] the Hebrew tribes, as they emerged from their desert homes and entered the fertile crescent, shared the beliefs and practices which were characteristic of all the Semitic nomads. As they came in contact with other peoples, Sumerians, Hurrians, Amorites, Egyptians, and Canaanites, their religion was modified, but it never quite gave up its animistic past. The Old Testament itself is full of references to many ancient religious practices, the original meaning of which cannot be recovered from the obscurity of antiquity.

The Bible contains no contemporary sources for the history of the Hebrew religion in the patriarchal period. The book of Genesis (the word means "beginning"), which contains the stories of the patriarchs, was not composed until after a long period of oral tradition.[2] This has led many scholars to treat the accounts in Genesis as unreliable to a considerable degree for the historical period which they describe. However, recent archaeological discoveries in Palestine reveal an extraordinary correspondence between the general cultural conditions portrayed in Genesis and those exposed by excavations. James Muilenberg points out the basic agreement between the archaeological "diggings" and the biblical materials:

> Pre-Mosaic religion has its home in Palestine. Only against the background of Canaanite religion are we able to make any estimate of the religion of the patriarchs. The biblical traditions of the book of Genesis do not suggest any sharp dif-

ference between the worship of the patriarchs and the worship of the Canaanites. The most telling witness of the inscriptions from widely separated places (Mari, Ras Shamra, Nuzi, Bogasköy, Tell el-Amarna, and elsewhere in Egypt) is in fundamental harmony with the Canaanite milieu and Canaanite character of the pre-Mosaic religion. All this is amply reinforced by the later biblical record (such as Deut. 26; Ezek. 16; the Priestly Code, etc.). Complex and late as our literary sources may be in their present form, the background against which Mosaic religion came into existence is without question Palestinian and Canaanite.[3]

The belief that trees were sacred was evidently a part of the Hebrew religion in the age of the patriarchs. Abraham received a divine manifestation in connection with the "terebinth of Moreh,"[4] an evergreen tree in Shechem which, from ancient times, had been regarded as a tree at which divine teaching was given. The terebinth of Mamre, in Hebron,[5] was a holy place where Abraham built an altar. The account of the divine appearance to Moses at the burning bush[6] shows that he regarded a tree, or tree-like plant, as the abode of the deity. One of the most instructive passages is II Samuel 5:23,24 (see also I Chronicles 14:15):

And when David inquired of the Lord, he said, "You shall not go up; go around to their rear and come upon them opposite the balsam trees. Then when you hear the sound of marching in the tops of the balsam trees, make haste, for at that moment the Lord has gone forth before you to fall upon the camp of the Philistines."[7]

Water was regarded as sacred by the Hebrews, especially springs, wells, and streams. The sanctuary in the desert, Kadesh, where the Hebrews stayed for a generation just before reentering Canaan was evidently selected because of the presence of an oracle well.[8] Several sacred wells are mentioned in th Old Testament; in one of the oldest fragments of poetry in the Bible, the well is addressed as if it were a living being.[9] Rivers were held in high esteem; the river Kishon was in all probability named after the god Kish.[10] Sanctuaries in the patriarchal period were often marked by sacred stones. At Bethel, Jacob took one of the stones of the place as a head rest; the next morning, he set it up as a sacred pillar, poured oil on it, and worshiped the deity he regarded as dwelling in the stone.[11] Cairns, or piles of stones, some times were regarded as personified witnesses of covenants between individuals.[12] "Ebenezer" means "stone of help;" there were two such stones mentioned in the Old Testament.[13]

Several mountains in Palestine were considered sacred. The most important was Sinai (Horeb),[14] a center of moon worship from very ancient times. Others were Nebo, Peor, Pisgah, Carmel, and the Mount of Olives. The sanctity of a mountain or hill was shown by the building of "high places" later as centers of worship in imitation of the mountain sanctuaries; perhaps this was the motive back of the construction of numerous "ziggurats," or towers, in the valley of the Tigris-Euphrates river.

There are remnants of totemism to be discerned in the Old Testament. The early Hebrews had many animal clan names and tribal names.[15] Sometimes they give evidence of believing themselves to be descended from a god; this is shown by the names compounded with a divine name.[16] There are indications of animal cults persisting into Old Testament times from an earlier totemistic stage; after referring to hints of this in Ezekiel 8:10,12 and in Isaiah 65:6 and 66:3,17, W. Robertson Smith concludes: "Here, therefore, we have a clear case of the re-emergence into the light of day of a cult of the most primitive totem type, which must have been kept alive in obscure circles of private or local superstition, and sprang up again on the ruins of the national faith, like some noxious weed in the courts of a desecrated temple."[17]

Among the Hebrews certain Semitic tabus persisted; in the Old Testament a good many things are "unclean," a ritual term for something that must not be touched or eaten. In Leviticus 11 and Deuteronomy 14:7-20 there are lists of animals which may not be eaten, probably those animals sacred to the heathens; the pig was tabu because it was the sacred animal of other cults, notably the Ashtart cult.[18] One of the most interesting stories of the strength of tabu is in II Samuel 6:6-10; while bringing the ark into the city of Jerusalem, Uzzah attempted to steady it; when he touched the sacred object, he was instantly stricken dead.[19]

Ancestor worship was evidently in vogue among the early Hebrews; this is shown by the reverence for graves which was common in the Old Testament.[20] It is also shown by the persistence of mourning customs which were roundly denounced by many of the later prophets and reformers.[21]

Religion in the patriarchal period, while it is still animistic, has moved along into a stage more correctly described as polytheism. The Hebrews then believed in a variety of supernatural beings, both benevolent and hostile; to them they had to make a very careful adjustment. Some of these spirits were in animal form, such as the seraphim, se'irim, and Azazel; others were in human form, as Lilith. Seraphim, literally "burning ones," were demons of the wilderness;[22] they were serpents, generally held by Semites as the incarnation of demons, who attacked the Hebrews in their wilderness wanderings.[23] In one direction these seraphim developed later into angelic beings.[24] The se'irim ("hairy ones") were originally gods worshiped in the form of he-goats; these degenerated into demons.[25] Azazel was originally a god of the flocks, for whom the ritual of the scape-goat in Leviticus 16:7-28 was performed; he became degraded later to the status of a demon and ended up as a synonym for Satan. Of the demons in human form, Lilith was regarded as one who flew at night, a sort of Lorelei who sought for her prey among unsuspecting males.

Necromancy persisted down into the Old Testament period and may well be considered an important part of the practice of the Hebrews during the period of the patriarchs.[26] The most obvious illustration of it is that of the witch of Endor, whom King Saul consulted in order to try and contact the spirit of Samuel.[27]

The Old Testament is full of examples of the use of magic as an attempt to placate the spirits and to secure blessings for those who made use of magical arts. Divination (Genesis 30:27; 44:5,15), sorcery (Exodus 22:18; Deuteronomy 18:10; II Kings 17:17), augury (II Kings 21:6; II Chronicles 33:6; Isaiah 2:6; Jeremiah 27:9; Micah 5:12), and witchcraft are condemned, bearing witness to the hold these practices had upon the common people. Rain-making by magical means is mentioned in I Samuel 12:16-18, I Kings 17:1, and I Kings 18:42-45. The story of the plagues visited on Egypt (Exodus 7:14-12:28) shows that Moses and Aaron were supplied with a much more potent magic than the professional magicians of Pharaoh's court. For King Saul, the music of David was regarded as having the magical power of driving away evil spirits or demons.[28]

For an understanding of Hebrew religion before the time of Moses, one of the most important Biblical passages is Exodus 6:2-4: "God spoke to Moses, saying to him, 'I am the Lord; I appeared to Abraham, Isaac, and Jacob as God Almighty ("El Shaddai"), but did not make myself known to them by my name Yahweh (the Lord)." This means that the religion of the patriarchs was an "El" religion. El was the chief god in the Canaanite pantheon; his name had existed in nine places in Canaan long before the Hebrews arrived there, such as Jezreel, Bethel, Penuel, etc. Muilenburg points out how similar the characteristics of El in Canaanite worship are to those of the El mentioned in the book of Genesis.[29] Among the Canaanites El was worshiped at Shechem, Jerusalem, Ugarit, and elsewhere; in Ugaritic poems he is described as dwelling in a distant cosmic locale, the "Source of the Two Deeps." "A developed cult of El Elyon which existed at Jerusalem has left its impress upon more than one Old Testament passage. . . . The chief interest in the cult represented by these various names (El Elyon, El Bethel, El Shaddai, El Roi, etc.) was in nature. The mystery of life as it manifested itself in the fertility of the soil was articulated in the worship on the *bâmôth* or high places. . . . Offerings and gifts were made on the high places and other sanctuaries, as at Bethel, Beersheba, Hebron, Shechem, and Jerusalem. Festivals were probably celebrated at certain seasons of the year, all of them nature celebrations. . . . The God pictured in Genesis is not like the God who reveals himself to Moses in the book of Exodus."[30]

And yet the Elohim of the book of Genesis, the gods of the fathers, are beginning to be differentiated from the gods of the Canaanites. Muilenburg follows Albrecht Alt (*Der Gott der Väter*, Stuttgart: W. Kohlhammer, 1929) in insisting that the tradition in Genesis has not only an original historical germ, but one which was also susceptible of further development.[31] Each of the patriarchs sees the deity revealed to him in a very special and a highly personal way; the names of the deities are directly connected with the patriarchs: the shield of Abraham (Genesis 15:1); the El "of my father," the El of Abraham, and the Awe of Isaac (Genesis 31:42); the El of Abraham and the El of Nahor (the gods of their ancestors) (Genesis 31:53), and the Mighty One of Jacob (Genesis 49:24). "These were family or clan gods with family names and associations in which the intimate relationships of the family (father, brother, etc.) were applied to the deities, as is reflected in many of the biblical names. They were personal gods and they bore the names of those to whom they first appeared: the God of Abraham, the God of Isaac, and the God of Jacob (Exod. 3:6). These were ancient tribal deities which later coalesced into one in the revelation to Moses."[32]

SUGGESTIONS FOR FURTHER STUDY

G. A. BUTTRICK, ed., *The Interpreter's Bible,* I, pp. 292-297.

F. C. EISELEN, E. LEWIS, AND D. G. DOWNEY, eds., *The Abingdon Bible Commentary,* pp. 165-166.

J. FINEGAN, *Light from the Ancient Past,* pp. 146-149.

E. W. K. MOULD, *Essentials of Bible History,* pp. 116-130.

W. O. E. OESTERLEY AND T. H. ROBINSON, *Hebrew Religion: Its Origin and Development,* pp. 18-127.

Chapter Seven

THE BIRTH OF THE HEBREW NATION:
MOSES AND THE EXODUS
FROM EGYPT

In spite of the fact that there is no archaeological evidence for the escape from Egyptian slavery of a group of Hebrews under the leadership of a man named Moses, there is good circumstantial evidence that the events recorded in the Book of Exodus are substantially correct. As we have seen,[1] some of the Hebrew tribes probably migrated to Egypt in connection with the Hyksos invasion toward the end of the eighteenth century B.C.; this was the sort of movement of peoples which had been occurring for centuries among the semi-nomadic Semitic tribes known as the Habiru. The favorable status of the Hebrews in Egypt under the Hyksos, as reflected in the Joseph stories in Genesis, came to an end in 1570 B.C. with the establishment of the powerful eighteenth dynasty and the eventual expulsion of the Hyksos. With the coming of the nineteenth dynasty in *ca.* 1350 B.C. the pharaohs of Egypt would have "had no knowledge of Joseph,"[2] and would have subjected the Hebrews to further oppression. Though there is some difference of opinion, the pharaoh of the exodus was probably Ramses II (*ca.* 1301-1234 B.C.).[3] if that is true, the exodus itself occurred *ca.* the year 1290 B.C.[4]

Growing fear that the Hebrews might be allies of an increasing number of Semite invaders from Palestine and the Arabian desert led the Egyptian pharaohs to take measures to curb their growing power; one of these was the killing of male Hebrew infants.[5] In this setting was born one of the most heroic figures in the history of the world, Moses. "No more illustrious name adorns

54

the pages of early history. Like Washington, he was the father of his nation. But he was more: judged by his influence upon future generations, he stands out as the greatest spiritual light in the history of antiquity."[6] As well as being the father of the Hebrew nation, he was the founder of the Hebrew faith, Jahwism, and the founder of the law. So great did he become in the estimate of later Jews that they ascribed to him the authorship of their earliest code of laws, the Book of the Covenant,[7] and, in fact, the entire Pentateuch.

The second chapter of Exodus tells the very beautiful story of the rescue of Moses and his adoption by the daughter of a pharaoh.[8] In spite of being reared at the royal court, he seems never to have forgotten his Hebrew ancestry. He is next presented as a grown man, murdering an Egyptian slave master and fleeing across the Sinai peninsula to the "land of Midian,"[9] which was located near the northern end of the Gulf of Akabah. There he became acquainted with a nomadic tribe, probably that of the Kenites, who were at the time making their home among some Midianites in the region near Mt. Sinai (Horeb).[10] He married the daughter of Jethro (Reuel), a priest, and settled down to a stable life as keeper of his flock. One day he led the flocks "to the western side of the desert, and came to the mountain of God, Horeb. Then the angel of the Lord appeared to him in a flame of fire, rising out of a bush."[11] This was a profound religious experience which led Moses to return to Egypt to lead his people from the oppression of the pharaoh. This experience marks the beginning of Jahwism, the religion of Israel, for God said to Moses:

> I am who I am, . . . Thus shall you say to the Israelites: " 'I am' has sent me to you." . . . Thus shall you say to the Israelites: "Yahweh (the Lord), the God of your fathers, the God of Abraham, Isaac, and Jacob, has sent me to you." This has always been my name, and this shall remain my title throughout the ages. Go and assemble the elders of Israel, and say to them, "The Lord, the God of your fathers, the God of Abraham, Isaac, and Jacob, has appeared to me. . . ."[12]

After receiving his divine commission Moses is joined by his brother Aaron and the two set off for Egypt to try and lead the Hebrew slaves in one of the greatest walk-outs in history. After receiving the approval of the leaders among the children of Israel,[13] the two brothers appear before pharaoh with a courteous but insistent request that the Hebrews be allowed to leave Egypt as a people to take part in a three days' celebration of an ancient religious festival;[14] if the pharaoh had granted this request, he would have been admitting what he had tried to get the Hebrew slaves to forget: that they were politically and culturally autonomous. Instead the pharaoh laid heavier work on the Hebrews, causing their own foremen to feel unkindly toward Moses and Aaron; then Moses turned to Jahweh in prayer and emerged from his meditation ready to grapple with the challenge.[15] Now there follows a series of calamities visited on the Egyptians which finally led to the pharaoh's reluctant consent and set the stage for the birth-night of the Hebrew nation.[16] Fleming James compares the account in Exodus with what has taken place in many a struggle of working people for better conditions:

First, the organizer comes in from the outside and forms the union; then a committee go to the management with their demands; these are curtly rejected; recognition of the union is denied; punitive pressure is applied to the workers in the form, let us say, of the "stretch-out," where the amount of work expected of each operative is increased; the union is thus proved powerless and the leaders discredited; the charge is made that the workers listen to the agitators because they have not enough to do. The workers then turn on the organizers and demand that they make good, and a grim fight ensues in which power is matched against power. Nor is the analogy fanciful for tradition insists that what Moses undertook to do was to emancipate a group of workers. No one need wonder therefore that throughout the Old Testament the successors of Moses were ever championing the poor, the oppressed, the foreigner. This was the bias which he imparted to Israel's religion and that bias still remains. The flaming social passion of many a modern Jew goes back all unconsciously to the man who dared to face the Pharaoh three thousand years ago.[17]

In the confusion attending the last of the plagues,[18] the Hebrews left Egypt in the night; so hurried was their departure that the last meal was composed of small cakes of unleavened bread. Tradition connects the institution of the Passover with this critical event; for pious Jews, this has always been a perpetual reminder of their miraculous deliverance from slavery and of their birth as a nation. The sacrificial lamb was symbolic of the suffering from which the Hebrew people had been freed; the cakes of unleavened bread represented the bitter years of their bondage in Egypt.

After the Israelites had been permitted to leave Egypt, the pharaoh changed his mind and dispatched a body of soldiers to bring them back. The fourteenth chapter of Exodus tells how the Egyptian soldiers overtook the fleeing Hebrews near a body of water called "the sea of reeds;"[19] then "the Lord moved the sea away by means of a strong east wind all night, and turned the sea into dry land. . . . The Israelites proceeded on dry ground. . . . As morning broke, . . . the water returned, and covered the chariotry and cavalry belonging to the whole army of Pharaoh. . . ."[20] The Israelites always looked back upon this apparently miraculous deliverance from the pursuing Egyptians as the birth night of a nation. The Song of Moses[21] is a national ode commemorating this great event; in all their history, the Israelites considered the exodus as a demonstration of Jahweh's presence with them.

The escape from Egypt was only preliminary to the work which Moses had cut out for him. His next task was to lead his people safely across the long distances of rock and sand characteristic of the Sinai peninsula toward the land of Midian.[22] This journey was beset with all kinds of hardships: food and water ran out; the tribesmen had to fight their wild desert kinsmen, the Amalekites; the people complained bitterly, some of them even longing for the advantages of Egypt. One of the significant episodes which occurred on the journey was the coming of Jethro to the Israelites to meet his son-in-law Moses; the account of this meeting in Exodus 18 seems to substantiate the claim of many scholars that Jahweh, the God whose name Moses had discovered in the "burning bush" episode, was the same as the god of the Kenites. Since Kenites and Israelites were distantly related, perhaps Israel under Moses recovered, in the religion known as Jahwism, what was originally part of a common possession.

Eventually Moses brought the children of Israel to the vicinity of the mountain of God, Sinai-Horeb. It was here that Moses accomplished the task of blending together into a single political unit the various tribes he had led out of Egypt; he wisely saw that the only force which could successfully do this would be that of a religious revolution. With the enactment of a solemn covenant Israel and Jahweh adopted each other; he became their god and they became his people.[23] This covenant was actualized in a ceremony in which, under the guidance of Moses, the people pledged their spiritual allegiance openly to Jahweh; a sacred meal was eaten by the leaders[24] and a blood covenant performed.[25] The covenant also resulted in a code of laws: though the decalogue itself[26] reflects conditions characteristic of the agricultural civilization of a later day in Palestine, it may contain some prescriptions which go back to Moses, and the Book of the Covenant,[27] with its humane spirit, is regarded by many scholars as the oldest codification of Hebrew law in existence, perhaps going back to Moses himself.

After about a year's stay near Sinai,[28] the Hebrew tribes became nomads again, wandering in the wilderness for a generation or more in search of adequate supplies for their flocks and herds and themselves. During the period of the wilderness wandering, their central rendezvous was Kadesh, at one and the same time an oasis and a sanctuary, the place where Moses and Jethro set up a scheme of social administration for the Hebrew tribes.

Moses considered advancing directly into Palestine from Kadesh, the distance northward from Kadesh being less than a hundred miles. But of the twelve spies he sent to survey the situation, only Caleb and Joshua brought back a favorable report.[29] The people made a belated and half-hearted attempt to enter Palestine from the south, but were decisively repulsed.[30] Next, they tried to go through the territory of Edom, hoping to get east of the Dead Sea and enter Palestine from a point north of that sea from which they could cross the Jordan River into Palestine; but the king of Edom was in no mood to cooperate.[31] So they were forced to move southward toward the head of the Gulf of Akabah, and thence northward on the east side of the Mount Seir range into the land of Moab. Various warlike tribes tried to oppose their progress, but eventually they "camped in the steppes of Moab on the other side of the Jordan at Jericho."[32] It was here that Moses died, and Hebrew leadership passed to Joshua.

In Moses we meet "the first of the truly great ones of Israel. Of all the forces,—economic, political, and social—which helped to shape the history of the Hebrews in this period, the greatest was the genius of Moses. He was the real creator of the Hebrew nation and the founder of the Hebrew faith. He has through the ages been revered as the lawgiver of Israel and the first of the prophets. He was 'the man of God'[33] and the statement, 'there hath not arisen a prophet since in Israel like unto Moses, whom Yahweh knew face to face,'[34] accurately represents Hebrew sentiment in later centuries. . . .'[35]

SUGGESTIONS FOR FURTHER STUDY

W. F. Albright, "The Biblical Period," in L. Finkelstein, ed., *The Jews: Their History, Culture, and Religion*, pp. 6-13.

A. E. Bailey, *Daily Life in Bible Times*, pp. 56-95.

A. E. Bailey and C. F. Kent, *History of the Hebrew Commonwealth*, pp. 25-46.

G. A. Barton, *Archaeology and the Bible*, pp. 375-426.

H. M. Battenhouse, *The Bible Unlocked*, pp. 80-96.

M. Buber, *Moses.*

G. A. Buttrick, ed., *The Interpreter's Bible*, I, pp. 273-275, 833-843.

F. C. Eiselen, E. Lewis, and D. G. Downey, eds., *The Abingdon Bible Commentary*, pp. 61, 62, 249-252.

J. Finegan, *Light from the Ancient Past*, pp. 105-109, 129-133.

F. James, *Personalities of the Old Testament*, pp. 1-44.

C. S. Knopf, *The Old Testament Speaks*, pp. 76-98.

E. W. K. Mould, *Essentials of Bible History*, pp. 96-106.

H. C. Snell, *Ancient Israel: Its Story and Meaning*, pp. 12-33.

Chapter Eight

RELIGION IN THE MOSAIC AGE

Because of the contribution of Moses in introducing the Hebrew tribes who were in slavery in Egypt to a new name for God, Jahweh, the religion of the time of Moses has been designated as Jahwism. Many of the religious beliefs and practices which characterized the Hebrews before Moses persisted,[1] along with many survivals of primitive animism, but there are so many new and creative factors in Hebrew religion as a result of the life and work of Moses that the religion of his times may well be regarded as the beginning of that which later became distinctive in Judaism. The religion which Moses proclaimed was not monotheism but henotheism, or monolatry; Jahweh was to be worshiped by the children of Israel to the exclusion, as far as they were concerned, of all other deities, but there was no thought of denying the reality and existence of other deities. Other peoples had their gods—Dagon for the Philistines, Chemosh for the Moabites, Ashur for the Assyrians, Marduk for the Babylonians, etc.—but for the Hebrews the one and only god was Jahweh.[2]

Though Moses may have gained a great deal from the religion of Egypt while he was being brought up in the court of the pharaoh,[3] the name and characteristics of the God whom he discovered in the desert of Midian were those of a Kenite deity;[4] Jahweh had had an independent existence before his adoption of Israel as his people. When this god manifested himself to Moses in the theophany of the burning bush Moses was convinced that he was the same god who had called upon Abraham in Harran and had been with Isaac and Jacob. When Moses successfully led the Israelites out of Egypt into the region near the mountain sacred to Jahweh (Sinai-Horeb), they gave this god recognition as their deliverer and entered into a covenantal relationship with him.

What were the characteristics of Jahweh in the Mosaic period? James Muilenburg believes that the most striking aspect of his nature is his holiness. "He is a zealous, jealous mighty God who thunders with his voice and sends forth lightning and fire. There is something fearful, terrifying, even demonic in him. The whole mountain quakes at his descent, and the people tremble before the awfulness of the theophany. This utterly holy character of Yahweh makes him and everything associated with him taboo."[5] In contrast with the nature gods of the Semite world, Jahweh had no feminine consort at his side; no other god is to be worshiped beside him. He demands an exclusive worship; everywhere else it was the common belief that the more gods one worshiped the better. He will not tolerate any likeness of himself, at least none which bears the mark of human handiwork;[6] he is invisible to human eyes.

Jahweh was a mountain god,[7] a nature deity, manifesting himself in the volcanic activity of the mountain,[8] and in the storm, earthquake, and wind which raged upon the mountain.[9] He was conceived as a fire god, revealing himself in a burning bush[10] and in a "pillar of fire" guiding the wanderers in the wilderness.[11] He was a wilderness guide.[12] As a god of war, he helped the Israelites to victory over their enemies.[13]

While in the wilderness the Israelites developed two new features of their worship. The first was the result of the problem of finding a means of communication with Jahweh after they left Sinai. When they were near the mountain, Moses climbed it and God talked to him; when they began to wander again they provided a portable meeting-place for Jahweh and his people, the so-called "tent of meeting."[14] It was pitched just outside the camp by a special group of ritualistically proper persons, members of the tribe of Levi, from whom, according to tradition, came the priests of later days.

Within the tent of meeting was placed the Ark of the Covenant. Evidently it was a box, or chest, carried by the Israelites all through their wilderness wanderings, entering Canaan with them, and finally coming to rest in the temple built by Solomon in Jerusalem. But what was in the ark, what its function was, and what it signified to those for whom it was a very sacred and holy object are matters of conjecture. It was certainly closely connected with Jahweh himself; perhaps it was considered the throne of this invisible god, or perhaps it contained some object or objects of a sacred nature.[15] It was used as an instrument for discovering the will of Jahweh; the stones in it may have come from Mount Sinai and thus signified his presence with his people. It became a tabu; it was such a holy object that only the priests were allowed to touch it, for fear of being killed by its mystic power.

In connection with the tent of meeting and the ark, a special group of Israelites was set aside for a special function—to care for the shrine of the deity and to perform ritualistic services in front of the sacred box. This group became the priesthood; it was the duty of the priests to care for the sacred emblems, to regulate the approach of the devout worshipers of Jahweh, and to interpret his will to those who came to inquire what it was. Old Testament traditions as a whole connect the origin of the priesthood with Moses and Aaron.[16] The Hebrews came to Moses and the later priests not only with religious problems but also with affairs of a social nature; decisions were made by the priests through the use of the sacred lot as an indication of the will of Jahweh. The objects used in this process were the "Urim" and "Thummim" and the "ephod." Just how these objects were used is not known; the "ephod" seems to have been a sort of apron worn by the priest, in the pockets of which the sacred stones were kept.[17] Ritual requirements for the ordinary worshiper at the time of Moses were very simple, in contrast with the elaborate and costly ceremonies of later Israel.[18] It was probably in the wilderness period that the primitive nomad festival of Pesach was merged with the Passover: Exodus 12:21-27 gives the earlier and simpler form of the celebration, while Exodus 12:1-20 gives the regulations in force some years later.

Without doubt, many of the decisions made in the tent of meeting would be ethical in character; it was this factor which made Hebrew religion unique in the ancient world. All through the history of Israel there persisted the tradition that Jahweh demanded high moral standards of his followers. These standards are embodied in the ten commandments; whether in their present form they are as old as Moses is unknown, but they do represent rather fairly the general moral standard characteristic of the Israelites in the days preceding the conquest of Canaan. To the nomad purity of blood and sanctity of life were matters fundamental to the tribe; the former was safeguarded by the seventh commandment

(Exodus 20:14) and the latter by the sixth (Exodus 20:13). In addition, the Israelites possessed a very strong respect for tradition, for the standing and authority of the elders of the tribe; this was embodied in the fifth commandment (Exodus 20:12). In summary, Mould lists the virtues of the Hebrew nomads:

> . . . Notable among their virtues were: (1) Loyalty to one's own family, or clan, no doubt often solidified by group conflicts. Such loyalty was probably accompanied by a spirit of vengeance, at times raw and unrestrained. Such loyalty meant (2) the readiness of the individual to sacrifice himself for the accepted group *mores.* Josh. 7 is a dramatic picture of group *mores* in action. (3) Fidelity to a covenant. (4) Courage in war. (5) Hospitality. (6) Generosity. (7) An elemental, but strongly felt sense of justice. (8) Integrity of character and devotion to the people's welfare on the part of the men who judged their fellows (Exodus 18:21). (9) Temperance in matters of sex, due no doubt to the physically exacting character of desert life, which is free from the temptations that accompany the more complex and luxurious life of settled agriculturist and commercial communities.
>
> All these moral virtues were regarded as necessary accompaniments of the one supreme religious virtue, i.e., exclusive devotion to Yahweh their God and fidelity to the Sinai covenant.[19]

Mosaic religion may thus be seen as a transition from the primitive to the more developed ethical type of religion. But, as has always been the case in the history of religions, the people were not prepared for the practice of Jahwism in its purity. This is illustrated by the story of the apostasy of Aaron at the foot of Mount Sinai; a molten image of a calf was fashioned and the people worshiped it (Exodus 32). This was roundly condemned by Moses, but it became a precedent for the institution of bull worship later in the northern kingdom.[20]

Another incident which may reflect the vestige of a more primitive belief was the fashioning of a bronze serpent by Moses for the purpose of curing the Israelites of snake bite.[21] This sacred object was carried by the people wherever they went and was set up in the courtyard when the temple was built by Solomon, where it stayed until taken down by the order of the reforming king Hezekiah.[22]

SUGGESTIONS FOR FURTHER STUDY

G. A. Buttrick, ed., *The Interpreter's Bible,* I, pp. 297-305.

F. C. Eiselen, E. Lewis, and D. G. Downey, eds., *The Abingdon Bible Commentary,* p. 166.

J. Finegan, *Light from the Ancient Past,* p. 142.

H. T. Fowler, *The Origin and Growth of the Hebrew Religion,* pp. 23-35.

C. S. Knopf, *The Old Testament Speaks,* pp. 91-98.

E. W. K. Mould, *Essentials of Bible History,* pp. 130-136.

J. B. Noss, *Man's Religions,* pp. 481-489.

W. O. E. Oesterley and T. H. Robinson, *Hebrew Religion: Its Origin and Development,* pp. 110-115, 134-153.

H. H. Rowley, *The Re-discovery of the Old Testament,* pp. 108-124.

E. D. Soper, *The Religions of Mankind,* pp. 270-272.

Chapter Nine

THE CONQUEST OF CANAAN

When Moses died the Israelites were on the eastern border of the land of Canaan, a territory they believed had been promised to them by Jahweh himself. Their next objective was the conquest and settlement of this land. In spite of the fact that this period was one of the most formative in the history of the Hebrew people, it is one of the most difficult ones to reconstruct. It is not possible to work out the precise order of events nor to speak with any accuracy of specific dates; it was a process which took many years. If we accept the traditional view of the length of the wilderness wanderings as forty years, the Israelites entered Canaan *ca.* 1250 B.C., but it was not until the times of Samuel (he crowned Saul the first king *ca.* 1020 B.C.) that the country may be said to have been under the control of the Hebrews and it was not until the reign of David (*ca.* 1004-961 B.C.) that the last vestige of Philistine and Canaanite opposition was successfully met.

There are several reasons why the period is a difficult one to reconstruct. In the first place, the Biblical materials (Joshua, Judges, and I Samuel) relating to the conquest were not written as history, though there is often good historical material in them; the writers, working under the influence of the Deuteronomic reform (621 B.C.) were apologists rather than historians; they selected incidents which would support their contention that the Hebrew tribes should never have made friendships with the original inhabitants of Canaan, but should have annihilated them and their religion. The philosophy of history which motivated these men is described in Judges 2:11-14 (and repeated in Judges 3:7,12; 4:1; and 6:1):

Then the Israelites did what was evil in the sight of the Lord, by serving the Baals and forsaking the Lord, the God of their fathers, who had brought them out of the land of Egypt, and by running after alien gods, from among the gods of the peoples that surrounded them, and by paying homage to them, so that they provoked the Lord to jealousy. Thus they forsook the Lord, and served the Baals and Ashtarts. Then the anger of the Lord blazed against Israel, so that he delivered them into the power of plunderers who plundered them, and he sold them into the power of their enemies around them, so that they were no longer able to withstand their enemies.

The second reason for the difficulty is that the authors of the books of Joshua, Judges, and I Samuel were not the originators of many of the stories; these they took either from oral tradition or earlier written works, now lost, and added to them their theological interpretations. "Thus, the vivid, spectacular, exciting exploits of the heroes and heroines of these books are probably very old stories, which some scholars think almost contemporaneous accounts. But the explanations that victory or defeat, peace or war, followed inexorably and immediately upon undivided loyalty to Yahweh or worship of the Canaanite gods is the work of the later writer."[1]

A third reason is the sharp contrast between the books of Joshua and Judges as to the nature of the conquest. The book of Joshua represents the conquest as an enterprise quickly completed; under the leadership of the vigorous Joshua, Jericho is taken and the entire southern part of Palestine is brought under the control of the Hebrews.[2] The book of Judges, on the other hand, pictures it as a gradual process, carried on by groups acting more or less independently over a long period of time. It is the latter approach to the subject which is more in harmony with the recent finds of archaeological research. Excavations at Jericho, Ai, and Hazor, the discovery of the Tell-el-Amarna correspondence in Egypt, the recovery of Hittite archives from Asia Minor and the Nuzi texts from the upper Euphrates valley, and the study of the ancient Assyrian Code of Laws have all added to our information and understanding of the period of the conquest.

From all sources, one might well conclude that the seminomadic Israelite tribes entering Palestine found many people there ahead of them—Canaanites, Amorites, Hittites, Philistines, etc.—and that the process of settlement of the land was by infiltration and inter-marriage as well as by military campaigns. The Israelites were not united to enter Canaan in one sudden "blitzkrieg;" the conquest was the work of various tribes or groups of tribes at various times.

Chief of all the foes to threaten Israel after she had gained a precarious footing in Palestine were the Philistines; it was not until they had been mastered by Saul and David that the period of the conquest may be said to be over.

In attempting to overthrow and dispossess the people who were already in the land of Canaan, particularly the Amorites and the Canaanites, the Israelites were attacking a people on a higher level of civilization, with greater resources in material and in military art. Thus, at first, the invading nomads were able only to master the hill country and the poorer parts of the land. For many generations there were just three sections of Palestine under Hebrew control: Hebron and the surrounding territory in the south, the center of the tribe of Judah and a place which may have been inhabited by Hebrews who did not go to Egypt; settlements about Bethel in the center; and a home for some of the tribes among the southern foothills of the Lebanon range.[3] And yet, in spite of the superiority of their foes, the Israelites were ultimately successful in winning the land. Dr. Mould lists four reasons why the Hebrew invaders were successful:

. . . (1) The power of the Canaanites to resist invasion was at a minimum. Just prior to the Hebrew invasion, Canaan had been the scene of a devastating war between Egyptians and Hittites in which the nineteenth dynasty Egyptians were endeavoring to win back the territory in Palestine and Syria which had been lost by the impotent monarchs of the closing years of the eighteenth dynasty. This war, incidentally, left the Canaanites so weakened that they could offer no forceful resistance to the determined invaders.[4] Moreover, the Philistines had since 1196 B.C. been pressing in upon Canaan, settling the coastal plain, and giving the Canaanites added trouble at the very time the Hebrew tribesmen were pushing in from the east. And of course the Canaanite princes were always engaged in feuds among themselves. (2) The Hebrews used tactics which rendered the Canaanite chariots and heavy armor worse than useless, for they refused to fight except in rough, broken territory where ambush and sudden raid could be most successfully employed. (3) Few Canaanites lived in the hill region and the dwellers on the plains were only remotely concerned about what went on in the mountains. . . . (4) None of the great powers was in a position to interfere with Canaan. The Hittite war had been disastrous for all concerned.

The Hittites retreated to the north. Egypt's days of aggression were over. Assyria did show her teeth when Tiglath-pileser I (*circa* 1115-1102) made an advance as far west as Phoenicia (1104 B.C.), but for two centuries after that there was no further show of aggression in the west. Thus all factors in the situation were favorable to the Hebrews.[5]

The conquest of Canaan affected profoundly the way of life of the Hebrews. They gave up their seminomadic life of the desert to become farmers in the oasis of Palestine. From the relative obscurity of the desert they became inhabitants of a great international corridor, a land-bridge between two continents. In the course of time, they gave up their relatively simple tribal organization to adopt one more like that of the Canaanites: a sort of confederation of city-states; in time this led to the monarchy. The clash and fusion of Hebrew and Canaanite transformed Hebrew religion for all time.

The religion of Canaan before the Israelite invasion was Baalism. Originally the Baals were spirits closely associated with the soil, local deities attached to the land rather than to clans. The word "Baal" (plural "Baalim") means "lord" or "owner"; Canaanites believed every spot of fertile ground owed its fertility to the fact that a supernatural being dwelt there and made it what it was. The "Baal" was considered the owner of the property, the lord of his domain. This lord would withhold his gifts from those who refused to recognize his lordship and denied him his due loyalty. Baalism was in a stage of degeneracy toward the end of the second millennium, as evidenced in the cult of ritualistic prostitution and sacrifice of infants.[6] The numerous baals each had their places of worship—on the hilltops, in the valleys, at springs, or at wells; each city built a sanctuary on elevated ground in honor of its patron baal. The priests in charge of these "high places" conducted the worship in an open-air court facing the shrine of the god. There would be an image of the god in the center and a stone pillar, or "mazzebah", near the altar outside. Perhaps there would also be a wooden pole or column, called the "asherah", representing the god's consort ("baalah"). Bull images and bronze snakes[7] were also popular representations of the fertility power of the god. Sacrifices were offered at the shrines and three festivals were observed, in spring, early summer, and fall, all giving prominence to

Astarte, the sister of Baal and the goddess of fertility. It was in connection with Astarte that the Canaanites practiced temple prostitution. "In the divine marriage between Astarte and Baal, which the Canaanites celebrated in the autumn, she was literally the soil become a wife, and he was the husband of the land who fertilized her."[8]

How would the culture and religion of Canaan affect the religion of the Israelite invaders? Here is an imaginary example:

A Hebrew stakes out a claim in the hollow to the south of Bethel and begins to till the soil. He buys or steals his seed from a Canaanite neighbor, sows it by guess, and sits down to wait for the harvest. Somehow the harvest does not come; the grain turns yellow before it heads. He goes anxiously to his Canaanite friend, who asks him: "Did you make sacrifices to the Baal who owns the field and lives in the big tree at the end of it?" The Hebrew confesses that since he is a Jehovah-worshiper he did not. Whereupon he is told that he may expect no crops till he sacrifices to Baal. Not being rich enough to stand a second loss, he takes his friend's advice next season, allows the Canaanite to teach him the correct method of worship and incidentally to give him some valuable points on how and when to sow and how to take care of his field. Next harvest-time there is a bumper crop. The Hebrew shows his joy by buying the Canaanite's daughter as a wife for his son, and by becoming a constant worshiper at the Baal-tree. Of course he worships Jehovah, too, for old time's sake; but he understands that the god whom it pays to cultivate, now that he has become a farmer, is Baal.[9]

There were those among the Hebrews, such as the Nazirites and the Rechabites, who refused to accept Baalism. There were others who found it natural to acknowledge agricultural divinities in an agricultural territory. Neither extreme was to be permanent. At times it seemed as if the Canaanite deities would be supreme; at other times the Hebrew tribes went back to Jahwism. But "ultimately Yahweh displaced the Canaanite deities at these shrines, and thus the people came slowly to think of him and to worship him in connection with the personal and local affairs of their daily life. It was impossible for the mass of the people even to come to know the great and awful Deity of Sinai's thunder clouds, the God of all Israel, as concerned in their ordinary life and industry, except by the road they traveled of first mingling with his worship that of the agricultural Canaanites."[10]   Thus gradually did the conviction arise among the Israelites that the Jahweh whom Moses had contacted on Sinai also controlled the processes of agriculture, that he could well become the god of the soil of Palestine. Jahweh eventually became the sole object of worship, but all the titles and attributes of the baals were transferred to him.

Many of the sanctuaries where Jahweh was worshiped during the period of the conquest and settlement of Canaan were taken over from the native inhabitants. Of these, the two greatest were Shechem and Shiloh. Shechem had long been Canaanite; here there was a temple to their god, Baal-berith ("Lord of the Covenant"); here, according to Joshua 24, a covenant was established, laws promulgated, and a union consummated among some of the Hebrew tribes.[11] At Shiloh, the Ark of the Covenant was brought; here Eli was the head of the sanctuary, and worship was observed with elaborate cultic sacrifices.[12] At another sanctuary in the far north, Dan, the priests there claimed continuity with Moses. In this period the Levites emerge as a priestly class.

During the period of the conquest political leadership among the Hebrew tribes was in the hands of "judges;"[13] though they may at times have adjudicated disputes, their function was much wider than that. They were men who felt themselves called to the leadership of their people in times of disaster. It is impossible to determine the dates of these leaders or the order in which we should study them; the authors of the book of Judges seem to have selected their stories as samples taken from each section of Palestine and in connection with each of the enemy peoples who opposed the Hebrew settlement in the land. For example, Deborah and Barak are in the north where they stir a few of the tribes to fight the Canaanites under Sisera.[14] Gideon is associated with central Canaan, where he repels a Midianite invasion.[15] To the East of the Jordan, Othniel expelled the Arameans,[16] Jephthah suppressed the Ammonites,[17] and Ehud, the left-handed Benjaminite, freed the Hebrews from the Moabites.[18] In the southwest, the enemy is the Philistine race: Shamgar[19] and Samson are concerned with meeting aggression from that direction.[20] All of these enemies were successfully defeated except for the Philistines; the seriousness of their threat to the Hebrews is indicated by their capture of the Ark of the Covenant at Ebenezer (I Samuel 4) and the probable resultant destruction of the shrine at Shiloh (Jeremiah 7:12). The presence of the Philistine menace made a final unification of the tribes imperative, and the monarchy was the result.

Though we may not speak with any degree of certainty of any extended literary works among the Hebrews before the monarchy, it was during the period of the conquest that many of the songs and stories which had been handed down orally from generation to generation found their way into their first literary form. Probably the earliest books of Hebrew literature of which we have any record were two collections of poems called the "Book of the Wars of Jahweh" and the "Book of Jashar;" both of these are no longer extant, but some of the material from them is quoted in the later Old Testament literature.[21] Imbedded in the Old Testament books from Genesis through II Samuel are lyric songs, didactic, prophetic, and cultic poems, proverbs, riddles, and wise sayings.

One of the most ancient bits of poetry in the Old Testament, in spirit if not in age, is the Song of Lamech, breathing a spirit of primitive thirst for revenge and brutal boastfulness:

> Adah and Zillah, hear my voice,
> You wives of Lamech, give ear to my words:
> I kill a man for wounding me,
> And a boy for striking me.
> If Cain is to be avenged sevenfold,
> Then Lamech seventy and seven fold![22]

Perhaps as old as the time of Moses is the Song of Miriam.[23] "A much later poet worked it out in more detail, beginning with this same refrain but unfolding its theme at length, and then attributing the whole not to Miriam but to Moses (Ex. 15:1ff.), the greater personality, as often happens in literary history."[24] Also of great antiquity are the Song to the Well,[25] and the Song of Deborah.[26] Perhaps the oldest proverb that has come down to us in poetic form is the one which David quoted:

> Out of the wicked comes wickedness,
>   But my hand shall not be against you.[27]

Riddles were popular among the invading Israelites; the one Samson propounded at his wedding may have been in circulation when he lived:

> Out of the eater came something to eat,
> And out of the strong came something sweet.[28]

SUGGESTIONS FOR FURTHER STUDY

W. F. ALBRIGHT, "The Biblical Period," in L. Finklestein, ed., *The Jews: Their History, Culture, and Religion,* pp. 13-23.

A. E. BAILEY, *Daily Life in Bible Times,* pp. 113-143.

A. E. BAILEY AND C. F. KENT, *History of the Hebrew Commonwealth,* pp. 59-84.

G. A. BARTON, *Archaeology and the Bible,* pp. 449-454.

H. M. BATTENHOUSE, *The Bible Unlocked,* pp. 97-111.

J. A. BEWER, *The Literature of the Old Testament,* pp. 1-15.

G. A. BUTTRICK, ed., *The Interpreter's Bible,* I, pp. 175-178, 275-279, 305-310; II, pp. 539-852.

F. C. EISELEN, E. LEWIS, AND D. G. DOWNEY, eds., *The Abingdon Bible Commentary,* pp. 62, 63, 166, 167.

J. FINEGAN, *Light from the Ancient Past,* pp. 133-149.

H. T. FOWLER, *The Origin and Growth of the Hebrew Religion,* pp. 36-50.

C. S. KNOPF, *The Old Testament Speaks,* pp. 98-130.

E. W. K. MOULD, *Essentials of Bible History,* pp. 137-164, 170-184.

J. B. NOSS, *Man's Religions,* pp. 489-496.

W. O. E. OESTERLEY AND T. H. ROBINSON, *Hebrew Religion: Its Origin and Development,* pp. 122-127, 154-174.

H. C. SNELL, *Ancient Israel: Its Story and Meaning,* pp. 34-51.

Chapter Ten

THE UNITED KINGDOM

A. *Samuel, Saul, David, and Solomon.*

The transition between the rather chaotic and disunited condition of the Hebrew tribes during the period of the conquest of Canaan to the more settled aspect of the monarchy is evident in the life of Samuel. One of the great characters of Hebrew history, Samuel has been called the "last of the champions," seer, prophet, priest, and maker of kings. He was held in honor by the Hebrews of central Canaan. Dedicated by his pious mother Hannah to the service of Jahweh, Samuel was brought up in the company of Eli the priest at the sanctuary of Shiloh.[1] In spite of the crushing defeat of Israel by the Philistines, in which the Ark of the Covenant was captured,[2] the death of Eli and his two sons, and the complete destruction of Shiloh,[3] Samuel seems never to have lost his faith in Jahweh. From his new residence at Ramah, he was the only bond of union holding the embattled Israelites together.[4] His chief concern was that Israel should be freed from the Philistines; it was this need, plus the worthlessness of his own sons,[5] which led his fellow countrymen to request a king. "The Philistine victories brought it home to the Hebrews that only by thorough organization and strong leadership could they hope to cope with their foes. It now became evident that either the Hebrews must get together against the efficiently organized Philistines or face complete and permanent subjugation. They determined upon national unity under a king."[6] It was a critical time for the religion of Jahwism; the capture of the ark meant that Jahweh had been vanquished by the Philistine god Dagon. Had it not been for the counter disasters which befell the Philistines,[7] faith in Jahweh might well have been permanently impaired.

Samuel's principal achievement was the inauguration of the Hebrew monarchy; he selected and anointed both Saul and David. In the Bible there are two contrasting and seemingly contradictory views of the establishment of the monarchy; a later historian, a member of the Deuteronomic reform party who wrote just before 621 B.C., thinking of the despotism of some of the kings, such as Solomon and Ahab, considered the monarchy a retrogression from the democratic freedom of Israel's early days;[8] the earlier writer represents the selection of a king as a real forward step, taken with the full approval of, and indeed upon the initiative of, Samuel.[9] These two points of view have been blended into one story. Samuel's first choice was Saul, son of Kish, of the tribe of Benjamin; in spite of Samuel's reluctant support, many of the Israelites withheld their allegiance and did not accept Saul as king until he had shown himself to be a successful military leader.

Saul's first act was the relief of Jabesh-gilead from a threatened attack by the Ammonites;[10] his success increased his prestige at home and secured for him a valuable military base to the east of the Jordan River. Then he could go to the sanctuary of Gilgal and be anointed king by Samuel before his followers,[11] because he had fulfilled the requirements stated in I Samuel 8:20:

> . . . There shall be a king over us, that we also may be like all the nations, and that our king may judge us and go forth before us and fight our battles.

The Philistines may have looked upon Saul as a local ruler under their authority; they had posts in various places among the central hills and government officials at various spots. Conflict between the Hebrews and the Philistines was begun when Jonathan, Saul's son, killed an official at Gibeah,[12] later Saul's capital; this fired the reluctant Hebrew forces with renewed vigor and, taking advantage of a reduced garrison at the Philistine stronghold of Michmash, they attacked and drove the Philistines back to the coastal plain.[13] Thus, Saul's authority was complete in the central highlands and to the east of the Jordan River, but he was never able to conquer the area around Jerusalem nor the Plain of Esdraelon. Though Saul (ca. 1020-1004 B.C.) made a good beginning toward the political unification of the Hebrew tribes, his reign was little more than that of a powerful military chieftain.

Saul got along fairly well as long as he had the support of Samuel, but the time came when the two disagreed.[14] No king could long remain in power in those days with the chief religious leader against him; Samuel showed his dislike for Saul by selecting a new king from the tribe of Judah, David the Bethlehemite.[15] From then on Saul's life deteriorated rapidly; his hatred for David, who had been brought to the royal court as a harpist, is portrayed in I Samuel 18-24, 26. When the Philistines resumed their aggressive efforts to resubjugate the Hebrews, they moved in from the north, having mastered the Plain of Esdraelon. With David an outlaw,[16] Saul was no match for his enemies; at the battle of Gilboa, the Hebrew army was defeated and both Saul and Jonathan were killed.[17]

The real unity of the Hebrews in Palestine begins with David. The successor of Saul was destined to bring Israel to the height of its political power and to found a dynasty that would endure for four hundred years. So many memories have been preserved around his name that we have more material about him, both legendary and historical, than any other character in the Old Testament, except Jeremiah. In spite of his faults, which are plainly apparent in the Old Testament record of his life, he became to later generations of Israelites the ideal king; in their periods of national despair they looked to his return, either in his own person or in a mighty "son," to deliver the nation from oppression and make it supreme over the nations. "No more romantic story is to be found in the world's literature than that of the shepherd boy of Bethlehem who won a king's favor, then lost it and became a hunted outlaw, only to be made king himself and to place his little people on a proud imperial height; then sinned deeply and saw nemesis work itself out in his house till he died a heart-broken old man in the midst of the splendor he had created. It is no wonder, as Kittel says (*Great Men and Movements in Israel*, N.Y.: Macmillan, 1929), that the minstrels and storytellers of Israel delighted to tell of him."[18]

Anointed by Samuel as the next king, David appears at Saul's court as a musician, called upon to play his harp to restore balance to the deranged mind of King Saul. Revealing his military prowess by daring exploits against the Philistines in the Shephelah region,[19] David became a great favorite of the king, a firm friend of the king's son Jonathan, and a darling of the populace.[20] However,

Saul's favor soon changed to insane jealousy, and he sought to kill him; giving him the seemingly impossible task of killing a hundred Philistines, the king was forced to give his daughter Michal to David in marriage when the latter was successful. This only added fear to jealousy; David was finally compelled to flee the court for his life. For several years David lived as an outlaw in the Negeb, in the wilderness of Judea, and in the Shephelah. To escape Saul's wrath, David and his followers attached themselves to the Philistines; fortunately for both David and the Philistines, he did not take part in any military action as their ally.[21]

When Saul died, the people of Judah called upon David to be their king.[22] The city of Hebron became his capital, and for seven and a half years his rule was confined to the area surrounding Hebron. The people of central Canaan turned to one of Saul's sons, Ishbaal,[23] as their ruler; his capital was Mahanaim in Gilead, east of the Jordan. Warfare raged between these two petty principalities until the death of Ishbaal; this must have pleased the Philistines, of whom both David and Ishbaal were probably vassals. When Ishbaal died, Saul's family line came to an end; representatives from all the tribes went to Hebron and asked David to be their king, but not without conditions:

> Then all the tribes of Israel came to David to Hebron and said as follows: "Behold, we are your bone and your flesh. Also formerly when Saul was king over us, it was you who led out and brought in Israel, and the Lord said to you, 'You shall shepherd my people Israel, and you shall be a leader over Israel.' " So all the elders of Israel came to the king at Hebron, and King David made a covenant with them in Hebron before the Lord, and they anointed David king over Israel.[24]

As soon as David was king over all the tribes, the Philistines launched an attack, and were promptly defeated. In fact, David put an end once and for all to the Philistine menace.[25]

Now David could turn his attention to consolidating and expanding his kingdom. One of the first things he did was to capture the city of Jerusalem from the Jebusites and make that his capital city.[26] This was a very wise move; Hebron would never have made a satisfactory capital over all of Palestine because it was too far south and not adequately defensible from military attack. Jerusalem was on neutral ground between the powerful tribe of Judah in the south and the equally strong tribes in the north; since it had never been under the control of any of the Israelite tribes, it became the "city of David," and was peopled largely by his personal retainers. Albright speaks of this act of David as "sheer political genius."[27] Through conquests over the Edomites, Moabites, Ammonites, Arameans, and Philistines, David extended the nominal boundaries of his kingdom as far north as central Syria and as far east as the valley of the Euphrates; his kingdom was the nearest approach ever made to the development of an empire in the western horn of the fertile crescent. David's realm constituted the greatest political state the Hebrews ever had; never again were they destined to rule as extensive an area with as strong a sense of security.

King David did not neglect the internal organization of the government. He developed a highly organized system of internal administration. For foreign wars he relied on a kind of militia in which every Hebrew was bound to serve. In addition, he maintained a permanent military establishment, composed of professional soldiers, recruited for the most part from non-Israelites (particularly Philistines). To support these expenses, David took tribute from subject nations and developed some kind of local taxes. Mention is made in the Bible of certain important officials whom David appointed to administer affairs of state: the scribe, a sort of secretary of state who handled royal correspondence;[28] the recorder, evidently a sort of chancellor, to remind the king of affairs which needed his attention;[29] "the king's friend," a trusted adviser;[30] two high priests, evidently also officials of state;[31] an overseer of labor gangs;[32] the chief of staff of the army;[33] and the commander of the king's bodyguard of six hundred picked men.[34] In the villages and towns the elders still exercised a certain amount of local self-government, but the king had the power of changing local decisions; one of David's chief functions was as a judge in matters of sufficient importance to be brought before him.

In spite of the admirable qualities of David, which have been heralded in story and song, and in spite of the glory of his empire, there were sown in his reign the seeds which resulted later in dissension, division, and moral deterioration. Like many other leaders in history David lived too long; from a position where he was universally admired and loved he descended to a disappointed and lonely old age. David adopted many of the customs of the oriental monarchs around him. One of these was the institution of a harem; at Hebron he had six wives,[35] and at Jerusalem he took several others.[36] The harem inevitably became a hotbed of intrigue. Some of his wives were doubtless princesses from neighboring nations whom David wished to keep as allies; it was the custom in those days to make treaties of alliance between nations by intermarriage of members of royal families. Solomon carried this custom to such an extreme that it contributed to the disruption of the kingdom.

David's despotism was revealed in the sordid story of his adultery with Bathsheba and his murder of her husband, Uriah the Hittite.[37] In a very interesting way, C. S. Knopf treats this whole incident as a striking example of Hebrew dramatic writing, with a marvelous plot structure, literary power, and climactic objective.[38] This violation of the rights of the common man would have passed unnoticed in any other oriental kingdom, but in Israel it was a violation of the democratic and moral basis on which the kingdom had been founded. The prophet Nathan arose to champion the rights of the people and to condemn the king for his action; that the prophet was not executed immediately is evidence for the fact that the government of David was still regarded as a limited monarchy. The corrupting influence of the harem is further revealed in the realistic story of Amnon's crime against his half-sister Tamar and Absalom's murder of Amnon according to the ancient custom of blood revenge.[39] David's domestic difficulties assumed political proportions in the revolt of his beloved son Absalom;[40] this was the first of a series of rebellions which saddened David's later years. The final episode in the endless series of difficulties in David's harem was the struggle over the succession to the throne.[41] Joab and Abiathar favored David's oldest surviving son, Adonijah; Nathan, Zadok, Benaiah, and others favored Solomon, son of Bathsheba. In the battle of wits, Solomon and his supporters were successful; Solomon was installed as king while his father was still alive.

It is not easy to evaluate the permanent contribution of David, because of the wealth of legendary idealization that has grown around his name. But all can agree that next to Moses David was the greatest man Israel had yet produced. "He was the real creator of the monarchy. He perfected the Hebrew national unity. To be sure he also introduced the forces which ultimately destroyed that unity, but never was the nation so much of a unit as in David's day. In no small measure this was due to the charm and vigor of a winsome personality, which evoked loyalty among his followers. He was a man of force, and he was also, generally speaking, fair and just. He was an aggressive warrior. He silenced all the nation's foes, and pushed the domain of the Hebrews to the widest bounds it ever knew. Internally he perfected a strong, centralized government with a capital city which was a credit to the nation."[42]

Solomon succeeded to the throne left vacant by the death of his father David. An able ruler might have carried on the new Hebrew empire, but the young autocrat was quite unfit for the task. He began his reign with a baptism of blood;[43] Adonijah, Joab, and Shimei were murdered, and Abiathar was banished to Anathoth. Almost from the beginning of his reign, the empire began to shrink. Edom revolted first; then the Aramean kingdom of Damascus, under Rezon I, secured its independence.[44] To make up for the subsequent loss of income Solomon increased taxes and reduced to slavery the descendants of the Amorites, Hittites, and other non-Hebrew people who lived in Canaan.[45] He expanded David's system of national organization, but he sowed the seeds of discord by leaving Judah out of his scheme of dividing the country into twelve administrative districts for the purpose of taxation.

Solomon is best known by the magnificent building program he initiated in Jerusalem and at other strategic points throughout his kingdom. On a hill in the eastern section of the city of Jerusalem, Mount Moriah, Solomon constructed the most significant of all his buildings, a temple to Jahweh.[46] On the terraces below the temple there were the king's palace (on which he spent thirteen years), the palace for his chief wife, the daughter of an Egyptian pharaoh of the twenty-first dynasty, the house of the forest of Lebanon, the hall of pillars, and the throne hall.[47] He strengthened the defenses of Jerusalem and constructed six fortresses elsewhere. He built cities for his chariots and horses.[48] He engaged in extensive commercial enterprises which brought in great wealth. He established a merchant marine in the Red Sea, with its base at Elath, at the head of the Gulf of Akabah, and hired Phoenician sailors to man the ships.[49] He supervised the mining of copper (and probably iron) from ore in the land of Edom, arranging for the ore to be hauled to and refined in a smelter at the head of the Gulf of Akabah.[50]

Far more than his father, Solomon played the part of the typical oriental despot. He outdid David in the extent of his harem;[51] he used intermarriage with royal princesses to make alliances which proved profitable politically, culturally, and economically. The most important of his marriages was that with the daughter of the pharaoh of Egypt; there is some indication that the Egyptian ruler considered Solomon a vassal, for the pharaoh captured Gezer, the last Canaanite stronghold, and gave it to Solomon.[52] The cost of maintaining his harem was enormous:

> Solomon's provision for one day was thirty kors (a kor was roughly equivalent to six bushels) of fine flour, and sixty kors of meal, ten fat cattle and twenty pasture fed cattle and a hundred sheep, besides harts and gazelles and roebucks and fatted fowls.[53]

In spite of the fact that Solomon was noted, especially during the early years of his reign, as a clever judge (I Kings 3:16-28) and as a maker of epigrams (I Kings 4:32),[54] his shortsighted imperialism, with its endless burden of taxation, led to revolt in Ephraim. Inspired by Ahijah, a prophet of Shiloh, and led by Jeroboam, overseer of labor gangs in Ephraim and later first king of the northern kingdom, the revolution was nipped in the bud. But the inevitable dissolution of the kingdom, which was the natural result of Solomon's despotic oppression, was only temporarily averted.

Perhaps Solomon did impart to the writers of wisdom literature something of an original impulse, because it is very clear that he was a patron of the intellectual life of his time. He must always be remembered as a great builder of public buildings, with a genius for government organization and a cosmopolitan interest in other countries. But, as H. C. Snell says:

> . . . We cannot regard the display, luxury, and extravagance of his court as evidence of a sound policy of government, particularly when much of its cost was wrung from the hard hands of peasants . . . The Temple, it is true, was important in the life of Israel, but it was built at too heavy a cost when it required the slavery of thousands of Israel's workmen. . . .

Finally, by substituting autocracy for democracy, to bring a stable kingdom to the point where it is ready to go to pieces is an inglorious act—and this is the folly for which Solomon must bear the responsibility.

. . . His worst delinquency was probably his disloyalty to the highest and best elements of Hebrew religion.

"Now when Solomon was old, his heart was not perfect with the Lord his God, as was the heart of David his father; and his wives turned away his heart after their gods. Solomon also went after Astarte, the goddess of the Sidonians, and after Milcom, the abomination of the Ammonites. . . . Then Solomon built a high place for Chemosh, the god of the Moabites, in the mountain over against Jerusalem. . . . And so he did for all his foreign wives, burning incense and sacrificing to their gods. Thus the Lord was angry with Solomon, because his heart was turned away from the Lord, the God of Israel (I Ki. 11:4-9)."

. . . Some credit should go to him for the building of the Temple, perhaps, and for the rapid advance in Hebrew culture during his reign, but both these achievements had their dark side.

Unfortunately there is little else that can be said for him. No deeds of heroism or self-denial are recorded in his reign. The sketch of his career cannot, therefore, be concluded with eulogy: he must go down in the annals of history as one who had the natural gifts and an unusual opportunity for distinctive service but who largely failed to justify either.[55]

B. *Literature During the United Kingdom.*

As we have seen,[56] there was little attention given to literature during the period of wilderness wandering and the subsequent conquest and settlement of Canaan. But with the establishment of the kingship, the peace which followed David's successful wars, and the luxury of Solomon's reign, there was ample leisure for some of the Hebrews to turn to cultural and literary pursuits. The seventy years during which David and Solomon ruled a united Israel were a time of extraordinary material and cultural progress; population doubled, and art, architecture, and music flourished. The popularity of literary pursuits may be measured by David's reputation as a psalmist and Solomon's fame as poet and author of proverbs and fables.

The reign of David must have been rich in poetry. The Oracles of Balaam may be as late as the reign of David,[57] for in them are mentioned the victories of Saul and the glories of David's rule. One of the earliest poems of David's time is the song of the women celebrating Saul's and especially David's victory over the Philistines.[58] Equally brief was Sheba's rhythmic call to rebellion in David's old age.[59] David himself has been celebrated in tradition as a poet, but we are not sure we have anything he wrote; two secular poems probably do come from his pen: the dirge over Saul and Jonathan[60] and the dirge over Abner.[61] David probably also composed religious hymns and psalms,[62] but if any of them are in the Old Testament book of Psalms it is not possible to point them out. The beautiful parable of Nathan (II Samuel 12:1-4), written in prose but poetic in diction, may have been written in David's time, though some would date it later.

From the reign of Solomon we have the dedicatory sentences he used when the temple was dedicated.[63] To the united kingdom, or shortly after, also probably belong the Blessing of Noah,[64] the Blessing of Moses,[65] and the Blessing of Jacob.[66]

The glorious career of David stimulated the beginning of historical literature in Israel. He appointed both a recorder (Jehoshaphat) and a scribe (Seraiah),[67] among whose duties may have been the care of the royal archives.[68] Solomon employed two secretaries besides the recorder;[69] perhaps they were responsible for the composition of the "Book of the Records of Solomon."[70] A parallel book of official records was prepared by the priests of the temple of Jerusalem; nowhere referred to in the books of I and II Kings, there are good reasons for assuming the existence of special temple records similar in nature to the royal records.[71]

Some time shortly after David's death, one of the men who had known David well and who possessed first hand knowledge of the affairs of his time[72] wrote the story of the founding of the kingdom. This was Israel's first great literary production in prose. It was an account of the events which took place at the court of David which was so graphic and convincing that it could come only from an eyewitness of the events described; literary and historical critics alike regard it as exceedingly reliable. The later Deuteronomic historians incorporated it in their work. Mould speaks of its uniqueness in the world's literature. "Nothing like it, which might have served as a pattern, is known to have existed in the literature of any other nation at the time. Here, then, we stand at a creative moment in the development of human literature."[73]

The interest in literary activities stimulated by the prosperity during the reigns of David and Solomon resulted in the first step in a long process of literary development which eventually culminated in the formation of the Pentateuch. Since 1880, most scholars have accepted the Graf-Wellhausen theory of the composition of the first five books of the Old Testament; this theory states that the Pentateuch attained its present form about 400 B.C. and that it was a combination of at least four literary sources—documents designated by the letters "J," "E," "D," and "P." "This theory in its simplest form may be summarized as follows: the J document (*ca.* 850) and the E document (*ca.* 700) were combined as JE by a redactor (RJE) about 650; the Deuteronomic Code of 621 (D) was added by RD about 550, and the Priestly Code (*ca.* 500-450) by RP about 400, when the Pentateuch attained substantially its present form."[74] In recent years, scholars have distinguished at least two strands of material in the J document: a very simple narrative, J[1], embodying the tradition of the southern tribes; and a later elaboration by another writer, J[2], who added to J[1] the stories of the Joseph tribes and reconciled the two traditions as best he could. The earlier of these, J[1], has been dated by Cuthbert A. Simpson about the year 1000 B.C.[75] The occasion for it may have been David's moving of his capital city from Hebron to Jerusalem, for the compiler of J[1] is interested in recording the events which brought greatness to Hebron and its sanctuary—a greatness now threatened by Jerusalem.

Of all the Hebrew inscriptions uncovered recently by archaeologists, the only one which can be attributed with confidence to the reign of Solomon or immediately afterwards is a school exercise, called the Gezer Calendar, containing a little ditty listing the periods of the agricultural year:

> His two months are (olive) harvest; his two months are grain-planting; his two months are late planting; his month is hoeing up of flax; his month is barley harvest; his month is harvest and festivity; his two months are vine-tending; his month is summer-fruit.[76]

"To the schoolboy in question and to his teacher we owe a debt of gratitude, since this priceless little document furnishes us invaluable data for the history of Hebrew script and spelling."[77]

C.   Religion During the United Kingdom.

It was under the rule of David and Solomon that Jahwism became a state religion. Though not completely devoid of all animistic tendencies, the religion of the Hebrews entered the second of the three stages through which the great religions of the world eventually pass: the nationalistic. With the development of an empire, Jahweh became a national god and took his place on a par with the national gods of the peoples surrounding Palestine. He could be said to possess all three of the requirements which characterized a national deity: a land (Canaan), a capital city (Jerusalem), and a house in which to live (the temple). It was still not monotheism, but henotheism; the other nations had their gods—Chemosh of Moab, Melek of Ammon, Rimmon of Syria, Ashur of Assyria, Marduk of Babylonia, Dagon of Philistia, etc. Outside of Palestine one was expected to worship the particular god of that area. Even in Palestine itself these gods exercised distinctive powers within their own limited spheres; for example, Solomon built temples to the gods of his wives.[78] But as far as the Hebrews were concerned, within the confines of the Hebrew nation, Jahweh was exclusively their god.

Along with the worship of Jahweh, local and minor deities were reverenced without any feeling of inconsistency. For the most part, the Canaanite baalim had been assimilated into the Jahweh cult, but the use of "baal" in personal names seems to point to the persistence of the worship of this agricultural deity.[79] Worship of the ashteroth, the cult of the mother-goddess of all the Semites, continued under the kings.[80] The use of teraphim (household gods) persisted.[81] The ephod, originally a sort of apron worn by the priests in the pockets of which were placed the sacred stones used in consulting the oracle of Jahweh,[82] became in the kingship a sort of idol.[83] Jahweh could tolerate all these practices, but when Solomon built shrines to the national gods of Phoenicia, Moab, and Ammon, his action was regarded as an insult to the prerogatives of the national god of the Israelites, Jahweh.[84]

Just as in the period of the conquest,[85] the high places were popular centers of worship. Samuel and Saul met each other for the first time at one of these high places.[86] At a "great high place" in Gibeon, Solomon had his famous theophany in which he begged Jahweh for wisdom.[87] Even after the temple was built, "The high places were not removed."[88] In addition to the temple in Jerusalem, several of the shrines were regarded as sacred during this period: Mizpah (I Samuel 10:17-24), Gilgal (I Samuel 11:14, 15; 15:33), Nob (I Samuel 22:11-19), and Bethel (I Samuel 7:16; I Kings 12:32, 33).

One of the first things David did after he made Jerusalem his capital city was to transfer the Ark of the Covenant from the home of Abinadab, whence it had been taken from Kirjath-jearim, to the house of Obed-edom for three months, and then to the tent David had constructed as a shelter for it.[89] Under Solomon, the ark was housed in a permanent building, the temple envisaged by David and actually erected by his successor. If the cubit mentioned in I Kings 6 and 7 is considered to be eighteen inches, the temple was ninety feet long, thirty feet wide, and forty-five feet high. Insignificant in size when compared with the cathedrals of Europe and America, it was built as a dwelling place for Jahweh and not for the comfort and convenience of his worshipers. Worship went on in the courts in front of the temple; the temple itself was reserved for Jahweh and his priests. The temple faced the east.[90] There were two rooms: the westernmost, thirty feet by thirty feet in size, was called the Holy of Holies; this was the most sacred part of the shrine, in which were placed the Ark of the Covenant and the two huge cherubim whose wings overshadowed the ark;[91] the easternmost, the Holy Place, was sixty feet by thirty feet; in it there were an altar of cedar, upon which was placed the "bread of the presence," and the ten lampstands. Somewhere, either in the Holy Place or the courtyard, was set up the bronze snake the Israelites had carried with them since the days of their wilderness wanderings.[92] Directly in front of the temple was the altar of burnt offering, the heart of worship for the cult of Jahweh.[93] To the south of the altar was the "brazen sea," resting on twelve bulls, three facing in each direction;[94] ten other bronze basins were scattered throughout the court to provide water for use in the ritual. Also in the court were two upright columns, symbols of deity from ancient days.[95]

Worship during the reigns of Saul, David, and Solomon was a matter of joy and feasting. If we can judge from the description of the ceremonies which took place when David brought the ark into Jerusalem (II Samuel 6:12-21), worship was accompanied by the clamor of trumpets and shouting voices, the ecstatic leaping and dancing of those in the procession,[96] the slaughter of great numbers of sacrificial animals, and royal gifts at the conclusion of the ceremony. But there was a darker side; II Samuel 21:1-14 records the fact that David had seven sons of Saul killed to appease Jahweh and thus end a three years famine; Saul was forced to resort to necromancy in his despair when "the Lord did not answer him either by dreams or by Urim or by prophets,"[97] to talk with the spirit of Samuel.

David appointed two priests to stand at the head of the Jahweh cult, Zadok and Abiathar; this was the beginning of an official ecclesiastical organization. Solomon appointed two additional priests, Azariah, son of Zadok, and Zabud, son of Nathan.[98] In addition to this official state priesthood, there seems also to have been a private priesthood; David himself acted as priest when the Ark of the Covenant was brought into his capital city;[99] II Samuel 20:26 mentions Ira the Jairite as also a priest to David, but just what his functions were is not known; David's sons also assumed the role of priests.[100]

Among the chief religious personalities of the United Kingdom were the prophets, particularly Gad, Nathan, and Ahijah of Shiloh. Other prophets, known as prophetic guilds, or sons of the prophets, had appeared on the scene as early as the time of Samuel. The significance of this movement, which was to constitute the most profound contribution of the Hebrews to the history of religion, will be dealt with in some detail in subsequent chapters.

SUGGESTIONS FOR FURTHER STUDY

W. F. ALBRIGHT, "The Biblical Period," in L. Finkelstein, ed. *The Jews: Their History, Culture, and Religion,* pp. 23-29.

A. E. BAILEY, *Daily Life in Bible Times,* pp. 161-181.

A. E. BAILEY AND C. F. KENT, *History of the Hebrew Commonwealth,* pp. 85-138.

H. M. BATTENHOUSE, *The Bible Unlocked,* pp. 112-145

J. A. BEWER, *The Literature of the Old Testament,* pp. 15-18, 21-29.

G. A. BUTTRICK, ed. *The Interpreter's Bible,* I, pp. 178-180, 279-282, 310-315; II, pp. 853-1176; III, pp. 1-111.

J. FINEGAN, *Light from the Ancient Past,* pp. 149-154.

H. T. FOWLER, *The Origin and Growth of the Hebrew Religion,* pp. 51-56.

F. JAMES, *Personalities of the Old Testament,* pp. 75-165.

C. S. KNOPF, *The Old Testament Speaks,* pp. 131-162.

E. W. K. MOULD, *Essentials of Bible History,* pp. 158-164, 185-216.

R. H. PFEIFFER, *Introduction to the Old Testament,* pp. 135-141.

H. C. SNELL, *Ancient Israel: Its Story and Meaning,* pp. 52-90.

Chapter Eleven

THE DIVIDED KINGDOM

When Solomon died (*ca.* 922 B.C.), he was succeeded by his son Rehoboam. At Shechem, Rehoboam was met by representatives of all the Hebrew tribes, who had assembled to exercise their ancient right to choose their king.[1] With Jeroboam, son of Nebat, back from his Egyptian exile,[2] the people expressed their democratic right of complaint:

> Your father (Solomon) made our yoke galling. Now then lighten the galling service of your father and his heavy yoke which he laid upon us, and we will serve you.[3]

Rehoboam considered the request for three days. He first asked the advice of the old men; some of them may have remembered the days before the kingship became so autocratic; they regarded the king as a public servant. But Rehoboam turned to the young men of the court who, like himself, had been brought up amid the luxury of Solomon's harem; they thought the king should be an oriental despot and that common people had no rights a monarch was required to respect. So, on the appointed day

> . . . The king answered them harshly, and rejected the counsel of the old men which they offered him. So he spoke to them according to the counsel of the young men, saying, "My father made your yoke heavy, but I will add to your yoke; my father chastised you with whips, but I will chastise you with scorpions." So the king did not listen to the people, . . . Now when all Israel saw that the king had not listened to them, the people replied to the king, saying, "What portion have we in David? Yea, we have no heritage in the son of Jesse. To your tents, O Israel! see now to your own house, O David!" So the Israelites went to their tents.[4]

In this way, the ten northern tribes seceded and made Jeroboam their king. Rehoboam sent Adoram, overseer of labor gangs, to suppress the revolt, but he was stoned to death; Rehoboam fled in haste to the comparative safety of Jerusalem,[5] and the disruption of the kingdom was complete.

Dr. Mould mentions four causes for the dissolution of the Hebrew kingdom:

1. Economic. Undoubtedly the most active immediate cause of the disruption was the discontent of the people over excessive taxation and forced labor. The heavy burden of expense laid upon the people because of Solomon's enormous harem, his elaborate and luxurious court, and his pretentious building enterprises was more than his little kingdom could finance. . . .

2. Political. Solomon's imperialism outraged the people's traditional instincts for freedom and democracy. Saul had been a choice of the people. So had David. But the people had no say as to the succession of Solomon, and they were given no voice in the selection of Solomon's successor. The northern tribes had already lost prestige to Judah, when the royal succession passed from the house of Saul to the house of David. For the succession to become hereditary at this time would forever preclude the possibility of any other tribe's, especially the leading northern tribe of Ephraim, having the honor of furnishing the king. The slumbering jealousy was fanned into flame by the favoritism of David and Solomon toward Judah. . . .

3. Social. Jealousy, grounded in the differing racial traits and inherited customs of the northerners (the Joseph tribes) and the southerners (the men of Judah), was age-old and deep-seated. The south was conservative; the north was progressive and independent, ready to experiment. . . .

4. Moral and Religious. Solomon's idolatries must have been an offense to loyal Yahweh worshipers in the south as well as in the north. . . . Another factor making for religious jealousy and resentment was that the costly temple in Jerusalem, built largely by northern labor and taxes, was of little use to the northern people on account of distance and difficulties of travel. Moreover, so far as the Jerusalem temple affected their interests at all, apart from the increased taxes for its maintenance, it was mainly to cast in the shade their own local shrines.[6]

The division of the Hebrew kingdom gave the northern tribes the advantage. Israel's territory was five times that of Judah; Israel's population was twice that of the southern kingdom.[7] Israel was by far the wealthier of the two, because she possessed more natural resources and more fertile farm lands and because through her ran the great trade routes connecting Egypt with Syria and Mesopotamia. However, the little kingdom of Judah was destined to outlast the northern kingdom by one hundred and forty-one years.

In religion, the temple remained in Judah the center of the Jahweh cult; though local shrines were not ordered demolished until the reform of 621, the temple grew in importance in the life of the people. In the north, Jeroboam reorganized the worship of Jahweh around two ancient centers, Dan in the north and Bethel in the south;[8] here Jahweh was worshiped under the form of bulls of gold. Bethel became the royal sanctuary and evidently became a place of splendor and attractiveness to offset the appeal of the temple at Jerusalem. In spite of his undoubtedly worthy intentions, Jeroboam sponsored in the north a religious syncretism which set religion back ethically; he alienated the very prophet who had helped him in the revolution, Ahijah, who was led to pronounce doom on Jeroboam and his family line, the worst fate that could befall any Hebrew.[9]

The immediate result of the disruption of the kingdom was warfare between the two little principalities for fifty years. Rehoboam was faced with the additional difficulty of a military invasion of the southern kingdom by the pharaoh of Egypt, Sheshonk I (Shishak), founder of the twenty-second dynasty; this was evidently started at the behest of Jeroboam, but the invading forces turned against Israel as soon as they had sufficiently harassed Judah. Luckily for both Hebrew kings, the Egyptians and their Libyan and Ethiopian allies were more interested in plunder than in conquest; to pacify the Egyptian ruler, Rehoboam had to pay a huge indemnity.

Friction between Israel and Judah was finally brought to an end by the rise of a common peril: a powerful Syrian state with its headquarters at Damascus. All of these little states in the western horn of the fertile crescent were free alternately to quarrel with one another and to ally themselves with one another only because mighty Egypt and Assyria were relatively weak. When

Assyria finally emerged from her quiescence, Israel and Syria were destined to collapse and Judah was to survive only at the expense of heavy indemnity.

In Judah, the family of David retained the throne from 922 to 586 B.C., except for the brief period when Queen Athaliah usurped the throne (842-837 B.C.). In the northern kingdom, it was a different story: changes of dynasty were frequent, and only two royal families lasted into a third generation. Jeroboam's son Nadab was assassinated in the second year of his reign by Baasha; Baasha's son Elah was murdered by Zimri in the second year of his reign. Zimri killed all male members of the house of Baasha,[10] but was himself burned to death in his palace by Omri (ca. 876 B.C.).

As king, Omri gave to Israel a brief period of importance. He made an alliance with Ethbaal, priest-king of Phoenicia, by marrying his son Ahab to Ethbaal's daughter Jezebel; this proved to be of commercial advantage to Israel, but religiously and politically it was to prove disastrous, as we shall see later. Evidence of Omri's greatness is seen in the fact that in Assyrian inscriptions for a century and a half after his death the northern kingdom is referred to as the "Land of Omri."[11] Omri's son Ahab was an even greater king, because he took part in a successful coalition of several small kingdoms against the rising power of Assyria; Ahab and his queen, Jezebel, will be remembered chiefly because of their arch adversary, the fiery Gileadite prophet Elijah. Ahab and Jehoshaphat of Judah entered into a military alliance against Ben-hadad of Syria; in a battle at Ramoth-gilead, Ahab was slain.[12]

Within a dozen years after Ahab's death, Jehu led a revolt against Jehoram of Israel, killing Jezebel and massacring every member of the house of Omri-Ahab. No revolution is described in the Bible with such a wealth of detail as that one; apparently it had back of it the blessing of the prophets of Jahweh, notably Elijah and Elisha,[13] but its excesses were condemned a century later by the prophet Hosea.[14] This brought an end to the commercial, political, and religious alliance between Israel and Phoenicia, and led to her subordination to Assyria and Syria both.

Under Jehu's grandson, Jeroboam II, Israel reached the highest prosperity she had known since the division of the monarchy. But, as is clear in the prophetic oracles of Amos and Hosea, the prosperity was based upon a great gulf between the rich and the poor, judicial corruption, moral degeneracy, and religious syncretism. The end predicted by the prophets was not long in coming. When Assyria once more recovered her strength, Tiglath-pileser III invaded Syria in 743 B.C. and incorporated a number of the little states in that area in the Assyrian Empire. Collapse in Israel was hastened by internal disunion. Zechariah, son of Jeroboam II, was murdered by Shallum, and Shallum by Menahem, who paid tribute to Assyria; probably Shallum represented an anti-Assyrian party in Israel and Menahem a pro-Assyrian group. Menahem's son Pekahiah was assassinated by Pekah, who was evidently anti-Assyrian. Pekah tried to revive the coalition of Palestinian states against Assyria; Rezin of Syria joined him, but Ahaz of Judah appealed for help to Tiglath-pileser and the latter attacked the coalition. Pekah was slain in a conspiracy headed by Hoshea, a tool of Assyria and the last king of the northern kingdom. Israel might have kept its independence a while longer, but Hoshea, in 724 B.C., because of Egyptian intrigue, suddenly turned anti-Assyrian. First Shalmaneser V and then Sargon II laid siege to Samaria, and the end came in 721 B.C. Sargon's records mention 27,290 Israelites taken away into captivity; they were scattered in different parts of the Assyrian Empire, in accordance with a deportation policy initiated by Tiglath-pileser III; colonists from other parts of the realm were imported into the northern kingdom.[15]

Judah was the only state in the western part of the fertile crescent to outlive the kingdom of Assyria, but it was not without a heavy toll of tribute. Hezekiah narrowly escaped annihilation at the hands of Sennacherib, successor of Sargon II, in 701 B.C., but many people were taken prisoners and an enormous indemnity was levied on the little kingdom.[16]

For the greater part of the seventh century, Judah was under the rule of Manasseh, son of Hezekiah; for his religious policy he was more sharply criticized by the Deuteronomic reform party than any of his predecessors.[17] But Manasseh was able to keep the peace against decadent Egypt and crumbling Assyria. In 621 B.C., Josiah of Judah, grandson of Manasseh, undertook to free himself of Assyrian religious and political overlordship by instituting a reform based on the discovery of Deuteronomy 12-26 in the temple. In 612, Nineveh, the capital city of the Assyrian Empire, was destroyed by a combined force of Medes, Babylonians, and Scythians. This led to a brief period of Egyptian control in Palestine; because of some breach of faith, Pharaoh Necho lured Josiah to Megiddo and killed him there (608 B.C.). But the real threat to the independence of the little kingdoms in Palestine and Syria was the rising power of the Neo-Babylonian Empire.

At Carchemish (605 B.C.), Necho of Egypt was defeated by the Babylonian army. Jehoiakim of Judah accepted the new regime, until pressure from Egypt made him come out openly against the Babylonians (sometimes referred to as Chaldeans). Nebuchadnezzar, the only really able king in the Neo-Babylonian Empire, moved on Judah in 597 B.C. and effected the first of three successive deportations.[18] He left a third son of Josiah, Zedekiah, in control of Jerusalem; for four years he was loyal to the Babylonian king, but in 588 he became a tool of an Egyptian conspiracy. Babylonian punishment was swift and terrible; Nebuchadnezzar moved his army into Judah and laid siege to Jerusalem and, after a year and a half of resistance, the city was sacked and the temple burned (586 B.C.). So thorough was the destruction that for one hundred and fifty years Jerusalem lay a mass of desolate and uninhabitable ruins. Over the people left in Judah, Nebuchadnezzar placed Gedaliah as governor with his headquarters at Mizpah; he was murdered in 581 by Ishmael, who fled to Egypt, taking the prophet Jeremiah with him.[19] Jeremiah mentions that Nebuchadnezzar engineered a third deportation in 581 B.C., carrying off seven hundred and forty-five Jews into exile.[20]

It is quite possible that the religion of Jahweh would have been eliminated by these tragic events of history had it not had within it elements of vitality which helped it to outlast the exigencies of political collapse. Many of the religions contemporary with Jahwism have disappeared, chiefly because they were tied too closely to a political and economic system which has long since disappeared. Jahwism persisted, and became the Judaism of today, because within it there were creative thinkers who helped the Hebrew people rethink their religious faith and rise above what seemed to be the end of their culture. Chief among these creative thinkers were the Old Testament prophets.

SUGGESTIONS FOR FURTHER STUDY

W. F. ALBRIGHT, "The Biblical Period," in L. Finkelstein, ed., *The Jews: Their History, Culture, and Religion,* pp. 29-45.

A. E. BAILEY, *Daily Life in Bible Times,* pp. 182-211.

A. E. BAILEY AND C. F. KENT, *History of the Hebrew Commonwealth,* pp. 139-351.

H. M. BATTENHOUSE, *The Bible Unlocked,* pp. 149-207.

G. A. BUTTRICK, ed., *The Interpreter's Bible,* I, pp. 282-287; III, pp. 111-338.

F. C. EISELEN, E. LEWIS, AND D. G. DOWNEY, eds., *The Abingdon Bible Commentary,* pp. 64-70.

J. FINEGAN, *Light from the Ancient Past,* pp. 154-163, 169-189.

C. S. KNOPF, *The Old Testament Speaks,* pp. 163-281.

E. W. K. MOULD, *Essentials of Bible History,* pp. 217-270.

H. C. SNELL, *Ancient Israel: Its Story and Meaning,* pp. 91-178.

Chapter Twelve

THE BIRTH OF HEBREW PROPHECY

The highest type of religious thinking which we find in the Old Testament is that which grew up in connection with a group of men called the prophets. It was this segment of the religious life of the Hebrews, more than any other group, which kept Jahwism from being swept into a naturalistic syncretism similar to Canaanite Baalism. The prophets represent the religion of Israel at its best; the great prophets, Amos, Hosea, Isaiah of Jerusalem, Micah, Jeremiah, and Deutero-Isaiah, were the spokesmen of the progressive idealism of their day. It was prophetism which constituted the chief Judaistic root of Christianity.

The great prophets did not appear suddenly; there was a long period of preparation. The earliest references to a group of prophets in the Old Testament are in the account of Samuel's choice of Saul to be king over Israel:

> Then Samuel . . . said, ". . . Afterward you (Saul) will come to the hill of God, where there is a Philistine post; and furthermore when you come there to the city, you will meet a band of prophets coming down from the high place with a lyre, a tambourine, a flute, and a harp before them; and they will be prophesying ecstatically. Then the spirit of the Lord shall suddenly seize upon you, and you shall prophesy ecstatically with them and you shall be changed into another man. . . ."[1]

The word "prophesy" in this connection seems to denote the behaviour of those who were beside themselves.[2] Like the dancing dervishes of the orient, these early prophets were ecstatics, who felt that when they were in a state of religious frenzy they were full of the spirit of Jahweh and had access to his truth. This ecstatic prophetism was similar to that which existed in other contemporary religions; in fact, many scholars, including Hugh E. W. Fosbroke, conclude that "ecstatic prophetism was no part of Israel's desert life, but had established itself in Canaan before Israel's entrance into the land and was part of the heritage, religious and cultural, which the nomad tribes appropriated."[3]

The ecstatic prophets during the period of the Hebrew kingdom banded themselves together in groups known as "sons of the prophets." This phrase implies nothing as to their family relationship; it indicates that they were persons endowed with the spirit of the prophets, members of the prophetic guild, the entire body of prophets as a whole.[4] Often called seers,[5] they were credited with the power to see things hidden from the eye of the common man.

The meaning of the word "prophet" itself gives us a clue to the significance of the prophet as one who had the confidence of Jahweh. It is a Greek word meaning "one who speaks for, or on behalf of, another," an accurate translation of the Hebrew word "nabi'," "to speak out," or "speak forth." C. S. Knopf suggests that a change of one letter in the root makes the Hebrew word signify boiling, bubbling. "Certainly the Hebrew prophets were distinctly religious enthusiasts who bubbled over, often boiled hotly, and bravely spoke out for God."[6] The idea of foretelling or prediction was not intrinsic in the word itself, but was a later development of the word for biblical usage. The prophet was a speaker for God; as such, together with his keen insight into historical situations and circumstances, he often did see the ultimate outcome of events and predicted what impends before it happens. But his chief function was to declare to the people the will of Jahweh.[7]

Alongside of, and perhaps associated with, the ecstatic bands of prophets were men of a more rational spirit, the real predecessors of the great prophets. The first of these was a woman, Deborah, one of the few women in the history of Judaism to function as a religious leader.[8] The embodiment of both patriotism and religion, she inspired a military leader to act and encouraged a few of the Hebrew tribes to support him in a successful battle against the Canaanites. The next outstanding figure among the prophets was Samuel; though called a seer, the last of the judges, a maker of kings, and a priest, part of his varied life seems to have been concerned with informing the Israelites of the will of God and inspiring them to resist the encroachments of the Philistines. During the reign of David there were two important individual prophets: Gad and Nathan. Gad is mentioned twice in the books of Samuel: as a supporter of David in his outlaw period, the prophet urges David to stay no longer in the land of Mizpeh, but to return to Judah;[9] later, Gad serves as the spokesman of the wrath of Jahweh directed against King David for having taken a census.[10] In Nathan we meet a fearless prophet who does not flinch from reproving and denouncing David for his sin with Bathsheba and his murder of her husband.[11] Nathan is connected with two other incidents during the reign of David: In II Samuel 7:1-17 he counsels David that he should not build a temple to Jahweh, but should leave that task for his son; in I Kings 1, Nathan takes part in a harem intrigue which results in the placing of Solomon, son of David and Bathsheba, as David's successor on the throne. In the time of Solomon, Ahijah the Shilonite inspired Jeroboam to lead an abortive attempt to revolt against the tyranny of Solomon's oriental despotism;[12] with the disruption of the kingdom, however, Ahijah turns against Jeroboam.[13] It was a prophet, Shemaiah, who dissuaded King Rehoboam from venturing on a suicidal civil war;[14] this indicates that the prophetic party in Judah may have been friendly, at least at first, to the revolution started by Jeroboam. It was another prophet, Jehu, son of Hanani, who was a hostile critic of Baasha, King of Israel.[15]

During the reign of Ahab, King of Israel, there appeared a cleavage in the ranks of the prophets which persisted until the exile. On the one hand there were the great masses of professional prophets, usually in the pay of the king, who gave their advice to the king, usually along lines favorable to the royal point of view; on the other hand, there were the independent individual prophets who did not hesitate to denounce the king if they felt the royal will was contrary to the will of Jahweh. This cleavage is graphically portrayed in the Old Testament story of the prophet Micaiah, son of Imlah:

Now for three years Syria and Israel continued without war. But in the third year Jehoshaphat, king of Judah, came down to the king of Israel, and the king of Israel said to his servants, "Do you know that Ramoth-gilead belongs to us, yet we are inactive instead of taking it from the hand of the king of

Syria?" Then he said to Jehoshaphat, "Will you go with me to fight against Ramoth-gilead?" "I am as you are, my people as your people, my horses as your horses," said Jehoshaphat to the king of Israel. Jehoshaphat said further to the king of Israel, "Inquire today, I pray, for the word of the Lord." Then the king of Israel assembled the prophets, about four hundred men, and said to them, "Shall I go to battle against Ramoth-gilead, or shall I forbear?" "Go up," they said; "for the Lord will deliver it into the hand of the king." But Jehoshaphat said, "Is there not here another prophet of the Lord through whom we may inquire?" Then the king of Israel said to Jehoshaphat, "There is another man through whom we might inquire of the Lord, Micaiah, the son of Imlah, but I hate him; for he never prophesies good concerning me, but only evil." "Let not the king say so," said Jehoshaphat. So the king of Israel called a eunuch and said, "Bring quickly Micaiah, the son of Imlah." Now the king of Israel and Jehoshaphat, the king of Judah, were sitting each on his throne, arrayed in their robes, at the entrance of the gate of Samaria, and all the prophets were engaged in ecstatic prophecy before them. Then Zedekiah, the son of Chenanaiah, made for himself horns of iron and he said, "Thus says the Lord: 'With these you shall gore the Syrians until they are destroyed.'" So all the prophets prophesied, saying, "Go up to Ramoth-gilead and prosper; for the Lord will deliver it into the hand of the king." Now the messenger who went to call Micaiah spoke to him, saying, "See, now, the prophets with one accord have spoken good to the king; let your word, I pray you, be like the word of one of them and speak good." "As the Lord lives," said Micaiah, *"What the Lord says to me, that will I speak."* Now when he came to the king, the king said to him, "Micaiah, shall we go to Ramoth-gilead to battle, or shall we forbear?" "Go up and prosper," he said to him, "for the Lord will deliver it into the hand of the king!" But the king said to him, "How many times must I adjure you that you speak to me nothing but the truth in the name of the Lord?" "I saw all Israel scattered on the mountains," he said, "like sheep without a shepherd; and the Lord said, 'These have no master; let them return each to his home in peace.'" Then the king of Israel said to Jehoshaphat, "Did I not say to you that he would not prophesy good concerning me, but only evil?" . . . .

Then the king of Israel said, "Seize Micaiah and take him back to Amon, governor of the city, and to Joash, the king's son, and say, 'Thus says the king: "Put this fellow in the prison and feed him with bread and water scantily until I return victorious." ' " Whereupon Micaiah said, "If you do indeed return victorious, the Lord has not spoken by me."[16]

The outstanding prophets of the time of Ahab and the period immediately following his death were Elijah and Elisha. Elijah the Tishbite was the leader of the Jahweh party in the northern kingdom against the encroachments of Tyrian Baalism, which had come into Israel as a direct result of Omri's commercial and political alliance with Phoenicia.[17] His chief antagonist was Queen Jezebel, whom Ahab had married as a part of the treaty with Phoenicia and who completely dominated her husband. Jezebel was an ardent worshiper of Baal-Melkart, the national god of Tyre; she was a religious fanatic, bent on propagating her religion in Israel, even if it meant supplanting the worship of Jahweh. She built temples to Baal everywhere she could and gave the priests of Baal prominence at court. She worshiped sacred poles and pillars, and introduced sacred prostitution, magic, and wild, ecstatic cultic dances. She might have succeeded in completely submerging the religion of Moses had it not been for the strict Jahweh party and Elijah.

Elijah is the greatest of the pre-literary prophets.[18] He was the champion of the older Hebrew traditions, such as loyalty to the nation's god and the inalienable rights of the Hebrew individual and the Hebrew family. He is one of the most dramatic personalities in the Bible, a vigorous desert soul; so important did he become in later Jewish thought that many believed he would come again as a forerunner of the Messiah.[19] He protested against the combining of Tyrian Baal worship with the worship of Jahweh; in the story of the trial of the respective powers of Jahweh and Baal on Mount Carmel Elijah makes good his contention that Jahweh is real and Baal-Melkart is not.[20] He protested against a growing emphasis on external forms of worship, even within Jahwism itself; the theophany Elijah experienced on Mount Sinai emphasized the coming of the presence of Jahweh in "the sound of a gentle whisper," rather than in wind, earthquake, or fire.[21] He protested against the injustice of Ahab's judicial murder of Naboth, contending for the privilege even of the humblest citizen to enjoy his own inheritance against the encroachments of the king.[22] Motivated by the age-old principle of blood revenge,

Elijah called down upon Ahab the worst curse of which a Hebrew could conceive—the extermination of his family line; however, when Ahab repented, the doom was postponed. In all these activities, Elijah "anticipated the social and moral earnestness that was to find unparalleled expression in the great writing prophets of a hundred or more years later."[23]

When Elijah died, his reforming work was continued by his disciple Elisha. He helped Hazael to overthrow Ben-hadad, king of Syria, evidently for the purpose of hastening the downfall of the house of Omri in Israel;[24] he instigated the revolution of Jehu, which resulted in the bloody purge of every member of the family of Ahab.[25] Tyrian Baalism was checked, but in its excesses Jehu's revolution killed off the capable leaders of the northern kingdom and brought an end to the Israelite-Phoenician alliance, which had been so profitable commercially and culturally. Baalism could still be practiced as a local cult, but the work of Elijah and Elisha resulted in the fact that the right of Jahweh to supremacy in Palestine was never afterward denied or even doubted. This was a great step forward, but Canaanitish rites still continued to be practised, much to the disgust of the great prophets of the eighth century.

SUGGESTIONS FOR FURTHER STUDY

G. A. Buttrick, ed., *The Interpreter's Bible*, I, pp. 201-204, 312-317.

F. C. Eiselen, E. Lewis, and D. G. Downey, eds., *The Abingdon Bible Commentary*, pp. 150-153.

F. James, *Personalities of the Old Testament*, pp. 166-195.

C. S. Knopf, *The Old Testament Speaks*, pp. 135, 136, 169-202.

E. W. K. Mould, *Essentials of Bible History*, pp. 227-239.

J. B. Noss, *Man's Religions*, pp. 496-499.

W. O. E. Oesterley and T. H. Robinson, *Hebrew Religion: Its Origin and Development*, pp. 182-189.

H. H. Rowley, *The Re-discovery of the Old Testament*, pp. 133-144.

J. M. P. Smith, *The Prophets and Their Times*, pp. 1-54.

Chapter Thirteen

THE EIGHTH CENTURY PROPHETS

A. *The Prophetic Activity of Amos.*

During the eighth century B.C. there appeared among the Hebrews four great prophetic characters: Amos of Tekoa, Hosea of Ephraim, Isaiah of Jerusalem, and Micah of Moresheth-gath. It was due to their creative religious genius that there emerged the conception of Jahweh as an ethical deity whose demands are ethical and whose worship must also be ethical. These men made such an indelible impression on the Hebrew religion that it cannot at all be understood apart from their contribution.

The first of these eighth century prophets was a herdsman and a pruner of sycamore trees, a native of Tekoa, a small town about twelve miles south of Jerusalem. Some time toward the middle of the eighth century (*ca.* 752 B.C.), when Uzziah was king in Judah and Jeroboam II ruled in Israel, Amos walked from his native Judah to the northern kingdom, to the royal shrine at Bethel, and there, on a feast day, he blazed forth in an impassioned address, one of the finest examples of oratory in the Bible.[1] His occupation as a herdsman had given him plenty of time to reflect upon the religious and social problems of his day; his reflections generated within him a consuming passion for righteousness and social justice, which was augmented when he noted the economic exploitation of the lower classes by the rich landlords in the northern kingdom. While he thought about the increasing laxity in religion and morals, the loss of integrity, justice, mercy, and spiritual religion, he began to proclaim the visions he had had foretelling the doom imminent over the Kingdom of Israel.

Amos begins by denouncing one of Israel's hereditary enemies:

Thus says the Lord:
"For the three transgressions of Damascus,
And for the four, I will not turn it back;
Because they have threshed Gilead
With threshing-tools of iron."[2]

A thrill of fierce pleasure must have run through his hearers at
Bethel. So Amos goes on in the same vein; Gaza, Tyre, Edom,
Ammon, Moab—all neighboring nations surrounding Israel who
had in some way incurred her wrath—will be doomed. Then, he
draws the circle closer to his audience:

Thus says the Lord:
"For the three transgressions of Judah,
And for the four, I will not turn it back;
Because they have rejected the instruction
of the Lord,
And have not kept his statutes;
But their lies have led them astray,
After which their fathers walked.
So I will send a fire upon Judah,
And it shall devour the palaces of Jerusalem."[3]

Perhaps there are fewer applauders. Finally, the prophet turns
on the people before him:

Thus says the Lord:
"For the three transgressions of Israel,
And for the four, I will not turn it back;
Because they have sold the innocent for silver,
And the needy in exchange for a pair of sandals;[4]
They who trample upon the heads of the poor,
And thrust aside the humble from the way."[5]

Israel, the most privileged nation of all, would feel the effects
of the wrath of Jahweh more than any of the others, because of the
enormity of her sins. Amid all the tyranny and oppression, the
people of Israel were making religion a mockery by worshiping
Jahweh with false piety:

> Thus says the Lord:
> "I hate, I spurn your feasts,
> And I take no pleasure in your festal gatherings.
> Even though you offer me burnt-offerings,
> And your cereal-offerings, I will not accept them;
> And the thank-offerings of your fatted beasts I will
> not look upon.
> Take away from me the noise of your songs,
> And to the melody of your lyres I will not listen.
> But *let justice roll down like waters,*
> *And righteousness like a perennial stream.*"[6]

What would be the end of all this sinning? Amos promised his audience that the Day of Jahweh would come. Many of the Israelites believed the Day of Jahweh would be a glorious day, when Jahweh would destroy all their foes and usher in a new age of glorious prosperity; Amos challenges that concept and insists that the Day of Jahweh will be a day of doom in which Jahweh will punish Israel:

> "Woe to you who desire the day of the Lord!
> What, then, does the day of the Lord mean to you?
> It is darkness, and not light;
> As though a man were fleeing from a lion,
> And a bear should meet him!
> Or as if he entered his house and rested his hand
> upon the wall,
> And a serpent bit him!
> Is not the day of the Lord darkness and not light,
> And blackness, with no brightness in it?"[7]

The instrument of Jahweh's wrath will be mighty Assyria; Amos does not mention this dread enemy by name, but his hearers know when he said: "So I (Jahweh) will carry you into exile beyond Damascus."[8] He describes in detail the fate of the nation:

> Therefore thus says the Lord God:
> "The foe shall surround the land,
> And strip you of your strength;
> And your palaces shall be plundered."

Thus says the Lord:
"Just as a shepherd rescues from the mouth of a lion
two shank-bones or a piece of an ear, so will the Israelites
be rescued, who dwell in Samaria, along with the corner of
a couch and the leg of a bed."

"Hear and testify against the house of Jacob,"
Is the oracle of the Lord God, the God of hosts,
"That on the day when I punish Israel for its offenses,
I will inflict punishment upon the altars of Bethel,
And the horns of the altar shall be cut off and fall
                    to the ground.
And I will smite both winter house and summer house,
And the ivory houses shall be ruined;
And many houses shall come to an end."
                    The oracle of the Lord.

"Hear this word, you cows of Bashan,
You who are on the mount of Samaria,
Who oppress the weak, who crush the needy,
Who say to their lords, 'Bring that we may drink.'

"The Lord God has sworn by his holiness,
That there are days coming upon you,
When they will drag you away with hooks,
And what is left of you with fish-hooks;
And through the breaches you will go, each
                    straight ahead,
And you will be cast upon the refuse heap."
                    The oracle of the Lord.[9]

There is only the barest suggestion of hope to relieve the message
of doom in the Book of Amos: there will be a remnant which
will be spared, a small group of loyal worshipers of Jahweh, around
whom we can build a new day.

For thus says the Lord God: "The city that sent forth a
thousand shall have but a hundred left; and the one that
sent forth a hundred shall have but ten left, for the house of
Israel."

            Hate evil, and love good
            And establish justice at the gate;
            Perhaps, the Lord, the God of hosts,
            Will be gracious to a remnant of Joseph.[10]

The reaction to the words of Amos was immediate and intense. The Priest at Bethel, Amaziah, sent word to Jeroboam II that Amos was a dangerous radical.[11] Then he told Amos to go back home to Judah and never return to Bethel. Amos' reply set him apart from the professional prophets of the king's court:

> Then Amos replied to Amaziah, saying,
> "I am no prophet, nor am I a member of a prophetic order;
> But I am a shepherd and a dresser of sycamores.
> And the Lord took me from behind the flock,
> And the Lord said to me,
> 'Go prophesy to my people Israel.' "[12]

What happened next we are not told. Perhaps Amos returned to the hills of Tekoa to write down and publish his oracles of judgment, and to inspire the long line of prophets who were to follow in his train. In any case, he is one of the great heroes in the long struggle for the emancipation of human beings from tyranny. Fleming James succinctly summarizes Amos' contribution:

> . . . In certain respects we have gone beyond him. His belief that God in a supernatural way reveals to individuals what is about to take place in history does not seem to apply to our time. His vivid sense of God's wrath both shocks us and leaves us cold. His conviction that calamities are to be interpreted as signs of divine displeasure appalls us. His scathing denunciations, though there is that in us which makes us enjoy them, strike us as possibly unfair, probably ineffective and certainly harsh. This same harshness, unrelieved by any tender passages, prevents his book from feeding the inner life; it is exhilarating but not devotional. One does not brood over it on his knees.
>
> And yet it *is* exhilarating. How clearly he puts first things first. . . . He is one of the great emancipated spirits of the race. And he is one of its most passionate champions of the poor. Wherever men have gone to the Bible for encouragement in the long struggle for the liberation of the underprivileged, they have found it chiefly in Amos and in those successors whom he deeply influenced—Isaiah and Micah.[13]

B. *Hosea, Prophet of Love and Mercy.*

Only a few years after Amos, possibly in 746 B.C., the prophet Hosea began to speak. Unlike Amos, Hosea was a native of Israel who proclaimed what he believed to be the truths of Jahweh in his own country; but like Amos, Hosea denounced the luxury and corruption, both political and religious, which harassed the declining years of the northern kingdom. In contrast to Amos, who is known as the prophet of the righteousness of God, Hosea must be called the prophet of the love and mercy of God; the former placed his emphasis on external conduct, while the latter goes deeper and searches the inner springs of action.

At first, Hosea was also a prophet of doom. He did not share the self-satisfied feeling of his contemporaries during the unparalleled peace and material prosperity which characterized Israel during the closing years of the reign of Jeroboam II. He observed the people celebrating the seasonal festivals to Jahweh and the baalim in the happy confidence that divine approval was upon all their acts, but, like Elijah, Hosea was confident that Jahweh did not approve the worship of the baalim. The dynasty of Jehu will fall; the dominion of the house of Israel will come to an end,[14] said the prophet. But something happened to change him from a prophet of doom to a prophet of love: his personal domestic tragedy; the facts of this story are to be found in Hosea, chapters 1 and 3:

> In the beginning, when the Lord spoke through Hosea, then the Lord said to Hosea,
> "Go, and take to yourself a harlotrous wife, and harlotrous children;
> For the land has committed great harlotry, turning from following the Lord."
> So he went and took Gomer, the daughter of Diblaim, and she became pregnant and bore him a son (Jezreel). . . .
> When she became pregnant again and bore a daughter, he said to him,
> "Call her 'She-who-is-unpitied'; for I will not again have pity upon the house of Israel, that I should ever forgive them. . . ."
> Then she weaned "She-who-is-unpitied," and became pregnant, and bore a son. And he said,

> "Call him, 'Not-my-people';
> For you are not my people,
> And I am not your God."[15]

Then Gomer left her home and her children, perhaps going after other lovers; finally, her husband sees her in a slave market. The prophet continues the tragic story:

> "The Lord said to me again,
> 'Go, love a woman that is beloved of a paramour, and is an adulteress; even as the Lord loves the Israelites, though they turn to other gods and are lovers of raisin-cakes.'[16]
> "So I bought her for myself for fifteen shekels of silver and a homer and a half of barley. Then I said to her,
> 'Many days you must dwell as mine;
> You must not play the harlot, nor have a husband; nor will I myself come near you.' . . ."[17]

Thus, for a long time Gomer must have remained a common servant in Hosea's household. But, if we can judge by the author's religious ideas later, she once again became his loyal and devoted wife.

The important factor in Hosea's domestic life, aside from its poignant tragedy, is what it taught him about Jahweh. He began to see that Gomer's conduct was parallel to the nation's conduct toward Jahweh; Israel had gone after other gods. In his inability to cease loving his wayward wife, Hosea found it an easy step to believe that Jahweh continued to love erring Israel. If a mere human being like himself could continue to feel affection and pity for the sins of a headstrong wife, surely God himself could not be less understanding and forgiving to a nation that had forsaken him. As Hosea forgave Gomer the prophet entered into the feeling he thought Jahweh must have in forgiving his guilty children, the people of Israel.

Hosea's most valuable contribution to the religion of the Hebrews was his concept that Jahweh was a god of love. He shows how the patience of God in previous centuries was like that of a loving husband and a tender father.

> "Therefore I (Jahweh) am going to persuade her (Israel),
> And lead her to the wilderness,

And speak to her heart.
Then I will give back her vineyards there,
And the valley of Achor as a door of hope.[18]
And she shall respond there as in the days of her youth,
As in the day when she came up from the land of Egypt.[19]
On that day it shall come to pass," is the oracle of the Lord,
"That you will call me, 'My husband,'
And you will no longer call me, 'My Baal.' . . .
And I will betroth you to myself for ever;
I will betroth you to myself in righteousness and justice,
And in kindness and mercy.
And I will betroth you to myself in faithfulness;
And you shall know the Lord.
It shall come to pass on that day," is the oracle of the Lord,
"That I will answer the heavens,
And they shall answer the earth;
And the earth shall answer the grain, the wine, and the oil;
And they shall answer Jezreel;
And I will sow her for myself in the land,
And I will pity 'Her-who-is-unpitied';
And I will say to 'Not-my-people,' 'You are my people';
And he shall say, 'My God!'"[20]

Never before had the relationship between God and his people been expressed with such strong emotional fervor.

"When Israel was a child, I (Jahweh) came to love him,
And from Egypt I called him.
The more I called them,
The more they went away from me;
They sacrificed to the Baals,
And made offerings to idols.
But it was I who taught Ephraim to walk;
I took them up in my arms;
But they did not know that I cared for them.
With human lines I led them,
With loving cords;
And I became for them like him who lifts the yoke from
                    their jaws;
And I bent toward them and fed them.

How can I give you up, O Ephraim!
How surrender you, O Israel!

How can I treat you like Admah!
How make you like Zeboim!
My mind turns against me;
My sympathies also grow hot.
I will not carry out my fierce anger;
Nor will I again destroy Ephraim;
For I am God and not man,
The holy one in the midst of you;
And I will not destroy.[21]

Hosea saw in the worship of his day a gross misrepresentation
of the nature of Jahweh. He condemned idolatry unsparingly;[22]
he made fun of the idea that men could make God with their own
hands[23] and that an ox or a calf should symbolize Jahweh to his
people:

> "Of their silver and their gold they made
> Idols for themselves, that they might be cut off.
> I loathe your bull, O Samaria;
> My anger blazes against them;
> How long will they be incapable of innocence?
> For from Israel is it;
> A mechanic made it;
> And it is not God.
> Indeed, Samaria's bull
> Shall become splinters.[24]

> "And now they sin more and more,
> In that they make for themselves molten images,
> And of their silver, through their skill, idols,
> Wholly the product of mechanics.
> 'To such,' they say, 'sacrifice.'
> Men kissing calves!"[25]

Bethel, the royal sanctuary, he nicknames "Bethaven."[26] To
Hosea, such pagan concepts and immoral practices made him firmly
convinced that the people and their religious leaders did not really
know God.[27] He has Jahweh say to them:

> "What shall I do with you, O Ephraim?
> What shall I do with you, O Judah?
> For your piety is like a morning cloud,
> Or like the dew that leaves early.

> Therefore will I hew them by the prophets;
> I will slay them by the words of my mouth,
> And my judgment will go forth like the light.
> For I delight in piety, not sacrifice;
> And in the knowledge of God, rather than burnt-offerings."[28]

Thus Hosea's doctrine of God is not one of an indulgent deity or one whose moral discrimination is blurred; like Jesus of Nazareth, this Hebrew prophet was able to hate sin without despising the sinner. He regarded the disasters and the suffering which follow wrongdoing as evidence for God's loving guidance, rather than his anger, which makes use of tragedy to prevent worse disasters.

> "Therefore, lo, I (Jahweh) am going to hedge up her way
>   with thorns;
> And I will erect a wall against her,
> So that she cannot find her paths.
> And she shall run after her lovers,
> But not overtake them,
> And seek them, but not find them.
> And she shall say, 'I will go back to my first husband,
> For it was better with me then than now.' "[29]

Israel must be chastened through suffering, but she will not be forsaken. Jahweh could no more reject Israel than Hosea could cast off Gomer. "That is the message of Hosea, the triumphant love of God, triumphant over wrath and judgment. What binds Israel and Yahweh is stronger than what separates them. Like Gomer, Israel will pass through a long period of discipline and purgation, 'without king, and without prince, and without sacrifice, and without pillar, and without ephod or teraphim' (3:4), but there will be a new covenant, a new marriage in which they will live together on the basis of a covenant God and a covenant people in justice and righteousness and mercy and love, and in faithfulness. Then Israel will know Yahweh as Yahweh knows her. Hosea sees the reality of the divine judgment and he sees how deep and terrible Israel's infidelity is, but he sees even more clearly the covenant faithfulness that outlasts judgment and a mercy that reconciles and restores and redeems a wayward and faithless people."[30]

Like Amos, Hosea made his contribution to the advancing concepts in religion which made Judaism persist through the years and which gave Christianity its rich Jewish heritage. Later prophets looked back to Hosea for the impulse toward their own creative thoughts. Isaiah of Jerusalem, Jeremiah, Ezekiel, and Deutero-Isaiah re-echoed his teachings of the love of God and of the necessity of knowing God's character and will. When Jesus sought justification for putting human need before ritual prescriptions it was the word of Hosea which he quoted: "It is mercy, not sacrifice, that I care for."[31]

As far as external contemporary events were concerned, the words of Amos and Hosea seem to have fallen on deaf ears. And yet both men had their disciples, who either encouraged the prophets to write down their oracles or wrote them down themselves as they remembered hearing them from the orations of the spokesmen of Jahweh. As a result of the inspiration of Amos and Hosea, an unknown prophetic writer in the northern kingdom began to engage in the preparation of a history of the Hebrew people, beginning with the story of Abraham. This so-called "E" (Ephraimitic) document made use of "Elohim" as the name for God, "Horeb" as the name for the sacred mountain in place of Sinai, and Shechem as the place where the conquest of Palestine began rather than Jericho. E's masterpiece is the story of Joseph (Genesis 37:5-48:22). Completed about 700 B.C., the "E" document reflects the political events of the eighth century. It was added to the "J" document by editors of the Kingdom of Judah when that kingdom was facing extinction (ca. 586 B.C.).[32]

C. Isaiah of Jerusalem, Prophet of Holiness.

Almost a contemporary of Amos and Hosea, Isaiah of Jerusalem began his prophetic activity "in the year that King Uzziah died."[33] Judah, like Israel under Jeroboam II, had been prosperous during the long reign of Uzziah, but Isaiah regarded it with aversion. Coming from the privileged class in the city of Jerusalem, brilliant of mind, poetic of temperament, Isaiah absorbed enough of the message of Amos to make him critical of conditions in both the northern and southern kingdoms. To Amos' concept of the righteousness of God and Hosea's idea of the love and mercy of God Isaiah added the notion of the holiness of God. Unlike Amos and Hosea, who spoke briefly and were never heard again, Isaiah was active in Jerusalem and Judah for some forty years. He was consulted, but not always willingly, by Ahaz and Hezekiah and with the latter he helped to institute a religious reform.

All the major emphases of Isaiah's teachings are present in the account of the theophany with which his career begins.

In the year that King Uzziah died, I saw the Lord sitting upon a throne, high and uplifted, with the skirts of his robe filling the temple. Over him stood seraphim, each having six wings, with two of which he covered his face, with two he covered his loins, and with two he hovered in flight. And they kept calling to one another, and saying,

"Holy, holy, holy, is the Lord of hosts;
The whole earth is full of his glory."

And the foundations of the thresholds shook at the sound of those who called, and the house filled with smoke.
Then said I,

"Woe to me! for I am lost;
For I am a man of unclean lips,
And I dwell among a people of unclean lips;
For my eyes have seen the King,
The Lord of hosts."

Then flew one of the seraphim to me, with a red-hot stone in his hand, which he had taken with tongs from the altar; and he touched my mouth with it, and said,

"See! this has touched your lips;
So your guilt is removed, and your sin forgiven."
Then I heard the voice of the Lord, saying,
"Whom shall I send,
And who will go for us?"
Whereupon I said,
"Here am I! send me."[34]

In this experience the holiness of God impresses itself upon him above everything else; the "holy one of Israel" becomes Isaiah's name for Jahweh. To the prophet, God's holiness meant his remoteness, his unapproachableness, his overwhelming majesty, his piercing glory; he also added to this concept an ethical emphasis: Jahweh is morally perfect, transcendent, and his justice and righteousness make holiness the supreme reality it is.[35] Jahweh is king, so exalted, so powerful, so extended in his sway that even the mightiest of empires, Assyria, falls under his farseeing control;[36] Jahweh is the determiner of the destiny of all nations, even Assyria.[37] Though he does not deny the existence of other gods, Isaiah moves still further along the road to monotheism; his idea of God is big enough to bend Assyria, the mightiest nation on the earth, to his righteous purpose.

Isaiah lived during the troublous times which marked the downfall of the northern kingdom.[38] During the early part of his career, Tiglath-pileser III of Assyria (745-727 B.C.) instituted his famous policy of shifting conquered populations from one part of the empire to another; though Judah was not ruthlessly destroyed, as was Israel, she became a vassal of Assyria in 734 B.C. and paid heavy tribute. In spite of Isaiah's advice not to trust in foreign alliances, King Ahaz negotiated with Tiglath-pileser III for help against a coalition headed by Rezin of Damascus and Pekah of Israel;[39] the prophet thought this would be ultimately disastrous for Judah and immediately destructive of the northern kingdom:

> Woe to the proud crown of the drunkards of Ephraim,
> And the fading flower of his glorious beauty,
> That rests on the heads of those overcome with wine!
> See! the Lord has one who is mighty and strong,
> One like a storm of hail, or a destroying tempest,
> Like a storm of mighty, overwhelming waters,
> That beats down to the earth with violence.
> And the proud crown of the drunkards of Ephraim
> Will be trampled under foot;
> And the fading flower of his glorious beauty,
> That rests on the head of a fertile valley,
> Will be like the early fig before summer,
> Which, as soon as a man sees it,
> While it is still in his hand, he swallows.[40]

As Isaiah anticipated, the successor of Tiglath-pileser, Shalmaneser V (727-722 B.C.), and his successor, Sargon II (722-705 B.C.), brought the northern kingdom to an end.

Shortly after the fall of Samaria, Ahaz died and was succeeded by Hezekiah (720-692). Again the prophet Isaiah recommended that the king should be wary of foreign alliances; belonging neither to the faction which curried favor with Egypt nor to the group which was pro-Assyrian, Isaiah urged Judah to rely on Jahweh, but since the nation had given its pledged word to Assyria it ought certainly to be true to that alliance. In spite of warnings, Hezekiah intrigued with Egyptian-supported small states in Palestine and Syria and with the anti-Assyrian Merodach-baladan of Babylon. A revolt broke out at Ashdod in 711, which was immediately crushed by Sargon; Judah was mercifully spared by not having any soldiers in the battle. Isaiah began to dramatize the danger of further reliance upon Egypt:

> In the year that the commander-in-chief came to Ashdod, when he was sent by Sargon, king of Assyria, and fought against Ashdod, and took it (now at that time the Lord had commanded Isaiah, the son of Amoz, saying, "Go and untie the sackcloth from your loins, and put off your sandals from your feet," and he had done so, going naked and barefoot), the Lord said, "As my servant Isaiah has gone for three years naked and barefoot, as a sign and symbol against Egypt and Ethiopia, so will the king of Assyria lead off the captives of Egypt and the exiles of Ethiopia, young and old, naked and barefoot, with buttocks uncovered, to the shame of Egypt. Then men will be dismayed and put to shame because of Ethiopia their hope and Egypt their pride. And the inhabitants of this coast-land will say on that day, 'See! this is the fate of those on whom we set our hope and to whom we fled for help to save us from the king of Assyria; how then can we escape?' "[41]

On another occasion, Isaiah referred to Egypt as "Rahab Sit-still;"[42] this exhibits Isaiah's contempt for Egypt and the pro-Egyptian party in Judah. He cries out against them:

> Woe to those who go down to Egypt for help,
> And rely on horses;
> Those who trust in chariots, because they are many,
> And in horsemen, because they are very numerous;
> But look not to the Holy One of Israel,
> Nor consult the Lord!
>
> Now the Egyptians are men, and not God;
> And their horses are flesh, and not spirit.[43]

Sargon II was succeeded on the throne of Assyria by the ruthless Sennacherib (705-681 B.C.). In 701, the Assyrian monarch quelled all resistance among the small allies of Egypt and moved on Jerusalem as the center of the anti-Assyrian coalition. The situation inside the city of Jerusalem became desperate, and Hezekiah sought to strengthen the defenses. One of the things he did was to stop the upper spring of Gihon and build a conduit for bringing every drop of water from this spring inside the walls of the city to the pool of Siloam, in order that Jerusalem might not be without an adequate supply of water during a siege.[44] Sennacherib gave his own version of his military invasion of Judah on a clay cylinder:

> As for Hezekiah the Jew, who did not submit to my yoke, 46 of his strong, walled cities, as well as the small cities in their neighborhood, which were without number,—by escalade and by bringing up siege engines, by attacking and storming on foot, by mines, tunnels and breaches, I besieged and took. . . . Himself, like a caged bird, I shut up in Jerusalem, his royal city. . . .[45]

In despair, Hezekiah sent for the prophet Isaiah; this time, Isaiah counseled fidelity to Jahweh as the only hope for the nation and people of Judah. Because Jahweh had been "blasphemed" by the king of Assyria, Jahweh was against Assyria and for Jerusalem.[46] Further, Isaiah promised that Assyrians would never take the city of Jerusalem:

> "Therefore thus says the Lord concerning the king of Assyria: 'He shall not enter this city, or shoot an arrow there; neither shall he come before it with shield, or cast a mound against it. By the way that he came, by the same he shall return; but he shall not enter this city,' is the oracle of the Lord. 'For I will defend and save this city for my own sake, and for my servant David's sake.' "[47]

For some mysterious reason, Sennacherib raised the siege of Jerusalem and took his troops back to Assyria.[48]

About Isaiah's private life we know very little. He was married and had two sons, whom he named according to some of his basic teachings; one was named "Shear-jesheb" ("a remnant will abide") and the other "Maher-shalal-hash-baz" ("quickly booty, speedily prey," or, in more recent language, "it won't be long now"). He was very familiar with the temple; in it he had his theophany

and in it later he denounced the drunken priests and prophets.[49]
He drew a group of disciples around him, to whom he intrusted his
writings.[50] There is a strong tradition that he died a martyr's death
during the early years of the reign of Manasseh (692-638 B.C.).

Isaiah's message, like that of Amos, is primarily one of judgment.
He denounced the popular conception of religion which rated
ritual above righteousness:

"Of what use is the multitude of your sacrifices to me,"
          says the Lord;
"I am sated with burnt-offerings of rams and the fat of
          fed beasts;
In the blood of bullocks and lambs and he-goats
          I take no delight.
When you come to visit me,
Who demands this of you—
          the trampling of my courts?
Bring no more worthless offering!
          the odor of sacrifice is an abomination to me.
New moon and sabbath,
          the holding of assemblies—
Fasting and festival
          I cannot endure.
Your new moons and your appointed seasons,
          my whole being hates;
They are a burden upon me;
          I am weary of bearing them.
So, when you spread out your hands,
          I will hide my eyes from you;
Even though you make many a prayer,
          I will not listen.
Your hands are full of bloodshed—
          wash yourselves clean;
Put away the evil of your doings
          from before my eyes;
Cease to do evil,
          learn to do good;
Seek justice,
          restrain the oppressor;
Uphold the rights of the orphan,
          defend the cause of the widow!"[51]

He criticized the economic and social sins of his day:

> The Lord will bring an indictment
> Against the elders and princes of his people.
> "It is you that have ravaged the vineyard;
> The plunder of the poor is in your houses.
> What mean you by crushing my people,
> And grinding the face of the poor?"
> Is the oracle of the Lord, the God of hosts.[52]

> Woe to those who rise up early in the morning
> To run after strong drink;
> Who sit late into the twilight
> Till wine inflames them;[53]

> Woe to you who join house to house,
> And add field to field,
> Till there is no more room,
> And you are left to dwell alone
> In the midst of the land![54]

> Your rulers are unruly,
>   and associates of thieves;
> Every one of them loves a bribe,
>   and runs after gifts;
> They uphold not the rights of the orphan,
>   and the cause of the widow comes not to them.[55]

The women of Judah have become bold and vampishly wanton.[56] The very distinction between right and wrong, good and evil, has become blurred:

> Woe to those who call evil good,
> And good evil;
> Who count darkness as light,
> And light as darkness;
> Who count bitter as sweet,
> And sweet as bitter![57]

Isaiah's message of judgment reaches its climax in his picture of the imminent day of Jahweh.[58] However, this great prophet did not look forward to the future without hope; a remnant, though an inconspicuous minority, will survive the judgment; they will be as a precious cornerstone of sure foundation.[59] It was in this idea of a remnant that we find the heart of Hebrew ethical idealism; the remnant was to be a group of spiritually minded people upon whom Jahweh could build the ideal order of the future. An ideal person, the Messiah, would be raised up to rule God's righteous people in the ideal age; contained in many places in his writings, though possibly not from Isaiah's own hand, are passages of hope and vision which paint a rosy picture of a warless world and the beneficent rule of a prince of peace. Perhaps the most familiar is in Isaiah 2:2-4:

> It shall come to pass in days to come,
> That the mountain of the Lord's house will be
> Established as the highest mountain,
> And elevated above the hills.
> All the nations will stream to it,
> And many peoples will come and say:
> "Come, let us go up to the mount of the Lord,
> To the house of the God of Jacob;
> That he may instruct us in his ways,
> And that we may walk in his paths;
> For from Zion goes forth instruction,
> And the word of the Lord from Jerusalem."
> Then shall he judge between the nations,
> And arbitrate for many peoples;
> And they shall beat their swords into plowshares,
> And their spears into pruning-hooks.
> Nation shall not lift up sword against nation,
> Nor shall they learn war any more.[60]

This Isaianic figure of the Messiah influenced the thought of later generations and lived on in the minds of the people. In this figure Jesus of Nazareth doubtless saw himself foreshadowed; certainly the early Christian Church saw in its Lord the fulfilment of Isaiah's dream of an ideal king.

D. *Micah of Moresheth-gath, a Prophetic Summarizer.*

Contemporary with Isaiah, and perhaps influenced by his writings, was the prophet Micah. In contrast to the city-born and city-bred Isaiah, Micah is a farmer, and his writings reflect his peasant sympathies. He began his ministry just prior to the fall of the northern kingdom, but he did most of his work in the stormy decade at the end of the eighth century. Sennacherib's army was ravaging the countryside—perhaps Micah's own farm was in the path of the Assyrian's "scorched earth" policy—and like a farmer Micah blames all his country's disasters on the city of Jerusalem. Cities like Samaria and Jerusalem embody the evil of the time.[61]

Micah does not add anything new to what his three predecessors among the prophets of the eighth century had said, but he takes the essence of the teachings of Amos, Hosea, and Isaiah and incorporates them into one brief statement, which many would regard in some respects as the greatest statement in the Old Testament:

> With what shall I come before the Lord,
> And bow myself before God most high?
> Shall I come before him with burnt-offerings,
> With calves a year old?
>
> Will the Lord be pleased with thousands of rams,
> With myriads of streams of oil?
> Shall I give my first-born for my transgression,
> The fruit of my body for the sin of my soul?
> You have been told, O man, what is good,
> And what the Lord requires of you:
> Only to do justice (Amos), and to love kindness (Hosea)
> And to walk humbly with your God? (Isaiah)[62]

Micah condemns unsparingly the social injustices of his contemporaries, singling out particularly the landlords who devise ways to fleece the peasants of their holdings:

> Woe to them who devise wrong,
> And work out wickedness upon their beds.
> In the morning light they do it,
> Because it is in their power.
> They covet fields and seize them,
> And houses and carry them off.
> So they crush a yeoman and his house,
> A man and his possessions.[63]

Next are the rulers:

> Then I said,
> "Hear now, you heads of Jacob,
> And rulers of the house of Israel,
> Is it not your place to know justice,

> You who hate the good, and love wickedness,
> Snatching their skin from upon them,
> And their flesh from upon their bones?"[64]

Then he speaks of the "prophets who lead my people astray, who preach prosperity when their mouth is filled; but if one does not put something in their mouths, they declare war against him!"[65]

> Her chiefs pronounce judgment for a bribe,
> And her priests declare oracles for hire,
> And her prophets divine for cash.
> Yet they lean upon the Lord, saying,
> "Is not the Lord in the midst of us?
> No misfortune can befall us."

> Therefore, because of you,
> Zion shall be plowed like a field,
> And Jerusalem shall become a ruin,
> And the temple hill a high place in a forest.[66]

Perhaps to a later hand belongs the messianic passage in Micah 5:2-4 which locates the birth place of the expected Messiah in Bethlehem.

Micah's words helped to influence King Hezekiah to begin a religious reform.[67] He removed the high places where the old fertility cults were still carried on; he cut down the sacred pillars and wooden poles which had been symbols of the Baalim in Canaanite religion; he broke into pieces the bronze serpent, supposedly constructed by Moses in the wilderness.[68] But the reform was short-lived, and a reaction set in under Manasseh, prophet-hating successor of Hezekiah.

SUGGESTIONS FOR FURTHER STUDY

A. E. BAILEY, *Daily Life in Bible Times,* pp. 182-211.

G. A. BARTON, *Archaeology and the Bible,* pp. 463-477.

H. M. BATTENHOUSE, *The Bible Unlocked,* pp. 162-186.

J. A. BEWER, *The Literature of the Old Testament,* pp. 74-120.

G. A. BUTTRICK, ed., *The Interpreter's Bible,* I, pp. 204-211, 317-324.

F. C. EISELEN, E. LEWIS, AND D. G. DOWNEY, eds., *The Abingdon Bible Commentary,* pp. 628-653, 759-767, 775-783, 791-797.

J. Finegan, *Light from the Ancient Past,* pp. 158-160.

H. T. Fowler, *The Origin and Growth of the Hebrew Religion,* pp. 70-98.

E. J. Goodspeed, *The Story of the Old Testament,* pp. 1-25.

F. James, *Personalities of the Old Testament,* pp. 210-281.

C. S. Knopf, *The Old Testament Speaks,* pp. 203-234.

E. A. Leslie, *The Prophets Tell Their Own Story,* pp. 13-158.

E. W. K. Mould, *Essentials of Bible History,* pp. 242-259, 299-303, 314-330.

J. B. Noss, *Man's Religions,* pp. 499-510.

W. O. E. Oesterley and T. H. Robinson, *Hebrew Religion: Its Origin and Development,* pp. 190-210.

R. H. Pfeiffer, *Introduction to the Old Testament,* pp. 415-488, 566-573, 577-584, 589-594.

J. M. P. Smith, *The Prophets and Their Times,* pp. 55-130.

Chapter Fourteen

THE DEUTERONOMIC REFORM

For seventy years after the prophetic proclamation of Micah there was no great prophet in Judah. They were evidently suppressed during the long reign of Manasseh (692-638 B.C.).[1] The people themselves went back to the gay festivities associated with the high places of the Canaanitish form of Jahweh worship, while Manasseh officially sponsored Assyrian cults for reasons of state. The Deuteronomic historian who composed II Kings gives a catalogue of Manasseh's religious policies:

> . . . He did that which was evil in the sight of the Lord, according to the abominations of the nations which the Lord dispossessed before the Israelites. For he built again the high places which Hezekiah his father had destroyed, and he erected altars for the Baal, and made a sacred pole as Ahab, king of Israel, had done, and worshiped all the host of the heavens and served them. He also built altars in the house of the Lord of which the Lord had said,
> "In Jerusalem will I put my name."
> Moreover he built altars for all the host of the heavens in the two courts of the house of the Lord. Likewise he caused his son to pass through the fire and practiced augury and witchcraft and he used to appoint necromancers and wizards. . . .
> He also set up the carved image of an Asherah that he had made, in the temple. . . .[2]

This did not mean that the worship of Jahweh had been given up, but only that there were other gods subservient to him—a kind of monarchical monotheism, a step backward in the development of Hebrew religion toward real monotheism.

We can guess, however, that the religious apostasy of Manasseh

122

did not pass without some protest. Judging by the reform which was finally brought out during the reign of King Josiah, the disciples of the eighth century prophets worked secretly, preparing to assume leadership in a more auspicious time. "Their cardinal principle was an exclusive, ethical, and spiritual monotheism. Yahweh alone is God, He alone is to be worshiped, all foreign cults are to be exterminated; and His own cult is to be purged of all images and all other heathen elements, however much they may have become part of Israel's worship. . . . To their first principle of the unity of God these reformers added therefore the second, the unity of the sanctuary. It followed, to their thinking, quite inevitably: if Yahweh was one, He had only one sanctuary where He might be worshiped and His oracle might be consulted. . . . Only, this worship must be pure, whole-hearted, and sincere, based on a true moral life, and free from all impure heathen elements. . . . This was a distinct compromise between the prophetic and the priestly views."[3]

The program of this reform party was put in written form, perhaps by one of the successors of the eighth century prophets. We have this superb literary product contained in our present Book of Deuteronomy, chapters 5-26 and 28; chapters 5-11 form the introduction and chapter 28 the conclusion, while chapters 12-26 comprise a law code, later known as the Deuteronomic Code. These men believed they were giving the people of Judah the great principles of the religion of Moses; they declared their work was written by Moses in order to enhance the authority of their laws.[4] Much of their work was an expansion of the earlier Book of the Covenant,[5] worked over in the light of the teachings of Amos, Hosea, Isaiah, and Micah, and brought up to date by the historical situation in the middle of the seventh century.

The Deuteronomic Code was brought out of hiding in the year 621 B.C., in connection with a religious reform begun in the eighteenth year of King Josiah, grandson of Manasseh; it was probably the basis for the reform and the instrument which touched it off. In that year, while some repairs were being made in the temple, Hilkiah the high priest found "a book of the law."[6] He put it into the hands of Shaphan the scribe, who read it to King Josiah. The king was prostrate when he heard the words of heavy judgment pronounced on the kingdom because of its foreign cults and evil practices. The prophetess Huldah, wife of one of the palace officials, evaluated the pamphlet as an authentic message from Jahweh, but she said judgment would not come to the nation during Josiah's reign.[7] Then the king summoned the people to a great assembly and led them as together they made a solemn covenant to keep zealously the statutes written in the newly discovered code. The stage was now set for the reformers to go to work.

> Then the king commanded Hilkiah, the high priest, and the second priest and the keepers of the threshold to bring out of the temple of the Lord all the vessels that were made for the Baal and the Asherah and for all the host of the heavens; and he burned them outside Jerusalem in the limekilns by the Kidron, and carried their ashes to Bethel. He also did away with the idolatrous priests, whom the kings of Judah had ordained to offer sacrifices in the high places in the cities of Judah and in the sanctuaries around Jerusalem; and those who offered sacrifices to the Baal, to the sun, the moon, and the constellations, and all the host of the heavens. Moreover he brought the Asherah from the house of the Lord outside Jerusalem to the Brook Kidron and burned it at the Brook Kidron, and ground it to powder, and cast the powder of it upon the graves of the common people. Furthermore he tore down the houses of the devotees of the fertility cult which were in the house of the Lord, . . . He also tore down the high places of the Satyrs, which stood at the entrance of the gate of Joshua, the governor of the city, . . . He also defiled Topheth, which is in the valley of Ben-Hinnom, that no man might make his son or his daughter pass through the fire to Molech. He took away the horses which the kings of Judah had given to the sun, at the entrance of the house of the Lord, . . . and he burned the chariots of the sun. The altars which were on the roof, the upper chamber of Ahaz which the kings of Judah had made, and the altars which Manasseh had made in the two courts of the house of the Lord, the king demolished and beat them down there, and cast the dust in the Brook Kidron. Moreover the high places that were east of Jerusalem, to the south of the hill of destruction, which Solomon, the king of Israel, had built for Ashtart, the abomination of the Sidonians, and for Chemosh, the abomination of Moab, and for Milcom, the abomination of the Ammonites, the king defiled. He shattered the sacred pillars, and cut down the sacred poles, and filled their places with the bones of men.[8]

Josiah ordered the same iconoclasm to be used all through Judah as far north as Bethel; he had his officials range through Samaria and destroy the temples of the high places that were in all the cities, slaying the priests upon the altar.

Undoubtedly the Deuteronomic Reform was a great landmark on the road to monotheism. The theology of the group of prophets who brought it to fruition is contained in the famous *Shema,* the keynote of the entire reform and one of the truly great verses in the Bible:

"Listen, O Israel; the Lord is our God, the Lord alone; so you must love the Lord your God with all your mind and all your heart and all your strength. . . ."[9]

At the beginning of the Deuteronomic Code stands the law of the single sanctuary; of prime importance to the reformers, this law involved the destruction of all other sanctuaries and the centralization of all worship in one place;[10] the Canaanites should have been exterminated back in the period of the conquest and all their sanctuaries and instruments of worship destroyed. This was not a very popular move, for it meant abolishing the rural and village priesthoods and giving the Jerusalem priesthood absolute control over Jahwism; literally, it meant that no animals could be killed at the local shrine for meat, but the code separated sacrifice from secular slaughter and allowed the latter anywhere provided the blood was not eaten.[11] The code also provided that tithes of crops and animals could be converted into money and brought to Jerusalem, there to be used to buy animals for the sacrifices.[12] Cities of refuge were designated where those who unintentionally killed someone might flee from those who would take their lives according to the law of blood revenge; up until this time, the altars of the now-forbidden local sanctuaries were asylums for these criminals.[13] Lay-judges were appointed to handle judicial matters at local shrines, but the priests at Jerusalem had the final decision in case of doubt.[14]

The Deuteronomic Code is distinguished throughout by a spirit of fairness, humaneness, and social justice. It is the message of the eighth century prophets in a concrete form. It pointed the way toward the elimination of poverty, but until that day should come it urged kindness in the treatment of the poor.[15] The orphan, the widow, the resident alien, the Levite (who had been thrown out of work with the abolition of the local shrines), the slave, and the casual passer-by were to be treated justly and kindly.[16] A unique system of poor relief was recommended:

"When you reap your harvest in your field, and forget a sheaf in the field, you must not go back to get it; it is to go to the resident alien, the orphan, and the widow, that the Lord your God may bless you in all your enterprises. When you beat your olive trees, you must not go over them a second time; that is to go to the resident alien, the orphan, and the widow. When you pick the grapes of your vineyard, you must not go over it a second time; that is to go to the resident alien, the orphan, and the widow. . . ."[17]

Things absolutely necessary for daily life, such as a handmill or an upper millstone, were not to be taken as security for a loan.[18] Every seventh year was to be one of remission, during which no debts could be collected.[19] Day laborers were to be paid daily, evidently because their need was often so desperate;[20] one who lent to a widow could not exact her clothing as security.[21] Justice was prescribed in the law courts; bribes were forbidden, along with any favoritism of the social status of litigants.[22] Lost property was either to be returned to its owner or carefully guarded until he could come and get it; every opportunity was to be seized to lend a helping hand to a neighbor in emergencies.[23]

The Deuteronomic Code was the first piece of Hebrew literature to be elevated to the status of holy scripture. It was the first "Bible," or authoritative, canonical book. Before this time, when men wanted to know the will of God, they inquired of a living prophet, priest, or seer; now a sacred document became a convenient substitute for consulting a person. In one sense, Deuteronomy is the real beginning of the Old Testament, for it was the first of a collection of writings later to be regarded as having special sanctity. After perfecting the Book of Deuteronomy, they began to survey their nation's history as an illustration and confirmation of their basic point of view: Jahweh was powerful and well-disposed toward his people, but his support and defense of them depended on their loyalty to him, the covenant they had made with him. Their philosophy of history was that there was a direct connection between their national prosperity and obedience to their national

God; calamity, such as foreign invasion, was considered punishment for their unfaithfulness to the covenant. With this thought in mind, they wrote what has come to be known as "The Deuteronomic History of the Hebrews."[24] Beginning with Moses, their history was brought down to their own day; then succeeding members of the reform group carried the story down to the Babylonian exile. The resulting literary product comprised the following books: Deuteronomy, Joshua, Judges, I and II Samuel, and I and II Kings. They used earlier materials, such as court records, temple annals, and the two parallel accounts of the kingdom under David and Solomon, one of which was evidently from the pen of an eyewitness.[25] The reign of every king they subjected to the strictest theological scrutiny; they were more interested in whether a king followed their idea of true religion or not and whether he opposed pagan practices or not than in describing what he accomplished as an administrator, builder, or warrior.[26]

Essentially the Deuteronomic Reform was based on the concept of love: Jahweh's love for Israel and Israel's loving response to Jahweh. He had taken the initiative and chosen them to be his people, not because they had any particular genius for religion, any native endowment, any ethical purity, or any merit at all, but rather because he loved them. Echoing the teachings of the prophet Hosea, Deuteronomy states:

". . . For you are a people consecrated to the Lord your God, the Lord your God having chosen you out of all the peoples that are on the face of the earth to be a people of his very own. It was not because you were the greatest of all peoples that the Lord set his heart on you and chose you (for you were the smallest of all peoples), but it was because the Lord loved you, and would keep the oath that he swore to your fathers, that the Lord brought you out by a strong hand, and rescued you from a state of slavery, from the power of Pharaoh, king of Egypt. . . ."[27]

The whole book of Deuteronomy is suffused with the sense of a covenant relationship between God and his people; because of God's love for her, Israel should be a holy people and should practice holiness both in the ritual purity of the cult and in the humanitarianism of the code of law. But this doctrine of love lacked the universality it was to have later in the teachings of Jesus; love was confined to fellow Israelites. Even though the Deuteronomic code recommends consideration for the resident alien, the nationalistic intensity of the reformers constituted one of the serious drawbacks in the religion they sought to strengthen. With Deuteronomy began the movement which made of Judaism the religion of a single sanctuary, a single city, a single nation, and a single book. This was not in the spirit of any of the great prophets; the absolutizing of the cult in terms of a narrow nationalism led to the criticisms of Jeremiah and the challenges later of Jesus of Nazareth.

Dominant in the Book of Deuteronomy and the succession of books which were produced by the reformers and their disciples was an unfortunate concept of the sovereignty of God; the divine justice seemed to demand that loyalty to God would produce good consequences and disloyalty bad.

> ". . . Be assured, then, that the Lord your God is God, a trustworthy God, who to a thousand generations keeps loving faith with those that love him and keep his commands, but one who immediately requites anyone who hates him, by destroying him, never delaying with anyone who hates him, but requiting him immediately. So be careful to observe the charge, the statutes and ordinances, that I am enjoining on you today."[28]

The code provided penalties for failure to obey many of the ordinances, but in the event of a great national disaster the principle of retribution would apply: "if the people were faithful to their God, he would be faithful to them and ensure their peace and prosperity. If they were unfaithful to him, he would reciprocate and punish them with war and disaster."[29] This has been one of the most influential ideas of the character of God in the history of religion: that if one does what God desires, he will prosper; but if he not, he will suffer. They attributed to God through this doctrine a completely human motive: jealousy; they extended the effects of his jealous action beyond the immediate culprits and pictured Jahweh as "punishing children for the sins of their fathers, to the third or fourth generation of those who hate me, but showing kindness to the thousandth generation of those who love me and keep my commands."[30]

The doctrine of retribution did not pass unchallenged, even in the writings of Old Testament religious leaders contemporary with and later than Deuteronomy. The book of Ezekiel contains a vigorous denial of the thought that any son should be punished for the sin of his father, or any father for the sin of his son:

> The word of the Lord came to me, saying,
> "What mean you by quoting this proverb in the land of Israel:
> 'The fathers eat sour grapes,
> And the children's teeth are set on edge'? As I live," is the oracle of the Lord God," you shall have no more occasion to quote this proverb in Israel. Behold, all lives are mine—the life of the son is mine equally with that of the father—the person who sins shall die."[31]

The book of Job is almost entirely constituted of a protest against the idea that the suffering of an individual is valid evidence of his wickedness—or of his father's.

The Deuteronomists saw in two outstanding national catastrophes confirmation of their theory of retribution: the fall of Samaria (721 B.C.)[32] and the fall of Jerusalem (586 B.C.).[33] Both had paid the supreme penalty of their failure to abide by the covenant. On a tragic note of ruin, the Deuteronomic literature closes. Its legacy to the religion of the Hebrews was a mixed one; the lofty spiritual teachings scattered throughout their writings must be taken along with survivals of ancient tribal religion. But for Bible readers today Deuteronomy and the books influenced by Deuteronomy stand among the chief of the Hebrew religious classics.

SUGGESTIONS FOR FURTHER STUDY

H. M. BATTENHOUSE, *The Bible Unlocked*, pp. 187-195.

J. A. BEWER, *The Literature of the Old Testament*, pp. 121-135, 214-233.

G. A. BUTTRICK, ed., *The Interpreter's Bible*, I, pp. 324-326; II, pp. 309-826, 853-1176.

F. C. EISELEN, E. LEWIS, AND D. G. DOWNEY, eds., *The Abingdon Bible Commentary*, pp. 318-438.

H. T. FOWLER, *The Origin and Growth of the Hebrew Religion*, pp. 99-113.

E. J. Goodspeed, *The Story of the Old Testament,* pp. 41-46, 68-78.

F. James, *Personalities of the Old Testament,* pp. 282-299.

C. S. Knopf, *The Old Testament Speaks,* pp. 251-254.

L. B. Longacre, *The Old Testament: Its Form and Purposes,* pp. 13-57.

E. W. K. Mould, *Essentials of Bible History,* pp. 330-335.

J. B. Noss, *Man's Religions,* pp. 510-513.

W. O. E. Oesterley and T. H. Robinson, *Hebrew Religion: Its Origin and Development,* pp. 211-215.

R. H. Pfeiffer, *Introduction to the Old Testament,* pp. 178-187, 232-238, 293-412.

J. M. P. Smith, *The Prophets and Their Times,* pp. 145-148.

Chapter Fifteen

THE PROPHETS OF THE DECLINE AND FALL OF JUDAH

A. *Zephaniah, Nahum, and Habakkuk.*

Almost contemporary with the Deuteronomic reform, although apparently not connected with it, the prophet Zephaniah lived and worked in the city of Jerusalem. He seems to have been roused to activity by the same series of events with which Jeremiah first dealt;[1] both prophets reflected the terror in the kingdom of Judah which was caused by the rumor that a barbarous horde from beyond the Caucasus, the Scythians, were about to overrun Palestine and all the western horn of the fertile crescent.[2] Zephaniah was a native of Jerusalem,[3] and was connected with the royal family by blood.[4] He sees in the threatened Scythian invasion Jahweh's punishment of a sinful nation, the advance guard of the awful Day of Jahweh which had been predicted by Amos· and Isaiah.[5] The keynote of the book is stated in 1:2,3:

"I will utterly sweep away everything
  From upon the face of the ground," is the oracle of the Lord.
"I will sweep away man and beast;
  I will sweep away the birds of the air, and the fish of the sea.
  And I will cause the wicked to stumble,
  And I will cut off mankind from off the face of the ground,"
  Is the oracle of the Lord.

This awful day was to bring destruction to the entire civilized world; even Assyria, the Canaanite nations, Judah, Egypt, and Ethiopia were all to meet their doom. The prophet uses the blackest imaginable coloring to portray the Day of Jahweh:

Near at hand is the great day of the Lord;
Near and speeding fast!
Near at hand is the bitter day of the Lord,
On which the warrior will cry in terror!
A day of wrath is that day;
A day of trouble and distress,
A day of desolation and waste,
A day of darkness and gloom,
A day of cloud and thundercloud;
A day of the trumpet and battle-cry,
Against the fortified cities,
And against the lofty battlements.

"And I will bring trouble upon mankind so that they shall
     walk like blind men";
Because they have sinned against the Lord.
And their blood shall be poured out like dust,
And their flesh like dung.
Neither their silver nor their gold
Will be able to rescue them.
On the day of the wrath of the Lord, and in the fire of his zeal,
All the earth shall be consumed;
For a complete destruction, indeed a frightful one, will he make
Of all the inhabitants of the earth.[6]

However, Zephaniah's doctrine of the day of Jahweh is softened
by his belief that a remnant will remain; in holding this he was
following the preaching of Amos and Isaiah.[7] This small group in
society he addresses as "you meek of the earth, who do his will,"
and exhorts them to "seek righteousness, seek humility; perhaps
you may be hidden on the day of the anger of the Lord."[8]

Just prior to the destruction of Nineveh (ca. 612 B.C.), the
prophet Nahum gloats over the prospect of its downfall. He may
have belonged to the anti-Assyrian party in Judah—those who
favored a strong alliance with Babylonia in the days of the decline
of the Assyrian Empire.[9] His book is an expression of the religious
and political mind of the court party in Judah toward the end of
the reign of Josiah. The language is vivid and dramatic:

Woe to the city, bloody throughout,
Full of lies and booty!
Prey ceases not.
The crack of the whip, and the noise of the rumbling wheel,

And the galloping horse, and the jolting chariot;
The charging horseman, and the flashing sword,
And the glittering spear, and a multitude of slain,
And a mass of bodies, and no end to the corpses!
They stumble over the corpses![10]

Nahum has no word of warning or criticism of the sins of Judah;
because of this he undoubtedly found himself in opposition to
Jeremiah.[11]

Habakkuk is often called the philosopher among the prophets.
We know nothing about his life, but scholars think the book which
bears his name was written *ca.* 604 B.C. Its three brief chapters
contain some of the finest statements of truth in all religious
literature. Habakkuk begins by complaining to Jahweh that wickedness is running riot everywhere in the land;[12] so far Jahweh
has done nothing to correct the iniquitous state of affairs in Judah.
Jahweh replies that he is about to do something: he will bring
forth the terrible Chaldeans (Babylonians) who will destroy
everything:

> "For behold, I am raising up the Chaldeans,
> That savage and impetuous nation,
> That marches through the breadth of the earth,
> To seize habitations that are not his own.
>
> "Terrible and dreadful is he (the Chaldean nation);
> Judgment and destruction go forth from him.
> Swifter than leopards are his horses,
> And keener than wolves of the desert.
> His horses prance,
> And his horsemen come from afar;
> They swoop down like a vulture hastening to devour.
>
> "Wholly for violence does he come;
> Terror marches before him;
> And he gathers up captives like sand,
> He makes scorn of kings,
> And rulers are a joke to him!
> He laughs at all fortresses,
> And heaps up dirt and captures them.
>
> Then he changes like the wind and passes on,
> And he makes strength his god."[13]

But Habakkuk has difficulty in thinking that the righteous Jahweh would use the dread Chaldeans to cause the righteous among his chosen people to suffer. After challenging Jahweh to stop the Chaldeans and preserve the righteous, Habakkuk takes his position on a watchtower and waits for the outcome.[14] Jahweh speaks:

> Then the Lord answered me, saying,
> "Write the vision clearly upon the tablets,
> That one may read it on the run.
> For the vision is a witness for the appointed time,
> And speaks of the end, and does not lie,
> If I tarry, wait for it;
> For it will surely come without delay.
>
> "Verily, the wicked man—I take no pleasure in him;
> But the righteous lives by reason of his faithfulness."[15]

Thus the prophet concludes that the real life of the upright man is not in outward circumstances or material prosperity, but in his moral integrity; he must walk and live by his trust and faithfulness to God. Of Habakkuk's contribution to the history of religion J. M. Powis Smith says:

> The difference between this prophet's affirmation that piety pays and that of his predecessors is that he has pondered over this problem and thought it through . . . It is a reasoned faith rather than one that has been placidly accepted without question at the hands of tradition . . . But Habakkuk differs from his predecessors also in the deeper content he reads into the reward of piety . . . Just as in some great passages in Jeremiah, there is here a contrast between material benefits and the deep and abiding worth of the things of the spirit, in a personal experience of God.
>
> This contribution of Habakkuk constitutes a new phenomenon in the history of prophecy. Heretofore, the prophets have been content to say, "Thus says Yahweh." . . . But here is something different. This prophet is asking questions. He is daring to call in question a traditional dogma. . . . He is seeking for light upon a difficult question, and he looks for that light to come from Yahweh, the source of all his light. Thus he furnished to the Scriptures of his race and of the

world an illustration and example of the recognition of the right of inquiry and investigation in the field of ethics and religion. . . . He has established for all time the principle that the search for truth is an essentially religious procedure.

This bit of prophecy is an illustration of a familiar truth, viz., that faith is always an achievement, not a mere inheritance. The Hebrews, of the Exilic and post-Exilic periods at least, had to fight for their faith. It was difficult to believe in Yahweh as the supreme God where Yahweh's people were rapidly losing all place and power in the political world. . . . It is the glory of Judaism that men like Habakkuk kept faith alive in the hearts of the people during a series of national calamities that might well have crushed the life out of it. The faith of Judaism grew richer and stronger the more severely it was tried.[16]

B. *Jeremiah of Anathoth, Prophet of Individualism*

Jeremiah was the greatest character of the period of the decline and fall of Judah; some would go further and say that Jeremiah was the greatest character of the Old Testament. We know more about him biographically than any other of the personalities of the Old Testament; this is largely because he had a close friend, Baruch, who acted as his secretary and biographer. Baruch's work is incorporated in the Book of Jeremiah.[17]

Jeremiah was born *ca.* 650 B.C. as the son of a priestly family of Anathoth, a small country village located about four miles northeast of Jerusalem.[18] He took life seriously, even as a young man; he never married, for he could not bear to bring children into the world in such a troublous time.[19] He was forced to leave Anathoth because his fellow townsmen plotted against his life; from then on he carried on his public prophetic work in Jerusalem.[20] His public career began in the year 626 B.C., when the Scythians were threatening to invade Palestine.[21] Against his own will, Jahweh persuaded him and consecrated him in a great spiritual experience which gave him a consciousness of prophetic mission unequalled among the prophets:

> The word of the Lord came to me, saying,
> "Before I formed you in the womb, I knew you,
> And before you were born I set you apart,

> I appointed you a prophet to the nations."
> Then said I,
> "Ah, Lord God! I cannot speak;
> For I am only a youth."
> But the Lord said to me,
> "Do not say, 'I am only a youth';
> For to all to whom I send you shall you go,
> And all that I command you shall you speak.
> Do not be afraid of them;
> For I am with you to deliver you,"
> Is the oracle of the Lord.
> Then the Lord stretched forth his hand, and touched
>   my mouth. And the Lord said to me,
> "See! I put my words in your mouth;
> This day I give you authority over the nations
>   and kingdoms,
> To root up and to pull down, to wreck and to ruin,
> To build and to plant."[22]

His call was accompanied by a series of visions;[23] like the other prophets, Jeremiah was a man of mystical religious experiences.

In Jerusalem, Jeremiah's work centered in the temple.[24] In his book we have glimpses of dramatic incidents which happened there. On one occasion, toward the beginning of the reign of Jehoiakim,[25] Jeremiah preached a sermon in which he foretold the total destruction of the temple; this so infuriated a mob of priests, prophets, and people that they plotted to kill him. Government officials intervened and saved him from death. Some remembered a similar prophecy made by Micah during the reign of Hezekiah and the fact that he was not punished.[26] Also, Jeremiah gained the support of Ahikam, son of Shaphan, a prominent leader.[27] On another occasion, Jeremiah took a group of Rechabites into the temple and tried to get them to drink wine; when they would not, Jeremiah contrasted their faithfulness to their religious conviction with the faithlessness of the people of Judah, who would be punished because of their disloyalty to Jahweh.[28] One day Jeremiah appeared in the temple with a wooden yoke around his neck, symbolizing his belief that national bondage would result from the anti-Babylonian policies of King Zedekiah;[29] a prophet Hananiah took the yoke off Jeremiah's neck and smashed it on the pavement; on the next day Jeremiah appeared in the temple wearing a yoke or iron. One sermon of Jeremiah's so irritated the priest Pashur that he had Jeremiah confined to the stocks for twenty-four hours.[30]

Because of his criticism of official policies, Jeremiah was seldom in favor with king and court. When King Jehoiakim heard that Baruch was reading Jeremiah's sermons publicly in the temple courts he ordered them burned.[31] When the captives were deported in 597 B.C., Jeremiah was left behind; he wrote a letter to the exiles shattering their belief that they would be able to return in a short time.[32] When, during the siege of Jerusalem by the Babylonians just before the collapse of Judah, Zedekiah and the slave-owners repudiated an earlier promise to free their slaves, Jeremiah denounced them in scathing terms; they had evidently freed the slaves during the battle as a pious gesture to invoke Jahweh's assistance, but had re-enslaved them when the Babylonian army temporarily lifted the siege to meet a threat from an Egyptian force.[33] During this same lull in the fighting, Jeremiah tried to leave Jerusalem to look after some property in his native Anathoth;[34] he was arrested at the city gate and charged with an attempt to desert to the Babylonians.[35] This he denied, but he was cast into prison. Once King Zedekiah sent for him and asked him for a message from Jahweh; Jeremiah repeated what he had said before: Zedekiah would be captured by Nebuchadnezzar. Subsequently Jeremiah was cast into a dungeon in the prison yard in which the mud was deep and where he was without food; when an Ethiopian eunuch, Ebed-melech, reported this to Zedekiah, the king ordered Jeremiah pulled up out of the dungeon and let loose in the prison yard.[36] Soon after, Zedekiah sent for Jeremiah secretly and asked his advice; again Jeremiah urged the king to surrender to the Babylonians and warned him that continuous resistance would result in utter destruction for himself, the city of Jerusalem, and the people of Judah.[37]

When the city of Jerusalem finally fell,[38] Jeremiah was released from prison and allowed to stay in Judah with Gedaliah the governor.[39] The short-lived peace was broken by civil war and the murder of Gedaliah. Jeremiah advised the assassins and rebels against going to Egypt, but they went and took Jeremiah with them.[40] Jeremiah continued the same type of preaching among the Jews in Egypt which they had been accustomed to hear from him in Jerusalem, and he died there, probably as a martyr.[41]

Jeremiah restated with remarkable clarity the ethical teachings of the great prophets who had preceded him. One day he stood at the entrance of the temple courtyard and spoke to everyone who approached him as follows:

> Thus says the Lord of hosts, the God of Israel: "Amend your ways and your doings, that I may establish your home in this place. Trust not in deceptive words, such as 'The temple of the Lord, the temple of the Lord, the temple of the Lord is this!' For if you but amend your ways and your doings—if you practice strict justice toward one another, if you do not oppress the resident alien, the orphan, and the widow, nor shed innocent blood in this place, nor run after other gods to your own hurt—I will establish your home in this place, in the land which I gave to your fathers for all time. But, as it is, you trust in deceitful words, that are of no avail. What? Steal, murder, and commit adultery, swear falsely, offer sacrifices to the Baal, and run after other gods, whom you do not know, and then come and stand before me in this house which bears my name, and say 'We are safe'—only to practice all these abominations! Has this house which bears my name become a robbers' cave in your eyes? . . . "[42]

Jeremiah believed that mere ritual was futile. Jahweh says:

> ". . . What care I for the frankincense that comes from Sheba,
> Or the sweet cane from a distant land?
> Your burnt-offerings are not acceptable to me,
> And your sacrifices bring me no pleasure."[43]

The prophet is constantly stressing the need for a religion which issues in right conduct and Godlike acts.

> ". . . Though you wash yourself with lye and use much soap,
> Your guilt stands ingrained in my sight," is the oracle
> of the Lord God.[44]

> "If you return, O Israel," is the oracle of the Lord,
> "return to me;
> If you put your detestable things out of my sight,
> and waver not;

If you swear, 'As the Lord lives,' in truth,
               in honesty, and in uprightness;
Then shall the nations invoke blessings on one another
               through him, and in him shall they glory."[45]

He spares no group:

"Because from the least to the greatest of them each one
               traffics in ill-gotten gain;
And from prophet to priest each one deals in falsehood."[46]

"I have given heed and listened, but none speaks the truth,
None repents of his wickedness, saying 'What have I done?'
Each runs his own wayward course,
Like a horse plunging headlong in battle."[47]

For I have seen your adulteries, and your lustful neighings,
Your lewd intrigues, and your infamous deeds,
               on the hills in the open field.
Woe to you, O Jerusalem! how long will it be till
               you are made clean?"[48]

Some of his ethical teachings sound very much like the Deuteronomic Code, which he probably favored at first:

Thus says the Lord: "Do justice and righteousness; deliver the despoiled from the hand of the oppressor; commit no wrong or violence against the resident alien, the orphan, and the widow; and do not shed innocent blood in this place. . ."[49]

Like Amos, he criticizes the rich landowners:

"Woe to him that builds his house by unrighteousness,
His upper chambers by injustice;
That makes his neighbor serve him without pay,
And gives him not his wages;

But your eyes and your thoughts
Are set on nought but your ill-gotten gain,
On the shedding of innocent blood,
And the practice of outrage and violence."[50]

Jeremiah's idea of God is very similar to that of Isaiah; both prophets stopped short of an absolute monotheism, yet Jeremiah believed that Nebuchadnezzar was Jahweh's servant,[51] and thus an essential part of Jahweh's world plan and world outlook.

When Judah has been chastised "for seventy years," the other nations of the world, including Babylon, will be disciplined even more severely.[52] Jeremiah had a deep and abiding faith in God and in a future in which the children of Israel would be restored to Jahweh's favor and bound to him in an unbreakable covenant.

"At that time," is the oracle of the Lord, "I will be the God of all the families of Israel, and they shall be my people."

> Thus says the Lord:
> "The people that escapes from the sword
> Shall find grace in the wilderness;
> When Israel goes to seek rest,
> The Lord from afar shall appear to him.
> With an everlasting love have I loved you,
> Therefore with kindness will I draw you to me.
> Once more will I build you, and you shall be built,
> O virgin of Israel!
> Once more shall you take your timbrels,
> And go out in the dances of those who make merry.
> Once more shall you plant your vineyards
> On the hills of Samaria;
> The planters shall plant, and shall raise their praises;
> For a day shall come when the vintagers shall call
> On the hills of Ephraim:
> 'Arise, and let us go up to Zion,
> To the Lord our God!'"[53]

The covenant will be a new and better one because it will be written "on their hearts":

"Behold, days are coming," is the oracle of the Lord, "when I will make a new covenant with the house of Israel and with the house of Judah, not like the covenant which I made with their fathers on the day that I took them by the hand to lead them out of the land of Egypt—that covenant of mine which they . . . broke, so that I had to reject them—but this is the covenant which I will make with the house of Israel after those days," is the oracle of the Lord: "I will put my law within them, and will write it on their hearts; and I will be their God, and they shall be my people. And they shall teach no more every one his neighbor, and everyone his brother, saying,

'Know the Lord'; for all of them shall know me, from the least of them to the greatest of them," is the oracle of the Lord; "for I will pardon their guilt, and their sin I will remember no more."[54]

Jeremiah spoke of Jahweh as a father. God speaks:

> "Have you not now been calling to me,
>   'My father! the comrade of my youth!
> Will he keep up his anger forever,
>   will he retain it to the end?'
> Thus have you spoken, but have done
>   all the evil that you could."[55]

His mercy extends to both the northern and southern kingdoms:

> So the Lord said to me, "Apostate Israel has proved herself more in the right than faithless Judah. Go, then, and proclaim these words toward the north:
>   'Return, apostate Israel,' is the oracle of the Lord;
>   'I will frown no more upon you.
>   For I am full of kindness,' is the oracle of the Lord;
>   'I will not keep up anger forever.'
> . . . But at that time they shall call Jerusalem 'The throne of the Lord,' and all the nations shall gather there, to celebrate the name of the Lord in Jerusalem, and they shall no more follow the stubborn promptings of their evil minds. In those days the house of Judah shall join the house of Israel, and they shall come together from the land of the north to the land that I gave your fathers for a heritage.
>
>   "I thought, 'How I would rank you among the sons,
>   And give you a pleasant land,
>   The goodliest heritage of all the nations!'
>   And I thought, 'Surely you will call me "Father,"
>   And will not turn back from me.'
>   But as a woman is faithless to her lover,
>   So were you faithless to me, O house of Israel,"
> Is the oracle of the Lord.[56]

Jahweh is a god of truth,[57] kindness, justice, and righteousness.[58]

The most creative idea in all of the writing, preaching, and thinking of the prophet Jeremiah was his doctrine of the individual. He has often been called the prophet of individualism. The earlier prophets had concentrated on the public, socially experienced relationship between Jahweh and his chosen people, the Hebrews; this had been the basis of the old covenant. Jeremiah advanced the new idea of a subjective experience of relationship between Jahweh and the individual. As a result of the notion of retribution, which had been strongly emphasized by the Deuteronomic reform, the individual enjoyed only those blessings which were his as a result of belonging to the nation, and he had to share the responsibility for the sins of the group. Now Jeremiah gives expression to the truth of individual moral responsibility.

> "In those days they shall say no more,
> 'The fathers have eaten sour grapes,
> And the children's teeth are set on edge';
> But everyone shall die for his own guilt—everyone
> shall have his own teeth set on edge. . . ."[59]

This truth upon which Jeremiah seized had great importance for the future of religion; if God can be approached directly it would become increasingly evident that the temple sacrifices were no longer, necessary for the highest spiritual experiences.

Jeremiah's loneliness and sensitivity to the sufferings of his people have earned for him the epithet of "the weeping prophet." Tradition ascribes to him the authorship of the book of Lamentations; actually, the five dirges which comprise that book were written a long time after the exile, but they reflect the same general attitude toward life which was characteristic of Jeremiah. In the purity of his affection and in the depth of his sorrow Jeremiah was a forerunner of Jesus of Nazareth; in fact, some people in the Galilee of the first century A.D. saw in Jesus the reincarnation of Jeremiah.[60]

C. Ezekiel, Prophet-Priest in Exile.

Ezekiel was the son of Buzi, a Jerusalem priest and a member of the family of the Zadokites, whom the Deuteronomic reform had established as the official priesthood of the land. Ezekiel was evidently growing up in Jerusalem during the height of Jeremiah's activity, and although the two never met and were radically different in temperament and outlook Ezekiel seems to have been influenced by the uncompromising courage of the older man. In 597 B.C. Ezekiel was one of the ten thousand or more Jews carried into captivity by King Nebuchadnezzar.[61] In Babylonia, on the banks of the river Chebar, the great canal of the city of Nippur, in the year 592 B.C. Ezekiel had a mystic vision which constituted his call to preach.[62] For twenty-two years or more he was active as a prophet and "watchman to the house of Israel."[63]

Prior to the fall of Jerusalem in 586 B.C., the message of Ezekiel was predominantly one of doom. He portrayed the tragic sins of his people; their guilt is so deep and dark that the fall of Judah cannot be averted. He surpasses Hosea and Jeremiah in the depth of his despair; he could see nothing but sin among the Hebrew people from the very start. Even in Egypt "they rebelled against me; they did not cast away each one the detestable things which they loved, nor did they forsake the idols of Egypt."[64] The history of Israel was one of continuous infidelity and apostasy; even at birth Judah was corrupt, the child of an Amorite father and a Hittite mother.[65] Israel's sin is so terrible to Ezekiel because he so profoundly appreciates the holiness and righteousness of Jahweh. In his indictment against Jerusalem social wrongs bulk more largely than ritual sins and all classes are held equally guilty.

Again the word of the Lord came to me, saying,

"O mortal man, say to her: 'You are a land on which no rain or shower shall fall on the day of my indignation. For the rulers in the midst of the land are like a roaring lion that rends his prey; they devour men's lives, they seize treasure and wealth, they make many widows in the midst of her. Her priests also violate my law, and profane my holy things; they make no difference betwen sacred and secular, and teach no difference between unclean and clean; they shut their eyes to my sabbaths, so that I am profaned among them. The princes in the midst of her are like wolves that rend the prey, shedding blood, and destroying lives, to get dishonest gain. Her prophets also daub their walls with whitewash, showing them empty visions, and giving them lying divinations, saying, "Thus says the Lord God," when the Lord has not spoken.

The common people practice oppression, and commit robbery; they wrong the poor and needy, and treat the resident alien with injustice. . .' "[66]

After the fall of Jerusalem the message of Ezekiel changed from one of doom to one of hope. Unlike his fellow exiles, to whom the news of this great calamity brought the death of all their high hopes, Ezekiel felt relieved. The judgment of Jahweh had been carried out; there was no need of further warning. God will not permit his honor to be profaned among the nations; he will vindicate his holy people before the whole world. Israel, now dead and buried in exile, will be restored to the Holy Land; both the northern and southern kingdoms will be reunited into one. The spirit of Jahweh will give life to the nation.[67]

Ezekiel adds to the developing concept of God among the Hebrew people by describing Jahweh as a shepherd. False shepherds, those who feed themselves and not the sheep, are condemned.

The word of the Lord came to me, saying,

"O mortal man, prophesy against the shepherds of Israel; prophesy, and say to them, 'Thus says the Lord God: Woe to the shepherds of Israel, who have attended themselves! Should not shepherds attend to the flock? . . . So my flock was scattered for want of a shepherd, and became food to all the beasts of the field; my flock wandered over all the mountains, and over every high hill; my flock was scattered over all the face of the earth, with none to seek or search for them.' "[68]

God himself becomes the good shepherd.

"For thus says the Lord God: 'Behold, here am I, and I will seek and search for my flock . . . I will lead them out of the nations, and gather them from the lands; and I will bring them to their own country, and tend them on the mountains of Israel, in the valleys, and in all the best places of the land . . . I myself will tend my flock and I myself will lead them to their pasture,' is the oracle of the Lord God. 'I will seek out the lost, I will bring back the strayed, I will bind up the wounded, I will strengthen the sick; and I will watch over the fat and strong ones, tending them rightly.' . . .

"Therefore thus says the Lord God to them: 'Behold, here

am I, and I will judge between the fat sheep and the lean
sheep . . . And I will set up one shepherd over them, to tend
them, even my servant David, who shall tend them, and be
a shepherd to them. I will make with them a covenant of
peace, and I will remove wild beasts out of the land, so that
they may live securely in the steppes, and sleep in the woods.
And I will bless them round about my hill, and will send
down the showers in their season—showers of blessing shall
they be . . . And they shall no longer be a prey to the nations,
nor shall the beasts of the earth devour them; but they shall
live securely, with none to make them afraid. I will provide
for them a soil renowned for fruitfulness, and they shall no
longer be consumed with hunger in the land, and no longer
bear the reproach of the nations. Thus they shall know that
I, the Lord, am their God, and that they, the house of Israel,
are my people,' is the oracle of the Lord God. 'And you my
flock are the flock of my pasture, and I the Lord am your
God,' is the oracle of the Lord God."[69]

Because of his combination of the characteristics of a prophet
and a priest, Ezekiel has been called the father of Judaism. He
restated the doctrine of individual moral responsibility, a principle which Jeremiah had preached.[70] On the literary side, he
introduced a new type of writing, the allegory; this was used
extensively later in Jewish writings, as in the book of Jonah.[71]

SUGGESTIONS FOR FURTHER STUDY

H. M. BATTENHOUSE, *The Bible Unlocked*, pp. 195-207, 216-220.

J. A. BEWER, *The Literature of the Old Testament*, pp. 136-183.

G. A. BUTTRICK, editor, *The Interpreter's Bible*, I, pp. 326-330.

HAROLD C. CASE, *Jeremiah*.

F. C. EISELEN, E. LEWIS, and D. G. DOWNEY, eds., *The Abingdon
Bible Commentary*, pp. 677-745, 798-814.

H. T. FOWLER, *The Origin and Growth of the Hebrew Religion*,
pp. 114-129.

E. J. GOODSPEED, *The Story of the Old Testament*, pp. 26-40,
47-67.

F. JAMES, *Personalities of the Old Testament*, pp. 300-359.

C. S. KNOPF, *The Old Testament Speaks*, pp. 241-243, 246-281.

E. A. LESLIE, *Jeremiah*.

E. A. Leslie, *The Prophets Tell Their Own Story*, pp. 159-260.

E. W. K. Mould, *Essentials of Bible History*, pp. 303-304, 335-344, 367-368.

J. B. Noss, *Man's Religions*, pp. 513-519, 523-525.

W. O. E. Oesterly and T. H. Robinson, *Hebrew Religion: Its Origin and Development*, pp. 216-232, 248-258.

R. H. Pfeiffer, *Introduction to the Old Testament*, pp. 482-565, 594-601.

J. M. P. Smith, *The Prophets and Their Times*, pp. 131-216.

Chapter Sixteen

THE EXILE

A. *Consequences for the Religion of the Hebrews*

The fall of the southern kingdom[1] had profound consequences for the religion of ancient Israel. It was at one and the same time the most tragic catastrophe the Hebrew people had ever experienced and also the most beneficial for the future of Judaism. The destruction of the temple, which had been exclusively dedicated to the worship of Jahweh, the cessation of the sacrifices on the altar of burnt offering, the termination of the royal family of David after more than four hundred years of continuous rule,[2] and the deportation of the important people of the realm turned many away from the worship of Jahweh. The nation was gone; therefore many assumed that the god of the nation was also through. After all, Marduk of the Babylonians seemed to have more power than Jahweh of the Hebrews. So profound was this change in national status that historians drop the name Hebrews and speak of the people who survived the fall of Jerusalem in 586 B.C. as Jews. "The Hebrews who entered the exile a nation emerged from it a religious community. The exile may be thought of as the bridge across which Israel journeyed in its historical and racial pilgrimage from the soil to the soul."[3] Among these people, to lead them on their journey, emerged spiritual geniuses, of whom the greatest was the unknown prophet of a universal god, Deutero-Isaiah; it was with them that the further and final development of Judaism lay.

It was very providential that the Babylonian exile was not as disastrous to the Jewish captives as the Assyrian deportation had been to their compatriots of the northern kingdom.[4] Nebuchadnezzar was a fairly benevolent type of despot; his hostility had been directed against the continuance of Hebrew national sovereignty. There is clear evidence in the Old Testament that the communal life of the Jewish exiles in Babylon was very much like that to which they had been accustomed in Palestine. Nebuchadnezzar allowed them to live together and follow their old ways of life and culture without disturbance; this tolerant policy made for the continuance of the worship of Jahweh.[5] The Jews were settled in a rich alluvial plain, intersected by irrigation canals, a section far superior to Palestine from an agricultural standpoint; it was located between Babylon and Nippur, two of the greatest cities of the world. So those who settled down and took advantage of the economic and agricultural opportunities throve wonderfully well.

At first, however, it was difficult to feel at home. Many of the Jews were so bitter in their homesickness and sorrow, and so full of love for Jerusalem and hatred for their enemies, the Babylonians and the Edomites, who had gloated over Judah's fall, that they sang the kind of song found in Psalm 137. We are impressed by the beauty and pathos of its opening words and repelled by the savage cruelty of its closing expressions, but it reveals how impossible some of them considered their status to be.

> By the rivers of Babylon,
> There we sat down, and wept,
> When we remembered Zion.
> Upon the poplars in the midst of her,
> We hung up our harps.
> For there our captors
> Demanded of us songs,
> And our tormentors, mirth;
> "Sing us some of the songs of Zion."
>
> How could we sing the songs of the Lord
> In a foreign land?
> If I forget you, O Jerusalem,
> May my right hand fail me!
> May my tongue cleave to my palate,
> If I do not remember you;
> If I set not Jerusalem
> Above my highest joy!

> Remember, O Lord, against the Edomites,
> The day of Jerusalem!
> They who said, "Raze it, raze it,
> To its very foundation!"
> O daughter of Babylon, destructive one,
> Blessed be he who requites to you
> The treatment that you dealt out to us!
> Blessed be he who seizes your little ones,
> And dashes them to pieces upon a rock!

"But the mood of irreconcilability with their lot passed. Economically the situation became better than tolerable. Those who farmed the rich soil found themselves harvesting big crops. Stoney Judah had never yielded such. Many Jews, freed from farming, entered government service, as soldiers and officials. Others, turning their economic opportunities to advantage, became merchants and traders, following a direction which many of their ethnic brethren were even now pursuing in Egypt and Syria, and were to pursue increasingly down the centuries. . . ."[6] The only restriction Nebuchadnezzar placed on the Jewish exiles was that they were not to return to Palestine; if they observed this and paid their taxes, their lot was not an unhappy one. During the exile the Jews changed from a provincial to a cosmopolitan people.

With the temple gone, many Jews felt that direct access to Jahweh was no longer possible; the temple services, with their external aspects centering around the altar of burnt offering, were now wanting and substitutes for those had to be found among those Jewish exiles who desired to remain loyal to Jahweh. Spiritually minded prophets of an earlier day[7] had pointed toward the possibility of a non-sacrificial type of worship; during the exile this was to become a reality. But it was not easy to find something which would take the place of the sacrificial system, a system which had touched the people in endless ways in everyday life as well as in their worship proper. Yet they began to gather together on the Sabbath day in their homes, read to each other their historical and prophetical writings as well as the scrolls of the Torah, and remind themselves of their ancient feasts. Out of these gatherings there developed a lasting Jewish institution, the synagogue. One of the chief features of these Sabbath meetings of the Jews in Babylonia came to be an exposition and interpretation of some portion of their sacred literature for the correction or comfort of the hearers; these talks were the predecessors of the sermon so familiar to Christian church-goers and synagogue worshipers today. Public prayer also became a prominent feature of the Sabbath services, along with the singing of psalms which had been used in the temple worship and songs which had been composed during the exile. Prophets and priests are both mentioned among the exiles; they would have been the leaders in worship. As a day set apart for worship every week the Sabbath became supremely important during the exile;[8] among their non-Jewish neighbors, it would help to make the Jews a people set apart.

Together with the Sabbath great stress came to be laid upon the rite of circumcision. The neighbors of the Jews in Babylonia and Egypt evidently knew nothing of such a custom; thus it became another distinctive mark of a Jew. This heightened the consciousness among the Jewish exiles that they were different from, even superior to, the peoples around them. They began to observe more strenuously the ancient laws regarding purification and forbidden food; the original meaning of such laws would have been forgotten, but the observance of them was another means of separating the Jews from their neighbors.

During the exile, the priesthood began to turn its energies, heretofore occupied with the temple sacrificial system and cultic rites, toward the elaboration of precepts for the regulation of the everyday life of the people. Some time after 570 B.C., an unknown author, akin to Ezekiel in thought and form of expression, compiled a small law book technically called the Holiness Code. Now comprising chapters 17-26 of the book of Leviticus, the Holiness Code mediated between Deuteronomy and the later Priestly Code, in which it was afterwards incorporated. The laws in it deal mainly with ceremonial purity, qualifications for the priesthood, religious festivals, and related themes. The author was dominated by the beliefs that Jahweh is holy and that his people must be holy; his idea of holiness was physical remoteness, not moral perfection; hence Jahweh's people must separate themselves from everything which the priests of Jahweh regarded as tabu. Jahweh is made to state these ideas clearly:

You must be holy to me; for I, the Lord, am holy, and have separated you from other peoples to be mine.[9]

But in spite of the cultic holiness of the Holiness Code it enumerates some notable social-ethical principles,[10] such as:

> You must not cherish hate against your fellow-countryman;
> you must be sure to reprove your fellow, but not incur sin
> because of him. You must not avenge yourself, not bear a
> grudge against the members of your own race, but you must
> love your fellow (neighbor) as one of your own, since I am
> the Lord.[11]

Of course the author of the Holiness Code meant this to apply only to the fellow Jew, but his emphasis upon the inner disposition rather than the outward deed marks an advance upon earlier concepts of neighborliness.

B. *Deutero-Isaiah, Unknown Prophet of a Universal God*

The reign of Nebuchadnezzar, the greatest king of the Neo-Babylonian (Chaldean) Empire, came to an end with his death in 561 B.C. It had been a long and prosperous period; the king concentrated on Babylonia, rebuilding cities, erecting and repairing temples, and reconditioning canals. But after his death political anarchy set in, resulting in the rapid decline of the empire. After a succession of weak rulers, Nabonidus, a Babylonian of priestly descent, seized the throne in 555 B.C.; busy with military campaigns in the western horn of the fertile crescent, he left affairs in Babylon in the hands of his son Belshazzar.[12] It was during the reign of Nabonidus that the Chaldean Empire fell to the invading Medes and Persians under the leadership of Cyrus the Great (538 B.C.).

The Babylonian populace seems to have welcomed Cyrus as a friend and benefactor; the gates of the city had been opened to the Persian army by the priests of Babylon, who were evidently disgusted by Nabonidus' enthusiasm for non-Babylonian forms of worship. None would have watched the rise of Cyrus nor gloried in his conquest of Babylon more eagerly than the Jewish exiles. While the Babylonian rulers were benevolent despots, they had effectively silenced any hopes of a restoration of the Jewish community in Palestine. Cyrus inaugurated a new policy in the treatment of conquered peoples; he was more tolerant and considerate of his subject people, particularly in the realm of religion.[13] Whenever he found exiles in his realm he permitted them to return to their native lands and resume their native customs and religion. In the very year of his conquest of Babylonia, Cyrus issued an edict of freedom; while no Jews made the trip to Palestine for another two or three years, they always considered this edict a great turning point in their history;[14] it "marked the literal dawn of a new day, the birth of a new people and of a new religion. Without it there probably would have been no Hebrew Bible, no Judaism, and, so far as we can humanly estimate, no Christianity."[15]

Among those who watched the rise of Cyrus was a young Jew whose name is unknown but whose writings have been preserved in the Book of Isaiah. For want of a better title, he has usually been given the cumbrous name of Second or Deutero-Isaiah, because his oracles were affixed to the writings of the earlier Isaiah of Jerusalem.[16] To him, Cyrus was the one chosen of Jahweh to give his people their freedom and to send them on the way to the building of an ideal state. Though he knew how to rebuke his fellow Jews, he stirs them up to a new hope and assures them that Jahweh's plan is one of deliverance and restoration for his people. He begins with a note of hope:

"Comfort, O comfort my people," says your God;
"Speak to the heart of Jerusalem, and call to her,
That her time of service is ended, that her guilt is
        paid in full,
That she has received of the Lord's hand
        double for all her sins."[17]

He tells how there will be a highway miraculously prepared for Jahweh, for he will go straight through the Syrian desert and lead his exiled people home to Jerusalem and Judah.

Hark! one calls:
"In the wilderness clear the way of the Lord,
Make straight in the desert a highway for our God.
Let every valley be raised up,
And every mountain and hill brought low;
Let the uneven ground become a plain,
And the rugged heights a valley.

Then shall the glory of the Lord be revealed,
And all flesh shall see it together;
For the mouth of the Lord has spoken."[18]

He called upon Jerusalem to watch for the coming of Jahweh.

On a high mountain get you up,
    O heralds of good news to Zion!
Lift up your voices with strength,
    O heralds of good news to Jerusalem!
Lift it up, fear not;
Say to the cities of Judah,
    "Behold your God!"
See! the Lord God is coming with might,
    his own arm having won him the kingdom;
See! his reward is with him,
    and his recompense before him.
Like a shepherd he tends his flock,
    with his arms he gathers them;
The lambs he carries in his bosom,
    and gently leads those who give suck.[19]

With the teaching of Deutero-Isaiah on the nature and personality of God we reach the zenith of Hebrew religious belief. Monotheism has been implicit in the teachings of the earlier prophets, but this unknown prophet was the first to set forth in unmistakable and explicit terms the truth of monotheism itself. Jahweh is the only god:

Thus says the Lord, the King of Israel,
His Redeemer, the Lord of hosts:
"I am the first, and I the last;
Apart from me there is no God.[20]

I am the Lord, and there is no other;
Beside me there is no God.
I will gird you, though you knew me not,
That men may know, from the east
And from the west, that besides me there is none.
I am the Lord, and there is no other . . ."[21]

Jahweh is the omnipotent creator of the heavens and the earth.

Have you not known? Have you not heard?
The Lord is God everlasting,
The Creator of the ends of the earth.
He does not faint, nor grow weary;
His insight is unfathomable.[22]

My hand laid the foundations of the earth,
My right hand spread out the heavens;
When I call to them, they stand up together.[23]

He is called "the God of all the earth."[24] And yet he is Israel's
God in a very special sense, that she might lead other people to
him.[25] He is in control of history,[26] eternal God, the "first and
the last."[27] As creator, the cosmic forces and the nations are
to him small and insignificant.

Who has measured the waters in the hollow of his hand,
And ruled off the heavens with a span,
And enclosed in a measure the dust of the earth,
And weighed the mountains with a balance,
And the hills in scales?
Who has directed the mind of the Lord,
And instructed him as his counselor?
With whom took he counsel for his enlightenment,
And who taught him the right path?
Who taught him knowledge,
And showed him the way of intelligence?
Lo! the nations are like a drop from a bucket,
Like fine dust in the scales are they counted.
Lo! the coast-lands weigh no more than a grain;
And Lebanon itself is not sufficient for fuel,
Nor its beasts enough for burnt-offering.
All the nations are as nothing before him,
Blank ciphers he counts them.[28]

Deutero-Isaiah identified the gods of the other nations with their
idols; his superbly sarcastic picture of the worship of wooden
images drove that practice out of Hebrew religion once and for
all; never again were the Jews to forsake the worship of the one
true spiritual god.[29]
Deutero-Isaiah spoke very strongly of the need for redemption.

This was to be the first prerequisite for the restoration of the Hebrew nation; Jahweh wants his people to return to him.

> Remember these things, O Jacob,
> Israel, for you are my servant!
> I formed you, my servant you are,
> O Israel, who will not be forgotten by me.
> I have blotted out your transgressions like a mist,
> Your sins like a cloud;
> Return to me, for I have redeemed you.[30]

Reminiscent of Hosea,[31] Deutero-Isaiah believes that Jahweh has tender regard for the exiles and will lead them back to Jerusalem.[32] But the redemption is to include all mankind, Gentiles as well as Jews; Israel's restoration is only the means leading to the salvation of the whole world.

> He says, "It is too slight a thing for your being my servant
> That I should but raise up the tribes of Jacob,
> And restore the survivors of Israel;
> So I will make you a light of the nations,
> That my salvation may reach to the end of the earth."[33]

> The Lord has made bare his holy arm in the eyes of all
>   the nations;
> And all the ends of the earth shall see the salvation
>   of our God.[34]

> "I the Lord have called you in righteousness,
> And have grasped you by the hand;
> I have kept you, and have made you a pledge to the people,
> A light to the nations;
> In opening blind eyes,
> In bringing prisoners out of the dungeon,
> Those who sit in darkness out of the prison. . . ."[35]

Nothing which the people have done has called forth Jahweh's plan to pardon and protect them; it results solely from his loving nature. In this concept the prophet reveals a warmth of feeling and a depth of appreciation of the love of Jahweh unmatched elsewhere in the Old Testament.[36]

Throughout the prophetic oracles of Deutero-Isaiah appears the figure of the suffering servant; this is the prophet's most original religious conception. Of whom was he speaking? Some say the servant of Jahweh is to be identified with some individual figure of past or contemporary history; others maintain it refers to the ideal messianic figure of the future, the one which Jesus fulfilled; but an increasing number of scholars takes the position that the suffering servant is to be identified with Israel as a nation. She has been selected by Jahweh, not for special favors, but for special service, to bring the saving knowledge of Jahweh and his holy will to all mankind. The suffering servant is the theme of the so-called "servant songs," four in number, but the term is also mentioned elsewhere.[37] The election of Israel is mentioned in the first of the "servant songs;" this is not inconsistent with the thought of Jahweh as the universal God for all men, for Israel is chosen so that she might make known to the Gentiles the character and will of God.

> See! my servant, whom I uphold;
> My chosen one, in whom I delight.
> I have put my spirit upon him,
> He shall bring forth justice to the nations.
> He shall not cry, nor shout,
> Nor make his voice heard in the streets;
> A bent reed shall he not break,
> And a flickering wick shall he not quench.
> Faithfully shall he bring forth justice;
> He shall not flicker or bend,
> Till he establish justice in the earth,
> And the coast-lands wait for his teaching.[38]

In the second of the songs the privilege and honor of Israel in being chosen by Jahweh are brought out even more clearly.[39] With the third of the "servant songs" there is no clear indication of the means whereby the servant is to accomplish his mission:

> I gave my back to the smiters,
>   and my cheek to the pluckers of hair;
> My face I hid not
>   from shame and spitting.[40]

His mission is not to be effected through honor and prestige, but through dishonor and suffering. This idea is carried to the heights in the fourth and last "servant song:"[41]

For he grew up like a sapling before us,
Like a root out of dry ground;
He had no form or charm, that we should look upon him,
No beauty, that we should admire him.
He was despised, and avoided by men,
A man of sorrows, and acquainted with pain;
And like one from whom men hide their faces,
He was despised, and we esteemed him not.

Yet it was our pains that he bore,
Our sorrows that he carried;
While we accounted him stricken,
Smitten by God and afflicted.
He was wounded for our transgressions,
He was crushed for our iniquities;
The chastisement of our welfare was upon him,
And through his stripes we were healed.[42]

The great truth that would then dawn upon all mankind following the servant's suffering and death was that he had been going through these vicariously. Innocent himself of any sin, he had borne the penalty of their transgressions; because of his willingness to suffer, Jahweh will give him the victor's crown.

The fruit of his suffering shall he see, and be satisfied;
Through his affliction shall my servant, the Righteous One,
Bring righteousness to many,
And he shall bear their guilt.
Therefore will I divide him a portion with the great,
And with the strong shall he share the spoil;
Because he poured out his lifeblood to the utmost,
And was numbered with the transgressors,
While he bore the sin of many,
And made intercession for the transgressors.[43]

Though it is probable that Deutero-Isaiah did not intend any of his "servant" passages to refer to the Messiah as a great individual who would be the future saviour of his people, some of his descriptions of the suffering servant were so concrete and individualized that later generations concluded that he was speaking of a person who would some day redeem the world through his suffering. The early Christians found in Jesus of Nazareth the embodiment of the ideal of the servant of Jahweh. Jesus evidently saw in the mission of service claimed by the servant the meaning of his own work; he found the basic philosophy of his life illustrated in Deutero-Isaiah, if he did not actually take it from this unknown prophet: "Yet I am like a servant among you"; "For the Son of Man himself has not come to be waited on, but to wait on other people, and to give his life to free many others."[44] On Calvary, Jesus made the doctrine of vicarious sacrifice a historical reality.

SUGGESTIONS FOR FURTHER STUDY

W. F. ALBRIGHT, "The Biblical Period," in L. Finkelstein, ed., *The Jews: Their History, Culture, and Religion,* pp. 45-50.

A. E. BAILEY, *Daily Life in Bible Times,* pp. 212-246.

A. E. BAILEY and C. F. KENT, *History of the Hebrew Commonwealth,* pp. 252-276.

G. A. BARTON, *Archaeology and the Bible,* pp. 481-485, 547-548.

H. M. BATTENHOUSE, *The Bible Unlocked,* pp. 211-216, 220-225.

J. A. BEWER, *The Literature of the Old Testament,* pp. 183-188, 200-213.

G. A. BUTTRICK, ed., *The Interpreter's Bible,* I, pp. 330-335.

F. C. EISELEN, E. LEWIS and D. G. DOWNEY, eds., *The Abingdon Bible Commentary,* pp. 653-677.

J. FINEGAN, *Light from the Ancient Past,* pp. 190-200.

H. T. FOWLER, *The Origin and Growth of the Hebrew Religion,* pp. 129-138.

F. JAMES, *Personalities of the Old Testament,* pp. 360-389.

C. S. KNOPF, *The Old Testament Speaks,* pp. 282-288, 295-299.

E. W. K. MOULD, *Essentials of Bible History,* pp. 345-367, 372-376.

J. B. NOSS, *Man's Religions,* pp. 520-523, 525-528.

W. O. E. OESTERLEY and T. H. ROBINSON, *Hebrew Religion: Its Origin and Development,* pp. 233-247, 259-272.

R. H. PFEIFFER, *Introduction to the Old Testament,* pp. 239-250, 449-480.

J. M. P. SMITH, *The Prophets and Their Times,* pp. 217-240.

Chapter Seventeen

POST-EXILIC JUDAISM: THE JEWS IN THE PERSIAN PERIOD

A. *The Restoration of Jerusalem.*

As we have seen,[1] when Cyrus the Great brought an end to the Neo-Babylonian Empire, he reversed the policy of previous conquerors in dealing with exiles. The first step he took toward implementing a more magnanimous treatment of subject peoples was the issuance, in 538 B.C., of an edict permitting exiles to return to their native lands and resume their native customs and forms of worship. There are three versions of the decree of Cyrus given in the Old Testament;[2] in addition, Cyrus left his own account of his conquest of Babylon and his decree of release on a clay cylinder inscribed in cuneiform, now found in the British museum:

> . . . The gods (whose sanctuaries were in ruins) . . . I brought back to their places, and caused them to dwell in a habitation for all time. All their inhabitants I collected and restored them to their dwelling places. . . . May all the gods, whom I brought into their cities, pray daily before Bel and Nabu for long life for me, and may they speak a gracious word for me. . . .[3]

Not many Jewish exiles took advantage immediately of the edict of freedom. After almost a half century of living in Babylonia many of them had been bound to the new land by ties of marriage and friendship and by commercial associations. Also, the journey to Palestine was dangerous and expensive, while conditions in Judah were hardly likely to inspire anyone to make a permanent home there. The wall of Jerusalem had been breached and black-ened in spots; the temple, even though it had remained in use, would appear as a ruin and the palace buildings and the other principal structures of the city would have been in a dilapidated condition. However, a small band of returning exiles, under the leadership of Sheshbazzar, a prince and a descendant of the royal line of David,[4] made the long trip to Jerusalem and heroically began the restoration of the lost fortunes of Judah; this event occurred *ca.* 535 B.C. Just who was in the group, besides the leader, how many there were, and what they accomplished are not known; Sheshbazzar himself disappeared from the scene of history. These first exiles evidently made a beginning in restoring the temple and the city of Jerusalem, but for some reason the work was inter-rupted and suspended for almost two decades.

In the year 520 B.C., a fresh expedition of returning exiles was led back to Palestine by Zerubbabel, a grandson of the unfortunate King Jehoiakin[5] and hence a lineal descendant of King David, a person with Messianic possibilities, and Joshua, a priest of the highly revered Zadokite branch of the Levite tribe. In the group were also two prophets, Haggai and Zechariah, who kept urging the cautious Zerubbabel to rebuild the temple.[6] This group may have been spurred to a renewal of the rebuilding of Jerusalem by disorder and unrest in the Persian Empire following the accession of Darius in 522; there was a glimmering of hope that Zerubbabel would reestablish the royal line of David and rule an independent kingdom in Judah.

The first act of the returning exiles in Jerusalem was the erec-tion of an altar on the site of the ruined temple and the reinsti-tution of regular morning and evening sacrifices. The temple area was cleared of debris and the foundation stones were laid for the reconstruction of the temple. But the Persian governor of Syria stopped the work, perhaps because he feared the Jews were planning a revolt. After appealing to Darius, who checked the state decrees of Cyrus, the Jews resumed the work, this time with direct Persian help, and the temple of Zerubbabel was dedicated in 515.[7] Just what happened to Zerubbabel is not known; he dropped out of sight and was never mentioned again. Perhaps he tried to set up a Davidic kingdom in Jerusalem,[8] something even the tolerant Persians would not have permitted. His disappear-ance left the priest Joshua in control of the Jewish community in

Palestine; from that time on the Jews regarded themselves as a theocracy ruled by the priesthood.

The result of the failure of the restored Jerusalem community to recapture the lost fortunes of the house of David was a decline in the restoration of Judah. For approximately sixty years the little priestly state of Judah did not influence greatly currents of Jewish life in other parts of the world. Sacrifices were carried on in the restored temple in the midst of the ruins of Jerusalem. None of the historical narratives in the Old Testament cover this period, but two anonymous prophetic voices uttered their messages: the authors of Isaiah 56-66 and the Book of Malachi. The former takes the point of view that the glorious restoration of Israel, which he pictures even more magnificently than Deutero-Isaiah, has been delayed because of the ritual and moral transgressions of the people and of their leaders. Malachi is more optimistic; though he accuses his fellow Jews of slackening zeal, cynicism, and lack of respect for Jahweh, he believes that Jahweh has not forsaken his people; the Day of Jahweh will be a terrible one for the wicked but a joyful one for the righteous:

"For behold, the day shall come burning like an oven,
    And all the arrogant and every doer of wickedness
        shall be stubble,
    And the day that comes shall burn them up," says the
        Lord of hosts,
"So that it will leave them neither root nor branch.

But for you who revere my name, there will arise
    The sun of righteousness, with healing in its wings.
    And you shall go forth skipping like calves from the stall,
    And you shall trample upon the wicked;
    For they shall be dust under the soles of your feet,
    On the day that I am about to make," says the
        Lord of hosts.[9]

Malachi's reference to a "messenger" who shall "prepare the way before me"[10] was a prediction which made a great impresson on Jewish and Christian thought of a later time.[11]

Many faithful Jews in Babylonia were disturbed by the state of affairs in Palestine. One of these was a young Jew who was a favorite cup-bearer to the Persian king Artaxerxes I (465-424

B.C.) at his palace in Susa. It may have been in December, 445, that this young man, named Nehemiah, learned from his brother Hanani and other Jews who had recently come from Jerusalem how bad the situation there really was. They said to him:

> The survivors who are left from the captivity there in the province are in great misery and reproach, and the wall of Jerusalem is broken down and its gates have been destroyed by fire.[12]

When Artaxerxes discovered Nehemiah's concern he sent the young cup-bearer to Jerusalem with the powers of a governor to superintend the rebuilding of the city's walls and to reorganize the community. It was in 440 that Nehemiah arrived in Jerusalem; he began the work of rebuilding the city wall early in August, 439; the complete task of restoring the city was finished by December, 437.

Nehemiah was one of the great characters of the Old Testament; he should be ranked along with Moses and David as one of the creative personalities of Hebrew history. Our knowledge of him is derived from the so-called memoirs of Nehemiah, written by his own hand,[13] and later incorporated into the larger work of the Chronicler. Because of this unique autobiography we know him as we know few others of the Old Testament personalities. In spite of opposition, Nehemiah gave to the Jewish people a new confidence; under his wise leadership a stable, semi-autonomous government was established with Jerusalem as the center; in time this district under Jewish control grew in extent until it included approximately half of the territory which had been in the kingdom of Judah in 586 B.C. When the city of Jerusalem was strengthened, Nehemiah turned his attention to measures of urgent social and religious reform. He abolished an evil system of usury by which the rich oppressed the poor.[14] He reorganized the temple by restoring the traditional tithe; temple income on grain, wine, and oil had fallen off so much that Levites and singers had been forced to desert the temple service and make a living in the fields.[15] He renewed a strict observance of the Sabbath by the closing of the city gates and by forbidding the day to be spent in the pursuit of trade.[16] Then Nehemiah began to work on a problem which distressed him very much: the growing Jewish custom of mixed marriages; though he was not as strict as Ezra was some years later, he still recommended drastic treatment:

> In those days also I saw the Jews who had married women of Ashod, of Ammon, and of Moab, and their children spoke half in the language of Ashod, and none of them could speak in the Jews' language, but according to the language of each people. Therefore I contended with them and cursed them and beat some of them and pulled out their hair and made them swear by God, saying,
>
> "You shall neither give your daughters to their sons nor take their daughters as wives for your sons or for yourselves. Did not Solomon, king of Israel, sin by these means? Yet among many nations there was no king like him, and he was beloved by his God, and God made him king over all Israel; nevertheless foreign wives were the cause of his sin; and shall it be reported of you that you do all this great evil, and break faith with our God in marrying foreign women?"[17]

Thus, Nehemiah was not without his faults, but few Old Testament characters show a more manly vigor and single-minded devotion to a cause. With Ezra, he forms the connecting link between the Jews of Palestine and those of the dispersion; it was largely due to these two men that the Jewish community with a Jewish religion was preserved.

Although there is no unanimity of opinion regarding the dates of Ezra and Nehemiah, nor even concerning the question of which one precedes the other, many scholars believe that Nehemiah terminated his work a generation, possibly, before Ezra came on the scene. There are more conflicting interpretations concerning the career and significance of Ezra than about any other character in the history of religion. Some go so far as to deny that there was such a man and to assert that the book which bears his name was a figment of the imagination of the Chronicler who wrote about a century after the events he was describing.[18] In support of this contention is the very peculiar omission of the name of Ezra from the list of Israel's famous men compiled by ben Sirach *ca.* 175 B.C.;[19] also, in II Maccabees there is an account of Nehemiah's work, but not Ezra's.[20] At the other extreme there is the fantastic story in II Esdras 14, in which Ezra reproduces from memory the twenty-four books of the Hebrew scriptures after they had been lost; it is this line of tradition which saw in Ezra the restorer of the Law—really a second Moses. The truth probably lies somewhere between the two extremes.

Assuming there was such a person as Ezra, he journeyed to Jerusalem early in the reign of Artaxerxes II, perhaps in the year 397 B.C. Bringing with him a caravan of fifteen hundred men, perhaps five thousand in all, including priests and Levites,[21] Ezra inspired new life to the community of poor and struggling Palestinian Jews. A priest and a scribe, he brought with him to Palestine the exilic ideal of a separate and ritually sanctified Jewish community, as it had been taught by the prophet Ezekiel. This ideal was embodied in an edited and recodified revision of the legislative history of the Hebrew people, now known as the Torah, or Pentateuch, the first five books of the Old Testament. This revision included the three earlier codes of law—the Book of the Covenant (Exodus 20:22-23:19), the Deuteronomic Code (Deuteronomy 12-26), and the Holiness Code (Leviticus 17-26)—but with additional material contributed by a group of priests who had been working in Babylonian Judaism for almost a century. Ezra's chief purpose in coming to Palestine was to reorient the Palestinian Jews toward a strict interpretation of the Torah:

> For Ezra had set his heart to seek the law of the Lord to keep it, and to teach in Israel statutes and ordinances.[22]

Toward this end, he read portions of the Torah before all the people assembled "in front of the Water Gate;"[23] Ezra stood on a raised platform and paused occasionally so that his priestly assistants could instruct people by sections in the meaning of the Torah—both suggestive of similar features in the later worship of the synagogue.

Ezra first applied the drastic measures of his reform to the institution of marriage. The edict of Nehemiah[24] had not put a stop to the practice of interracial marriages, so Ezra recommended the expulsion of foreign wives and the children of mixed marriages.

> Now when these things had been completed, the princes approached me and said,
> "The people of Israel and the priests and the Levites have

not separated themselves from the peoples of the lands, from their abominations, even from the Canaanites, the Hittites, the Perizzites, the Jebusites, the Ammonites, the Moabites, the Egyptians, and the Amorites. For they have taken wives from their daughters for themselves and their sons, so that the holy race has mixed itself with the peoples of the lands, and the hands of the princes and the rulers have been foremost in this inconsistency."

Now when I heard this thing, I tore my garment and my mantle, and pulled the hair from my head and my beard, and sat down appalled. . . .

Then all the men of Judah and Benjamin assembled at Jerusalem. . . .; and all the people sat in the open square in front of the house of God, trembling on account of the occasion itself and also because of the pouring rain. Thereupon Ezra the priest arose and said to them,

"You have broken faith and have married foreign women to increase the guilt of Israel. Now therefore make confession to the Lord, the God of your fathers, and do his will and separate yourselves from the peoples of the land and from the foreign wives."[25]

In spite of the religious exclusivism evident in Ezra's decree, it is possible that the times demanded such a narrow-minded concept of religion for the preservation of Judaism and its literature. Then Ezra organized a complete system of religious worship centering in the institutions of the temple, the sacrifices, and the Levitical priesthood. He has been called the father of Judaism; upon the foundation of the old pre-exilic faith he superimposed the clear-cut legalistic religion later known as Judaism. "The chief figures of the reorganized faith were priests; its infallible guide was a book of the Law (the Torah); its concern was directed toward matters of ritual: what was clean and unclean, purifications and expiations, permissions and prohibitions, and the general obedience to scriptural law. . . ."[26] The Jews were well on the way toward becoming a religiously as well as racially exclusive group. Ezra and his retinue, following in the spirit of Nehemiah, gave Judaism the stamp it was to bear through all the ages down to our own time.

B. *The Priestly Code and the Pentateuch.*

An unknown priestly author from among the Babylonian Jews began *ca.* 500 B.C. to compile the laws and usages which had grown up among the Jewish exiles; his purpose was to convince his people of the authority and the importance of the religious institutions of Israel, through which alone, according to his way of thinking, salvation could be achieved. Combining history with law, he gathered together many ancient sources which had not yet found a place in earlier documents; following a grandiose scale, he begins with the creation of the world and carries the story down to the establishment of the priestly system under Moses. The document which he completed before 450 B.C. is known as the Priestly Code, or "P," and it was one of the basic source documents which were put together *ca.* 400 B.C. to make up the Pentateuch.[27] His work may be divided into two parts: the first consists of narratives beginning with the creation and ending with the exodus from Egypt under the leadership of Moses (Genesis 1:1—Exodus 15:21); the second consists mainly of legal codes and completes the story with the settlement in the land of Canaan (Exodus 15:22—Deuteronomy 34:12).

The work of the priestly author and editor is well illustrated by the passage with which their work begins—Genesis 1:1-2:4. The priestly emphasis is at once apparent, for the climax of the whole march of God's creative activity is the institution of the Sabbath. The first to be divinely ordained, the Sabbath is so sacred that God himself observes it. "In all this one hears the clear voice of the priest, who thus confirms the Sabbath as one of the supreme institutions of Judaism. In observing it one is doing something that is being done by God himself."[28] After recounting the details of the flood the priests emphasize the laws prohibiting murder and the eating of blood for all mankind.[29] Circumcision was given a central place in the stories relating to Abraham.[30] In the story of the exodus from Egypt "P's" interest centered in the institution of the Passover.[31] Thus did these priestly writers use history merely for the purpose of teaching the origin of the sanctity of the various rites and institutions which the priesthood was trying to make acceptable after the exile.

The priestly writers viewed all of life religiously, or, rather, according to the theological presuppositions of the priesthood. Their ideal was the theocracy; the Jewish people were to be ruled by their religious leaders. They were interested in instruction in the Torah, primarily on the ritualistic side. Religious worship was organized into a complete system centering in the institutions of the temple, the sacrifices, and the Levitical priesthood. The priests believed that the Jews could be made acceptable to Jahweh only through ritual holiness; ceremonial precepts were required for the regulating of all of life and for reminding the people of Jahweh's demands.

The priestly code enumerates in orderly fashion the regulations of the cult; the only valid worship was the service at the central sacrifice. The worship consisted chiefly of sacrificial offerings. There were, first of all, the solemn offerings for general worship and for the forgiveness of sin; then there were the festive offerings for fellowship, supplication, and thanksgiving. The most important of the solemn offerings was the burnt offering, a daily temple sacrifice; closely akin to it were the sin offering, given for a wrong which could not be undone, and the trespass or guilt offering, presented for wrong doing which could be righted by a gift or an act of restitution. All the solemn sacrifices were combined into one great ritual on one day of the year, the Day of Atonement, celebrated on the tenth day of the seventh month (Tishri, September-October); then the high priest entered the Holy of Holies and removed the uncleanness of the priests, the sanctuary, and the people. The sin-offerings made on that day atoned for the omissions of sin-offerings on the part of individuals.[32] The people themselves shared in the festive offerings, with the traditional peace offerings, meal offerings, and additional offerings of libation and incense; the celebrated festivals were the Passover (the fourteenth day of the first month, Nisan, our March-April), Pentecost (on the fiftieth day after Passover), and the Feast of the Tabernacles (four days after the Day of Atonement).

Before the year 400 B.C., perhaps in Babylonia, the priestly code was added to JED to make JEDP, the Pentateuch.[33] The redactor, or redactors, designated by the letters R^P, showed real genius in the fusion of the sources which were available to them. "They saw profoundly into the needs of their times. Judaism demanded such an imposing edifice of revelation, and succeeding centuries have amply vindicated their work by the place that the Torah has assumed in the subsequent development of the religion. . . . For these great compilers and editors and theologians deserve a place in the development of Judaism which may surpass even that of their great predecessors. Indeed, when the Pentateuch is seen in its diversity and its unity, we have before us one of the loftiest achievements of the human race, and for faith, a holy Scripture; it is a history of Israel's religion; it is the Torah of Israel; the revelation of God."[34]

The Pentateuch constituted the second official Bible of the Hebrew people.[35] This priests' Bible accomplished what the Deuteronomists had tried to do prior to the exile: develop a people who would live strictly according to the will of Jahweh. In the Torah the foundations were laid for the Judaism which developed after the exile and which has survived until now.

C. *Exclusivists vs. Inclusivists*: the Books of Esther and Joel in Contrast with the Books of Ruth and Jonah

The religious exclusivism evident in the decrees of Ezra and Nehemiah against mixed marriages[36] continued to dominate Judaism during the declining years of the Persian Empire. It was reflected in the sharply bitter books of Esther and Joel, both of which fostered an uncompromising aloofness toward the Gentile world.

Though variously dated from *ca.* 800 B.C. to *ca.* 350 B.C., the general religious outlook of the Book of Joel seems to demand a post-exilic date. The author was not a great religious genius but he was a remarkable poet; a great disaster accompanying a plague of locusts sets him to reflecting on the Day of Jahweh. Unlike Amos,[37] Isaiah,[38] and Zephaniah,[39] in whose writings the Day of Jahweh was considered to be a judgment on Israel, Joel insists that this terrible day will witness a judgment of vengeance upon the foes of the Jews.[40] His writings definitely link him with the more vengeful and radically exclusive group in Judaism:

> Proclaim this among the nations:
> Hallow war! Arouse the warriors!
> Let the fighting men approach and ascend!
> Beat your plowshares into swords,

> And your pruning hooks into lances![41]
> Let the weakling say, "I am a warrior."
> Haste and come, all you nations,
> And gather yourselves there from every side.
> Bring down thy warriors, O Lord!
> Let the nations rouse themselves and come up
> To the valley of Jehoshaphat;
> For there I will sit to judge
> All the nations from every side.
> Put in the sickle,
> For the harvest is ripe!
> Go in, tread;
> For the wine-press is full!
> The vats overflow!
> For their wickedness is great.[42]

He passionately called his people to repentance,[43] and promises them forgiveness and a prosperous future,[44] but he ends his book by gloating over the destruction of Judah's enemies:

> "Egypt shall become a waste,
> And Edom shall be a barren steppe;
> Because of the wrong done to the children of Judah,
> In that they shed innocent blood in their land.
> But Judah shall abide forever,
> And Jerusalem throughout the ages.
> And I will avenge their blood; I will not
>   leave it unpunished."
> For the Lord dwells in Zion.[45]

Dates for the composition of the Book of Esther vary from "not long after the fall of the Persian Empire,"[46] to "toward the close of the third century B.C.,"[47] or even as late as *ca.* 125 B.C.[48] But all scholars are fairly well agreed that it is an interesting historical romance exuding an atmosphere of exultant and bitter patriotism. It is not a religious book; the name of God nowhere appears in its ten chapters. Its spirit of hate and vindictiveness represents an all-time low in Jewish ethical thinking. Its place in the canon of Jewish scriptures seems to have been determined by its purpose to explain the origin of the ancient Jewish yearly festival of Purim; observed on the fourteenth day of the month Adar (February-March), Purim may have been a Persian festival which the Jews appropriated, and the Book of Esther may have been written to popularize this non-religious holiday among the Palestinian Jews. Jews still observe the day with the exchange of gifts and general merry-making. The book was popular because it fitted in very well with the Jews' natural desire for revenge on their enemies. The individual Jew must disregard his own life when the existence of the nation is at stake. Mordecai tells Esther:

> "Think not to yourself that you will escape inside the royal palace any more than all the rest of the Jews. For if you remain altogether silent at this time, then relief and deliverance will rise up for the Jews from another quarter, but you and your father's house will perish; and who knows whether you have not come to the kingdom for such a time as this?"

To which Esther replies:

> "Go, assemble all the Jews that are to be found in Shushan (Susa, the Persian capital) and fast for me, and neither eat nor drink for three days, night or day. I also and my maidens will likewise fast, and then I will go to the king, which is not according to the law; and if I perish, I perish."[49]

There are more copies of Esther in existence today than of any other book in the Old Testament, because copies of it are given to Jewish boys when they reach the age of thirteen. The book was never quoted in the New Testament; the contrast between it and the teachings of Jesus may help to explain why the ethical teachings of Jesus may have encountered such bitter opposition in Jewish circles of his day.[50]

Some time close to the end of the Persian period, between 400 and 350 B.C., a beautiful little didactic romance was produced by a Jew of broad sympathies, who was evidently a member of a small minority which was reacting against the rigorous policy of Ezra and Nehemiah and their successors in excluding foreign wives. The writer's aim was to show that Jahweh's blessings had rested, in days gone by, upon Moabite and Israelite alike; a foreigner, Ruth, became the noble ancestress of the great king David. He was trying to show that loyalty, piety, and goodness were evident in other people besides Jews; these qualities were fully as important as pure Jewish descent. "So out of the memory of a Moabite strain in the ancestry of David came this story of the devotion and piety of a Moabite girl to her Jewish mother-in-law. If the children of such marriages were unclean in the sight of Ezra, what of David himself, whose grandfather was a child of just such a mixed marriage? And were not women like Ruth worthy to stand with the women of Israel?"[51] Let exile (Naomi), native (Boaz), and foreigner (Ruth) learn to live together in harmony; perhaps in three or four generations there may be another David and another united kingdom of Israel. Ruth's altruistic character is reflected in the beautiful words she speaks to Naomi:

> Do not press me to leave you, to turn back from following you; for wherever you go, I will go; and wherever you lodge, I will lodge; your people shall be my people, and your god my god; wherever you die, I will die, and there will I be buried. May the Lord requite me and worse, if even death separates me from you.[52]

A little bit later than the composition of the Book of Ruth, the Book of Jonah similarly was a didactic romance, or allegory, which argues appealingly for a liberal attitude toward non-Jews. It has been called the first missionary book in the history of the world's religions. The author used the name of a prophet who lived in the northern kingdom during the reign of Jeroboam II and made him stand for the narrow, nationalistic tendency among the Jews of his day. When told to go to Nineveh and preach to the hated Assyrians, Jonah set out in the opposite direction to get as far away as he could from his responsibility. By this the author meant his readers to compare Jonah's rebellion with the spiritual blindness which was creeping upon the Jewish priestly leaders with their policy of exclusiveness against foreigners. Even while witnessing the success of his Assyrian mission, Jonah resented God's mercy toward them.[53] The book of Jonah shows that the prophetic doctrine of Deutero-Isaiah—that Israel's mission was to be the servant of Jahweh and to reveal his universal solicitude for all people—had not entirely disappeared in post-exilic Judaism. It represents the highest level reached by Jewish thought concerning the character of God prior to the teachings of Jesus of Nazareth. If the Jews had listened to the author of the Book of Jonah, Judaism might well have become the great universal religion of the world.[54]

SUGGESTIONS FOR FURTHER STUDY

W. F. ALBRIGHT, "The Biblical Period," in L. Finkelstein, ed., *The Jews: Their History, Culture, and Religion,* pp. 50-55.

A. E. BAILEY and C. F. KENT, *History of the Hebrew Commonwealth,* pp. 277-285.

G. A. BARTON, *Archaeology and the Bible,* pp. 486-490.

H. M. BATTENHOUSE, *The Bible Unlocked,* pp. 226-247.

J. A. BEWER, *The Literature of the Old Testament,* pp. 60-86. 234-279, 282-284, 302-307, 395-399, 403-405.

G. A. BUTTRICK, ed., *The Interpreter's Bible,* I, pp. 185-200, 335-336; II, pp. 827-852; III, pp. 549-874.

F. C. EISELEN, E. LEWIS, and D. G. DOWNEY, eds., *The Abingdon Bible Commentary,* pp. 134-144, 278-317, 377-380, 477-482, 768-774, 787-790, 815-831.

H. T. FOWLER, *The Origin and Growth of the Hebrew Religion,* pp. 139-149.

E. J. GOODSPEED, *The Story of the Old Testament,* pp. 79-87, 93-99, 107-116, 151-154.

F. JAMES, *Personalities of the Old Testament,* pp. 390-478.

C. S. KNOPF, *The Old Testament Speaks,* pp. 288-295, 301-311, 331-336.

E. W. K. MOULD, *Essentials of Bible History,* pp. 368-372, 376-383, 407-410.

J. B. NOSS, *Man's Religions,* pp. 529-536.

W. O. E. OESTERLY and T. H. ROBINSON, *Hebrew Religion: Its Origin and Development,* pp. 273-286, 296, 301.

R. H. PFEIFFER, *Introduction to the Old Testament,* pp. 127-389, 573-576, 586-589, 717-719, 732-747, 813-838.

J. M. P. SMITH, *The Prophets and Their Times,* pp. 241-257, 271-291.

H. C. SNELL, *Ancient Israel: Its Story and Meaning,* pp. 193-225.

Chapter Eighteen

JUDAISM DURING THE HELLENISTIC PERIOD

A. *The Rule of Alexander the Great and His Successors*

Ca. 400 B.C. the Persian Empire began to show signs of decay. Under the benificent rule of Artaxerxes II (404-358 B.C.), the Jewish community in Palestine regained much of its old time prosperity.[1] But the ruthless Artaxerxes III (Ochus, 358-338 B.C.) put down a revolt in Phoenicia, Egypt, and Palestine; Jericho was destroyed and the Jewish community was oppressed for about a decade.[2] The reputation of the Persian kings was redeemed somewhat by Darius III (335-333 B.C.), but he had the misfortune to begin to rule just as Alexander of Macedon started his conquest of the world.[3] Alexander's brief reign (he died in 323 in Babylon after penetrating as far as the Indus River) started cultural and religious forces moving which were to last for many years after his death. The Greek philosopher Aristotle had been Alexander's tutor; this may have led the young monarch to try to spread Greek civilization eastward until every one should be a part of the Hellenistic culture he had known as a boy. From now on it is to serve as a background for the understanding of Biblical literature especially in the New Testament period. Alexander treated the Jews kindly, giving them a section in his new cosmopolitan city of Alexandria, built on the Mediterranean coast near the western apex of the Nile delta. Many Jews became loyal supporters of the Greek regime and began to urge assimilation of Hellenistic ideas and ideals.

After the death of Alexander his empire broke up into three main parts. The section comprising Greece, Macedonia, and an adjoining strip of Asia Minor does not figure in Bible history. A second part comprised roughly the western section of the old Persian Empire; it passed under the control of a line of kings known as the Seleucids, with their capital city at Antioch in Syria. The third was in Egypt, with Alexandria as its capital and with the Ptolemies as its rulers. For the next century and a quarter Palestine was a bone of contention between the Seleucids and the Ptolemies; it changed hands seven times between 323 and 298 B.C. After a thirty year truce, Palestine changed hands so frequently between 264 and 248 B.C. that no accurate account of the number is possible. From 248 to *ca.* 218 B.C., Palestine was an Egyptian province, but struggle between the Seleucids and the Ptolemies began all over again. Finally, from 198 to 165 B.C., Palestine was under the exclusive control of the ruthless Seleucids.

The Jews in Palestine had a hectic time during the period following the death of Alexander the Great. Under the reign of Ptolemy II (Philadelphus, 285-247 B.C.), the Jews were treated with respect and reciprocated by studying Greek literature and philosophy. About that time, certain Jewish scholars, under royal patronage, began to translate the Hebrew scriptures into the Greek language. Later known as the Septuagint, this work of some seventy authorities was the first historical attempt at Biblical translation; it became the Bible of the Hellenistic, or Greek-speaking, Jews throughout the Greek world, and later throughout the Roman empire. Under later Ptolemies the Jews in Palestine were not so fortunate; concerned only with the collection of exhorbitant taxes, the Egyptian rulers made the high priest in Jerusalem a civil and secular official as well as a religious one. This led to opportunities for abuse of the high priestly office; of the nine men who held this office in Judah in the Greek period only one was worthy of his high trust.

With the coming of the Seleucids into sole control of Palestine, the Jews were subjected to the determined Hellenizing influence of the kings of Syria. Under Antiochus the Great and his successors, two attitudes toward the pervading Hellenistic culture arose among the Jews: one group, known as the Chasidim, or pious, was wholly opposed to any contact between Jew and Greek; the liberal group welcomed Hellenism for its broad civilizing influence and for the chance it gave for the spread of the Jewish faith. The first group developed into the party of the Pharisees, and the second became known later as the Sadducees. At about this time also there was developed by the priests a group of Hebrew elders called the Sanhedrin, or senate; originally designed to correspond to the authority of the senators in the Greek free cities, it is doubtful if the Sanhedrin was ever a very effective check on the power of the high priests.

B. *Wisdom Literature*: *Proverbs, Ecclesiastes, and Job.*

During the Hellenistic period, no prophets are mentioned in Hebrew literature; their ethical pronouncements were repeated and applied by the teachers of wisdom, the so-called "wise men," or sages, who were the educators of their day.[5] Not concerned with the ceremonies of the priests nor with the immediate demands of the prophets, the wise men sought to apply religious wisdom to the practical affairs of daily life and conduct. A very ancient aspect of Hebrew culture,[6] wisdom received pronounced impetus from Greek civilization, in which the traveling philosopher was a common phenomenon. The Hebrew sages were not philosophers in the Greek sense; the Hebrew mind was never speculative regarding questions of ultimate reality. The wise man among the Jews was more concerned with the practical problem of human destiny than with the theoretical problem of human origin. Yet the wisdom literature in post-exilic Judaism filled the same role in its culture as philosophy did in Hellenism.

The literary products of the Hebrew wise men include some of the Psalms,[7] the books of Proverbs, Ecclesiastes, and Job, together with fragments scattered elsewhere throughout the Old Testament,[8] the books of Ecclesiasticus and the Wisdom of Solomon in the Apocrypha, and the book of IV Maccabees in the Pseudepigrapha. The Book of Proverbs is a compendium of several collections of previously independent materials,[9] the whole thing having been put together *ca.* 250 B.C. It contains many short statements of truth, or maxims, unrelated to one another and covering the whole range of human experience. "The large number and variety of these proverbs give them a special interest because of the way they reflect the life of their day. In them one finds himself in a small-town community with its men, women, and children; its rich and poor, its servants and masters; its lazy and industrious; its good and its bad. Here one sees the speculator who holds his grain for higher prices (11:26), the simple fellow who believes everything he hears (14:15), the man who is strong enough through his self-control (16:32), the man who conducts whispering campaigns (18:8), the fellow who is so lazy he won't even lift his food to his mouth (19:24), the bargain hunter who beats down the price and then boasts of how little he paid (20:14), the woman who would talk you to death (21:9; cf. 27:15, 16), and many others that are hit off with the same aptness and humor. It is a wonderful portrait gallery and, if read with a little imagination, is one of the most entertaining books in the Old Testament."[10] The acrostic poem at the end of the book (31:10-31) is a literary composition in praise of the model wife; unacceptable to the modern woman, the passage reveals the dominance of the male sex characteristic of all Jewish life and religion.[11] From a religious point of view, the most praiseworthy parts of the book of Proverbs are chapters 3, 4, and 8:1-9:6.

The book of Ecclesiastes is a wisdom book written some time between 250 and 200 B.C. It is a miscellany of wisdom, part of it in prose, part in poetry. The unknown author wrestles with a very deep philosophical question: Is life worth living? What is the meaning of it all? Is there any purpose? Not a very profound or systematic philosopher, the author, named "koheleth," or "collector of wisdom teachings," pours forth one long drawn out and bitter lament of pain and disappointment, because there was no escape from present misery either in this life or in the life to come. In all his search for the meaning of existence, koheleth finds nothing of enduring value; he tries practical wisdom (1:12-18), pleasure (2:1-11), labor and the accumulation of great riches (2:18-26; 6:1-12), and fame (8:10-9:6), but concludes from each the same gloomily skeptical exclamation: "Vanity of vanities, all is vanity!"[12] He points out the cyclical character of nature and life;[13] he concludes that the total of human misery is a constant quality, so that it is hopeless to do anything about it. Koheleth's basic philosophy of life is thus stated:

There is nothing good for man but that he eat and drink and find satisfaction in his work. This too have I seen, that it is from the hand of God.[14]

One must have regard for the fitness of things:

> For everything there is an appointed time;
> And there is a time for every purpose
> > under the heavens:
> A time to be born, and a time to die;
> A time for planting, and a time for uprooting;
> A time to slay, and a time to heal;
> A time to tear down, and a time to rebuild;
> A time to weep, and a time to laugh;
> A time to mourn, and a time to dance;
> A time to scatter stones, and a time to
> > gather stones;
> A time to embrace, and a time to refrain
> > from embracing;
> A time to seek, and a time to count as lost;
> A time to keep, and a time to throw away;
> A time to tear, and a time to sew;
> A time to keep quiet, and a time to talk;
> A time to love, and a time to hate;
> A time for war, and a time for peace.[15]

For koheleth, God exists and is powerful, but his pessimistic skepticism leads him to assert that God does not care for the righteous and is of a capricious nature. There is no immortality:

> For there is one fate for both man and beast—the same fate for them; as the one dies, so dies the other; the same breath is in all of them, and man has no advantage over the beast; for everything is vanity. All go to one place; all are from the dust, and all return to the dust.[16]

however, in another connection koheleth gives expression to the so-called reabsorption theory of immortality:

> The dust returns to the earth as it was, and the spirit returns to God who gave it.[17]

The Book of Ecclesiastes was so skeptical and heterodox that it would never have found its way into the canon if it had not been edited and revised in the interest of orthodox religion. By a series of interpolations, a later editor reinterpreted offensive sections and modified the skepticism implied in them; for example, the concluding section of the book,[18] in which koheleth advised young men to enjoy life before it was too late, was tempered by the following insertions:

> But know that for all these things God will bring you into judgment . . . Remember your Creator in the days of your vigor, . . .[19]

while the pious editor brought the entire work to a close with the following orthodox pronouncements:

> The conclusion of the matter, all having been heard: Fear God and keep his commands; for this concerns all mankind, that God brings every work into judgment with regard to everything concealed, whether it be good or evil.[20]

Other additions of the unknown editor strengthened the impression that Solomon, patron of all wise men in the history of Judaism, was the author of the book of Ecclesiastes; this did much to overcome objections to including the book in the canon.[21]

Without doubt, the book of Job is the greatest of the Hebrew wisdom books and one of the great classics in the literary history of the human race.[22] In poetry except for the opening and closing sections,[23] the book is not history, but a highly wrought work of semidramatic literary art. The central character of the drama is a Hebrew patriarch named Job.[24] In the light of the tremendous suffering of this righteous man, the unknown author produced a sustained treatise on the problem of human suffering. His book can best be understood as an attempt to contradict the conventional Hebrew belief in retribution: that prosperity and adversity were rewards and punishments direct from God.[25] This view is very clearly stated in the first Psalm:

> How happy is the man who has not walked in
>   the counsel of the wicked,
> Nor stood in the way of sinners,
> Nor sat in the seat of scoffers!
> But his delight is in the law of the Lord.
> And in his law does he study day and night.

For he is like a tree planted by streams of water,
That yields its fruit in its season,
And whose leaf does not wither;
And whatever it bears comes to maturity.

The wicked are not so;
But are like the chaff which the wind
          drives away.
Therefore the wicked will not stand in
          the judgment,
Nor sinners in the assembly of the righteous.
For the Lord knows the way of the righteous.
But the way of the wicked will perish.

This popular view was maintained by the friends of Job and denied by Job himself; to his friends, Job's poverty and suffering were the direct result of sin.[26]

The book of Job proposes several solutions for the problem of suffering. The first is contained in the prologue; suffering is a test of character; the righteous man must suffer in silence and preserve his integrity and purity of heart.[27] A second attitude toward Job's undeserved fate is contained in the main part of the book: a dialogue between Job and his three friends (chapters 3-27). Eliphaz, Bildad, and Zophar all insist vehemently that Job's suffering is punishment for sin, but Job stubbornly insists upon his own uprightness and integrity and protests loudly against his affliction. In Job's reply to Bildad, the author says:

My lips do not speak untruth,
Nor my tongue utter deceit.
Far be it from me that I should justify you;
Till I die I will not put my integrity from me.
I will hold onto my innocence and will not
          let it go.
My conscience does not reproach any of
          my days.[28]

One of the high points in the book of Job and, for that matter, in the entire Old Testament, is the sketch of Job's personal character in chapters 29-31. In this section, Job's character is portrayed as the embodiment of the ethical ideals of the Hebrew prophets. Then, after the speeches of Elihu,[29] there is the grand climax of the book of Job in a theophany (38:1-42:6) in which God himself answers Job's questions out of a whirlwind. The nature poems in this section present still a third attitude toward the problem of suffering: suffering is a part of the inexplicable mystery of God's universe. Reminiscent of Isaiah 40-55,[30] God is described as a being of awe-inspiring majesty, in whose presence mere man is insignificant. Life is a mystery; its essential worth must be accepted by man's act of faith.

The book of Job has been variously dated all the way from 500 B.C. to 165 B.C. The story itself was a part of the folk lore of the Hebrew people. Very late in the Greek period, an editor added the prose epilogue in which the conventional view of retribution is reaffirmed; Jahweh gives Job twice as much as he had originally.[31]

C. *The Literary Activity of the Chronicler*

The Hellenistic period of Hebrew history also witnessed the appearance of the latest of Israel's historical writings. *Ca.* 250 B.C., an unknown author, or possibly a group of like-minded authors,[32] produced the biblical books of I and II Chronicles, Ezra, and Nehemiah. Technically called "the Chronicler," the author, or authors, made great use of material found elsewhere in the Old Testament, such as I and II Samuel, I and II Kings, and the memoirs of Ezra and Nehemiah. What he wrote is not history; he used historical facts only to illustrate the particular theological purpose he had in mind. His mind was thoroughly steeped in the dogma that in the past the prosperity of the nation had been due to the fact that the Judean kings had supported the temple, the cultus, and the ceremonial law; conversely, adversities suffered by the nation must have been due to apostasy from the sacrificial cultus. He rewrote the story of the kingdom of Judah as if the developed religious law of his own day (the priestly code) had been in force through its whole history. The four books he produced constitute the third official Bible of the Hebrew people.[33]

The Chronicler was most eager to tell the story of the chosen people, the Hebrews, beginning with David, but he also wanted to give the impression of a much more inclusive range by beginning at the beginning—that is, with Adam. To get from Adam to David in ten chapters is no mean task, but he accomplished it by compiling a very interesting genealogical list extending from Adam to Saul.[34] Then he is free to devote the next nineteen chapters to an idealized portrait of his great hero, David.

The work of the Chronicler shows the operation of three controlling ideas. The first of these is the extreme degree to which he carried the doctrine of retribution;[35] he applied it even if he had to revise what he found in his source materials. In the case of Saul, I Chronicles 10 is based on I Samuel 31, but the Chronicler adds his interpretation of Saul's death. In I Samuel 31:4, Saul took his own life by falling on his sword; in I Chronicles 10:13,14, it is stated that Jahweh took Saul's life "for his faithlessness wherein he was faithless toward the Lord because of the word of the Lord which he did not observe, and also because he consulted a medium, resorting to it and not to the Lord." The same sort of revision is evident in the Chronicler's handling of the census taken by David; in II Samuel 24 it was Jahweh who "incited" David to count his people and then punished him by sending on the realm a three days' pestilence; but in I Chronicles 21 it was Satan who moved David to number Israel and then sent the plague.

Another of the Chronicler's controlling ideas is revealed by the manner in which he emphasized the supremacy of God by making God's action so great a factor in historic events that the part taken by human beings seems almost negligible. God becomes the active agent in history. This is illustrated by an account of the invasion of Judah by Moabites, Ammonites, and the men of Mount Seir in the days of King Jehoshaphat.[36] When informed of the threatened attack, Jehoshaphat evidently forgets an army he had in Jerusalem[37] and orders a fast throughout Judah; then he goes to the temple to pray; the next morning the choir leads the army and the people out to the battleground and they stand on one side while God does the work. The enemies of the Hebrews turn against each other until all are killed; so much booty is left that it takes three days to collect it; then the choir leads everyone back to Jerusalem.[38]

In the third place, the writings of the Chronicler reveal his opinion that David's kingdom was the true Israel, the true representative of God's purposes, and that the disruption of the kingdom in 922 B.C.[39] was a ghastly mistake on the part of Jeroboam and the ten northern tribes. In fact, after telling the story of the split,[40] the Chronicler turns his whole attention to the history of the kingdom of Judah and the family line of David. In the career of his hero, David, he omits any item which might detract from the power and the glory of an ideal king.[41]

An interesting feature of the Chronicler's style is his love for large numbers. A total of 339,600 warriors comes to Hebron to make David king;[42] David pays 600 gold shekels for the site of the future temple;[43] David uses a great deal of wealth in preparing for the building of the temple;[44] on different occasions, the number of animals used in the sacrifices totals many thousands.[45]

Quite unintentionally, the Chronicler preserves for posterity detailed descriptions of elaborate liturgical temple services, characteristic of the worship of the third century B.C., but projected back into the period of David, in which priests, Levites, and guilds of singers took part; I Chronicles 15 and 16 give clues as to how the Psalms were used in public worship.[46] His interest in the liturgical and ecclesiastical features of Judaism far outweighs his concern with the ethical aspects of religion. He mentions some of the prophets sympathetically, but "he seems to have learned little from the mighty men of old who bore that name. Royal wealth and splendour, which they denounced, he extolled. But it is most of all in his silences that he stood over against them. He is ever speaking of kings, but when does he say anything about their duty to govern well? He glories in the beauty of the temple services, but lets fall no word concerning clean hands and a pure heart. He is strong for valid orders, but omits mention of the moral responsibilities of the ministry . . ."[47] In his ecclesiastical narrowness, the Chronicler belongs to the exclusivist group in Jewish life.[48]

D. *The Psalter*: *The Hymn-book of the Second Temple.*

Though some of the individual psalms may date as early as 1000 B.C., during the time of David,[49] and though Hebrew tradition ascribed to David the authorship of all of the Psalms, the collection of Psalms which stands at the beginning of the Hagiographa, or Writings, the third major division of the Jewish Bible, was not completed in its present form until late in the Greek period. It is impossible to date accurately any of the individual psalms, for ascriptions of authorship in the titles of psalms are late scribal conjectures or traditions. The Psalter is actually a collection of collections; there are discernible within it five smaller collections of psalms, each section ending with a doxology.[50] The Book of Psalms is brought to an end with the one hundred and fiftieth, itself a doxology.

A psalm is a religious poem. The psalter has been called the "hymn-book of the second temple;" though some of the psalms would hardly suit this purpose, the title would be applicable to most of them. Some of the collections used in the Psalter were evidently designed as hymnals for guilds of singers in the temple; mention is made of Psalms of Asaph,[51] Psalms of the Sons of Korah,[52] Songs of Ascents,[53] and Psalms of David.[54] Other evidence that the Psalter is the result of a process of accretion may be found in the various duplications and repetitions among the Psalms; for example, Psalm 53 and Psalm 14 are identical; Psalm 70 duplicates Psalm 40:13-17; Psalm 108 is the same as Psalm 57:7-11 combined with Psalm 60:5-12.

That the Psalms were used liturgically in the temple worship is attested by the Chronicler.[55] Those which have refrains were evidently intended for antiphonal use; the leader might be an individual or a small chorus; the response might be sung by a second individual, a second small chorus, or the worshiping congregation; the entire group would participate in the "Hallelujahs" and the "Amens."[56] Of all the Psalms with refrains, Psalm 107 is the most elaborate. In Psalm 46, the refrain strikes the keynote of the psalm;[57] Martin Luther caught the essential spirit of this psalm in his great hymn "A Mighty Fortress Is Our God," the first line of which was inspired by the first words of the psalm: "God is our refuge and strength." Psalm 24 is perhaps the best illustration of a liturgical psalm; the first two verses constitute a hymn of praise, forming a suitable opening for any festal program; verses 3-6 show a question and answer pattern, with the questions asked evidently by those approaching the sanctuary and the replies given by the priest; verses 7-10 reflect a processional of some sort with a sacred object, perhaps the ark, being carried up to the temple, the doors of which are opened to the worshipers:

> Lift up your heads, O gates!
> And lift yourselves up, O ancient doors,
> That the king of glory may come in!
> Who, then, is the king of glory?
> The Lord strong and mighty,
> The Lord mighty in battle!
>
> Lift up your heads, O gates!
> And lift yourselves up, O ancient doors,
> That the king of glory may come in!
> Who, then, is the king of glory?
> The Lord of hosts,
> He is the king of glory!

The so-called "Hallel" Psalms were sung in celebration of the Passover, half before and half after the paschal meal.[58] One of these, Psalm 117, is the shortest of all the Psalms and also the briefest chapter in the Bible; however, its two verses contain all the essentials of a hymn: a summons to praise and a basis of praise. The Songs of Ascents (Psalms 120-134) were sung by pilgrims, either going up to Jerusalem for one of the annual festivals, or returning from one of them. Psalm 150 presents the most complete summary in existence of the musical instruments used in the temple worship:

> Hallelujah!
> Praise God in his sanctuary!
> Praise him in his mighty firmament!
> Praise him for his mighty deeds!
> Praise him for his abundant greatness!
> Praise him with the blast of the horn!
> Praise him with lyre and lute!
> Praise him with drum and dance!
> Praise him with strings and pipe!
> Praise him with clanging cymbals!
> Praise him with crashing cymbals!
> Let everything that breathes praise the Lord!
> Hallelujah!

Many of the Psalms reveal the close connection between the religious piety of the Hebrews and their respect for the Torah. This is seen in a remarkable way in Psalm 119, the longest chapter in the Bible. The unknown author set for himself an almost impossible task: he took the twenty-two letters of the Hebrew alphabet in their order and wrote a strophe of eight verses for each letter, beginning each verse of a strophe with the same letter. Then, in each of the one hundred and seventy-six verses the author uses some word that stood for the Torah; among these are the words "law," "commands," "decrees," "precepts," statutes," "word," "ordinances," "message," etc. Also, he puts into each verse something about his personal relationship to the Torah.. Another section which praises the Torah is Psalm 19:7-14; there are six terms for the law in the first three verses:

> The law of the Lord is perfect, renewing the life;
> The decree of the Lord is trustworthy, making wise
>   the simple;
> The precepts of the Lord are right, rejoicing the heart;
> The command of the Lord is pure, enlightening
>   the eyes;
> The fear of the Lord is clean, enduring forever.
> The judgments of the Lord are true; they are also right;

In verse 10 the author sums up the Torah's supreme value:

> They are more valuable than gold, and much fine gold;
> Also sweeter than honey, and the droppings of the
>   honey-comb.

Many of the Psalms remind the reader of the wisdom books of the Old Testament. Psalm 1 reflects a judgment on men and their behavior reminiscent of the Book of Proverbs; in its view that each kind of behaviour has its inevitable consequence of reward or punishment, this Psalm upholds the doctrine of retribution.[59] Psalms 112, 49, 73, 32:8-11, 34:11-22, and 37 also contain wisdom teachings. Among all the Psalms, there is only one secular song: Psalm 45, a wedding poem composed by a court poet for the marriage festival of a king with a foreign princess.[60] Some of the Psalms are called imprecatory Psalms; such Psalms as 109 and 149 do not measure up ethically to Christian standards or to the best in the Old Testament; Psalm 137 reflects the bitterness and heartbreak of the pious Jew in the midst of the Babylonian exile.

From the start of the Christian movement, Psalms were used in the worship. The New Testament offers abundant evidence to show how popular the Psalter was among pious Jews and how often they were used in Christian meetings. When Paul advises the Ephesians to "speak to one another in Psalms, hymns, and sacred songs,"[61] he doubtless had in mind some of these hymns in the Jewish Psalter. The Psalms have always been of great religious inspiration to the Christians of every age; the Psalter has probably been the best known of all the Old Testament writings to the average Christian. Those Psalms which have been of the greatest devotional value are the first, the nineteenth, the eighth, the twenty-ninth, the very familiar twenty-third, the twenty-fourth, the twenty-seventh, the thirty-first, the thirty-fourth, the forty-second, the forty-sixth, the sixty-third, the eighty-fourth, the nine-tieth, the ninety-first, the ninety-fifth, the ninety-sixth, the ninety-eighth, the one hundredth, the one hundred and third, the one hundred and eighteenth, the one hundred and twenty-first, the one hundred and twenty-second, the one hundred and thirtieth, the one hundred and thirty-sixth, the one hundred and thirty-ninth, and the one hundred and forty-eighth. The words of the fortieth psalm might serve as a motto for most of the Psalter:

> I waited patiently for the Lord, and he
>> paid heed to me and heard my plea.
> So he drew me up from the pit of ruin,
>> from the miry swamp;
> And he set my feet upon a rock,
>> establishing my steps.
> And he put a new song in my mouth,
>> praise to our God.
> Many will see and be afraid,
>> and will trust in the Lord.[62]

SUGGESTIONS FOR FURTHER STUDY

G. A. BARTON, *Archaeology and the Bible*, pp. 491-515.
H. M. BATTENHOUSE, *The Bible Unlocked*, pp. 248-255.
J. A. BEWER, *The Literature of the Old Testament*, pp. 285-301, 308-391.

G. A. Buttrick, ed., *The Interpreter's Bible,* I, pp. 336-339; III, pp. 339-548, 875-1198; IV.

F. C. Eiselen, E. Lewis, and D. G. Downey, eds., *The Abingdon Bible Commentary,* pp. 439-476, 483-621.

E. J. Goodspeed, *The Story of the Old Testament,* pp. 100-106, 122-126, 133-137, 143-150, 155-160.

F. James, *Personalities of the Old Testament,* pp. 479-553.

C. S. Knopf, *The Old Testament Speaks,* pp. 318-328, 336-339, 346-352.

E. A. Leslie, *The Psalms.*

E. W. K. Mould, *Essentials of Bible History,* pp. 401-407.

W. O. E. Oesterley and T. H. Robinson, *Hebrew Religion: Its Origin and Development,* pp. 287-289, 311-316, 333-341.

R. H. Pfeiffer, *Introduction to the Old Testament,* pp. 619-707, 724-731, 782-812.

H. S. Snell, *Ancient Israel: Its Story and Meaning,* pp. 226-238.

Chapter Nineteen

THE MACCABEAN AGE

A. *Apocalypticism*: *The Book of Daniel.*

Following the exile, during the Persian and Hellenistic Periods of Jewish history, a new type of writing appeared among the Jews. A great many unknown writers felt that the rebukes of the prophets before the exile had been vindicated and that the nation had suffered sufficiently for its sins. They proclaimed a message of comfort and reassurance which urged the people to look forward to a new day. These successors of the prophets are known as apocalyptists.[1] Israel's prophetic consciousness was deepened in the light of the destruction of the nation and the sad years of suffering and tragedy which followed. Many of the prophetic messages were brought up to date by attaching to some earlier threat or rebuke a word to show that, in the light of the later hope, the bitter warnings of the past had been succeeded by promises of a brighter future. For example, the prophet Amos had warned his contemporaries of a day of disaster;[2] the disaster came, and years afterward, there was added to the collection of the words of Amos a new word:

> "On that day I will raise up the fallen hut of David,
> And I will wall up its ruins,
> And raise up its breaches,
> And rebuild up its beaches,
> In order that they may possess the remnant of Edom
>   and all the nations,
> Over whom my name is called."
>   The oracle of the Lord, who does this.

"Behold the days are coming," is the oracle of the
    Lord,
"When the plowman shall overtake the reaper,
    And the treader of grapes him who sews the seed;
    And the mountains shall drip new wine,
    And all the hills shall melt;
    And I will restore the fortune of my people Israel,
    So that they shall rebuild the ruined cities,
    And dwell in them and plant vineyards,
    And drink their wine,
    And make gardens, and eat their fruit;
    And I will plant them upon their own soil,
    And they shall never again be rooted up
From off their soil which I have given them."
            Says the Lord, your God.[3]

Many of the anonymous apocalyptic writers among the Jews
wrote full-size books; the Apocrypha[4] and the Psuedepigrapha[5]
contain several apocalypses, while in the Old Testament itself
the Book of Daniel is the largest and most familiar example of
this type of writing.[6] Though differing somewhat in setting and
circumstance, all the apocalypses reveal some common elements.
In the first place, they all emphasize the sovereignty of God; all-
wise and all-powerful, God breaks through the orderliness of the
natural world to bring about his will and purpose among men.
Secondly, all the apocalyptists believe that the end of the world
is near; God will soon effect his final purpose in the world, and
his justice and sovereignty will be vindicated in history. One age
is about to end, and a new one will dawn soon. In the third place,
when the Day of Jahweh comes, it will be a day of judgment, at
which time the righteous will receive their reward and the wicked
their punishment; it will settle once and for all the conflict between good and evil. The apocalyptic writers believed that God
knew and determined the course of history and that he had revealed his secrets to his servants, the apocalyptic seers, in visions
of things to come.

The apocalyptic Book of Daniel was called forth by the stirring
times at the outbreak of the Maccabean rebellion. Always restive
under the tyrannical policy of enforced Hellenization by the Seleucid kings,[7] the Hebrews were in for real trouble with the accession of Antiochus IV Epiphanes.[8] He set about with vigor to

Hellenize Palestine and to compel the Jews to give up their own religion and adopt a Hellenistic cult. He forbade the Jews to perform the rite of circumcision, to keep the Sabbath, or to read the Scriptures. He went so far as to erect, on the site of the altar of burnt offering in front of the Jerusalem temple, an altar to Olympian Zeus, on which he offered, in 168 B.C., the flesh of swine as a sacrifice.[9] It was this act which precipitated the Maccabean uprising.[10] Under the leadership of Judas Maccabeus, "the Hammerer," Jerusalem was recovered and the temple purged of its defilement. The regular Jewish temple service was reinstituted with great rejoicing on the part of the Jews.[11]

The author of the Book of Daniel was an unknown Jew, perhaps a member of the Chasidim, or pious Jews,[12] who was faithful to Jewish custom and loyal to the strict anti-Hellenizing Judaism of the time. The purpose of the book was to stimulate Jewish resistance to the encroachment of Antiochus Epiphanes; instead of a direct reference to their hated enemy, the author tells the story of the tragic episode leading up to the Maccabean Revolt in apocalyptic dress. Any more direct reference to the Seleucid king would have been suicide; the veiled figures of apocalyptic permitted safe condemnation of the monster. By using a great hero of their past as an example of a sincerely devout young Jew, unswerving in his piety and gifted above all others of his time in the interpretation of events, the author wishes to encourage the Jews to continue steadfastly loyal to true Judaism in spite of persecution and suffering. He believes that within a short time the trouble will be over, the tyrant dead, and the glorious age of deliverance and triumph for the Jewish people will come.

The first six chapters of the Book of Daniel consist of stories of Daniel and his three friends, Shadrach, Meshach, and Abednego; their loyalty to Jewish custom in the midst of a foreign situation resulted in their proving to be superior to the other young men at the court of Nebuchadnezzar in health, wisdom, and skill. Daniel interprets King Nebuchadnezzar's dreams and predicts the destruction of the four pagan empires (Babylonia, Media, Persia, and Greece) and the establishment of the kingdom of saints of the Most High (the Jewish nation under the leadership of the Maccabees). History is thus narrated under the apocalyptic form of prediction:

... In the days of those kings the God of the heavens shall set up a kingdom which shall never be destroyed, nor shall the kingdom be left to another people; it shall break in pieces and annihilate all these kingdoms, but it shall stand forever, as you saw how a stone was hewn from a mountain without hands, which broke in pieces the iron, the bronze, and clay, the silver, and the gold . . .[13]

Thus are the Jews assured that they will triumph over Antiochus Epiphanes and establish a kingdom of their own.

Daniel and his three friends are forced to undergo suffering; the latter are thrown into a furnace of fire, while Daniel is cast into a den of lions. Both metaphors aptly describe the situation in Judea at the time of the Maccabean resistance to Seleucid tyranny; as God protected Daniel and his three friends and restored them to the favor of a pagan monarch, so would God protect his people. Just as God reduced Nebuchadnezzar to the level of a beast[14] and decreed the death of Belshazzar and the destruction of his kingdom[15] so would he deal with the tyrants of the Maccabean age.

The second part of the Book of Daniel, chapters seven through twelve, is devoted to a series of visions witnessed and described by Daniel, dealing with world empires. In chapter seven Daniel sees four beasts, symbolic of the same four kingdoms mentioned in chapter 2: the first is a lion with eagle's wings (Babylon); the second is a bear with three ribs of his victims between his teeth (Media); the third is a leopard with four heads and four wings (Persia); the fourth and most terrible is more elaborately described (2:7, 8):

Then, in the visions of the night, I looked, and lo! there was a fourth beast, dreadful and terrible, exceedingly strong, with great iron teeth, which devoured and tore in pieces, trampling what remained under its feet. It was different from all the beasts that were before it; and it had ten horns. As I watched the horns, lo! there came up among them another horn, a little one, before which three of the first horns were plucked up by the roots; and lo! in this horn there were eyes like the eyes of a man, and a mouth speaking great things.

This fourth beast evidently stands for the Seleucid Empire; its ten horns could well be the ten kings from Alexander the Great to Demetrius (176 B.C.); the eleventh horn stands for Antiochus Epiphanes, who in 176 B.C. actually did eliminate his three immediate predecessors ("plucked up by the roots"). The eleventh horn is to "wear out the saints of the Most High," (Daniel 7:25) but after a period under his domination they will take away his dominion and consume and destroy it for all time (verse 26); it will be replaced by an everlasting kingdom of their own (verse 27). In the remaining chapters the author portrays the history of the Greek kingdoms and forecasts what he expects will happen to Antiochus Epiphanes.[16] The purpose of these visions was to teach that God has a program of history which cannot be thwarted and which he can make known to his servants.

In the midst of the apocalyptic imagery of the Book of Daniel there are some factors which have been very influential in the history of religion. The author is convinced of the greatness of God and of the ultimate triumph of his kingdom. He believes that the time of God's coming is near at hand; it will be ushered in by a representative of the kingdom of the saints of the most high "one like a man," who is given authority by God, "the Venerable One."

> I watched
> Till thrones were placed,
> And a Venerable One took his seat;
> His clothing was white as snow,
> And the hair of his head like pure wool;
> His throne was a flame of fire,
> Whose wheels were blazing fire;
> A stream of fire went forth,
> And flowed from before him;
> A thousand thousands ministered to him,
> And ten thousand times ten thousand stood
>   before him;
> The court took its seat,
> And the books were opened.
>
> Then in the visions of the night I looked,
> And lo! with the clouds of the heavens
> There came one like a man,
> Who advanced toward the Venerable One,

And was brought near his presence.
To him was given dominion, and glory, and kingly
power,
That all peoples, and nations, and tongues should
serve him;
His dominion was to be an everlasting dominion,
that should not pass away,
And his kingdom one that should not be overthrown.[17]

For the most part God does his work through angelic inter-
mediaries. In Daniel for the first time there is mention of patron
angels, determining the destinies of individual nations.[18] Angels
are personified and given names.[19] When God comes to judge
the earth the righteous will receive their reward and the wicked
their punishment; to earlier Old Testament teachings of life
after death, the Book of Daniel adds a clear concept of the resurrection of the dead, though evidently no non-Israelites are to be
included and not even all Israelites:

And many of those who sleep in the land of dust shall
awake, some to everlasting life, and others to everlasting
reproach and contempt. Then those who are wise shall shine
like the brightness of the firmament, those who have led the
multitude to righteousness like the stars forever and ever.[20]

"The influence of Daniel has been widespread and profound.
The fact that the faith of the Jewish community was kept alive
through a time of deep distress was due to the combined effects
of the Maccabean revolution and the reading of this book. So
much a classic did it become that even after the crisis of Syrian
persecution had passed, it retained its popularity and served to
prepare its readers for other emergencies in the later days, e.g.,
the Roman war of 68-70 A.D. Jesus quoted its familiar words in
commenting on the approach of that time of fresh calamity (Mt.
24:15; Mk. 13:14). It has remained through the centuries one of
the favorite portions of holy Scripture."[21]

B. *The Decline of the Jewish State.*

As we have seen,[22] Judas Maccabeus and his followers restored to the Jews their worship in the temple. The land might have remained at peace had it not been for the ambition of the Maccabees to increase their territory and drive the Syrian garrison out of Jerusalem. After campaigns against Edom, Gilead, and Philistia, the Jews attacked the citadel in Jerusalem. Word was sent to the governor in Antioch, Lysias, and he came with a large army against the Maccabeans in Jerusalem; it looked as if the Maccabean cause was doomed, but a sudden shift in Syrian politics required Lysias' return to Antioch. In a surprisingly favorable peace, Lysias reconfirmed the religious freedom of the Jews, but kept unchanged the political status of the Jews as subjects of Syria and retained a garrison in the citadel in Jerusalem.

Under the governorship of Demetrius, a much stronger Syrian army appeared to harass the fortunes of the Maccabees. In a battle in the year 159 B.C. Judas Maccabeus was killed and the cause of Jewish freedom was thwarted. The Hellenizers among the Jews now joined the Syrians in a dreadful persecution of the Chasidim, or Pious, the Puritan party among the Jews. The latter went into hiding and for a while fought a guerilla type of warfare under the leadership of Jonathan, brother of Judas Maccabeus. More of the diplomat than Judas, Jonathan was able to secure a treaty with the Syrians which made him virtual ruler of all Judea, except Jerusalem; later, by playing one claimant to the Syrian throne against another, Jonathan was appointed high priest and was consecrated to that office at the feast of Tabernacles in 152 B.C. Jonathan was treacherously slain by the Syrian general Tryphon in 141 B.C., but his brother and successor, Simon, the last of the Maccabees, secured complete political independence for Judea from the Syrian king, Demetrius II. He recovered the citadel of Jerusalem from the Syrians and established himself as high priest, thus founding the high-priestly and princely house of the Hasmoneans.[23] Thus was begun a period of Jewish independence which lasted until the coming of the Romans in 63 B.C.

In 134 B.C. Simon was murdered by his son-in-law Ptolemy, whom he had placed over the important fortress of Jericho, and was succeeded by his son John, commonly known as John Hyrcanus (134-103 B.C.). Making use of Syrian dissensions he broadened the territory of Judea by conquering Idumea and Edom.

During his reign two main sections of the Jewish people crystallized into the parties known as Pharisees and Sadducees; the latter were the consistent supporters of the Hasmoneans in their political as well as in their religious efforts; the former, successors of the Chasidim, concentrated on the religious aspect of Judaism and tried to keep the temple worship pure.

John Hyrcanus was the last of the really great Hasmoneans. With his death in 103 B.C. there began a period of conflict and decline; the last forty years of Jewish independence present a sad picture of personal jealousies and lust of power. The oldest son of John, Aristobulus, assumed the high priesthood, imprisoning three of his brothers and putting the fourth to death. After less than a year, he died and his widow secured both high priesthood and the kingship for one of her brothers-in-law, Alexander Jannaeus (102-76 B.C.), whom history has justly surnamed "the brute." His licentious brutality alienated the Pharisees, who stirred up the people against him, but he put down all opposition ruthlessly. When he died, Alexander's wife Alexandra took over the kingdom; she appointed Hyrcanus to be high priest. Queen Alexandra[24] and Hyrcanus both joined the party of the Pharisees, and their reign of nine years (76-67 B.C.) has been called the golden age of Pharisaism. A younger brother of Hyrcanus, Aristobulus, had cast his fortunes with the Sadducees; on Alexandra's death bitter fighting broke out between the brothers. At first Aristobulus was successful and ruled three years as Aristobulus II (66-63 B.C.), but the vigorous Idumean named Antipater enabled Hyrcanus to come from retirement and continue the struggle against his brother at least on equal terms.

The general confusion in Judea led at last to the interference of Rome. In the year 63 B.C. Pompey entered Jerusalem as an ally of Hyrcanus; after three months of fighting, Aristobulus was defeated and the city of Jerusalem captured. Hyrcanus II became the high priest and was given the title of ethnarch. Hyrcanus had a certain amount of authority in his own country, but always under the watchful eyes of Antipater, who represented the interests of Rome. Judea was nominally incorporated into the province of Syria; the brief spell of Jewish independence had come to an end. From 63 B.C. until the end of the Bible period Palestine was under the rule of Rome.[25] Henry M. Battenhouse has a very good summary of the reasons for the decline of the Jewish state:

The collapse of the Jewish state was the result of its moral and spiritual decay. The age lacked worthy political and religious leadership. Its early heroism gave way to later fratricidal feuds; its spiritual ideals were trampled under foot by men of lust and greed. But for the loyalty of the faithful few who upheld them, they might have been allowed to perish in a mire of blood. This noble minority, largely unknown by name, was Israel's spiritual saviour. The Messianic dream which it cherished depended for its sustenance upon the lives and homes of saintly and spiritually gifted individuals. Though prophecy had practically disappeared, the apocalyptic hope, sustained by prophetic predictions and an undying national consciousness, survived. More and more it turned Israel's attention heavenward and toward the distant future. Popular religion, on its practical side, became increasingly legalistic. It became a punctiliously observed cult of obedience. On its mystical side it tended rapidly toward a cosmic supernaturalism. The Persian and Greek philosophical influences succeeded in making themselves appreciably felt. The Pharisees, strict puritans though they were, adopted the angelology and demonology which had entered Hebrew thought through contact with the East. The doctrines of the resurrection and a future universal judgment were definitely accepted. The prophetic urge to moral reform was noticeably absent. Piety was gradually reduced to the simple formula of watching and praying. The priest devoted himself to the sacrificial ritual; the scribe became the faithful interpreter of the law; the synagogue, now well established, nurtured the popular Messianic hope. Lastly, the sage, the practical religious philosopher, continued his fruitful inquiry into truth and life in order to discover their hidden and ultimate meaning . . .[26]

SUGGESTIONS FOR FURTHER STUDY

A. E. BAILEY and C. F. KENT, *History of the Hebrew Commonwealth,* pp. 295-317.

H. M. BATTENHOUSE, *The Bible Unlocked,* pp. 256-269

J. A. BEWER, *The Literature of the Old Testament,* pp. 410-419.

G. A. BUTTRICK, ed., *The Interpreter's Bible,* I, pp. 288-290, 339, 340.

F. C. EISELEN, E. LEWIS, D. G. DOWNEY, eds., *The Abingdon Bible Commentary,* pp. 71, 746-758.

H. T. Fowler, *The Origin and Growth of the Hebrew Religion,*
    pp. 153-166.

E. J. Goodspeed, *The Story of the Old Testament,* pp. 138-142.

C. S. Knopf, *The Old Testament Speaks,* pp. 339-345.

E. W. K. Mould, *Essentials of Bible History,* pp. 414-420, 425-428.

R. H. Pfeiffer, *Introduction to the Old Testament,* pp. 748-781.

J. M. P. Smith, *The Prophets and Their Times,* pp. 292-318.

H. C. Snell, *Ancient Israel: Its Story and Meaning,* pp. 239-263.

PART III

THE BEGINNINGS
OF
CHRISTIANITY

Chapter Twenty

PREPARING THE WAY

A. *The Graeco-Roman World.*

Christianity is a historical religion. It did not grow up in a vacuum and in antithesis to the world in which it appeared. Like all institutions, it had its roots in the past and partook in its origin of the strengths and weaknesses of its antecedents. Of course it is true that there was much in early Christianity that was new; the world into which this new religion came was hungering for something different and soul-satisfying, and Christianity came, as Paul puts it, "when the proper time came."[1] But we cannot estimate the beginning of the Christian religion aright unless we understand the historical circumstances in which it appeared and the difficulties it had to encounter. Christianity's founder, Jesus of Nazareth, was a historical individual who lived in Palestine over nineteen hundred years ago; he is to be included among those historical founders of religion who left so strong an impression upon their contemporaries that they were remembered by their followers long after their death.[2] The careful student cannot separate Christianity and its founder from the framework of the age in which they appeared. The efforts of many generations in many places helped to prepare the way for the coming of the Christian religion.

As we have seen,[3] the religious development of Judaism helped to prepare the way for Christianity; one cannot understand the lives of Jesus, Paul, and the early Christian leaders without remembering that they were Jews. But the world into which Christianity was thrust was more than can be contained in the narrow confines of Palestinian Judaism; it was culturally Greek and politically Roman. These two factors blend into each other to such a degree that it is more satisfactory to combine them and speak of the Graeco-Roman world.

After the conquests of Alexander the Great (336-323 B.C.)[4] Greek culture spread throughout the entire known world. The period between the death of Alexander and the year 200 A.D. may be referred to as the Hellenistic Age,[5] for even the art, science, literature, and philosophy of the early centuries of the Roman Empire were essentially Hellenistic. With the scattering of Greek armies, the journeys of Greek colonists and salesmen, and the wanderings of Greek philosophers and religious leaders, people throughout the entire Mediterranean basin accepted the veneer if not the reality of Hellenistic civilization. The chief agent for the spread of this Hellenizing process was the Greek city; Alexander is said to have founded more than seventy of them, of which the most famous is Alexandria in Egypt. These flourishing centers of commerce and culture attracted the best minds for the development of the arts and the sciences; in almost every center grammar schools were to be found, while at some of them were established great seats of learning.[6]

The Greek language was spoken and read by the educated classes everywhere. From the fourth century B.C. on there arose a Greek dialect known as the "koiné," or common, or Hellenistic Greek, which became the "lingua franca," or universal language, of the entire Roman Empire. It was in this language that the books of the New Testament were written. It was the language of culture, commerce, diplomacy, and administration; inscriptions in koiné testify to its use in a wide area from the Tagus River in Spain to the Indus River on the border of western India.[7] Even the Hebrew Bible was not to escape the influence of Hellenization; it had been translated into Greek in Egypt during the reign of Ptolemy Philadelphus of Egypt (285-247 B.C.);[8] this was the version of the sacred scriptures which the early Christians used; when the authors of the New Testament books quoted the Old Testament they invariably used the Greek of the Septuagint. Greek was the language of worship in the Jewish synagogues throughout the dispersion; we find Paul speaking to Jews and God-fearing Gentiles in the synagogues in the Greek language, the one they would all have understood.

Greek culture created a new tradition of education. As a result of its influence, education became general; tutors, professors, and private chaplains occupied positions of social distinction and were paid more generously than some of their contemporaries. Wealthy Romans sent their sons to Athens to finish their education; Cicero, Horace, and Philo were among those who studied there. Alexandria soon took the place of Athens as the seat of learning in the later Roman Empire; famous for its museum and library of some 700,000 volumes, it attracted scholars from all countries.[9] It was at Alexandria that Christianity later was to contact the best in pagan thought; under Clement and Origen Alexandria became the intellectual capital of Christianity. Under Greek influence, books became more numerous and cheap; writing materials became more common and the facilities of production by slave copyists more general. When Christianity emerged into the Graeco-Roman world it met an environment which was rather well educated.

Greek philosophy helped prepare the way for the coming of the Christian religion; for twelve hundred years creative thinkers had sought to solve the problems of man and the universe. Through the use of reason in the attainment of truth, the Greek philosophers made a unique contribution to civilization and to religion. Socrates, Plato, and Aristotle are numbered among the great giants of the history of human thought. Christianity originated as an oriental religion, in which the revelation of the divine will to the prophets was of supreme importance; but before a half century of its history had passed, the Christian religion had to meet all the aspects of Hellenistic culture, including its philosophy. In the second century, leadership in the Christian church passed to men who knew Greek philosophy and who knew how to combine creatively the best in Hebrew thought with the best in Greek thought.

There were some schools of Greek philosophy, such as Epicureanism, which proved inimical to the Christian gospel.[10] There were others which helped to pave the way for the spread of Christianity; of these the most important was Stoicism. Founded by Zeno (340-265 B.C.), its representatives in the early days of Christianity were Seneca (4-65 A.D.), Epictetus (60-110 A.D), and the emperor Marcus Aurelius (121-180 A.D.). In its emphasis on the brotherhood of man, the primacy of virtue as man's chief end, the duty of self-control, and the reign of moral law, Stoicism was close to much that was in Christian teaching; but it was a creed of despair and it despised the Christian virtues which spring from belief in the love of God. The Stoic idea of conscience informed by the divine reason as the guide of life is not very much different from Christian ethical teaching; echoes of this are found in parts of the letters of Paul.[11] The Stoic idea of the Logos also was influential on Christian thought, particularly in the fourth gospel. First used by Heraclitus (*ca.* 540-475 B.C.) and continued by later Greek philosophers, the Logos was taken to be the same as the divine reason in the universe. The Jewish philosopher of Alexandria, Philo (*ca.* 20 B.C.-50 A.D.), spoke often of the Logos as the synthesis of the Jewish Messiah with the Greek notion of the supreme reason. Philo may have mediated such a concept to the author of the fourth gospel, for in the Gospel of John the Logos is the divine creator of the universe, an eternal light shining in darkness for the illumination of all mankind.

> The similarity of this concept of the Fourth Gospel to the Stoic Logos has often been pointed out. The author was probably familiar with the Stoic idea and certainly many of his Greek readers would be. He adopted a concept which all educated Greeks knew. Whether he intended to do it or not, he laid a bridge from Christian faith to Greek philosophy which was shortly to become a highway . . .

> Another New Testament passage which shows affinity with Stoic thought is Heb. 4:12. The Logos of God, this writer states, is living and powerful, and sharper than any sword in penetrating every recess of personality and judging all the desires and thoughts of the human heart. This idea is certainly close to the omnipresent and omniscient Logos of Stoicism, yet it is not identical with it. The Logos here is the mind or intelligence of God, not God himself, as it would be in Stoicism.[12]

The echo of a Stoic idea that the world was created out of fire and would be dissolved by fire is found in II Peter 3:10.

Christianity came into a world which was not irreligious; in fact there was a multiplicity of religions. Paul tells the men of Athens, as he addresses them in the Areopagus: "From every point of view I see that you are extremely religious."[13] There were, first of all, the traditional cults in honor of the Olympian gods, of whom the chief was Zeus. Even though the Hellenistic period witnessed the decline of worship of these ancient Greek gods, many festivals were celebrated as splendidly as ever, temples continued to receive votive gifts, and many of the gods were still consulted through their oracles, as the one to Apollo at Delphi. Both private persons and state officials came from all over the world to consult the pronouncements of the priestesses of Apollo at Delphi; vapors believed to be the breath of the god arose from the cavern and caused the priestesses to go into a trance and mutter words believed to be directly from the god. It is quite possible that the mentally ill girl met by Paul at Philippi on his second missionary journey was considered by many to be a walking oracle of Apollo.[14]

The primitive Greek polytheism gave little satisfaction to personal religious feeling and to the quest for immortality. Hence there arose a second kind of religious phenomenon in the Hellenistic Age: the mystery cult. The existence of numerous mystery cults at the time Christianity was born is evidence of the pathetic yearning of the ancient world for regeneration and salvation. Similar to Christianity in many ways and perhaps influential to Christian growth, these mystery cults claimed to meet the needs of the common man; they had been first introduced into Greece from the Orient as early as the seventh century B.C. They had replaced the idea of a religion attached to a tribe or a city-state with the revolutionary concept of a religion open to all men. Membership in the cults was free and spontaneous, to be attained by initiation rather than by birthright.

Like Christianity, most of the mystery cults were founded on some story of the life and death and resurrection of a god. Out of Egypt came the cult of Isis and Osiris; it spread over the Mediterranean world from the third century B.C. on and became very popular even in Athens and Rome. According to its theology, Isis was the earth-mother and Osiris (sometimes called Serapis), her brother-husband, was the vegetation spirit. Osiris had an evil brother, Seth, who murdered Osiris and concealed his body. Isis was aided by other deities in finding his body and restoring it to life. Originally an interpretation of Egyptian agriculture and intended to insure the fertility of the soil and the regularity of the harvest through the annual overflowing of the Nile River, the cult developed into a religion of personal redemption. Those who were initiated into its sacred rites were assured that they could be like Osiris and triumph over death; sometimes the adventures of the dying and rising god were depicted before the eyes of the neophytes in the form of a mystery play.

Also similar to Christianity was the fact that most of these mystery cults required of each new member the rite of initiation, preceded by a variety of purificatory ceremonies. Initiation included a witnessing of the mystery at the heart of the cult, i.e., a dramatization of the career of the god, and participation in a sacred meal. By such means the devout worshiper believed that he was united to the very nature of the god himself and through eating the flesh of the sacred animal the god himself dwelt within him.[15] The cult of Mithra, coming out of Persia, probably took over from the ancient Asiatic mother-cult of Cybele-Attis the interesting initiatory rite of the taurobolium; according to the Christian poet Prudentius (died *ca.* 410 A.D.), who seems to have been one of the few outsiders who ever witnessed such an event, the devotee would enter a pit covered with perforated planks, while upon the planks was stationed a bull adorned with a band of gold. The breast of the bull was pierced with the consecrated spear, and the blood dripped through upon the initiate in the pit. "He exposed his head and all his garments to be saturated with the blood; then he turned around and held up his neck that the blood might trickle upon his lips, ears, eyes, and nostrils; he moistened his tongue with the blood, which he then drank as a sacramental act. Greeted by the spectators, he came forth from this bloody baptism believing that he was purified from his sin and 'born again for eternity.' "[16]

Mithraism was the strongest rival of Christianity for the allegiance of the Graeco-Roman world. Coming from Persia, it became exceedingly popular with Roman soldiers. Only men were allowed to be initiated into its mysteries. Originally associated with the bright sky, Mithra in Roman times was identified with the sungod, called "Sol invictus Mithra." Mithraists regarded the winter solstice as the time for the rebirth of their god; on or about December 21 the sun seemed to recover its strength after the days of decreasing sunlight in late summer and autumn. Mithra's birthday was celebrated on December 25; when Christianity finally won out over its rival, it was customary to use the old festival day for the celebration of the birth of Christ.

In Greece itself, the most popular mystery cult was the one which centered at Eleusis. With its rituals based on the cycle of the seasons, the cult emphasized the alternating death and birth of life witnessed in fall and spring. To its initiates it assured a blessed immortality. The rituals were centered around Demeter, the spirit of fertility, Persephone, her daughter, the spirit of vegetation, and Pluto, who brought death to all living things every autumn. The Eleusinian cult became a state cult in Athens, and its popularity had become world-wide by the first century of our era. Rivaling the Eleusinian mysteries was the cult of Dionysus (Bacchus), the god of wine; the devotees believed that they could worship the power of life in nature and become possessed by the presence of the god just as the imbibers of wine worked themselves into a frenzy. The god entered their lives through eating the raw flesh and drinking the blood of a sacred animal, sometimes a bull, a goat, or a fawn; the animal had to be devoured in haste, lest some of the divinity should escape, giving the feast a frenzied character.[17] The cult of Orpheus in Greece was a variant form of the Dionysian, with a stronger emphasis upon theological speculation.

When Christianity entered the stage of history, it was destined to triumph over the other oriental mystery religions which were its rivals. Instead of being based upon a mythical story of the life, death, and resurrection of a god, Christianity was founded by a historical personality.[18] In place of the esoteric mysticism of the cults, Christianity introduced the concept of love as a new moral force applicable to the entire human race. Christianity triumphed over all other cults because it most effectively brought a satisfying message to the widespread sorrow of the ancient world. The gospels showed that this new religion offered more abundantly and more assuredly the two values most earnestly craved in the Graeco-Roman world: healing in this life and immortality after death.[19]

The spread of the mystery cults meant the decline of the classical Graeco-Roman polytheism. Many of the Roman emperors were disturbed by this development; they began to repair old temples and build impressive new ones, but the decline continued. The emperor Augustus inaugurated a religious revival under which he claimed to have repaired eighty-two temples in the city of Rome itself; his interest was mainly due to political reasons, for he regarded the decline of the worship of the old gods to be a loss of patriotism. To preserve further the religious character of patriotism, Augustus instituted the imperial cult by elevating Julius Caesar to a divine status and decreeing that the emperor should be worshiped even during his lifetime. This cult was never intended to displace the mystery cults or other national religions, but it was the best means the emperors knew to give cohesion to their vast empire.[20] The cult of the emperors was the culmination of a long period of development, particularly in the orient, during which the kings of Babylonia and Assyria, the pharaohs of Egypt, and even the kings of the Hebrews were regarded as incarnations of deity; the Greeks had elevated many of their heroes and thinkers to the status of divinity. Alexander and his successors, the Ptolemies of Egypt and the Seleucids of Syria, had not stood in the way of divine honors being paid to them. And finally, the emperors of Rome opened the door for their own entrance to the pantheon of gods. To the Jews the state worship of the emperor was the blasphemy of blasphemies; on their side, the Roman authorities could tolerate the national messianism of the Jewish religion, but could not permit the contention of the Christian missionaries that Jesus was the sovereign of the new heavenly kingdom and the ruler of a new imperial cult designed to supplant all rivals.[21] It was this contrast which led the Christian Church to suffer so much at the hands of the Roman rulers, as is ably pointed out by Mould:

Domitian regarded himself as divine, and imperial orders issued in his name began with the formula, "Our lord and god." During the reign of Domitian the demand that the emperor be worshiped made serious trouble for the Christians and precipitated a wide-spread persecution.

The act of emperor worship consisted in sprinkling a few grains of incense or a few drops of wine on an altar which stood before an image of the emperor. Perhaps at our long remove from the situation we see in the act nothing different from standing at attention with removed hat before a statue of Abraham Lincoln or lifting the hand in salute to the flag or to some distinguished ruler of state, an expression of courtesy, respect, and patriotism. Possibly a good many people in the first century felt just that way about it but not so the Christians. They viewed the whole matter as one of religious worship, acknowledging the emperor as a deity and therefore being disloyal to God and Christ, and they refused to do it. Because they refused they were regarded as politically disloyal. The reason why Christians were persecuted was precisely that they were considered enemies of the state because they would not join in emperor worship. It was such worship that helped bind into a real unity the widely divergent elements that made up the Roman empire. Emperor worship and the Christians' attitude toward it are basic to an understanding of two books of the New Testament which arose in times of persecution, *viz.*, Revelation and I Peter.[22]

At the time of the genesis of the Christian religion, the Graeco-Roman world was literally one world. After four centuries of intermittent fighting, Roman political and military genius had welded her vast empire into a solid unity. Rome administered her vast holdings with skill and efficiency; the "Pax Romana" (Roman peace) brought the benefits of order and organization to the many races and nations under Roman control. A vast network of splendid roads was constructed; originally built for the travel of officials of state and for the movement of armies, the roads were used by Christian missionaries to extend the gospel all over the known world. The highways had been made safe for travel and the seaways had been swept free of pirates. People from all over the empire mingled together in the great centers of commerce and trade, thus making for a cosmopolitanism which characterized the growth of Christianity as portrayed in the Book of Acts.[23] The unity of the empire aided in the dissemination of the Christian conviction of the oneness of humanity and the brotherhood of man. Citizenship in such an empire was highly prized; the privileges of Roman citizenship operated advantageously in the life of Paul;[24] they included freedom from dishonorable punishment, such as flogging and crucifixion, the right of trial, and the right of appeal to the emperor.

However, there was a darker side to life in the Graeco-Roman world. Society was divided sharply into classes; there were at the top the aristocrats of wealth and position, who were the only ones to benefit from increased trade and commerce; there were at the bottom the very poor; the absence of any important middle class deepened and widened the terrible gap between the rich and the poor. Economic and social conditions were further aggravated by the presence of an enormous number of slaves, which had been increased by captives taken in war; in some centers in the Roman empire slaves outnumbered freemen by as many as three to one.[25] Eventually slavery was to be one of the causes of the downfall of the Roman Empire; it inoculated society with a moral poison from which it never recovered. Slaves were treated with very little humanitarianism; they furnished most of the material for the gladiatorial combats. Many slaves, such as those who came from Greece, were often of high birth and of a culture far superior to that of their masters, but they, like their fellow slaves, owed absolute obedience to their masters. Christianity grew rapidly among the slaves and the lower classes, though it did not at first try to exterminate the institution of slavery.[26]

The amusements of the period showed the low level of morals prevailing throughout the Roman Empire. The government provided for the populace, especially in the cities, dramatic productions and spectacles in the amphitheater which were morally degrading. "Gladiatorial games were introduced in 264 B.C. . . . The combatants were slaves, criminals or captives; . . . Exhibitors vied with each other in the numbers exposed to slaughter. Caesar put 320 pairs up at once; Agrippa caused 700 pairs to fight in one day in Berytus; under Augustus 10,000 fought; Titus, 'the darling of the human race,' put up 3,000; Trajan amused Rome for 123 days by exhibiting 10,000 captives in mutual slaughter. Rome's holiest, the vestals, had seats of honour in the arena. Claudius liked to witness the contortions of dying gladiators . . . To witness the murder of men in cold blood grew monotonous, and the Romans always loved novelty in their pleasures. Pompey introduced combats of men with wild beasts: . . . Every excess of cruelty and novelty was tried . . ."[27]

It was in such a world that Christianity was first planted. With its gospel of redemption, it appealed to all classes of men in all stations of life. Its concern for human welfare, expressed in the fellowship of Christian brothers under one Father-God, united orientals and occidentals in one community, breaking down barriers between rich and poor, slaves and freemen, masters and servants. "It gave an assurance of salvation for the immortal soul, it appealed to the imagination and emotions, in its sacred rites it answered the current longing for realism, it satisfied intellectual demands, as they arose, it awakened conscience by its insistence on rewards and punishments, it sounded a strong ethical note, and in its doctrine of the one true God it gave men a sufficiently large conception of Deity to meet the needs of an enlarging world and an imperialistic age."[28]

B. *Judaism at the Time of Jesus.*

The Christian movement began in Palestine; its antecedents were all Jewish, and its chief problems at first grew out of its relationship to its Palestinian background. Judaism gave to the new religion the personalities of John the Baptist, Jesus, the twelve disciples, Paul, and all the early Christian leaders. In its origin it must be considered a Jewish phenomenon. It is important, therefore, to consider the Jewish aspect of the world in which the books of the New Testament were written and into which the religion of the Nazarene was thrust.

The political history of the Hebrew people had a great deal to do with the development of their religion. After being under the domination of Egyptians, Babylonians, Assyrians, Persians, and Greeks at various times in history, the Jews finally enjoyed a period of independence under the Maccabees and the Hasmonean kings.[29] This came to an end with the coming of the Romans in 63 B.C.; from that year until his violent death in 43 B.C., the real power in Palestine was Antipater. After three years of confusion, Antipater's son, Herod the Great, was declared by the Romans "king of the Jews," and he enjoyed a period of relatively independent rule until 4 B.C. His policy was loyalty to Rome no matter who was in power at Rome; hence he was able to maintain himself under both Antony and Augustus.

Herod proved himself a ruler of ability and energy; though he did not succeed in winning the respect and affection of the Jews —he was an Idumean and was sarcastically called a "half-Jew"— he did restore outward glory and splendor to Palestine. He built Caesarea on the coast, which became his capital; he constructed palaces and temples, theaters and castles, baths and aqueducts. Even in Jerusalem he built a theater and an amphitheater, in which he celebrated games in honor of the emperor Augustus; he also built a palace for himself and a citadel at the north end of the temple enclosure, the tower of Antonia. The temple itself did not escape his plans for improvement; in the year 20-19 B.C. he began the reconstruction of the temple, which was still in progress forty-six years later[30] and was not actually completed until after 62 A.D., just a few years before its final destruction in 70 A.D. The last years of Herod's reign were saddened by family tragedy; one of his wives, Marianne, a Hasmonean princess, he murdered, along with her two sons and his oldest son Antipater. Despised and hated by the people of Palestine, his career of murder led Augustus to coin a Greek pun: "It is better to be Herod's pig ("hyn") than his son ("hyion").[31] To guarantee sincere mourning when he died, Herod ordered all the principal men of the nation to be massacred at the hour of his death; fortunately his orders were not carried out. Thus the picture of Herod in the Gospel of Matthew as a cruel tyrant who ordered all the male children of Bethlehem, "who were two years old or under,"[32] to be slaughtered is not overdrawn; it was in the reign of this Herod that Jesus of Nazareth was born.[33]

Herod's kingdom was divided among his three sons: Archelaus was given Judea; Philip was made tetrarch of Iturea and Trachonitis;[34] and Herod Antipas became ruler over Galilee and Perea. In 6 A.D. the rule of the barbarous and incompetent Archelaus was brought to an end; from then until 40 A.D., Judea was ruled by Roman procurators.[35] Philip seems to have been the most respectable of the sons of Herod, and he ruled his territory north and east of the Sea of Galilee with justice and peace.[36] Herod Antipas (4 B.C.-39 A.D.) was clever and vainglorious like his father;[37] he rebuilt the city of Sepphoris, near Nazareth,[38] and constructed a new city on the Sea of Galilee, Tiberias, as his capital.[39] He caused a great scandal by marrying Herodias, the wife of one of his half-brothers.[40] It was natural that Jesus would clash with such a person, or at least with his subordinate officials.[41] Herod was present in Jerusalem when Jesus was tried, but contributed nothing toward solving Pilate's dilemma.[42] In 39 A.D. the emperor Caligula removed Herod Antipas from power and exiled him to Lyons in southern Gaul, giving his dominions to Herod Agrippa I, who had been made ruler of Iturea and Trachonitis three years after the death of Philip (34 A.D.).[43] Following the death of Herod Agrippa, the emperor Claudius reorganized Palestine into a Roman province (44-66), but the procurators[44] failed to reconcile the Jews to Roman rule; in fact, some of them helped to precipitate the disastrous war of 66-70.

Even under Roman rule, national feeling among the Jews, with its keen memory of the heroic period of independence under the Maccabees and the Hasmoneans,[45] was kept alive, particularly by the group among them known as the Zealots. This culminated finally in a suicidal rebellion against Rome, which was begun in 66 A.D. and ended in 70 with the complete destruction of the city of Jerusalem and the demolition of the temple by the soldiers of the Roman general Titus. The Hebrew temple has never been restored;[46] at first it seemed a calamity without remedy, but, as so frequently in Hebrew history, wise leaders among the Jews helped their people make a necessary adjustment; the synagogues replaced the temple; a study of the ritual laws became a substitute for the cult; and repentance followed by good works took the place of sacrifices offered in expiation of sin. Twice again did the Jews rebel futilely against Rome; under Trajan (98-117), thousands of Jews were killed in Cyprus, Mesopotamia, Egypt, and Cyrene (115-116); under Hadrian (117-138), the revolt led by Simon bar Cocheba was the last outburst of patriotic hope for national independence. After that normative Judaism began to consolidate its life as a community primarily on a religious basis; the teachers of the written and oral law, the scribes, the Pharisees, and the rabbis, became the leaders of Israel, and the era of rabbinical Judaism or Talmudism was begun.

In the period just prior to New Testament times, the great parties in Judaism were developed. The scribes were the professional interpreters of the Torah; they are first mentioned by the Chronicler (*ca.* 250 B.C.)[47] as one of the professional guilds of Judaism; Ezra is referred to as "the priest, the scribe, learned in matters of the command of the Lord and his statutes in Israel."[48] The first scribe whose name is known was Jesus ben Sirach (*ca.* 180 B.C.). Sirach has given us a good description of the work of the scribes:

A scribe attains wisdom through the opportunities of leisure,
And the man who has little business to do can become wise.

He searches out the wisdom of all the ancients,
And busies himself with prophecies;
He observes the discourse of famous men,
And penetrates the intricacies of figures.

He searches out the hidden meaning of proverbs,
And acquaints himself with the obscurities of figures.

He will reveal instruction in his teaching,
And will glory in the Law of the Lord's agreement.[49]

The scribes were the educators of the day; they were often called
lawyers,[50] or doctors of the law.[51] Though most of them were
Pharisees, the terms "scribes" and "Pharisees" were not synonymous.[52]

The Pharisees were probably the successors of the Chasidim,
going back in their origin to the anti-Hellenizing party in Palestine under the Seleucid kings.[53] In New Testament times they
were more numerous than a sect; the word "brotherhood" may
more strictly be applied to them, for they were the largest and
most influential group in Jewish society. Lagrange defines them
correctly as "a fraternity boasting a unique acquaintance with
the Law of God, both written and oral, and organized for the purposes of observing this Law with even greater exactitude, and of imposing it on others."[54] The Pharisaic ideal was a worthy one: to
live a life in full accord with the will of God. In this objective,
the Pharisees and Jesus were basically in agreement; the sharp
distinction between them was largely one of method. The Pharisees
believed that the good life could be attained by following the min-
utest regulations of both written (Torah) and oral (Mishna)
law; when the laws were perfectly kept, thought the Pharisees, the
Messiah would appear and free the Jews from Roman domination.
Jesus criticized sharply the immense body of oral interpretation
which the Pharisees had been developing through the years around
the Torah.[55] The gospels are full of references to the customs of the
Pharisees,[56] all of them showing the narrowness, censoriousness,
self-righteousness, and conceit of these pious laymen. That not all
Pharisees were of this sort is evidenced by the fact that Jesus attracted some of them.[57] The Pharisees devoted themselves without
stint to the work of instructing the people in the Law and in
bringing religion to bear upon the popular life. However, they
were impatient with the Jews who found their legal restrictions
upon life burdensome, and they tended to hold themselves aloof
from the common people.[58]

Though there were many Pharisaic schools, there were two

which were particularly popular at the time of Jesus. They had been founded by two famous rabbis during the reign of Herod the Great: Shammai and Hillel. The first was in favor of a rigorous orthodoxy, while the second represented a more liberal tendency among the Pharisees. Hillel's grandson and successor was the famous Gamaliel, who was the teacher of Paul.[59] Shammai was conservative, exclusive, and anti-foreign; Hillel was moderate and patient toward Gentiles.

His (Hillel's) patience was proverbial and his tact unfailing. Men might wager that they could make him lose his temper, to their own loss. Proselytes rebuffed by Shammai never annoyed Hillel. He understood that the heathen with an interest in Judaism was first concerned with the ultimate, the essential message of the religion, not its minutiae. When a heathen, discouraged by Shammai, once appeared before Hillel and asked: What in a nutshell does Judaism teach? Hillel did not interpret the question as impertinence. He grasped what had escaped his less patient colleague, and replied, "What is hateful to thee never do to thy fellow man. This is the entire Torah; all else is commentary." Then he added, "Go master it."

The liberal spirit so manifest in this incident is no less a characterization of the man as teacher and jurist. He welcomed everybody to his school, rich and poor, prominent and humble, pious and negligent. His followers never approved of the exclusive character of Shammai's academy. Furthermore, unlike Shammai, Hillel attempted to express the larger intent of Scripture rather than its limited implications. And as a jurist he had none to equal him in his generation . . .[60]

One section of the school of Shammai seems to have consisted of extremists, bitter and narrow-minded and open to the charge of formalism and hypocrisy.[61]

The Sadducees also emerged as a distinct group at the time when the Seleucid kings were trying forcibly to Hellenize the inhabitants of Palestine.[62] They were friendly to foreign rulers, whether Greek or Roman; they wanted the Jews to accept the influences coming from the cultures of the other people with whom they came into contact. The Sadducees represented the old aristocratic families, and they dominated the temple priesthood.[63] They wanted to keep on good terms with Rome in order to retain their own power. Unlike the Pharisees, the Sadducees accepted only the written Torah and rejected the Mishna; they denied the doctrine of resurrection;[64] they disbelieved in spirits and angels. The Pharisees considered them to be worldly-minded and completely lacking in real religious conviction. In the New Testament the Sadducees are mentioned only in connection with the city of Jerusalem; when the temple was destroyed in 70 A.D. the Sadducees became a small sect with no further noticeable influence over the Jewish people. Presumably the Sadducees did not oppose Jesus until he cleansed the temple during the last week of his life.[65]

The Zealots started out as the fanatical left-wing section of the Pharisees, sharing with them their religious views but advocating direct action against Rome. Josephus[66] connects the appearance of the Zealots as a party with a movement that followed the deposition of Archelaus *ca.* 6 A.D.[67] The leaders were Judas of Gamala[68] and a Pharisee named Zadduk; they recruited active opposition to a census ordered by Quirinius, governor of Syria. The Romans speedily suppressed the revolt, but the Zealot faction persisted. One of the twelve disciples of Jesus was a Zealot.[69] It was this group which kept alive the spirit of rebellion among the Jews and finally precipitated the disastrous Jewish wars of 66-70 A.D.[70]

Philo and Josephus both mention a Jewish monastic order living in celibate communities on the shores of the Dead Sea and called the Essenes. They were so unlike anything in normative Judaism that scholars have tried to show that their essential beliefs and customs derived from Greek Pythagoreanism, or from Orphism, or from both, at a time when they were being fused together. They are not mentioned in the New Testament and probably did not influence early Christianity in any appreciable degree. Some have speculated that John the Baptist and Jesus may have belonged to this order; John the Baptist does present some similarities to an ascetic order, but he probably was not an Essene; Jesus was most certainly not an Essene, for he did not recommend fleeing from the world. In matters of doctrine the Essenes represented an extreme Pharisaism; they were strict in the observance of the Sabbath and stressed ceremonial purity through frequent lustrations.

The accidental discovery (in 1896) in Cairo of Hebrew documents acquainting us with a body of reform Jews called the Covenanters of Damascus and their publication in 1910 show how varied the sectarian movements in Judaism were near the beginning of our era. Turning their back on the temple and rejecting the belief that the Messiah would come from the tribe of Judah, they comprised an association of pious legalists who interpreted the Law after their own manner. They resembled the Pharisees, but they were dissatisfied with their ineffective religious leadership and with the corruption of the Sadducean priesthood in Jerusalem. They urged their fellow Jews to repent and to adopt a very strict type of living which alone, they felt, could deliver the nation from its unhappy state.[71]

These six groups do not cover all the people in Palestine during the New Testament period. Mention has already been made of the Herodians[72] and the "am-haares."[73] The former were the supporters of the dynasty of Herod; pro-Hellenistic, they are pictured in the gospels as making common cause with the anti-Hellenistic Pharisees against Jesus. The "am-haares" were the people of the land, the common people. Though many of them seem to have believed in religion and revered the scribes, priests, and Pharisees, they were discouraged with the prospect of being very religious themselves because of the hopelessness with trying to keep the Law and its exacting burden of requirements. The Pharisees looked upon these people as "sinners," similar in status to the outcastes in modern Hinduism. They were the Jews who could not recite the Shema, nor the morning and evening prayers, who did not wear the ritual fringes on their garments nor the phylacteries on their wrists and heads, who ate without first washing their hands, and who did not pay the tithe on any property which they might have in their possession. It was in these "sinners" that Jesus was primarily interested.[74]

There was one group of people in Jewish society to whom religion was a genuine, earnest experience, who looked forward anxiously to the coming of a Messiah, and who were filled with a quiet devotional spirit. These may well be called the pietists. They came from almost every one of the sects, parties, schools, and movements of Judaism. A great many of them were from the am-haares, like Joseph and Mary; some were connected with the temple, like Zechariah and Elizabeth, Symeon and Hannah. Some were Pharisees, like Nicodemus; others were scribes, like the one who was "not far from the Kingdom of God."[75] At least one was a member of the Sanhedrin: Joseph of Arimathea; some were rich, like the rich young ruler; others were poor. It was from among them that a new religion was to spring, a religion which would more satisfactorily meet their spiritual needs.[76]

By the time of the rise of Christianity by far the greater part of the Jewish people lived outside the boundaries of Palestine; they were called the Diaspora, or Dispersion, Jews. The process of dispersion began with the fall of the northern kingdom in 721 B.C.[77] and was accelerated by the end of the southern kingdom in 586 B.C.[78] The Jews had established important colonies in Babylonia and Egypt, and in Graeco-Roman times they were so numerous in every land that the geographer Strabo, whom Josephus quotes, remarks: "It is difficult to find a place in the habitable earth that has not admitted this tribe of men and is not possessed by them."[79] Their diffusion is indicated by a famous list of peoples in Acts 2:9-11:

> Parthians, Medes, Elamites, residents of Mesopotamia, of Judea and Cappadocia, of Pontus, and Asia, of Phrygia, and Pamphylia, of Egypt and the district of Africa about Cyrene, visitors from Rome, Jews and proselytes, Cretans and Arabs— we all hear them in our native tongues the mighty deeds of God.

Though the Jews were profoundly affected by their environment wherever they lived, they were even more loyal to their religious traditions than were the Palestinian Jews. Adopting Greek language in their synagogue services, translating their scriptures into Greek, and borrowing to some extent Greek organizational forms in their communal institutions, they became intense propagandists for their faith. They were very successful, for proselytes and God-fearers were found in large numbers in every country of the Diaspora.[80] These later became the most fruitful group of prospects for Christianity.[81] The liberal attitude of the Dispersion Jew helped to prepare the way for the coming of a broad universalistic religion which would be free from the barriers of race connection. Such a religion was Christianity. It was a Hellenistic Jew, Paul of Tarsus, who helped to remove the barriers of circumcision and race and to proclaim a universalism which could form the basic principle of a genuinely worldwide religion.

C. *Jewish Literature of the New Testament Period*

What the Jews were reading and thinking at the beginning of the Christian religion is revealed by a study of their literature. Most important were the writings which they considered sacred scripture; of these, the first to be canonized was the Torah.[82] The first five books of the Old Testament evidently stood alone at first as distinct from other Jewish writings. In the prologue to the book of Ecclesiasticus, written by the grandson of the author,[83] there is quite definite testimony to the existence of collections of writings regarded with particular reverence as having been handed down from the fathers; mention is made of three groups: the Law, the Prophets, and the other Writings (Hagiographa).[84] Jewish writers after the exile treat the Torah with exceptional reverence;[85] for the author of I Maccabees, writing some time between 90 and 70 B.C., the Torah is not only a set of rules but something for which men would fight and die. The Torah was that part of sacred writing which was first and best translated into Greek, and it was the first literature to be read systematically in the services of the synagogue. It was also the only section of Hebrew literature which the Samaritans recognized as canonical following their split with the Jerusalem Jews at the time of Nehemiah.[86] Thus, by the end of the third century B.C. the text of the Pentateuch may be considered to have been fixed in somewhat its present form. The New Testament writers, while they are not conscious of any fixed canon of sacred writings, do recognize the Torah as having some special sanctity and authority. The Jews became known as the people of a book; later the word "Torah" often was used to refer to the entire Hebrew Bible. Jesus was brought up in a devout family which reverenced the Torah.[87] The Jews never regarded any other part of the Scriptures to be as holy as the Torah.

The second group of Hebrew writings to be considered as sacred scripture was the collection called "The Prophets," which became the second division of the entire Hebrew Bible. This group of books was divided into the "Former Prophets" (the historical books from Joshua to II Kings, with the exception of Ruth) and the "Latter Prophets" (Isaiah, Jeremiah, Ezekiel, and the twelve so-called minor prophets, "minor" because their books were brief). The process of canonization of these books was begun *ca.* 250 B.C., and their place in the canon was quite thoroughly recognized in the period between 180 and 130 B.C. When the book of Daniel was written,[88] the author gives evidence that he knows of a group of books which includes the words of Jeremiah and is considered as scripture.[89] The author of Ecclesiasticus, Jesus ben Sirach, writing about 180 B.C., names the prophetic books in the order in which they are now found in the Hebrew Bible, mentioning the "Twelve Prophets" as if such a collection were well known in his day.[90] From this time on, the Bible of the Jews was conveniently called "the Law and the Prophets."[91] Together with the book of Psalms, which was evidently the first book of the Writings to be canonized, the Law and the Prophets constituted the Bible of Jesus.[92]

The third part of the Hebrew Bible is called the Hagiographa (or "Writings"), a collection of miscellaneous books, some of which may have begun to win recognition as early as parts of the prophetic collection. The Hagiographa comprises three poetical books: Psalms, Proverbs, and Job; five "rolls":[93] Song of Songs, Ruth, Lamentations, Ecclesiastes, and Esther; and the remaining books Daniel, Ezra, Nehemiah, and I and II Chronicles. It is thought that the stimulus for the canonization of this material was provided by the persecution of the Jews under Antiochus Epiphanes,[94] who forbade them to possess or use their sacred scriptures and destroyed all he could find. From II Maccabees 2:14 "it may safely be inferred that the losses incurred in the religious revival inaugurated by the war led to a demand that steps should be taken to preserve the relics of the national literature and to gather it together into an authoritative edition."[95] The canon of the Hagiographa was evidently determined by the time of Josephus (37-ca. 100 A.D.); in his *Against Apion* he mentions four books, in addition to the Torah and the Prophets, which contain hymns to God and maxims of life for men.[96] Even though no formal act of ratification took place until the Council of Jamnia in 90 A.D., it is unlikely that anything new was added to the canon during the troublous times of the last century B.C. and the first century A.D. Though the fourteen books of the Apocrypha found their way into the Greek translation of the Old Testament known as the Septuagint,[97] none of them were ever included in the Palestinian canon of the Hebrew Scriptures.

Thus, all the books eventually included in the Old Testament canon had probably met with some kind of recognition by the end of the second century B.C. They gradually made their way to universal acceptance in the synagogue. It is doubtful if they were ever formally canonized by any judicial or ecclesiastical authority, although the council meeting at Jamnia, a Jewish seat of learning near Jaffa, did decide to include the Song of Songs and the book of Ecclesiastes, both of which evidently had some difficulty in making the list. It was a long time before all of the Jews accepted all of the books as canonical; the Sadducees did not accept such an artificial limitation, and the Essenes had books of their own which they promised to preserve. The greatest doubt was felt about the book of Esther; it was omitted entirely from some lists of sacred books in the first century A.D., possibly because of its insistence upon a feast not mentioned in the Torah or because of the absence of all mention of the name of God.[98]

Outside of Palestine there never was any formally fixed canon of Scriptures. The Jews read from among many books. Even in Palestine itself, the contemporaries of Jesus were familiar with books other than the canonical ones. Among the Christians, the authors of the New Testament quote from all the books of the Old Testament proper except Obadiah, Nahum, Ezra, Nehemiah, Esther, the Song of Songs, and Ecclesiastes, and, although they do not quote directly from any book in the Apocrypha or Pseudepigrapha, some of the New Testament writers allude to certain passages in them.[99] The Septuagint, which included the fourteen books of the Apocrypha, became the Bible of the early Christians; translated from Greek into Latin by Jerome, the Septuagint has served as the basis for the Old Testament of the Roman Catholic Church. Protestant translators at the time of the Reformation went back to the canon of Palestinian Judaism, which did not have the Apocrypha, thus obscuring the literary and religious value of some of these books through neglect.[100]

The term "Apocrypha" is derived from a Greek word meaning "something hidden." Originally it was used to mean literature hidden from the eyes of the uninitiated and intended only for the wise; later it was applied in a derogatory sense to the literature of secondary value and still later to literature considered false and heretical. Unfortunately, many Christians regard the Old Testament Apocrypha under one or both of the last two designations; as a matter of fact, some would prefer the story of Judith to that of

Esther, and the book of Ecclesiasticus is superior to the pessimistic Old Testament book of Ecclesiastes. All the books of the Apocrypha were written by Jewish authors whose names, except for Jesus, the son of Sirach,[101] are unknown; their writings came into being between 200 B.C. and 90 A.D. For one reason or another, these fourteen books were excluded from the Palestinian canon: some had been composed in Greek (Wisdom of Solomon and II Maccabees 2:19-15: 39); some were manifestly later than the time of Ezra (I and II Maccabees and Ecclesiasticus); some did not strike the popular fancy and hence ceased to be copied soon after their translation into Greek.

The books of the Apocrypha may be classified according to the kinds of literature they represent. I and II Maccabees are books of history. I Maccabees is a first-class historical work covering the Jewish struggle for independence from 175 to 135 B.C.; it was written about 100 B.C. by a Palestinian Jew who was devoted to the faithful, nationalistic, non-Hellenizing Judaism of the Hasmonean period. The greater part of the book centers in the exploits of Judas, apparently the most remarkable figure of the rebellion. II Maccabees, written in Greek *ca.* 100 B.C. by a Pharisee, is not a sequel to I Maccabees but a duplicate account of the period from 175 to 161 B.C. Not as reliable for historical purposes as I Maccabees, II Maccabees has value more in the field of religious belief. The Roman Catholic doctrine of prayers for the dead finds support in II Maccabees 12:43,44, while 15:11,12 has been used to bolster belief in the intercession of the saints.

There are several books of religious fiction in the Apocrypha. I Esdras is a repetition of the story of the rebuilding of the Jerusalem temple in the Persian period, based on II Chronicles, Ezra, and Nehemiah. The only original section of the book is an interesting discussion by three pages at the royal Persian court as to which is the strongest: wine, the king, or women; the one who speaks in praise of wisdom (with an appended story glorifying truth) wins the contest.[102] The book of Tobit was written in Aramaic probably some time between 190 and 170 B.C. in Alexandria; it is the story of a very pious Jew of Galilee who was taken captive by the Assyrians, supposedly in 721 B.C.,[103] and carried off to Nineveh. The purpose of the author was to inculcate religious faith and ethics of the sincerely devout type of Judaism. In Tobit 4:15 there is the earliest occurrence of the golden rule in all extant Jewish literature: "Do not do to anyone else what you hate;" this is also the briefest form in which it has ever been stated, exactly four words in the Greek. The story of Judith (taken from a Hebrew word meaning "Jewess") was written by an orthodox Jew toward the middle of the second century B.C.; like Esther,[104] Judith performs a courageous feat for her people by cutting off the head of the Babylonian general Holofernes.[105] The purpose of the book is to create faith in and loyalty to the Jewish religious institutions. The book of Baruch was written by an unknown Alexandrian Jew some time between 150 and 50 B.C.; partly prose and partly poetry, the book contains various religious ideas centering around the condition of Jewish exiles in Babylonia; some of the contents resemble the wisdom literature of the Old Testament. The Prayer of Manasseh, written in Alexandria *ca.* 100 B.C., is one of the finest prayers in the apocryphal literature; it was put in the mouth of Manasseh during the time he was supposed to be a captive in Babylon.[106] Obviously such a prayer could not have been offered by Manasseh, who was characterized by the Deuteronomic authors of II Kings as the arch idolater of history.[107] The other works of fiction in the Apocrypha are three additions to the book of Daniel (the story of Susanna, the Song of the Three Holy Children, and Bel and the Dragon) and an additional section of the book of Esther.

Two of the apocryphal books belong under the general classification of wisdom literature. The book of Ecclesiasticus, composed in Palestine by Jesus ben Sirach some time between 190 and 170 B.C., is one of the most delightful of the wisdom books produced by the Jews. Like the Old Testament book of Proverbs, it contains numerous proverbs, maxims, and practical observations on human conduct. Wisdom is personified and regarded as eternal and pre-existent.[108] The author presents choice passages on friendship (6:5-17), on the pursuit of wisdom (6:18-37), on free will (15:11-20), against gossip (19:4-17), on physicians (38:1-15), on the works of the Lord (42:15-43:33), and in praise of famous men (44:1-15). The Wisdom of Solomon was written by an Alexandrian Jew some time between 100 and 50 B.C.; very familiar with Greek philosophical thought as well as Judaism, the author reveals in his book the fusion of Jewish and Greek thought which went on among the Dispersion Jews in the Graeco-Roman age. In a passage on immortality (1:12-6:11), the Wisdom of Solomon gives a direct answer to the cynicism and skepticism of Ecclesiastes[109] and a refutation of Epicureanism; chapters 13-15 contain the fullest and most effective criticism of idols in all Jewish literature.

The fourteenth and last book in the Old Testament Apocrypha is the one called II Esdras; this is an apocalyptic book written about twenty years after the tragic destruction of Jerusalem in 70 A.D. Many of the ideas in II Esdras influenced the thinking of Christian apocalyptic writers: the sinful state of man arising from the fall of Adam (7:116-131), the period of woes preceding the coming of the Messiah (4:52-5:13; 6:11-28), the destruction of the enemies of the righteous by the Messiah and the restoration of the lost tribes to Palestine (13:25-40); after four hundred years Messiah and all living creatures will die, there will be silence for seven days, and then will come a general resurrection and the day of judgment (7:29-44); only a few will be saved (7:45-61; 7:132-8:3; 9:13-22).[110]

In addition to the thirty-nine books in the canonical Old Testament and the fourteen books in the Old Testament Apocrypha, certain other Jewish books of the New Testament period have survived. These books are called the Pseudepigrapha.[111] There is no recognized fixed limit to this group of books; new titles are constantly being added as fragments of ancient books are uncovered by archaeologists.[112] Many of them have been very influential on later Christian thought. The writings of the early church fathers mention a good many other books which could be classified among the Pseudepigrapha which are no longer extant.[113]

Some of the pseudepigraphical books are works of religious fiction. The book of Jubilees, originating in Palestine some time between 135 and 105 B.C., is a reworking of the book of Genesis from the standpoint of late Jewish legalism. The author believes that the Torah represents the full revelation of God to man; its ethical, social and ritual demands are part of a changeless and perfect order. Its strong emphasis upon strict observance of the Sabbath (2:25-33; 50:6-13) shows an important trend in Jewish thought at the time of Jesus.[114] The angelology and demonology of the book are results of the influence of Persian dualism upon the Jewish religion.[115] The Letter of Aristeas is a fictional account of the translation of the Pentateuch into Greek; written in Alexandria some time between 130 and 70 B.C., the book has for its chief purpose the glorification of the Torah and the priesthood; the author wants to present Jewish institutions in their most favorable light and to give general approval to the translation of the Torah into Greek. It contains statements of the golden rule and other ethico-religious thoughts current among the Dispersion Jews of the second century B.C. A book called the Sibylline Oracles, books three to five of which are largely Jewish in origin, was compiled during the period between 125 B.C. and 130 A.D.; the unknown author issued these writings as if they were the authentic utterances of the first sibyl of Erythrae.[116] He very cleverly puts into the mouth of the Greek sybil a prediction of the rise of the Jews and Judaism to world primacy.

Many of the writings in the Pseudepigrapha are apocalyptic in nature. I Enoch is a series of apocalyptic writings, Palestinian in origin, dating from about 200-75 B.C. It is very important for understanding the background of the early Christian movement, for in it are contained some of the ideas of the nature of the Messiah which were current among the Jews at the time of Jesus. The Messiah appears as a lamb and transforms the righteous into his likeness (I Enoch 90:37,38); he is called the Christ (48:10; 52:4), the righteous one (38:2; 53:6), the elect one (40:5; 45:3,4), but most frequently the Son of Man (46:2-6; 48:2-10; 62:5-14; 63:11; 69:26-29; 71:14-17).[117] This Son of Man appears with God in the last judgment: "And there I saw One who had a head of days (i.e., an aged head), and his head was white as wool, and with him was another being whose countenance was like the appearance of a man, and his face was full of graciousness, like that of one of the holy angels."[118] There is an elaborate angelology worked out in I Enoch 20 and a solution of the problem of evil through demonology in I Enoch 6. God will overthrow the wicked and transform the earth by means of a great cataclysm; the new age will be good and eternal.[119] There is a view of the resurrection in I Enoch in which all of the righteous will be restored to life and only those of the wicked who have not been punished in this life.[120] The judgment will be followed by the messianic kingdom, which is conceived in I Enoch as an everlasting state of material prosperity on the present earth; the new Jerusalem will be in the center of this kingdom.[121] Parts of I Enoch 91-104 contain worthwhile wisdom teachings.

II Enoch was written some time between 1 and 50 A.D., probably in Alexandria. In a dream the hero is conducted by two divine messengers through the seven heavens, thus revealing the cosmology of the Jews of the first century A.D.[122] The most important part of the book is a compendium of wisdom teachings in chapters 42-66. The Assumption of Moses was composed in Palestine in Aramaic during the lifetime of Jesus (6 B.C.-27 A.D.); the author agrees with the point of view of Jesus toward the Pharisees; they should not blend political ideas with the Messianic hope. While believing in the coming of the kingdom, this author has no room for a Messiah. The author of Jude (verse 9) refers to this apocalyptic book in support of his plea for a proper respect for authority. II Baruch originated in Palestine in the last decade of the first century A.D.; the principal topic of the book is the judgment, with its warning of the wicked and its encouragement of the righteous. III Baruch was written early in the third century of our era; in it the friend and biographer of Jeremiah is supposedly taken by an angel through five of the seven Jewish heavens.

Some of the pseudepigraphical books contain legendary history or biography. III Maccabees is a piece of fiction written by an Alexandrian Jew concerning an alleged persecution of the Jews of Palestine by Ptolemy IV Philopator (221-203 B.C.); the author lived shortly after or before the beginning of the Christian era. The Testaments of the Twelve Patriarchs was written in Hebrew about 140-110 B.C.; inspired by Genesis 49 and Deuteronomy 33, the author puts across his wisdom teachings by representing each of Jacob's twelve sons on his deathbed giving a last will and testament. The purpose of the book is to emphasize devotion to the basic Old Testament virtues; the author condemns the sins of hatred, lying, envy, lust, covetousness, retaliation, selfishness, etc., and commends the virtues of love, forgiveness, truthfulness, chastity, temperance, patience, self-control, etc. Perhaps the remarkable part of the book is the Testament of Gad; the author shows a very high degree of ethical sensitivity as he sets forth his teaching on forgiveness:

> My children, hearken to the words of truth to work righteousness, and go not astray through the spirit of hatred . . .
> Beware therefore, my children, of hatred . . . For as love

would quicken even the dead, and would call back them that
are condemned to die, so hatred would slay the living, and
those that had sinned excusably it would not suffer to live . . .
Hatred therefore is evil, for it constantly mates with lying,
speaking against the truth; and it makes small things to be
great, and causes the light to be darkness, and calls the sweet
bitter, and teaches slander . . . and all covetousness.

And now, my children, I exhort you, love each one his
brother, and put away hatred from your hearts; love one another
in deed, and in word, and in the inclination of the soul . . .
Love one another from the heart; and if a man sin against thee,
speak peaceably to him, and in thy soul hold not guile; and if
he repent and confess, forgive him . . .[123]

This book circulated as a pamphlet of popular devotion in Galilee during the lifetime of Jesus, showing that in the second century
B.C. there was in Palestine a deeply spiritual religious life. The
Martyrdom of Isaiah, written in Palestine *ca.* 100 A.D. as a part of
a larger work, the Ascension of Isaiah, gives the legend of Isaiah's
death by being sawn asunder in a tree trunk.[124] The Paralipomena
of Jeremiah may well be Christian in origin except for the first
eight chapters; this writing purports to contain teachings of Jeremiah which were not included in his book in the canonical Old
Testament. The Lives of the Prophets is a series of biographical
sketches of the four major and twelve minor prophets and some of
the pre-literary prophets; legendary stories are added, particularly
in the lives of Isaiah, Jeremiah, Ezekiel, Daniel, Jonah, and Habakkuk. The Testament of Job is an Aramaic addition to the book of
Job, composed probably in the last century B.C. The Life of Adam
and Eve (Apocalypse of Moses) is a fictitious work apparently composed in Aramaic in the first century of the Christian era just before the destruction of Jerusalem in 70 A.D. It shows the work of
Christian redactors, with whom these and other Jewish legends
were very popular.

At least one book in the Pseudepigrapha, the Psalms of Solomon,
contains some of the Hebrew hymns which had not been included
in the canonical book of Psalms when that collection was made.[125]
The Pharisaic author composed these eighteen religious poems
some time between 48 B.C. and the beginning of the Christian era.
They are ascribed to Solomon,[126] and they comprise mainly peti-

tions to God for help, comfort, and vindication. Chapter 17 is one of the principal messianic passages in Jewish literature:

> Behold, O Lord, and raise up unto them their king, the son of David,
> At the time in which thou seest, O God, that he may reign over Israel thy servant . . .
> And he shall gather together a holy people, whom he shall lead in righteousness,
> And he shall judge the tribes of the people that has been sanctified by the Lord his God.
> And he shall not suffer unrighteousness to lodge any more in their midst,
> Nor shall there dwell with them any man that knoweth wickedness,
> For he shall know them, that they are all sons of their God . . .
> All nations shall be in fear before him,
> For he will smite the earth with the word of his mouth for ever.
> He will bless the people of the Lord with wisdom and gladness,
> And he himself will be pure from sin, so that he may rule a great people.
> He will rebuke rulers, and remove sinners by the might of his word.[127]

IV Maccabees is an Alexandrian production dating from about the beginning of the Christian era. It is a homily or diatribe on philosophical and religious matters after the manner of the Cynics and the Stoics. The Jewish author fully accepts Greek philosophy while remaining thoroughly loyal to the Jewish faith. The theme of the book is the supremacy of devout reason over the passions (a Stoic principle). One of the tracts of the Mishna,[128] called the Sayings of the Jewish Fathers, circulated separately as a treatise by itself; there are six chapters quoting a total of sixty-five Jewish teachers ranging in time from 200 B.C. to 200 A.D. It represents the point of view of the Pharisaic scribes, loyally devoted to the Torah and Jewish religious ethics.

In the ruins of a synagogue in Cairo in 1896 there was discovered a fragmentary text of a document which was evidently produced *ca.* 196 B.C. by a sect of Jews in Damascus called the Zadokites.[129] The fragment contained chiefly a series of laws; the people who wrote it accepted the Torah as final authority, but they also considered the Prophets as canonical scripture. They describe their belief in the coming of a Messiah who would be a descendant of Aaron[130] and would be preceded by a "Star" or "Lawgiver" and "Teacher of Righteousness."

SUGGESTIONS FOR FURTHER STUDY

S. Angus, *The Environment of Early Christianity.*

S. Angus, *The Mystery-Religions and Christianity.*

S. Angus, *The Religious Quests of the Graeco-Roman World.*

A. E. Bailey, *Daily Life in Bible Times*, pp. 230-328.

A. E. Bailey and C. F. Kent, *History of the Hebrew Commonwealth,* pp. 295-356.

G. A. Barton, *Archaeology and the Bible*, pp. 571-578.

H. M. Battenhouse, *The Bible Unlocked*, pp. 269-300.

G. A. Buttrick, ed., *The Interpreter's Bible*, I, pp. 32-45, 390-436; VII, pp. 75-113.

S. J. Case, *The Evolution of Early Christianity.*

R. H. Charles, *Religious Development Between the Old and New Testaments.*

R. H. Charles, ed., *The Apocrypha and Pseudepigrapha of the Old Testament.*

C. T. Craig, *The Beginning of Christianity*, pp. 25-52, 215-225.

A. Dupont-Sommer, *The Dead Sea Scrolls*, pp. 45-52.

F. C. Eiselen, E. Lewis, and D. G. Downey, eds., *The Abingdon Bible Commentary*, pp. 91-98, 187-213, 839-852.

J. Finegan, *Light from the Ancient Past*, pp. 209-220.

T. R. Glover, *The World of the New Testament.*

J. Goldin, "The Period of the Talmud," in L. Finkelstein, ed., *The Jews: Their History, Culture, and Religion*, pp. 70-215.

E. J. Goodspeed, *The Story of the Apocrypha.*

C. Guignebert, *The Jewish World in the Time of Jesus.*

M. R. James, *The Lost Apocrypha of the Old Testament: Their Titles and Fragments.*

J. Klausner, *From Jesus to Paul*, pp. 3-205.

M. E. Lyman, *The Christian Epic*, pp. 1-12.

E. W. K. Mould, *Essentials of Bible History*, pp. 420-424, 428-482.

R. H. Pfeiffer, *History of New Testament Times, with an Introduction to the Apocrypha.*

D. W. RIDDLE and H. H. HUTSON, *New Testament Life and Literature*, pp. 1-44.

E. SCHURER, *A History of the Jewish People in the Time of Jesus Christ.*

C. C. TORREY, *The Apocryphal Literature: A Brief Introduction.*

Chapter Twenty-One

THE LIFE AND TEACHINGS OF JESUS

A. *Sources for the Life of Jesus: The Synoptic Gospels*

Christianity had its origin in the life and teachings of Jesus of Nazareth. In spite of the fact that Jesus probably did not intend to establish a new religion, his followers after his death, notably the apostle Paul, broke away from the parent stock of Judaism and founded a new faith based on their memories of Jesus. Though none of the twenty-seven books of the New Testament were written during the lifetime of Jesus, it is appropriate to begin our study of the Christian religion with a consideration of the events of his life and the salient features of his teachings. Even though all the letters of Paul and possibly some of the other New Testament writings antedate the gospels, they were put at the head of the list of Christian writings because they dealt with the career and significance of Jesus. It is all-important for us to know the historic Jesus, the central personality of the Bible, the climax of the religious development through which his people had been passing ever since their early days in Palestine.

There are no contemporary records of the life and teachings of Jesus. He and his followers would not have found their way into any Roman *Who's Who;* events in a remote and obscure land like Palestine, a land whose lawlessness and bloodshed in the first century of our era can hardly be believed, would have caused no ripple of excitement in the great city of Rome. In a time when Jews all over the Roman Empire were being subjected to outrages at the hands of mobs and even to banishment from Rome itself,[1] the crucifixion of a mere carpenter, who was considered no more than a rabble-rouser by his fellow Jews, was not likely to attract attention. Even the words used by the early Christians ascribing divinity to Jesus would not have excited Roman curiosity and interest; they would have been similar to the phrases and words they had already used of their own emperors.

Probably the earliest Latin author to refer to Jesus was Pliny the Younger, the governor of the rich province of Bithynia.[2] He wrote to the emperor Trajan *ca.* A.D. 112 that the pagan temples were almost deserted because of the adoption of Christianity by so many of the inhabitants. He reported that he had encouraged many of them to abandon their faith; those who did so affirmed that they were in the habit of meeting on a certain fixed day before daylight, when they sang hymns to Christ as if he were a god and partook of food together.[3] More important yet is the witness of the Roman historian Tacitus, who described in his *Annales* (A.D. 115) the persecution of the Christians under Nero (*ca.* A.D. 64); in the course of describing the way Nero tried to free himself from the suspicion that he ordered Rome to be set on fire, Tacitus reports:

> Neither by works of benevolence nor the gifts of the prince nor by means of appeasing the gods did the shameful suspicion cease, so that it was not believed that the fire had been caused by his command. Therefore, to overcome this rumor, Nero put in his own place as culprits, and punished with most ingenious cruelty, men whom the common people hated for their shameful crimes and called Christians (Tacitus was no friend of the Christians). Christ, from whom the name was derived, had been put to death in the reign of Tiberius by the procurator Pontius Pilate. The deadly superstition having been checked for a while began to break out again ("rursum erumpebat"), not only throughout Judaea, where this mischief first arose, but also at Rome, where from all sides all things scandalous and shameful meet and become fashionable . . .[4]

As far as is known, there was no Palestinian Jewish literature contemporary with Jesus. The Mishna, put into written form *ca.* 200 A.D., and the Talmud, compiled some centuries later,[5] do contain some polemical references to Jesus, but their purpose is to depreciate the gospels and they clearly depend upon them. Joseph Klausner, in his *Jesus of Nazareth,* has summarized statements about Jesus in the Talmud:

There are reliable statements to the effect that his name was Yeshu'a (Yeshu) of Nazareth; that he "practised sorcery" (i.e., performed miracles, as was usual in those days) and beguiled and led Israel astray; that he mocked the words of the Wise; that he expounded Scripture in the same manner as the Pharisees; that he had five disciples (named Mattai, Nakkai, Netzer, Buni, and Todah, only the first and last of which are reminiscent of names which appear in the gospels); that he said that he was not come to take away from the law or to add to it; that he was hanged (crucified) as a false teacher and beguiler on the eve of the Passover which happened on a Sabbath; and that his disciples healed the sick in his name.[6]

In spite of the fact that much of his evidence may be discounted because of his later conversion to Christianity, the Jewish historian Josephus[7] gives an extended reference to Jesus in his *The Antiquities of the Jews*. He says that Pontius Pilate was procurator of Judaea for ten years (probably 27-37 A.D.), during which time he tried to placate the Jews by turning Jesus over to them for crucifixion. He calls Jesus a wise man and Christ. "And when Pilate, at the suggestion of the chief men among us, had condemned him to the cross, those that had previously followed him did not forsake him, for he appeared to them alive on the third day, as the divine prophets had foretold these and many other wonderful things concerning him. And the tribe of Christians, so named from him, is not extinct at this day (*ca.* 90 A.D.)."[8]

Thus, in the light of the paucity of references to Jesus in non-Christian sources, we are driven to rely upon Christian literature as the chief witness to the life and teachings of Jesus. It was only through those who believed in his name that any information was preserved concerning what he did and what he said. But before anything was written down, information about Jesus passed through several years of oral tradition; for at least twenty years following the crucifixion nothing, as far as we now know, was written down concerning Jesus. His companions kept no diaries; there were no stenographers present to record his words; his followers kept no hastily scribbled notes of his basic teachings; he wrote nothing himself. All of this is quite strange in the light of modern practice, for now every man in the public eye is watched carefully and there is a faithful transcription made of every word he utters. But the Jews contemporary with Jesus were not inclined to literature and they did not write biographies; for them the individual existed only for the glory of the Hebrew race. Also, the followers of Jesus fully expected his early return; therefore, why write anything down in the short interim between his leaving them and his return?[9] Then too, the Jews were trained to make use of their memories; It was customary for rabbis to have their pupils commit their teachings to memory. While Jesus was not a rabbi, he may have occasionally made use of the technique of memorization; in any case, retentive memories preserved the only record of the words and deeds of Jesus. The testimony of living witnesses who had actually known Jesus in the flesh was enough to establish the church; as long as they were alive written documents seemed unimportant and unnecessary.[10]

During the period of oral tradition the needs of the churches supplied the bases on which the original gospel materials were preserved and utilized; such matters as evangelism, worship, the creation and maintenance of moral standards, and defense against hostile criticism determined the forms in which the statements of Jesus and the narratives of his life were invested before Christian teachers began to create the first written records. The study of oral tradition is usually called "form-criticism"; according to this point of view, the forms of the traditions which were later incorporated into the gospels were determined by the needs of the churches. Paul seems to have benefited by the oral tradition; by the time he wrote his letters a certain amount of fixity in the gospel materials seems to have been attained, and some parts may have already been committed to writing.

> For I myself received from the Lord the account that I passed on to you, that the Lord Jesus the night he was betrayed took some bread and gave thanks for it and then broke it in pieces, . . .[11]
> For I passed on to you, as of first importance, the account I had received, that Christ died for our sins, as the Scriptures foretold, . . .[12]

The early Christian preachers did not seem to need a connected narrative of the life of Jesus; the sayings and incidents originally circulated independently of one another. With the exception of the story of the passion, most of the incidents and stories in the career of Jesus were repeated without reference to time and place; the passion story had a connected sequence almost from the beginning.

Most of the form critics[13] distinguish among several classifications of the materials which were preserved during the period of oral tradition. First of all there are paradigms, or apothegms, or pronouncement stories, usually dialogues of Jesus, often controversial, sometimes associated with a miracle, which lead up to a striking pronouncement by Jesus capable of general application; good examples of this are the story of the plucking of the ears of corn (Mark 2:23-38) and the question about tribute to Caesar (Mark 12:14-17). Secondly, there are the miracle stories, which emphasize the power of Jesus; such a story as the stilling of the waves (Mark 4:35-41) shows the early Christian teacher in competition with the wonder tales of other religious heroes. In the third place, there are the sayings, further subdivided into various headings such as short parables, poetic stanzas, maxims, etc.; these sayings may have been preserved for the benefit of young converts. Then there are the legends, or epiphany stories, which bring out the divine significance of Jesus; among these would be included the nativity stories and the stories about associates of Jesus. Finally, there are the longer parables, which constitute a definite literary form; most of them were preserved independently of their original context. In this way form criticism helps the modern student of the gospel materials to realize that there were scores of units of material preserved during the period of oral tradition, all of which had a long history in the life of the church before they were recorded in the gospels.

As the years passed and those who had known Jesus died, many leaders in the early church began to realize that they would soon have no permanent means of spreading the gospel unless they wrote something down concerning Jesus and his teachings. Memories began to fail and oral repetition became unsatisfactory, particularly for those who heard of the preaching of Jesus only at second or third remove. Furthermore, the expected return of Jesus seemed to be delayed; still expecting it to occur some time in the future,[14] Christian preachers began to see that they would need some written documents to which to appeal until the Day of the Lord came.[15] There was a need for an authoritative handbook, a notebook for ready reference, which would contain materials about Jesus which would be useful for the church leaders in each Christian community. So there developed in each prominent center of evangelistic activity a body of Christian tradition which gradually began to assume a written form. There were six of these leading cities, each entrusted with the guardianship of varying versions of the gospel story: Jerusalem, Caesarea, Antioch, Ephesus, Corinth, and Rome.

It was probably in the year 50 A.D. that the literary activity began which was to culminate later in the production of the gospels. In that year,[16] probably at Antioch in Syria, the document known as "Q,"[17] made up chiefly of teaching material, but containing a few bits of narrative, was written. The existence of such a document, or one like it, is supported by strong Christian tradition; a second century bishop, Papias of Hierapolis, writing *ca.* 140 A.D., said:

> Matthew arranged the Discourses (Logia) in the Hebrew language and each one interpreted them as he was able.[18]

While many attempts have been made to reconstruct from the gospels of Matthew and Luke the exact content of Q, such an attempt will probably never be possible; for one thing, the two authors probably had Q before them in different versions. Therefore, all we can safely attribute to the lost source is that group of sayings which Matthew and Luke have in common. These are divided by Albert E. Barnett[19] into narrative episodes, discourse similar in both Matthew and Luke, and discourse materials common to both Matthew and Luke but in which differences are as noteworthy as resemblances. The narrative episodes are:

Luke	Matthew
3:17-19, 16-17 — 3:7-12 (cf. Mark 1:7,8)—John the Baptist	
4:1-13 — 4:1-11 (cf. Mark 1:12,13)—temptation of Jesus	
7:1-10 — 8:5-10, 13—centurion's servant	
7:18-20, 22-28, 31-35 — 11:2-11, 16-19—message from John	
10:13-15 — 11:21-24—denunciation of cities in Galilee	
11:14-23 — 12:22-27 (cf. Mark 3:22-27)—Beelzebub controversy	

Discourse materials similar in Matthew and Luke are as follows:

Luke   Matthew

6:37,38,41,42 — 7:1,2,3-5—judging
6:43-45 — 7:16-18,20; 12:33-35—a tree is known by its fruit
6:47-49 — 7:24-27—two builders
9:57-60 — 8:19-22—Jesus' demand for supreme loyalty
10:2 — 9:37, 38—an abundant harvest, but few reapers
10:3-12 — 10:16,9,10a,11-13,10b,7,8,14,15—instructions
10:23,24 — 13:16,17—rare privilege of the disciples
11:9-13 — 7:7-11—asking, searching, knocking
11:24-26 — 12:43-45—danger of spiritual emptiness
11:29-32 — 12:38-42—sign of Jonah
11:33 — 5:15—a lighted lamp belongs on its stand
11:34,35 — 6:22,23—a sound eye
11:42,43, 46-48 — 23:23,6,7a,4,29-31—denunciations
11:49-51 — 23:34-36, 13—the guilt of Jesus' contemporaries
12:2-9 — 10:26-33—faith and fearlessness
12:10 — 12:32—to revile the holy spirit is unpardonable
12:22-32 — 6:25-33—the banishment of anxiety
12:33,34 — 6:19-21—heavenly treasure
12:39-46 — 24:43-51—the Son of Man comes unexpectedly
12:51-53 — 10:34-36—Jesus brings discord, not peace
12:54-56 — 16:2,3—interpretation of signs
13:18,19 — 13:31,32 (cf. Mark 4:31,32)—parable of mustard
13:20,21 — 13:33—yeast
13:26,27 — 7:22,23—acquaintances who are strangers
13:28,29 — 8:11,12—universalism of the kingdom
13:34,35 — 23:37-39—lament over Jerusalem
14:11 — 23:12—humility the way to exaltation
14:26,27 — 10:37,38—loyalty to Christ comes first
14:34,35 — 5:13—salt that loses its strength is thrown away
16:13 — 6:24—no servant can belong to two masters
16:16 — 11:12,13—the Kingdom supersedes Torah and Prophets
16:17 — 5:18—every "dotting of an 'i'" will be fulfilled
16:18 — 5:32—divorce and adultery
17:1,2 — 18:6,7—hindrances to humble people
17:6 — 17:20—vital efficacy of faith
17:23,24 — 24:26,27—lightning symbolizes Son of Man
17:26,27 — 24:37-39—danger of engrossment in worldly interests
17:34,35 — 24:40,41—the days of the Son of Man
17:37 — 24:28—a dead body attracts the vultures

The following are verses of discourse which are common to Matthew and Luke where resemblances are enough to establish some sort of kinship, but where the differences are equally striking:

Luke	Matthew
6:20-23 — 5:3-6, 11, 12—the beatitudes	
6:27-33,35,36 — 5:44,39,40,42; 7:12; 5:46,47,45,48—love	
6:39,40 — 15:14b; 10:24,25a — disciple and teacher	
6:46 — 7:21—ascription of lordship implies obedience	
11:2-4 — 6:9-13—model prayer for disciples	
11:39-41,44 — 23:25-27—false emphasis on externals	
12:58,59; 5:25,26—prompt reconciliation with adversaries	
13:23,24; 7:13,14—entrance by the narrow door	
14:15-24; 22:1-10—parables of the supper and the marriage	
15:4-7 — 18:12-14—parable of the lost sheep	
17:3,4; 18:15,21,22—forgiving an offending brother	
19:11-27; 24:14-30—parables of the pounds and the talents	
22:30b — 19:28b—the disciples will judge Israel	

In addition to these, there were probably other sayings and narrative incidents of Jesus which may have stood in one version of Q but not in another.[20] "Q was therefore not a fixed book, but a collection which was always more or less fluid. We may conceive of a missionary carrying about with him a notebook of Jesus' Sayings and inserting in it from time to time any new saying that might come to his knowledge. But while Q was thus constantly changing and expanding, it would retain its general character as a manual of the Lord's teaching . . ."[21]

The final stage in gospel production was reached ca. 70 A.D. with the compilation and editing of the Gospel of Mark. It is one of the almost universally accepted results of gospel criticism that Mark is the earliest of the four canonical gospels and one of the sources for the Gospels of Matthew and Luke.[22] This earliest gospel was composed some time between 65 and 70 A.D.; the product of the Christian community in Rome, it is the first complete literary narrative of the life of Jesus. Written just after the persecution of the Christians by Nero, Mark emphasizes the heroic bravery of Jesus in the face of all his sufferings. To the Christians who were hiding out in the catacombs, this gospel would have been a source of courage and comfort, particularly in the section devoted to the passion of Jesus (chapters 11-16). According to the tradition of the early church, the author of the earliest gospel was John Mark, a companion of Paul[23] and an interpreter of Peter. The oldest ecclesiastical tradition regarding the origin and authorship of the Gospel of Mark is that given by Papias,[24] bishop of Hierapolis, *ca.* 140 A.D.; Eusebius quotes him in his *Church History* (325 A.D.) as follows:

> This also the presbyter used to say: "Mark, indeed, who became the interpreter of Peter, wrote accurately, as far as he remembered them, the things said or done by the Lord, but not however in order." For he (Mark) had neither heard the Lord nor been his personal follower, but at a later stage, as I said, he had followed Peter, who used to adapt the teachings to the need of the moment, but not as though he were drawing up a connected account of the oracles of the Lord; so that Mark committed no error in writing certain matters as he remembered them. For he had only one object in view, namely to leave out nothing of the things which he had heard, and to include no false statements among them.[25]

Irenaeus, bishop of Lyons in southern France, wrote *ca.* 180 A.D.:

> After the deaths (of Peter and Paul) Mark, the disciple and interpreter of Peter, himself also handed down to us in writing the things which Peter had proclaimed.[26]

Mark's Roman origin is indicated by several facts. In the first place, Mark wrote for a Gentile community, for he frequently adds a translation of Aramaic words and often feels it necessary to explain certain Jewish customs and practices.[27] Then, there are various latinisms scattered throughout the gospel.[28] Also, there is mention in Mark 15:21 of Rufus, a prominent Roman Christian,[29] and the son of Simon of Cyrene. The persistent tradition in the early church linking both Peter and Paul to Rome points to the imperial city as the place where this gospel was written.[30] Above all, the fact that the Gospel of Mark maintained its existence while other early records were lost indicates a Roman origin; no other church would have had enough power to influence all Christian opinion. The date of the Gospel of Mark—*ca.* 70 A.D.— is determined by studying the gospel itself; in chapter thirteen, which is called the

"little apocalypse," there is treatment of the destruction of Jerusalem and the terrifying events of the Jewish wars of 66-70.[31]

The Gospel of Mark begins abruptly, without any infancy stories,
genealogy, or childhood occurrences. There is no mention of his
parents, no hint about his boyhood or early life, no suggestion about
his age, and no characterization of him. The author is evidently
not concerned with backgrounds and interpretations; he wants
Jesus to speak for himself through his own words and works.
More than a third of his work deals with Jesus' last week in Jerusalem, his passion, death, and resurrection; these events take a
central place of importance. He found the healing and wonder-
working of Jesus to be of great significance. The gospel is a literary
product of great simplicity and objectivity, with a graphic style
of writing sometimes colloquial and rough.[32] "Professor Burkitt
once spoke of Mark's portrait of Jesus as of 'a stormy and mysterious
personage.' It is certain that the tender and humanitarian aspects
of Jesus' ministry to men are not emphasized here as they are in
Luke. His place in history as the fulfillment of the high hopes of
the past has no stress here as it has in Matthew. This is a bold
and somewhat austere portrait presenting Jesus as the man of
Power."[33] The gospel ends almost as abruptly as it begins—in the
middle of the story of the resurrection.[34]

About a generation after the composition of the gospel according
to Mark, an unknown Christian, who was perhaps a Hellenistic
Jew living at Antioch in Syria, prepared a more complete and
comprehensive gospel narrative. Matthew's name adhered to it
because he may have been connected with one of the documents
which served as the nucleus for the gospel itself.[35] Writing some
time between 90 and 95 A.D., the author was well versed in the
Hebrew Scriptures and was profoundly impressed by the correspondence between the incidents in the life of Jesus and the
prophecies and psalms of the Old Testament. He saw in the
fall of Jerusalem (70 A.D.) punishment for the Jewish nation for
its rejection of Jesus as the Messiah.[36]

The author of the gospel according to Matthew made use of
several sources. His narrative framework is substantially that of
Mark; of the 678 verses in the earliest gospel, 623 of them are
in Matthew; however, Matthew freely changes the details of individual stories, embellishes, abridges, and summarizes the narrative,

and rearranges the order of materials in Matthew 4:22 through 13:53. His second source is the document Q; the discourses of Jesus which are in both the gospels of Matthew and Luke were taken from Q,[37] but Matthew retains a number of Q sayings which Luke omits and his copy of Q may have been more extensive than the one used by Luke. In addition, Matthew is dependent for about a quarter of the gospel's contents upon sources peculiar to itself. In the first place, there is in the gospel of Matthew some material which is very Judaistic and particularistic in tone and feeling, representing, says Streeter,[38] the material the author of Matthew derived from the church at Jerusalem. As many as 260 verses in the gospel may be said to have a Jewish Christian, anti-Gentile tone; they may reflect the influence of the desires of the party of James, brother of Jesus, who was the head of the Jerusalem church and the leader of the Judaizing party in Christianity.[39] Some of this material was probably taken by the author of Matthew from a Jerusalem document designated by the letter "M." Sherman E. Johnson assigns to the M document sections of the Sermon on the Mount (Matthew 5:17-24, 27, 28, 33-37; 6:1-7, 16-18; 7:15; perhaps also 5:4, 5, 7-10 and 7:13, 14), sections dealing with the mission of Jesus and that of his disciples (10:5, 6, 23, 25, 41; 13:52; and 15:24), the legal and ethical sections (12:5-7; 16:19; 18:19, 20; and 25:31-46; perhaps also 18:21-35), and the sayings directed against the Pharisees (23:2, 3, 5, 8-10, 15-22, 24; perhaps also 21:28-32).[40] Then there was a small body of Antiochene tradition incorporated in Matthew 1 and 2; of this material, the only section in written form would have been the genealogy in Matthew 1:1-17. For some of the material incorporated in his gospel, Matthew was dependent upon no written source; he seems to have a predilection for stories of a legendary character, which came to him orally from his Antiochene sources, such as the dream of Pilate's wife (Matthew 27:19), Pilate's washing of his hands (Matthew 27:24, 25), and the earthquake and ghostly apparitions at the death of Jesus (27:51-53). Perhaps the birth stories in chapters one and two should also be placed in this category.

The Christian church considered the Gospel according to Matthew the most important of all the gospels by placing it at the beginning of the collection of gospels. Its arrangement of material made it admirably suited for purposes of catechetical instruction of new converts to the Christian religion. Unlike the other gospel writers, the author of Matthew followed a systematic plan, alternating discourse with narrative; into the narrative framework, which he borrowed from Mark, Matthew inserts, at stated intervals, five great discourses, puts a prologue at the beginning, and adds an epilogue at the end. Each of the five divisions of the gospel ends with the phrase "When Jesus had finished this discourse."[41] Each section is partly discourse, partly narrative. The gospel of Matthew may be thus outlined as follows:

I. Prologue: chapters 1 and 2. Infancy stories, genealogy.

II. Narrative: Chapters 3 and 4. The period of preparation, including the ministry of John the Baptist, the baptism, and the temptation experiences.
Discourses: chapters 5-7. The sermon on the mount.

III. Narrative: chapters 8 and 9. Mighty works in Galilee.
Second Discourse: chapter 10. Instructions to the twelve disciples before their mission.

IV. Narrative: chapters 11 and 12. Rejection in Galilee.
Third discourse: chapter 13. Teachings and parables on the kingdom of heaven addressed to the crowds.

V. Narrative: chapters 14-17. Events bringing the Galilean ministry to a close. Peter's confession. Transfiguration.
Fourth Discourse: chapter 18. Last instructions to the disciples in Galilee.

VI. Narrative: chapters 19-22. Journey to Jerusalem and events during the early part of Passion Week.
Fifth Discourse: chapters 23-25. Jesus' last public teachings.

VII. Epilogue: chapters 26-28. Events leading up to the death of Jesus, crucifixion, resurrection, post-resurrection events.

Here we have a marvelous combination of the chronological and the topical, showing great artistry and care on the part of the author.

The fact that the gospel of Matthew contains the famous "sermon on the mount" in its most complete and unified form[42] would account further for its prominence in the early church. The sermon is actually a compendium of the basic teachings of Jesus; some have spoken of it as the "constitution of the kingdom of God," the classical exposition of the Christian ethic. Matthew is also the most comprehensive gospel, with a catholicity of outlook and a breadth of interest which help the reader to understand all the various phases of Jesus' life and teaching. Then, too, the pre-occupation of the author with the church gives the gospel something of an official ecclesiastical nature; a number of Jesus' parables are handled in such as way as to make them apply to the needs and conditions of the church.[43] It has ably presented the Christian faith to all ages and conditions of men.

Writing at approximately the same time the Gospel according to Matthew was being composed—i.e., some time between 90 and 95 A.D.—and evidently being unacquainted with Matthew's gospel, a Gentile Christian composed a two-volume history of the beginnings of Christianity.[44] According to tradition, this author was Luke, a physician[45] and a companion of Paul.[46] There is no clear indication as to the place of composition; Antioch, Rome, and Ephesus are the principal possibilities; Streeter favored Rome as the location of Luke-Acts,[47] while Barnett favors Ephesus.[48] The author's purpose in writing is clearly stated in his preface to the gospel:

Many writers have undertaken to compose accounts of the movement which has developed among us, just as the original eye-witnesses who became teachers of the message have handed it down to us. For that reason, Theophilus, and because I have investigated it all carefully from the beginning, I have determined to write a connected account of it for Your Excellency, so that you may be reliably informed about the things you have been taught.[49]

By attempting to inform Theophilus "reliably" Luke does not necessarily claim for his writing superior historical accuracy; instead, he probably wrote to allay suspicion and hostility. Luke wants the Roman official world to understand that Christianity was definitely not a subversive movement; in both volumes of his work he shows that the crucifixion of Jesus was due to the animosity of the Jews and not to the intervention of the Roman authorities and that the growing Christian movement was not based upon an anti-Roman bias. One interesting suggestion is that Theophilus was a member of Nero's court, which was scheduled to try Paul's case, and that Luke was endeavoring to brief Theophilus in defense of Paul by giving him an account of the life and teachings of Jesus along with his record of the missionary journeys of Paul and the other early Christian leaders;[50] if this is true, an earlier date for the composition of Luke-Acts would have to be postulated. Along with this apologetic defense of Christianity against heathen prejudice, Luke wrote his two volumes as a missionary document to convince earnest and intelligent Gentiles of the superiority of Christianity; for that reason, Luke avoids many of the theological questions which were agitating Christian leaders in his day and tries to make his work interesting and persuasive.

As to the sources which Luke had at his command to write his gospel, he suggests in his preface a number of written records upon which he could draw. Among them would be the gospel according to Mark,[51] the document Q,[52] and others available only to Luke. Luke's treatment of this material in Mark is much more free than that of Matthew; he does not hesitate to abridge and alter Mark's record when such a treatment makes his information more compact and his story more smoothly natural and interesting. He utilized sections of Q which had been omitted by the author of Matthew; aso, Luke may have had a somewhat different version of Q than the one used by Matthew; these facts help us to understand some of the differences which appear in the two gospels as they record the teachings of Jesus.[53] S. MacLean Gilmour voices the opinion of many modern scholars when he asserts that the order and wording of Q are best preserved in Luke's gospel; as in his use of Mark, Luke employed blocks of material from Q without extensive systemization or conflation, and followed the order of his material as he found it, whereas Matthew freely edited both Mark and Q.[54] Then, in addition to Mark and Q, Luke used various special sources from which he drew the rich collection of narratives, parables, and sayings appearing only in his gospel; a great deal of this material came from oral tradition, but some of it evidently had a documentary source or sources. This special tradition in the main body of Luke's gospel was designated by Streeter as "L;"[55] it represents gospel material from the territory surrounding Caesarea, which Luke may have collected while Paul was languishing in prison for two years.[56] Much of the so-called Perean period in the ministry of Jesus (Luke 9:51-18:14), which is found only in the Gospel of Luke, may well have come from Luke's special source L; this would include such special sections as the parables of the lost coin and the lost sheep (15:8-32), and the good Samaritan (10:25-37).[57]

Though Luke was not a scientific historian, we do have in his gospel at least two references which help scholars determine the chronology of events in the life of Jesus. The most important of these is in Luke 3:1, 2: "In the fifteenth year of the reign of the emperor Tiberius, . . . the message from God came to Zechariah's son John in the desert." This is the only fixed date of gospel chronology; the emperor Augustus had died and been succeeded by Tiberius in 14 A.D.; thus the fifteenth year of Tiberius would correspond to A.D. 28-29.[58] Since Jesus began his ministry with the imprisonment of John the Baptist, we may assume that Jesus began to preach in Galilee in *ca.* 29 A.D.[59] The other chronological reference in Luke is in 2:1-5, where the author dates the birth of Jesus with "the first census, taken when Quirinius was governor of Syria." Here Luke's historical accuracy is subject to considerable criticism: the first census when Quirinius was governor of Syria did not take place until 6 A.D.[60] However, Quirinius did carry on a military expedition against the Homonadenses, a tribe in the Cilician Taurus country, while he was a military official in Syria during the lifetime of Herod the Great, between 9 and 6 B.C.;[61] probably Luke confused this expedition with the census taken after Quirinius became governor.

The Gospel according to Luke is the most humanitarian of all the gospels; the author understands and sympathizes with human traits and feelings. The parables which are unique in his gospel deal mostly with human situations and human feelings. "This characteristic interest of Luke in human concerns finds its highest expression in his interpretation of Jesus. The Master in Luke's story is not primarily the figure of mystery and wonder that he is in Mark, nor yet as in Matthew the Messiah of Jewish thought taking up his role as also the Saviour of the Gentile nations, but is rather here the embodiment of divine compassion and sympathy. . . . It is characteristic of Luke to represent Jesus' healings as a manifestation of his compassionate interest in people. . . . Only

Luke reports the parables in which a member of the despised race of Samaritans is the exemplar of charitable service, in which a publican contrasts favorably in his worship with a Pharisee, and in which a rich man is condemned to hell merely for indifference to the sufferings of the beggar at the gate. . . . These aspects of Jesus' ministry—its compassion, its concern for the poor and un-privileged, its tolerance—as manifested both in act and teaching seem to be of special interest to Luke . . ."[62] The very birth of Jesus, according to Luke, is heralded by the song of angels and the visit of lowly shepherds; the hymns and stories in Luke's opening two chapters are among the most beautiful in the world's sacred literature.

B. *Outline of Events in the Life of Jesus*

None of the gospels were written as biographies of Jesus; their primary aim was to serve as handbooks for the preaching and gov-ernment of the new religion. The word "gospel" means "good news." The authors, editors, and compilers of the gospels were interested in the religious effects which their materials would produce among their readers and hearers. The gospels were pieces of religious propaganda, written, according to the author of the fourth gospel, "so that you may believe that Jesus is the Christ, the son of God, and through believing you may have life as his fol-lowers."[63] Yet, in spite of this, it is possible to arrange the material in the synoptic gospels in some sort of a general chronological sequence.

1.   Infancy and Childhood: Matthew 1 and 2; Luke 1:1-2:39

In the opening chapters of Matthew and Luke there are several stories about the birth of Jesus and two genealogical accounts of his ancestry. The purpose of the infancy narratives is interpretative and inspirational rather than historical; there is very little infor-mation in them which would help us to understand the later career of Jesus, but they express so effectively the adoration and affection which Jesus' followers had for him that they have be-come for all time a fitting description of the very essence of what Jesus means to the world. "These infancy narratives, . . . bring home the truth of the assertion that divinity attends the origin of all life, that life at its fountain is always pure, that it comes from God, that it is essentially a holy thing, and that its origin is miraculous."[64] "The reason why these stories are hallowed is not because of the light they throw on Jesus' biography, but because of their sublime interpretation of the *meaning* of his life—that he was, indeed, the God-sent Savior of the world."[65]

There is no indication in any of the gospels as to the precise date for the birth of Jesus. Matthew indicates that he was born while Herod the Great was ruling;[66] Herod died in March or April of the year 4 B.C. Since Herod, before he died, had ordered the slaughter of "boys in Bethlehem and in all that neighborhood who were two years old or under,"[67] Jesus was evidently in his second year at that time; this would push the date of his birth back to 5 or 6 B.C. Luke's mention of the "census" taken when Quirinius was "governor" of Syria[68] seems to favor a date for the birth of Jesus no later than 6 B.C. All things considered, 6 B.C. seems to be the most satisfactory year for the birth of Jesus.[69] There is also no evidence for the particular day of the year upon which Jesus was born; the early church celebrated the event on January 6, now called Epiphany in most calendars of the Christian year. The observance of December 25 as the birthday of Jesus dates from no earlier than the fourth century A.D.; this day may have been selected because of a celebration of the birthday of *Sol Invictus* on that same day by the devotees of the cult of Mithra, from which many Christians had been converted.[70]

The gospels of Matthew and Luke locate the birth of Jesus at Bethlehem, as predicted in Micah 5:2.[71] The sojourn of the holy family in that small town located about seven miles south of Jerusalem was brief;[72] all four gospels agree that Nazareth was Jesus' home town.[73] In his public ministry, he was never called "Jesus of Bethlehem," but " Jesus of Nazareth."[74] According to both genealogies (Matthew 1:17; Luke 3:23-28) and the birth story in Luke (2:4) Jesus descended from David; this fact was very important to the gospel writers, for Jewish Messianic expectation of an ideal ruler coming from the family of David had to be fulfilled in the person of Jesus. Paul goes further than the gospels in affirming Jesus' Davidic descent.[75]

2.   Youth and Early Manhood in Nazareth: Luke 2:40-52.

Specifically we know next to nothing concerning the childhood and young manhood of Jesus in Nazareth. Only one of the four gospels mentions any incident in his life between infancy and the beginning of his public life when he was about thirty. When Jesus was twelve years old, he and his parents traveled to Jerusalem for the passover festival.[76] Therefore, biographers of Jesus are forced to reconstruct the probable events in his life during the so-called "hidden years."[77] From the writings of Josephus[78] and the Jewish Scriptures, both oral and written, much can be ascertained concerning the training of the average Jewish boy of Jesus' day;[79] it is helpful to assume that Jesus followed somewhat the same pattern as other devout Jewish boys of his time.

The family of Joseph the carpenter in Nazareth was moderately poor but self-respecting. There were five boys, including Jesus, and at least two girls.[80] Joseph probably died while Jesus was still a young man; no mention is made of the father after the visit to Jerusalem when Jesus was twelve. Since the eldest son of the Hebrew family usually followed the father's occupation, we may safely assume that Jesus took over the duties of maintaining the carpenter shop and began to support the rest of the family by his toil. His job may have included more than simply working with wood; a carpenter's task then often covered the duties now undertaken by a contractor. If that is true, Jesus must have supervised the construction of simple dwellings, storehouses for grain, and barns; he probably made furniture and fashioned tools, yokes, plows, and similar articles. His teachings include stories which reflect his craft.[81] It is interesting to speculate that Jesus may have helped in the reconstruction of Sepphoris, which was only an hour's walk north of Nazareth.[82]

The home in which Jesus lived was one in which Jewish religion was honored and in which its feasts and festivals were observed. Joseph and Mary probably belonged to that class in Jewish society which can be designated as pietists.[83] In their home there would be reading and committing to memory of the Jewish Scriptures; this is borne out by Jesus' familiarity with his own sacred writings in his later teaching and preaching. Jesus would have been sent to the synagogue school, where he would have learned to write the Shema[84] and other sacred literature in the Hebrew of the Old

Testament. He learned to speak in Aramaic, the vernacular of the Jewish people in Palestine in the first century. Unlike Paul, Jesus probably did not have any formal training as a rabbi; instead, he had an eager and inquiring mind, even as a youth of twelve,[85] and an unusually keen interest in religion. He must have been a careful observer of nature; in the hills around Nazareth he first became acquainted with the lilies of the field, the birds of the air, the sower, and the other features of the landscape which played so great a part in his teachings later. "The shop and the market lay claim upon much of his time. He associates with his fellow Galileans in worship and in toil. Day after day he is seen at his bench, and every Sabbath finds him in his place in the village synagogue. Years pass, dream years, years of holy communion, happy years of obscurity, over which history has drawn the kindly and unruffled mantle of silence. Then, when he is thirty years of age, he answers the divine summons."[86]

3. The Public Ministry.

a. The Period of Preparation

i. Baptism by John the Baptizer: Mark 1:1-11; Matthew 3; 1-17; Luke 3:1-22.

All four gospels describe a great crisis which took place in the life of Jesus during the movement inaugurated by his cousin John the Baptizer. John had been preaching and baptizing in the river Jordan, attracting great numbers of people by his unusual clothing and manner of life and his uncompromising message of the need for repentance. John had taken the purificatory rite of baptism, which had been associated with the priestly ceremony of the sacrificial ablution, and made it a symbol of individual repentance and of committment to a new ethical life fit for the kingdom of God. His stern message reminded his hearers of the prophet Elijah; he warned the nation of approaching destruction and announced in ringing terms the coming of someone mightier than himself. Like many of his fellow countrymen, Jesus was convinced that John was an authentic messenger of God, such as the one predicted by Malachi.[87] Messianic expectancy ran high; perhaps Jahweh's people were about to be delivered from their oppressors. Accordingly Jesus went from Nazareth to the place where John was baptizing in order to become a fellow-worker with him in the movement toward spiritual recovery.

Jesus was baptized by John, not because his life needed any spiritual or moral rebirth, but to bear testimony to his faith in John's message and to assume his part in bringing John's ideal to an immediate realization. The baptism of Jesus was for Jesus a profound spiritual experience; he became keenly conscious, perhaps for the first time, that God had called him for a special task—to teach God's people his divine will and to deliver them from their enemies. As a result of his baptism Jesus had a deep sense of divine approval and consecration to a God-given ministry.

ii.   Temptation Scene in the Wilderness: Mark 1:12, 13; Matthew 4:1-11; Luke 4:1-13

Thinking over the tremendous task with which he was faced— to convince his fellow countrymen that the real solution to their national problems was love and forgiveness for their enemies— Jesus was driven to a place of solitude for a period of intense thought and prayer. In the gospels this period is described as the "temptation" of Jesus, but he was not "tempted" toward moral evil; perhaps a better word would be "testing." In his imagination, Jesus examines one by one the various plans of action which would be possible for one who desired to be a divinely appointed leader of his people. How was he to establish the kingdom of God into which he had just been initiated by baptism? He rejected the plan, acceptable to some of his contemporaries, by which he would have devoted his powers to the seeking of material things (turning stones into bread) rather than spiritual goals; armed revolution semed to Jesus to be futile as well as morally wrong. He rejected the point of view of the apocalyptists of his day, which would have required the Messiah to violate the laws of God by jumping off the high roof of the temple: Jesus had no spectacular "tricks" to perform in order to win for himself a shallow superficial following; men must work with God to build his kingdom, not wait for God to perform a miracle to preserve them from the consequences of their own sinning. Then, by refusing to do homage to evil in order to get all the kingdoms of the world, Jesus rejected the policy of assimilation, which would have merged Jewish culture into the larger stream of Graeco-

Roman culture; Jesus felt the Jewish people had a divine mission to perform—to lead the rest of the world to the true God.

Jesus emerged from his spiritual retreat with the conviction that the Jewish nation could be saved from certain destruction only if the Jews accepted God as the father of all mankind; even the hated Romans were their brothers. The period of decision had tested the quality of Jesus' sonship and the nature of the methods he would use to fulfill his divine mission. The victory was decisive, but other periods of conflict and trial were to come up later in his ministry.[88]

b.   The Campaign in Galilee: Mark 1:14-9:50; Matthew 4:12-18:35; Luke 4:14-9:50.

The period of quiet preparation following the baptism of Jesus was broken by the news that John the Baptizer had been arrested and imprisoned by Herod Antipas.[89] Immediately Jesus decided to carry on John's work; he selected his home province of Galilee and started out by preaching on the same text John had used: "The time has come and the reign of God is near; repent, and believe this good news."[90] Jesus regarded himself as John's successor, but he adopted an utterly different way of life and used far more normal and wholesome methods. John was an ascetic, preaching a stern and apocalyptic message of doom; Jesus was a man among men, accepting the common social life of his time, and preached the glad good news of God's readiness to forgive.[91] Jesus selected twelve men to be his intimate disciples; of these, three, Simon, James, and John, became an inner circle of close followers.[92] Though all these twelve completely misunderstood the implications of Jesus' Messianic leadership—one was to betray him, another to deny him—it was in their training in mission work by Jesus which was to bear fruit in the founding of the Christian religion.

It was in Galilee that most of the episodes in the public ministry of Jesus took place. The gospels do not begin to record all the healings which Jesus performed, nor do they mention all the words he must have spoken during this period; there is a great deal more that we would like to know about his movements and activities; as the author of the fourth gospel admits, "there are many other things that Jesus did, so many in fact that if they were

all written out, I do not suppose that the world itself would hold
the books that would have to be written."[93] Jesus made Capernaum
his headquarters; this was the home city of the four fishermen
who became his first disciples: Andrew, Simon, and James and
John Zebedee;[94] Many of Jesus' activities centered in the home of
Simon and Andrew.[95] Mark has compressed in a few verses a variety
of episodes which give us a vivid picture of the opening days of
Jesus' Galilean campaign; Jesus was occupied nearly every day
with just such teachings and healings.[96]

Just how long Jesus spent on his campaign in Galilee is not
known. The actual events as recorded in the synoptic gospels
would have taken only six or seven weeks, but a longer time of
eighteen months or even two years is necessary to account for the
movements of Jesus between scenes of activity and for the influence he exerted on both friends and foes.[97] There is nothing
in the history of the world to compare with the tremendous consequences which came from so short a public life!

The synoptic gospels record the startling fact that opposition
to Jesus set in very early in his public career. The first chapter
of the earliest gospel cannot end without stating that "Jesus
could no longer go into a town openly, but stayed out in un-
frequented places, . . ."[98] Then there follows a series of controversies which Jesus had with the authorities in Galilee (Mark
2:1-3:6), which seems to answer a question which the early Christians found very puzzling: How was it that Jesus, the Messiah, had
to face a shameful death at the hands of his enemies? Why did
a man who went about doing good and proclaiming the advent
of the kingdom of God come to such an untimely end? The
scribes, Pharisees, and Herodians combined to engineer a death
plot against Jesus; among the things which caused them offense
was Jesus' claim to forgive sins (Mark 2:6-10), his association with
tax collectors and "sinners"[99] (Mark 2:15-17), the neglect of
fasting by Jesus and his disciples (Mark 2:18-20), their working
on the Sabbath (Mark 2:23-28), and Jesus' healing on the Sabbath
(Mark 3:1-6). Scribes came up from Jerusalem to add to Jesus'
difficulties;[100] his relatives tried to put an end to his public
appearances, "for they said that he was out of his mind;"[101] but
"the mass of the people ("am-haares") liked to hear him."[102] In
Mark 7:1-23 there is a further group of incidents and sayings

showing the breach between Jesus and the religious leaders of his nation; chief among them were the argument over ceremonial hand-washing and the discussion concerning the oath corban.[103]

The crowning episode in Jesus' Galilean ministry is the story of the feeding of the five thousand; it is the only miracle story recorded in all four gospels.[104] It marks the high tide of Jesus' popularity in Galilee and of his influence over the populace. Though it is impossible to reconstruct the exact historical situation, the fact that a great crowd of people followed him and wanted to make him a king[105] seemed to indicate the ultimate success of the movement. Jesus had to withdraw hurriedly into a secluded spot to avoid being made the kind of Messiah he had once repudiated. However, the increase of Jesus' popularity with the crowd was matched by the increasing enmity of the scribes; their propaganda, along with Jesus' refusal to fulfill the popular revolutionary Messianism, finally took away from Jesus the support of the multitude. He began to see that his Galilean ministry had been a failure.

Jesus now decided upon a bold strategy; to go to Jerusalem and challenge the rulers of the nation to accept his solution of their problems. However, before he does this he wants to prepare his disciples for the tragedy which may lay in wait for them in the capital city. He takes them to the vicinity of Caesarea Philippi, about twenty-five miles due north of Capernaum. On the way, he asks them a question: "Who do people say that I am?" They reply: "John the Baptist; others say Elijah, and others that you are one of the prophets." Then he asks them: "But who do you say that I am?" With his characteristic impetuosity Peter answers for the twelve: "You are the Christ." That Peter shared some of the contemporary points of view concerning the coming of a physical Messianic leader is evident from what followed; when Jesus told them that he must go through much suffering and be killed, Peter began to scold him for those words; then Jesus delivered to Peter one of the most scathing of all indictments: "Get out of my sight, you Satan! for you do not side with God, but with men."[106] This episode is considered the turning-point in the career of Jesus; he begins now to speak about himself, especially the suffering and death which he feels await him in Jerusalem. He still hopes his journey to Jerusalem will produce the desired results but he remembers what had happened to prophets in former times.[107]

Six days after Peter's confession at Caesarea Philippi, Jesus took Peter, James, and John with him up on a high mountain, perhaps snow-capped Mount Hermon, and there the face of Jesus, while in rapt communion with his heavenly father, seemed to be transfigured before them. The vision included, perhaps only for Peter, the figures of Moses and Elijah, the representatives of the Torah and the prophets; it is as if Peter's bold confession—"You are the Christ"—was now substantiated by the presence of the greatest figures in the history of their religion. Whatever actually happened on the Mount of Transfiguration will perhaps be hidden from the investigations of the Bible historian, but it was a great spiritual experience for Jesus; he came down from the mountain prepared for martyrdom and assured of his divine Messiahship. The three disciples were convinced that Jesus was the Son of God, but they were still puzzled by many aspects of the experience.[108]

c.   Journey to Jerusalem: Mark 10:1-52; Matthew 19:1-20:34;
Luke 9:51-19:27

Soon after the confession of Peter and the Transfiguration, Jesus and his disciples began the fateful journey to Jerusalem. The accounts in Mark and Matthew are brief; the incidents of the journey are more fully recounted in Luke.[109] The most direct road from Galilee to Jerusalem was through Samaria, but Jesus was turned aside from his intention of going through Samaria by discourtesy on the part of the inhabitants of the first town he came to.[110] So he and his disciples crossed the Jordan, traveled southward through Perea, and recrossed the Jordan at Jericho for the final stages of the journey to Jerusalem.

In the accounts of this last journey we note a change in the mood of Jesus; he no longer walks with his disciples, but he goes out in front of them, alone; for the most part he is silent, and when he does speak it is of the fate which awaits him in Jerusalem. The disciples continue to think of the Messianic kingdom as one of physical success and political glory.

As they went on their way up to Jerusalem, Jesus walked

ahead of them, and they were in dismay, and those who still
followed were afraid. And he took the Twelve aside again and
began to tell them what was going to happen to him. "See!"
he said, "we are going up to Jerusalem, and the Son of Man
will be handed over to the high priests and scribes, and they
will condemn him to death and hand him over to the heathen
and they will ridicule him and spit on him and flog him and
kill him; and three days after he will rise again." And Zebedee's
two sons, James and John, came up to him and said, "Master,
we want you to do for us whatever we ask." He said to them,
"What do you want me to do for you?" They said to him,
"Let us sit one at your right hand and one at your left, in
your triumph." Jesus said to them, "You do not know what
you are asking for. Can you drink what I am drinking, or
undergo the baptism that I am undergoing?" They said to
him, "Yes, we can." Jesus said to them, "Then you shall
drink what I am drinking, and you shall undergo the baptism that I am undergoing; but as for sitting at my right or
at my left, that is not mine to give, but belongs to those for
whom it is destined."[111]

Jesus continued to give offense to the Jewish authorities, first
by a sharp answer to a question concerning divorce,[112] then by
accepting, in Jericho, the hospitality from the rich little district
superintendent of taxation, Zacchaeus.[113]

4. Closing Scenes and Crucifixion.

a. The Triumphal Entry: Mark 11:1-11; Matthew 21:1-11; Luke 19:28-44

We are now ready to move with Jesus and his disciples into
the last week of his earthly life. Though there are some difficulties
in ascertaining the correct order of events, as among the different
accounts in the four gospels, all the gospel writers agree, by
the bulk of space they give to the incidents of Passion Week, that
this was by far the most significant week in the life of Jesus.[114]
Early Christians remembered with horror the death of their
beloved master and all the events which precipitated it.

Jesus had evidently planned to declare himself as the Messiah
at the approaching feast of the Passover. By previous arrangement, he had borrowed an ass, upon which he was to ride into

the city of Jerusalem; this followed a suggestion in Zechariah 9:9, a description of the Messiah which was not taken seriously by the militaristic Messianists of Jesus' day:

> Exult greatly, O daughter of Zion;
> Shout with joy, O daughter of Jerusalem.
> Lo, your king comes to you;
> Vindicated and victorious is he;
> Humble, and riding upon an ass,
> Even upon a colt, the foal of an ass.

He followed the road along the Mount of Olives, from which the Messiah was expected to appear. "In this way he half revealed and half concealed his claim to be the Messiah, and at the same time made clear that his kingdom was not of this world."[115]

Jesus' entry into the city has often been described as the triumphal entry, but it was scarcely that—for Jesus. A large and enthusiastic crowd heralded him as "the prophet of Nazareth in Galilee";[116] they saw in his approach to the city a sign that the kingdom of David was about to appear. But Jesus' mind was full of foreboding; he saw in the acclaim of the mob an uncertain and perhaps untrustworthy beginning of his challenge to the nation. No reference is made to this incident in the later trials of Jesus by the authorities, as would have been the case if it had been a "triumphal" entry. Because of the lateness of the hour, Jesus simply looked around in the temple area and went out with his disciples to spend the night in Bethany.[117]

b. Cleansing the Temple: Mark 11:12-25;
Matthew 21:12-22; Luke 19:45-48.

Entering the temple the next morning, Jesus and his friends went directly to the court of the Gentiles. This was the location of the market in cattle, sheep and birds which had been established for the convenience of the pilgrims from the Dispersion who came to Jerusalem for the sacrificial festivals.[118] Also, there were the tables where money-changers operated; the priests had ruled that the fees of the temple had to be paid in special Jewish coins, not in the coins of the empire of Rome. The whole system had grown into a great scheme of exploitation for the benefit of the Sadducean priesthood; no wonder Jesus became so incensed with what he saw that he "began to drive out of it those who were buying or selling things in it, and he upset the money-changers' tables and the pigeon-dealers' seats, and he would not allow anyone to carry anything through the temple;"[119] no wonder Jesus accused the priests of turning the temple into a robbers' cave[120] instead of "a house of prayer for all nations."[121] This "raid" of the temple on the part of Jesus and his followers alienated for the first time the powerful party of the Sadducees; they had taken no part in earlier opposition to Jesus, but now they joined with the Pharisees and the Herodians in a combination which had to wait only for the support of the mob to secure the death of Jesus.

c. Last Public Teachings: Mark 11:27-13:37; Matthew 21:23-25:46; Luke 20:1-21:38.

One or two days of Passion Week, perhaps Tuesday and/or Wednesday, were spent by Jesus in the temple area giving expression to his last public utterances. Representatives of all the official classes in Jewish society—scribes, elders, and priests—tried to trap Jesus into damaging admissions by their dialectical skill. Mark groups five of these controversies into one section: "What authority have you for doing as you do? And who gave you a right to do as you are doing?" (Mark 11:28) "Is it right to pay the poll tax to the emperor or not? Should we pay it, or refuse to pay it?" (Mark 12:14, 15) "At the resurrection, which one's (of seven husbands) wife will she be?" (Mark 12:28) "How can the scribes say that the Christ is a son of David?"[122] In all of these discussions, Jesus showed that he is the master of the situation by refusing to be trapped; he reduces his adversaries to silence and confusion.

During the day, the enemies of Jesus found it impossible to arrest him. Then something happened which capped the climax of all the tragic events of Passion Week: one of the twelve, Judas Iscariot, came to the priests with a propostion—for a certain sum of money he would lead them to his rendezvous in the Garden of Gethsemane and point him out to them. This was a great advantage to the priests, for they could now proceed to arrest Jesus with the greatest secrecy, guided by a disciple. The motive of Judas has been a subject of endless speculation among Christians: perhaps he thought he was forcing Jesus to assert his Messianic character by putting him in a position where only supernatural agencies would have been able to help him; perhaps he was bitterly disappointed that Jesus was not a Son of David Messiah and had not declared himself in favor of the revolutionary schemes of the Zealots. Certainly the betrayal was not motivated by greed for thirty pieces of silver, a paltry sum.[123]

d.   The Last Supper in the Upper Room: Mark 14:1-31; Matthew 26:1-35; Luke 22:1-38

On Thursday evening Jesus and his disciples gathered in an upper room, possibly in the Jerusalem home of John Mark,[124] for the last supper. In the synoptic gospels it is described as if it were the passover feast, although there is no reference to bitter herbs in the meal and some of the disciples, as well as the men who arrested Jesus later that night, were bearing arms. In the fourth gospel, the supper was a meal of preparation for the Passover, called a "Qiddush"; in this case, the Johannine point of view is probably more correct than the synoptic. "Canon Box has told us lately that it was customary for rabbis and their pupils to meet on the eve of great feast-days, and greet the coming of 6 P.M. with a simple meal of bread and wine and the passing around of the loving-cup; . . ."[125] In any case, the Passover was in the minds of Jesus and the twelve with its remembrance of the miraculous deliverance of the nation from Egypt and the suffering of the Hebrews through the years. Jesus had carefully made in advance the necessary preparations for the farewell meal.

The story of the last supper is significant because of its bearing upon the supreme rite of Christian worship, the Eucharist. So simple was Jesus' action, so fond was the disciples' memory of his words, that the early Christians found themselves remembering his institution of the Lord's Supper every time they assembled themselves together for a fellowship meal. The earliest account of the rite is given by Paul:

. . . The Lord Jesus the night he was betrayed took some bread and gave thanks for it and then broke it in pieces, saying, "This is my body which takes your place. Do this in

memory of me." He took the cup, too, after supper, in the same
way, saying, "This cup is the new agreement ratified by my
blood. Whenever you drink it, do so in memory of me."
For until the Lord comes back, every time you eat this
bread and drink from the cup, you proclaim his death . . .[126]

Then the event grew, by various ritualistic devices, into a stated
ceremony and became separated from the common meal with
which it was at first associated; periodically Christians remember
Jesus and the meaning of his life and death, and consecrate themselves once again to him and to one another in spiritual fellowship.

During the meal Jesus announced the presence of a betrayer
in the midst of the twelve. Then, "after singing the hymn[127] they
went out of the city and up the Mount of Olives."[128]

e. Gethsemane: Mark 14:32-42; Matthew 26:36-46; Luke 22:39-46

It was late at night when Jesus and the remaining eleven disciples
left the upper room, making their way downward into the valley
of the Kidron and then up the lower slope of the Mount of Olives
to a secluded thicket of olive trees known as the Garden of Gethsemane.[129] To eight of the disciples Jesus said: "Sit down here while
I pray." Then he took Peter, James, and John with him further
into the garden, stopping with them after a little while and saying
to them: "My heart is almost breaking. You must stay here and
keep watch." He went on a little way further and threw himself
upon the ground in what the church later called an "agony" of
prayer. He must have been thinking of the hypocrisy of the scribes,
the pride of the priests, the cruelty of the elders, the untrustworthi-
ness of the multitudes, the treachery of Judas, and even the lack
of understanding on the part of those closest to him as he prayed:
"Abba! (that is, Father) "anything is possibe for you! Take this
cup away from me! Yet not what I please but what you do!" Returning to the disciples, he found them asleep; in his hour of
trial they were of no help at all! His agony was all the more poignant because he suffered alone. He finally said to them: "Are you
still sleeping and taking your rest? Enough of this! The time has
come."[130]

The experience of Jesus in Gethsemane was another crisis, or "testing" time, in his life.[131] There was a chance he could escape into the desert under cover of darkness, but would that be following the will of his heavenly father? The agony of Jesus was a "great spiritual conflict involving a personal and an adventurous decision. It was a soul battle fought with the weapon of faith. In the supremest sense Jesus here risked his life on God. As in the wilderness after the baptism, and again on the mount of the transfiguration, so now he was face to face with a crisis. He had, from the first moment of his call, sought resolutely to do the Father's will. He must do it now even unto the draining of the bitter cup of death. To do the will of God, as interpreted by Jesus, meant to share with Him the burden of human redemption from sin and guilt. Love alone was equal to so stupendous a task. The test of love is its capacity for self-sacrifice; its fruit or reward is spiritual peace and tranquillity. Jesus came from the garden fully prepared for the cross."[132]

   f. Betrayal and Arrest: Mark 14:34-52; Matthew 26:47-56;
Luke 22:47-53.

While Jesus was still speaking to the tired disciples, Judas arrived with a detachment of temple police and gave Jesus the kiss of betrayal, the prearranged signal for his arrest.[133] Jesus shows no sign of fear, but rebukes his enemies soundly:

   Have you come out to arrest me with swords and clubs as
   though I were a robber? I have been among you day after day
   in the Temple teaching, and you never seized me . . .[134]

When his disciples saw that Jesus was not going to resist arrest, they "left him and made their escape."[135] This cowardly desertion of their once beloved leader seems to us the height of ingratitude, but it was probably the flight of the eleven which saved Jesus' cause from extinction. Because the disciples were not caught by the authorities and subjected to the same tragic treatment as their leader, the founding of Christianity became possible later.

   g. The Trials and Scourging: Mark 14:53-15:20;
Matthew 26:57-27:31; Luke 22:54-23:25.

Since none of the disciples were present at any of the trials of Jesus, the accounts of them in the gospels are confusing. Of course, they are not trials in the usual sense of the word, for the Jewish authorities had already determined upon their course of action and wanted to give only the appearance of legality to the proceedings. If they were to get rid of Jesus before the Passover they would have to work fast; there were only about eighteen hours from the time of his arrest until 6 P.M. Friday.

There was first a preliminary examination of Jesus in the house of Annas, father-in-law of Caiaphas, the high priest, and recently high priest himself. Caiaphas tried to get Jesus to make damaging admissions, but Jesus refused to commit himself. It was in the courtyard of Annas' house that the famous denial of Jesus by Peter took place. As soon as daylight came, the priests hastily assembled representatives of the Jewish Sanhedrin for a more formal hearing; with Caiaphas presiding, false witnesses were produced who maintained that Jesus had spoken against the temple.[136] Throughout the questioning Jesus kept quiet, until the high priest asked him directly: "Are you the Christ?" to which Jesus replied: "I am!"[137] This convinced the court that Jesus was guilty of blasphemy and gave them a pretext for taking him before the Roman tribunal of Pilate; a self-styled Messiah could always be regarded as an enemy to Rome. "And they all condemned him as deserving to be put to death";[138] then Jesus was taken to Pilate.[139]

The trial before Pilate was also a miscarriage of justice. The governor's Roman sense of justice led him to the realization that Jesus was not guilty of any crime, but his chief official responsibility in Palestine was to preserve order, and in order to achieve that he had to cooperate with the Jewish leaders, particularly on religious matters. Jesus was brought by the Jews to the broad pavement in front of Pilate's palace, just to the northwest of the temple area; the charge against him was threefold: "Here is a man whom we have found misleading our nation, and forbidding the payment of taxes to the emperor, and claiming to be an anointed king himself."[140] According to Luke, when the crowd sensed the fact that Pilate considered Jesus innocent they protested, and someone mentioned that he was a Galilean. Upon hearing this, Pilate decided to send Jesus to Herod Antipas, who happened to be a visitor in Jerusalem at the time. Herod did nothing, but he "and his guards made light of him and ridiculed him, and they put a gorgeous robe on him and sent him back to Pilate."[141] The closing scene in the series of trials took place on the porch of Pilate's hall. Momentarily, he tried to meet the growing fury of the crowd by offering them a compromise: he would release to them a prisoner at the Passover, hoping they would want Jesus; instead they asked for Barabbas, whose first name may also have been Jesus, who had achieved great popularity by taking part in a serious anti-Roman riot. When Pilate asked them what he should do with Jesus, the crowd shouted: "Crucify him!" And Pilate attained a shameful immortality by pronouncing the death sentence.

Brutal hands were laid on Jesus; he was flogged before Pilate, and then taken into the courtyard to be ridiculed by the soldiers. The flogging, or scourging, was a customary part of the ritual of preparing criminals for execution by crucifixion; the instrument used was a whip with several thongs, each loaded with acorn-shaped balls of lead or sharp pieces of stone. Frequently the victim died under the extreme torture; if they lived, the terrific pain would have dulled them to the even more cruel suffering of crucifixion itself.

h. The Crucifixion: Mark 15:21-47; Matthew 27:32-66; Luke 23:26-56

A more terrible death than crucifixion can hardly be imagined. There was no physical pain which was not involved in the agony of death on the cross. It was a Roman invention, reserved for condemned political prisoners and the worst outlaws. Death usually was due to starvation or exposure or both. John 20:25 intimates that Jesus was nailed to the cross, but often victims were tied to it; this was less immediately painful, but served simply to prolong the suffering. Jesus was taken from the judgment hall to the place of execution, which was called Golgotha.[142] It was customary for a condemned man to carry the horizontal beam of the cross himself; Jesus may have started out "carrying the cross by himself,"[143] but his physical strength did not permit him to continue under its burden for very long; the soldiers forced a passer-by, Simon of Cyrene, to carry it for him.[144] When the group reached the place of execution, Jesus' cross was set up between those of two outlaws.[145] Mark says it was nine o'clock in the morning when Jesus was placed on the cross;[146] he hung there until three, when death very mercifully came.[147]

While Jesus hung on the cross, he is reported to have given

expression to seven "words" or sayings; there are three of these in Luke's gospel, three in John, and one in Mark.[148] Whether historically verifiable or not, these words throw light on the real suffering of Jesus on the cross and summarize his whole life and mission. In the light of his previous teachings on prayer[149] and his prayer in Gethsemane,[150] we would expect Jesus to say from the cross: "Father, forgive them; for they know not what they do"[151] and "Father, I intrust my spirit to your hands!"[152] The most difficult of Jesus' seven last words to interpret is the one given in Matthew and Mark: "My God, my God, why have you forsaken me?"[153] Many have assumed that the words mean that God had abandoned Jesus to the pains of hell; such a view contradicts all that Jesus taught about the nature of God. Others maintain that Jesus was quoting familiar words of the twenty-second psalm, which begins with a cry of despair and ends on a note of triumph; if so, why did Jesus pick the verse of that psalm least adapted to a declaration of unshaken faith? It is more probable that the saying represents another testing experience in the career of Jesus; he gives expression to a feeling of utter desolation, a sense of abandonment and despair, but he endures unto the end.

When Jesus died, Joseph of Arimathea, a member of the Sanhedrin, requested from Pilate the privilege of burying him in a rock-hewn tomb prepared by Joseph as the burial place of his own family.[154] His death seemed to bring an end to the movement he had inaugurated; the Roman Empire had disposed of another rebel! But later history was to reverse this verdict and agree with the captain of the Roman soldiers who crucified him: "This man was certainly a son of God!"[155] The death of Jesus was more than that of an ordinary martyr; it was the pledge of the larger success of the ideals for which he had laid down his life. In his death we see the loving fatherhood of God completely revealed; it shows how far God's love will go toward redeeming his wayward children.

5. The Resurrection and Post-resurrection Appearances:
Mark 16; Matthew 28; Luke 24; John 20, 21;
I Corinthians 15:3-8

The day following the crucifixion of Jesus was the Sabbath of Passover week. The disciples of Jesus spent the day in deep grief over the death of their leader and with a sense of humiliation that they had failed him in his great hour of need. To all intents and purposes, their hopes for a Messianic Kingdom lay buried with Jesus in his borrowed tomb. Then, suddenly, on Sunday morning, the city of Jerusalem was astir with the astounding report that Jesus had risen and appeared to several of the disciples and to the devout women who had come to the tomb bearing spices to anoint his body. From the point of view of history, we shall probably never know the exact details of what happened on that exciting morning; but of this we must be sure: the disciples were convinced that Jesus was not dead, but was a living and present force in their lives. From this event sprang the Christian Church. For the first time his followers sensed the full meaning of his life and teachings. From fear-stricken cowards and deniers they were transformed into heroic apostles. It was not possible for a tomb to hold Jesus. While our Christianity does hold the cross central, it does not deify a corpse; it is not the worship of a dead prophet, but a vital faith based on a present and ever-living reality, his spirit.

The earliest account of the appearances of Jesus after his resurrection is given by Paul; perhaps his letter to the church at Corinth contains the key to the mysterious nature of the appearance of Jesus as recorded in the four gospels.

For I passed on to you, as of first importance, the account I had received, that Christ died for our sins, as the Scriptures foretold, that he was buried, that on the third day he was raised from the dead, as the Scriptures foretold, and that he was seen by Cephas (Peter) and then by the Twelve. After that he was seen by more than five hundred brothers at one time, most of whom are still alive, although some of them have fallen asleep. Then he was seen by James, then by all the apostles, and finally he was seen by me also, as though I were born at the wrong time.[156]

Paul seems to regard all these appearances as being of the same nature as his own; at his own conversion on the road to Damascus Paul "saw" the Lord and "heard" his voice.[157] To Paul, the appearances of Jesus to Peter, James, and the other disciples were inward, spiritual experiences which convinced them that Jesus was a living personality, giving them courage to carry on the work which Jesus had started among them. The faith of the church came as the result of a realization on the part of the early Christians of the living and life-giving presence of Jesus.

C. *The Teachings of Jesus*

1. Jesus' Method as Teacher

Even more important for the modern Christian than a study of the life and times of the historic Jesus is an investigation of his teachings. It was as a teacher that Jesus began his work in Galilee: "Then he went all over Galilee, teaching in their synagogues and proclaiming the good news of the kingdom . . ."[158] He was always teaching—in the synagogue at Nazareth, in the temple courtyard in Jerusalem, by the side of the lake, on the road, or at table in the house of a friend. Sometimes there were crowds hanging on every word; sometimes he spoke to one person. Wherever he was, Jesus was always speaking to men concerning the kingdom of God and their relationship to God as sons. What he was is inextricably bound up with what he said. Theologians and religious leaders have differed through the years concerning the nature of his personality, but leaders in all religions—Jewish and Gentile, Christian and non-Christian—bow reverently before his teachings. History accords him first place among the great teachers of the world.

Much of his success as a teacher springs from his teaching method. The ordinary teacher has a more or less complete system of ideas which he wishes to impart to his pupils, but Jesus had no such; he was not a classroom lecturer giving a course in the philosophy of religion. He was more interested in men and life than in ideas and logical expositions. He never prepared an address to be delivered on a formal occasion; all his teaching was marked by the greatest naturalness and informality. He taught as occasion demanded, dealing with all the great questions of life—God and his kingdom, man and sin—as they arose in the experience of his hearers. Jesus' teachings were practical; he lifted common needs and duties to the plane of eternal values. His creed as a teacher may be seen in the parable of the sower:

I am a sower. There are some souls on whom my words fall, that are like the beaten ground where no seed can take root. Then there are folks who accept the truth at once, but have no depth of understanding or purpose; they shout today but forget tomorrow. They are like that place in the field where a little soil covers the rock, where the wheat springs up quickly only to wither away. And there are the divided souls. They are interested in my words, but they have other interests, too, roots of selfishness and sin that are in them; and these other interests crowd out what I say. All this I see, but I see something more. I see the good soil, the simple earnest folks who take my words into honest hearts. And I know the seed; it has life in it. I know the power of truth: and I know that it will bring forth thirty, sixty, a hundredfold.[159]

The teachings of Jesus have been frequently misinterpreted because his teaching method has been largely misunderstood. Like the oriental he was, his language was picturesque, not literal, full of figures of speech, illustrations, striking expressions, and parabolic stories. This is very apparent when collections of his words like the sermon on the mount[160] are read. A large part of the simplicity and power contained in the teachings of Jesus is due to the fact that he taught by using pictures; his illustrations came out of common life and experience. He took bird and beast, grain and weed and flower, salt and seed and candle, men at work and children at play, and made these common things speak to men of high truths. His figures of speech included metaphors, similes, paradoxes, and hyperboles.[161] The most unique feature of his teaching method was his abundant use of the parable.[162] In spite of the apparent implication of some of the gospel writers,[163] Jesus' purpose in using parables was to make his teachings simple and easily understood; Jesus came to reveal truth, not conceal it, and he did this so clearly and naturally that "the mass of the people liked to hear him."[164] Very often Jesus used in his teachings a balanced poetical form; this is evident in the first half of Matthew 7 and in the close of that chapter, where a parable forms two stanzas of equal length; in each of these, a long line states the theme, four short lines follow, and another long line states the conclusion:

Everyone, therefore, who listens to this teaching of mine and
acts upon it,

Will be like a sensible man who built his house on a rock.
> And the rain fell,
> And the rivers rose,
> And the winds blew,
> And beat about that house,
And it did not go down, for its foundations were on rock.
And anyone who listens to this teaching of mine and does not
> > act upon it,
Will be like a foolish man who built his house on sand.
> And the rain fell,
> And the rivers rose,
> And the winds blew,
> And beat about that house,
And it went down, and its downfall was complete.[165]

Jesus was indebted to the Jewish scriptures for the content of much of his teaching, but he used it discriminatingly; his was not the scribal method of hairsplitting, but the free method of interpretative insight. He chose the Old Testament passages which fit in with his own spirit and message—the moral and spiritual instead of the legal and ceremonial. He restated the essential meaning of the Old Testament in terms of his own discernment of spiritual truth; sometimes he revises or rejects, using the formula: "You have heard that they were told, . . . But I tell you . . ."[166] No wonder his independence brought him into conflict with the acknowledged authoritative religious leaders and teachers of his people, those who gave their lives to the study and interpretation of the Torah. "And they were amazed at his teaching, for he taught them like one who had authority, and not like the scribes."[167] Jesus' authority came from deep within his own inner life; what made his words so permanently significant was the fact that he himself was the best illustration of his own teachings. The scribes taught by means of negative legal prescriptions; Jesus welcomed men to a new life with God by persuading them to make positive commitments to his way of life.[168]

2. Jesus' Teaching about God.

Central in Jesus' teaching was his idea about God. His special term for God was "Father." This concept was not a new thing among the Jews; the fatherhood of God had been mentioned in the Old Testament, the Apocrypha, and the Pseudepigrapha. Jeremiah had spoken of God as "My Father."[169] What Jesus brought was not a new set of theological ideas; what was new and unique about his teaching of God was his emphasis and the depth and vividness of his experience of God. He gave the word "Father" new content; he took the Old Testament view of God seriously enough to apply it to his life and to see God's mercy, power, and love everywhere revealed in his universe. Nowhere does Jesus argue systematically for the existence of God or seek to present his metaphysical attributes; in a typically Jewish way, Jesus assumes that God does exist, that he is one, and that he created the world. Then he goes on to assert that God is directly active in history and that nothing is too small to escape his attention and care.

To Jesus, God was all-powerful and absolutely holy. "So you are to be perfect, as your heavenly father is."[170] "Why do you call me good? No one is good but God himself."[171] Jesus' consciousness of the majesty and holiness of God led to an element of reverence and worship which was of profound significance in the life of Jesus. But, not only was God morally perfect in the thought of Jesus; he was also infinite in love. God is not engaged in passive self-contemplation; he cares for every man, woman, and child; each individual has a unique and personal value in God's sight. "You are worth more than a great many sparrows."[172] "The Sabbath was made for man, not man for the Sabbath."[173] God does not distribute his blessings on the basis of merit, but because of the overflowing goodness of his divine grace.[174] He loves even those opposed to his will;[175] he is always ready to forgive.[176] "There will be more joy in heaven over one sinful person who repents, than over ninety-nine upright people who do not need any repentance."[177] God approves the penitent cry of the tax-collector: "O God, have mercy on a sinner like me!"[178] In this kind of God, who was everlastingly merciful, Jesus placed his entire confidence; he surrendered his will to him all through his public ministry, and was able triumphantly to say from the cross: "Father, I intrust my spirit to your hands!"[179]

For Jesus, the parental love of God was not synonymous with mere optimistic sentimentalism or moral indifference. The fatherhood of God carries with it a sense of responsibility for the maintenance of uncompromising righteousness and judgment for wrong-doing. "It is not everyone who says to me 'Lord! Lord!' who will get into the Kingdom of Heaven, but only those who do the will of my Father in heaven."[180] Man's attitude toward God is to be more than trust; it is also to contain reverence and awe. God is in heaven, and his name is to be revered.[181] God's love is through and through ethical; men cannot receive its blessings unless they are willing to share with others its benefits.[182] The primary thing which God desires from men is love with all their heart, soul, strength, and mind.[183] "Jesus taught that love lies at the heart of the universe, and if we will only see it, the deepest love pulsates through the world; that God calls men into fellowship with and likeness to himself, so that the divine life may become ever more realized in the world; that the divine blessings are freely given to men not on their deserts but because of God's nature, but that the results of continued moral refusal are inexorable."[184]

3. Jesus and the Kingdom of God.

No phrase stands out in the teachings of Jesus any more promi-nent than "the kingdom of God."[185] His first sermon in Galilee was based on the words "The time has come and the reign (king-dom) of God is near: repent, and believe this good news."[186] Jesus' ministry ended with a reference to this same kingdom in his last word to his disciples before he led them out to Gethsem-ane.[187] Nowhere does Jesus describe precisely what he meant by this phrase; just as with other words he used, he took what was familiar with everybody and gradually gave them his own meaning. There was common agreement, among the Jews of Jesus' day, that such a kingdom existed and that it had a three-fold nature: an eternal fact from the time God created the heavens and the earth; a present manifestation in the lives of men; and a complete consummation still to come in the future.[188] Thus, there was nothing original about the phrase "the kingdom of God"; what Jesus did was to give it a new content.

The heart of Jesus' preaching about the kingdom was the pronouncement that it was near; it was coming whether men re-pented or not, but if they repented they would then enter the kingdom. In this respect, Jesus shared the eschatological expectations of his fellow Jews. Much of what he said lends support to this point of view: "I tell you, some of you who stand here will certainly live to see the reign of God come in its might."[189] "I tell you, these things will all happen before the present age passes away."[190] "I tell you, I will never drink the product of the vine again till the day when I shall drink the new wine in the Kingdom of God."[191] However, Jesus also believed that in some respects the kingdom had already come; he had none of the hopeless pessimism of the Jewish apocalyptists who could do nothing but complain about the evil of their age and wait for something catastrophic to occur.[192] He said: "The Kingdom of God is within you."[193] He regarded his ministry of healing as fulfillment of the Messianic prophecies.[194] God was not waiting until some future time to act; he was here, caring for all his creation. As far as the actual time for the consummation of the age, a question which worried the apocalyptists, Jesus left that with God, admitting that he did not know "either the day or the hour."[195] What was new, then, in Jesus' teaching concerning the kingdom of God was his bold affirmation that his own ministry constituted a preliminary realization of the rule of God.

New also was Jesus' description of the constituency of the kingdom; he promised entrance to an entirely different group of people than most expected. The kingdom was for the poor, not the rich;[196] little children could enter, but not the wise scribes;[197] tax collectors and prostitutes would go in ahead of the Pharisees.[198] The kingdom would not be confined to Jews, for "many will come from the east and from the west and take their places at the feast with Abraham, Isaac, and Jacob, in the Kingdom of Heaven."[199] Those who enter the kingdom will bear the mark of the persecuted.[200] Then, too, Jesus took the whole idea of the kingdom of God, which had been a part of the hope of the Jewish people for many generations, with a new seriousness; because God was about ready to assert his full sovereignty on the stage of history, there was a stirring sense of urgency to everything Jesus did and said. "But you must make his kingdom, and uprightness before him, your greatest care."[201] It was better to enter the kingdom without an eye, or a hand, or a foot than to go to Gehenna with a whole body.[202] "For I tell you that unless your uprightness is far superior to that of the scribes and Pharisees, you will never even enter the Kingdom of Heaven!"[203] Complete obedience, not lip service, was a prime requisite for the kingdom.[204] God demands wholehearted commitment: "No one who puts his hand to the plough, and then looks back, is fitted for the Kingdom of God."[205] Entrance into the kingdom was worth any sacrifice.[206]

Around the concept of the kingdom of God many parables of Jesus center. Twelve of them are introduced by phrases with the kingdom emphasis, such as "The reign of God is like . . ."[207] They reveal the belief of Jesus concerning the nature of the kingdom: it was a fellowship already existing on this earth, into which Jesus urged men to enter at once; it was essentially in the hearts of men, although it would soon extend its influence on outward conditions; beginning small, it would grow with time; it was a gift which God was ready to impart to men if they would accept it.[208] Jesus' own words are as follows:

It is like a mustard seed, which, when sown in the ground, though it is the smallest of all the seeds in the world, yet once sown, comes up and grows to be the largest of all plants, and produces branches so large that the wild birds can roost under the shelter of it.[209]

The reign of God is like a man scattering seed on the ground, and then sleeping at night and getting up by day, while the seed sprouts and comes up, without his knowing it. The ground of itself is productive, putting forth first a blade, then a head, then fully developed wheat in the head. But as soon as the crop will let him, the man goes in with his sickle, for the harvest time has come.[210]

The Kingdom of Heaven is like yeast, which a woman took and buried in a bushel of flour until it had all risen.[211]

The Kingdom of Heaven is like a hoard of money, buried in a field, which a man found, and buried again. And he was overjoyed and went and sold everything he had and bought the field.[212]

Again, the Kingdom of Heaven is like a dealer in search of fine pearls. He found one costly pearl, and went and sold everything he had, and bought it.[213]

Again, the Kingdom of Heaven is like a net that was let down into the sea, and inclosed fish of all kinds. When it was full, they dragged it up on the beach, and sat down and sorted the good fish into baskets and threw the bad away. That is what will happen at the close of the age . . .[214]

The kingdom of God, the rule or reign of God, was both personal and social, both individual and institutional. The kingdom was considered to be a fellowship of those committed to the will of God; in it, each individual was to be motivated entirely by the spirit of God and the society to which each person belonged was to become the ideal order. Jesus makes the spiritual worth of man as a self central in his definition of citizenship in the kingdom: "Do not worry about life, wondering what you will have to eat or drink, or about your body, wondering what you will have to wear. Is not life more important than food, and the body than clothes?"[215] Jesus' objective in teaching was that all who heard him might become "true sons of your Father in heaven."[216] Jesus stressed the inward motive lying behind the external act.[217] Real prayer and worship are based on inner feeling rather than outward ritualistic acts.[218] And the kingdom was also a society in which brotherhood was to be the rule of life, revealing itself in love and service for those who need.[219] All of human life and activity was to come under the sovereign will of God; not only must persons follow the ideal of personality as revealed in Jesus, but all social institutions, which are after all only lengthened shadows of persons, must succumb to the ideal of fellowship which Jesus intended for his disciples to demonstrate.[220]

SUGGESTIONS FOR FURTHER STUDY

A. E. Barnett, *The New Testament: Its Making and Meaning,* pp. 93-180.

H. M. Battenhouse, *New Testament History and Literature,* pp. 33-105, 173-253.

H. M. Battenhouse, *The Bible Unlocked,* pp. 301-398.

D. M. Beck, *Through the Gospels to Jesus.*

I. R. Beiler, *Studies in the Life of Jesus.*

W. R. Bowie, *The Master: A Life of Jesus Christ.*

B. H. Branscomb, *Jesus and the Law of Moses.*

B. H. Branscomb, *The Message of Jesus.*

B. H. Branscomb, *The Teachings of Jesus.*

W. E. Bundy, *Jesus and the First Three Gospels.*

G. A. Buttrick, ed., *The Interpreter's Bible,* VII, pp. 60-74, 114-175, 229-917; VIII, pp. 1-434.

G. A. Buttrick, *The Parables of Jesus.*

S. J. Case, *Jesus: A New Biography.*

S. J. Case, *The Historicity of Jesus.*

E. C. Colwell, *An Approach to the Teaching of Jesus.*

C. T. Craig, *The Beginning of Christianity*, pp. 55-114.

W. B. Denny, *The Career and Significance of Jesus.*

F. C. Eiselen, E. Lewis, and D. G. Downey, eds., *The Abingdon Bible Commentary*, pp. 867-879, 891-920, 953-1059.

J. Finegan, *Rediscovering Jesus.*

H. E. Fosdick, *The Man from Nazareth.*

G. H. Gilbert, *The Student's Life of Jesus.*

T. R. Glover, *The Jesus of History.*

E. J. Goodspeed, *A Life of Jesus.*

E. J. Goodspeed, *The Story of the New Testament*, pp. 49-69.

T. S. Kepler, ed., *Contemporary Thinking about Jesus.*

C. M. Laymon, *The Life and Teachings of Jesus.*

M. E. Lyman, *Jesus.*

M. E. Lyman, The *Christian Epic*, pp. 13-25, 67-137.

J. Moffatt, *An Introduction to the Literature of the New Testament*, pp. 177-282.

E. W. K. Mould, *Essentials of Bible History*, pp. 483-517

H. F. Rall, *The Life of Jesus.*

H. F. Rall, *The Teachings of Jesus.*

D. W. Riddle and H. H. Hutson, *New Testament Life and Literature*, pp. 56-94, 149-171.

E. F. Scott, *The Ethical Teaching of Jesus.*

E. F. Scott, *The Literature of the New Testament*, pp. 18-87.

J. A. Scott, *We Would Know Jesus.*

V. G. Simkhovitch, *Toward the Understanding of Jesus.*

B. H. Streeter, *The Four Gospels.*

Chapter Twenty-two

THE SPREAD OF THE NEW RELIGION:
THE BOOK OF ACTS

The fact that Christianity today has more adherents than any other of the world's living religions should not blind us to the fact that it was once a new faith. The obscure Jews who launched the new religion were not conscious that they were beginning a movement which would grow, like a mustard seed,[1] into such tremendous proportions. The eleven disciples and the other intimate followers of Jesus had survived the terrible tragedy of the crucifixion and had become convinced by his appearances to them that he was spiritually alive and that their activities as disciples must be resumed. It was from these experiences that the Christian religion was created.[2]

There is only one extant historical account of the beginnings of the Christian Church: the fifth book of the New Testament, entitled "the Acts of the Apostles."[3] It was originally intended by the author to be volume two of his two-volume history of the origins of Christianity.[4] The two volumes are linked together by the opening words of the Book of Acts:

In my first volume, Theophilus, I dealt with all that Jesus did and taught from the beginning . . .[5]

The author of both volumes has traditionally been considered to be Luke, the physician and companion of Paul,[6] but there has been considerable opposition to this in recent years.[7] If Luke-Acts is a literary unit, the date of composition would be some time between 90 and 95 A.D., as has already been noted.[8] The author makes use of various written sources and possibly oral traditions in his work; the demarcation between these is difficult to determine because he puts the stamp of his own style on his source materials and freely edits by abbreviation or expansion the stories which were made available to him. In the last part of Acts—from 15:35 to the end—the author employs in several passages the pronoun "we," indicating that the author is either traveling along with Paul or using a travel diary of one who had been a traveling companion of Paul.[9]

The book of Acts is the oldest handbook of Christian missions. The author's aim was not to present exhaustive details about the rise and spread of Christianity but to select a number of outstanding incidents which would vividly reveal the way in which Christianity succeeded in expanding from Jerusalem to Rome. He tells us nothing about the beginning of the new religion in north Africa or even how it started in Rome; he leaves out many interesting incidents in the life of Paul.[10] He had to confine himself to his main purpose: to show by a judicious choice of incidents the process by which the religion of Jesus grew from humble beginnings to a world-wide power. The general outline of his work is revealed early in the first chapter; the early Christian preachers were to be

. . . witnesses for me (Christ) in Jerusalem and all over Judea and Samaria and to the very ends of the earth.[11]

The book falls into six distinct sections, each of them closing with a formula which summarizes the progress made previously and which points forward to the section following:

I. The Origin of the Church at Jerusalem (1:1-6:7).
   A. Introduction: The risen Jesus and the apostles (1:1-26).
   B. Pentecost (2:1-47).
   C. Acts of Peter and John (3:1-4:31).
   D. The Jerusalem Church (4:32-5:11).
   E. Acts of the twelve (5:12-6:7).

II. The Spread of Christianity Through Palestine (6:8-9:31).
   A. The acts of Stephen (6:8-8:3).
   B. The acts of Philip (8:4-13, 26-40).
   C. More acts of Peter and John (8:14-25).
   D. The conversion of Saul of Tarsus (9:1-31).

III. The Expansion from Palestine to Antioch in Syria
     (9:32-12:24).
     A. Acts of Peter (9:32-11:18).
     B. The rise of the Gentile question (11:19-30).
     C. The church and Herod Agrippa I (12:1-24).

IV. The Expansion of the Church from Syria to Asia Minor
     (12:25-16:5).
     A. The acts of Barnabas and Paul (12:25-14:28).
     B. The Jerusalem Conference (15:1-35).
     C. Paul and Silas return to Asia Minor (15:36-16:5).

V. The Work of Paul in Macedonia and Greece (16:6-19:20).
     A. Paul's preaching in Macedonia (16:6-17:15).
     B. Paul in Athens and Corinth (17:16-18:17).
     C. Paul returns to Jerusalem via Ephesus (18:18-22).
     D. Paul in Ephesus (18:23-19:20).

VI. The Gospel Reaches Rome (19:21-28:31).
     A. Paul's journey from Ephesus via Macedonia and Achaia
        to Jerusalem (19:21-21:17).
     B. Paul's arrest in Jerusalem (21:18-23:22).
     C. Paul's Imprisonment at Caesarea (23:22-26:32).
     D. The voyage to Rome (27:1-28:16).
     E. Arrival in Rome (28:17-31).

According to the book of Acts, institutional Christianity began fifty days after the tragic Passover supper with an experience which took place in connection with the Jewish festival of ingathering on the day of Pentecost. Peter and the ten other loyal disciples, accompanied by a larger disciple group of about a hundred and twenty persons, met in the same upper room of hallowed memory, awaiting the time of the earthly return of Jesus. Then, suddenly, as if from one heart, the feeling spread among the disciples that Jesus had returned and that he was spiritually present among his faithful followers. This is called the baptism of the holy spirit.

On the day of the Harvest Festival, they were all meeting together, when suddenly there came from the sky a sound like a violent blast of wind, and it filled the whole house where they were sitting. And they saw tongues like flames separating and settling one on the head of each of them, and they were all filled with the holy Spirit and began to say in foreign languages whatever the Spirit prompted them to utter.[12]

The group became so ecstatically joyful that they began to speak "in other tongues";[13] these words are symbolic of the remarkable significance of this experience for the early Christians; henceforth this day was to be remembered as the birthday of the Christian church. They themselves were "all amazed and bewildered," and disinterested observers said of them: "They have had too much new wine!"[14] Then Peter stood up and made a remarkable address; for the first time a disciple declared that Jesus was the saviour of the world.[15] This discourse became the basis of the statement of faith in Jesus which was standard for the apostolic age:

> He is Jesus, whom God raised from the dead, and to whose resurrection we are all witnesses. So he has been exalted to God's right hand, and has received from his Father and poured over us the holy Spirit that had been promised, as you see and hear . . . Therefore the whole nation of Israel must understand that God has declared this Jesus whom you crucified both Lord and Christ.[16]

The result of the sermon was a vast increase in membership:

> So they welcomed his message and were baptized and about three thousand people joined them that day. And they devoted themselves to the teaching and the society of the apostles, the breaking of bread, and prayer.[17]

The book of Acts presents an interesting picture of the social life of the first Christian community. As loyal Jews, the first Christians observed the age-old temple sacrifices: "Day after day they all went regularly to the Temple."[18] However, their daily meetings for religicus worship began to take on a new significance: "They broke their bread together in their homes, and they ate their food with glad and simple hearts, constantly praising God and respected by all the people. And every day the Lord added people who were saved to their number."[19] The custom of breaking bread together reminded them of the suffering and death of their beloved Christ and pledged them to new consecration to the task of bringing in his kingdom. Very early it developed into the sacrament later known as the Eucharist (literally "giving thanks"), also called Holy Communion or Lord's Supper. At first celebrated daily, the Eucharist was celebrated later only on the first day of the week, which accordingly became known as the Lord's Day. The common meal preceding the Lord's Supper was the love-feast, or Agapé, in which all members of the Christian community joined in a religious service of song and prayer or sacred benediction.[20] The apostles continued the same type of ministry for which they had been trained by Jesus himself: preaching, teaching, and healing; Peter seems to have been particularly successful in the ministry of healing.[21] Their new-found religious ecstasy had economic implications: "The believers all shared everything they had with one another, and sold their property and belongings, and divided the money with all the rest, according to their special needs."[22] Though sometimes the early church in Jerusalem is referred to as a communistic society, it was more strictly a type of life patterned closely after the family, with the strong caring for the weak and everyone sharing in mutual burden-bearing; not every Christian gave up all his possessions.[23] Peter was extremely harsh to Ananias and Sapphira, not because they had not turned over all the money from the sale of their property into the church treasury, but because they had retained part of the proceeds of the sale and thereby pretended to be more generous than they really were.[24] Barnabas' free gift of his property was a spontaneous act of generosity which others were urged to imitate; through their gifts the early Christians were expressing the brotherhood of all believers:

There was but one heart and soul in the multitudes who had become believers, and not one of them claimed anything that belonged to him as his own, but they shared everything they had with one another. The apostles gave their testimony to the resurrection of the Lord Jesus with great power, and God's favor rested richly upon them. No one among them was in any want, for any who owned lands or houses would sell them and bring the proceeds of the sale and put them at the disposal of the apostles; then they were shared with everyone in proportion to his need. Joseph, a Levite, and a native of Cyprus, whom the apostles had named Barnabas, which

means Son of Encouragement, sold a piece of land that belonged
to him, and brought the proceeds and put them at the disposal
of the apostles.[25]

At first, the primitive church in Jerusalem enjoyed comparative
peace; there were only two occasions upon which a mild hostility
asserted itself.[26] Peter and his companions were arrested, but they
were released after being ordered "not to speak or teach at all
about the name of Jesus."[27] During the second hearing of Peter
and the apostles before the Sanhedrin the famous rabbinic teacher
Gamaliel[28] gave expression to a famous statement on tolerance:

> Men of Israel, take care what you propose to do with these
> men . . . Keep away from these men and let them alone, for
> if this idea or movement is of human origin, it will come to
> naught, but if it is from God, you will not be able to stop it.
> You may actually find yourselves fighting God![29]

Real opposition to the new religion began with a relatively minor
incident:

> In those days, as the number of disciples was increasing,
> complaints were made by the Greek-speaking Jews against the
> native Jews that their widows were being neglected in the
> daily distribution of food.[30]

The matter was corrected when the twelve apostles appointed
seven men to be in charge of welfare work.[31] One of these men
was Stephen, a Greek-speaking Jewish Christian himself; not
content with being a mere administrator, this able man began
to preach in one of the city's Hellenist synagogues, where "Libyans,
Cyreneans, and Alexandrians, and men from Cilicia and Asia
undertook to debate with Stephen, . . ."[32] The burden of Stephen's
message was the culmination of the progressive divine revelation
to Israel in the person and message of Jesus Christ; he pled for
a more spiritual type of religious worship, in which the temple
ritual would be replaced by the inward experience of the worshiper.[33] For his criticism of the Torah and the temple, Stephen
was hailed before the Sanhedrin: infuriated with his address,
the members dragged him out of the city and stoned him.[34] The
heroic death of the first Christian martyr was witnessed by Saul

of Tarsus; he watched the clothes of those who threw the first stones.[35] Then there followed a terrific persecution of the Greek-speaking Jewish Christians; they were dispersed throughout Judea and Samaria, planting for the first time the seeds of the new religion in foreign soil.[36]

In the period following the death of Stephen, leadership of the fanatical anti-Christian Jews passed into the hands of the zealous Hellenistic Pharisee named Saul of Tarsus.

> But Saul harassed the church. He went into one house after another, and dragging out men and women, put them in prison.[37]

He even extended his field of operations outside of Palestine proper; while on a trip to Damascus he was converted:

> Now Saul, still breathing murderous threats against the Lord's disciples, went to the high priest, and asked him for letters to the synagogues in Damascus, so that if he found any men or women there who belonged to the Way (the followers of Jesus were called by this designation before they were called Christians), he might bring them in chains to Jerusalem.[38]

During the next ten or twelve years, Hellenist Jewish Christians spread everywhere, establishing new evangelistic frontiers where-ever they went. Philip preached in Samaria, Ashdod, and Caesarea.[39] Even Peter, though reluctantly at first, began preaching at Lydda, Joppa, and Caesarea.[40] But it was at Antioch that the most outstanding Hellenist, Barnabas, a native of Cyprus, achieved the most remarkable evangelistic success for the new religion.

> The fugitives from the persecution that had broken out over Stephen went all the way to Phoenicia, Cyprus, and Antioch, but they told the message to none but Jews. There were some men from Cyprus and Cyrene among them, however, who when they reached Antioch spoke to the Greeks also, and told them the good news about the Lord Jesus. The Lord's hand was with them, and there were a great many who believed and turned to the Lord. The news about them came to the ears of the church in Jerusalem, and they sent Barnabas

all the way to Antioch. When he reached there and saw the favor God had shown them, he was delighted, and encouraged them all to be resolute and steadfast in their devotion to the Lord, for he was an excellent man, full of the holy Spirit and faith. So a considerable number of people came over to the Lord. Then Barnabas went over to Tarsus to seek out Saul, and found him and brought him to Antioch. The result was that for a whole year they met with the church, and taught large numbers of people, and it was at Antioch that the disciples first came to be known as Christians.[41]

Thus was the religion of Jesus well on the way toward becoming the leading religion of the Roman empire.

The primitive Jewish Christian community in Jerusalem had been spared from any destructive results which might have accrued to it from the persecution of the Hellenists.[42] During the decade following the death of Stephen, the Jerusalem Christians became more conciliatory in their attitude toward Judaism and softened the points of sharp difference which had separated them so sharply from their orthodox Jewish neighbors at the time of the crucifixion of Jesus. But all of this was changed in the year 44 A.D.:

About that time King Herod laid violent hands upon some who belonged to the church. He had John's brother, James, beheaded, and when he saw that this gratified the Jews, he proceeded to arrest Peter too, at the time of the festival of Unleavened Bread. He had him seized and put in jail, with four squads of soldiers to guard him, meaning after the Passover to bring him out before the people . . .[43]

Herod's sudden death brought the short-lived persecution to an end, but Palestinian Christianity was never the same again. The future of Christianity lay outside of Palestine.[44] When Jerusalem was destroyed in 70 A.D., most of the small group of Jewish Christians still remaining there fled from Judea. After the war the Christians in Palestine declined still more; in the second century they became known as the heretical sect of the Ebionites.[45]

At this point the main interest in the development of the Christian religion shifts from Palestine to the great Gentile world. The hero of the book of Acts from chapter thirteen until the end of the book is the apostle Paul; since the details of his life will be given in the next chapter, any further discussion of the contents of the book of Acts will come up in connection with the events of his life.

SUGGESTIONS FOR FURTHER STUDY

H. M. BATTENHOUSE, *New Testament History and Literature*, pp. 257-279.

H. M. BATTENHOUSE, *The Bible Unlocked*, pp. 399-430.

G. A. BUTTRICK, ed., *The Interpreter's Bible*, VII, pp. 38, 47, 48, 176-186; IX, pp. 1-352.

C. T. CRAIG, *The Beginning of Christianity*, pp. 133-155.

F. C. EISELEN, E. LEWIS, and D. G. DOWNEY, eds., *The Abingdon Bible Commentary*, pp. 1094-1134.

E. J. GOODSPEED, *The Story of the New Testament*, pp. 70-74.

M. E. LYMAN, *The Christian Epic*, pp. 52-66, 137-156.

J. MOFFATT, *An Introduction to the Literature of the New Testament*, pp. 282-314.

E. W. K. MOULD, *Essentials of Bible History*, pp. 518-581.

D. W. RIDDLE and H. H. HUTSON, *New Testament Life and Literature*, pp. 95-105.

E. F. SCOTT, *The Literature of the New Testament*, pp. 88-106.

Chapter Twenty-three

THE LIFE AND LETTERS OF PAUL

A. *Outline of Events in the Life of Paul the Apostle.*

1. Childhood and Training.

Next to Jesus, the most important personality in the New Testament was the apostle Paul. Some would go so far as to refer to him as the co-founder of the Christian religion; at least, we must admit, with Battenhouse, that "the life of Jesus was the spring, and the life of Paul the vital fructifying stream, of the great historic institution called the Christian Church."[1] Much of the literature in the New Testament was either written by him or influenced by his ideas; he wrote nine letters: First and Second Thessalonians, Galatians, First and Second Corinthians, Romans, Philippians, Colossians, and Philemon; four other letters are based on his life and thought: Ephesians, First and Second Timothy, and Titus. The authors of the Gospels of Mark and Luke are traditionally considered to have traveled with him and to have been his companions in his prison days in Rome.[2] The Gospel of John bears the imprint of his theological ideas. Seventeen chapters in the book of Acts are devoted to his life (chapters 9, 13-28). Had it not been for his mission to the Gentiles, culminating in the significant decision reached at the Jerusalem Conference in A.D. 49-50 favorable to the Gentile mission,[3] the Christian religion would have remained a reforming sect within Judaism and might have died out along with the other Jewish parties in the period following the disastrous Jewish Wars of 66-70.[4] In the spirit of Jesus Paul transformed Christianity from a small Jewish sect into a world religion.

Paul was born in the city of Tarsus, a famous educational center in the province of Cilicia, 129 miles west of Antioch and 515 miles northwest of Jerusalem.[5] Advantageously located on the Cydnus River twelve miles inland from the coast, Tarsus was in a strategic position on the Roman road leading northward into Asia Minor through the Taurus Mountains by way of the famous pass known as the Cilician Gates. It had been a free city for a hundred years prior to Paul's birth; this meant that it had the right to control its own finances, legal jurisdiction over its own citizens and visitors who were sojourning there, freedom from the Roman land tax, and freedom from a garrison of Roman soldiers. Philosophers, travellers, Roman soldiers, merchants, and men of leisure all mingled in the market places and public halls of this cosmopolitan city.

The exact date of Paul's birth cannot be accurately determined. A recent scholar suggests that he could have been born at any time between 10 B.C. and 10 A.D.[6] His parents were evidently loyal Dispersion Jews, for Paul refers to his Hebrew background several times; for example, he says:

> I was circumcised when I was eight days old. I am a descendant of Israel. I belong to the tribe of Benjamin. I am a Hebrew, and the son of Hebrews.[7]
>
> I am an Israelite myself, I am descended from Abraham, and I belong to the tribe of Benjamin.[8]

Paul nowhere mentions his parents by name, nor whether he had any brothers or sisters. Since Paul was a citizen of Rome by birth,[9] we may assume that his father was a Roman citizen. The spirit of his family was strongly Pharisaic; Paul later spoke of himself as a Pharisee and the son of Pharisees.[10] The author of Acts speaks of a nephew of Paul, warning the apostle of a plot against his life;[11] we infer from this that he may have had a married sister in Jerusalem moving in high circles close to the Sanhedrin itself.[12] In his pious Jewish home and in the Tarsus synagogue Paul would have received an emphatically religious training; he would have become acquainted with the Jewish Scriptures—the Torah, the Prophets, and the Writings[13]—and he would have heard them constantly interpreted, debated, and praised.

While Paul was still a young boy, perhaps about fifteen years old, he was taken to Jerusalem to receive instruction in the law and prepare himself to be a rabbi.[14] Though not required of all students preparing for the rabbinate, Jerusalem was the best place to get such training, for the temple was located there and the two schools of Pharisaic thought, those following Hillel and those following Shammai, had their representative teachers in the temple courtyards.[15] It was natural for Paul, because he came from the Hellenistic background of the city of Tarsus, to select the more liberal school of Hillel; Paul's teacher was Gamaliel, grandson of Hillel and the most illustrious representative of that school.[16] The young Cilician may have been one of several hundred pupils who listened to the great teacher every day in their accustomed meeting-place in the temple courtyard. The method of instruction in a Jewish school was memorization;[17] the teacher would repeat a passage of Scripture over and over again until the scholars could not help but commit it to memory. How long it took Paul to complete the course of instruction is not known; sometimes it took twelve years before it could be said that a student was ready to become a rabbi. Many of the ideas which Paul learned in the school of Gamaliel and many of the rabbinic modes of thought are manifest in the letters he wrote as a Christian apostle.

2. Zealous Persecutor of the Christians.

Though there is no direct evidence as to Paul's whereabouts immediately after the completion of his course of training, some scholars think he returned to Tarsus for further training and study. Thus, he was probably not in Jerusalem during the public ministry of Jesus.[18] In his home city he would have learned the occupation by which he earned his living all during his later missionary journeys: the weaving of cloth from Cilician goats' hair, from which tents, carpets, shawls, and shoes were made.[19] At the end of this time we find Paul back in Jerusalem, a zealous Jewish worker, perhaps the rabbi of the Cilician synagogue in that city.[20] His arrival found the city in a great religious upheaval; a group of Jews, calling themselves followers of a certain Jesus of Nazareth, were proclaiming the recent advent of the Messianic era, and hundreds had confessed their faith. Such a movement seemed to threaten the security and supremacy of Judaism; Paul and other Jewish leaders took alarm, and Paul soon became the leader of the anti-Christian forces. Though probably not a member of the Sanhedrin, because he was a Dispersion Jew, Paul admits later:

When they were put to death, I cast my vote against them, and many a time in all the synagogues I had them punished, and tried to force them to say impious things. In my extreme rage against them I even pursued them to distant towns.[21]

Paul first appears on the stage of history as a young man named Saul,[22] at whose feet the killers of Stephen, the first Christian martyr, cast their clothes.[23] Stephen's unjust death at the hands of an angry mob increased Saul's determination to persecute the new religion with his whole soul; in good conscience, he regarded it as a movement dangerous to his beloved Pharisaism and he desperately tried to wipe the entire sect out of existence. For some months Paul was engaged in this work, and it was eminently successful; of it Luke says:

A great persecution of the church in Jerusalem broke out that day, and they were all scattered over Judea and Samaria except the apostles. Some pious men buried Stephen and loudly lamented him. But Saul harassed the church. He went into one house after another, and dragging out men and women, put them in prison.[24]

Paul tried to get the followers of Jesus to renounce their loyalty to him; if they did not, he caused them to be put to death. Then Paul received word that a group of Christians were flourishing unmolested in the city of Damascus, about a week's journey north of Jerusalem:

Now Saul, still breathing murderous threats against the Lord's disciples, went to the high priest, and asked him for letters to the synagogues in Damascus, so that if he found any men or women there who belonged to the Way, he might bring them in chains to Jerusalem.[25]

Thus the stage is set for a revolutionary spiritual experience in the life of Paul: his conversion to Christianity.

3.   Paul's Conversion

There are three accounts of this transforming experience in Paul's life in the book of Acts,[26] one in Paul's letter to the Galatians,[27] and two in his second letter to the church at Corinth.[28]

These accounts agree in some of the details, but differ in others; the important thing is the change the experience wrought in the life of Paul; it was a mystical religious experience, or theophany, which completely transformed Paul's life.[29] Paul's conversion is a radical turning point in his career; the unbeliever becomes a believer, and the persecutor becomes the propagandist for the faith. Paul emphasizes its significance before King Herod Agrippa II:

> I was once going to Damascus on this business, authorized and commissioned by the high priests, when on the road at noon, your Majesty, I saw a light from heaven brighter than the sun flash around me and my fellow-travelers. We all fell to the ground and I heard a voice say to me in Hebrew, "Saul! Saul! Why do you persecute me? You cannot kick against the goad!" "Who are you, sir?" said I. The Lord said, "I am Jesus, whom you are persecuting. But get up and stand on your feet, for I have appeared to you for the express purpose of appointing you to serve me and to testify to what you have seen and to the visions you will have of me. I will save you from your people and from the heathen, to whom I will send you to open their eyes and turn them from darkness to light and from Satan's control to God, so that they may have their sins forgiven and have a place among those who are consecrated through faith in me." Therefore, King Agrippa, I did not disobey that heavenly vision, but first to the people of Damascus and Jerusalem and then all over Judea, and even to the heathen I preached that they must repent and turn to God and live as men who have repented should.[30]

Paul was so dazed by his tremendous conversion experience that his companions had to lead him into Damascus by the hand.[31] He was taken to the house of a certain man named Judas on Straight Street; here he was visited by a brave Jewish Christian by the name of Ananias,[32] who baptized Paul and helped him regain his senses. Almost at once, Paul began publicly to proclaim Jesus as the Christ; this must have amazed his former Jewish associates as much as it did his new Christian friends.

4. The Period of Obscurity

Immediately after his conversion, according to Paul himself,[33] the new Christian recruit retired into Arabia, one section of which,

Arabia Petraea, was just to the south and east of Damascus. The reasons why Paul went into this region, the exact location of his visits, and the length of his stay are not known; we may presume that he retired to the desert for meditation and prayer, but there are cities in Arabia Petraea in which Paul may have preached.

After his Arabian sojourn, Paul returned to Damascus and began his active career as a Christian preacher in earnest. At first the synagogues were open to him; he was so successful that his former Pharisaic allies began to regard him as a dangerous renegade. Luke recites this story:

> Saul stayed for some time with the disciples in Damascus, and began at once to declare in the synagogues that Jesus was the Son of God. Everyone was astonished and said, "Is not he the man who made such havoc of the people in Jerusalem who call upon that name, and who came here especially for the purpose of arresting such persons and taking them before the high priests?" But Saul grew more and more powerful, and bewildered the Jews who lived in Damascus by his proofs that Jesus was the Christ. After some time had passed, the Jews made a plot to kill him, but Saul found out about the plot. They watched the city gates day and night, in order to kill him, but disciples took him one night and let him down over the wall, lowering him in a basket.[34]

Paul's work in Arabia and among the Jews of Damascus, during this so-called "obscure period" in his life,[35] may well have resulted in some of his painful and humiliating experiences he mentions in his third letter to the church at Corinth:

> Five times I have been given one less than forty lashes, by the Jews.[36]

Safely out of Damascus, Paul went to Jerusalem to confer with Peter,[37] and to preach boldly his new convictions in the center of Pharisaic Judaism.[38] Paul also met Barnabas, a Jewish Christian from the island of Cyprus, who was later to be his companion on a missionary journey,[39] and James, brother of Jesus and head of the Jerusalem Christian community.[40] The Greek-speaking Jews in Jerusalem tried to kill him, so the Christian friends of Paul took him to Caesarea, where he took ship for his native city of Tarsus.[41]

Then there follows a period of eight or ten years of missionary apprenticeship, during which time Paul preached considerably in "the districts of Syria and Cilicia."[42] Probably this should be referred to as Paul's first missionary journey. His work was very successful and was evidently chiefly among the Gentiles; later Paul refers to the churches in Syria and Cilicia,[43] many of which would have been founded during this period. It is possible also that some of the many hardships enumerated by Paul in II Corinthians 11:23-33 occurred during these years:

> . . . With far greater labors (than his critics at Corinth), far more imprisonments, vastly worse beatings, and in frequent danger of death. Five times I have been given one less than forty lashes, by the Jews. I have been beaten three times by the Romans, I have been stoned once, I have been shipwrecked three times, a night and a day I have been adrift at sea; with my frequent journeys, in danger from rivers, danger from robbers, danger from my own people, danger from the heathen, danger in the city, danger in the desert, danger at sea, danger from false brothers, through toil and hardship, through many a sleepless night, through hunger and thirst, often without food, and exposed to cold . . .

These were years during which Paul's thought of Christianity was maturing; his experience in evangelistic work would have been preparing him for the larger and better known missionary tours of later years. He became perfectly assured in his own mind that his work among the Gentiles was indeed a work of God.

As we have already seen,[44] it was Barnabas who brought Paul out of a relative obscurity at Tarsus to work with him among the Greeks at Antioch. During that time, news came to the Christians at Antioch of a great famine which seemed to be causing much suffering among the Christians in Jerusalem; a collection was taken, and Barnabas and Paul were commissioned to take it to the home church.[45] Upon their return to Antioch, Barnabas and Paul brought back with them a young man named John Mark, who was destined to play an important role in the growing church.[46] In Antioch the three men found the church prepared with a new program for them: an ambitious plan to evangelize the world for Christ; with this in mind, three of the "prophets and teachers"— Symeon called Niger, Lucius of Cyrene, and Manean, the intimate friend of Herod Antipas—laid their hands on two others of their group—Barnabas and Paul—and set them apart for further work among the Gentiles in a field of activity which was destined to extend from Syria to Spain.[47]

5.   Missionary Tour to Cyprus and Galatia.

Though there is considerable disagreement among scholars concerning the exact chronology of events in the life of Paul, it was probably in the year 47 A.D. when Paul, Barnabas, and John Mark set out from Seleucia, the harbor of Antioch, for the island of Cyprus.[48] The three missionaries traversed Cyprus from Salamis, the eastern seaport, to Paphos, the Roman capital city in the western part of the island; the only event of their stay on Cyprus which Luke cares to record took place at Paphos. Paul met the Roman proconsul, Sergius Paulus, and began to tell him God's message, but he was interrupted by a Jewish sorcerer, Bar-Jesus, who gave himself the Arabic title Elymas (meaning "wise"); in his role as court fortune-teller, or man of science, Elymas opposed the apostles out of fear that they might supplant him in the favor of the proconsul. Paul was aroused to all the anger of which his soul was capable and spoke so sharply to the fortune-teller that the latter was struck with a temporary blindness:

> You monster of underhandedness and cunning! You son of the devil! You enemy of all that is right! Will you never stop trying to make the Lord's straight paths crooked? The Lord's hand is right upon you, and you will be blind and unable even to see the sun for a time.[49]

The proconsul was tremendously impressed, but it is not certain whether he became a Christian or not.

From Paphos the missionary party set sail for Perga in Pamphylia on the coast of the mainland of Asia Minor. Here John Mark left them and went back to Palestine, for what reason is not known.[50] Paul and Barnabas went north out of the low-lying coastland to the highlands of Galatia, perhaps to get relief from the malaria-infested climate of the coastal regions; after a journey of about a hundred miles, the two intrepid travellers found themselves in Antioch in Pisidia. The first Sabbath found Paul and Barnabas among the worshipers in the Jewish synagogue; the elders of the synagogue asked them to address the people, a courtesy extended to all visitors from Palestine by Dispersion Jews. Paul got up and spoke to those assembled; he began by summarizing the outstanding events in Hebrew history which had culminated in the life, death, and resurrection of Jesus the Messiah;[51] he ended by offering his hearers a forgiveness and reconciliation in the risen Jesus which was superior than anything offered by the law of Moses. Such words were gladly received. "As they were going out, the people begged to have all this said to them again on the following Sabbath, and after the congregation had broken up, many of the Jews and the devout converts to Judaism went away with Paul and Barnabas, and they talked with them, and urged them to rely on the favor of God."[52] The success of Paul and Barnabas aroused the jealous animosity of the Jewish leaders; on the next Sabbath, they contradicted everything the two apostles said; then Paul and Barnabas spoke out boldly for a universal gospel:

> God's message had to be told to you first, but since you thrust it off and judge yourselves unworthy of eternal life, we now turn to the heathen. For these are the orders the Lord has given us: "I have made you a light for the heathen, to be the means of salvation to the very ends of the earth!"[53]

The non-Jews in the audience were delighted with these words, but the Jews "stirred up the well-to-do religious women and the leading men of the town, and they started a persecution against Paul and Barnabas, and drove them out of their district."[54]

The apostles left Antioch and traveled eighty or ninety miles eastward along the Roman road to Iconium; they were so successful that a great many Jews and Greeks believed in their message, but hostile Jews stirred up a crowd of both Jews and Greeks and forced Paul and Barnabas to escape a possible stoning.[55] They made their way southward to the town of Lystra, a journey of about six hours from Iconium; here there seem to have been not enough Jews to have a synagogue, so the apostles evidently preached on the streets or in the courtyards. Multitudes came to hear them. The cure of a lame man aroused the crowd to frenzy, and they hailed Paul and Barnabas as Hermes and Zeus respectively.[56] The apostles could hardly restrain the people from offering sacrifices to them. "But some Jews came from Antioch and Iconium, and

won the people over, and they stoned Paul and dragged him out
of the town, thinking that he was dead. But the brothers gathered
about him, and he got up and reentered the town."[57] The next
day, Paul and Barnabas traveled in a southeasterly direction to the
Roman town of Derbe, where they gained a number of recruits
for the Christian gospel.[58]

From Derbe the missionaries might easily have continued to
travel southeastward along the Roman roads to Tarsus and Antioch
in Syria. Instead, they chose to go back the way they had come,
through Lystra, Iconium, Antioch in Pisidia, and Perga in Pamphylia. What their reception was in each town can only be imagined,
but Luke records:

> Then they returned to Lystra, Iconium, and Antioch, re-
> assuring the disciples and encouraging them to stand by the
> faith and reminding them that we have to undergo many
> hardships to get into the Kingdom of God. They appointed
> elders for them in each church, and with prayer and fasting
> they committed them to the Lord in whom they had believed.
> Then they crossed Pisidia and entered Pamphylia. They told
> their message in Perga, then went on to Attalia, and from
> there they sailed back to Antioch, where they had first been
> commended to God's favor for the work which they had now
> finished. When they arrived there, they called the church to-
> gether, and reported how God had worked with them, and how
> he had opened the way to faith for the heathen. There they
> stayed for a long time with the disciples.[59]

6. The Apostolic Council in Jerusalem

At Antioch, Paul and Barnabas resumed their work among
the vast Greek population of that city. Things went along smoothly
until

> some people came down from Judea and began to teach the
> brothers that unless they were circumcised as Moses prescribed,
> they could not be saved. This created a disturbance and a
> serious discussion between Paul and Barnabas and them, and
> it was agreed that Paul and Barnabas and some others of their
> number should go up to Jerusalem to confer with the apostles
> and elders about this question.[60]

The meeting which took place in Jerusalem between the apostles to the Gentiles and the leaders among the Jerusalem Christian community was the first of its kind in the history of Christianity and the most momentous; it was not an ecclesiastical council with power to legislate for the various bodies represented, but it was rather a friendly conference of a younger church with the mother church in Jerusalem. The issue at the Conference was presented in the form of three questions: Can a Gentile become a Christian without first adopting Judaism? But wouldn't a Gentile be a better Christian by observing the Jewish ceremonial law? Does becoming a Christian absolve a Jew from his formal legal and ceremonial obligations? Representing the strict Judaistic point of view was James, the brother of Jesus; advocating the freedom of the Gentile believers were Paul and Barnabas; also present at the Conference were Peter and John, foremost leaders of the church in Jerusalem, and Titus, a Greek convert whom Paul had brought with him as evidence that his Gentile mission had been favored by God.

According to Galatians 2:1-10, the meeting of the apostles in Jerusalem was a stormy one; Luke does not record any seeming disharmony in his account.[61] Some scholars have suggested that Paul's record in Galatians refers to a private discussion among the leaders held probably before the milder public meeting.[62] In the earlier session, both parties to the dispute probably presented their points of view in as strong a light as possible. James and the Judaizers might have pointed out that Jesus had been a Jew and had not formally abrogated the Torah for his followers; Jesus himself had kept the Torah;[63] the disciples in Jerusalem, including the apostles themselves, had not separated themselves from the temple and Jewish ceremonial regulations.[64] Paul would have stoutly maintained that Gentiles could become Christians without being sons of Abraham through the covenant of circumcision and would have pointed to Titus as a good example of that fact. Peter would have tried to preserve harmony between the two extremes; manifestly the blessing of God rested upon Paul's work among the Gentiles. The result was that Paul was extended the right hand of fellowship by James, Peter, and John.[65]

In the public meeting, Peter took the initiative, telling the council of his own experience with Gentiles and pleading with them not to lay on the Gentiles a burden which the Jews themselves could not bear.[66] Then Paul and Barnabas told of their experiences in Antioch, Cyprus, Galatia, and the other places where they had preached. When they had finished, James recommended the decision of the council; he agreed that the Gentiles should not be troubled further, but he proposed a decree which was to be sent to the churches at Antioch and in Syria and Cilicia in the form of a letter to be delivered by Judas Barsabbas and Silas. The decree was a compromise measure dealing with unessential matters: Gentile converts were urged to "avoid whatever has been sacrificed to idols, the tasting of blood and of the meat of animals that have been strangled, and immorality."[67] It did not touch the specific question which the Antioch church had brought to Jerusalem; the real answer to that was in the right hand of fellowship which Peter, James, and John extended to Paul and Barnabas: the cause of Gentile freedom was triumphant.[68] The importance of this outcome cannot be overemphasized; the decision to admit Gentiles into the Christian religion directly, rather than through Jewish ceremonial requirements, led to the emergence of Christianity as a separate and distinct and universal religion; if the early Christians had agreed that all converts must submit to circumcision and the Jewish food laws, then the Christian religion would have remained a Judaistic sect and would have disappeared from history before the end of the first century, as Jewish Christianity did disappear.[69]

An unfortunate incident took place in Antioch soon after the apostolic council in Jerusalem. Peter went from Jerusalem to Antioch and, in the spirit of the Jerusalem council, ate with the Gentile believers; but when some Judaizing disciples came from Jerusalem, Peter "began to draw back and hold aloof, for fear of the party of the circumcision. The other Jewish Christians followed his example in concealing their real views, so that even Barnabas was carried away by their pose."[70] Paul rebuked Peter sharply and openly for his conduct.[71] This shows that the elder apostles, while they were willing to admit that the Gentiles ought to be free from Judaistic restrictions, were not ready to free Jewish Christians from such requirements. The letter of the Jerusalem church contemplated a certain amount of social intercourse between Jewish and Gentile Christians, but not table fellowship, which was a mark of perfect ceremonial equality.[72] This reveals the weakness of the compromise reached at Jerusalem; from this point on, Paul opposes

Jewish legalism with all the virility of which he is capable; justification by faith in Jesus Christ absolutely excludes the works of the law.[73]

7.   Paul Takes the Gospel to Europe.

Some months after the Apostolic Council, Paul said to Barnabas:

> Come, let us go back and revisit the brothers in each of the towns where we made the Lord's message known, to see how they are doing.[74]

Barnabas was agreeable to making the journey, but he suggested to Paul that they take with them his cousin John Mark, as they had done on the previous journey. "But Paul did not approve of taking with them a man who had deserted them in Pamphylia instead of going on with them to their work.[75] They differed so sharply about it that they separated, and Barnabas took Mark and sailed for Cyprus. But Paul selected Silas and set out, the brothers commending him to the Lord's favor."[76]

Paul and Silas set out from Antioch in Syria, this time by land, first visiting churches in Syria and Cilicia.[77] The two travelers probably followed a winding highway which frequently led through hills overlooking the Mediterranean Sea through the Syro-Cilician gates, a narrow pass between Mount Ananus and the sea, to Issus, in Cilicia, only forty or fifty miles from Antioch; another hundred miles would have brought them to Tarsus, Paul's home city, where there must have been a group of Christians ready to welcome him and his companions.[78] After several more days of riding, Paul and Silas would have gone through the Cilician gates into the region in which the Galatian churches were located, most of which Paul had already visited twice before.[79] At Lystra, Paul selected as his secretary a young man named Timothy, the son of a Jewish Christian mother and a Greek father; Paul had him circumcised, in order to establish his Jewish status and to save him embarrassment in his future work.[80] From Lystra, the party of three doubtless visited Iconium and Antioch in Pisidia, though Luke does not mention them by name.

From Antioch in Pisidia Paul's thought naturally turned toward the province of Asia. It was part of his missionary strategy always to select the great centers of population and commerce as the chief fields of his evangelistic labors; only two hundred miles west of Pisidian Antioch was the important city of Ephesus, the chief city of the whole region. But for some unknown reason, "the holy Spirit prevented them from delivering the message in Asia."[81] Then Paul sought to enter Bithynia, a Roman province lying on the south shore of the Black Sea,[82] but again "the Spirit of Jesus would not permit it."[83] So, finding doors closed to the gospel message in Asia and Bithynia, Paul, Timothy, and Silas continue northwestward to Troas, only a few miles south of the Troy made famous by Homer, on the shores of the Aegean Sea. At Troas, Paul had a mystical experience one night, in which "a Macedonian was standing appealing to him and saying, 'Come over to Macedonia and help us.' "[84] It has been conjectured by some scholars[85] that the Macedonian in Paul's vision was Luke; beginning with Acts 16:10, the personal pronoun suddenly changes from "they" to "we," suggesting that Luke was Paul's companion as he set sail from Troas across the Aegean Sea to Macedonia.[86]

Paul started for Macedonia immediately after the vision.

> As soon as he had this vision, we made efforts to get on to Macedonia, concluding that God had called us to tell them the good news.[87]

This was a very significant step in the career of Paul; it meant that he was introducing Christianity into Europe, where it was destined to make such a tremendous contribution to civilization and culture. Within the next few centuries the Christian religion would leave Asia, the continent of its origin, almost entirely and enter the new spiritual climate of Europe. As Paul crossed the Hellespont with Luke, Timothy, and Silas, the Christian gospel took a westward direction which was to determine its history from then on.

On the second day after they left Troas, the missionary party landed at Neapolis, the port of Philippi, and walked the remaining ten miles to Philippi. This city had been a fortress of Philip of Macedon, the father of Alexander the Great; though not the capital of Macedonia, it was the most important city in it; Augustus had made it a Roman colony in 42 B.C., the very year in which Octavius (later Augustus) and Antony had defeated at Philippi the armies of the murderers of Julius Caesar, Brutus and Cassius.

There were not enough Jews in Philippi to have a synagogue; so, as Luke records in his diary:

> On the Sabbath we went outside the gates, to the bank of the river where we supposed there was a praying place, and we sat down and talked with the women who gathered there. One of our hearers was a woman named Lydia, a dealer in purple goods, from the town of Thyatira. She was a believer in God, and the Lord touched her heart, and led her to accept Paul's teaching. When she and her household were baptized, she appealed to us, and said, "If you are really convinced that I am a believer in the Lord, come and stay at my house." And she insisted upon our coming.[88]

Paul and his fellow-workers preached in Philippi for "a number of days;"[89] the usual opposition from hostile Jews was missing. The church they established in Philippi was composed largely of Gentile members; they became especially devoted to Paul in later years and to them he wrote his most intimately affectionate letter.[90] However, before very long the apostles ran into trouble with certain commercial interests in the city; some men were deriving financial profit from a slave-girl who had the gift of ventriloquism and used it to make prophetic utterances. Paul put a stop to her soothsaying, thus making her masters extremely indignant. Seeing their business venture brought to a halt,

> they seized Paul and Silas, and dragged them to the public square, to the authorities, and brought them before the chief magistrates. "These men," they said, "are Jews, and they are making a great disturbance in our town. They are advocating practices which it is against the law for us as Romans to adopt or observe." The crowd also joined in the attack on them, and the magistrates had them stripped and beaten. After beating them severely, they put them in jail, and gave the jailer orders to keep close watch of them. He, having had such strict orders, put them into the inner cell, and fastened their feet in the stocks.[91]

Then, about midnight, one of the earthquakes not unusual in that region shook the jail to its very foundations, while Paul and Silas were praying and singing hymns of praise to God. When the jailer saw that the prisoners might be escaping, he was about to kill himself with his sword, when Paul reassured him that none of the criminals had escaped. The jailer was so impressed with Paul and Silas that he and all the members of his family became Christians immediately. On the next morning the magistrates sent word that Paul and Silas were to be released, but this did not satisfy Paul; he said:

> They had us beaten in public without giving us a trial, and put us in jail, although we are Roman citizens! And now, are they going to dismiss us secretly? By no means! Have them come here themselves and take us out![92]

So the authorities came themselves and took Paul and Silas out of jail, but begged them to leave town. After a brief farewell visit with the little group of new converts assembled in Lydia's house, Paul, Timothy, and Silas leave Philippi.[93]

From Philippi, Paul, Silas, and Timothy set out westward along the Via Egnatia, the great Roman highway running east and west through Macedonia. They passed through Amphipolis, the capital of the eastern section of the province, and Apollonia, and came to Thessalonica, a great seaport town at the head of the Thermaic Gulf and the capital of the entire province of Macedonia.[94] The gospel was preached by Paul in the Jewish synagogue for three Sabbaths, according to Luke,[95] but his ministry in Thessalonica must have lasted considerably longer than that; some Jews and a great many proselytes were converted, and these formed the nucleus of a virile Christian Church; then, Paul must have stayed in Thessalonica long enough for aid to have been sent to him from Philippi "more than once."[96] His success in Thessalonica was very great; a few months later, in writing to the Thessalonian Christians, Paul reminds them of how joyfully they had received him:

> And you followed the example set by us and by the Lord, for though our message brought you great trouble, you welcomed it with joy inspired by the holy Spirit, so that you set an example to all the believers in Macedonia and Greece. For the Lord's message has rung out from you not only over Macedonia and Greece, but the story of your belief in God has gone everywhere, so that we never need to mention it. For when people speak of us, they tell what a welcome you gave us, and how you turned from idols to God . . .[97]

But Paul's success inspired some Judaizers to stir up a mob of criminal loafers; they stormed the house of a man named Jason, who had had the courage to take Paul, Silas, and Timothy into his home; unfortunately for Jason, the missionaries were not at home. The mob dragged Jason and some other converts before the authorities, charging them with disturbing the peace and with disloyalty to the emperor; their words indicate the success which these Christian evangelists were having everywhere:

> The men who have made trouble all over the world have come here too, and Jason has taken them in. They all disobey the emperor's decrees, and claim that someone else called Jesus is king.[98]

Jason had to promise that there would be no further trouble from the apostles; accordingly, that same night Paul and his companions left Thessalonica.[99]

Paul's next missionary station was the populous city of Beroea, modern Verroia, more than fifty miles west of Thessalonica, on the great Via Egnatia. Here, for the first time, Paul was truly welcomed in a Jewish synagogue.[100] Many were converted, both Jews and Greeks; among the Gentile converts were several leading men and women, perhaps members of the Stoic school of philosophy.[101] But Judaizers came to Beroea from Thessalonica and stirred up the populace against Paul; leaving Silas and Timothy to continue the work of teaching the new converts, Paul went on alone, urging his two associates to come to him as soon as possible; several Christians went with him all the way to Athens,[102] a distance of some two hundred miles by water.

Evidently Paul had not intended to pursue any missionary activity in Athens; he was just waiting for Silas and Timothy to catch up with him. But he was so shocked by the many evidences of idolatry which he saw in Athens that he was impelled to speak, both in the synagogue and in the public square.[103] Because Paul kept speaking about "Jesus and the resurrection," which sounded to the Greeks like the names of a new god and goddess, some of them arranged for this "rag-picker"[104] to deliver a public address in the portico of the Agora, the civic center of Athens, where the council held its meetings.[105] Paul's famous speech in Athens was a literary and philosophical masterpiece, marked by a depth of religious insight and a liberality of thought in regard to the Gentiles which must have impressed his hearers tremendously.[106] Paul revealed his familiarity with Greek poets, and quoted approvingly the sentiment of Aratus: "For we are also his offspring."[107] However, this able address won very few converts; Luke mentions only two by name: "Dionysius, a member of the council, and a woman named Damaris."[108] Paul later revealed his consciousness of a sense of failure at Athens by writing to the Corinthian Christians:

> And I, brethren, when I came to you, came not with excellency of speech or of wisdom, declaring unto you the testimony of God.
> For I determined not to know any thing among you, save Jesus Christ, and him crucified.
> And I was with you in weakness, and in fear, and in much trembling.
> And my speech and my preaching was not with enticing words of man's wisdom, but in demonstration of the Spirit and of power:
> That your faith should not stand in the wisdom of men, but in the power of God.[109]

Without waiting for Silas and Timothy to come to him, Paul left Athens for Corinth, a journey of about fifty miles.[110]

Corinth was the capital and the chief commercial city of the province of Achaia. It was strategically located on an isthmus which connected upper and lower Achaia, with two good harbors: Cenchreae, on the Aegean Sea, and Lechaeum, on the Corinthian Gulf; to avoid sailing around the dangerous southern tip of Greece, cargoes were either carried from the Corinthian Gulf to the Aegean Sea or the ships were dragged on rollers across the isthmus. Eighteen hundred feet above the city towered the Acrocorinth, with its famous Temple of Aphrodite and its thousand sacred prostitutes, a symbol of the wild nature of pagan worship in the city. Corinth had been made a Roman colony by Julius Caesar in 46 B.C.; its population was made up of many peoples and races, among whom were many Jews. Though there were some traveling philosophers, the city was noted for its flourishing commerce and trade, its licentiousness, and its immorality. When Paul began his work in this turbulent city, he did not expect to stay long;

he wanted to return to Macedonia.[111] Yet he stayed there longer than any other city on his missionary journeys, with the exception of Ephesus; arriving some time near the spring of A.D. 50, Paul remained in Corinth eighteen months. He found a Pontian Jew, named Aquila, and his wife, Priscilla, and he made his home with them because they were of the same trade.[112] When he was settled in their home, Paul began preaching in the Jewish synagogue every Sabbath, but his word lacked vigor until Silas and Timothy brought him heartening news from Macedonia,[113] some three months after Paul's arrival in Corinth. Then Paul's preaching grew bolder, resulting in opposition from hostile Jews; ". . . as they contradicted and abused him, he shook his clothes in protest, and said to them, 'Your blood be on your own heads! I am not to blame for it! After this I will go to the heathen.' So he moved to the house of a devout proselyte named Titus Justus, which was next door to the synagogue. But Crispus, the leader of the synagogue, believed in the Lord, and so did all his household, and many of the people of Corinth heard Paul and believed and were baptized."[114] Paul had some success among his own people, but his greatest number of converts in Corinth came from the Gentiles, most of whom were slaves and freedmen.[115] From the letters Paul wrote to the Christians in Corinth two or three years later we may infer that the church which he established in that seaport city was the most vigorous and perhaps the largest of all his churches. Paul speaks of four different factions[116] and of many spiritual activities.[117] Several persons were appointed to carry their part of the collection to Jerusalem.[118] The church in Corinth caused Paul more grief, and also more satisfaction, if we can judge from his correspondence with it, than any other. Finally, in the summer or autumn of 51 A.D., hostile Jews brought Paul to trial before a newly appointed Roman governor, Gallio, brother of the famous Stoic philosopher Seneca; the charge was that Paul was persuading men to worship God in ways contrary to those prescribed by the law of Moses.[119] Gallio refused to hear the case:

If some misdemeanor or rascality were involved, Jews, you might reasonably expect me to listen to you. But as it is only a question of words and titles and your own law, you must look after it yourselves. I refuse to decide such matters.[120]

The Gentile audience then proceeded to beat up Sosthenes, the leader of the synagogue,[121] without any interference from Gallio. Early in 52, Paul left Corinth, taking Priscilla and Aquila with him as far as Ephesus.[122]

Paul walked from Corinth to Cenchreae, the eastern harbor of Corinth, where he had his hair cut short in fulfillment of a Nazirite vow.[123] Then he sailed the two hundred and fifty mile stretch across the Aegean Sea to Ephesus; here he was well received in the Jewish synagogue and was asked to stay longer, but after promising to return to them, Paul hastened to sail from Ephesus to Caesarea.[124] After a brief visit with James and Peter in Jerusalem, Paul returned to Antioch, full of wonderful news for his missionary colleagues concerning the extraordinary success he had experienced in carrying the gospel to Europe and establishing it in the chief centers of Greece and Macedonia.[125]

8.   Paul at Work in Ephesus.

According to Luke, Paul spent some time in Antioch,[126] resting from his arduous journeys and renewing acquaintances among his fellow workers. Then, "he started out again, and traveled systematically through Galatia and Phrygia, reassuring all the disciples."[127] He probably visited the Galatian churches in which he and Barnabas had first preached the gospel and which he and Silas and Timothy had visited three years earlier.[128] From Antioch in Pisidia, Paul traveled in a westerly direction toward Ephesus, probably following the valley of the Cayster river. Arriving in Ephesus, Paul was ready to fulfill the promise made earlier[129] and to begin a ministry of three years,[130] the longest time he spent in any one place on his missionary journeys.

The city of Ephesus offered to Paul the greatest opportunity of his missionary career; it was the most important city in which Paul founded a church.[131] Ephesus had been the capital of the Roman province of Asia from the time it had been organized (133 B.C.). Located three miles from the Aegean Sea on the Cayster river, it was surpassed only by Rome in size, wealth, and general influence throughout the empire. It was the religious center of Asia Minor at the time of Paul; Hellenistic mystery cults met and mingled there. Paul found in Ephesus a remnant of the followers of John the Baptizer;[132] there were wandering Jewish exorcists[133] and followers of the cult of magic.[134] But most important of all was the cult of the local goddess Artemis (Roman Diana); the temple dedicated to her, which was already three centuries old in Paul's day, was one of the seven wonders of the ancient world.[135] This impressive building was a bank and an art museum as well as a temple;[136] at its center was a great meteorite, roughly in the shape of a goddess, which was regarded as having fallen from heaven as a replica of Artemis.[137] The worship centering around the temple was very primitive; as one authority on the period has said:

> The goddess worshiped in this temple . . . was in reality a primitive nature deity whose worship was a recognition of the earth's power of fecundity. Her most sacred image was a block of wood or ivory, so old that it was fabled to have fallen from heaven, rudely carved in part into a head and a bust covered with breasts, the symbol of fertility.[138]

One of the principal industries connected with the temple was the manufacture of images and other objects connected with the worship of Artemis; these were made out of terra cotta, marble, and silver.[139] There was also a magnificent open-air theater, which had a capacity for over twenty-four thousand spectators;[140] in the vast stadium, men fought with beasts for the amusement of the multitude.[141]

In Ephesus, Paul began as usual in the Jewish synagogue, where he was allowed to speak uninterruptedly for three months; then he secured the famous lecture hall of Tyrannus for two years.[142] Paul made a great many converts among his own people, but the greater part of his success was among the Gentiles. His influence was felt not only in Ephesus, but "everyone who lived in Asia, Greeks as well as Jews, heard the Lord's message."[143] Visitors to Ephesus from other parts of the province were drawn to Paul's evangelistic addresses and returned to their homes with his gospel message; through these able assistants, Paul was able to reach prominent centers of population without actually visiting them himself.[144] His success was matched by the growing number of his adversaries; he tells the Corinthians:

> . . . I have a great and promising opportunity here, as well as many opponents.[145]

> For I do not want you, brothers, to misunderstand the distress that I experienced in Asia, for I was so utterly and unendurably crushed, that I actually despaired of life itself.[146]

The extent of his influence in Ephesus is indicated by Luke's story of the collapse of magic; Paul confounded the Jewish exorcists and influenced many magicians to burn their books on magic.[147] Paul was able to supplement his public appearances with visits to the homes of interested people, both Jews and Gentiles.[148] He worked at his trade of tent making and earned more than enough for his own needs, so that he could contribute to the support of others.[149] One of the imprisonments Paul mentions in II Corinthians 11:23 may well have occurred at Ephesus.

It was while he was at Ephesus, perhaps during the year 53 or 54, that Paul had his correspondence with the troublous church at Corinth. This literary activity involves at least four letters, of which three are preserved in the New Testament, visits by Timothy and Titus, and perhaps a hasty journey by Paul himself. The first letter is the so-called "lost letter," mentioned by Paul in I Corinthians 5:9.[150] Then Paul wrote his second letter, our present I Corinthians, following it later with a letter answering certain slanders they had raised against him (II Corinthians 10-13); delivered by Titus, the third letter improved the situation at Corinth, leading Paul to write a fourth and last letter, II Corinthians 1-9, probably from Macedonia while impatiently awaiting Titus' return. The final letter was followed almost immediately by Paul's arrival in Corinth.

As in Philippi,[151] Paul's work in Ephesus was brought to an abrupt close by a group of Gentiles whose business had suffered because of his preaching. Opposition to him was led by a silversmith named Demetrius, who gathered his fellow laborers together and inspired them to action with an impassioned speech:

> Men, you know that this business is the source of our prosperity, and you see and hear that not only in Ephesus but almost all over Asia, this man Paul has persuaded and drawn away numbers of people, telling him that gods made by human hands are not gods at all. There is danger, therefore, not only that this business of ours will be discredited, but also that the temple of the great goddess Artemis will be neglected and

the magnificence of her whom all Asia and the world worship will be a thing of the past![152]

They went out and stirred up a mob in the city streets, and in great confusion all rushed toward the theater, chanting "Great Artemis of Ephesus!" over and over again.[153] Most of those in the theater did not know why they were there.[154] A Jew named Alexander failed in his attempt to quiet the mob, but after two more hours of shouting, the recorder stopped the riot with a speech and sent the mob home.[155] Though Paul had been exonerated, he felt that his work at Ephesus was over, and he made his preparations to leave for Macedonia.[156]

9. Paul's Second Trip to Europe and Return.

When Paul left Ephesus he had an ambitious project in mind; to revisit Macedonia and Greece, to go to Jerusalem with a collection for the poor of that city, and after that to travel to Rome and Spain.[157] Accordingly we find him, in *ca*. A.D. 55, traveling northward from Ephesus toward Troas, where he found a good opportunity to preach the gospel but could not put his heart into it because of his anxiety over the situation in Corinth.[158] He crossed over into Macedonia, where Titus finally met him, perhaps in Philippi, and brought him good news from Corinth.[159] Paul spent some time in Macedonia, "giving the people a great deal of encouragement;"[160] he sent Titus and two other brothers on to Corinth to arrange for the collection there,[161] while he followed them himself in a short time.[162] Paul stayed in Corinth three months, where he was entertained by Gaius.[163] Here he wrote the most systematic letter and the most complete statement of his theology in all his writings: his famous letter to the Romans; he had not yet visited the church in the capital city of the empire, but in Corinth his thoughts and plans turn westward and he tells the Christians in Rome that he hopes to preach the gospel in that city.[164]

Paul had hoped to return to Jerusalem with the collection in time to participate in the celebration of Pentecost in the spring of 56 A.D. For this reason, he told the Roman Christians, he could not continue westward at this time:

Just now I am starting for Jerusalem, to take help to God's people. For Macedonia and Greece have determined to make a contribution for the poor among God's people in Jerusalem . . . So when I have finished this matter and see this contribution safely in their possession, I will start for Spain, and come to you on the way . . .[165]

At first he planned to sail directly to Syria, but "the Jews made a plot against him, and he made up his mind to return by way of Macedonia."[166] The committee of seven men designated by the churches to carry their contribution to Jerusalem went across the Aegean Sea, where they waited for Paul at Troas.[167] Paul went by land to Philippi, from which Macedonian city he and Luke sailed after the days of unleavened bread, early in April,[168] and joined the rest at Troas. There was a delay of a week at Troas, during which time an interesting episode took place; while Paul was preaching late one night, a young man named Eutychus fell out of an upstairs window and was presumed dead; Paul revived him, and the entire company assembled again in the upstairs room and continued the conversation until dawn.[169]

From Troas the party sailed along the western coast of Asia Minor for several days. Stopping at Miletus, about thirty-five miles from Ephesus at the mouth of the Maeander river, Paul summoned the elders of the Ephesian church to come and see him, and he delivered to them a movingly beautiful farewell address.[170] The speech presents a vivid picture of the personality of Paul—the apostle as an evangelist, pastor, teacher, prophet, toiler, man of courage, man of prayer, noble companion, affectionate and loyal friend. In it, Paul reveals the apprehensive feelings he had concerning the fate in store for him in Jerusalem; he is afraid, as he had told the Romans,[171] that some kind of suffering awaited him in the stronghold of Judaism.

. . . I am here now on my way to Jerusalem, for the Spirit compels me to go there, though I do not know what will happen to me there, except that in every town I visit, the holy Spirit warns me that imprisonment and persecution are awaiting me. But my life does not matter, if I can only finish my race and do the service intrusted to me by the Lord Jesus, of declaring the good news of God's favor. Now I know perfectly well that none of you among whom I went about preaching the Kingdom of God will ever see my face again . . .[172]

After these words, Paul knelt down with the elders and prayed.

They all wept aloud, and throwing their arms about Paul's neck they kissed him affectionately, for they were especially saddened at his saying that they would never see his face again. Then they accompanied him to the ship.[173]

After sailing among some of the other islands in the Aegean Sea off the west coast of Asia Minor, Paul and his party finally reached Tyre.[174] Here they stayed a week, meeting with the Christian disciples in their homes; these friends "warned Paul not to set foot in Jerusalem,"[175] but he would not be dissuaded. After a touching farewell with all their families on the beach, Paul went on board his ship and sailed for Caesarea. Here again Paul was warned not to go to Jerusalem, this time by a prophet named Agabus,[176] but Paul stated his intentions of dying, if necessary, for his master's sake. With this, his followers gave up trying to restrain him, and they made preparations for the journey by land to Jerusalem.

10.   Arrest in Jerusalem and Imprisonment in Caesarea

When Paul and his followers reached Jerusalem, they were gladly received at first.[177] On the day after his arrival, Paul gave a full report of his work before James and the other leaders of the Jerusalem church.[178] They rejoiced with him over the growth of the gospel in Gentile lands, but they informed Paul that the Jewish converts to the church had also grown in numbers and that unfavorable reports had been circulating concerning Paul and his teaching; they said to him:

You see, brother, how many thousand believers there are among the Jews, all of them zealous upholders of the Law. They have been told that you teach all Jews who live among the heathen to turn away from Moses, and that you tell them not to circumcise their children nor to observe the old customs. What then? They will be sure to hear that you have come. So do what we tell you. We have four men here who are under a vow. Join them, undergo the rites of purification with them, and pay their expenses so that they can have their heads shaved. Then everybody will understand that there is no truth in the stories about you, but that you yourself observe the Law . . .[179]

Paul readily consented to the proposition, in order to show that the charges circulating against him were false.[180] The ceremonies lasted a week and were almost over when some Ephesian Jews caught sight of him in the temple; they had seen him out in the city in the company of Trophimus, a Gentile from Ephesus, so they concluded that Paul was taking an uncircumcised Greek into the temple, a deadly offense. So they seized him, and shouted:

Men of Israel, help! This is the man who teaches everybody everywhere against our people and the Law and this place, and besides he has actually brought Greeks into the Temple and desecrated this sacred place.[181]

The mob dragged Paul into the Court of the Gentiles and was trying to kill him, when word came to the Roman troops stationed in the Castle of Antonia, located at the northwest corner of the temple area, that there was a riot; immediately Claudius Lysias, the colonel of the regiment, gathered some officers and men and hurried down into the Court of the Gentiles and rescued Paul.[182] The Roman soldiers did not intervene out of sympathy with Paul, but because it was their chief duty to preserve order; the colonel may have thought that the riot might be a continuation of a recent rebellion led by an Egyptian.[183]

Claudius Lysias arrested Paul for disturbing the peace, binding him with chains to a soldier on either side; then he asked the bystanders what he had done, but, making no sense out of the confusing and contradictory statements made by the mob, the Roman colonel ordered Paul to be taken up the stairs to the Castle itself, while the crowd shouted: "Kill him!"[184] At the top of the stairs, Paul begs the startled Lysias for permission to speak to the crowd; granted, Paul delivers one of his famous speeches, in which he recounts how he had persecuted the disciples of Jesus and then been converted on the road to Damascus.[185] They listened respectfully until Paul mentioned that his mission had been to the heathen; then they shouted:

Kill him and get him out of the world! A creature like that ought not to be allowed to live![186]

Whereupon the Roman colonel hastened Paul into the Castle, giving orders to have him lashed in order to extricate from him the reason for all the disturbance. Just as they were ready to apply the whip, Paul announced that he was a Roman citizen; this put a stop to such ignominious punishment.[187]

On the next day, Claudius Lysias took Paul before the Jewish Sanhedrin, not because it had any legal jurisdiction over Paul, but because the Roman colonel wished to determine for himself whether Paul was guilty or innocent. Paul began his defense by saying that he had done everything "with a perfectly clear conscience."[188] Somehow the presiding high priest, Ananias,[189] felt that Paul's statement was worthy of censure and ordered those standing nearest him to strike Paul on the mouth. This provoked Paul to give vent to some very un-Christlike words:

God will strike you, you white-washed wall! Do you sit there to try me by the Law, and order them to strike me in violation of the Law?[190]

Then Paul proceeded to take advantage of the well-known hostility between Sadducees and Pharisees over the question of the resurrection, by asserting that he was a Pharisee and hence believed in the resurrection; this created such an uproar that Lysias once again had to rescue Paul by taking him back into the Castle;[191] the Roman colonel must have been convinced that the Sanhedrin was not capable of passing judgment on Paul.

The next move on the part of Paul's enemies was a conspiracy on the part of more than forty of them to kill Paul; they resolved not to eat nor drink until they had accomplished their intention. They hoped to get Paul out of the Castle on the pretext of giving him another hearing before the Sanhedrin, but Paul's nephew warned Paul and the colonel of the ambush, and the latter decided to take Paul under armed escort to Caesarea, the capital of the Roman province of Judea and the residence of the Roman procurator Felix.[192]

Five days after his arrival at Caesarea, the high priest Ananias and other Jews from Jerusalem appeared before Felix with an attorney, a Roman named Tertullus. After a few words of flattery directed toward the procurator, Tertullus preferred against Paul in behalf of his Jewish opponents:

> ... We have found this man a pest and a disturber of the peace among Jews all over the world. He is a ringleader of the Nazarene sect, and actually tried to desecrate the Temple, but we caught him . . .[193]

Paul's reply was courteous, direct, and sincere; he denied that he was an insurrectionist; he admitted that he belonged to the sect of the Nazarenes, but that did not seem to him to be contrary to the law; he did not desecrate the temple; and he pointed out that the Sanhedrin had found nothing against him.[194] This convinced the procurator of Paul's innocence, but for some unknown reason he decided to defer his decision until he could consult further with Claudius Lysias.[195] This is the beginning of Paul's two years of imprisonment at Caesarea; he was kept under guard, but he was allowed to live in his own quarters and enjoyed many privileges, such as visits from his friends.[196] Luke records nothing of any of Paul's activities during these two years except that Felix summoned him several times, hoping to get money out of Paul;[197] on one occasion, Drusilla, the wife of Felix, was present, and Paul frightened the procurator by mentioning a future day of judgment.[198]

Some time between 58 and 60 A.D., the inept Felix was succeeded by the abler Festus, who was appointed procurator of Judea by the emperor Nero.[199] Unfamiliar with Jewish affairs, the new governor conferred immediately with authorities in Jerusalem, but he would not agree to transferring Paul from Caesarea to Jerualem for trial. Instead, Paul's enemies came once more to Caesarea and laid their charges against him before Festus.[200] Paul categorically denied all the charges, and, when asked by Festus if he would willingly stand trial in Jerusalem, he made his famous appeal to the emperor, which was the right of every Roman citizen: "I am standing before the emperor's court, where I ought to be tried. I have done the Jews no wrong, as you can easily see. If I am guilty and have done anything that deserves death, I do not refuse to die; but if there is no truth in the charges that these men make against me, no one can give me up to them; I appeal to the emperor."[201] Having heard Paul's appeal, Festus had nothing left to do but grant it.[202]

While arrangements were being made for Paul and a few other prisoners to be transported to Rome, Festus was paid a state visit by Herod Agrippa II and his sister Bernice.[203] Festus told Agrippa about Paul and how difficult it was for him to find a suitable accusation against the apostle to send along with him to the emperor. Agrippa expressed a desire to hear the prisoner; accordingly, Paul was brought before the two rulers and all their royal retinue.[204] After being given permission to speak, Paul delivered a lengthy address, which, like the one he gave on the Castle stairs,[205] contained an account of his life as a Pharisee and recounted his mystical experience on the road to Damascus.[206] At the end of this recital, Agrippa pronounced Paul innocent: "He might have been set at liberty, if he had not appealed to the emperor."[207] And to Rome he must be sent.

11. The Voyage to Rome.

Luke's story of Paul's journey as a prisoner to Rome, with its vivid narrative of the shipwreck, is one of the most dramatic passages in the Bible.[208] Paul and the other prisoners were placed in the custody of Julius, a kind-hearted Roman centurion, an officer of the imperial regiment.[209] Because of delays in Caesarea, it was early September, possibly in the year 58, before they were placed aboard a ship leaving Caesarea for the coastwise ports of Asia Minor.[210] In addition to Luke, Paul had Aristarchus, a Christian from Macedonia, as a companion.[211] At Myra in Lycia, Julius transferred the group to an Alexandrian ship bound for Italy; this was one of a fleet of grain vessels taking cargoes of wheat from Alexandria to Rome.[212] Because of adverse winds, the captain sailed southward along the island of Crete and, after a voyage of some three hundred and twenty-five miles from Myra, found shelter in the harbor of Fair Havens, located about midway of the length of Crete on the southern shore.[213] Here Paul recommended that the party spend the winter,[214] but Julius followed the majority opinion, including those of the pilot and the captain, which was that Phoenix, a harbor some sixty miles to the west, was a much more attractive place to winter.[215] With a favorable south wind, they set sail, keeping close to the coast of Crete, but as soon as they tried to get around Cape Matala, a violent north-easter swept down from the mountains and drove them out to sea. It looked as if the gale would sweep the little boat across to the northern shores of the continent of Africa; they could not secure the ship's small boat on shipboard until they passed near the small island of Cauda.[216] Luke continues:

> . . . The next day, as the storm continued to be violent, they began to throw the cargo overboard, and on the next, they threw the ship's tackle overboard with their own hands. For a number of days neither the sun nor the stars were visible, and the storm continued to rage, until at last we gave up all hope of being saved. Then, when they had gone a long time without food, Paul got up among them, and said,
> "Gentlemen, you ought to have listened to me and not to have sailed from Crete and incurred this disaster and loss. Even now, I beg you to keep up your courage, for there will be no loss of life among you, but only of the ship. . . For I have faith in God that it will be just as I was told. But we are to be stranded on some island."[217]

Paul was again shown to be the master of the situation by an episode which occurred about the middle of the fourteenth night after they left Crete; the sailors had lowered the lifeboat, pretending that they were going to cast off anchors from the bow, but really intending to abandon the ship. Paul exposed their plan to Julius, who ordered his soldiers to cut the boat's ropes and let it drop into the sea.[218] That same night, Paul persuaded all on board to take food, and they did so, following his example.[219]

Next morning, the ship was wrecked on the north shore of the island of Malta, about fifty-eight miles south of Sicily, in a place now known as St. Paul's Bay.

> . . . When daylight came they could not recognize the coast, but they saw a bay with a beach and determined to run the ship ashore there if possible. So they cast off the anchors and left them in the sea, at the same time they undid the lashings of the steering oars, and hoisting the foresail to the wind, they made for the beach. But they struck a shoal and ran the ship aground. The bow struck and could not be moved, while the stern began to break up under the strain. The

soldiers proposed to kill the prisoners, for fear some of them
might swim ashore and escape, but the officer wanted to save
Paul, and so he prevented them from doing this, and ordered
all who could swim to jump overboard first and get to the
land, and the rest to follow on planks or other pieces of
wreckage. So they all got safely to land.[220]

Paul and his fellow-travelers were obliged to stay on the island
of Malta for three months following the shipwreck, perhaps until
the early part of February, 59. The inhabitants treated them
kindly, building a fire to warm them and dry their clothes;
while helping them in this operation, Paul was bitten by a snake.
The superstitious aborigines thought he was a murderer and
was receiving his just punishment; but after they saw Paul shake
the creature off into the fire, while he himself was unharmed, they
changed their minds and decided he was a god.[221] The governor
of Malta, Publius, entertained them hospitably; Paul reciprocated
by healing his father of a severe illness and curing others who were
afflicted with various diseases.[222]

The ship on which Paul, Julius, and the rest left Malta was bound
from Alexandria to Rome, just like the one which had been wrecked,
and had spent the winter in one of the harbors on Malta. After
touching Syracuse and Rhegium, the party landed on Italian soil
at Puteoli, just north of the modern city of Naples. After a week
visiting the Christians in Puteoli, Paul proceeded to travel the
remaining one hundred and twenty-nine miles to Rome by land;
some of the Roman Christians came out of the capital city to meet
him, one group going down the Via Appia thirty miles to Three
Taverns and another group traveling forty miles to Appius' Forum.
Their gracious welcome of the weary apostle seemed to make all
his past efforts worthwhile.[223]

12. The Closing Years of Paul's Life.

For events in the life of Paul after his arrival in Rome the Book
of Acts is of very little help; in fact, the closing years of his life,
like those of his youth, are hidden from our view. Luke does tell
us that Paul met with Jewish leaders, that most of them did not
accept the gospel, and that he then turned to the Gentiles.[224] He
tells us further that Paul stayed "for two full years in rented lodg-

ings of his own,"[225] he was guarded by a soldier, apparently being bound to him by a chain, but aside from that he was at liberty to preach and write, and receive all whom he wished.[226] But with that the Book of Acts breaks off. The letters Paul wrote from his Roman imprisonment—Colossians, Philemon, and Philippians—give us more information than Acts concerning this period. From them we learn who his companions were: Timothy,[227] Mark, Aristarchus, Demas, Luke,[228] Epaphras,[229] Tychicus,[230] Onesimus,[231] and Epaphroditus.[232] He tells the Philippians that he has been successful in preaching the gospel:

> Now I want to assure you, brothers, that what has happened to me has actually resulted in furthering the preaching of the good news. Thus it is generally known throughout the Imperial Guard and elsewhere that it is for the sake of Christ that I am in prison, and so most of the Christian brothers have been exceedingly encouraged by my example to declare God's message without fear of the consequences.
>
> Some of them, it is true, are actually preaching the Christ from jealousy and partisanship, but there are others who are doing it out of good-will. These latter do it from love for me, for they know that God has put me where I am to defend our right to preach the good news. But the others are preaching the Christ not sincerely but for their own ends, imagining that they are making my imprisonment harder to bear.
>
> But what difference does it make? All that matters is that, in one way or another, from false motives or honest ones, Christ is being made known; I am glad of that . . .[233]

Paul is uncertain about the outcome of his own case; he is ready to die for Christ, yet he could see that for his work it was necessary for him to live, and he hopes to visit Philippi again as well as continue to hear news from them.[234]

What happened to Paul in 61 A.D., at the end of two years' imprisonment in Rome? Scholars are still divided in their answers to that question. In the main, there are three possible solutions, depending on whether the pastoral letters are considered genuinely Pauline or not. Those who accept I and II Timothy and Titus as authentic letters of Paul's commonly assume either that Paul was acquitted at an initial hearing before Nero's tribunal, followed by further extensive missionary travels, or that it was impossible for his enemies to obtain enough evidence against him to bring him to trial at all and that the case against him fell by default.[235] In support of the point of view that Paul was never brought to trial at all, William H. P. Hatch presents four considerations:

> (a) It would have been necessary to bring Paul's accusers and the witnesses in the case from Jerusalem to Rome; (b) the offenses charged against the apostle were allegedly committed several years earlier; (c) these alleged offenses were mostly infractions of the Mosaic Law, with which the Roman authorities did not concern themselves; (d) according to the author of Acts, the Jews in Rome knew of no evil that Paul had done (Acts 28:21), and they were not hostile to him.[236]

George Holley Gilbert[237] believes that Paul was brought to trial and acquitted. In either case, Paul would be free to travel about and carry on further missionary work. He may have visited Ephesus and Macedonia (I Timothy 1:3; 3:14; 4:13; II Timothy 1:18), Miletus (II Timothy 4:20), Troas (II Timothy 4:13), Corinth (II Timothy 4:20), Crete (Titus 1:5), perhaps Nicopolis (Titus 3:12), and possibly Spain.[238] After this, it is assumed that Paul was rearrested, perhaps on a charge of sedition against the state, condemned, and executed in 64 A.D. during the Neronian persecution. According to this point of view, I Timothy and Titus were written during the interval when Paul was free to travel and II Timothy during his second imprisonment, which was altogether unlike the first. Only Luke was with him (II Timothy 4:11; cf. 1:15; 4:10,16). He was probably in extreme peril and his confinement, unlike the first, was full of discomfort and pain (II Timothy 1:8,12,16; 2:3,9-12). Paul's words are full of foreboding:

> My life is already being poured out, and the time has come for my departure. I have had a part in the great contest, I have run my race, I have preserved my faith. Now the crown of uprightness awaits me, which the Lord, the upright judge, will award me on that Day, and not only me but also all who have loved and hoped for his appearing.[239]

The end is in sight; he implores Timothy:

Do your best to come to me soon, . . . Get Mark and bring him with you, for he is of great assistance to me,[240] . . . When you come, bring the cloak that I left with Carpus at Troas, and the books, especially the parchments . . . Do your best to come before winter.[241]

"Whether Paul lived to greet Timothy and to read in the precious books which Timothy was directed to bring, cannot be determined. Nothing is known of the time or circumstances of the final trial . . . Thus the close of Paul's life is veiled from our eyes, but no cloud dims, or ever can dim, the splendor of the services of that life for God and for humanity."[242]

If the pastoral letters are not Paul's—a position held by most modern scholars, because the theological ideas and the indications of a more complex ecclesiastical organization in them reflect a date later than Paul's time—then there is no evidence, at least in the New Testament, of any further missionary activity on the part of Paul. Even if the pastorals contain certain genuinely Pauline fragments, as seems likely, any references in the fragments to Paul's missionary activity are probably variants of situations in Paul's life before his voyage to Rome. Luke concludes his story of Paul's farewell address to the Ephesian elders at Miletus with the words: "They all wept aloud, . . . for they were especially saddened at his saying that they would never see his face again."[243] Macgregor affirms that "it is difficult to believe that Luke would have given us so solemn and affecting an account of the farewell, had he not known that in fact Paul did not return . . . Complete silence as to an acquittal, not only by all other sources but above all by Luke himself, seems conclusive evidence of condemnation. For Luke the account of such an acquittal would have provided a magnificent climax to a story throughout which he has been consistently concerned to stress the favorable impression which Paul always made on Roman authority.[244] Had he known that Paul had been triumphantly exonerated, it is inconceivable that he should have omitted to tell us so. Such a triumph, moreover, must have been widely known in the church; yet it is not mentioned by one single early writer. This consideration alone almost compels us to pronounce Paul's alleged acquittal to be a fiction, and to conclude that his two years' captivity ended with conviction and death."[245] Luke does not mention Paul's condemnation and trial, because to do so would have defeated the purpose he had in mind in writing Luke-Acts: to commend Christianity to the Roman world; if the chief hero of his story were known to have been killed as an enemy of the state, the Romans would not have been attracted to the new religion.

Of this much we are certain: Paul was beheaded in Rome during the reign of Nero. When I Clement was written—*ca.* A.D. 95—the Corinthian church was informed that Paul and Peter were the greatest martyrs of the Roman church. Irenaeus, whose information depends upon Polycarp, links the name of Paul with that of Peter as martyrs of the faith. Ignatius of Antioch, in his letter to the Ephesians, Tertullian of Carthage, Origen of Alexandria, Eusebius of Caesarea, the father of church history,[246] Dionysius of Corinth (*ca.* 170), and Gaius of Rome (early in the third century)[247] all bear witness to the unanimous tradition in antiquity that Paul suffered the fate of martyrdom in Rome under Nero. It probably occurred before the great Neronian persecution of 64 A.D., perhaps in the year 62. As Paul knelt with bowed head before the Roman executioner, it looked as if it might be the end; but in the light of subsequent history of the movement he did so much to spread, it was only the beginning. He was now able to have fellowship with his beloved Lord and illustrate what he had written earlier to the Roman Christians:

> . . . Who can separate us from Christ's love? Can trouble or misfortune or persecution or hunger or destitution or danger or the sword? . . . But in all these things we are more than victorious through him who loved us. For I am convinced that neither death nor life . . . will be able to separate us from the love God has shown in Christ Jesus our Lord![248]

B. *The Letters of Paul*

1. The Pattern of the Letters

When Paul began to write letters, probably in the spring of 50 A.D.,[249] he was not adopting a new literary device. Many thousands of ancient letters have been recovered from the rubbish heaps of Egypt. Some of them were written between emperors and high government officials;[250] some were written by great authors, such as Cicero and Epicurus; most of them were ordinary letters written from one person to another as occasion required. Though the imperial post carried only official communications of the empire, the protection of roads necessary to make it function properly encouraged individuals to send and receive letters, entrusting them to travelers for delivery as they made their way from city to city. In Paul's case, Titus, Tychicus, Epaphroditus, and Onesimus were among those who bore his letters with them as they traveled.

In form, Paul's letters follow the epistolary style of the time. The writer's name came first—just the reverse of our modern letters—and was followed by the name of the person to whom it was addressed. "Paul, a prisoner for Jesus Christ, . . . to our dear fellow-worker Philemon;"[251] "Paul, a slave of Jesus Christ, . . . to all those in Rome whom God loves;"[252] "Paul, by the will of God called as an apostle of Jesus Christ . . . to the church of God at Corinth"[253] are typical ways in which Paul opens his letters. Paul omits the place and date of writing; after all, his readers would know. Sometimes in these salutations two or three writers are named; this does not mean that they took an active part in composing the letter, but that they join him in greeting the addressee.[254] In contrast with the short "Dear Sirs" and other forms of greeting in modern letters, Paul's salutations are usually lengthy and involve some doctrinal ideas; the longest one is at the beginning of his letter to the Romans:

> Paul, a slave of Jesus Christ, called as an apostle, set apart to declare God's good news, which he promised long ago through his prophets in the holy Scriptures, about his Son, who was physically descended from David, and decisively declared Son of God in his holiness of spirit, by being raised from the dead—Jesus Christ our Lord, through whom we have received God's favor and been commissioned in his name to urge obedience and faith upon all the heathen, including you who have been called to belong to Jesus Christ—to all those in Rome whom God loves, who are called to be his people; God our Father and the Lord Jesus Christ bless you and give you peace.[255]

Following the salutation, there is in all of Paul's letters, with the exception of Galatians, a paragraph of thanksgiving, in which Paul expresses affectionate interest in the person or church to whom he is writing. This section of his first letter to the church at Thessalonica begins with the words "We always thank God for you all when we mention you in our prayers, . . ."[256] In his personal letter to Philemon, Paul reveals a keen insight into human nature, when he finds a great deal about Philemon for which he can be grateful, before he asks him to do him a favor:

> I never mention you in my prayers without thanking my God for what I hear of the love and faith you have in the Lord Jesus and all his people, and I pray that through coming to know every good thing about us as Christians they may effectually share your faith. I have been greatly pleased and encouraged over your love, for the hearts of God's people have been cheered, my brother, by you.[257]

Then there is a section in the letters in which Paul deals with the specific matters which have occasioned the letters;[258] this is the theological part of his letters, in which Paul relates all the questions under discussion to the basic beliefs of the Christian faith.[259] Next, in most of the letters, before the conclusion, Paul writes a section of practical ethical advice and exhortation without any apparent specific relationship with the church to which he is writing.[260] Paul's letters close with a paragraph of personal greetings[261] and a benediction.[262]

As a rule, Paul's method of writing his letters was by dictating his words to an amanuensis, a professional letter writer. This is apparent from reading his letters; except for Romans and chapters thirteen and fifteen of I Corinthians, which bear the mark of careful preparation, the letters are rough and wordy, as might be expected from having them hurriedly dictated. He did not realize that he was writing materials which would some day be considered sacred scripture; he did not feel the necessity of correcting and polishing letters which to him were concerned only with personal and church problems of a temporary nature. Sometimes at the end of a letter, Paul would himself take the pen from the amanuensis and add something in his own hand.[263] Usually the letters of Paul were intended to be read aloud in the assemblies of the churches to which they were addressed; this may help to explain why, in many respects, their style is that of spoken language, "the characteristic formlessness of which can be traced in Paul's writings, e.g. in the interjected corrections of himself (as in I Corinthians 1:16), in incomplete sentences (Romans 5:12), and in the heaping up of pointed expressions (e.g. Colossians 2:20-23) the reference of which was comprehensible to the readers, but which we should only be able to explain with complete certainty if we knew the tone and gestures employed by Paul when he dictated . . ."[264]

Traditionally the number of Paul's letters in the New Testament has been considered to be fourteen: Romans, I and II Corinthians, Galatians, Ephesians, Philippians, Colossians, I and II Thessalonians, I and II Timothy, Titus, Philemon, and Hebrews. Paul's authorship of the book of Hebrews was never taken quite seriously; both in language and content it shows that it is not the work of the apostle and was never intended so to be understood.[265] The pastoral letters—I and II Timothy and Titus—cannot be regarded as Pauline in authorship, at least in their present form; however, they probably grew out of fragmentary notes of his, which scholars can still detect.[266] Of the remaining ten, the letter to Ephesians is now considered by many scholars to be pseudonymous, largely because it was intended to be a circular letter and because it duplicates much of what Paul has already said in his letter to the Colossians.[267] Thus, there are nine letters in the New Testament which almost every scholar admits come directly from the pen of Paul: I and II Thessalonians, Galatians, I and II Corinthians, Romans, Philippians, Colossians, and Philemon; four others may be in part Pauline: Ephesians, I and II Timothy, and Titus. Besides these, Paul wrote many other letters which have been lost; to some of these he makes reference in his extant letters;[268] it is possible that some fragments of these have found their way into the letters we still have.[269]

2.   Letters Written from Corinth *ca.* 50 A.D.

As we have already seen,[270] Christian literature began in the spring of the year 50 A.D., just after Paul arrived in the city of Corinth to begin his stay of eighteen months in that Greek city. A scant twenty years after the crucifixion of Jesus, Paul wrote I Thessalonians, the earliest of his letters and the oldest Christian writing which now survives. In it we see Paul's concern for a primitive Christian community in actual operation: his memories of fellowship with those who had been Christians a very short time; his fears for their faith; the problems he sought to solve for them; the doctrines he had stressed when he had first preached to them;

and the attitudes he now assumes toward them. The church in
Thessalonica had been the second one founded by Paul on the
continent of Europe;[271] he was pleased with the results of his work
there, but he was anxious for the welfare of those of whom he had
had to take leave too soon. From Athens Paul had sent Timothy to
Thessalonica to strengthen them in the faith and to encourage them
to stand fast in all their troubles.[272] Timothy brought to Paul in
Corinth a report that the Christians in Thessalonica were getting
along fine; this led Paul to write his earliest letter, encouraging
the Thessalonians in their faith and giving them further counsel
and instruction in Christian living. He expresses his joy thus:

> But now that Timothy has just come back to me from you,
> and brought me good news of your faith and love, and told me
> how kindly you think of me and that you long to see me just
> as much as I long to see you, I feel encouraged, brothers, about
> you, in spite of all my distress and trouble, at your faith, for
> now I can really live, since you are standing firm in the
> Lord . . .[273]

The content of I Thessalonians is summarized in a single verse:
"We beg you, brothers, warn the idlers, cheer up the despondent,
keep hold of the weak, be patient with everybody."[274] The "weak"
were apparently those who had been converted from "paganism"
to Christianity and had attempted to carry over into their new pattern of living certain characteristics from their former way of life.
Paul's advice to them is:

> It is God's will that you should be consecrated, that you
> abstain from immorality, that each of you learn to take a wife
> for himself from pure and honorable motives, not to gratify his
> passion, like the heathen who know nothing of God. No one
> is to wrong or defraud his brother in this matter, for the Lord
> avenges all such things, as we told you before, in the most
> solemn terms. God has not called us to an unclean life, but to
> a pure one. So whoever disregards this is not disregarding man,
> but God, who gives you his holy Spirit.[275]

The "despondent" may have been those who were worried because
the end of the world had not come as soon as Paul had said it
would; some of their fellow Christians had died, and they were

afraid they would not share in the joyous event when it came. To their anxieties Paul gave this answer:

> We do not want you to be under any misapprehension, brothers, about those who are falling asleep. You must not grieve for them, as others do who have no hope. For if we believe that Jesus died and rose again, then by means of Jesus God will bring back with him those who have fallen asleep. For we can assure you, on the Lord's own authority, that those of us who will still be living when the Lord comes will have no advantage over those who have fallen asleep. For the Lord himself, at the summons, when the archangel calls and God's trumpet sounds, will come down from heaven, and first those who died in union with Christ will rise; then those of us who are still living will be caught up with them on clouds into the air to meet the Lord, and so we shall be with the Lord forever. Therefore, encourage one another with this truth.[276]

The "idlers" were those who had quit work because of the imminence of the return of Jesus; Paul advises them to

> surpass yourselves in striving to live quietly and mind your own affairs, and work with your hands, as we directed you, so that you may have the respect of the outsiders and not be dependent upon anybody.[277]

Paul expresses his gratitude that the Thessalonian Christians had been enduring persecution,[278] but had stood firm in their faith.[279] He includes in the letter some concise exhortations to upright moral living:

> We beg you, brothers, to respect those who work with you and who lead you in the service of the Lord, and teach you. Hold them in the highest esteem and affection for what they do. Live at peace with one another. We beg you, brothers, warn the idlers, cheer up the despondent. Keep hold of the weak, be patient with everybody. Take care that none of you ever pays back evil for evil, but always try to treat one another and everybody with kindness. Always be joyful. Never give up praying. Thank God for whatever happens. For this is what God through Christ Jesus wants you to do. Do not stifle the Spirit. Do not disregard the utterances it inspires, but test

them all, retaining what is good and avoiding every kind of evil.[280]

A few weeks after Paul had written I Thessalonians, some one brought him word that conditions in Thessalonica had grown worse. Letters were being circulated with Paul's name on them which contradicted all he had taught concerning the end of the age and said that the Day of the Lord had already come.[281] Some had misunderstood Paul's message in his first letter; consoled by his words that Jesus would return soon, some were preparing themselves by quitting work; others were disorderly. So Paul wrote II Thessalonians to try to comfort and encourage the faithful, clear up all misconceptions concerning the return of Christ, and to strengthen the discipline of the church. After he tells them that the Lord will surely come, but the time is not yet at hand,[282] Paul gives expression to a common sense philosophy of labor:

> We charge you brothers, in the name of the Lord Jesus Christ, to keep away from any brother who lives in idleness, instead of following the teaching you received from us. For you know yourselves what you must do to follow my example, for I was not idle when I was with you; I did not eat anybody's bread without paying for it, but with toil and labor I worked night and day, in order not to be a burden to any of you. Not that I had not a right to my own support, but to give you in my own conduct an example to imitate. When I was with you, I gave you this rule: "If anyone refuses to work, give him nothing to eat." For we hear that some of you are living in idleness, mere busybodies, not doing any work. Now with the authority of the Lord Jesus Christ we charge and exhort such people to keep quiet and do their work and earn their own living. But you, brothers, must not get tired of doing right.[283]

While Paul was still at Corinth,[284] in the year 50 or 51 A.D., he may have written his famous letter to the Galatians. The most autobiographical of Paul's letters, Galatians is one of the principal sources of our knowledge of Paul and of his religion. If the so-called "South Galatian Theory" is correct, the Galatians were the Christians in the cities of Antioch in Pisidia, Iconium, Lystra, and Derbe, which Paul had first visited with Barnabas on an earlier missionary journey and which he had revisited before he had begun his European campaign.[285] Paul had heard that these new Christians had been violently upset by conservative Judaizers who were contradicting his gospel and who were preaching that, in addition to believing that Jesus was the Messiah, converts to Christianity must also observe the customs and laws of Moses.[286] Then there were the antilegalists in Galatia who thought that Paul was introducing a new form of slavery to law by insisting that new converts crucify their old sinful nature and produce the fruit of the Spirit.[287] Paul replies to these critics in a letter which is one long outburst of indignant remonstrance; out of the white heat of his convictions Paul declares his "religious independence from men and dependence on God. It is the Magna Charta of the Christian faith, repudiating all authorities, institutions, customs, and laws that interfere with the direct access of the individual to his God."[288] His enemies had questioned Paul's right to be an apostle; hence, his salutation vindicates his apostolic authority and states the theme of the letter:

> Paul, an apostle not from men nor sent by any man, but by Jesus Christ and God the Father who raised him from the dead— . . .; blessing and peace to you from God our Father and the Lord Jesus Christ, who to save us from the present wicked world gave himself for our sins at the will of our God and Father. To him be glory forever and ever! Amen.[289]

In his description of the contrast between law and grace, Paul gives expression to one of the most formative ideas in the history of religion: justification by faith:

> For there is a curse upon all who rely on obedience to the Law, for the Scripture says, "Cursed be anyone who does not stand by everything that is written in the Book of the Law and obey it."[290] That no one is accepted as upright by God for obeying the Law is evident because the upright will have life because of his faith,[291] and the Law has nothing to do with faith; it teaches that it is the man who does these things that will find life by doing them. Christ ransomed us from the Law's curse by taking our curse upon himself (for the Scripture says, "Cursed be anyone who is hung on a tree"[292]) in order that the blessing given to Abraham might through Jesus Christ reach the heathen, so that through faith we might receive the promised Spirit.[293]

Acceptance with God does not depend upon the Jewish law, or upon this law with grace added, but upon faith in Jesus Christ.[294] The law was all right in its time and place as "our attendant on our way to Christ, so that we might be made upright through faith. But now that faith has come, we are no longer in the charge of the attendant."[295] The law was powerless to bestow God's spirit and make men his children; only Christ could free men from the curse of the law and make men sons and heirs of his heavenly father.[296] Paul reminds his Galatian converts that that was the burden of his message when he was with him; in passionate language, Paul sees the integrity of his gospel threatened and pleads for its renewal in the hearts of the Galatians.

I am amazed that you are so quickly turning away from him who called you by the mercy of Christ, to some different good news—not that there is any other, only that there are some people who are trying to unsettle you and want to turn the good news of the Christ around. But even if we or an angel from heaven preach to you good news that contradicts the good news we have preached to you—a curse upon him![297] We have said it before, and I repeat it now—if anyone is preaching to you good news that contradicts the good news you have already received, a curse upon him![298]

Galatians is the first apology for the Christian religion, and one of the greatest ever written. Paul has to defend his gospel and his right to be considered an apostle by claiming direct communication with the living Christ and having his right to preach recognized by the pillars of the church in Jerusalem.

For I tell you plainly, brothers, that the good news that I preached is not a human affair. I did not receive it from any man, and I was not taught it, but it came to me through a revelation of Jesus Christ.[299]

Paul then gives an account of his relations with the Jerusalem church during the years immediately after his conversion, including the apostolic council in Jerusalem and its aftermath.[300] The apostles finally agreed to recognize the equality of all men before the grace of God.

> For in union with Christ Jesus, neither circumcision nor the want of it counts for anything, but only faith acting through love . . .
> For neither circumcision nor the want of it is of any importance, but only a new creation.[301]

Paul then felt he had a perfect right to say:

> Let nobody interfere with me after this, for I bear on my body the scars that mark me as a slave of Jesus.[302]

In his letter to the Galatians, Paul expounds on his great doctrine of Christian freedom; freedom in Christ fulfills the intention of the moral law. Christ's followers were no longer in slavery but had received full adoption as sons:

> . . . So, brothers, we are children not of a slave but of one who is free.
> This is the freedom with which Christ has freed us. So stand firm in it, and do not get under a yoke of slavery again.[303]

But this freedom was not to be equated with irresponsibility, nor Christian liberty debased into license. The Christian freeman must not fall below the moral standards of the legalist; rather, he must exceed the requirements of the old Mosaic law.[304] The new life which the spirit created was more strenuous than the old slavery; in Christ one had resources to discharge this heavier responsibility and produce the fruit of the spirit: "love, joy, peace, patience, kindness, goodness, faithfulness, gentleness, self-control."[305] Paul unites Christian freedom to daily crucifixion with Christ and unbroken companionship with his spirit:

> I have been crucified with Christ, and it is no longer I that live, but Christ that lives in me.[306]
> Those who belong to Jesus the Christ have crucified the physical nature with its propensities and cravings.[307]

He makes it clear that freedom from the demands of the Mosaic law does not involve an approval of license:

> For you, brothers, have been called to freedom; only do not make your freedom an excuse for the physical, but in love be slaves to one another . . .

I mean this: Live by the Spirit, and then you will not indulge your physical cravings. For the physical cravings are
against the Spirit, and the cravings of the Spirit are against
the physical; the two are in opposition, so that you cannot do
anything you please. But if you are guided by the Spirit, you
are not subject to law . . .[308]

As a corollary to his doctrine of Christian freedom, Paul develops
in Galatians his concept of the unity of all men in Christ and of
the church as the divine instrument to illustrate and promote it.
He criticizes sharply those who have attempted to upset this basic
unity:

But if you bite one another and eat one another, take care,
or you will be destroyed by one another.[309]
. . . These men who are trying to force you to let yourselves
be circumcised want to present a good appearance externally
to save themselves from having to stand persecution for the
cross of Jesus the Christ. Why, even those who let themselves
be circumcised do not observe the Law themselves! But they
want you to let yourselves be circumcised so that they can boast
of that physical fact about you![310]

There could be no class distinction in the church of Christ:

For in Christ Jesus you are all sons of God through your
faith. For all of you who have been baptized into union with
Christ have clothed yourselves with Christ. There is no room
for "Jew" and "Greek"; there is no room for "slave" and
"freeman"; there is no room for "male" and "female"; for in
union with Christ Jesus you are all one. And if you belong
to Christ, then you are true descendants of Abraham and his
heirs under the promise.[311]

By insisting that his Gentile converts did not have to submit to
the painful initiatory rite of circumcision, Paul helped the new
religion to break, once and for all, with the restrictions of a narrow
nationalistic Judaism. Christianity was to become a universal
religion, open to all who would believe in Christ, largely because of
Paul's dramatic break with his own religious heritage in Pharisaic
Judaism.

In the course of his doctrinal statements, Paul gives in Galatians some excellent ethical teachings, especially in Galatians 5:13-6:10:

> . . . For the whole Law is summed up in one saying: "You must love your neighbor as you do yourself."
> . . . The things our physical nature does are clear enough— immorality, impurity, licentiousness, idolatry, sorcery, enmity, quarreling, jealousy, anger, selfishness, dissension, party-spirit, envy, drunkenness, carousing, and the like. I warn you as I did before that people who do such things will have no share in the Kingdom of God . . .
> . . . Let us not in our vanity challenge one another or envy one another. But if a man is caught doing something wrong, brothers, you are spiritual, and you must set him right, in a spirit of gentleness. Think of yourselves, for you may be tempted too. Bear one another's burdens, and in that way carry out the law of the Christ. For if anyone thinks he is somebody when he is really nobody, he is deceiving himself . . . For everyone will have to carry his own load.
> . . . Do not be deceived. God is not to be sneered at. A man will reap just what he sows . . . Let us not get tired of doing right, for at the proper time we shall reap, if we do not give out. So then whenever we have an opportunity, let us do good to all men, especially to those who belong to the family of the faith.

The last part of the Galatian letter seems to have been written by Paul in his own larger handwriting.[312] In this way, he stressed some matters which he had already dictated to his amanuensis. He ended this great revolutionary statement of religious ideals and attitudes with a brief benediction.[313]

3. Paul's Correspondence with the Church at Corinth

While Paul was bringing his long Ephesian ministry to a close, word was brought to him from across the Aegean Sea that conditions among the Christians in the port city of Corinth were far from ideal.[314] This led to a correspondence with them which was to bulk larger than that with any other church. No church gave Paul as much trouble as the one in Corinth, but his attempts to keep this unruly church in order led to the fullest and most interesting of all his writings. As James Stalker once said (*The Life of St. Paul,* section 129), "the letters of Paul take the roofs off the meeting places of the early Christians and let us look inside, and this is peculiarly true of the letters to the Corinthians."[315] Communication was frequent between Ephesus and Corinth; Paul learned from travelers that some of the new converts in Corinth were still practising their old pagan vices, particularly those of an immoral nature. This impelled Paul to write a short letter to the church in Corinth, urging the loyal Christians there "not to associate with immoral people."[316]

Whether Paul's first letter to the Corinthians had its desired effect or not is not known. Very shortly, other Corinthian visitors to Ephesus brought him further news concerning conditions in the church there. "Chloe's people"[317] informed Paul that the Corinthians were breaking up into cliques and factions.[318] They may also have told him that the Corinthian Christians were going to heathen law courts for settlement of their business differences.[319] Also, Paul may have discovered from them the distressing news that the solemn religious character of the Lord's Supper was being lost in feasting and drunkenness.[320] In spite of the content in his initial letter, immoral behavior was continuing among the Corinthian Christians; one man was guilty of incest by taking his widowed stepmother in marriage.[321] Then, one day, three members of the Corinthian Church—Stephanas, Achaicus, and Fortunatus—came to Paul at his dwelling place in Ephesus and presented him with a letter from the community of Christians in Corinth.[322] This letter raised a number of new questions; the Corinthians were concerned about problems of marriage,[323] the purchase of meat in markets attached to pagan temples,[324] the regulation of public worship, including the dress of the women who attended and the control of those who spoke ecstatically,[325] and the collection for the poor people of the mother church in Jerusalem.[326] The letter may also have contained information concerning a group in Corinth who denied the resurrection.[327] Undoubtedly the situation in Corinth was so complex that only a personal visit from Paul himself would clear up the difficulties; but Paul was engrossed in his work in Ephesus and could not leave.[328] Instead, he wrote a second letter to the church in Corinth, our First Corinthians, in a spirit of pastoral helpfulness and concern, despatching it by Stephanas, Achaicus, and Fortunatus.

Though not a doctrinal letter in the same sense that Romans and Galatians are, I Corinthians presents Paul at his very greatest as a practical religious thinker; every part of the letter deals with some aspect of the gospel of Jesus Christ. Besides occasional utterances, this letter contains two of the mountain-peak chapters of the Bible: in I Corinthians 15, Paul presents a sustained analysis of his doctrine of the resurrection; I Corinthians 13 is perhaps the greatest single chapter in all sacred literature: Paul's great hymn to love. The letter begins with a discussion of the factionalism in the church at Corinth, the most serious of the matters of which "Chloe's people" had informed Paul. In the first four chapters, Paul tries to show that all party divisions should be transcended by a common loyalty to Christ.

But I urge you all, brothers, for the sake of our Lord Jesus Christ, to agree in what you say, and not to allow factions among you, but to be perfectly united in mind and judgment. For I have been informed, my brothers, by Chloe's people, that quarrels are going on among you. What I mean is this, that one of you says, "I am a follower of Paul," another, "And I, of Apollos," another, "And I, of Cephas (Peter)," and another, "And I, of Christ." Christ has been divided up![329]
. . . For when there are still jealousy and quarrels among you, are you not worldly and living on a merely human level? For when one man says, "I am a follower of Paul," and another, "I am a follower of Apollos," are you not simply human? What is Apollos? Or what is Paul? Just servants through whom you came to have faith, as the Lord gave each of us opportunity. I did the planting, Apollos the watering, but it was God who made the plants grow. So neither the planter nor the waterer counts for anything, but only God who makes the plants grow. The planter and the waterer are all one, though each of us will be paid for his own work. For we are fellow-laborers for God, and you are God's farm, God's building.[330]
. . . For no one can lay any other foundation than the one that is laid, that is, Jesus Christ himself.[331]
Let no one of you deceive himself. If any one of you imagines that he is wiser than the rest of you, in what this world calls wisdom, he had better become a fool, so as to become really wise. For this world's wisdom is foolishness to God . . . So no one should boast about men. For it all belongs to you—Paul, Apollos, Cephas, the world, life, death, the present, the future —all of it belongs to you. But you belong to Christ, and Christ belongs to God.

> The right way for a man to think of us is as Christ's servants, and managers authorized to distribute the secret truths of God . . .[332]

In chapters 5 and 6 Paul deals very sharply with immorality in Corinth; concerning the man who is guilty of incest, Paul is surprised that his fellow Christians have not been "overwhelmed with grief at having to expel" him from their midst; Paul himself has "already passed judgment upon the man who has done this, and . . . I have handed the man over to Satan, for his physical destruction, in order that his spirit may be saved on the Day of the Lord."[333] Paul regards litigation between Christians in courts presided over by heathen judges as a lamentable breakdown in brotherhood; it is better to take wrong and be unjustly defrauded than to be quarreling Christians before the world.[334] On immorality in general Paul concludes:

> . . . Do you not know that wrongdoers will not have any share in God's kingdom? Do not let anyone mislead you. People who are immoral or idolaters or adulterers or sensual or given to unnatural vice or thieves or greedy—drunkards, abusive people, robbers—will not have any share in God's kingdom. . .
> . . . Fly from immorality! Any other sin a man commits is something outside his body, but the immoral man sins against his own body. Or do you not know that your body is a temple of the Holy Spirit that is within you, which you have received from God? Besides, you are not your own; you have been bought and paid for. Therefore, honor God with your bodies.[335]

As to marriage, Paul affirms that it is better for single men, widows, and single women to avoid marriage; it is not because marriage is a sin, but because the unmarried man or woman is freer to do the Lord's work. Paul's views on marriage are based on his Jewish background and, more significantly, upon his belief in the imminence of the end of the existing world order. Married couples are not to separate; engaged couples may marry if physical attraction is getting too strong for them.

> . . . It is an excellent thing for a man to remain unmarried. But there is so much immorality that every man had better have a wife of his own, and every woman a husband of her

own . . . I should like to have everyone be just as I am my-self; . . .

To all who are unmarried and to widows, I would say this: It is an excellent thing if they can remain single as I am.[336] But if they cannot control themselves, let them marry. For it is better to marry than to be on fire with passion. To those already married my instructions are—and they are not mine but the Lord's—that a wife is not to separate from her husband . . . And a husband must not divorce his wife . . .[337]

Paul took the same attitude toward slavery: "Everyone ought to remain in the station in which he was called."[338] Then Paul handles a matter which seems very unpromising from the point of view of Christianity today—meat purchased in markets attached to pagan temples—but which was of crucial significance to many in Corinth who had just come into the Christian church from paganism. Portions of the animals used as sacrifices in pagan temples were consumed in the liturgical rites themselves; other portions were consumed by devout worshipers in sacramental temple feasts; still a third kind of meat was sold to the public for food, and to many devout pagans this meat was also holy. Paul says that under no conditions should Christians eat meat sacramentally in a pagan temple;[339] in a private home, Christians could eat whatever food was served, unless someone in good conscience objected to eating meat which he considered holy.[340] In dealing with this extremely delicate matter, Paul gives expression to a far-reaching moral law of respect for the consciences of others:

. . . Food is not going to affect our standing with God. We are none the worse if we do not eat it, and none the better if we do. But you must take care that this right of yours does not prove a hindrance to the overscrupulous. For if somebody sees you, who are intelligent about this matter, attending a dinner in an idol's temple, will not he, with his sensitive conscience, be led to eat meat that is offered to idols? . . . Therefore, if what I eat makes my brother fall, I will never eat meat again, rather than make my brother fall.[341]

Paul's Jewish training is again revealed when he describes how women should behave and dress in church; in his opinion, any woman without a veil covering her face, head, and shoulders would be taken for an immoral street-walker; Christian women should keep the veil as evidence of male supremacy:

> . . . Christ is the head of every man, while a woman's head is her husband, and Christ's head is God. Any man who offers prayer or explains the will of God with anything on his head disgraces his head, and any woman who offers prayer or explains the will of God bareheaded disgraces her head, for it is just as though she had her head shaved . . . For a man ought not to wear anything on his head, for he is the image of God and reflects his glory; while a woman is the reflection of man's glory. For man was not made from woman, but woman from man, and man was not created for woman, but woman was for man.[342] That is why she ought to wear upon her head something to symbolize her subjection, out of respect to the angels, if to nobody else . . .[343]

In his next topic, Paul turns to questions growing out of disorderly behavior in the observance of the Lord's Supper. In that day, the Supper was a real meal, during which the participants observed the bread and wine memorial; in Corinth it had degenerated into a kind of carousal, where fellowship with Christ and one another was impossible:

> But while I am on this subject, I cannot approve of your meetings, because they are doing you more harm than good. For, in the first place, when you meet as a congregation, I hear that you divide into sects, and in a measure I believe it . . . Each of you hurries to get his own supper and eat it, and one goes hungry while another gets drunk. Have you no houses to eat and drink in?[344]

This gives Paul an occasion to tell the Corinthians the story of the Last Supper;[345] each repetition of it ought to lead to serious self-examination:

> . . . Anyone who eats the bread or drinks from the Lord's cup in a way that is unworthy of it will be guilty of profaning the body and the blood of the Lord. A man should examine himself, and only when he has done so should he eat any of the bread or drink from the cup . . .[346]

Continuing, Paul considers the troublesome matter of spiritual gifts; the Christians in Corinth were evidently envious of one another; also, ecstatic utterances were disrupting public worship.[347] In his discussion, Paul gives expression to some of his supremely inspiring utterances.

> Endowments vary, but the Spirit is the same, and forms of service vary, but it is the same Lord who is served, and activities vary, but God who produces them all in us all is the same.[348]
>
> For just as the body is one and yet has many parts, and all the parts of the body, many as they are, form one body, so it is with Christ . . . Now you are Christ's body, and individually parts of it. And God has placed people in the church, first as apostles, second as inspired preachers, third as teachers, then wonder-workers; then come ability to cure the sick, helpfulness, administration, ecstatic speaking . . . But you must cultivate the higher endowments.[349]

Then, in chapter thirteen, Paul breaks forth in a great paean in praise of love, which he considers the greatest gift of all, the supreme endowment of the Christian, the noblest ideal of Christian behaviour.[350] He applies this great principle to the problem of ecstatic utterance in chapter fourteen:

> . . . The man who is inspired to preach is more useful than the one who speaks ecstatically—unless he can explain what he says so that it may do the church some good.[351]
>
> . . . Thank God, I speak in ecstasy more than any of you. But in public worship I would rather say five words with my understanding so as to instruct others also than ten thousand words in an ecstasy.[352]
>
> . . . When you meet together, suppose every one of you has a song, a teaching, a revelation, an ecstatic utterance, or an explanation of one; it must all be for the good of all. If there is any ecstatic speaking, let it be limited to two or three people at the most, and have one speak at a time and someone explain what he says. But if there is no one to explain it, have him keep quiet in church, and talk to himself and to God. . .[353]

Paul reserves to the close of his letter his great description of the future life; historically, chapter fifteen is the most important part

of I Corinthians, for in it there is the earliest and most important
testimony to the resurrection of Jesus and to its place in the early
church's doctrine;[354] but more significantly, the chapter contains
Paul's ideas of the nature of the resurrection of Jesus and the character of the resurrection body of all who die. Evidently there were
those in Corinth who did not believe that Jesus could have risen
from the dead; Paul insists that he did, not in the body which
was buried in the tomb, but in a "glorious body"[355] which Paul
had seen on the road to Damascus in a blaze of light.[356]

> . . . For I passed on to you, as of first importance, the account
> I had received,[357] that Christ died for our sins, as the Scriptures
> foretold, that he was buried, that on the third day he was
> raised from the dead, as the Scriptures foretold, and that he
> was seen by Cephas, and then by the Twelve . . . Finally he
> was seen by me also, . . .[358]
>
> . . . If Christ was not raised, there is nothing in our message;
> there is nothing in our faith either, and we are found guilty
> of misrepresenting God, . . . If Christ was not raised, your
> faith is a delusion; you are still under the control of your
> sins . . .[359]
>
> But the truth is, Christ was raised from the dead, the first
> to be raised of those who have fallen asleep . . .[360]

Another group in Corinth, following Greek ways of thinking,
believed that men would possess no body in the after life; all
would be pure spirit, without personal identity. For their benefit,
Paul stands firm on the Jewish position, though without the crude-
ness of the typical Pharisaic doctrine of the resurrection; the present
earthly body will disappear, and its place will be taken by a
"spiritual body."

> . . . It is so with the resurrection of the dead. The body is
> sown in decay, it is raised free from decay. It is sown in humilia-
> tion, it is raised in splendor. It is sown in weakness, it is raised
> in strength. It is a physical body that is sown, it is a spiritual
> body that is raised. If there is a physical body, there is a spiritual
> body also . . . For the trumpet will sound, and the dead will
> will be raised free from decay, and we shall be changed. For
> this perishable nature must put on the imperishable, and this
> mortal nature must put on immortality . . . But thank God!
> He gives us victory through our Lord Jesus Christ . . .[361]

The letter ends with business and personal matters.

> About the collection for God's people . . . on the first of every week each of you is to put aside and store up whatever he gains, so that money will not have to be collected after I come. When I come I will send whatever persons you authorize with credentials, to carry your gift to Jerusalem. And if it seems worth while for me to go myself, they can go with me.[362]

Paul then tells them that he plans to stay in Ephesus until Pentecost; then he will journey to Corinth through Macedonia and perhaps spend the winter with them.[363] The farewell greeting is in Paul's own hand.[364]

One might well expect that I Corinthians would produce the reforms Paul so desperately hoped would occur among the Corinthian Christians, but such was far from the case. Conditions in Corinth grew from bad to worse; all the parties opposed to Paul united in opposition to him. The efforts of Timothy, whom Paul had sent to Corinth to prepare the Christians there for the arrival of I Corinthians,[365] had proved to be fruitless. Certain Jewish Christians had succeeded in undermining the influence of Paul.[366] One Corinthian Christian in particular seemed to be the leader in a full-scale revolt against Paul;[367] he gathered around him all those whom Paul had condemned in I Corinthians and developed a sweeping criticism of Paul and his supposed apostolic authority. Then, Paul himself may have made an unexpected journey to Corinth; later he refers to it as a "painful visit;"[368] if so, his opponents met him with open insult. Heartsick and depressed, Paul returned to his work in Ephesus, with a warning that he would return and set matters right. But before he could arrange to visit Corinth again he wrote a "stern letter," with the purpose of bringing the Corinthian Christians to their senses and restoring their obedience to him. Later, he refers to the "stern letter" several times:

> . . . For I was in great trouble and distress of mind when I wrote you, and I shed many tears as I did it, yet it was not to hurt your feelings, but to make you realize the extraordinary affection I have for you.[369]
> . . . For that is why I wrote you—to find out how you would stand the test, and see if you would obey me absolutely.[370]

Paul despatched this letter by Titus, planning to meet him in Troas and hear of the reception it had in Corinth.[371] Upon completion of his ministry in Ephesus, Paul hurried to Troas; not finding Titus there, he crossed over to Macedonia and intercepted Titus at Philippi or Thessalonica.[372] Titus brought Paul a welcome report that his letter had brought the Corinthians to their senses; once again, Paul was their gladly acknowledged apostle.

The "stern letter" has been preserved, in whole or in part, in II Corinthians 10-13. It is a letter of severe rebuke, written out of the agony of Paul's soul. It is one long apologia, in which Paul answers every one of the slanders which his enemies at Corinth had raised against him. He had been accused of being weak when he was actually with them and courageous only when he is far away; they will see how bold he can be.

> . . . I beg you not to make me take as bold an attitude when I come, as I count on taking toward some people who suspect me of acting from worldly motives . . . I destroy arguments and every obstacle that is raised against the knowledge of God, and I take captive every thought and make it obey Christ, and am prepared to punish any trace of disobedience when you have made your obedience perfectly clear . . .[373]

They had said he was arrogant and boastful; Paul admits that he may have boasted too much, but he thinks he has a right to.

> . . . If anyone is sure he belongs to Christ, let him think again and understand that I belong to Christ, just as much as he. For suppose I do boast a little too much of my authority— which the Lord gave me to build you up, not to pull you down— I will not have to blush for it. I do not want to seem to scare you with my letters. For they say, "His letters are impressive and telling, but his personal appearance is insignificant and as a speaker he amounts to nothing." Such people had better understand that when I arrive and take action I will do just as I say I will in my letters when I am far away . . .[374]

His critics had tried brazenly to supplant him and assume the leadership over the Christians in Corinth; Paul affirms that they are still under his proper missionary jurisdiction,

. . . for I was the first to come all the way to you with the good news of the Christ. I do not indulge in extravagant boasts over work done by others, but I do hope that as your faith increases, my influence may be immensely enlarged through you, and I may preach the gospel in the lands beyond you without having to boast over work already done in another's field . . .[375]

His enemies had criticized his authority as an apostle; in his answer, Paul presents one of the finest autobiographical sections in all his writings:

I wish you would put up with a little folly from me. Do put up with it! I feel a divine jealousy about you, for I betrothed you to Christ, to present you as a pure bride to her one husband . . . For when somebody comes along and preaches another Jesus than the one I preached, or you receive a different spirit from the one you received, or a different gospel from the one you accepted, you put up with it well enough! For I think that I am not in the least inferior to these superfine apostles of yours. Even if I have no particular gifts in speaking, I am not wanting in knowledge . . .[376]

And I shall go on doing as I do, so as to cut the ground from under those who want to make out that in their boasted apostleship they work on the same terms that I do. Such men are sham apostles, dishonest workmen, masquerading as apostles of Christ . . .[377]

I repeat, no one should think me a fool, but if you do, show me at least the patience you would show a fool, and let me have my little boast like the others . . . For you like to put up with fools, you are so wise yourselves! For you put up with it if a man makes you his slaves, or lives on you, or takes you in or puts on airs, or gives you a slap in the face . . . But whatever anyone else dares to boast of—I am playing the part of a fool— I will dare to boast of too. If they are Hebrews, so am I! If they are Israelites, so am I! If they are descended from Abraham, so am I! If they are Christian workers—I am talking like a madman!—I am a better one![378]

So I am perfectly willing to boast of all my weakness, so that the strength of Christ may shelter me. That is why I am pleased with weaknesses, insults, hardships, persecutions, and difficulties, when they are endured for Christ's sake, for it is when I am weak that I am strong.

I have been making a fool of myself, but you forced me to do it, when you ought to have been expressing your approval of me. For I am not a bit inferior to your superfine apostles, even if I am nobody! The signs that mark a true apostle were most patiently shown when I was among you, in signs, wonders, and marvels . . .[379]

The Corinthians were disturbed because Paul had accepted no financial support from them for his preaching;[380] they thought that he had taken money from other churches, notably Philippi, thus giving the Corinthians' church a lower standing than others. Paul defends himself by saying:

. . . And when I was with you and wanted money, I did not burden any of you, . . . So I kept myself, as I shall always do, from being a burden to you in any way . . .[381]

. . . And I do not intend to burden you now; for it is not your money but yourselves that I want; for children are not expected to lay up money for their parents, but parents for their children. And I will be glad to spend all I have and all I am for your sake. Are you going to love me the less for loving you so intensely? But granting that I did not burden you myself, I was clever about it, you say, and took you in by a trick. Yet did I make anything out of you by anybody that I sent to you?[382] . . .

Paul concludes this letter with an appeal to repent before he pays them a visit:

. . . For I am afraid that perhaps when I come I may find you not as I want to find you, and that you may find me not as you want to find me. I am afraid that perhaps there may be quarreling, jealousy, bad feeling, rivalry, slander, gossip, conceit, and disorder, and that when I come back my God may humiliate me before you, and I may have to mourn over many who have kept on in their old sins and have never repented of the impurity, immorality, and sensuality in which they have indulged.

. . . Those who have kept on in their old sins and all the rest I have warned, and I warn them now while I am still away, as I did on my second visit, that if I come back I will spare nobody —since you demand proof that Christ really speaks through me

. . . That is what I pray for—the perfecting of your characters. That is why I write this while I am away from you, so that when I come, I may not have to be harsh in my use of the authority the Lord has given me, for it was to build you up, not to pull you down.

Now brothers, goodbye! Be what you ought to be, listen to my appeal, agree with one another, live in peace, and God the source of love and peace will be with you . . .[383]

Surprisingly enough, the "stern letter," Paul's third letter to the Corinthians, accomplished what he had been hoping and praying for; when Paul met Titus in Macedonia, the latter brought him good news that the Corinthians wanted to see him and be reconciled to him once again.[384] So, with a heart overflowing with gratitude, Paul wrote his fourth Corinthian letter, which has been preserved in II Corinthians 1-9.[385] The keynotes of his message are love, faith, and thanksgiving; from the very first sentence, the letter breathes a serene air of harmony, understanding, and comfort:

Blessed be the God and Father of our Lord Jesus Christ, the merciful Father, and the God always ready to comfort! He comforts me in all my trouble, so that I can comfort people who are in trouble with the comfort with which I myself am comforted by God . . .[386]

Then Paul reviews and reinterprets the relations he has just had with the Christian community at Corinth. He recommends that they restore the man who led the opposition against Paul to a place in their affections once again:

. . . For that individual, this censure by the majority of you is punishment enough, so that you must now turn around and forgive and comfort him, or he may be overwhelmed by his remorse. So I beg you to restore him to his place in your affections . . . When you forgive a man, I forgive him too . . .[387]

Then there is a long section in which Paul states the ideals of the Christian missionary; this is one of the great treasures of Christian literature:

Yes, I am the fragrance of Christ to God, diffused among

those who are being saved and those who are perishing alike;
to the one, a deathly, deadly odor, to the other a vital, lifegiving
one. Who is qualified for this task? I am! For I am no peddler
of God's message, like most men, but like a man of sincerity,
commissioned by God and in his presence, in union with Christ
I utter his message.

Am I falling into self-recommendation again? Do I, like some
people, need letters of recommendation to you or from you?
You are my recommendations, written on my heart, for everybody to read and understand. You show that you are a letter
from Christ delivered by me, written not in ink, but in the
Spirit of the living God, and not on tablets of stone, but on
the human heart.[388]

So since by the mercy of God I am engaged in this service,
I never lose heart. I disown disgraceful, underhanded ways. I
refuse to practice cunning or to tamper with God's message.
It is by open statement of the truth that I would commend
myself to every human conscience in the sight of God . . . For
it is not myself but Christ Jesus that I am proclaiming as Lord;
I am only a slave of yours for Jesus' sake. For God who said,
"Let light shine out of darkness," has shone in my heart, to
give me the light of the knowledge of God's glory, that is on
the face of Christ.[389]

But I have this treasure in a mere earthen jar, to show that
its amazing power belongs to God and not to me. I am hard
pressed on every side, but never cut off; perplexed, but not
driven to despair; routed, but not abandoned; struck down, but
not destroyed; never free from the danger of being put to
death like Jesus, so that in my body the life of Jesus also
may be seen . . .[390]

So I never lose heart. Though my outer nature is wasting
away, my inner is being renewed every day. For this slight,
momentary trouble is piling up for me an eternal blessedness
beyond all comparison, because I keep my eyes not on what is
seen but what is unseen. For what is seen is transitory, but
what is unseen is eternal. For I know that if this earthly tent
that I live in is taken down, God will provide me a building in
heaven to live in, not built by human hands but eternal . . .[391]

. . . It is Christ's love that controls me, . . .[392]

. . . So if anyone is in union with Christ, he is a new being;
the old state of things has passed away; there is a new state of
things. All this comes from God, who through Christ has recon-

ciled me to himself, and has commissioned me to proclaim this
reconciliation—how God through Christ reconciled the world to
himself, refusing to count men's offenses against them, and
intrusted me with the message of reconciliation.

It is for Christ, therefore, that I am an envoy, seeing that
God makes his appeal through me. On Christ's behalf I beg
you to be reconciled to God. He made him who knew nothing
of sin to be sin, for our sake, so that through union with him
we might become God's uprightness.[393]

In II Corinthians 6:1-10 Paul gives another catalogue of hardships
similar to the one in II Corinthians 11:23-33.[394] Because of the love
he has for the Corinthians, he wants them to reciprocate.[395] Then
he again tells them how overjoyed both he and Titus felt in Macedonia when they knew of their changed attitude; Paul had now
had his confidence in them restored.[396] In chapters eight and nine
Paul urges the Corinthian Christians to be generous in contributing
to the collection for the poor people of Jerusalem:[397]

. . . Just as you excel in everything else—faith, expression,
knowledge, perfect devotion, and the love we have awakened
in you—you must excel in this generous undertaking too.

I do not mean this as a command. I only want to test the gen-
uineness of your love by the devotion of others. You know how
gracious the Lord Jesus Christ was. Though he was rich, he
became poor for your sake, in order that by his poverty you
might become rich . . . For you were the first not only to do
anything about this, but to want to do anything, and that was
last year. Now finish doing it, so that your readiness to under-
take it may be equaled by the way you finish it up, as well as
your means permit . . .[398]

Remember this: The man who sows sparingly will reap
sparingly, and the man who sows generously will reap generously. Everyone must give what he has made up his mind to give,
not reluctantly or under compulsion; God loves a man who is
glad to give . . . The way you stand the test of this service
must do honor to God, through your fidelity to what you profess as to the good news of Christ, and through the liberality
of your contributions for them and for all others; . . . Thank
God for his indescribable gift![399]

4. Paul's Letter to the Church at Rome.

Late in the year 55 A.D., or early in 56, during the three months' visit Paul paid to the church in Corinth soon after his correspondence with it,[400] he had the leisure to compose what has since proved to be his most important letter: Romans. It was addressed to a group of Christians in a city which he had never visited; they belonged to a church which Paul had not founded. Paul had now arrived at a great turning point in his missionary career; he had traversed the eastern provinces of the Roman Empire and was ready to turn his attention westward. He wants to visit the Roman Christians on his way to Spain and to secure from them cooperation for his new field of work.

> . . . I have completed the preaching of the good news of Christ all the way from Jerusalem to Illyricum . . .

> . . . Now that there is no more work for me in this part of the world, and as I have had a great desire for many years to come to see you, when I go to Spain I hope to see you on my way there, and to have you see me off on my journey, after I have enjoyed being with you for a while. Just now I am starting for Jerusalem, to take help to God's people . . . So when I have finished this matter, and see this contribution safely into their possession, I will start for Spain, and come to you on the way, and I know that when I do come to see you, I will come with Christ's fullest blessing.[401]

Also, Paul wants to inform the Roman Christians of the meaning of the salvation in Christ, which is the main theme of the letter, in contrast with Jewish law and in relation to the calling and destiny of the Jewish nation; there may have been some misunderstanding and suspicion on the part of the Roman church of Paul's gospel which he sees the need of meeting.

> . . . I long to see you, to convey to you some spiritual gift that will strengthen you; in other words, that you and I may be mutually encouraged by one another's faith. I want you to understand, brothers, that I have often intended to come to see you (though thus far I have been prevented) in order to produce some results among you, as well as among the rest of the heathen . . .[402]

Just how Christianity was first brought to Rome is not known. There had been a strong Jewish community in that capital city of the empire since the days of Pompey.[403] "Visitors from Rome"[404] were in Jerusalem on the day of Pentecost; perhaps some of them took the gospel home with them. Roman visitors to Ephesus, Corinth, or Antioch, or commercial travelers from those cities or others like them had evidently helped to carry the gospel to Rome.[405] There is a persistent tradition in the early church, beginning as early as 95 A.D. with a passage in I Clement (5:3ff.), that Paul and Peter both suffered martyrdom in Rome.[406] That Paul and Peter were both visitors of the church in Rome is highly possible, but the further tradition that Peter established the Roman church is highly improbable; Peter probably did not go to Rome until after the Jerusalem Council[407] of 49 A.D., whereas Christianity in Rome was well established by that date. John Knox points to the most probable ancient account of the beginnings of Christianity in Rome by quoting from a fourth-century writer known as "Ambrosiater":

It is established that there were Jews living in Rome in the times of the apostles, and that those Jews who had believed (in Christ) passed on to the Romans the tradition that they ought to profess Christ but keep the law. . . One ought not to condemn the Romans, but to praise their faith; because without seeing any signs or miracles and without seeing any of the apostles, they nevertheless accepted faith in Christ, although according to a Jewish rite.[408]

According to this source, none of the apostles had been at Rome before Paul's visit; the church there had not been founded by any of the apostles at all, but by "lay" Christians. The early church in Rome had a definitely Jewish cast; this is substantiated by the quotation from "Ambrosiater" and by the fact that Roman Christianity later had a soberer, more conservative cast than Pauline Christianity.[409] Then, too, Paul in his letter to the Romans speaks of "we Jews,"[410] "our ancestor Abraham,"[411] and "our forefather Isaac."[412] However, the original Jewish-Christian nucleus in Rome had given way to a predominantly Gentile majority by the time Paul wrote his letter to them, but the contrast between the Roman church and those which Paul founded, such as the one at Corinth, may have led the Roman Christians to regard Paul suspiciously;

knowing that, Paul may have decided to write them a correct version of his "gospel."

After a long salutation, in which Paul presents his apostolic credentials,[413] and a paragraph in which he explains why he is interested in the church at Rome, he states the theme of the letter:

> . . . For I am not ashamed of the good news, for it is God's power for the salvation of every one who has faith, of the Jews first and then of the Greeks. In it God's way of uprightness is disclosed through faith and for faith, just as the Scripture says, "The upright will have life because of his faith."[414]

The remainder of the letter is actually an enlargement of this theme: the salvation available in Jesus Christ. Both Jews and Gentiles are sinners before God and subject to the final judgment; because the Jew has not kept his law his responsibility is increased and his despair deepened.[415] The way of salvation is not the way of obedience to the Torah but the way of justification in response to faith in Jesus Christ:

> . . . For no human being can be made upright in the sight of God by observing the Law. All that the Law can do is to make man conscious of sin. But now God's way of uprightness has been disclosed without any reference to law, though the Law and the Prophets bear witness to it. It is God's way of uprightness and comes through having faith in Jesus Christ, and it is for all who have faith, without distinction. For all men sin and come short of the glory of God, but by his mercy they are made upright for nothing, by the deliverance secured through Christ Jesus . . .[416]

Paul takes four chapters, five through eight, to set forth the meaning and character of the new life to which justification through Christ admits us; this is the most significant section of the letter:

> So as we have been made upright by faith, let us live in peace with God through our Lord Jesus Christ, by whom we have been introduced through faith to the favor of God that we now enjoy, and let us glory in our hope of sharing the glory of God. More than that, we ought to glory in our troubles, for we know that trouble produces endurance, and endurance,

character, and character, hope, and hope will not disappoint us. For, through the holy Spirit that has been given us, God's love has flooded our hearts.[417]

Reconciliation is the end-result of the promised salvation.

> For when we were still helpless, at the decisive moment Christ died for us godless men. Why, a man will hardly give his life for an upright person, though perhaps for a really good man some may be brave enough to die. But God proves his love for us by the fact that Christ died for us when we were still sinners. So if we have already been made upright by his death, it is far more certain that through him we shall be saved from God's anger! If, when we were God's enemies, we were reconciled to him through the death of his Son, it is far more certain that now that we are reconciled we shall be saved through sharing in his life! More than that, we actually glory in God through our Lord Jesus Christ, to whom we owe our reconciliation.[418]

In chapter six, Paul shows that, along with emancipation from sin, man is given a new power leading to a higher life.

> . . . If we have died with Christ, we believe that we shall also live with him, for we know that Christ, once raised from the dead, will never die again; death has no more hold on him. For when he died, he became once for all dead to sin; the life he now lives is a life in relation to God. So you also must think of yourselves as dead to sin but alive to God, through union with Christ Jesus.[419]

The man of faith is freed from the law:

> What follows, then? Are we to sin, because we live not under the law but under mercy? Certainly not! . . . But now that you have been freed from sin and have become slaves of God, the benefit you get is consecration, and the final result is eternal life. For the wages sin pays is death, but the gift God gives is eternal life through union with Jesus Christ our Lord.[420]
>
> Then what shall we conclude? That the Law is sin? Certainly not! Yet, if it had not been for the Law, I should never have learned what sin was; . . .

. . . We know that the Law is spiritual, but I am physical, sold into slavery to sin. I do not understand what I am doing, for I do not do what I want to do; I do things that I hate. But if I do what I do not want to do, I acknowledge that the Law is right. In reality, it is not I that do these things; it is sin, which has possession of me . . . I find the law to be that I who want to do right am dogged by what is wrong. My inner nature agrees with the divine law, but all through my body I see another principle in conflict with the law of my reason, which makes me a prisoner to that law of sin that runs through my body. What a wretched man I am! Who can save me from this doomed body? Thank God! it is done through Jesus Christ our Lord! So mentally I am a slave to God's law, but physically to the law of sin.[421]

Paul's letter to the Romans reaches its climax in the magnificent eighth chapter, which contains a description of the victorious life of the spirit.[422]

So there is no condemnation any more for those who are in union with Christ Jesus. For the life-giving law of the Spirit through Christ Jesus has freed you from the Law of sin and death. For though it was impossible for the Law to do it, hampered as it was by our physical limitations, God, by sending his own Son in our sinful physical form, as a sin-offering put his condemnation upon sin through his physical nature, so that the requirement of the Law might be fully met in our case, since we live not on the physical but on the spiritual plane . . . For to be physically minded means death, but to be spiritually minded means life and peace . . . But if Christ is in your hearts, though your bodies are dead in consequence of sin, your spirits have life in consequence of uprightness. If the Spirit of him who raised Jesus from the dead has taken possession of you, he who raised Christ Jesus from the dead will also give your mortal bodies life through his Spirit that has taken possession of you.

. . . For all who are guided by God's Spirit are God's sons . . . The Spirit itself testifies with our spirits that we are God's children, and if children, heirs also; heirs of God, and fellow-heirs with Christ, if we really share his sufferings in order to share his glory too.

For I consider what we suffer now not to be compared with the glory that is to burst upon us . . .

... We know that in everything God works with those who love him, whom he has called in accordance with his purpose, to bring about what is good. For those whom he had marked out from the first he predestined to be made like his Son, so that he should be the eldest of many brothers; and those whom he has predestined he calls, and those whom he calls he makes upright, and those whom he makes upright he glorifies.

Then what shall we conclude from this? If God is for us, who can be against us? Will not he who did not spare his own Son, but gave him up for us all, with that gift give us everything? Who can bring any accusation against those whom God has chosen? God pronounces them upright; who can condemn them? Christ Jesus who died, or rather who was raised from the dead, is at God's right hand, and actually pleads for us. Who can separate us from Christ's love? Can trouble or misfortune or persecution or hunger or destitution or danger or the sword? ... But in all these things we are more than victorious through him who loved us. For I am convinced that neither death nor life nor angels nor their hierarchies nor the present nor the future nor any supernatural forces either of height or depth will be able to separate us from the love God has shown in Christ Jesus our Lord![423]

In chapters nine through eleven, Paul presents a serious and sustained discussion of a concern which was very poignantly real to him: the fact that his beloved Jewish nation was refusing to accept the gospel of Jesus Christ. This rejection of Christ on the part of Israel is actually God's rejection of Israel. The Jewish nation has missed the point of God's revelation of himself, but their failure has only been temporary; it is true that they did not immediately accept Christ, but their failure meant that the heathen were given the opportunity to receive the benefits of the gospel. Now that the gospel has been enthusiastically accepted by non-Jews, the eyes of the Jews themselves are now open to their heritage in the gospel of Christ. In these chapters, Paul sets forth in detail his doctrine of predestination, which has led to so much disagreement in later theological writings. Paul concludes his letter to the Romans by pointing out some miscellaneous ethical and social implications of the Christian faith. It involves a new attitude of mind:

I appeal to you, therefore, brothers, by this mercy of God, to offer your bodies in a living sacrifice that will be holy and acceptable to God; that is your rational worship. You must not adopt the customs of this world but by your new attitude of mind be transformed so that you can find out what God's will is—what is good, pleasing, and perfect.[424]

This change should find its concrete expression in the relationship which the individual sustains with his fellow Christians:

> By the favor that God has shown me, I would tell every one of you not to think too highly of himself, but to think reasonably, judging himself by the degree of faith God has allowed him. For just as there are many parts united in our human bodies, and the parts do not all have the same function, so, many as we are, we form one body through union with Christ, and we are individually parts of one another . . . Your love must be genuine. You must hate what is wrong, and hold to what is right. Be affectionate in your love for the brotherhood, eager to show one another honor, not wanting in devotion, but on fire with the Spirit. Serve the Lord. Be happy in your hope, steadfast in time of trouble, persistent in prayer. Supply the needs of God's people, be unfailing in hospitality.[425]

The love of the Christian should include his enemies:

> Bless your persecutors; bless them; do not curse them. Rejoice with those who rejoice, weep with those who weep. Live in harmony with one another. Do not be too ambitious, but accept humble tasks. Do not be conceited. Do not pay anyone back with evil for evil. See that you are above reproach in the eyes of everyone. If possible, for your part, live peaceably with everybody. Do not take your revenge, dear friends, but leave room for God's anger, for the Scripture says, "Vengeance belongs to me; I will pay them back, says the Lord."[426] No! If your enemy is hungry, feed him! If he is thirsty, give him something to drink! For if you do, you will heap burning coals upon his head![427] Do not be conquered by evil, but conquer evil with good.[428]

Romans 13:1-7 contains Paul's philosophy of the relationship of the Christian to the state; in writing to Christians in the capital city, Paul does not dare give any hint that the church might be disloyal to the appointed government; Christians should be good citizens and assist political institutions in their divinely appointed tasks. At the time when Paul wrote Romans the Roman government would have appeared to him as a friend; one wonders if he would have written so amicably a few years later:

> Everyone must obey the authorities that are over him, for no authority can exist without the permission of God; the existing authorities have been established by him, so that anyone who resists the authorities sets himself in opposition to what God has ordained, and those who oppose him will bring down judgment upon themselves . . . The magistrates . . . are God's agents to do you good . . . They are God's servants, to execute his wrath upon wrongdoers. You must obey them, therefore, not only to escape God's wrath, but as a matter of principle, just as you pay your taxes; they are God's ministers, devoting themselves to this service. Pay them all what is due them—tribute to the man entitled to receive it, taxes to the man entitled to receive them, respect to the man entitled to it, and honor to the man entitled to it.[429]

All of life should be regulated by Christian love,[430] which is the fulfillment of the Torah; such love is especially necessary because of the imminence of the Day of the Lord.[431] In chapter 14 Paul deals with a problem which he had faced in the church at Corinth; he recommends loving sympathy for the Christian whose conscience will not permit him to eat meat:

> Treat people who are overscrupulous in their faith like brothers; do not criticize their views . . . The man who will eat anything must not look down on the man who abstains from some things, and the man who abstains from them must not criticize the one who does not, for God has accepted him . . . None of us lives only to himself, and none of us dies only to himself; if we live, we are responsible to the Lord, and if we die, we are responsible to him; so whether we live or die, we belong to the Lord . . .

> . . . Nothing is unclean in itself; a thing is unclean only to the man who regards it as unclean . . . You must not, by what you eat, ruin a man for whom Christ died. The thing you have a right to do must not become a cause of reproach. The Kingdom of God is not a matter of what we eat or drink,

but of uprightness, peace, and happiness through the possession of the holy Spirit . . . It is true, everything is clean, but it is wrong for a man to hurt the consciences of others by what he eats. The right thing to do is to eat no meat at all and to drink no wine or do anything else if it hurts your brother's conscience . . .[432]

It is the duty of us who are strong to put up with the weaknesses of those who are immature, and not just suit ourselves. Everyone of us must try to please his neighbor, to do him good, and help in his development . . .

Therefore, treat one another like brothers, in God's honor, just as Christ has treated you. I hold that Christ has become an agent of circumcision to show God's truthfulness in carrying out the promises made to our forefathers, and causing the heathen to praise God for his mercy; . . .[433]

Paul's letter to the Romans ends with the benediction of Romans 15:33; chapter 16 deals with matters entirely separate from what has gone before it. It starts with an introduction of Phoebe, a "helper in the church at Cenchreae,"[434] not far from Corinth, and continues with a long list of persons to whom Paul sends greetings.[435] There is a short paragraph of exhortation and warning,[436] which is an outburst of anger on the part of Paul which chapters 1 through 15 of Romans has not led us to expect; he mentions threats to the church's life which have not been alluded to elsewhere. Greetings from Paul's fellow-workers and a doxology complete the chapter.[437] It is unlikely that Paul would have had in Rome, a city he never visited, so many acquaintances as those to whom he here sends greetings; he not only seems to know twenty-five individuals and two families very well but he also knows the house-church groups into which the congregation to which he is writing is divided. Hence, scholars are inclined to believe that chapter 16 was not originally addressed to the church in Rome. However, they are not agreed on the solution to the problem. Some say that Romans 16 is a short letter which Paul wrote to the church at Ephesus; the paragraph of exhortation would have been entirely appropriate for Ephesus; also, some of the names mentioned point to Ephesus as the destination of the letter which Phoebe is bringing.[438] Other scholars maintain that "Rom. 16 was not a part of the original collection of Pauline letters, under either or any guise, but was added to Romans at some later stage in the evolution of the Pauline letter corpus, just as the three Pastoral epistles were added . . . When Rome took the lead in the fight against the heretics toward the middle of the second century and issued a new edition of the Pauline letters—enlarged to include the Pastoral epistles—as a weapon in that fight, the attaching of this note to the Roman letter would serve to strengthen the position of the Roman church by demonstrating that Paul was really intimately acquainted with its members despite the fact that he had not himself visited the city at that time . . ."[439]

5.   Letters Paul Wrote from His Roman Prison.

While Paul was in prison in the city of Rome he composed three of the letters which later found their way into the New Testament: Philippians, Colossians, and Philemon.[440] The first of these is a letter of gratitude directed to the Christian group at Philippi which he regarded with greater affection than any other of the churches he founded.[441] In it Paul becomes intimately autobiographical, letting the reader look into his personal and spiritual life. His Christian friends in Philippi, always generous in providing for Paul's material needs,[442] had sent Epaphroditus to Rome ahead of him, perhaps to provide his lodgings for him and to arrange for Paul's comfort and health. Epaphroditus was to stay with Paul as long as he neded him, but the young man became ill, and it became necessary for him to return to Philippi. Epaphroditus feared the church might criticize him for not accomplishing his mission; to guarantee him a comfortable homecoming, Paul sent this letter by Epaphroditus.

But I feel that I must send back to you Epaphroditus, my brother, fellow-laborer, and fellow-soldier, whom you sent to look after my needs. For he has been longing to see you all, and has been greatly distressed because you heard that he was sick. For he was sick, and nearly died, but God took pity on him, and not only on him, but on me, to save me from having one sorrow after another. So I am all the more eager to send him, so that you may have the pleasure of seeing him again, and I may feel more relieved. So give him a hearty Christian welcome, and value men like him very highly, for he came near dying for the Lord's work, and risked his life to make up for what was lacking in the service you have done me.[443]

After an unusually lengthy salutation, thanksgiving, and prayer,[444] Paul brings the Philippians up to date on what has been happening to him and how he has been longing to see them.[445] Then he states the central theme of the letter:

> Whatever happens, show yourselves citizens worthy of the good news of the Christ, so that whether I come to see you or am kept away and only hear news of you, I may know that you are standing firm with one spirit, one purpose, fighting side by side for faith in the good news . . .[446]

In urging them to follow the example set for them in Jesus Christ, Paul gives expression to the noblest passage in the letter:

> . . . Have the same attitude that Christ Jesus had. Though he possessed the nature of God, he did not grasp at equality with God, but laid it aside to take on the nature of a slave and become like other men. When he had assumed human form, he still further humbled himself and carried his obedience so far as to die, and to die upon the cross. That is why God has so greatly exalted him, and given him the name above all others, so that in the name of Jesus everyone should kneel, in heaven and on earth and in the underworld, and everyone should acknowledge Jesus Christ as Lord, and thus glorify God the Father.
> . . . Do everything without any grumbling or disputing, so that you will be blameless and honest, faultless children of God in the midst of a crooked and perverted age, in which you appear like stars in a dark world, offering men the message of life . . .[447]

Because there is a complete break in the sequence of thought between Philippians 3:1 and 3:2 and because 3:1 sounds like the conclusion of a letter in which Paul mentions having written to them before:

> Now, my brothers, goodbye, and the Lord be with you. I do not mind writing the same thing over and over to you; it is necessary for your safety.

some scholars say that our present letter to the Philippians is really a combination of two letters: the earlier one in Philippians 3:2-4:23 and the later in 1:1-3:1[448] Paul warns the Philippians against the formalism of Judaizers, in a passage reminiscent of Galatians.[449]

> Look out for those dogs, those mischief-makers, with their amputation! We are the true circumcision, who worship God by his Spirit, priding ourselves only on Christ Jesus, and not relying on physical advantages . . .
> . . . For the sake of Christ I have come to count my former gains as loss. Why, I count everything as loss compared with the supreme advantage of knowing Christ Jesus my Lord. For his sake I have lost everything and think it rubbish, in order to gain Christ and be known to be united with him, with any uprightness I may have not based on law but coming through faith in Christ—the uprightness that comes from God through faith. I want to know him in the power of resurrection, and to share his sufferings and even his death, in the hope of attaining resurrection from the dead.[450]

Paul then warns them against spiritual pride:

> Not that I have secured it (resurrection) yet, or already reached perfection, but I am pressing on to see if I can capture it, because I have been captured by Jesus Christ. Brothers, I do not consider that I have captured it yet, only, forgetting what is behind me, and straining toward what lies ahead, I am pressing toward the goal, for the prize to which God through Christ Jesus calls us upward . . .[451]

He criticizes those who take the opposite extreme of following after lawlessness.[452] In a practical, ethical section of the letter, Paul exhorts the Philippians to cultivate joy, harmony, unselfishness, and love:

> Now, brothers, let your minds dwell on what is true, what is worthy, what is right, what is pure, what is amiable, what is kindly—on everything that is excellent or praiseworthy. Do the things that you learned, received, and heard from me, and that you saw me do. Then God who gives peace will be with you.[453]

. . . I have learned how to be contented with the condition
I am in. I know how to live humbly and I know how to enjoy
plenty. I have learned the secret, in any and all conditions,
of being well-fed and of going hungry, of having plenty and
of going without. I can do anything through him who gives
me strength . . .[454]

While Paul was in Rome some one, perhaps Epaphras, who
may have been the minister of the church at Colossae,[455] or Onesimus, the runaway slave mentioned in Paul's letter to Philemon,[456]
brought him word that conditions were not satisfactory in the
church at Colossae. Colossae was a Phrygian town of secondary importance some one hundred miles east of Ephesus. Paul had never
been there, but Christianity had been established in that town,
perhaps by Epaphras himself, during Paul's long stay in Ephesus.[457]
Now Paul was informed that a strange heresy had arisen in the
province of Asia which was threatening to undermine the faith of
the Colossian Christians and undo everything Paul had established
in that entire area. This heresy, which was apparently one of the
roots of the Gnosticism of the second century, had a strongly Jewish
tinge; its adherents recommended abstention from certain articles of
food and observance of certain Sabbaths, new moons, and feasts.
Because of the influence of an oriental dualism, perhaps from
Zoroastrianism, God was considered to be so far from this evil world
that an ascending order of angels was necessary to establish contact
between God and man. The heretics were willing to assign a place
to Jesus Christ in their hierarchy of angelic beings, but if they had
been successful Christianity would have been submerged in a vague
and unprofitable syncretism. In this letter Paul tells the Colossian
Christians that Christ is supreme above all things in heaven and
on earth. After the usual salutation, Paul begins with a long paragraph of thanksgiving and prayer for the Colossians and then continues by making clear the place Christ has in Christian experience:

. . . (God) has rescued us from the dominion of darkness,
and has transferred us into the realm of his dear Son, by whom
we have been ransomed from captivity through having our
sins forgiven. He is a likeness of the unseen God, born before
any creature, for it was through him that everything was created
in heaven and on earth, the seen and the unseen, angelic

thrones, dominions, principalities, authorities—all things were created through him and for him. He existed before all things and he sustains and embraces them all. He is the head of the church, it is his body; for he is the beginning of the first-born from among the dead—that he might come to stand first in everything. For all the divine fulness chose to dwell in him, and through him to reconcile to God all things on earth or in heaven, making his peace through his blood shed on the cross . . .[458]

Paul tells them that the mystery of the incarnation of Christ can be the possession of all; there are to be no classes in the church. They are not to be misled by specious arguments:

> . . . I want you to be united by love, and to have all the benefit of assured knowledge in coming to know Christ—that divine mystery in which all treasures of wisdom and knowledge are to be found. What I mean is, let nobody mislead you by specious arguments . . .
>
> So just as you once accepted the Christ, Jesus, as your Lord, you must live in vital union with him. You must be rooted and built up in him and made strong in faith, just as you were taught to be, overflowing with it in your gratitude.
>
> Take care that nobody exploits you through pretensions of philosophy, guided by human tradition, following material ways of looking at things, instead of following Christ. For it is in him that all the fulness of God's nature lives embodied, and in union with him you too are filled with it. He is the head of all your principalities and dominions . . .[459]

Then Paul urges them not to be concerned unduly with those who make a great deal of external matters and who have philosophic pretensions and ascetic poses; "such practices pass for wisdom, with their self-imposed devotions, their self-humiliation, and their ascetic discipline, but they carry with them no real distinction, they are really only a catering to the flesh."[460] There follows a section of the letter containing some practical advice for Christian living:

> If, then, you have been raised to life with Christ, set your hearts on the things that are where Christ is, above, seated at God's right hand. Fix your thoughts on the things that are

above, not on those that are on earth. For you have died, and your life now lies hidden with Christ in God. When Christ, who is our true life, shall make his appearance, then you also will appear glorified with him.

So treat as dead your physical nature, as far as immorality, impurity, passion, evil desire, and greed are concerned; for it is really idolatry ... But now you too must put them all aside—anger, rage, spite, rough, abusive talk—these must be banished from your lips. You must not lie to one another. For you have stripped off your old self with its ways and have put on that new self newly made in the likeness of its Creator, to know him fully. Here, what matters is not "Greek" and "Jew," the circumcised and the uncircumcised, barbarian, Scythian, slave, freeborn, but Christ is everything and in us all.

As persons chosen by God, then, consecrated and dearly loved, you must clothe yourself with tenderness of heart, kindness, humility, gentleness, forbearance. You must bear with one another and forgive one another ... And over all these put on love, which completes them and fastens them all together. Let the ruling principle in your hearts be Christ's peace, for in becoming members of one body you have been called under its sway. And you must be thankful. Let the message of Christ live in your hearts in all its wealth of wisdom. Teach it to one another and train one another in it with thankfulness, with psalms, hymns, and sacred songs, and sing to God with all your hearts. And whatever you have to say or do, do it all as followers of the Lord Jesus, and offer your thanksgiving to God the Father through him.[461]

Paul includes special instructions for wives and husbands, children and fathers, slaves and masters.[462] The letter ends with personal greetings and news about his associates; Tychicus and Onesimus are to deliver this missive;[463] Epaphras and Paul are both concerned about the churches at Laodicea and Hierapolis; about the former Paul says:

... Remember me to the brothers in Laodicea and to Nympha and the church that meets at her house. When this letter has been read to you, have it read to the church at Laodicea also, and see that you read the letter that is coming from there ...[464]

Paul adds a farewell in his own hand.[465]

Paul's letter to Philemon is unique among his writings, for it is a purely private personal letter, addressed to a prominent Christian in Colossae;[466] but Paul intended it to be read before the entire group of Christians of Colossae and perhaps also of Laodicea. Philemon was a slave owner; one of his slaves, Onesimus, ran away from home and came to Paul in Rome; under the great missionary's persuasive influence, Onesimus became a Christian. In this new relationship, the slave felt honor bound to return to Colossae and surrender himself to his master. To make it easier for Onesimus, Paul writes this letter to Philemon, urging him to do the Christian thing and receive his erring slave back as a brother. Very adroitly, Paul thanks Philemon in advance for what he knows he will do:

> I never mention you in my prayers without thanking my God for what I hear of the love and faith you have in the Lord Jesus and all his people . . .
> So although as a Christian I feel quite free to order you to do what ought to be done, I prefer to appeal to you in the name of love . . . I appeal to you for my child Onesimus, whose father I have become here in prison. Once you found him useless, but now he has become useful to you and to me, and now that I send him back to you, it is like sending my very heart. I would have liked to keep him with me, to wait on me in your place while I am in prison for the good news, but I do not wish to do anything without your consent, so that your kindness might be voluntary, and not have the appearance of compulsion. For perhaps this is why you and he were parted for a while, that you might have him back forever, not as a slave any longer but more than a slave, a dear brother—dear especially to me, but how much dearer to you, both as a man and as a Christian! So if you regard me as a comrade, welcome him as you would me. And if he has caused you any loss or owes you anything, charge it to my account. I, Paul, write this with my own hand: I will repay it—not to mention the fact that you owe me your very self besides . . .
> I write you in full reliance upon your obedience; I know that you will do even more than I ask. And get ready to entertain me too, for I hope that I shall be restored to you, in answer to your prayers.[467]

We have no way of knowing whether Philemon took Paul's pointed suggestion or not, but we may safely assume, because of the supreme confidence with which Paul writes, that Philemon willingly granted Paul's request. Though Paul nowhere says anything in condemnation of the institution of slavery, but rather seems to accept it as a part of the laws and customs of the Roman Empire,[468] he did more than any one man to hasten its abolition. By insisting that the relation between master and slave was to be ruled by Christian love, and by recommending in his letter to Philemon that a slave owner receive a runaway slave as his Christian brother, Paul placed the entire business on a new footing. Brotherhood of all men in Christ finally led to the disappearance of slavery.

6. Letters Based on the Life and Thought of Paul: Ephesians, I and II Timothy, and Titus.

Though many scholars still hold to the Pauline authorship of the letter to the Ephesians, many others, beginning with the early years of the nineteenth century, have come to the conclusion that the book is pseudonymous.[469] In style and language, Ephesians shows peculiarities of vocabulary, changes in the meaning of characteristic Pauline words, and reveals an author with a much calmer temperament than Paul's. Though the author develops some of Paul's leading ideas, it is in his secondary doctrinal ideas that he reveals the peculiar bent of a different mind. In Ephesians, Paul boasts of his display of insight into the "secret of the Christ,"[470] an attitude not in accord with what we know of Paul in his own letters. Ephesians reveals its dependence on the letters of Paul, notably Colossians. The historical situation reflected in Ephesians is more nearly that of the last decade of the first century than that of Paul's life; "apostles and prophets" are mentioned as if they had belonged to an earlier generation:

. . . You are built upon the apostles and prophets as your foundation, and Christ Jesus himself is the cornerstone . . .[471]

Both the author and his readers are Gentiles.[472] The author and his readers have evidently had no previous acquaintance with one another;[473] this would certainly not have been the case if the author had been Paul and the readers the members of the church at Ephesus, where Paul stayed longer than any place else.[474] The great conflict with the Judaizers, which occupied Paul's energies all through his life, is not indicated in Ephesians; instead, the author fears that his hearers may be influenced by the type of heresy which invaded the church toward the end of the first century:

> . . . We must not be babies any longer, blown about and swung around by every wind of doctrine through the trickery of men with their ingenuity in inventing error . . .[475]

and that they might relapse into pagan practices:

> So what I mean and insist upon in the Lord's name is this: You must no longer live like the heathen, with their frivolity of mind and darkened understanding . . . You must lay aside with your former habits your old self which is going to ruin through its deceptive passions. You must adopt a new attitude of mind, and put on the new self which has been created in likeness to God, with all the uprightness and holiness that belong to the truth.
> So you must lay aside falsehood and each tell his neighbor the truth, for we are parts of one another. Be angry, but do not sin. The sun must not go down upon your anger; you must not give the devil a chance . . . You must give up all bitterness, rage, anger, and loud abusive talk, and all spite . . .
> But immorality or any form of vice or greed must not be so much as mentioned among you; that would not be becoming in God's people . . .
> Whatever anyone may say in the way of worthless arguments to deceive you, these are the things that are bringing God's anger down upon the disobedient. Therefore have nothing to do with them. For once you were sheer darkness, but now, as Christians, you are light itself. You must live like children of light, for light leads to perfect goodness, uprightness, and truth; you must make sure what pleases the Lord. Have nothing to do with the profitless doings of the darkness; expose them instead. For while it is degrading even to mention their secret practices, yet when anything is exposed by the light, it is made visible, and anything that is made visible is light . . .[476]

So we may conclude, with Francis W. Beare, that "the epistle is not the work of Paul. It was published under his name as a tribute of love and admiration by a disciple of great gifts, deeply imbued with the mind and spirit of the great apostle, closely acquainted with his letters, especially with the letter to the Colossians, and quite possibly acquainted with the apostle in person. If the writer had been in touch with Paul during his last imprisonment, he may well have written the letter to give expression to the ideas of Christ and the church which had been developing in the apostle's mind after the writing of the letter to Colossae; in that case he would feel, like Plato in the *Apology of Socrates,* that he was no more than a vehicle of his master's thoughts and might therefore legitimately address the church in his name."[477]

The letter to the Ephesians is a circular letter, addressed not to any one church in a particular locality but to all the churches in a region, such as the one surrounding Paul's missionary headquarters in Ephesus,[478] or to all churches throughout the world. The author is not concerned with local problems of administration and discipline; he emphasizes the unity of the church as a world society and what he has to say concerns all the Christian congregations alike. Edgar J. Goodspeed in his book *The Meaning of Ephesians* theorizes that the letter to the Ephesians was written by the unknown Christian who first brought together all of Paul's letters for publication, perhaps at Ephesus, under the stimulation of the appearance of Luke-Acts;[479] in spite of the fact that Goodspeed's theory represents an extreme position, more moderate writers, such as Beare, find elements of truth in the theory:

> . . . Ephesians is, and is meant by the author to be, a commendation of Paul's theology to the church of another generation . . . His interpretation will help them to understand Paul's writings, and to gain through them a deeper and wider comprehension of the gospel in its profoundest implications.
> The Epistle to the Ephesians is a very ambitious undertaking by a writer of great originality and power. The book is more than a summary of Pauline doctrine; more even than a commentary on the Pauline letters. It is an attempt to formulate a philosophy of religion, which is at the same time a philosophy of history, out of Pauline materials . . . [480]

Ephesians follows much the same line of argument as Colossians, but in the former there is no note of controversy; in Colossians Jesus is described as supreme above all earthly and heavenly beings;[481] in Ephesians Christ becomes the center and meaning of the whole universe and the pattern and hope of all human life:

Blessed be the God and Father of our Lord Jesus Christ, who through Christ has blessed us with every spiritual blessing in the heavenly realm. Through him he chose us out before the creation of the world, to be consecrated and above reproach in his sight in love. He foreordained us to become his sons through Jesus Christ, in fulfillment of his general purpose, so that we might praise the splendid blessing which he has given us through his beloved Son. It is through union with him and through his blood that we have been delivered and our offenses forgiven, in the abundance of his mercy which he has lavished upon us. He has given us perfect insight into his secret purpose and understanding of it, in following out the design he planned to carry out in Christ, and in arranging, when the time should have fully come, that everything in heaven and on earth should be unified in Christ, . . .[482]

God's universal purpose is accomplished in and through Christ:

. . . The God of our Lord Jesus Christ, the glorious Father, grant you the Spirit of wisdom and revelation, through the knowledge of himself . . . so that you may know . . . how surpassingly great his power is for us who believe; like the mighty strength he exerted in raising Christ from the dead, and seating him at his right hand in heaven, far above all hierarchies, authorities, powers, and dominions, and all titles that can be bestowed not only in this world but in the world to come. He has put everything under his feet and made him the indisputable head of the church, which is his body, filled by him who fills everything everywhere . . .[483]

. . . But now through your union with Christ Jesus you who were once far away have through the blood of Christ been brought near. For he is himself our peace. He has united the two divisions, and broken down the barrier that kept us apart, and through his human nature put an end to the feud between us, and abolished the Law with its rules and regulations, in order to make peace and create out of the two parties one new man by uniting them with himself, and to kill the feud between them with his cross and in one body reconcile them both to God with it. He came with the good news of peace for you who were far away and for those who were near; for it is through him that we both with one Spirit are now able to approach the Father. So you are no longer foreigners or strangers, but you are fellow-citizens of God's people and members of his family.[484]

The author presents a very beautiful prayer for the spiritual progress of his readers; this section ends with a doxology:

> For this reason I kneel before the Father from whom every family in heaven or on earth takes its name, and beg him out of his wealth of glory to strengthen you mightily through his Spirit in your inner nature and through your faith to let Christ in his love make his home in your hearts. Your roots must be deep and your foundations strong, so that you and all God's people may be strong enough to grasp what breadth, length, height, and depth mean, to understand Christ's love, so far beyond our understanding, so that you may be filled with the very fulness of God. To him who by the exertion of his power within us can do unutterably more that all we ask or imagine, be glory through the church and through Christ Jesus through all generations forever and ever. Amen.[485]

The chief doctrinal feature of the letter to the Ephesians is the idea that the church is the glorious society which embodies in human history the eternal purpose of God as revealed in Jesus Christ. Man can be reconciled to man and all humanity can be elevated into communion with God through the corporate life of the church. The unity of the church must be promoted:

> . . . Make every effort to maintain the unity of the Spirit through the tie of peace. There is but one body and one Spirit, just as there is but one hope that belongs to the summons you received. There is but one Lord, one faith, one baptism, one God and Father of all, who is above us all, pervades us all, and is within us all . . . And he has given us some men as apostles, some as prophets, some as missionaries, some as pastors and teachers, in order to fit his people for the work of service, for building the body of Christ, until we attain unity in faith, and in the knowledge of the Son of God, and reach mature manhood, and that full measure of development found in Christ . . . We must lovingly hold to the truth and grow up into perfect union with him who is the head—Christ himself . . .[486]

The author makes the marriage relationship the symbol of the union of Christ with his church.[487] He mentions the special duties of children, parents, slaves, and masters in the Christian fellowship.[488] All must put on the Christian armor and fight the Christian battle:

> Henceforth you must grow strong through union with the Lord and through his mighty strength. You must put on God's armor, so as to be able to stand up against the devil's stratagems. For we have to struggle, not with enemies of flesh and blood, but with the hierarchies, the authorities, the master-spirits of this dark world, the spirit-forces of evil on high. So you must take God's armor, so that when the evil day comes you will be able to make a stand, and when it is all over to hold your ground. Stand your ground, then, with the belt of truth around your waist, and put on uprightness as your coat of mail, and on your feet put the readiness the good news of peace brings. Besides all these, take faith for your shield, for with it you will be able to put out all the flaming missiles of the evil one, and take salvation for your helmet, and for your sword the Spirit, which is the voice of God . . .[489]

Toward the end of the first century or in the opening years of the second century,[490] an unknown Christian adopted a current literary convention and brought out three letters of his under the name of Paul containing a message he felt sure Paul would have given if he had then been alive. These letters—I and II Timothy and Titus—are called the "pastoral letters" because they deal from a pastoral point of view with matters of church government and are addressed to two young assistants of Paul, Timothy and Titus. The great majority of New Testament scholars now agree that these, letters cannot have been written by Paul, at least in their present form; there may be some genuine fragments from Paul's authentic correspondence, but the finished product is much later than Paul's time.[491] For one thing, the author of the pastoral letters considers religious faith to consist of an acceptance of a body of authoritative teaching rather than, as with Paul, a transforming inner experience; in this, the author reveals his interest in the formation of an orthodox doctrinal position in opposition to the various heretical sects which were beginning to increase in numbers and influence. He often speaks of "the faith," "the truth," "the teaching," etc.:

These are the instructions that I entrust to you, my son Timothy, and they are in accordance with the predictions made long ago about you. Fight the good fight with their aid, keeping hold of faith and a good conscience. For some people have let that go and have had their faith ruined, . . .[492]

The Spirit distinctly says that in later times some will turn away from the faith, and devote their attention to deceitful spirits and the things that demons teach through the pretensions of liars—men with seared consciences who forbid people to marry and insist on abstinence from certain kinds of food that God created for men who believe and understand the truth to enjoy and give thanks for it . . .[493]

. . . The household of God . . . is the church of the living God, the pillar and foundation of the truth . . .[494]

. . . Until I come, devote yourself to the public reading of Scripture, preaching, and teaching . . . Look out for yourself and for your teaching . . .[495]

Timothy, guard what has been intrusted to you. Keep away from the worldly, empty phrases and contradictions of what they falsely call knowledge, through professing which some people have made a failure of the faith. God bless you all.[496]

. . . I know whom I have trusted and I am sure that he is able to guard what I have intrusted to him for that Day. As your example in wholesome instruction, keep before you what you learned from me, in the faith and love that come through union with Christ Jesus. Guard that splendid trust through the holy Spirit that lives in our hearts.[497]

Also, Paul's emphasis upon the imminence of the return of Jesus is absent from the pastoral letters; the author expects the Christian movement to be in existence for quite a long time in the future.[498] Then, the vocabulary of the pastoral letters is that of Christian literature of the second century; further, the style of the author is much more smooth than the rugged abruptness characteristic of Paul's letters.[499] But above all, the ecclesiastical order presupposed in the pastoral letters cannot be associated with the period covered by the life of Paul. In Paul's day there was no official ministry; as long as he and the other apostles were alive, their leadership was taken for granted. The pastoral letters mention five kinds of church officials: superintendent (bishop, overseer), elder (presbyter), assistant (deacon), the wife of the assistant (deaconess), and widow. Between the time of Paul and the time the pastoral letters were written a great constitutional change had taken place in the life of the church involving the disappearance of the independent, spirit-filled, apostolic leadership and the coming of local pastoral leadership. The pastoral letters unfortunately do not present a list of duties of these officials and their relationships to each other, but they do give personal qualifications of candidates for these offices, with emphasis on moral considerations. For the superintendent the author recommends:

> Whoever aspires to the office of superintendent sets his heart on a fine work. A superintendent must be a man above reproach, only once married, temperate, sensible, a man of good behavior, hospitable, able to teach; not addicted to drink or pugnacious, but a man of moderation and peace, not avaricious, managing his own house well, and keeping his children under control and perfectly respectful . . . He must not be a new convert, or he may grow conceited and incur criticism from slanderous people. He must also be a man of good standing with outsiders, or he may get into disgrace and be entrapped by the slanderers . . .[500]

The qualifications for the office of elder are similar to those of the superintendent; in fact, in Titus the words "elder" and "superintendent" seem to be used interchangeably to designate officials of the same rank. Elders were to be

> men of irreproachable character, who have been married only once, whose children are Christians, free from any suspicion of profligacy or disobedience.[501]

The assistants were subordinate to the elder-bishop:

> . . . Assistants, in turn, must be serious, straightforward men, not addicted to wine or dishonest gain, but holding the divine truth of the faith with a clear conscience. They should first be tested, and afterward, if there is no fault to be found with them, they can serve as assistants . . . The assistants must be only once married, and manage their children and their

households well. For those who do good service as assistants gain a good standing for themselves and great confidence in their faith in Christ Jesus.[502]

The wives of the assistants were to "be serious, not gossips; they must be temperate, and perfectly trustworthy."[503] The author says about widows:

> . . . No one under sixty years of age should be put on the list of widows. A widow must have been married but once, and have a good reputation for Christian service, such as bringing up children, being hospitable to strangers, washing the feet of God's people, helping people in distress, or devoting herself to any form of doing good . . .[504]

To the ministers and church officials who would soon have supervision over the welfare of the Christian religion, the author of the pastoral letters recommends certain general considerations as to their duties. They were to teach sound doctrine:

> These are the things you must teach and preach. Anyone who teaches different views and does not agree with the wholesome instruction which comes from our Lord Jesus Christ, and with religious teaching is a conceited, ignorant person, with a morbid craving for speculations and arguments . . .[505]

They were to select other teachers carefully and train them to supervise the work of other teachers; the author was particularly concerned with the refutation of heretical teachings. Paul appears in the pastoral letters as the great opponent of heresy.

> . . . Stay on in Ephesus in order to warn certain people there not to teach strange views nor to devote themselves to fictions and interminable pedigrees; . . . The aim of your instruction must be love that springs from a pure heart and from a good conscience and from a sincere faith. Some people have failed in these things and been diverted into fruitless talk . . .
> . . . Law is not intended for upright men but for the lawless and disorderly, the godless and irreligious, the irreverent and profane, men who kill their fathers or mothers, murderers, immoral people, men sexually perverted, kidnappers, liars, perjurers, or whatever else is contrary to sound teaching . . .[506]

. . . Let worldly fictions and old wives' tales alone. Train yourself for the religious life . . .[507]

. . . Let no one look down on you because you are young, but set those who believe an example in speech, conduct, love, faith, and purity. Until I come, devote yourself to the public reading of Scripture, preaching, and teaching. Do not neglect the gift you have . . . Look out for yourself and for your teaching, . . .[508]

Remind men of these things. Charge them before God to avoid idle arguments which do no one any good and only bring destruction on those who listen to them. Do your best to win God's approval as a workman who has nothing to be ashamed of, but rightly shapes the message of truth. Leave worldly, empty phrases alone, for they lead people deeper and deeper into godlessness, and their teaching spreads like a cancer; . . . Fly from the cravings of youth, and go in pursuit of uprightness, faith, love, and peace, in company with those who call upon the Lord with pure hearts. Avoid foolish, crude speculations; you know they only lead to quarrels, and a slave of the Lord must not quarrel, but treat everyone kindly; he must be persuasive and unresentful, correcting his opponents with gentleness; for God may possibly let them repent and acknowledge the truth, and they may yet return to their senses and escape from the toils of the devil, who has caught them to make them do his will.[509]

. . . They are the kind of men who make their way into people's houses and make captives of poor, weak women, loaded down with their sins and under the control of all sorts of impulses, always ready to learn but never able to comprehend the truth . . . These people in turn oppose the truth; they are men of depraved minds and counterfeit faith . . .[510]

The prospective Christian leaders were to encourage their followers to become acquainted with the sacred writings; evidently by the time the pastoral letters were written some Christian writings had reached canonical status, perhaps in opposition to the heretic Marcion:

. . . But you must stand by what you have learned and been convinced of, and remember from whom you learned it, and how from childhood you have known the Scriptures which can give you the wisdom that through faith in Christ Jesus leads to salvation. All Scripture is divinely inspired, and useful in teaching, in reproof, in correcting faults, and in training in uprightness, so that the man of God will be adequate, and equipped for any good work.[511]

The future leaders of the church were to exercise wholesome discipline administered both for the benefit of the church and for the regeneration of the offender;

> . . . The things you learned from me before many witnesses you must commit to trustworthy men who will be capable of teaching others. Share my hardships like a good soldier of Christ Jesus . . . No one who competes in the games is awarded a crown unless he obeys the rules . . .[512]

> . . . Never ordain anyone hastily; do not make yourself responsible for the sins of others; keep your life pure . . .[513]

To all Christians the author's words of advice and counsel still ring true:

> . . . Strive for uprightness, godliness, faith, love, steadfastness, gentleness. Enter the great contest of faith! Take hold of eternal life . . . I charge you to keep his (Christ's) command stainless and irreproachable until the appearance of our Lord Jesus Christ, . . .[514]

In the words which the author places in the mouth of his great hero, Paul, we see his purpose to conserve and bring about deep appreciation for the great Pauline Christian tradition:

> My life is already being poured out, and the time has come for my departure. I have had a part in the great contest, I have run my race, I have preserved my faith. Now the crown of uprightness awaits me, which the Lord, the upright judge, will award me on that Day, and not only me but also all who have loved and hoped for his appearing.[515]

SUGGESTIONS FOR FURTHER STUDY

A. E. Barnett, *The New Testament: Its Making and Meaning,* pp. 21-92, 181-191, 275-292.

H. M. Battenhouse, *New Testament History and Literature,* pp. 279-357.

H. M. Battenhouse, *The Bible Unlocked,* pp. 431-509.

G. A. Buttrick, ed., *The Interpreter's Bible,* VII, pp. 187-213; IX, pp. 355-668; X; XI, pp. 1-573.

C. T. Craig, *The Beginning of Christianity,* pp. 156-178, 226-265.

F. C. Eiselen, E. Lewis, and D. G. Downey, eds., *The Abingdon Bible Commentary,* pp. 931-943, 1135-1294.

J. Finegan, *Light from the Ancient Past,* pp. 252-352.

G. H. Gilbert, *The Student's Life of Paul.*

E. J. Goodspeed, *An Introduction to the New Testament,* pp. 1-124, 210-239, 327-344.

E. J. Goodspeed, *Paul.*

E. J. Goodspeed, *The Meaning of Ephesians.*

E. J. Goodspeed, *The Story of the New Testament,* pp. 1-48, 125-131.

T. S. Kepler, ed., *Contemporary Thinking about Paul.*

J. Knox, *Chapters in a Life of Paul.*

M. E. Lyman, *The Christian Epic,* pp. 26-51, 234-245.

J. Moffatt, *An Introduction to the Literature of the New Testament,* pp. 59-176, 373-420.

E. W. K. Mould, *Essentials of Bible History,* pp. 582-588.

C. W. Quimby, *Paul for Everyone.*

C. W. Quimby, *The Great Redemption.*

H. F. Rall, *According to Paul.*

D. W. Riddle, *Paul, Man of Conflict.*

D. W. Riddle and H. H. Hutson, *New Testament Life and Literature,* pp. 106-148, 203-206.

B. W. Robinson, *The Life of Paul.*

E. F. Scott, *The Literature of the New Testament,* pp. 107-197.

PART IV

CHRISTIANITY
IN THE
POST-APOSTOLIC AGE

Chapter Twenty-four

THE CHURCH UNDER FIRE

A. *The Book of Hebrews*

Toward the end of the first century the Christian church found itself in conflict with the Roman government. Prior to the accession of the emperor Domitian (81-96 A.D.) there had been no consistent policy on the part of the state in opposition to Christians as such. Jewish religious leaders had put Jesus to death;[1] Jewish unfriendliness, though sporadic and occasional, had hampered the work of Paul and other apostles;[2] even Nero's persecution, though it had resulted in the martyrdom of Peter and Paul,[3] was confined to the city of Rome and did not threaten the life of the church as a whole. But by the year 90 A.D., persecution of the Christians by Domitian was deliberate, systematic, and empire-wide. The emperor demanded divine honors as a symbol of political loyalty to his rule;[4] for many subjects throughout the empire this constituted no religious problem, for they could recognize their political allegiance to Domitian by taking part in the emperor cult and then worship in whatever other cult they desired to. But for the Christians, with their strong monotheistic presuppositions, they could not take part in any rite which hinted at the existence of gods other than the one true God. There was thus conflict between the church and the state, with serious consequences for the Christian religion. The New Testament books of Hebrews and Revelation—and perhaps also I Peter—reflect this situation in the reign of Domitian.

That the book of Hebrews was written at a time when Christians were being subjected to persecution is evident from its contents:

> But you must remember those early days[5] when after you had received the light you had to go through a great struggle

with persecution, sometimes being actually exposed as a public spectacle to insults and violence, and sometimes showing yourselves ready to share the lot of those in that condition. For you showed sympathy with those who were in prison, and you put up with it cheerfully when your property was taken from you . . . You must not lose your courage, for it will be richly rewarded, but you will need endurance if you are to carry out God's will and receive the blessing he has promised . . .[6]

. . . Think of the opposition that he (Jesus) encountered from those sinners against themselves, if you would not grow weary and faint-hearted. You have not yet resisted unto death in your struggle with sin . . . You must submit to it as discipline. God is dealing with you as his sons. For where is there a son whom his father does not discipline? . . . Discipline is never pleasant at the time; it is painful; but to those who are trained by it, it afterward yields the peace of character. So tighten your loosening hold! Stiffen your wavering stand! . . .[7]

Therefore, the date of its composition would be *ca*. 90 A.D. The author is unknown; the traditional view that it should be included among the letters of Paul has been entirely abandoned.[8] The author differentiates himself from the first hearers of the gospel message; he thus does not belong in the group of first generation Christians contemporary with Paul:

. . . It was first proclaimed by the Lord himself, and it was guaranteed to us by those who heard him . . .[9]

In style and doctrinal position the book of Hebrews could not have been Paul's; Hebrews is a systematic treatment of a single theme, unlike Paul's energetic, miscellaneous, and informal letters; missing from Hebrews are the great Pauline concepts of justification by faith, mystical union with Christ, and present salvation in Christ. The author of Hebrews stresses the Jewish sacrificial system in contrast with the high priestly role of Jesus, a matter rarely referred to in Paul's letters.[10] But, in spite of the fact that the author's name is unknown, we can learn a great deal about him from his book itself. He was primarily a preacher; though Hebrews ends with personal messages, greetings, and a benediction, it opens like a sermon should: with a statement of the theme of the book:

It was little by little and in different ways that God spoke in old times to our forefathers through the prophets, but in these latter days he has spoken to us in a Son, whom he had destined to possess everything, and through whom he had made the world. He is the reflection of God's glory, and the representation of his being, and bears up the universe by his mighty word. He has effected man's purification from sin, and has taken his seat at the right hand of God's Majesty, showing himself to be as much greater than the angels as his title is superior to theirs . . .[11]

Other references scattered throughout Hebrews indicate that the author is a preacher; he seems to have been separated for a little while from his flock, but he has prepared a treatise, which he calls an "appeal,"[12] from various sermons and addresses he has delivered on different occasions, all woven into a unity serving to strengthen his main theme.[13] His message was to be read to his followers:

For it was not for angels that he destined the control of that world to be, that we are speaking of . . .[14]

But about you, dear friends, even though we say this, we are sure of better things that promise salvation . . .[15]

Now the main point in what I am saying is this: . . .[16]

And why should I go on? For my time would fail me if I told of Gideon, Barak, Samson, Jephthah, David, Samuel, and the prophets . . .[17]

The author was a man of great literary genius; the Greek style of the book of Hebrews is the best in the New Testament. He was a man of wide philosophical knowledge; he shows intimate acquaintance with the philosophy of Plato, perhaps as it was mediated by Philo, the noted Alexandrian Jew; the Platonic conception of the dualism between the ideal and the real world is evident when the author speaks of Jesus as "the reflection of God's glory"[18] and the service of earthly priests "only a shadow and imitation of that in heaven."[19] Prominent in the author's thought is the doctrine of the Logos, possibly derived also from Philo, which seems to lie behind some of his descriptions of Jesus:

In thus making everything subject to man, God left nothing that was not subjected to him. But we do not as yet see everything made subject to him, but we do see Jesus, who was "made for a little while inferior to angels, crowned with glory and honor" because he suffered death, so that by the favor of God he might taste the bitterness of death on behalf of every human being. For it was appropriate that he who is the great First Cause of the universe should, in guiding his many children to his glorious salvation, make their leader in it fully qualified through what he suffered . . .[20]

The author is thoroughly acquainted with the Jewish scriptures, though in the Greek translation known as the Septuagint rather than the original Hebrew text. In the typical Alexandrian way, the author uses the allegorical method in handling the Old Testament; this is evident in the way he treats Melchizedek.[21] To the author the Christian faith is the only adequate and final philosophy; the book of Hebrews is the first attempt to create a philosophy of the Christian religion. The word "Hebrews" in the title was intended to designate the first readers of this book as a community of Jewish Christians living in or near the city of Rome, but the title is no earlier than the third century and may have been the result of an inference from the importance of Judaism in the author's presentation of his main theme. Sometimes the words "Israel" or "Hebrews" were used to refer to all Christians, Jewish or Gentile. Barnett thinks that the Hebrews were "Hellenistic Christians whose Bible was the Greek Old Testament and whose knowledge of Judaism was, like the author's, entirely literary."[22] The Roman destination of the book is strengthened by the final greeting: "The brothers from Italy wish to be remembered to you. God bless you all!"[23]

The book of Hebrews was written to stimulate the consciences and renew the courage of Christians who were under the stress of persecution. The author warns them against deserting the faith; the faith once compromised can never be regained.

For it is impossible to arouse people to a fresh repentance when they have once for all come into the light and had a taste of the gift from heaven, and shared in the holy Spirit and felt the goodness of the word of God and the strong influences of the coming age, and yet have fallen back, for they

crucify the Son of God on their own account, and hold him up
to contempt . . .[24]

For if we choose to go on sinning after we have so fully
learned the truth, there is no sacrifice left to be offered for
our sins, but only the dreadful prospect of judgment and that
blazing indignation which is to devour God's enemies . . .[25]

He wants to remind them of the real foundation of the Christian
faith: Jesus Christ is the ideal high priest who offered the ideal
sacrifice in the ideal sanctuary, in contrast with the Old Testament
priesthood who offered up the imperfect sacrifice in the earthly
tabernacle. In the Old Testament we have the earthly shadows of
the heavenly realities. "The heavenly realities have been brought
down to earth in the transcendent person and work of Jesus Christ,
who as the Son of God has made the perfect revelation of the divine
will and purpose, and by his sacrifice has wrought out the perfect
redemption for mankind."[26] After proving Christ's supremacy over
the angels, the author of Hebrews demonstrates the superiority of
Christ over Moses.[27] In contrast with the Aaaronic priesthood of
the Old Testament, Jesus is the supreme high priest after the order
of Melchizedek;[28] the author works this out in some detail:

. . . And in proportion as Jesus was not appointed priest
without God's making oath to it, the agreement which he
guarantees is better than the old one, for God took no oath in
appointing the old priests, . . . The old priests too had to be
numerous, because death prevented their continuing in office.
But he continues forever, and so his priesthood is untransfer-
able. Therefore, he is able to save forever all who come to God
through him, because he lives and intercedes for them forever.
Such a high priest we needed—godly, blameless, unstained,
removed from sinful men and raised above the very heavens;
who does not need, as the old high priests did, to offer sacrifices
every day, first for his own sins and then for those of his people
—for this last he has done once for all, in offering up himself.
For the Law appoints to the high priesthood men full of im-
perfection; but this utterance about the making of the oath,
which came along after the Law, appoints a son, fully qualified
to be high priest forever.
. . . We have such a high priest as this, and he has taken his

seat in heaven at the right hand of God's Majesty, to officiate as priest in the sanctuary and in that true tent of worship which not man but the Lord himself set up . . . The priestly service to which Christ has been appointed is as much better than the old as the agreement established by him and the promises on which it is based are superior to the former ones . . .

But when Christ came, as the high priest of the better system under which we love, he went once and for all, through that greater, more perfect tent of worship not made by human hands nor a part of our material creation, into the sanctuary, taking with him no blood of goats and calves, but his own, and secured our permanent deliverance . . .

. . . He is taking away the old to put the new in its place. And it is through his doing of God's will that we have been once for all purified from sin through the offering of the body of Jesus Christ in sacrifice. Every other priest stands officiating day after day, offering over and over again the same sacrifices, though they were powerless ever to remove people's sins. But Christ has offered for all time one sacrifice for sin, and has taken his seat at God's right hand, from that time waiting for his enemies to be made his footstool. For by that one sacrifice he has forever qualified those who are purified from sin to approach God . . .[29]

Through Christ Christians can grasp the reality of things which have hitherto been vague and dim; he has brought the unseen realities within our reach, so that we now can take part in an eternal, invisible world. This thought is given its clearest expression in chapter eleven, the glorious chapter in praise of faith, one of the mountain-peak chapters of the Bible.[30]

Faith means the assurance of what we hope for; it is our conviction about things that we cannot see. For it was by it that the men of old gained God's approval.[31]

And why should I go on? For my time would fail me if I told of Gideon, Barak, Samson, Jephthah, David, Samuel, and the prophets, who by their faith conquered kingdoms, attained uprightness, received new promises, shut the mouths of lions, put out furious fires, escaped death by the sword, found strength in their times of weakness, proved mighty in war, put foreign armies to flight. Women had their dead restored to them by resurrection. Others endured torture, and refused to accept release, that they might rise again to the better life. Still others had to endure taunts and blows, and even fetters and prison. They were stoned to death, they were tortured to death, they were sawed in two, they were killed with the sword. Clothed in the skins of sheep or goats, they were driven from place to place, destitute, persecuted, misused—men of whom the world was not worthy wandering in deserts, mountains, caves, and holes in the ground.

Yet though they all gained God's approval by their faith, they none of them received what he had promised, for God had resolved upon something still better for us, that they might not reach the fulfillment of their hopes except with us.[32]

Christ himself is the supreme example of this faith; through him all the true servants of Christ can live in the higher spiritual realm.

Therefore, let us too, with such a crowd of witnesses about us, throw off every impediment and the entanglement of sin, and run with determination the race for which we are entered, fixing our eyes upon Jesus, our leader and example in faith, who in place of the happiness that belonged to him, submitted to a cross, caring nothing for its shame, and has taken his seat at the right hand of the throne of God . . .[33]

The book closes with a few practical admonitions:

Your love for the brotherhood must continue. Do not forget to be hospitable to strangers, for by being so some, without knowing it, have had angels as their guests. Remember those who are in prison as though you were in prison with them, and those who are ill-treated as being yourselves liable to the same trials. Marriage should be respected by everyone, and the marriage relation kept sacred, for vicious and immoral people God will punish. You must not be avaricious; . . .

Do not forget your former leaders, the men who brought you God's message.

Jesus Christ is the same today that he was yesterday, and he will be so forever. You must not be carried away with strange varieties of teaching. The true way to steadfastness of heart is through God's mercy, not through scruples about food, which have never done their adherents any good . . . But do not forget to be helpful and generous, for that is the kind of sacrifice that pleases God.[34]

B.   *The Apocalypse of John.*

During the reign of Domitian,[35] probably *ca.* 95 A.D., another Christian writer produced a book which reveals the serious effects of the conflict between church and state on the Christians of the last decade of the first century. Differing substantially from the point of view of the author of Hebrews, the author of Revelation takes an attitude of open hostility toward the Roman government; for him, the struggle between the church and the Roman empire was identical with the age-old conflict between good and evil, the prelude to the cataclysmic destruction of the world and the ultimate triumph of righteousness. Christians were suffering because of persecution at the hands of the authorities; there had already been one martyrdom in Pergamum,[36] and elsewhere Christians were being forced to pay the penalty of refusing to worship the emperor's statue.[37] The author has despaired of any permanent solution of the difficulties the church is facing; therefore, he turns the attention of his readers from this present world to a life beyond this age. He adopted the imagery of traditional apocalypticism in order to bolster the morale of the Christians, whose sufferings seemed to deny the efficacy of their faith. To strengthen their loyalty, he pointed them to the imminence of the kingdom of God, whose blessings would make their present difficulties seem insignificant. In a situation similar to the one which inspired a Jewish apocalypticist to compose the book of Daniel,[38] this Christian leader wrote the book of Revelation to affirm the supremacy of the lordship of Christ against the iniquitous demands of the emperor Domitian.

The author calls himself John,[39] but nowhere in the book does he present anything which warrants his being identified with any particular one of the several men by that name in the early church. He was evidently not John, the son of Zebedee, one of the twelve disciples of Jesus, for there are no personal reminiscences of Jesus in the book and he regards the twelve objectively and with a reverence which they would not have felt for one another.[40] As early as the middle of the third century A.D., Dionysius of Alexandria denied that the author of the book of Revelation was the apostle John;[41] for that reason, rejection of apostolic authorship and authority became frequent in the eastern part of Christendom and resulted in the omission of Revelation from the earliest forms of the Egyptian and Armenian versions of the New Testament. Dionysius also argued, and quite correctly, that the author of Revelation was not the same man who wrote the fourth gospel and I John; in grammar, diction, style, and theological outlook, Revelation is in contrast with the other writings in the New Testament bearing the name of John. The author of Revelation was a Christian prophet of Asia, perhaps a native of Ephesus,[42] who was spending his exile on the island of Patmos,[43] a rocky island in the Aegean Sea southwest of Miletus, a penal settlement to which undesirables were frequently banished. He is writing to "the seven churches of Asia"[44]—Ephesus, Smyrna, Pergamum, Thyatira, Sardis, Philadelphia, and Laodicea[45]—and he intends his message to be read publicly.[46]

The first three chapters of the book of Revelation constitute a sort of prologue to the main message of the book. A long time has elapsed since Paul's missionary activity in Asia,[47] and the "seven" churches do not reveal the same spiritual vitality of the period of their founding. To Ephesus John writes:

> . . . You show endurance; you have undergone much for my sake, and you have not grown weary. But I hold it against you that you do not love as you did at first. So remember how far you have fallen, and repent and do as you did at first, or else I will come to you and take your lampstand from its place, if you do not repent. But it is in your favor that you hate the practices of the Nicolaitans, as I do . . .[48]

The church at Smyrna is encouraged to endure the suffering they will undergo: "Prove faithful unto death and I will give you the crown of life."[49] The church at Pergamum also had Nicolaitans in their midst as well as false teachers; they were urged not to compromise the faith.[50] At Thyatira there was one influential woman, "that Jezebel of a woman,"[51] who was advocating the practices of the Nicolaitans; she and all those who followed her are to be punished. To the church at Sardis he wrote:

> . . . I know what you are doing; you are supposed to be alive, but you are dead. Wake up, and strengthen what is left, although it is already on the point of death, for I have found nothing you have done complete in the sight of my God. So remember what you received and heard, and obey it, and repent . . . He who is victorious will be clothed thus, in white

clothing, and I will not erase his name from the book of life, but I will acknowledge him as mine in the presence of my Father and his angels . . .[52]

The church at Philadelphia,[53] like the one at Sardis, was not attacked from within by heresy nor from without by persecution, but these two were the least satisfactory of the seven churches. The Christians at Laodicea had not rejected religion, but their half-hearted acceptance of it was even less commendable:

> . . . I know what you are doing, and that you are neither cold nor hot. I wish you were either cold or hot! As it is, since you are tepid and neither cold nor hot, I am going to spit you out of my mouth! Because you say, "I am rich, I have become wealthy, I need nothing," and you do not know that it is you that are wretched, pitiable, poor, blind, and naked, I advise you to buy of me gold that has been tested with fire, so that you may be rich, and white clothes to put on, to keep your shameful nakedness from being seen, and salve to put on your eyes, to make you see. I reprove and discipline all whom I love. So be earnest and repent. Here I stand knocking at the door. If anyone listens to my voice and opens the door, I will be his guest and dine with him, and he with me. I will permit him who is victorious to take his seat beside me on my throne, just as I have been victorious and taken my seat beside my Father on his throne . . .[54]

The main part of the book is a series of visions which picture the church of the future. In chapters four and five, the author tells how he sees, in his imagination, the throne of God, surrounded by hosts of angels; in God's hand was "a roll with writing on both sides, sealed with seven seals."[55] The roll was given to Jesus, while "myriads of myriads and thousands of thousands" of the angelic figures around the throne of God said:

> The Lamb that was slaughtered deserves to receive power, wealth, wisdom, might, honor, glory, and blessing.[56]

Then the author "heard every creature in heaven, on earth, underneath the earth, and on the sea, and all that they contain, say,

Blessing, honor, glory, and power to him who is seated on the throne and to the Lamb forever and ever!"[57]

As Christ breaks each of the seven seals, a calamity falls upon the earth. After the first one, the author sees a white horse, the rider of which carried a bow; "he was given a crown, and he rode forth as a victor to conquer."[58] Then, there appears a red horse, which symbolizes revolution.[59] From the breaking of the third seal comes a black horse; the rider has a balance in his hand, and a voice speaks of a time of inflation and famine:

Wheat at a dollar a quart, and barley three quarts for a dollar, but you must not injure the oil and wine![60]

A pale horse comes out of the fourth seal; the rider's name was death.[61] The fifth seal reveals the souls of those who have been martyred for the faith.[62] When the sixth seal is broken, disasters occur in the universe which had been predicted in the Old Testament as precursors of the Day of Jahweh.[63] Before watching the opening of the seventh seal, John introduces an interlude in the unfolding drama; he reassures the righteous people that they will not be harmed by all the plagues and disasters which will be sent on the earth. In Revelation 7:1-8 the number thus protected is given as one hundred and forty-four thousand—a traditional Jewish apocalyptic number symbolizing the completeness of Israel; in Revelation 7:9-17, the representatives of the Jewish tribes have become "a great crowd which no one could count from every nation, tribe, people, and language, standing before the Lamb, wearing white robes, with palm branches in their hands." Those who were robed in white were those who had passed through the fires of martyrdom:

. . . They will never be hungry or thirsty again, and never again will the sun or any burning heat distress them, for the Lamb who is in the center of the throne will be their shepherd, and will guide them to springs of living water, and God will wipe every tear from their eyes.[64]

When the seventh seal is broken, seven angels appear with seven trumpets;[65] the first four angels blow their trumpets, and four terrible calamities occur in the world of nature, affecting one third of the earth.[66] With the blowing of the fifth trumpet, an angel opens with a key the pit of the abyss, the place of punishment for all the fallen angels, and out swarms a very unusual cloud of locusts.

> . . . They were told not to harm the grass of the earth or any plant or tree, but only the men who did not have the mark of God's seal upon their foreheads.[67] They were not allowed to kill anyone, but only to torture them for five months . . . In those days men will seek death and never find it. They will want to die, but death will fly from them. In appearance the locusts were like war-horses armed for battle; on their heads were what appeared to be crowns like gold; their faces were like human faces; they had hair like a woman's; their teeth were like those of lions; their breasts were like iron breast-plates, and the noise of their wings was like the noise of a great number of chariots and horses rushing into battle. They had tails and stings like scorpions; it was in their tails that their power lay to harm men for five months . . .[68]

The sixth angel blows his trumpet and four angels are let loose to kill one third of all mankind; in their bloody work they used "twice 10,000 times 10,000" hosts of horsemen,[69] but repentance does not result from their destructive activity:

> . . . Yet what was left of mankind, those who escaped being killed by these plagues, did not repent of the works of their hands and give up worshiping demons and gold, silver, bronze, stone, and wooden idols, which cannot either see or hear or move, and they did not repent of their murders, or their magic arts, or their immorality, or their thefts.[70]

Before the seventh trumpet is blown, John interposes another interlude: he wants to show that the time is near when God's purposes will be fulfilled.[71] The blowing of the seventh trumpet announces the arrival of another terrible calamity, which the author sees in vivid detail. There was a woman "clothed in the sun, with the moon under her feet, and on her head a crown of twelve stars. She was soon to have a child, and she cried out with pain and agony in giving birth to it."[72] Standing ready to devour the child as soon as it was born was "a great fire-red dragon with seven heads and ten horns, with seven diadems on his heads. His tail swept away one third of the stars of heaven and flung them down upon the earth."[73] The child went up to God; the woman fled to the desert; the dragon pursued the woman, but was unable to catch up with her, so "he went off to make war on the rest of her children—those who obey God's commands and adhere to the testimony of Jesus."[74] Then the dragon summoned an animal to "come up·out of the sea," a terrible beast "with ten horns and seven heads, and with ten diadems on its horns, and blasphemous titles on its heads. The animal I saw was like a leopard, its feet were like a bear's, and its mouth was like a lion's mouth. The dragon gave it his own power and his throne and great authority."[75] The animal was worshiped by those whose names were not in the Lamb's book of life.[76] With it came a second animal;[77] it came up out of the land and "had two horns like a lamb, but it spoke like a dragon . . . It makes the earth and its inhabitants worship the first animal, . . .[78] telling the inhabitants of the earth to erect a statue to the animal . . . It is also allowed to impart life to the animal's statue so that the animal's statue can speak, and to have all who do not worship the animal's statue killed. And it makes everyone, high and low, rich and poor, freemen and slaves, have a mark stamped on their right hands or on their foreheads, and permits no one to buy or sell anything unless he bears the mark, that is, the animal's name or the number corresponding to its name.[79]

Chapter fourteen contains a third parenthesis, in which the author encourages his readers by giving them a picture of a later stage in God's plans; it contains two visions of the glorious church on earth and a judgment on Rome.[80] The dead who from this time on die as Christians will be blessed; they will "rest from their toil, for what they have done will go with them."[81] But the terrible things reserved for the wicked reveal the Old Testament concept of a God of vengeance under which the author of Revelation works.

Whoever worships the animal and its statue and lets its mark be put on his forehead or on his hand shall drink the wine of God's wrath, poured unmixed into the cup of his anger, and be tortured with fire and brimstone before the eyes of the holy angels and the Lamb. The smoke of their torture will go up forever and ever, and they will have no rest night or day— . . .[82]

So the angel swung his sickle on the earth and gathered the fruits of the earth's vine and flung them into the great winepress of God's wrath. The grapes were trodden in the winepress outside the city, and blood poured out of the winepress in a stream so deep that for 200 miles it came up to the horses' bridles.[83]

In another series of visions, John sees seven angels with seven bowls of wrath to be poured out on the earth; the calamities resulting from these prepare the way for the end of both Anti-Christ and Satan. Before the contents of the bowls are poured out, the righteous people offer praises to God:

Great and marvelous are your doings, Lord God Almighty! Upright and true are your ways, King of the Ages! Who will not fear and give glory to your name, Lord? For you alone are holy. All the heathen will come and worship before you, for the justice of your sentences has now been shown.[84]

Then plagues descend upon the earth to harass the heathens.[85] The city of Rome and the Roman empire are thoroughly destroyed.[86] The stage is set for the final battle between Christ and Satan:

Then I saw heaven thrown open and there appeared a white horse. His rider was called Faithful and True, and he judges and wages war in uprightness. His eyes blazed like fire. There were many diadems on his head, . . . The armies of heaven followed him mounted on white horses and clothed in pure white linen . . . On his clothing and his thigh he has this title written: King of kings and Lord of lords.

Then I saw an angel standing on the sun, and shouting in a loud voice to all the birds that fly in midair,

"Come! Gather for God's great banquet, and eat the bodies of kings, commanders, and mighty men, of horses and their riders—the bodies of all men, slaves and freemen, high and low."

Then I saw the animal and the kings of the earth and their armies gather to make war on him who was mounted upon the horse and upon his army. And the animal was captured and with it the false prophet who performed wonders on its behalf by means of which he led astray those who had let the animal's mark be put on them and who worshiped its statue. Both of them were flung alive into the fiery lake of burning brimstone. The rest were killed with the sword that came out of the mouth of him who sat on the horse, and all the birds gorged themselves upon their bodies.[87]

Then I saw an angel come down from heaven with the key of the abyss and a great chain in his hand. He seized the dragon, the ancient serpent, who is the devil and Satan, and bound him for a thousand years, and hurled him into the abyss and he closed it and sealed it over him, to keep him from leading the heathen astray any longer, until the thousand years are over; after that he has to be released for a little while.[88]

Christ will rule the earth for a thousand years in perfect peace. Then Satan will be released to have a final fling on the earth; but he and his heathen followers will be burned with fire from heaven and he will be flung into the "fiery, sulphurous lake, where the animal and the false prophet were, there to be tortured day and night forever and ever."[89] That sets the stage for the last judgment, an event toward which all the events recorded in the imagination of the author have been moving. All the dead are brought back to life to face judgment; "anyone whose name was not found in the book of life was flung into the fiery lake."[90] The book of Revelation ends with a very exalted picture of the new age, when the heavenly Jerusalem will descend to a new earth and all of God's people will live in it.

Then I saw a new heaven and a new earth, for the first heaven and the first earth had passed away, and there was no longer any sea. And I saw the new Jerusalem, the holy city, come down out of heaven from God, like a bride dressed and ready to meet her husband. I heard a loud voice from the throne say,

"See! God's dwelling is with men, and he will live with them. They will be his people and God himself will be with them, and he will wipe every tear from their eyes. There will be no death any longer, nor any grief or crying or pain. The old order has passed away."[91]

In spite of the puzzling symbolism of the book of Revelation and in spite of the fact that its religious and ethical teachings are below the level of other New Testament writings, it still has a permanent message for Christians of every age: God is ruling the world; material forces, however strongly intrenched, will in the end be destroyed; those who are in fellowship with Christ, though they are killed for the faith, will inherit eternal life.

SUGGESTIONS FOR FURTHER STUDY

C. H. ALLEN, *The Message of the Book of Revelation.*

A. E. BARNETT, *The New Testament: Its Making and Meaning,* pp. 192-213.

H. M. BATTENHOUSE, *New Testament History and Literature,* pp. 355-357, 369, 370.

H. M. BATTENHOUSE, *The Bible Unlocked,* pp. 516-519.

G. A. BUTTRICK, ed., *The Interpreter's Bible,* XI, pp. 575-763; XII, pp. 345-613.

C. T. CRAIG, *The Beginning of Christianity,* pp. 286-289, 319, 320, 327-329.

M. DIBELIUS, *A Fresh Approach to the New Testament and Early Christian Literature,* pp. 124-130, 194-197.

F. C. EISELEN, E. LEWIS, and D. G. DOWNEY, eds., *The Abingdon Bible Commentary,* pp. 1295-1326, 1364-1398.

E. J. GOODSPEED, *An Introduction to the New Testament,* pp. 240-264.

E. J. GOODSPEED, *The Story of the New Testament,* pp 75-94.

M. E. LYMAN, *The Christian Epic,* pp. 169-188, 199-213.

J. MOFFATT, *An Introduction to the Literature of the New Testament,* pp. 420-455, 483-514.

E. W. K. MOULD, *Essentials of Bible History,* pp. 590-592.

D. W. RIDDLE and H. H. HUTSON, *New Testament Life and Literature,* pp. 179-187.

E. F. SCOTT, *The Literature of the New Testament,* pp. 198-208, 274-284.

Chapter Twenty-five

THE JOHANNINE WRITINGS

A. *The Fourth Gospel*: *An Interpretation of Jesus*

In any study of the gospel sources for the life of Jesus, the Gospel of John should be considered separately from the synoptic gospels.[1] Even the casual reader is conscious of the fact that there are marked differences between the fourth gospel, on the one hand, and Matthew, Mark, and Luke on the other. As early as 200 A.D. Clement of Alexandria wrote: "John, . . . conscious that the outward facts had been set forth in the Gospels, was urged on by his disciples, and, divinely moved by the Spirit, composed a spiritual Gospel."[2] The author states his own purpose as being somewhat different from that of the other gospel writers;[3] from the materials he has before him he has selected those which have significance for the inward religious life of his readers; his aim is theological rather than historical; biographical data in the life of Jesus are noted, but the doctrine is always more important than the story.

> There are many other signs that Jesus showed before his disciples which are not recorded in this book. But these have been recorded so that you may believe that Jesus is the Christ, the Son of God, and through believing you may have life as his followers.[4]

There are thirty-six units of material on the life and teachings of Jesus in the synoptic gospels which are not to be found in John; these include genealogies, birth stories, baptism, temptation scene, transfiguration, and the agony in Gethsemane. The synoptists know of only one visit of Jesus to Jerusalem during his public ministry—the one during his last week; John records several visits of Jesus to the capital city, during which he delivers long contro-versial discourses in the temple court. John places Jesus' cleansing of the temple during the first of these visits rather than during Passion Week. The teaching of Jesus in the fourth gospel is far different in form and subject matter from anything in the first three gospels; John contains lengthy discourses which are doctrinal in tone rather than ethical; there are no parables in John, but the entire gospel is set in the form of a long parable of the timeless Christ. John is concerned with the religious significance of events; in the fourth gospel, the story of the feeding of the five thousand, one of the few incidents in all four gospels, is a concrete symbol of a teaching of Jesus: "I am the bread that gives life;"[5] the raising of Lazarus from the dead enforces a fundamental teaching of Jesus: "I myself am Resurrection and Life. He who believes in me will live on, even if he dies, and no one who is alive and believes in me will ever die . . ."[6]

Tradition, beginning with the second half of the second century, has attributed the authorship of the fourth gospel to John, son of Zebedee. The early church saw in the references to "one of his disciples whom Jesus especially loved,"[7] proof that the author was John, son of Zebedee. Chapter twenty-one, a postscript added to the original gospel, identifies the author with the beloved disciple: "It is this disciple (the one "who was very dear to Jesus") who testifies to these things and who wrote them down, and we (the unknown writer, or writers, of chapter twenty-one) know that his testimony is true."[8] But the original gospel, chapters 1-20, gives no indication as to who the author was; nowhere does he claim to have been an apostle; he employs Hellenistic rather than Jewish literary forms;[9] since the humanity of Jesus is subordinated in the fourth gospel to his theological significance, the author probably was not a personal disciple of the historic Jesus; he calls the opponents of Jesus "the Jews," rather than Pharisees, indicating a period in Christian history when the synagogue was actively opposing the church; for some of his materials, he drew upon the synoptic gospels, which were written by the year 95 A.D. Thus, the late date for the composition of the fourth gospel—some time between 95 and 115 A.D.—and the other considerations just men-tioned seem to be against the traditional view that the gospel was the work of John, the son of Zebedee. Furthermore, the picture of John in the synoptic gospels does not lend itself to the title of the disciple "whom Jesus especially loved;"[10] then, it is entirely probable that John died as a martyr to the faith in Palestine a long time before the fourth gospel was written.[11] But, in spite of the fact that the fourth gospel is anonymous, the author's personality can be discovered somewhat from the gospel itself. He was a religious genius of the highest order, to be ranked along with Paul and the unknown author of the book of Hebrews; he was well acquainted with rabbinical Judaism, both in its legalistic and in its mystical aspects, and he knew very well the currents of Hellenistic thought which flourished in the first decade of the first century. He probably lived in Ephesus; this great city had all the requirements which would help a great religious genius to produce a document like the fourth gospel. It had a powerful Jewish community, which had opposed Paul some sixty years earlier;[12] it was the reputed home of a sect which gave special honor to John the Baptizer;[13] it was at Ephesus that Heraclitus (*ca.* 540-475 B.C.) had first used the term "Logos," which became so prominent in the prologue of the fourth gospel. If the author of the fourth gospel also composed the three letters of John, as seems likely, some scholars identify him with John the Elder, prominent in the Ephesian church at the turn of the century;[14] this is corroborated by the evidence given by Papias, as reported in Eusebius' *Church History* III. 39. 4,5:

> If anyone chanced to arrive (Papias was bishop at Hierapolis, a city east of Ephesus near Colossae) who had been a follower of the elders, I would inquire as to the sayings of the elders— as to what Andrew or Peter said, or Philip or Thomas or James or John or Matthew, or any other of the Lord's disciples said; also as to what Aristion and the elder John, the Lord's disciples, say.[15]

In the poem with which the fourth gospel opens, called the prologue,[16] the author makes use of a Stoic word which would have gained the immediate attention of his readers in Ephesus: Logos. In Stoicism, the Logos was the ultimate principle of the world, the divine reason immanent in nature and man; beginning with Heraclitus, the Logos took the place of God. However, Philo, the Jewish philosopher of Alexandria, made the Logos subordinate to God; he attributed to it all the functions which belong in the

Old Testament to the concept of the Word of God, which is the expression of his creative energy.[17]   Whether directly from Philo or indirectly from the general cultural climate of Greek thought, the concept of the Logos made its entrance into Christian thought in writings like Colossians and Hebrews.[18] The author of the fourth gospel takes this familiar Greek concept and completely personalizes it; the Logos becomes intelligible only as we think of the historic Jesus. In his person Jesus combined the Greek Logos and the Hebrew Word. Though the word Logos drops out of the gospel as a technical word after the prologue, the ideas in the prologue are determinative of what is to follow in the remainder of the gospel.

> In the beginning the Word (Logos) existed. The Word was with God, and the Word was divine.
> It was he that was with God in the beginning. Everything came into existence through him, and apart from him nothing came to be. It was by him that life came into existence, and that life was the light of mankind. The light is still shining in the darkness, for the darkness has never put it out.
> So the Word became flesh and blood and lived for a while among us,[19] abounding in blessing and truth, and we saw the honor God had given him, such honor as an only son receives from his father . . .
> For from his abundance we have all had a share, and received blessing after blessing. For while the Law was given through Moses, blessing and truth came to us through Jesus Christ. No one has ever seen God; it is the divine Only Son, who leans upon his Father's breast, that has made him known.[20]

In the Gospel of John the reader is struck by the author's unique portrait of Jesus; the central theme of the entire book is stated in one great verse, sometimes referred to as the golden text of the Bible:

> For God loved the world so much that he gave his only Son, so that no one who believes in him should be lost, but that they should all have eternal life.[21]

Men are responsible for accepting or rejecting the one whom God has sent. Jesus is the Logos-Christ of the ages; his human career is a mere episode in the on-going eternal existence of the Logos. He passes through every human experience unhampered and unruffled; he seems to have more than human knowledge and a more than human power:

> Jesus saw Nathanael coming toward him, and he said of him,
> "Here is really an Israelite without any deceit in him!"
> Nathaniel said to him,
> "How do you know me?"
> Jesus answered,
> "While you were still under that fig tree, before Philip called you I saw you."[22]

Jesus knows the past of the Samaritan woman even before she tells him;[23] he announces, at the last supper, that Judas will betray him:

> . . . From now on I will tell you things before they happen, so that when they do happen you may believe that I am what I say . . .
> "I tell you, it is one of you that will betray me!" . . .
> "It is the one to whom I am going to give this piece of bread when I have dipped it in the dish." So he dipped the piece of bread and took it and gave it to Judas, Simon Iscariot's son . . .[24]

> . . . Jesus . . . knew everything that was going to happen to him . . .[25]

We miss in the fourth gospel the features of surprise, ignorance, mistake, and disappointment which are included in the synoptic record; there is no hint of any growth in Jesus' own understanding of his life and mission; he has been the Messiah since the beginning of time and is proclaimed as such by John the Baptizer even before his public ministry begins.[26] In the synoptic gospels Jesus performs miracles in order to help human misery and need; in the gospel of John they are "signs" of Jesus' spiritual power and glory; he performs them to compel belief on the part of his followers that he is the unique son of God. The first miracle recorded in the fourth gospel is the changing of water into wine at the wedding in Cana in Galilee, an event not appearing in the synoptic gospels; after telling about it, the author adds:

This, the first of the signs of his mission, Jesus showed at Cana in Galilee. By it he showed his greatness, and his disciples believed in him.[27]

Jesus' wonderful deeds are proof that God has sent him.[28] No external force seems to influence him; he is always in command of his own destiny:

> ... This is why the Father loves me, because I am giving my life, but giving it to take it back again. No one has taken it from me, but I am giving it ot my own accord. I have power to give it, and I have power to take it back again. These are the orders I have received from my Father.[29]

His death is his own free choice, his glorification;[30] he carries the cross himself.[31] The prayer life of Jesus is considered from a different point of view in John than in the synoptic gospels; in the latter, Jesus prays because he needs to renew his strength;[32] in the fourth gospel, Jesus does not need to pray for his own sake, but that he might confirm the faith for those who heard him pray. After a prayer, Jesus said:

> Father, I thank you for listening to me, though I knew that you always listen to me. But I have said this for the sake of the people that are standing around me that they may believe that you have made me your messenger.[33]

Yet, in spite of this suppression of anything that would suggest Jesus' common humanity, the author of the fourth gospel does stress the reality of Jesus' fleshly existence.[34] Jesus is subject to the laws of time and space; he travels from place to place;[35] he gets tired and thirsty;[36] he avoids trouble;[37] he experiences grief at the loss of a friend:

> When Jesus saw her (Mary, the sister of the deceased Lazarus) weep and the Jews who had come with her weeping too, repressing a groan, and yet showing great agitation, he said, "Where have you laid him?"
> They answered,
> "Come and see, Master."
> Jesus shed tears. So the Jews said,
> "See how much he loved him!"[38]

he answers indignantly the questions of the high priest.[39] But, all in all, John's picture of Jesus emphasizes the triumph of his spirit over the tragedy of the flesh:

> . . . And if I am lifted up from the ground, I will draw all men to myself.[40]

The fourth gospel contains the author's statement of faith in Jesus Christ; he is saying to the Christians of the first decade of the second century that their spiritual life should be centered in their relationship to Jesus. They are to honor Jesus as they honor his heavenly father; he is the way by which men can come to God.

> Jesus said to him,
> "I am Way and Truth and Life. No one can come to the Father except through me. If you knew me, you would know my Father also. From now on you do know him and you have seen him."[41]

> . . . For whatever the Father does, the Son also does. For the Father loves the Son and lets him see everything that he himself is doing, and he will let him see greater deeds than these, to make you wonder. For just as the Father awakens the dead and makes them come to life, the Son makes anyone whom he chooses come to life. For the Father passes judgment on no one, but he has committed the judgment entirely to the Son, so that all men may honor the Son just as much as they honor the Father. Whoever refuses to honor the Son refuses to honor the Father who sent him . . .[42]

In a series of "I am" sayings the author describes the role Jesus plays in the religious life of the Christian:

> Jesus said to them,
> "I am the bread that gives life. No one who comes to me will ever be hungry, and no one who believes in me will ever be thirsty . . . All that my Father gives to me will come to me, and I will never refuse anyone who comes to me, for I have come down from heaven not to do what I please but what pleases him who has sent me . . . For it is the purpose of my Father that everyone who sees the Son and believes in him shall have eternal life, . . .

. . . I am the bread that gives life. Your forefathers in the desert ate the manna and yet they died. But here is bread that comes down out of heaven, and no one who eats it will ever die. I am this living bread that has come down out of heaven. Whoever eats this bread will live forever, and the bread that I will give for the world's life is my own flesh!"[43]

Then Jesus spoke to them again and said,
"I am the light of the world. Whoever follows me will not have to walk in darkness but will have the light of life."[44]

So Jesus said again,
"I tell you, I am the door of the sheepfold. All who have come before me are thieves and robbers, but the sheep would not obey them. I am the door. Whoever enters through me will be saved, and will pass in and out and find pasture. A thief comes only to steal and kill and destroy; I have come to let them have life, and to let them have it in abundance. I am the good shepherd. A good shepherd will give his life for the sheep . . . I am the good shepherd. I know my sheep and my sheep know me, just as the Father knows me and I know the Father, and I am giving my life for my sheep. I have other sheep too that do not belong to this fold. I must lead them too, and they will obey my voice, and they will all become one flock, with one shepherd . . ."[45]

Jesus said to her (Martha),
"I myself am Resurrection and Life. He who believes in me will live on, even if he dies, and no one who is alive and believes in me will ever die . . ."[46]

The follower of Jesus may achieve eternal life now through fellowship with Jesus. At the last supper, he prayed to God:

Father, the time has come. Do honor to your son, that your son may do honor to you, just as you have done in giving him power over all mankind, so that he may give eternal life to all whom you have given him. And eternal life means knowing you as the only true God, and knowing Jesus your messenger as Christ . . .[47]

Those who believe in Christ are to maintain a continuous, mystical union with Christ, typified in the allegory of the vine and the branches:

I am the true vine, and my Father is the cultivator. Any branch of mine that does not bear fruit he trims away, and he prunes every branch that bears fruit, to make it bear more . . . You must remain united to me and I will remain united to you. Just as no branch can bear fruit by itself unless it remains united to the vine, you cannot unless you remain united to me. I am the vine, you are the branches. Anyone who remains united to me, with me united to him, will be very fruitful, for you cannot do anything apart from me. Anyone who does not remain united to me is thrown away like a branch and withers up, and they gather them and throw them into the fire and burn them. If you remain united to me and my word remains in your hearts, ask for whatever you please and you shall have it . . . If you keep my commands you will retain my love, just as I have observed the Father's commands and retain his love . . .[48]

Jesus prays for his followers:

Let them all be one. Just as you, Father, are in union with me and I am with you, let them be in union with us, so that the world may believe that you sent me. I have given them the glory that you gave me, so that they may be perfectly unified, and the world may recognize that you sent me and that you love them just as you loved me . . .[49]

Eternal life is a gift from above, as Jesus said to Nicodemus:

I tell you, no one can see the Kingdom of God unless he is born over again from above![50]

Through this new birth men are guided out of their original state in the darkness of sin into the light that comes from active faith in Jesus, the true light of the world.

He who comes from above is above all others . . . It is to what he has seen and heard that he gives testimony . . . Whoever does accept it has thereby acknowledged that God is true. For he whom God has sent speaks God's words, for God gives him his Spirit without measure. The Father loves his Son, and has put everything in his hands. Whoever believes in the Son possesses eternal life, but whoever disobeys the Son will not experience life, but will remain under the anger of God.[51]

By the time the fourth gospel was written more than two generations had gone by since the death of Jesus; many Christians were beginning to express serious doubts about his physical return—a doctrine which Paul had expounded.[52] Some of the later New Testament writers[53] tried to convince the doubters that Jesus would really be coming back. The author of the fourth gospel tries another method; he maintains that Jesus has already returned, not in material form, but as an inward spiritual presence in the hearts of his followers. There is no "second coming" because Jesus never left. Jesus was closer to the devout Christian after his physical death than he was during his lifetime; now he was the Christ of the ages, present everywhere, with whom they could have unbroken and complete communion.

> Your minds must not be troubled; you must believe in God, and believe in me. There are many rooms in my Father's house; if there were not, I would have told you, for I am going away to make ready a place for you. And if I go to make it ready, I will come back and take you with me, so that you may be where I am . . .

> If you really love me, you will observe my commands. And I will ask the Father and he will give you another Helper to be with you always. It is the Spirit of Truth . . . I am not going to leave you friendless. I am coming back to you. In a little while the world will not see me any more, but you will still see me, because I shall live on, and you will live on too. When that day comes you will know that I am in union with my Father and you are with me and I am with you . . .[54]

> I have told you this while I am still staying with you, but the Helper, the holy Spirit which the Father will send in my place, will teach you everything and remind you of everything that I have told you. I leave you a blessing; I give you my own blessing. I do not give it to you as the world gives. Your minds must not be troubled or afraid. You have heard me say that I am going away and am coming back to you; if you loved me you would be glad that I am going to the Father, for the Father is greater than I . . .[55]

The apocalyptic concept of the second coming was transformed in John into a spiritual experience of the living Christ.

. . . Yet it is only the truth when I tell you that it is better for you that I should go away. For if I do not go, the Helper will not come to you, but if I go I will send him to you. When he comes, he will bring conviction to the world about sin and uprightness and judgment; . . . I have much more to tell you, but you cannot take it in now, but when the Spirit of Truth comes, he will guide you into the full truth, . . . He will take what is mine and communicate it to you . . .

In a little while you will not see me any longer, and a little while after, you will see me again.[56]

Unlike the book of Revelation,[57] the fourth gospel pictures judgment as a continuous process going on here and now in the life of men rather than as an event in the future to be anticipated.

. . . For God did not send his Son into the world to pass judgment upon the world, but that through him the world might be saved. No one who believes in him has to come up for judgment. Anyone who does not believe stands condemned already, for not believing in God's only Son. And the basis of the judgment is this, that the light has come into the world, and yet, because their actions were wicked, men have loved the darkness more than the light . . .[58]

. . . I tell you, whoever listens to my message and believes him who has sent me, possesses eternal life, and will not come to judgment, but has already passed out of death unto life. I tell you, the time is coming—it is here already!—when those who are dead will listen to the voice of the Son of God, and those who listen to it will live . . .[59]

The highest tribute the author of the fourth gospel can pay to Jesus is to think of him in the same terms as he thought of God; Jesus and God are one in purpose and character.

. . . The Father and I are one.

. . . The Father is in union with me, and I am in union with the Father.[60]

. . . Whoever has seen me has seen the Father.[61]

B. *The Letters of John*

Soon after the composition of the fourth gospel, its author, or one of his disciples who was closely influenced by his style, wrote three letters which carry out the main thoughts of the gospel of John.[62] I John is a miscellany of meditations; a letter only in the sense that the author is "writing" rather than speaking,[63] it is a treatise written by an experienced church leader who shows concern for his constituents and who wants to advise them on matters of widespread interest. His remarks are spontaneous and unsystematically arranged, but they were designed to strengthen the spiritual life of the readers. The author wants them to be reminded that God has revealed himself perfectly in Jesus Christ; through Christ they may have fellowship with God. They can prove the validity of this inward experience by the way they live:

> . . . This is how we can be sure that we know him—by obeying his commands. Whoever says, "I know him," but does not obey his commands, is a liar, and there is no truth in his heart; but whoever obeys his message really has the love of God in perfection in his heart. This is the way we can be sure that we are in union with him; whoever says, "I am always in union with him" must live just as he lived.[64]

Right belief is also important as a test of the spirit of God:

> . . . You can tell the Spirit of God in this way: all inspiration that acknowledges that Jesus Christ has come in human form comes from God, and any inspired utterance that does not acknowledge Jesus does not come from God; it is the spirit of the Antichrist . . .[65]

But the final test is brotherly love; those who love share in the life of God himself; we learn of the divine love by the love which manifests itself in our daily intercourse as human beings:

> Dear friends, let us love one another, for love comes from God, and everyone who loves is a child of God and knows God. Whoever does not love does not know God, for God is love. God's love for us has been revealed in this way—that God has sent his only Son into the world, to let us have life through him. The love consists not in our having loved God, but in his

loving us and sending his Son as an atoning sacrifice for our sins.

Dear friends, if God has loved us so, we ought to love one another. No one has ever seen God; yet if we love one another, God keeps in union with us and love for him attains perfection in our hearts . . .

God is love, and whoever continues to love keeps in union with God, and God with him . . . There is no fear in love, but perfect love drives out fear . . . We love because he loved us first. If anyone says, "I love God," and yet hates his brother, he is a liar; for whoever does not love his brother whom he has seen cannot love God whom he has not seen. This is the command that we get from him, that whoever loves God must love his brother also.[66]

The author keeps in mind that some of his followers had been attracted to heretical teachings, the character of which was similar to the Gnosticism of the second century; these teachings he condemns. Some of the heretics were evidently Docetists, who believed that the incarnation of Jesus was only an appearance; against them the author speaks:

Who is such a liar as the man who denies that Jesus is the Christ? He is the real Antichrist—the man who disowns the Father and the Son. No one who disowns the Son can have the Father. Whoever acknowledges the Son has the Father too.

. . . All inspiration that acknowledges that Jesus Christ has come in human form comes from God, and any inspired utterance that does not acknowledge Jesus does not come from God; it is the inspiration of the Antichrist . . .

. . . For who is there that is victorious over the world except the man who believes that Jesus is the Son of God? It was he, Jesus Christ himself, who came in water and in blood; not in water only, but in water and in blood . . .[67]

The author asserts strongly that Jesus really lived.

It is what existed from the beginning, that we announce; what we have heard, what we have seen with our own eyes, what we have beheld, and touched with our hands; it is the very message of life—for life has been revealed, and we have seen it and testify to it and announce to you that eternal life that was with the Father and has been revealed to us—it is what we have seen and heard that we announce to you also, so that you may share our fellowship, for our fellowship is with the Father and with his Son Jesus Christ, and we write this to you to make your happiness complete.[68]

The heretics had evidently allowed no place for the idea of sin; some have declared that they were exempt from sin, because of their native kinship with God; these perfectionists are condemned:

. . . If we say, "We are without sin," we are deceiving ourselves, and there is no truth in our hearts. If we acknowledge our sins, he is upright and can be depended on to forgive our sins and cleanse us from everything wrong. If we say, "We have not sinned," we are making him a liar, and his message is not in our hearts.[69]

others had disregarded the moral law completely, and they come in for their share of the author's wrath:

Whoever commits sin disobeys law; sin is disobedience to law. You know that he appeared to take our sins away and that there is no sin in him. No one who keeps in union with him sins . . .[70]

The later church was to follow the judgment of thinkers like the author of I John and reject Gnosticism completely.

If we say, "We have fellowship with him," and yet live in darkness, we are lying and not living the truth. But if we live in the light, just as he is in the light, we have fellowship with one another, and the blood of Jesus his Son cleanses us from every sin . . .[71]

II John is a condensed version of I John, written to a church and its members.[72] The author, who refers to himself as John the elder, wants to warn the church against heretics; he urges the regular members to have nothing to do with them.

For many impostors have gone out into the world—men who do not acknowledge the coming of Jesus Christ in human

form. That is the mark of the impostor and the Antichrist . . .
If anyone comes to you without bringing this teaching, do
not let him come into the house or bid him good morning. For
anyone who bids him good morning shares in his wicked work.[73]

Apparently certain members of the congregation have just visited
the author and he is grateful that they "are guided by truth."[74]
Perhaps he sent this little greeting in their care as they returned to
their home church; he would prefer to come and see them.

Though I have a great deal to write to you, I would rather
not write it with paper and ink, but I hope to come to see
you, and talk with you face to face, so that your happiness may
be complete . . .[75]

The heart of his message is Christian love.

. . . And now I beg you, my lady—not as though I were
writing you any new command, but one which we have had
from the beginning—let us love one another. Love means this,
that we be guided by his commands. The command, as you
have heard from the beginning, is to be guided by love . . .[76]

In III John, the elder is writing to his friend Gaius, who may
have been a member of the church to which II John is addressed,[77]
commending him for extending hospitality to the evangelistic team
which John has sent, in contrast with the attitude of a man named
Diotrephes, who "refuses to welcome the brothers himself, and he
is interfering with those who want to do so, and has them put out
of the church."[78] The author promises to set things right when he
next visits the church.

So if I come, I will bring up the things that he (Diotrephes)
is doing, and how he is maliciously accusing me . . .
Dear friend, do not follow bad examples, but good ones.
I have a great deal to write to you, but I do not want to
write it with pen and ink; I hope to see you very soon and
we will talk face to face . . .[79]

This little letter reveals conditions in the organization of a local
church at the beginning of the second century. The period when

the traveling missionaries, among whom John may have been numbered, were the chief leaders in the expanding church had given way to a time when local elected officers were assuming more and more responsibility in the conduct of affairs. Diotrephes was evidently one of these local officials, perhaps a bishop, against whom the author feels himself in conflict. This trend was to lead to the development of the monarchical episcopate, which became the normal pattern of church organization by the end of the third century.

SUGGESTIONS FOR FURTHER STUDY

A. E. BARNETT, *The New Testament: Its Making and Meaning,* pp. 225-252.

H. M. BATTENHOUSE, *New Testament History and Literature,* pp. 361-365.

H. M. BATTENHOUSE, *The Bible Unlocked,* pp. 520-523.

G. A. BUTTRICK, ed., *The Interpreter's Bible,* VIII, pp. 435-811; XII, pp. 207-313.

E. C. COLWELL and E. L. TITUS, *The Gospel of the Spirit.*

C. T. CRAIG, *The Beginning of Christianity,* pp. 292-295, 302-304.

M. DIBELIUS, *A Fresh Approach to the New Testament and Early Christian Literature,* pp. 95-110, 209-213.

C. H. DODD, *The Johannine Epistles.*

F. C. EISELEN, E. LEWIS and D. G. DOWNEY, eds., *The Abingdon Bible Commentary,* pp. 1060-1093, 1350-1360.

E. J. GOODSPEED, *An Introduction to the New Testament,* pp. 296-326.

E. J. GOODSPEED, *The Story of the Bible,* pp. 106-124.

M. E. LYMAN, *The Christian Epic,* pp. 214-233.

J. MOFFATT, *An Introduction to the Literature of the New Testament,* pp. 475-482, 515-619.

E. W. K. MOULD, *Essentials of Bible History,* pp. 593-594.

D. W. RIDDLE and H. H. HUTSON, *New Testament Life and Literature,* pp. 190-196, 200-203.

E. F. SCOTT, *The Fourth Gospel, Its Purpose and Theology.*

E. F. SCOTT, *The Literature of the New Testament,* pp. 230-273.

R. H. STRACHAN, *The Fourth Gospel.*

Chapter Twenty-six

THE CATHOLIC LETTERS

Toward the end of the New Testament period, there are four writings which are sometimes grouped together as the Catholic or General letters: James, Jude, I Peter, and II Peter.[1] This is done because all four are not addressed to any particular community or person; however, the "general" nature of these books is not clearly perceivable. James and I Peter seem to be addressed to groups of churches rather than to the church at large; it is not certain for whom Jude and II Peter were intended; the four books are individually of such a different character that they cannot properly be studied as a unit. Each book presents problems peculiar to itself.

I Peter belongs among the writings in the New Testament which were produced during periods of persecution.[2] If Peter was the author, the date of the work would be *ca.* 64 A.D. and the persecution involved would be that under Nero. However, if I Peter is pseudonymous, as seems likely, the date of its composition would be placed between the years 95 and 117 A.D., and the persecution would be either the one under Domitian or the one under Trajan. In I Peter the opposition to the Christian religion is well organized and worldwide:

> Dear friends, do not be surprised that a test of fire is being applied to you, as though a strange thing were happening to you, . . .
>
> . . . For you know that your brotherhood all over the world is having the same experience of suffering . . .[3]

The situation reflected in I Peter is much more serious than it was under Nero; the latter accused the Christians of arson and confined his executions pretty largely to the city of Rome; however, in I Peter Christians suffer just because they are Christians:

> . . . If you are being abused for the sake of Christ, you are blessed, because the glorious Spirit of God is resting upon you. For no one of you must suffer as a murderer or thief or criminal or revolutionary, but if a man suffers for being a Christian, he must not be ashamed of it, but must do honor to God through that name . . .[4]

I Peter was written in Rome[5] "to those who are scattered as foreigners over Pontus, Galatia, Cappadocia, Asia, and Bithynia, whom God the Father has chosen and predestined by the consecration of the Spirit to be obedient to Jesus Christ, and to be sprinkled with his blood; . . ."[6] In spite of persecution, the author of I Peter recommends that the Christians accept graciously the blessings of the state under which they live.

> Submit to all human authority, for the Master's sake; to the emperor as supreme, and to governors, as sent by him to punish evil-doers, and to encourage those who do right. For it is the will of God that by doing right you should silence the ignorant charges of foolish people. Live like free men, only do not make your freedom an excuse for doing wrong, but be slaves of God. Treat everyone with respect. Love the brotherhood, be reverent to God, respect the emperor.[7]

The attitude of the book toward the problem of suffering is one of hope and triumph; the author tries to help his readers to understand their undeserved suffering and to attain the spirit in which they as Christians should meet it. Suffering is a means of purifying and ennobling the soul.

> Blessed be the God and Father of our Lord Jesus Christ! In his great mercy he has caused us to be born anew to a life of hope through Jesus Christ's resurrection from the dead, and to an imperishable, unsullied, and unfading inheritance, which is kept safe for you in heaven, and you by God's power are being protected through faith to receive a salvation that is now ready to be disclosed at the last time. Rejoice over this, although just now perhaps distressed by various trials; they

are to show that your faith when tested is found to be more precious than gold, which though it is perishable is tested with fire, and they will bring you praise, glory, and honor when Jesus Christ is revealed . . .[8]

Suffering results in a closer fellowship with Jesus.

. . . Come to him (Jesus) as to a living stone rejected by man, but chosen and prized in the sight of God, and build yourselves up as living stones into a spiritual house for a consecrated priesthood, so as to offer spiritual sacrifices that through Jesus Christ will be acceptable to God. . . But you are the chosen race, the royal priesthood, the consecrated nation, his own people, so that you may declare the virtues of him who has called you out of darkness into his wonderful light; . . .[9]

Those who suffer cease from sin and live in harmony with God.

Since Christ therefore has suffered in our physical nature, you must also arm yourselves with the same resolve. For he who suffers in his physical nature has done with sin, and no longer lives by what men desire, but for the rest of his earthly life by what God wills. . . .[10]

Jesus is cited as the great example of undeserved suffering.[11] Jesus is also "the chief shepherd," who, when he comes, will give the faithful "the glorious wreath that will never fade."[12] In connection with his treatment of Christ, the author brings in the strange doctrine of Jesus as preaching the gospel in the world of the dead, perhaps in the mysterious period of time between the crucifixion and the resurrection.

. . . For Christ himself died once for all, for sin, an upright man for unrighteous men, to bring us to God, and was physically put to death, but he was made alive in the Spirit. In it Enoch went and preached even to those spirits that were in prison, who had once been disobedient, . . .
. . . This is why the good news was preached to the dead also, that though they are judged in their physical nature as men are, they may yet live, like God, in the Spirit.[13]

I Peter expresses the author's confidence that the sufferings of the Christian will not be long; "the end of all things is near."[14] In the light of this, he gives some practical ethical advice:

> . . . Be serious and collected, therefore, and pray. Above all keep your love for one another strong, because love covers up a host of sins. Be ungrudgingly hospitable to one another. . .[15]

> I appeal therefore to those who are elders among you; . . . —be shepherds of the flock of God that is among you, not as though it were forced upon you but of your own free will, and not from base love of gain but freely, and not as tyrannizing over those in your charge but proving models for the flock; . . . You younger men must show deference to the elders. And you must all clothe yourselves in humility toward one another, for God opposes the proud, but shows mercy to the humble. . .[16]

All groups of Christians—servants, married women, married men—have their special responsibility as Christians.[17]

> Finally, you must all be harmonious, sympathizing, loving, tender-hearted, modest, not returning evil for evil, or abuse for abuse. You must bless people instead. . .[18]

Some time between 100 and 125 A.D. an unknown Christian writer composed a sermon and addressed it to "the twelve tribes that are scattered over the world." He refers to himself as "James, a slave of God and of the Lord Jesus Christ;"[19] but there is no indication as to which one of the four men in the New Testament by that name is intended. He certainly was not James, the son of Zebedee.[20] Tradition says that the author was James, the brother of Jesus, who became the head of the church in Jerusalem,[21] but the late date of the book and the absence of controversial issues with which we know James, the brother of Jesus, was associated seem to point to the conclusion that he did not write it. Thus, the book of James was probably a pseudonymous work written under the name of an earlier leader of the church in order to strengthen its chances of being read and included in the canon. It is a sermon, though not carefully organized, in which the author presents a series of wholesome counsels on the making of a good life. It is a compendium of wisdom sayings similar in form and content to Jewish wisdom literature, the diatribes of contemporary Stoic wandering preachers, and the sermon on the mount and the other ethical teachings of Jesus. Some have seen in the book of James a sharp criticism of Paul's doctrine of justification by faith; Martin Luther contemptuously called it "that Epistle of Straw,"[22] because he mistakenly thought its message was against Paul's teachings. The author does not try to oppose Paul, but he undertakes to correct some false inferences from the great doctrine of justification by faith. Effective faith involves commitment to ethical ideals and expression in Christian conduct. The preacher says:

My brothers, what is the good of a man's saying he has faith, if he has no good deeds to show? Can faith save him? If some brother or sister has no clothes and has not food enough for a day, and one of you says to them, "Goodbye, keep warm and have plenty to eat," without giving them the necessaries of life, what good does it do? So faith by itself, if it has no good deeds to show, is dead. But someone may say, "You have faith, and I good deeds." Show me your faith without any good deeds, and I will show you my faith by my good deeds. . . Just as the body without the spirit is dead, faith is dead without good deeds.[23]

James denounces the rich people again and again in his sermon:

My brothers, do you try to combine faith in our glorious Lord Jesus Christ with acts of partiality? For if a finely dressed man with a gold ring comes into a meeting, and a poor man in shabby clothes comes in also, and you pay attention to the man in the fine clothes and say to him, "Sit here; this is a good place!" and say to the poor man, "Stand up, or sit on the floor at my feet," have you not wavered and shown that your judgments are guided by base motives? Listen, my dear brothers. Has not God chosen the world's poor to be rich in faith, and to possess the kingdom that he promised to those who love him? But you humiliate the poor. Are not the rich your oppressors? Is it not they who drag you into court? Is it not they who slander the noble name you bear? . . .[24]

Come now, you rich people! weep aloud and howl over the

miseries that are going to overtake you! Your wealth has rotted, your clothes are moth-eaten, your gold and silver are rusted, and their rust will testify against you and eat into your very flesh, for you have stored up fire for the last days. Why, the wages you have withheld from the laborers who have reaped your harvests cry aloud, and the cries of the harvesters have reached the ears of the Lord of Hosts. You have lived luxuriously and voluptuously here on earth; you have fattened your hearts for the day of slaughter. You have condemned and murdered the upright. Will he make no resistance?[25]

The book of James contains a classic treatment of the tongue:

Not many of you should become teachers, my brothers, for you know that we who teach will be judged with greater strictness. For we all make many mistakes. . . So the tongue is a little organ and yet very boastful. What a great forest a spark will set on fire! And the tongue is a fire, a world of wrong the tongue proves in our bodies, soiling the whole body and setting fire to the whole round of nature, and set on fire itself by hell. For every kind of animal and bird, reptile and sea creature, can be tamed and has been tamed by man, but no human being can tame the tongue. It is an irreconcilable evil, full of deadly poison. . .[26]

The author's definition of religion, the only one in the Bible, reflects his ethical interests:

. . . A religious observance that is pure and stainless in the sight of God the Father is this: to look after orphans and widows in their trouble, and keep one's self unstained by the world.[27]

The book of James is full of short statements relating to Christian conduct and religious thought:

You must find the greatest joy, my brothers, in being involved in various trials, for you know that the testing of your faith leads to steadfastness, and steadfastness must have full play, so that you may be fully and perfectly developed without any defects.[28]

Blessed is the man who endures trial, for when he stands the test, he will be given the crown of life, which God has promised to those who love him. . . Every good gift and every perfect present is from heaven, and comes down from the Father of the heavenly lights, about whom there is no variation of changing shadow. . .[29]

You must understand this, my dear brothers. Everyone must be quick to hear, slow to speak, slow to be angry, for men's anger does not produce the uprightness God wishes. . .[30]

. . . For wherever jealousy and rivalry exist, there will be confusion and every low action. The wisdom that is from above is first of all pure, then peaceable, considerate, willing to yield, full of compassion and good deeds, wholehearted, straight-forward. The harvest uprightness yields must be sown in peace, by peacemakers.[31]

What causes wars and fights among you? Is it not your cravings, which are at war within your bodies? . . . There-fore, submit to God. Resist the devil and he will fly from you. Approach God, and he will approach you. Wash your hands, you sinners! Make your hearts pure, you doubters! Be miserable, grieve, and weep aloud! Turn your laughter into grief and your happiness into gloom. Humble yourselves before the Lord, and he will raise you up.

Do not talk against one another, brothers.

. . . So when a man knows what is right and fails to do it, he is guilty of sin.[32]

. . . Do not complain of one another, brethren, or you will be judged. . .[33]

If any one of you is in trouble, he should pray. If any one is in good spirits, he should sing a hymn. If any one is sick, he should call in the elders of the church and have them pray over him, and pour oil on him in the name of the Lord, and the prayer offered in faith will save the sick man; the Lord will restore him to health, and if he has committed sins, he will be forgiven. So confess your sins to one another and pray for one another, so that you may be cured. An upright man can do a great deal by prayer when he tries. . .[34]

The little letter of Jude is a book which was written in a time when the apostles belonged to a past generation.[35] The author calls himself "Jude, a slave of Jesus Christ, and the brother of James,"[36] but does not indicate anything more specifically detailed about his identity; hence, the book is probably the work of an unknown author who writes under the pseudonym of a famous man in the past. The letter is addressed to "those who have been called, who are dear to God the Father and have been kept through union with Jesus Christ; . ."[37] just who they were is not known. The author is concerned with the threat to the orthodox faith presented by the heretical teachings which were finding their way into the church; the heresy in question may have been of the Gnostic variety.[38]

Dear friends, I was just on the point of writing to you about our common salvation, when it became necessary for me to write and appeal to you to come to the defense of the faith that has once for all been intrusted to God's people. For some people have sneaked in among us—their doom was foretold long ago—godless persons, who turn the mercy of our God into an excuse for immorality, and disown our only Master and Lord, Jesus Christ.

. . . These dreamers defile the body, make light of authority, and deride majesty. . . These people deride anything they do not understand, and the things they know by instinct, like unreasoning animals, they use for their own destruction. . . They are stains on your religious meals, where they carouse together, boldly attending to no one but themselves; rainless clouds driven before the wind; leafless trees without fruit, doubly dead, and uprooted; wild sea waves foaming up their own shame; wandering stars doomed forever to utter darkness.

These men are grumblers, dissatisfied with life. They go where their passions lead, their talk is arrogant and they cultivate people in the hope of gain.
. . . These are the men who create division; they are animal and devoid of the Spirit. . . Those whom you pity in their uncertainty, save, snatching them out of the fire, and look on others with pity mixed with fear, loathing even the clothes the animal nature has stained.[39]

The date when Jude was written was *ca.* 125 A.D. In spite of its apocalyptic nature and its subchristian spirit of condemnation of heretics, Jude contains a doxology which is perhaps the most beautiful of all the benedictions in the New Testament:

> Now to him who is able to keep you from stumbling and to make you stand in his presence irreproachable and triumphant—to the one God our Savior be glory, majesty, power, and authority through Jesus Christ our Lord now and forever and ever. Amen.[40]

The period covered by the New Testament writings comes to a close *ca.* 150 A.D. with the composition of II Peter, chronologically the latest of the twenty-seven books in the New Testament. The author claims in no uncertain terms to be the apostle Simon Peter,[41] but the fact that he is a pseudonymous writer who deliberately used the name of the great apostle is indicated by his dependence upon Jude,[42] his reference to the letters of Paul as canonical scriptures,[43] and his mention of the death of the "forefathers,"[44] the apostolic founders of the church. II Peter was written at a time when Christians were doubting more and more the physical return of Jesus; the author wants to revive the old confidence in the visible and immediate return of Christ. He appeals to the transfiguration of Jesus[45] and the Stoic doctrine of the destruction of the universe by fire:

> But do not overlook this one fact, dear friends, that with the Lord one day is like a thousand years and a thousand years are like one day. . . The Day of the Lord will come like a thief; on it the heavens will pass away with a roar, the heavenly bodies will burn up and be destroyed, and the earth and all its works will melt away. . .[46]

The author, in the same highly apocalyptic spirit which had characterized the author of Jude, hurls a bitter invective not only against heretics but also against those who disbelieve in the second coming of Christ. In Jude, there is some hope for those who will repent;[47] the author of II Peter holds out no such hope for his enemies. The author maintains that Christians should continue to struggle for moral perfection:

> Thus he (Jesus) has given us his precious and splendid promises so that through them you may escape the corrupting

influences that exist in the world through passion, and come to share in the divine nature. For this very reason make every effort to supplement your faith with goodness, goodness with knowledge, knowledge with self-control, self-control with stead-fastness, steadfastness with piety, piety with a spirit of brother-hood, and the spirit of brotherhood with love. For if you have these qualities in their fulness, they will make you neither idle nor unproductive when it comes to the understanding of our Lord Jesus Christ. . .[48]

Therefore, dear friends, while waiting for this (the Day of the Lord), make every effort to be found by him unstained, irreproachable, and at peace. Look upon our Lord's patience as salvation, . . . So you, dear friends, now that you are fore-warned, must be on your guard against being led away by the errors of unprincipled men and losing your present firm-ness. You must grow in the blessing and knowledge of our Lord and Savior Jesus Christ. Glory to him now and for-ever.[49]

SUGGESTIONS FOR FURTHER STUDY

A. E. BARNETT, *The New Testament: Its Making and Meaning*, pp. 214-224, 253-274.

H. M. BATTENHOUSE, *New Testament History and Literature*, pp. 370-372.

H. M. BATTENHOUSE, *The Bible Unlocked*, pp. 515-516, 524-525.

G. A. BUTTRICK, ed., *The Interpreter's Bible*, XII, pp. 1-206, 315-343.

M. DIBELIUS, *A Fresh Approach to the New Testament and Early Christian Literature*, pp. 186-189, 205-209, 226-230.

F. C. EISELEN, E. LEWIS, and D. G. DOWNEY, eds., *The Abingdon Bible Commentary*, pp. 1327-1349, 1361-1363.

E. J. GOODSPEED, *An Introduction to the New Testament*, pp. 265-295, 345-355.

E. J. GOODSPEED, *The Story of the Bible*, pp. 95-105, 132-136.

M. E. LYMAN, *The Christian Epic*, pp. 157-168, 189-198, 246-256.

J. MOFFATT, *An Introduction to the Literature of the New Testa-ment*, pp. 318-372, 456-475.

E. W. K. MOULD, *Essentials of Bible History*, pp. 589, 592, 593, 594, 595.

D. W. RIDDLE and H. H. HUTSON, *New Testament Life and Liter-ature*, pp. 187-189, 196-199, 206-208.

E. F. SCOTT, *The Literature of the New Testament*, pp. 209-229.

NOTES

CHAPTER ONE

1. A textbook in the Philosophy of Religion, V. Ferm's *First Chapters in Religious Philosophy* (N.Y.: Round Table Press, 1937) devotes seventy-one pages to a discussion of the definition of religion. A sample list of definitions may be found in H. T. Houf's *What Religion Is and Does* (N.Y.: Harper's, 1945), pp. 4-6; E. D. Soper's *The Religions of Mankind* (N.Y.: Abingdon-Cokesbury, 1938), pp. 25-34; and E. S. Brightman's *A Philosophy of Religion* (N.Y.: Prentice-Hall, 1940), pp. 15-16, footnote 9.

2. Brightman, *op. cit.*, p. 16.

3. One Salomon Reinach has defined religion as "a sum of scruples which impede the free exercise of our faculties." *Orpheus: A History of Religion*, translated by Florence Simonds. N.Y.: Liveright Publishing Corp.

4. *What Religion Is and Does*, p. 7.

5. James 1:27: "A religious observance that is pure and stainless in the sight of God the Father is this: to look after orphans and widows in their trouble, and keep one's self unstained by the world." All quotations from the Bible are from Smith and Goodspeed's *The Complete Bible* (Chicago: University of Chicago Press, 1939).

6. Quoted in Soper, *op. cit.*, p. 27.

7. *Ibid.*

8. *Religion within the Limits of Reason Alone. The Critique of Pure Reason*, translated by N. K. Smith; Macmillan & Co., Ltd.; N.Y.: St Martin's Press, Inc.

9. *The Varieties of Religious Experience* (N.Y.: Longmans, Green and Co., 1902), p. 31. Reprinted by permission of Paul R. Reynolds & Son, 599 Fifth Ave., N.Y. 17, N.Y.

10. A. N. Whitehead, *Religion in the Making*. Quoted in Soper, *op. cit.*, pp. 28-29.

11. Quoted in W. K. Wright's *A Student's Philosophy of Religion* (N.Y.: Macmillan, 1935), p. 528.

12. *Op. cit.*, p. 17.

CHAPTER TWO

1. The ablest representative of this point of view was Andrew Lang. For a brief description of this theory and the views of Rudolf Otto, see Wieman, Henry Nelson, and Horton, Walter Marshall, *The Growth of Religion* (Chicago and New York: Willett, Clark and Co., 1938), pp. 18-21.

2. Schopenhauer said that the beginning of religion and philosophy may be found in the fact of death; his famous essay, "Man's Need of Metaphysics," is referred to in Brightman, *op. cit.*, p. 40. See also Soper, *op. cit.*, p. 38, for the beliefs of Lewis Browne and Paul Radin.

3. See Wieman and Horton *op. cit.*, pp. 8-11; Soper, *op. cit.*, pp. 42-44.

4. N.Y.: Macmillan, 1923.

5. Many Christians treat the Bible as a sort of fetish or sacred charm. Prayer is often regarded as a means of brow-beating God into obeying man's whims.

Belief in witchcraft is still prevalent in some sections of the United States. Other examples of magic in our modern life are the rabbit's foot, hesitancy to use the number thirteen, crossing one's chest before pitching a baseball, etc.

6. An English translation appeared later (N.Y.: Macmillan, 1926).

7. Op. cit., p. 46.

8. H. Richard Niebuhr, in his The Social Sources of Denominationalism (N.Y.: Henry Holt and Co., 1929), points out that economic and nationalistic factors had far more to do with the denominational varieties in America than theological concerns.

9. Introduction to Social Psychology, 13th edition. Quoted in Houf, op. cit., p. 10.

10. Matthew 22:37-40; Mark 12:30-33; Luke 10:27.

11. Notably Durkheim, op. cit.; Edward Scribner Ames, The Psychology of Religious Experience (Boston: Houghton Mifflin Co., 1910); and Joachim Wach, The Sociology of Religion (Chicago: University of Chicago Press, 1944).

CHAPTER THREE

1. Soper, op. cit., p. 60.

2. Primitive man noted that when a man ceased to breathe, his spirit, or soul, left the body. Also, when a body lost its blood, life seemed to flow out with it. This identification of spirit with breath and blood carries over into Bible times. The Hebrew word for "spirit" was "ruach," which may also be translated "breath." In Christianity, poets speak of the "spirit of God" as the "breath of God" (as in Edwin Hatch's hymn, "Breathe on Me, Breath of God"). The Hebrews regarded blood as the chief seat of life in the body; it became a living, almost a personal, entity and must not be eaten under any circumstances. In Christianity blood becomes a symbol of sacrifice.

3. The same sort of reaction is evident in quite parallel terms used by the American Indians ("manitu," "orenda," "wakan," etc.), the savages of Morocco, the pygmies of middle Africa, the Bantu of South Africa, and aboriginal people in many other parts of the world. "Taken together all such terms refer to the experienced presence of a powerful but silent force in things, especially any occult force which is believed to act of itself, as an addition to the forces naturally or usually present in a thing. It operates most evidently and freely through persons and in living or moving things. It is a force that is thought to be transmissible from objects in nature to man, from one person to another, or again from persons to things." (Noss, Man's Religions, N.Y.: Macmillan, 1949, p. 12).

4. Noss, op. cit., p. 14.

5. The Hebrew ritual of transferring the sins of the people to a scape-goat (Leviticus 16:20-22) is a carry-over from animistic worship of a goat god and a magical attempt to get rid of all the harmful effects of a group's mistakes.

6. It would be interesting and revealing to make a list of some common tabus in modern society. The Bible is full of references to tabus among the Hebrews: the ark of the covenant (I Chronicles 13:7-10); the Sabbath; reference to the name of God is avoided (Exodus 20:7); certain kinds of animals and birds cannot be eaten (Deuteronomy 14:3-8, 12-19, 21; Leviticus 11:4-8, 10-20, 23); leprosy (Leviticus 13:45, 46). Early Christians broke with some of these tabus (Jesus declared the Sabbath was made for man, not man for the Sabbath).

7. The story of the sacrifice of Isaac (Genesis 22:1-19) is an illuminating account of the transition from human sacrifice to the acceptance of an animal substitute.

8. Weapons, clothing, furniture, every sort of precious object (including, as in Egypt, chairs, servants, and even wives) are placed in the tomb. This cult of the dead resulted in ancestor worship in China and in the veneration of certain tombs among the Hebrews, such as the graves of Sarah (Genesis 23) and Joseph (Joshua 24:32).

9. The use of the Christmas tree and the maypole represents a survival of this kind of worship. As we shall see later, trees, particularly the evergreen, were held sacred among the Hebrews.

10. The Ka'bah stone at Mecca is a meteorite which every Moslem pilgrim kisses to acquire its saving virtues. Devoted worshipers of Artemis of the Ephesians had built a beautiful temple to house an ugly meteorite which was roughly in the shape of a goddess (Acts 19:35). Among the Hebrews, Bethel (Genesis 28:11-22) and Ebenezer (I Samuel 7:12) were sacred stones.

11. Among the early Hebrews there seems to have been a rather highly developed snake cult, particularly in the period of their wilderness wanderings (Numbers 21:4-9). In Egypt the figure of the serpent was worked into the representations of the sun-god Ra.

CHAPTER FOUR

1. *The Religion of the Semites* (London: A. and C. Black, Ltd., 1923), p. 187.
2. *Ibid.*, p. 190.
3. *Ibid.*, p. 195.
4. *Ibid.*
5. *Ibid.*, p. 170.
6. *Ibid.*, p. 212.
7. Oesterley, W. O. E., and Robinson, Theodore H., *Hebrew Religion: Its Origin and Development* (N.Y.: Macmillan, 1930), pp. 11, 39.
8. Referred to in *ibid.*, pp. 49-52.
9. Referred to in *ibid.*, pp. 56-57.
10. II Kings 4:23; Amos 8:5; Hosea 2:11; Isaiah 1:13; 66:23; Psalms 81:3; Ezekiel 45:17; 46:1, 3; Nehemiah 10:33; I Chronicles 23:31; II Chronicles 2:4; 8:13; 31:3.

CHAPTER FIVE

1. Its average extent from north to south was perhaps about 150 miles. From the Mediterranean Sea it extended inland to the desert an average distance of less than 75 miles. At no time in history did Palestine cover more than 10,000 square miles, slightly larger than the state of Vermont.
2. E. W. K. Mould, *Essentials of Bible History* (revised edition; N.Y.: The Ronald Press, 1951), p. 3.
3. The land was evidently known first of all as "Canaan"; the Old Testament uses this designation for it most frequently. The word "Palestine" was given it because of the Philistine ("Peleste") invasion of the southern coast of Canaan in the twelfth century B.C.
4. This expression was first used by J. H. Breasted (*Ancient Times*, Boston & N.Y.: Ginn & Co., 1916, p. 101).
5. *Op. cit.*, pp. 4-5.
6. E. E. Voigt, "The Land of Palestine," in F. C. Eiselen, E. Lewis, and D. G. Downey, eds., *The Abingdon Bible Commentary* (N.Y.: The Abingdon Press, 1929), p. 53.

7. Amos 4:7.

8. Genesis 42; I Kings 17.

9. Garstang found remains from the Chalcolithic Period in the eighth level of his excavations at Jericho. The fourth level at Teleilat Ghassul, a site just north of the Dead Sea near Jericho, is also Chalcolithic (see W. F. Albright, "The Old Testament World," in G. A. Buttrick, ed., *The Interpreter's Bible*, N.Y.: Abingdon-Cokesbury Press, 1952, I, p. 242).

10. See an interesting story of "giants," perhaps meaning tall non-Semites, in Genesis 6:1-4.

11. Numbers 13:29 contains an interesting historical allusion: "Amalek is living in the land of the Negeb, and the Hittites, Jebusites, and Amorites are living in the highlands, while the Canaanites are living along the sea and the banks of the Jordan." This was a report of the spies sent out by Moses and Aaron.

12. It is significant that Bathsheba's husband was Uriah "the Hittite" ((II Samuel 11:3). Abraham dealt with Hittites; they are called the "natives of the land" (Genesis 23:8). Ezekiel mentions them as part of the racial background of the Hebrew people (Ezekiel 16:3, 45).

13. The "Horites" of Genesis 14:6.

14. Mould, *op. cit.*, p. 30.

15. J. Finegan, *Light from the Ancient Past* (Princeton: Princeton University Press, 1946), pp. 99-100. Ikhnaton, a religious reformer, was more interested in introducing into Egypt the worship of the sun-god Aton than in holding on to his empire. The letters are a part of the Tell-el-Amarna correspondence.

16. *Ibid.*, p. 100.

17. C. S. Knopf, *The Old Testament Speaks* (N.Y.: The Ronald Press, 1933), p. 30.

18. A city in Lower Mesopotamia with a history going back to the days of Sumerian civilization (*ca.* 3000 B.C.). Excavations by British scholars at Ur from 1922 to 1934 have proved that Ur was at the height of its prosperity from *ca.* 2070 to *ca.* 1960 B.C., when it was destroyed by invading Elamites.

19. Genesis 11:31. The exact date for this migration will probably never be exactly determined, but it occurred some time near the end of the third millennium B.C.

20. Genesis 12:1.

21. The familiar story of the separation of Abraham and Lot was due to an insufficiency of food and water for their large "families" and numerous animals (Genesis 13:5-12).

22. Terah, Abraham, Isaac, and Jacob were eponymous heroes, i.e., individuals who in their experiences personify the fortunes of whole tribes or families. The migration of Terah, and later of Abraham, can, therefore, best be understood as a tribal movement. Yet, the historicity of the patriarchal tradition, as recorded in the Book of Genesis, is substantiated by recent archaeological discoveries. This leads W. F. Albright to say: "We now know that the age of the Patriarchs, between the twentieth and sixteenth centuries B.C.E., was unusually well adapted for just such movements as those described in the Book of Genesis. . . Numerous recent excavations in sites of this period in Palestine, supplemented by finds made in Egypt and Syria, give us a remarkably precise idea of patriarchal Palestine, fitting well into the picture handed down in Genesis. . . The picture of limited movements in the hill country of Palestine, of seasonal migration between the Negeb and central Palestine, and of easy travel in Mesopotamia and Egypt is, accordingly, so perfectly in accord

with conditions in the Middle Bronze Age (*ca.* 2100-1550 B.C.) that historical skepticism is quite unwarranted. . . ." ("The Biblical Period," in L. Finkelstein, ed., *The Jews: Their History, Culture, and Religion,* N.Y.: Harper's 1949, pp. 5-6).

23. T. H. Robinson, "History of the Hebrew and Jewish People," in F. C. Eiselen, E. Lewis, and D. G. Downey, eds., *The Abingdon Bible Commentary,* p. 61.

24. See especially Genesis 14.

25. *Op. cit.,* p. 60.

26. Not all the Hebrew tribes found their way into Egypt. The powerful tribe of Judah probably became settled in Canaan and never left it (Genesis 38).

27. Genesis 37-48.

CHAPTER SIX

1. See *supra,* chapter IV.

2. The earliest of the four documents comprising the Pentateuch (the first five books of the Old Testament) dates from the early monarchy (*ca.* the tenth century, B.C.). The other three are placed by scholars in the eighth, seventh, and fifth centuries B.C. Though containing earlier material, these documents reflect the conditions and theological presuppositions of a much later day.

3. J. Muilenburg, "The History of the Religion of Israel," in G. A. Buttrick, ed., *The Interpreter's Bible,* I, p. 296.

4. Genesis 12:6-8. This same terebinth is mentioned also in Genesis 35:4, Joshua 24:26, 27, and Judges 9:6.

5. Genesis 13:18; 18:1.

6. Exodus 3:2-5.

7. Oesterley and Robinson, *op. cit.,* p. 27, points out that "it is quite clear from this passage that the belief was held that Yahweh entered the trees. His presence being indicated by the rustling. One could not have a more direct indication of animistic belief."

8. In Genesis 14:7, Kadesh is called En-mishpat ("the spring of decision"). "En" means "spring" and place names with "en" in them are believed to have been originally sacred places.

9. Numbers 21:17, 18.

10. Judges 5:21.

11. Genesis 28:11-22.

12. Genesis 31:44-48.

13. I Samuel 4:1; 5:1; 7:12.

14. Called "the mountain of Jahweh" in Numbers 10:33.

15. Simeon means "hyaena"; Deborah means "bee"; Caleb means "dog"; etc.

16. Such as Ahijah (" my brother is Jah") and Abijah ("my father is Jah").

17. *Op. cit.,* p. 357.

18. Mould, *op. cit.,* p. 127.

19. Knopf suggests (*op. cit.,* p. 151) that "Uzzah's instinctive movement may have induced a sudden, split-second realization of his act. If Uzzah believed implicitly in the deadly tabu, and if fear and undue heart strain merged in one great psycho-physical convulsion, death might easily result." Similar cases have been observed among primitive people under domination of their witch doctors and medicine men.

20. The graves of Sarah (Genesis 23), Joseph (Joshua 24:32), Miriam (Numbers 20:1), and Rachel (Genesis 35:20) may have been considered as shrines for worship.

21. These included rending one's garments (Genesis 37:34; II Samuel 1:11; 3:31), slashing one's body and cutting off one's hair (Leviticus 21:1-5; Isaiah 15:2; Jeremiah 16:6; Ezekiel 7:18; Amos 8:10; Micah 1:16), putting on sackcloth (II Samuel 3:31; Isaiah 22:12; Ezekiel 27:31), fasting (I Samuel 31:13; II Samuel 1:12), and lamentation and wailing (Genesis 37:34; II Samuel 3:31-34; I Kings 13:30; Jeremiah 22:18). Deuteronomy 26:14 is evidence that the cult of the dead persisted as late as 621 B.C.

22. Deuteronomy 8:15 (cf. Isaiah 24:29; 30:6).

23. Numbers 21:6, 8 describes a case of imitative magic in which a "seraph" was set up on a pole to cure the Hebrews of the "burning" occasioned by the bites which these demons, who were in serpent form, had given.

24. Isaiah 6:1-6.

25. The "satyrs" in Isaiah 13:21 and 34:14.

26. Isaiah 8:19; 19:3; 29:4; II Kings 21:6. It was evidently a difficult practice to eradicate (Deutronomy 18:10-14 prohibits it emphatically).

27. I Samuel 28:3-25.

28. I Samuel 16:23.

29. Our knowledge of Canaanite religion has been greatly extended by the excavations begun in 1929 by C. F. A. Schaeffer at Ras Shamra (Ugarit) on the coast of northern Syria. The literature discovered in two large groups of tablets was found to be very similar in diction and style to the oldest Hebrew poetry. In spite of the contrast between the brutal coarseness of many of the narratives in this Canaanite setting and the religion of the Hebrews, "the rich new data from Ugarit are rapidly revolutionizing our entire approach to the history of Hebrew literature, and everything written on this subject before the late 1930's is already in need of revision." (W. F. Albright, "The Old Testament World," in G. A. Buttrick, ed., *The Interpreter's Bible,* I. p. 259.)

30. J. Muilenberg, *op. cit.,* pp. 296-297.

31. *Ibid.,* p. 297.

32. *Ibid.*

CHAPTER SEVEN

1. *Supra,* p. 47.

2. Exodus 1:9. The pharaoh mentioned in this verse may have been Seti I (ca. 1319-1301 B.C.), who began the building program in which the Hebrews were impressed as slaves. It is difficult to date the life of Moses and the exodus because the Bible does not mention any of the names of the pharaohs and the name "Moses" does not appear in Egyptian inscriptions.

3. Exodus 1:11 mentions the Hebrews building "Pithom and Raamses as store-cities for Pharaoh." We also know from Egyptian records that Ramses continued the reconstruction of Tanis, begun by Seti I, as the capital of Egypt. Situated on the Egyptian frontier toward Palestine, it was located near where the Hebrews had settled.

4. The children of Israel were settled in Palestine by the third quarter of the thirteenth century, B.C., for a stele of the pharaoh Merneptah (1234-1227 B.C.) reads: "The people of Israel is desolate, it has no offering; Palestine has become a widow for Egypt!" (W. F. Albright, *op. cit.,* p. 261.)

5. Exodus 1:15-22.

6. Battenhouse, H. M., *The Bible Unlocked,* (N.Y.: D. Appleton-Century Co., 1940), p. 82. Used by permission of the author.

7. Exodus 20:22—23:33.

8. While the story may be legendary, the word "Moses" is Egyptian in origin, meaning "to be born," or "child," or "son" (Ramses means "born of Ra," Thutmose "born of Thoth," etc.).

9. Exodus 2:15.

10. The location of this mountain is very uncertain. The traditional site is near the apex of the Sinai peninsula, but many scholars have sought to locate it in the land of Midian just east of the head of the Gulf of Akabah, while still others place it northwest of the Gulf of Akabah near the location of Kadesh, where the wandering Israelites stayed for a generation. The exact location may never be known; what is important is the religious significance of what happened there.

11. Exodus 3:1, 2. Many have tried to figure out what sort of a phenomenon is involved here. A "bush burning with fire without being consumed" may have been the result of sunlight playing on brightly colored leaves. Whether that is true or not, what happened to Moses is far more significant than what happened to the bush. Moses was experiencing a theophany, a manifestation of the presence and voice of God.

12. Exodus 3:14-16. The Hebrew for "I am who I am" is sometimes translated "He who causes to be," or "The Eternal" (Moffatt). This proper name of the Hebrew God, which Moses probably received from the Kenites, was written JHWH (or YHWH) in the Hebrew language. We are not sure how it was pronounced, but scholars think that it was something like "Jahweh" (or "Yahweh"). In time, the Hebrews came to hold this name in such reverence that they would not even speak it, least by mispronouncing it they do God dishonor. Thus, when they came upon "JHWH" in their Bible they said instead "adonai," which means "Lord." The American Standard Version made use of the hybrid word "Jehovah" (the consonants of "JHWH" and the vowel sounds of "adonai"). The Revised Standard Version uses "Lord."

13. No mean task in itself (Exodus 4:29-31).

14. Exodus 5:1-5. Perhaps the festival referred to was Pesach, the ancient spring celebration of the Semitic nomads, the predecessor of the Passover (see *supra*, p. 34).

15. Exodus 5:6—6:13.

16. Exodus 7:8—12:36.

17. *Personalities of the Old Testament* (N. Y.: Scribner's, 1947), p. 17.

18. Which may well have been an actual epidemic affecting only the Egyptian children following a series of violent seasonal phenomena. The Hebrew children escaped this, perhaps because of hardier bodies or healthier surroundings in Goshen.

19. Not "Red Sea," as the Septuagint has it. This was either the upper end of the Gulf of Suez or the chain of shallow pools farther north, known as the "Bitter Lakes."

20. Exodus 14:21-28, singling out the oldest, simplest, and most straightforward of the three documentary strands (the "J" document) woven together in chapter 14.

21. Exodus 15:1-18. This hymn was written no earlier than the period of the united kingdom. The Song of Miriam (Exodus 15:19-21) is much older and may have originated at the time of Israel's escape from Egypt.

22. Assuming that Mount Sinai was one of the peaks of the Mount Seir range in Midian (see *supra*, p. 421, footnote 10).

23. Exodus 19:3-6.

24. Exodus 24:11.

25. Exodus 24:6-8. For the usual intermingling of blood of the members of the clan, Moses substituted an orderly ritual of sacrifice: the blood of a sacred animal (in this case, an ox) was sprinkled on both the sacred altar and the waiting congregation.

26. Exodus 20:1-17; Deuteronomy 5:6-21.

27. Exodus 20:22—23:33.

28. Numbers 10:11, 12, 33. Numbers 33:16-36 gives their itinerary from Sinai to Kadesh, but positive identification of all of the places mentioned is impossible.

29. The clan of Caleb did conquer the area around Hebron in southern Palestine and later became a constituent part of the powerful southern tribe of Judah.

30. Numbers 13:17—14:45.

31. Numbers 20:14-21.

32. Numbers 22:1.

33. Deuteronomy 33:1; Joshua 14:6; Ezra 3:2; Psalm 90, title.

34. Deuteronomy 34:10.

35. Mould, *op. cit.*, p. 106. A German scholar, Volz (*Mose und sein Werk*, Tübingen, 1932), pays a fine tribute to Moses. He says there was "at the beginning of the Old Testament religion a genius who belonged to the greatest of mankind, who as a messenger of God and of the supersensible world far outstripped his own time, who succeeded in drawing his fellow-countrymen into his own life with God, who towered also over the centuries following, and whose power continued on in the following centuries of hardest struggle. . . . The genius of Moses brought wholly unique new comprehensions, whose consequences were not recognized even by himself. He could reutter the voice of God but he could not, as man, fully understand it. Only in the course of centuries was the divine possession of this genius fully absorbed; until finally his program, newly proclaimed by ever new leaders, became self-evident." (quoted in F. James, *op. cit.*, p. 44, footnote 2).

CHAPTER EIGHT

1. See *supra*, chapter VI.

2. The wording of the first commandment suggests henotheism: "Since I, the Lord, am your God, who brought you out of the land of Egypt, out of a state of slavery, you must have no other gods beside me." (Exodus 20:2, 3).

3. Just prior to the time of Moses, a pharaoh, named Amenhotep IV (Ikhnaton), who was on the throne of Egypt *ca.* 1377-1360, broke completely with the powerful cult of Amen and replaced it with a solar monotheism centering on the god of the sun disk, Aton. Some writers insist that this religious reformation was the source of Moses' later interest in the worship of a single deity, but a direct connection between the two cannot be proved. While Ikhnaton's short-lived monotheism may have influenced Jahwism to some extent, the latter was so far advanced ethically that it was far better qualified than Atonism to survive.

4. This so-called Kenite hypothesis was first set forth by Karl Budde (*The Religion of Israel to the Exile*, N.Y.: G. P. Putnam's Sons, 1899) and still is the most probable explanation of the origin of Jahwism. When Moses married into the tribe of Jethro, priest of the Kenite clan, he was adopted covenantally as a member of the clan whose god was Jahweh; Moses' theophany occurred in connection with the mountain sacred to this god. The Kenites were a

wandering tribe of smiths; this leads Oesterley and Robinson (*op. cit.*, pp. 138-139) to the interesting conjecture that their occupation would lead them naturally to think of their god as a god of the celestial fires manifested in the thunderstorm and of the terrestrial fires appearing in the earthquake and the volcano, all characteristic of Jahweh at the time of Moses.

5. *Op. cit.*, p. 301.

6. Exodus 20:4.

7. Exodus 3:1; 19:3 (cf. Psalm 121).

8. Exodus 19:16, 18; 24:17; Deuteronomy 4:11, 12.

9. I Kings 19:11, 12; Deuteronomy 33:2; II Samuel 22:7-16; Judges 5:19-23; Psalm 29.

10. Exodus 3:2.

11. Exodus 13:21, 22.

12. Exodus 33:13-16.

13. Exodus 17:8-16.

14. Described in Exodus 33:7-11. The more elaborate description of the ark and the tent of meeting (tabernacle) in Exodus 35-40 is an idealized picture of a later time, possibly a reflection back into the earlier time of the details of Solomon's temple.

15. Tradition states that the stones bearing the Law received by Moses on Sinai were placed in it, together with a pot of manna and Aaron's rod (Exodus 16:33; 40:20; Numbers 17:10). Carried into battle, the ark seemed to give strength to the Hebrew warriors. The old song for the taking up and setting down of the ark is considered one of the bits of poetry in the history of Israel and may date from the wilderness period:

"Arise, O Lord, that thy foes may be scattered,
That those who hate thee may flee before thee.

. . . .

Halt, O Lord, and bless the clans of Israel" (Numbers 10:35, 36)

Perhaps the sacred stones in the ark were the "Urim and Thummim," objects manipulated by the priests seeking to discover the will of God. (as to their possible use, see Mould, *op cit.*, p. 134).

16. But note Exodus 33:11, in which the Ephraimite (northern kingdom) writer of the "E" document assigns the position to Joshua.

17. Some think these stones were kept in the ark of the covenant (see *supra*, p. 423, footnote 15).

18. Most of the ritualistic prescriptions in the books of Exodus, Leviticus, and Numbers were composed after the temple was constructed. The pre-exilic prophets, representing the older nomadic traditions, all condemned the elaborate ceremonies of the later kingdoms of Israel and Judah. Their cry was: back to the desert (see Hosea 2:14-17; 12:9; 13:4, 5). A primitive account of what the worshipers in the desert might have observed is in Exodus 34:14-26.

19. *Op. cit.*, p. 136.

20. This incident may have been due to the influence of Egyptian bull worship, or the story in its present form may have come from the period after the conquest of Canaan and reflected the influence of the nature cults of that land.

21. Numbers 21:6-9. The construction of the bronze snake was attributed directly to Moses himself, at the behest of Jahweh. The passage does not say that worship was offered to it, but it did become an object of worship for many centuries. It is significant that the Hebrew expression for "serpent"

here is the same as that for "seraph" in the vision of Isaiah in the temple (Isaiah 6:1-13).

22. II Kings 18:4, where it is spoken of as "Nehushtan." The serpent cult has been considered by archaeologists to be a very ancient one in Palestine. Among objects found at Beth-shan ("shan" is probably the old Semitic name for the old Sumerian serpent deity) were a bowl with a serpent design, pottery model of a serpent, little clay shrines with coiled serpents at the base, and figures of the mother goddess and serpent (see C. S. Knopf, *The Old Testament Speaks*, pp. 97-98, footnote 59, and J. Finegan, *Light from the Ancient Past*, p. 142).

CHAPTER NINE

1. E. W. K. Mould, *op cit.*, pp. 137-138.

2. Joshua 10:28-43.

3. Judges 18 tells the story of the migration of the small tribe of Dan from a very uncomfortable location among Canaanite strongholds in the north of the Shephelah to the extreme north of Palestine, near the headwaters of the Jordan River.

4. In Exodus 23:28, Deuteronomy 7:20, and Joshua 24:12, there is mention of "hornets" (Smith and Goodspeed has "leprosy") as clearing the way in Canaan so that the Hebrews could take possession of the land. The hornet was the symbol of the pharaoh Thutmose III (*ca.* 1501-1447 B.C.) and may be taken to refer to Egypt in the passages noted.

5. *Op. cit.*, p. 142.

6. Recent discoveries at Ras Shamra (cf. *supra*, p. 420, footnote 29) tells us a great deal about Canaanite culture and religion. The majority of the documents unearthed are in the nature of mythological poems concerning Canaanite gods and heroes. The supreme god is known as El and his home is in the "Source of the Two Deeps"; his wife is Asherat-of-the-Sea, the counselor of the gods, and their son is Baal, the god of the rain and the storm. One of Baal's titles is "Zabul (Prince), Lord of the Earth," reminiscent of the name Baal-zebub (II Kings 1:2) and Beelzebub (Mark 3:22). "The religion was polytheistic, mythological, and ritualistic, and was centered to a large degree in interest in the fertility of the soil." (Finegan, *op. cit.*, pp. 148-149).

7. See *supra*, p. 424, footnote 22, Chapter VIII.

8. J. B. Noss, *op. cit.*, p. 494.

9. Bailey, A. E., and Kent, C. F., *History of the Hebrew Commonwealth* (N.Y.: Scribner's, 1935), p. 72. Also quoted in H. C. Snell, *Ancient Israel: Its Story and Meaning* (Salt Lake City, Utah: Stevens and Wallis, 1948), p. 44.

10. Fowler, H. T., *The Origin and Growth of the Hebrew Religion* (Chicago: The University of Chicago Press, 1935), p. 44.

11. Some scholars, such as Alt and Albright, hold that the Code of the Covenant (Exodus 20:22—23:33) contains the original Shechemite laws (see J. Muilenberg, *op. cit.*, p. 309). The final formulation of the Code of the Covenant probably dates from the reign of Solomon (see Bewer, J. A., *The Literature of the Old Testament*, N.Y.: Columbia University Press, 1945, pp. 30-42).

12. I Samuel 2:13, 14 gives us a vivid picture of the practice of the cult at Shiloh.

13. Perhaps "heroes" or "champions" would be closer to the meaning of the Hebrew word "shophetim."

14. Judges 4 and 5. The former is a prose account of a famous battle, while the latter is a poetic version of the same encounter. Most ancient of all the

war songs in the Old Testament, it may date from the period of the conquest itself (see J. A. Bewer, *op. cit.,* pp. 5-9).

15. Probably this helped the Canaanites as much as it did the Hebrews, contributing thus to the amalgamation of the two peoples (Judges 6:1-8:28).

16. Judges 3:7-11.

17. Judges 10:6—12:7. Jephthah's adherence to his dreadful vow made to Jahweh is an illustration of the savage nature of religion during the conquest.

18. After treacherously murdering King Eglon (Judges 3:12-20).

19. Judges 3:31.

20. Judges 13-16.

21. A fragmentary list of stations in Numbers 21:14, 15 is from the "Book of the Wars of Jahweh." Excerpts from the "Book of Jashar" are Joshua 10:12, 13; II Samuel 1:19-27; and I Kings 8:12, 13.

22. Genesis 4:23, 24.

23. Exodus 15:21 (see *supra,* p. 421, footnote 21, Chapter VII).

24. Bewer, *op cit.,* p. 2.

25. Numbers 21:17, 18 (cf. *supra,* p. 49).

26. Judges 5 (cf. *supra,* pp. 424, 425, footnote 14, Chapter IX).

27. I Samuel 24:13.

28. Judges 14:14.

CHAPTER TEN

1. I Samuel 1:1—4:1.

2. I Samuel 4:2—5:2.

3. See *supra,* p. 71, Chapter IX.

4. I Samuel 7:15-17.

5. I Samuel 8:1-5.

6. E. W. K. Mould, *op. cit.,* p. 159.

7. I Samuel 5:3—6:21. The Philistines were embarrassed with the presence of the ark in their midst, and returned it to the Hebrews. It finally found lodgement in a private home in Kirjath-jearim (I Samuel 7:1).

8. I Samuel 7:3—8:22; 10:17-27; 12.

9. I Samuel 9:1—10:16; 11:1-15; 13; 14.

10. I Samuel 11:1-13.

11. I Samuel 11:14, 15.

12. I Samuel 13:3.

13. I Samuel 13:4—14:52.

14. Apparently because Saul had spared Agag, king of the Amalekites, in a raid against his people (I Samuel 15). Not so soft-hearted as Saul, Samuel "hewed Agag in pieces before the Lord in Gilgal" (I Samuel 15:33). Probably the real reason for Samuel's turning against Saul was that the latter had assumed the priestly function (I Samuel 15:15, 21; cf. I Samuel 13:8-14).

15. I Samuel 16:1-13.

16. I Samuel 21:1—28:2; 29:1—30:31. David drew all the discontented members of Saul's realm to him and lived a sort of Robin Hood type of existence for several years. He was even an ally of the Philistines, but they did not trust him to the extent of letting him fight with them (I Samuel 29).

17. I Samuel 31. Saul fell on his own sword. The tragic death of Saul and Jonathan gave the occasion for David to compose a beautiful poem, the "Lament over the Death of Saul and Jonathan" (II Samuel 1:19-27).

18. F. James, *op. cit.,* p. 119.

19. In I Samuel 17 there is recorded the familiar story of David and Goliath. However, II Samuel 21:19 credits Elhanan, another Bethlehemite, with slaying Goliath.

20. But Saul's jealousy of David begins with David's successes in battle. The people began to sing (I Samuel 18:7):

"Saul has slain his thousands,
But David his ten thousands."

The friendship between David and Jonathan has become the classic example of human friendship.

21. Cf. *supra,* p. 425, footnote 16.

22. II Samuel 2:1-7, 11.

23. This name indicates that fusion between Jahwism and Baalism was far enough advanced by the time of David that personal names compounded with "baal" were not considered out of place among the loyal worshipers of Jahweh.

24. II Samuel 5:1-3. We may infer from what happened later (I Kings 12:16) that one of the rights David guaranteed the people was the right to anoint or refuse to anoint his sons as successors.

25. II Samuel 5:17-25; 8:1; 21:15-22; 23:9-17. The Philistines could tolerate David as a vassal king at Hebron, but not as king over all the tribes.

26. II Samuel 5:6-12.

27. "The Biblical Period," in L. Finkelstein, ed., *The Jews: Their History, Culture, and Religion,* p. 25.

28. I Chronicles 18:16; II Samuel 8:17; 20:25.

29. II Samuel 8:16; 20:24. He may also have kept the official royal chronicles.

30. II Samuel 16:16 (cf. also I Kings 4:5).

31. Zadok and Abiathar (II Samuel 8:17).

32. Adoram (II Samuel 20:24). He was stoned to death in the rebellion of 936 B.C. (I Kings 12:18).

33. The ruthless Joab (II Samuel 20:23).

34. Benaiah, the Judahite (II Samuel 8:18).

35. Not counting Michal (II Samuel 3:2-5).

36. II Samuel 5:13-16.

37. II Samuel 11:1—12:25.

38. *Op. cit.,* pp. 154-157.

39. II Samuel 13:1-39.

40. II Samuel 15:1—19:42. David mourned Joab's savage murder of Absalom.

41. I Kings 1:1—2:11.

42. E. W. K. Mould, *op. cit.,* pp. 194-195.

43. I Kings 2:12-46. Joab and Shimei had been cursed by David in his dying hour (I Kings 2:1-11); Adonijah was considered a rival for the throne, and Abiathar had been one of his supporters. Some scholars credit Abiathar with the composition of the history of the founding of the kingdom in II Samuel 9-20; I Kings 1 and 2.

44. In the ancient Near East, the accession of a new king was usually the signal for discontented subject states to try to revolt.

45. I Kings 9:20, 21.

46. Seven years were employed in completing the project (I Kings 6:1—8:66). The building was destroyed by Nebuchadnezzar in 586 B.C. A second temple was erected by the Jews shortly after their return from the Babylonian exile and completed in 516 B.C. A third temple, actually a remodeling of the second, was constructed by Herod the Great *ca.* 20 B.C. This was destroyed by the Ro-

mans in the Jewish Wars of 66-70 A.D. At the present time there is a Moham-
medan mosque, the Dome of the Rock, on the traditional site of Solomon's
temple.

47. I Kings 7:1-12.

48. Archaeological excavations at Megiddo since 1903 have uncovered extensive stables built by Solomon. There were stalls for two hundred horses.
"Stone pillars, with holes in their corners, separated the horses and served
as hitching-posts. Stone mangers were provided, and the ground on which the
horses stood was paved with rough stones to prevent hoofs from slipping."
(Finegan, *op. cit.*, p. 152).

49. I Kings 9:27.

50. Our knowledge of this source of income is due to recent archaeological
discoveries at Eziongeber (see Finegan, *op. cit.*, pp. 152-153).

51. Though the number of seven hundred wives and three hundred concubines
(I Kings 11:3) may be an exaggeration, it is safe to conclude that "King
Solomon was a lover of women; and he married many foreign wives. . . ."
(I Kings 11:1).

52. I Kings 9:16.

53. I Kings 4:22, 23.

54. His later reputation for wisdom was probably based on these two
traditions.

55. *Op. cit.*, p. 89. Used by permission of the author.

56. *Supra*, p. 71.

57. Numbers 23:1—24:25.

58. I Samuel 18:7; 21:11; 29:5 (cf. *supra*, p. 426, footnote 20).

59. II Samuel 20:1. This shows how strong tribal jealousy was even in David's
kingdom.

60. II Samuel 1:19-27, taken from the Book of Jashar (cf. *supra*, p. 71 and
p. 425, footnote 17).

61. II Samuel 3:33, 34.

62. See Amos 6:5. "The tradition of Davidic authorship of the Psalms was
established as early as the time of the Chronicler. He believed that David had
planned the temple and arranged for the singing and the music in the temple
services. To the Chronicler (whose work is in I and II Chronicles and Ezra-
Nehemiah) David was not a mighty warrior so much as a writer and singer
of psalms, and to him and to his chief musicians was therefore attributed the
authorship of many of them." (J. A. Bewer, *op cit.*, p. 342.) Psalms 18 and
24:7-10 are considered by some to be Davidic in origin, but the former is no
longer in its original form and the latter is part of a later psalm whose religion
is far in advance of the time of David.

63. I Kings 8:12, 13.

64. Genesis 9:25-27.

65. Deuteronomy 33:1-29.

66. Genesis 49:1-28.

67. II Samuel 8:16, 17.

68. These archives may have been similar to those kept by Ahab, king of
the northern kingdom some two centuries later than David, which have been
discovered by archaeologists in excavations of his capital city Samaria (see
Mould, *op. cit.*, p. 206; Finegan, *op. cit.*, pp. 155-156, believes these archives
were those of Jeroboam II, not Ahab). They consisted of broken bits of pottery
written upon with a carbon ink and a kind of brush pen. They related mostly
to matters of revenues and estates.

69. I Kings 4:3. Jehoshaphat was still recorder; the two scribes were Elihoreph and Ahijah.

70. I Kings 11:41. This is one of the "lost books," so-called because they are no longer extant. It was written shortly after the death of Solomon by his admirers, who had a first-hand knowledge of the events of Solomon's reign. Later it became a valuable source for the Deuteronomic historians who wrote I Kings. The custom of keeping records persisted among the later kings; the authors of I and II Kings frequently mention the "Book of the Chronicles of the Kings of Israel" (I Kings 14:19; 15:31; etc.) and the "Book of the Chronicles of the Kings of Judah" (I Kings 14:29; 15:7, etc.). Neither of these is extant. Had they been preserved, we would know a great deal more about the history of the Israelites than we do now.

71. The point of view of Bewer (op. cit., p. 44). Passages like I Kings 6 and 7, covering the details of Solomon's temple, must have come from some sort of official record. It would naturally have been burned in the destruction of the temple by Nebuchadnezzar in 586 B.C.

72. Possibly Abiathar. Cf. supra, p. 426, footnote 43.

73. Op. cit., p. 208.

74. R. H. Pfeiffer, Introduction to the Old Testament (N.Y.: Harper's, 1941), pp. 139-140. Divergent views of a minority of Old Testament scholars are presented by Pfeiffer, ibid., pp. 140-141.

75. "The Growth of the Hexateuch," in G. A. Buttrick, ed., The Interpreter's Bible, I, p. 194.

76. Translated by W. F. Albright; reprinted in J. Finegan, op. cit., p. 153.

77. W. F. Albright, op. cit., p. 29.

78. An early form of extraterritoriality, according to which, in modern international relations, the building and property of an embassy in a foreign country belong to the nation of which the ambassador is a citizen. The Deuteronomic historians who wrote the books of Kings condemned this custom unsparingly (I Kings 11:5, 33; II Kings 23:13).

79. Ishbaal (II Samuel 4:1; cf. supra, p. 426, footnote 23) and Meribaal (II Samuel 4:4) belonged to Saul's family line. One of David's sons was named Baaliada (II Samuel 5:16).

80. Solomon gave official state sanction to this cult when he erected a special shrine to Ashtart (Astarte) in Jerusalem (I Kings 11:5, 33). This was destroyed by Josiah in the Deuteronomic Reform of 621 B.C. (II Kings 23:13).

81. Evidently idols used in divination or necromancy, the teraphim were often small in stature (Genesis 31:34, where Rachel sits on her father's teraphim) or later, lifesize (I Samuel 19:16, where Michal hides one in David's bed so he can escape Saul's soldiers). They too were eliminated in Josiah's reform (II Kings 23:34).

82. See supra, p. 62.

83. I Samuel 21:8; Judges 8:27; 17:5; 18:14, 17, 20, 24. The Bible gives no data concerning its appearance, but it was evidently big enough to hide Goliath's sword behind it.

84. I Kings 11:4-13, 33.

85. Supra, p. 68.

86. I Samuel 9:13, 25.

87. I Kings 3:4-9.

88. I Kings 15:4 (cf. I Kings 3:2).

89. I Samuel 7:1, 2; II Samuel 6:1-23. Psalm 24:7-10 reenacted this historic procession as a part of the worship of the second temple.

90. Perhaps a carry-over from an ancient cult of the sun. Solomon's remarks at the dedication of the temple seem to imply an association of worship of the sun with the temple cult:

"The Lord established the sun in the heavens,
But he himself said that he would dwell in thick darkness;
'Build my house, a house of habitation for me,
That I may dwell therein forever.'" (I Kings 8:12, 13).

91. I Kings 6:23-28. The cherubim, child-like images with wings, were the bearers of deity (Psalm 18:10) and hence symbolized the very presence of Jahweh in this innermost room.

92. See *supra*, p. 63.

93. I Kings 8:64; 9:25.

94. I Kings 7:23-26. The use of representations of bulls in the temple area shows the strong implications for Jahwism of primitive bull worship.

95. Named Boaz and Jachin (I Kings 7:15-22). Cf. *supra*, p. 68.

96. David danced with such abandon that his wife Michal scolded him for it (II Samuel 6:16-23).

97. I Samuel 28:6.

98. I Kings 4:2, 5.

99. II Samuel 6:12-15.

100. II Samuel 8:18.

CHAPTER ELEVEN

1. Cf. *supra*, p. 426, footnote 24, Chapter X. For some unknown reason, Solomon had not been required to meet this test of approval.

2. Cf. *supra*, p. 80.

3. I Kings 12:4.

4. I Kings 12:13—16.

5. The prophets of Jahweh seemed to be in favor of the revolution, at least at first. Ahijah of Shiloh had been Jeroboam's associate in the revolt against Solomon (I Kings 11:26-40) and was still his supporter in 922 (I Kings 12:15). Shemaiah dissuaded Rehoboam from marching against the northerners with an army (I Kings 12:21-24). From now on, the "Kingdom of Israel" will refer to the northern kingdom and the "Kingdom of Judah" to the southern.

6. *Op. cit.*, pp. 218-220.

7. W. F. Albright (*loc. cit.*) estimates that the population of Palestine (of Israelites alone) in the united kingdom was approximately 800,000 This would make Israel's share in 922 approximately 535,000 and Judah's 265,000.

8. I Kings 12:25-33.

9. I Kings 13:1—14:20. The author of I Kings, probably a Judahite historian of the period immediately following the Deuteronomic Reform, attributes to Jeroboam's religious policy all the calamities which led to Israel's downfall in 721 B.C.

10. His name became a synonym for "killer." Jezebel called Jehu "you Zimri" (II Kings 9:31).

11. On the famous Black Obelisk of Shalmaneser III, discovered in 1846, Jehu is referred to as "son of Omri." Actually, it was Jehu who overthrew the Omride dynasty (cf. Finegan, *op. cit.*, pp. 171-173).

12. I Kings 22:34-40.

13. II Kings 8:29—10:36.

14. Hosea 1:4.

15. The Bible records the fall of Israel in II Kings 15:8-31; 17:1-41. The Deuteronomic historians regard it as a necessary result of earlier religious apostasy (cf. II Kings 17:7-12). The captives carried away by Sargon and absorbed by surrounding peoples have been aptly designated as "the ten lost tribes of the house of Israel." Those brought into Israel in 721 intermarried with the Hebrews left in the land and from this mixture developed the race later known as the Samaritans. Of mixed blood, the Samaritans were always despised by the inhabitants of Judah (cf. John 4:9).

16. II Kings 18:1—19:37. Just what happened to Sennacherib's army is not known. Perhaps bubonic plague caused the 185,000 deaths mentioned in II Kings 19:35.

17. Cf. II Kings 21:2-16. Though Manasseh ruled approximately fifty-four years, only eighteen verses in II Kings are allotted to him.

18. II Kings 23:31—25:30 recounts the tragic story of the fall of Judah. The authors blame it on the religious apostasy of Manasseh (II Kings 24:3). In 597 Nebuchadnezzar carried off some ten thousand people, including the king (Jehoiachin), princes, mighty men of valor, and artisans.

19. II Kings 25:22-26; Jeremiah 40:1-43:7. Jeremiah seems to have been the only person who kept his head in all this chaotic period.

20. Jeremiah 52:30.

CHAPTER   TWELVE

1. I Samuel 10:5, 6.

2. Cf. I Samuel 10:10; 18:10, 11; 19:24.

3. "The Prophetic Literature," in G. A. Buttrick, ed., *The Interpreter's Bible*, I, p. 202. The Bible itself speaks of prophets of the Phoenician Baal, who "performed a limping dance around the altar" and "proceeded to slash one another according to their custom, with swords and with lances until the blood gushed out upon them" (I Kings 18:26, 28). An Egyptian papyrus of the eleventh century B.C. speaks of the existence of such prophetism at Byblos in ancient Phoenicia.

4. In Smith and Goodspeed's *The Complete Bible,* the expression "sons of the prophets" is most frequently translated as "members of the prophetic order."

5. I Samuel 9:9. This function of the prophet was exercised when leaders among the Hebrews wanted to discover the will of Jahweh; there were various ways of doing this, but one of the most important was consulting the prophet's oracle.

6. *Op. cit.,* p. 135.

7. Moses is called the "nabi'" ("mouthpiece") of Jahweh in Exodus 4:16, and Aaron the "nabi" of Moses in Exodus 7:1.

8. See *supra,* pp. 70, 71.

9. I Samuel 22:5.

10. II Samuel 24:11-14. The conception of Jahweh in this incident is quite primitive. He is said to have been angered against Israel (though his reason is not mentioned); so he stirred David up to take a census. Then Gad appeared to speak to David in the name of Jahweh to oppose the census, offering the king a choice of three years of famine, three months of defeat in battle, or

three days of pestilence. David chose the pestilence, and seventy thousand died as a result of it. I Chronicles 21:1 blames the census on Satan.

11. II Samuel 12:1-15.

12. I Kings 11:29-40.

13. I Kings 14:1-18.

14. I Kings 12:21-24.

15. I Kings 16:1-7.

16. I Kings 22:1-28. Italics mine. The battle ended disastrously, as Micaiah had predicted, with victory for the Syrians and death for Ahab.

17. *Supra*, p. 91.

18. By "pre-literary prophets" is meant those who wrote no books, or whose writings, if any, have not been preserved. The prophets were essentially speakers, not writers. The fact that the words of some of them, like Amos and Hosea, have been preserved is one of the most fortunate aspects of Hebrew religious history.

19. Malachi 4:5, 6. Cf. Matthew 11:14; 16:14. Later Christians referred to John the Baptist as Elijah (John 1:25).

20. I Kings 18:20-40.

21. I Kings 19:8-13.

22. I Kings 21:1-29. This incident reveals Ahab's impotence in contrast with the fiery disposition of Queen Jezebel.

23. Smith, J. M. P., *The Prophets and Their Times* (Chicago: University of Chicago Press, 1941, Second Edition revised by W. A. Irwin), p. 53.

24. II Kings 8:7-15. Jehoram of Israel was unsuccessful against Hazael in another battle at Ramoth-gilead (II Kings 8:28, 29).

25. II Kings 8:29—10:36. In spite of the condemnation of Hosea (1:4) a hundred years later, Jehu's revolution did sever the ties which linked Jahwism to Tyrian Baalism.

CHAPTER THIRTEEN

1. Amos 1:3—2:5. The Book of Amos is the earliest book in the Old Testament, chronologically speaking.

2. Amos 1:3.

3. Amos 2:4, 5.

4. Referring to the extreme inflationary conditions characteristic of Israel during the prosperous reign of Jeroboam II. To purchase a pair of shoes, the poor people were forced to sell themselves as slave laborers for extended periods of time. The middle class in the northern kingdom had virtually disappeared.

5. Amos 2:6, 7.

6. Amos 5:21-24. Italics mine. The last two lines constitute the theme of the Book of Amos.

7. Amos 5:18-20.

8. Amos 5:27. This represents an enlargement of the scope of Jahweh's activities. In this way, Amos set the idea of God forward a long way toward monotheism (cf. Amos 9:7, where Amos affirms the fact that Jahweh guides other nations).

9. Amos 3:11—4:3. Another graphic description of the luxury-loving Israelites is in Amos 6:1-8.

10. Amos 5:3, 15. Cf. also Amos 9:9-15, evidently added by a later editor for whom the unmitigated pessimism of the Book of Amos was too unbearable.

11. Like Elisha, Amos had pronounced Jahweh's rejection of a royal family (Amos 7:9).

12. Amos 7:14, 15.

13. *Op. cit.*, pp. 227, 228.

14. Hosea 1:4, 5. Apparently Hosea's message was based on moral and religious convictions rather than on political considerations. Though he mentions Assyria (5:13; 7:11; 8:9; 9:3, 6; 10:6; 11:5; 12:1) and Egypt (7:11, 16; 9:3, 6; 10:6) it is as if they were both equal threats to Israel's security. Tiglath-pileser III had just begun to expand Assyria's power and Egypt was in a state of complete impotence at the beginning of the 23rd dynasty.

15. Hosea 1:2-4, 6, 8, 9. Scholars differ as to whether Gomer was an actual person or not, but the majority are inclined to believe that she was a real woman, perhaps a well-known sacred prostitute attached to one of the Baal shrines. Hosea's marriage to her would not have been considered morally culpable in the eighth century B.C. Sanctuary prostitutes were regarded as wives of the god and thus members of an honored profession. It was Gomer's later infidelities which were not so "sacred."

16. "Raisin-cakes" may have been articles of food figuring in some of the Canaanite vintage-festivals (cf. Jeremiah 7:18).

17. Hosea 3:1-3.

18. The Valley of Achor was the one which leads down from the hill-country of Judah to the Jordan valley by Jericho. Jahweh will allow Israel to make a new beginning—to enter Canaan a second time more hopefully.

19. Hosea regarded the wilderness experience as the happiest period in the life of the nation; it was then the nation acted most like a trusting child under a father's loving protection (cf. also Hosea 11:1-7; 12:9; 13:4, 5; see *supra*, p. 423, footnote 18, Chapter VIII).

20. Hosea 2:14-16, 19-23.

21. Hosea 11:1-4, 8, 9, Cf. also Hosea 13:4-8; 14:1-8.

22. Hosea 4:12, 17; 11:2; 14:3.

23. Hosea 8:6.

24. Hosea 8:4-6.

25. Hosea 13:2.

26. Hosea 4:15; 5:8; 10:5. The word may be translated "house of panting breath." Mould (*op. cit.*, p. 321) thinks the expression "carries the connotation of a place where tremendous efforts are put forth but with futile outcome. He means, of course, that all their zealous and costly worship before these images avails them not a thing in reality."

27. Hosea 4:6.

28. Hosea 6:4-6. The last verse of this quotation, along with Hosea 12:6, expresses most exquisitely Hosea's basic concept of Jahweh and religion in general.

29. Hosea 2:6, 7 (cf. also Hosea 2:9, 11-16; 5:11-15; 6:1, 4-6; 7:1).

30. J. Muilenburg, *op. cit.*, pp. 320, 321.

31. Matthew 9:13; 12:7 (cf. Hosea 6:6). Hosea may have lived to see the downfall of the northern kingdom in 721 B.C. (see *supra*, p. 92).

32. See *supra*, p. 83.

33. Isaiah 6:1. The year was 740 B.C., though some authorities place it in 751 B.C.

34. Isaiah 6:1-8.

35. Isaiah 5:16.

36. Isaiah 10:5-7.

37. Isaiah 14:24-27. When Assyria had served Jahweh's purpose, she will be annihilated.

38. See *supra*, p. 92.

39. Isaiah 7:1—8:10. Cf. II Kings 16. This fateful alliance with Assyria caused Ahaz to adopt Assyrian religious symbols for the temple at Jerusalem.

40. Isaiah 28:1-4.

41. Isaiah 20:1-6. This unusual behaviour seems to have persuaded Hezekiah and his counselors to stay out of such rebellions.

42. Isaiah 30:7. Moffatt translated this expression as "Dragon Do-nothing." Mould (*op. cit.*, p. 254) speaks of it as "Lady Brag-and-Stay-at-Home." Rahab is the Hebrew word for the monster of chaos.

43. Isaiah 31:1, 3.

44. II Kings 20:20; II Chronicles 32:30. The story of the discovery of this tunnel and the inscription on the right wall, about nineteen feet in from the Siloam entrance, may be found in G. A. Barton, *Archaeology and the Bible* (Philadelphia: American Sunday School Union, 1937), p. 476. See also J. Finegan, *op. cit.*, pp. 158-160, and Mould, *op. cit.*, pp. 53-55.

45. Finegan, *op. cit.*, p. 177.

46. II Kings 19:6 (Isaiah 37:6).

47. Isaiah 37:33-35. The prophets Micah (3:12) and Jeremiah (26:1-19) spoke unhesitatingly of the doom of Jerusalem. Jeremiah was almost put to death for contradicting Isaiah's message concerning the inviolability of the temple and the city of Jerusalem, but he was spared when someone remembered Micah had made a similar remark and was not killed (Jeremiah 26:18, 19).

48. II Kings 19:35. It may have been an epidemic of bubonic plague.

49. Isaiah 28:7-22.

50. Isaiah 8:16-18. Only part of the present book of Isaiah was written by Isaiah of Jerusalem (chapters 1-23 and 28-39).

51. Isaiah 1:11-17.

52. Isaiah 3:14, 15.

53. Isaiah 5:11.

54. Isaiah 5:8.

55. Isaiah 1:23.

56. Isaiah 3:16—4:1.

57. Isaiah 5:20.

58. Isaiah 2:5-22 gives a striking picture of this terrible day of judgment.

59. Isaiah 28:16. See also Isaiah 4:2-6; 6:13; 17:4-14; 28:5; 37:31, 32.

60. This same passage is also quoted in Micah 4:1-3. Other sections of Isaiah which refer to the Messiah are Isaiah 4:2-6; 9:2-7; 11:1-9; 32:1-8, 15-20.

61. Micah 1:5.

62. Micah 6:6-8. Some regard chapters 4-7 of the Book of Micah as having been added to the original oracles of Micah. Micah 4:1-3 is identical with Isaiah 2:2-4 (see *supra*, p. 118).

63. Micah 2:1, 2.

64. Micah 3:1, 2.

65. Micah 3:5.

66. Micah 3:11, 12.

67. Jeremiah 26:16-19; II Kings 18:1-6.

68. See *supra*, p. 63.

CHAPTER FOURTEEN

1. See *supra*, pp. 92, 116.

2. II Kings 21:2-7.

3. J. A. Bewer, *op. cit.*, pp. 122, 123.

4. Hence it is called the "second law" (Deuteronomy) of Moses. The authors did not mean to deceive the people by ascribing their work to Moses; it was as if they were saying: if Moses were here he would urge you to obey these laws. They thought they were bringing out more clearly and in a more modern form the essential truths of the religion of Moses—Jahwism.

5. Exodus 20:22—23:19, probably the oldest piece of Hebrew legislation now extant, dating at least as early as the reign of Solomon.

6. Probably Deuteronomy 12-26. It may have been "planted" in the temple by the reform party, to be brought forth at the psychological moment. It was wise strategy, for its effect was electric and far-reaching.

7. The whole story is in II Kings 22:1—23:27.

8. II Kings 23:4-14.

9. Deuteronomy 6:4, 5. When Jesus quoted this as the first and great commandment (Mark 12:28-30) he added the phrase "with all your soul." Devout Jews through the centuries have followed the prescriptions outlined by Deuteronomy (6:6-9): "These instructions that I am giving you today are to be fixed in your mind; you must impress them on your children, and talk about them when you are sitting at home, and when you go off on a journey, when you lie down and when you get up; you must bind them on your hand as a sign, and they must be worn on your forehead as a mark; you must inscribe them on the door-posts of your house and on your gates."

10. Deuteronomy 12:2-7.

11. Deuteronomy 12:20-26.

12. Deuteronomy 14:24-26. This is the beginning of that temple traffic in cattle, sheep, birds, and money which so horrified Jesus (Mark 11:15-18).

13. Deuteronomy 19:1-13. Blood-revenge was further limited to the actually guilty persons (Deuteronomy 24:16). See *supra*, p. 35.

14. Deuteronomy 17:8-13.

15. Deuteronomy 15:4-11.

16. Deuteronomy 14:28, 29; 16:9-17; 24:17; 26:12-15; 27:19.

17. Deuteronomy 24:19-21. Such a custom was called gleaning.

18. Deuteronomy 24:6. Grain was crushed in Bible times between two circular stones, the upper of which was rotated on the lower by means of a handle set near the edge. See A. E. Bailey, *Daily Life in Bible Times* (N.Y.: Scribner's, 1943), p. 136.

19. Deuteronomy 15:1-11.

20. Deuteronomy 24:14, 15.

21. Deuteronomy 24:17, 18.

22. Deuteronomy 16:18-20.

23. Deuteronomy 22:1-4.

24. L. B. Longacre, *The Old Testament: Its Form and Purpose* (N.Y.: Abingdon-Cokesbury Press, 1945), p. 41. Used by permission of Southwestern University, Georgetown, Texas.

25. See *supra*, pp. 82, 83.

26. For example, Jeroboam I (I Kings 12:25—14:20) and Manasseh (II Kings 21:1-18) were the arch villains of Hebrew history because they "did that which was evil in the sight of the Lord," whereas Josiah, because of his support of the Deuteronomic reform, "did that which was right in the sight of the Lord," like David (II Kings 22:1—23:27).

27. Deuteronomy 7:6-8.

28. Deuteronomy 7:9-11.

29. Longacre, *op. cit.*, p. 32.

30. Deuteronomy 5:9,10.
31. Ezekiel 18:1-4 (cf. Jeremiah 31:29,30).
32. See *supra,* pp. 91, 92.
33. See *supra,* p. 93.

CHAPTER FIFTEEN

1. Jeremiah 1:1, 2, 13-19; 4:5—6:26.
2. Zephaniah 1:14-18. Herodotus mentioned these raiders from the north (Book I, Sections 103-106) and said they dominated Asia for twenty-eight years. Apparently they began to threaten the peace of the western part of the fertile crescent *ca.* 626 B.C. and were stopped at the borders of Egypt by Pharaoh Psamtik I. Since they were primarily interested in plunder, the Scythians did little permanent damage to Judah, but they took part in the destruction of Nineveh (612 B.C.; *supra,* p. 92).
3. Zephaniah 1:10, 11 seems to indicate familiarity with the topography of of that city.
4. Zephaniah 1:1.
5. See *supra,* pp. 103, 104, 117.
6. Zephaniah 1:14-18. Verse 15 inspired one of the great hymns of the church, the "Dies Irae" of Thomas of Celano (*ca.* 1185-1255 A.D.).
7. See *supra,* pp. 104, 117, 118.
8. Zephaniah 2:3. A further reference to the hope of the remnant is in Zephaniah 3:11-13.
9. *Supra,* p. 93.
10. Nahum 3:1-3.
11. Nahum was similar in spirit to Hananiah (Jeremiah 27 and 28) Shemaiah the Nehelemite (Jeremiah 29:24-32), and others who encouraged Jerusalem's leaders with false hopes of victory and blocked Jeremiah's efforts to prevent the revolt of 586 B.C. (Jeremiah 14:13-15; 37:19).
12. Habakkuk 1:2-4.
13. Habakkuk 1:6-11.
14. Habakkuk 1:13—2:1.
15. Habakkuk 2:2-4 (cf. also Habakkuk 3:17-19). Verse 4 is very familiar to the Christian world because of its repetition in Hebrews 10:38, Romans 1:17, and Galatians 3:11. Martin Luther seized on these words as the watchword of his reform movement.
16. *Op. cit.,* pp. 160-162.
17. Jeremiah 19:1—20:6; 26-29; 32; 34-45.
18. Jeremiah 1:1. His family evidently belonged to the tribe of Benjamin rather than Judah; hence Jeremiah would have been well versed in the traditions of his exiled northern countrymen. He was profoundly influenced by the writings of the prophet Hosea.
19. Jeremiah 16:1-4. The Scythian menace (626 B.C.), the Deuteronomic Reform (621 B.C.), the fall of Nineveh (612 B.C.), and the tragic death of Josiah (608 B.C.) were only a few of the great events happening inside and outside of Judah during Jeremiah's early life.
20. Jeremiah 11:18-23. The plot against his life may have been caused by Jeremiah's indorsement of the Deuteronomic Reform, which would have put the local priests at Anathoth out of a job in favor of the central sanctuary in Jerusalem. Later Jeremiah recognized the dangers implicit in the views of

the Deuteronomists, particularly the doctrine of retribution (Jeremiah 31:29, 30; *supra*, p. 129).

21. Jeremiah 25:3. This was the same year which brought Zephaniah into the public eye (*supra*, p. 131). Jeremiah 1:13-19 and 2-6 seem to have these invaders in mind.

22. Jeremiah 1:4-10.

23. Jeremiah 1:11-19.

24. Jeremiah 7:1, 2.

25. Josiah had been succeeded by his son Jehoahaz, but after three months he was put in prison in Egypt by Pharaoh Necho. Another son of Josiah, Jehoiakim, reigned in his stead, under the watchful eye of Egypt (I Kings 23:30-35). Jeremiah courageously threatened Jehoiakim with a violent death and an indecent burial (Jeremiah 22:18,19; cf. Jeremiah 36:30), but Jeremiah's prediction did not materialize (II Kings 24:6; II Chronicles 36:8).

26. Jeremiah 26:16-19; Micah 3:12. Cf. *supra*, p. 433, footnote 47. Another prophet, Uriah, was killed by Jehoiakim for saying the same thing Jeremiah had said (Jeremiah 26:20-24).

27. Jeremiah 26:24. Jeremiah 26 is devoted to this temple address and its consequences.

28. Jeremiah 35. This probably took place during the first siege of Jerusalem by Babylonian troops under Nebuchadnezzar (*supra*, p. 93).

29. Jeremiah 27 and 28. After a reign of three months, Jehoiakim's successor, Jehoiachin, was carried off to Babylon in the captivity of 597 B.C. (II Kings 24:8-17). Jehoiachin's uncle, Zedekiah, Judah's last king, changed from pro-Babylonian to anti-Babylonian in 588 (*supra*, p. 93). Mould (*op. cit.*, p. 337) thinks the incident of the yoke took place in 593 B.C., when Egyptian agents were trying to induce Zedekiah to join a revolt against Babylon.

30. Jeremiah 19:14—20:6.

31. Jeremiah 36.

32. Jeremiah 29:1-23.

33. Jeremiah 34:8-22.

34. Jeremiah 32:6-15.

35. Jeremiah 37:11-21.

36. Jeremiah 38:1-13. Ebed-melech is the "good Samaritan" of the Old Testament. Jeremiah did not forget his kindness (Jeremiah 39:15-18).

37. Jeremiah 38:14-27.

38. See *supra*, p. 93.

39. Jeremiah 39-41.

40. Jeremiah 42 and 43.

41. Jeremiah 44.

42. Jeremiah 7:3-10. Did Jesus have these words of Jeremiah in mind when he said to those in the temple in his day: "You have made it a robber's cave." (Mark 11:17)?

43. Jeremiah 6:20 (cf. 7:21-26).

44. Jeremiah 2:22.

45. Jeremiah 4:1, 2.

46. Jeremiah 6:13.

47. Jeremiah 8:6 (cf. Jeremiah 9:2-6).

48. Jeremiah 13:27 (cf. also verses 23 and 25).

49. Jeremiah 22:3 (see *supra*, pp. 435, 436, footnote 20, Chapter XV).

50. Jeremiah 22:13, 17.

51. Jeremiah 27:4-7 (cf. also 25:9 and 43:10).

52. Jeremiah 25:11-26.

53. Jeremiah 31:1-6 (cf. also verses 15-25).

54. Jeremiah 31:31-34. Fleming James says of this passage: "The prophecy of the new covenant was one of the sayings which introduce a fresh era in man's thinking about God . . . There is nothing in the Old Testament more sufficient, more ineluctable, and more permanent. Any enduring fellowship between God and man must be built in this foundation or not built at all . . ." (*op. cit.*, pp. 328-329). Jeremiah purchased a piece of property at Anathoth even while the Babylonians were besieging Jerusalem in the confident expectation that Judah would once again be restored (Jeremiah 32:1, 2, 6-15, 36-44; cf. *supra*, p. 137).

55. Jeremiah 3:4, 5.

56. Jeremiah 3:11, 12, 17-20.

57. Jeremiah 5:3.

58. Jeremiah 9:24. Other passages clearly expressing Jeremiah's concept of God are 12:15-17; 14:8, 9; 16:19; 17:10; 20:12; 31:3, 20, 34.

59. Jeremiah 31:29, 30. Cf. also 17:10 and 12:1-6.

60. Matthew 16:14.

61. II Kings 24:8-17. See *supra*, p. 93.

62. Ezekiel 1:1—3:15. This unusual vision of a throne-chariot and a "semblance like that of a man sitting above it" (1:26) suggests an appearance of the glory of Jahweh similar to Isaiah's in the temple (Isaiah 6:1-8; cf. *supra*, p. 112). In describing it Ezekiel uses imagery derived from the religion of his Babylonian neighbors. Such visions and trances were a feature of this prophet's experience (see the vision of the valley of dry bones in Ezekiel 37:1-14 and others in Ezekiel 8:2-18; 10:1-22; 11:22-25); the most elaborate of his visions was the one concerning the new temple (chapters 40-47).

63. Ezekiel 3:17.

64. Ezekiel 20:8 (cf. also 11:1-12).

65. Ezekiel 16:3, 45.

66. Ezekiel 22:24-29.

67. This is the essential meaning of the vision of the valley full of dry bones (Ezekiel 37:1-14).

68. Ezekiel 34:1-6.

69. Ezekiel 34:11-31. Reminiscent of the language of Psalm 23, this is one of the most beautiful chapters in the Bible. Unlike Jesus, Ezekiel confined the glorious future to Israelites.

70. Ezekiel 18. Cf. *supra*, pp. 141, 142.

71. Ezekiel 17:1-10, 22-24, the allegory of the eagles and the vine, is typical of Ezekiel's style. The conclusion of it is similar to the earlier prophetic doctrine of the remnant (cf. *supra*, pp. 104, 117, 118).

CHAPTER SIXTEEN

1. For this story, see *supra*, p. 93.

2. Except for the six years when Queen Athaliah was in control and the infant Josiah was in hiding (II Kings 11:1-20).

3. H. M. Battenhouse, *op. cit.*, p. 211.

4. See *supra*, pp. 91, 92.

5. Jeremiah 29:1-7, in Jeremiah's letter to the exiles (see *supra*, p. 137), and Ezekiel 8:1, 14:1, and 20:1-3 indicate a freedom of action permitted the exiles by the Babylonians.

6. J. B. Noss, *op. cit.,* pp. 521-522.

7. Such as Jeremiah (6:16,20; 7:21,22) and Micah (6:6,7).

8. See Ezekiel 20:12-24.

9. Leviticus 20:26.

10. Leviticus 19:17, 18; 25:14, 17-25, 35-40, 44, 45, 47-50, 53, 55.

11. Leviticus 19:17,18—the highest point in the ethics of the Old Testament. Quoted by Jesus as the commandment next in importance to the Shema (Mark 12:31; cf. *supra,* p. 125).

12. See Daniel 5:1.

13. Cyrus himself was a loyal disciple of Zoroaster, the Persian religious genius who had lived about a hundred years earlier. Like all Zoroastrians, Cyrus worshiped one god, whom they knew as Ahura Mazda. During the next two centuries, Zoroastrianism was to have a profound effect on Judaism.

14. Cyrus would probably have welcomed a rehabilitated Judah, as a good buffer state for his projected conquest of Egypt.

15. H. M. Battenhouse, *op. cit.,* pp. 222-223.

16. See *supra,* pp. 111-118. With rare exceptions, critics are now agreed that the sixty-six chapters of the Book of Isaiah were not all written by Isaiah of Jerusalem. While some defend the unity of Isaiah 40-66, a great many scholars believe that chapters 40-55 were written *ca.* 540 B.C. and chapters 56-66 *ca.* 455 B.C. Still others would separate the apocalyptic chapters 24-27 from the section (1-39) usually assigned to Isaiah of Jerusalem and would date them *ca.* 340 B.C. (cf. *supra,* p. 433, footnote 50, Chapter XIII).

17. Isaiah 40:1, 2.

18. Isaiah 40:3-5.

19. Isaiah 40:9-11. George Frederic Handel made use of many of this Jewish poet's phrases for his famous oratorio, *The Messiah.*

20. Isaiah 44:6.

21. Isaiah 45:5,6 (cf. also 45:22 and 46:9).

22. Isaiah 40:28.

23. Isaiah 48:13 (cf. also 42:5).

24. Isaiah 54:5 (cf. also 45:12, 22, 23; 49:6).

25. Isaiah 43:15; 45:17; 54:7, 8; 42:6-9.

26. Isaiah 41:25; 45:1; 48:14.

27. Isaiah 44:6 (cf. also 41:4; 48:12); other references to various attributes of Jahweh and various titles given to him are in Isaiah 40:8; 41:17; 43:11, 14, 15; 45:7; 49:26; 50:10.

28. Isaiah 40:12-17.

29. Isaiah 44:9-20 (cf. also 40:18-26; 41:6, 7).

30. Isaiah 44:21, 22 (cf. also 45:17).

31. *Supra,* pp. 106-111

32. Isaiah 54:4-8.

33. Isaiah 49:6.

34. Isaiah 52:10.

35. Isaiah 42:6, 7.

36. Isaiah 48:11.

37. In Isaiah 41:8-16; 44:1, 2, 21; and 45:4 the term "servant" is identical with the word "Israel." In Isaiah 42:18-22; 44:26; and 50:10 there is nothing that would call for a different meaning. This leads J. M. P. Smith (*op. cit.,* p. 229) to assert: "Now, if the term 'Servant' everywhere in this prophecy means 'Israel' outside of the 'Songs,' it certainly is to be supposed that the meaning of the term will be the same inside of the 'Songs'; . . ."

38. Isaiah 42:1-4.

39. Isaiah 49:1-6.

40. Isaiah 50:6. The entire song is in 50:4-9.

41. Isaiah 52:13—53:12.

42. Isaiah 53:2-5.

43. Isaiah 53:10-12.

44. Luke 22:27; Mark 10:45. "The supreme servants of God who have greatly served mankind have ever been despised and rejected of men, men of sorrows and acquainted with grief, bearing the iniquities of many . . . The martyrs of religion, and of every other high devotion, men who have greatly risen above the level of their own age, have drawn others up toward their high vision only as they themselves have borne the iniquities . . ." (Fowler, H. T., *The Origin and Growth of the Hebrew Religion*, Chicago: The University of Chicago Press, 1935, pp. 136-137).

CHAPTER SEVENTEEN

1. *Supra*, pp. 151, 152.

2. II Chronicles 36:22, 23; Ezra 1:2-4; 6:3-5.

3. J. Finegan, *op. cit.*, p. 191. The praise of Cyrus in Isaiah 41:2-4 and the reference to him as the Lord's anointed in Isaiah 45:1 reveal the pleasurable reaction of the Babylonian Jews to his edict.

4. Ezra 1:8, 11 (cf. also Ezra 5:14, 16).

5. *Supra*, p. 430, footnote 18, Chapter XI.

6. Haggai 1:1-11; Zechariah 4:9.

7. Ezra 6:1-14. Opposition to the restoration of Jerusalem also came from the Samaritans and the poor "people of the land" (Ezra 3:8—4:5, 23).

8. Zechariah 6:11 seems to imply the crowning of Zerubbabel as king.

9. Malachi 4:1-3.

10. Malachi 3:1-3. Referred to as "Elijah the prophet" in Malachi 4:5.

11. Nehemiah 11:14; Mark 9:11-13; Luke 1:17.

12. Nehemiah 1:3.

13. Nehemiah 1:1—7:73; 11:1—13:31.

14. Nehemiah 5.1-19.

15. Nehemiah 13:10-14. Much to his disgust Nehemiah discovered, upon his return to Jerusalem from a trip to Susa, one family using part of the temple buildings for a dwelling; he ordered them out (Nehemiah 13:15-22).

16. Nehemiah 13:15-22.

17. Nehemiah 13:23-27. Ezra required the Jews to divorce their foreign wives (Ezra 10:10, 11). The exquisite book of Ruth was probably written as a protest against this anti-foreign policy of Ezra and Nehemiah.

18. Notably C. C. Torrey in his *Ezra Studies* (Chicago: University of Chicago Press, 1910). But this point of view has found little acceptance.

19. Ecclesiasticus 44-49. Nehemiah is mentioned in 49:13.

20. 1:18-36.

21. Ezra 8:1-14.

22. Ezra 7:10.

23. Nehemiah 8:1. Nehemiah 8:1—10:39 evidently belongs to the Memoirs of Ezra.

24. *Supra*, pp. 162, 163.

25. Ezra 9:1-3; 10:9-11.

26. J. B. Noss, *op. cit.*, p. 532. For detailed information regarding the sacrificial system of the priestly code, see Hastings, J., ed., *A Dictionary of the Bible* (N:Y.: Scribner's, 1911), IV, p. 357.

27. See *Supra*, p. 83. Ezra may have read parts of this code to the people of Jerusalem (*supra*, p. 164).

28. L. B. Longacre, *op. cit.*, p. 71.

29. Genesis 9:1-5.

30. See especially Genesis 17. "Circumcision, like the Sabbath, was one of the most significant religious institutions of Israel for P, because during the exile and in the dispersion both were distinguishing signs of the covenant, by which the Jews could be recognized" (J. A. Bewer, *op. cit.*, p. 260).

31. See Exodus 12:1-14, 28.

32. The ritual of the Day of Atonement is given in Leviticus 16.

33. See *supra*, p. 83.

34. J. Muilenburg, *op. cit.*, pp. 335, 336.

35. The first was the Bible of the Deuteronomists (*supra*, pp. 126, 127).

36. See *supra*, pp. 162, 163, 164, 165.

37. *Supra*, pp. 103, 104.

38. *Supra*, pp. 117, 118.

39. *Supra*, pp. 131, 132.

40. Joel 2:28—3:13.

41. Just the reverse of Isaiah 2:2-4 (*supra*, p. 118) and Micah 4:1-3 (*supra*, p. 433, footnote 62).

42. Joel 3:9-13.

43. Joel 2:12-17.

44. Joel 2:21-27; 3:1-18.

45. Joel 3:19-21.

46. J. A. Bewer, *op. cit.*, p. 303.

47. E. W. K. Mould, *op. cit.*, p. 408.

48. R. H. Pfeiffer, *op. cit.*, p. 742.

49. Esther 4:13-16.

50. Martin Luther said about the Book of Esther: "I am so hostile to the book and to Esther that I wish they did not exist at all; for they Judaize too much and have much heathen perverseness" (*Table Talk*, quoted in R. H. Pfeiffer, *op. cit.*, p. 747).

51. Goodspeed, E. J., *The Story of the Old Testament* (Chicago: University of Chicago Press, 1945), pp. 98, 99.

52. Ruth 1:16, 17.

53. Jonah 4:1-8.

54. The allegory of Jonah is similar to the parable of the Good Samaritan (Luke 10:25-37); the character of Jonah would correspond to the spirit of the priest and the Levite. Jahweh is made to say: "And should not I, indeed, have pity on Nineveh, that great city, in which are more than a hundred and twenty thousand infants, that cannot distinguish between their right hand and their left, and many cattle?" (Jonah 4:11).

CHAPTER EIGHTEEN

1. It was under Artaxerxes II that Ezra probably came to Jerusalem (see *supra*, p. 164).

2. Tradition says 40,000 inhabitants of the Phoenician city of Sidon died in this revolt. Psalms 74 and 79 may reflect the despair caused by these disasters.

3. Actually there was very little difference in Palestinian affairs at first caused by the demise of the Persians. The Jews simply changed masters, as they have done so often in their history. *Ca.* 332 B.C. the rift between the mixed Jews in Samaria and the "pure" Jews in Judah widened into a gulf that has never been bridged. The Samaritans established a rival sanctuary on Mount Gerizim (see John 4:20).

4. Simon the Just (*ca.* 180 B.C.), mentioned in Ecclesiasticus 50:1 as "the great priest."

5. The wise men are mentioned in Jeremiah 18:18, along with priests and prophets, as an essential part of Hebrew life.

6. Wisdom sayings are found in Egypt and Babylonia as early as the third millenium B.C. For a brief summary of wisdom literature among the Canaanites and the Hebrews before the exile, see W. A. Irwin, "The Wisdom Literature," *The Interpreter's Bible,* I, pp. 212-215.

7. Especially Psalms 1, 8, 15, 19, 37, 49, 73, 103, 107, and 119.

8. Such as Isaiah 28:23-29.

9. Pfeiffer, *op. cit.,* pp. 645-646, recognizes eight different collections brought together in the Book of Proverbs (chapters 1-9; 10:1—22:16; 22:17—24:22; 24:23-34; 25-29; 30; 31:1-9; and 31:10-31).

10. Longacre, *op. cit.,* pp. 131-132.

11. However, it also reveals the fact that monogamy was the accepted custom in post-exilic Judaism.

12. Ecclesiastes 1:2, *passim.*

13. Ecclesiastes 1:1-11.

14. Ecclesiastes 2:24 (cf. also 3:12, 13, 22; 5:18; 8:15; 9:7-10; 11:7-10).

15. Ecclesiastes 3:1-8.

16. Ecclesiastes 3:19, 20 (cf. also 2:14-17; 9:2, 3).

17. Ecclesiastes 12:7. Hebrew writers heretofore had not expressed any interest in the problem of immortality. It was to Greek speculators on the relationship of body and soul that later Christian writers turned for inspiration on their doctrine of immortality (see I Corinthians 15).

18. Ecclesiastes 11:9—12:8.

19. Ecclesiastes 11:9d; 12:1a.

20. Ecclesiastes 12:13, 14.

21. Koheleth is called "the son of David, who was king in Jerusalem" in Ecclesiastes 1:1 (cf. also 1:12).

22. Snell, *op. cit.,* p. 230, ranks Job with Virgil's *Aeneid* and Homer's *Iliad.*

23. Job 1; 2; 42:7-17.

24. Mentioned in Ezekiel 14:14, 20.

25. On retribution, see *supra,* pp. 128, 129, 142, and 145.

26. The persistence of this view is illustrated by an incident in the life of Jesus. A man born blind was once brought to him with the question: "Master, for whose sin was this man born blind? For his own, or for that of his parents?" (John 9:2).

27. Job 1:11, 12; 2:4-10. Job 23:10 expresses the same attitude: "When he knows my manner of life, when he has tested me, I shall come forth like gold."

28. Job 27:4-6.

29. Job 32-37. This fourth fault-finding friend adds nothing new to the views of the other three.

30. *Supra,* pp. 151-158.

31. Job 42:10.

32. Albright (op. cit., pp. 54, 55) believes that Ezra was the Chronicler. Hence the date for the composition of I and II Chronicles, Ezra, and Nehemiah would have to be ca. 400 B.C.

33. The earlier two being the Deuteronomic History of the Hebrews (supra, pp. 126, 127) and the Pentateuch (supra, p. 168).

34. I Chronicles 1-10. Most of the names were taken from the Book of Genesis. Saul is disposed of in a single chapter, the tenth.

35. Stated in Deuteronomy (supra, pp. 128, 129) and supported by the three friends of Job (supra, p. 178) and some of the Psalms (such as Psalm 1), the doctrine was challenged by Ezekiel (supra, p. 145), Jeremiah (supra, p. 142), and Job (supra, p. 179), and by some of the Psalms (such as Psalm 73).

36. II Chronicles 20.

37. Mentioned in II Chronicles 17:14-19, this army, according to the author, had a total of 1,160,000 soldiers. This is characteristic of the Chronicler's exaggerated use of numbers.

38. Other similar accounts are in II Chronicles 13:2, 3, 13-18, where God defeats Jeroboam's army of 800,000 and II Chronicles 14:9-12, where God puts to flight an army of a million Ethiopians.

39. Supra, pp. 88-90.

40. II Chronicles 10.

41. Such as David's desertion to the Philistines, his affair with Bathsheba, and Absalom's rebellion (supra, pp. 76, 78). This helps us to understand the Jews' belief, particularly strong in the late Old Testament period, that the Messiah would be another David, or a son of David.

42. I Chronicles 12:23-37.

43. I Chronicles 21:25. This is in contrast with the fifty silver shekels mentioned in II Samuel 24:24.

44. 100,000 gold talents and 1,000,000 silver talents (I Chronicles 22:14), to which he added personal gifts of 3000 gold talents and 7000 silver talents (I Chronicles 29:3, 4).

45. I Chronicles 29:21; II Chronicles 29:32-35; 34; 35:7-9.

46. I Chronicles 16:8-22 is identical with Psalm 105:1-15; I Chronicles 16:23-33 is the same as Psalms 96; while I Chronicles 16:34-36 equals Psalm 106:1, 47, 48. The Chronicler raised the Levites to a much higher position than they had been given in the priests' Bible of 400 B.C. (supra, pp. 166-168). Guilds of singers are mentioned, such as Asaph, Ethan, and Heman (II Chronicles 15:19), which are familiar names in the Psalms (Psalms 50 and 73-83 are a collection of psalms "of Asaph"; Heman is mentioned in the title of Psalm 88 and Ethan in the title of Psalm 89).

47. James, op. cit., p. 496.

48. Supra, pp. 168-170.

49. Supra, pp. 75-79.

50. Psalms 1-41; 42-72; 73-89; 90-106; 107-150. The fivefold division of the Book of Psalms corresponds with the Pentateuch, or fivefold division of the Torah.

51. Psalms 50, 73-83.

52. Psalms 42-49, 84, 85, 87, 88.

53. Perhaps processional hymns, Psalms 120-134.

54. Psalms 3-41, 51-72.

55. Supra, p. 182. Cf. especially supra, p. 442, footnote 46. R. H Pfeiffer, op. cit., p. 621, suggests that the Chronicler may well have been a member

of one of the festival choirs participating in worship because he seems to know the musical parts of the ritual so expertly.

56. In Psalm 136, the refrain "For his kindness is everlasting" is in each of the twenty-six verses. The leading voice gives a patriotic review of the way God had aided the nation in the past.

57. Psalm 46:7, 11. Longacre, *op. cit.*, p. 165, thinks that the refrain should also be inserted after verse 3.

58. Psalms 113-118. Psalms 115-118 were the ones sung after the paschal meal; more than likely these were the ones sung by Jesus and his disciples following the last supper in the upper room (Mark 14:26; Matthew 26:30).

59. Cf. *supra*, p. 442, footnote 35.

60. This is similar in style and content to the Song of Solomon, a collection of love and wedding songs which found itself included in the Old Testament canon.

61. Ephesians 5:19 (cf. also Colossians 3:16; James 5:13).

62. Psalm 40:1-3.

CHAPTER NINETEEN

1. The word "apocalypse" means "dream" or "revelation."

2. *Supra*, pp. 103, 104.

3. Amos 9:11-15. Cf. *supra*, p. 431, footnote 10. Apocalyptic additions or insertions may also be noted in Isaiah (2:2-4; *supra*, p. 118; 24-27; 34; 35), Micah 4:1-4 (*supra*, p. 433, footnote 62), Joel, Zechariah, and Ezekiel.

4. A title referring to the fourteen books in the Septuagint translation of the Old Testament which did not find their way into most Protestant translations of the Bible.

5. A word meaning literally "writings attributed to fictitious authors," but technically referring to Jewish writings of the period from 200 B.C. to 200 A.D. outside of the Old Testament and the Apocrypha.

6. The Apocalypse, or Book of Revelation, in the New Testament, is a Christian apocalyptic book.

7. *Supra*, pp. 174, 175.

8. Meaning "illustrious" or "brilliant." The Jews dubbed him secretly Epimanes, which means "crazy."

9. Called "the desolating abomination" in Daniel 11:31.

10. The story of this revolt is recorded in I Maccabees 1:10—9:73 and in II Maccabees.

11. I Maccabees 2-4; II Maccabees 8:1—10:8. This is still celebrated among the Jews by the festival of Hanukkah, occupying eight days every December.

12. See *supra*, pp. 174, 175.

13. Daniel 2:44, 45a.

14. Daniel 4:33.

15. Daniel 5:1-31.

16. Daniel 8:13, 14, 25; 9:25-27; 11:21-39; 12:7, 11. "The desolating abomination" referred to in Daniel 11:31 and elsewhere occurred in 168 B.C. when Antiochus Epiphanes desecrated the temple at Jerusalem (*supra*, p. 190).

17. Daniel 7:9, 10, 13, 14. The "one like a man" became in later apocalyptic writings a personal Messiah. It has no such meaning in the Book of Daniel. Also, since the author believes that these events will soon take place, the Book of Daniel is not a blueprint of history for any period other than his own, the Maccabean age.

18. Persia has a guardian angel (Daniel 10:13, 20), as do also Greece (Daniel 10:20) and Judah (the angel Michael, Daniel 10:21; 12:1).

19. In addition to Michael, there is Gabriel, an interpreter sent from heaven (Daniel 8:16; 9:21).

20. Daniel 12:2, 3 (cf. Isaiah 26:19).

21. Willett, Herbert L., "Daniel," in F. C. Eiselen, E. Lewis, and D. G. Downey, eds., *The Abingdon Bible Commentary*, p. 748.

22. *Supra*, p. 190.

23. In spite of the eulogistic report in I Maccabees 14 and Psalm 110, many of the orthodox Jews opposed making "men of blood" like Jonathan and Simon high priests.

24. Alexandra was the second queen to rule over the Jews in all their history, the first having been Athaliah, daughter of Jezebel (*supra*, p. 91).

25. Palestine has continued to be under the rule of some non-Jewish political power until the formation of the state of Israel in recent times (1948).

26. *Op. cit.*, p. 268.

CHAPTER   TWENTY

1. Galatians 4:4.

2. Shirley Jackson Case, in his *The Historicity of Jesus* (Chicago: The University of Chicago Press, second edition, 1928), ably presents all the arguments which refute those who, like Strauss (*Das Leben Jesu*, Tübingen, 1835 and 1836) and Bauer (*Christus und die Caesaren*, Berlin, 1877 and 1879) have denied that Jesus ever really lived (cf. also Case, *Jesus: A New Biography*, Chicago: The University of Chicago Press, 1927).

3. *Supra*, pp. 39-197.

4. *Supra*, pp. 173, 174.

5. The word "Hellenism" was first coined by the German scholar J. G. Droysen in a book the first volume of which was published in 1836 (*Geschichte des Hellenismus*, Gotha).

6. Tarsus, the birthplace of Paul, was a center of this sort. The great geographer Strabo (*ca.* 64 B.C.—19 A.D.) was a resident of Tarsus.

7. Adolph Deissman, in his *Bibelstudien*, published in Marburg in 1895, demonstrated decisively that the Greek of certain papyri discovered along the Nile River in Egypt was the same as that of the New Testament, the common (koiné) everyday vernacular speech of the first century A.D., the language of business, shop and home, personal letters, and everyday affairs. This fact has thrown more light on some of the difficult and obscure passages in the New Testament.

8. See *supra*, p. 174.

9. The library at Alexandria was destroyed by fire at the time of the conquest by Julius Caesar (47 B.C.). This was one of the greatest tragedies of antiquity, for many famous volumes, of which there were no other copies, went up in smoke. In 391 A.D., Christian fanatics burned its successor, a library housed in the temple of Jupiter Serapis.

10. The author of the Old Testament book of Ecclesiastes had much in common with Epicureanism (*supra*, pp. 176-178).

11. Romans 8:14-17; Galatians 2:20; 5:16-24.

12. S. V. McCasland, "The Greco-Roman World," *The Interpreter's Bible*, VII, p. 87.

13. Acts 17:22. The Athenians were so tolerant of all faiths that they had even erected an altar "to an unknown God" (Acts 17:23). Paul used this as an occasion to tell them about his God and the Christ who came to reveal his nature.

14. Acts 16:16-18. Cf. McCasland, *op. cit.*, pp. 91-92.

15. In many ways, baptism fulfills for Christians the same function which the rite of initiation did for the devotee of a mystery cult. Likewise the Eucharist, or Lord's Supper, is a memorial service with features similar in purpose to the sacramental meal in the cult. For a detailed study of this and other similarities and differences see S. Angus, *The Mystery-Religions and Christianity* (N.Y.: Scribner's, 1925).

16. *Ibid.*, pp. 94, 95. Used by permission of John Murray (Publishers) Ltd., London. Prudentius objected to this rite most vociferously because of its affinity in redemptive conception with the crucifixion of Jesus, of which it was viewed as a travesty.

17. While in Athens (Acts 17:15-34) Paul may have seen the great outdoor theater of Dionysus, located on the southeastern side of the Acropolis, with seats for fourteen thousand spectators. The works of Sophocles, Euripides, Aristophanes, and other Greek poets would have been presented on its stage. An altar to Dionysus stood in the center of the orchestra, and a chorus of highly trained singers and dancers performed in his honor.

18. *Supra,* p. 444, especially footnote 2.

19. Some have seen in the letters of Paul evidence of the language and spirit of the mystery cults, but it is doubtful that Paul himself was ever really influenced by the mystery religions. "Paul undoubtedly uses terms which are characteristic of the terminology of the mystery-religions, just as he used occasionally Stoic technical terms. But in both cases the language is charged with a new meaning and a new content." (E. H. Box, "The Historical and Religious Backgrounds of the Early Christian Movement," in F. C. Eiselen, E. Lewis, and D. G. Downey, eds., *The Abingdon Bible Commentary,* p. 851).

20. The deification of Caesar was fixed by law January 1, 42 B.C. Augustus was accorded divine honors in the eastern provinces, but declined such honors in Rome. His long and prosperous reign was conducive to the growth of emperor worship, and after his death his official apotheosis only confirmed what had been going on during his lifetime. Tiberius was not assertive of the right to divine honors, but Caligula did declare himself to be a god.

21. In his *The Evolution of Early Christianity* (Chicago: The University of Chicago Press, 1923), Shirley Jackson Case says: "Over against the divine Caesar, whether apotheosized at death or appearing as a deity upon earth, stood Jesus raised from the dead, exalted to lordship in heaven, having displayed miraculous powers upon earth, having been miraculously born or appearing as a pre-existent divine being manifest in the flesh. Jesus' authority was not less great or less divine in character than that of the most distinguished Roman emperor. Jesus was lord and his subjects were servants, which was not only the typical relation between monarch and people from ancient times in the Orient, but had become a familiar notion to the Graeco-Roman world in the Hellenistic age." (page 236).

22. *Op. cit.*, p. 563.

23. Jerusalem at Pentecost, as described in Acts 2:5-11, displayed a cosmopolitan character which would have prevailed in every large city of the Roman Empire.

24. Acts 22:25-29.

25. "The total number of slaves in the Graeco-Roman world at any period is variously estimated, as also their relative proportion to the free. Le Maistre reckons 60,000,000 in the Empire. In Pergamum there was one slave to every two freemen. In the city of Rome the proportion was undoubtedly much greater: Beloch reckons 280,000 slaves to 500,000 free; Gibbon reckons as many slaves as free in the time of Claudius, Blair guesses the number of slaves and of free to be about equal up to the destruction of Carthage, and after that the proportion to be 3 to 1, giving a population of over 20,000,000 slaves in Italy. Zumpt reckons over 650,000 slaves in Rome in 5 B.C." (S. Angus, *The Environment of Early Christianity*. N.Y.: Scribner's 1922, p. 38).

26. Though the effect of a document such as Paul's letter to Philemon would be to cut the ground out from under human slavery. Paul urges Philemon, a slaveowner, to welcome back a runaway slave, Onesimus, "not as a slave any longer but more than a slave, a dear brother—" (verse 16).

27. S. Angus, *op. cit.*, p. 43. Other emperors used armies of dwarfs, female gladiators, and even blindfolded men.

28. S. J. Case, *op. cit.*, pp. 368-369.

29. For this story, see *supra*, pp. 189, 190, 193-195.

30. John 2:20.

31. R. H. Pfeiffer, *History of New Testament Times* (N.Y.: Harper's, 1949), page 32, footnote 34. It is not clear whether these murders were due to Herod's jealous rage or to political dissension in his harem.

32. Matthew 2:16.

33. Matthew 2:1.

34. Luke 3:1.

35. A special interest for Christians attaches to one of these procurators, Pontius Pilate (26-36 A.D.), who condemned Jesus to death.

36. Jesus seems to have found a haven of retreat in Philip's realm after leaving Galilee. Philip built Caesarea Philippi, near the source of the Jordan River, near which the famous confession of Peter took place (Mark 8:27-33; Matthew 16:13-28).

37. Jesus called him "that fox" (Luke 13:32).

38. It is interesting to speculate that possibly Jesus and Joseph, as carpenters (or, more probably, contractors), may have taken part in the rebuilding of Sepphoris.

39. The Jews refused to live in Tiberias because of its mixed population and because it was built on the site of an ancient cemetery.

40. The gospel writers connect this story with the death of John the Baptist (Mark 6:14-28; Luke 3:19, 20; 9:7-9; Matthew 14:1-11).

41. Very early in his Galilean ministry, Jesus had to face a combination of Pharisees and Herodians (Mark 3:6), though the wife of one of Herod's officials (Luke 8:3) helped to support Jesus and his disciples. Jesus' teachings on divorce (Mark 10:2-12) may have been aimed directly at Herod's private life.

42. Luke 23:7-16.

43. This is the Herod mentioned in Acts 12:1-6 as being hostile to the early Christians. In 41 A.D., Claudius added Judea and Samaria to Herod's domain. He died from a mysterious disease (44 A.D.), which struck him down on a state occasion (Acts 12:19-23).

44. Of whom two are mentioned in the Book of Acts: Antonius Felix (52-60 A.D.; Acts 23:24—24:27) and Porcius Festus (60-62 A.D.; Acts 24:27—26:32).

45. *Supra*, pp. 189, 190, 193-195.

46. A Moslem mosque, the Dome of the Rock, now occupies the traditional site of the Jewish temple.

47. *Supra*, pp. 180-182.

48. Ezra 7:11.

49. Ecclesiasticus 38:24—39:8.

50. Luke 11:45, "experts in the Law."

51. Luke 5:17.

52. "The New Testament classes the Scribes with the Pharisees, who also represented in Israel the legalistic and exclusivist party, but who constituted 'neither a sect nor a school . . . It is perfectly natural that the Pharisees, whose aim was to live according to the Law, should have been regarded as the allies—or even the followers—of the Scribes, who were the interpreters of that Law . . . Nevertheless the Scribes must not be identified with the Pharisees, nor must the Pharisees be regarded as a party led by the Scribes, for there were Scribes who were not Pharisees at all . . ." (C Guignebert, *The Jewish World in the Time of Jesus*, N.Y.: E. P. Dutton and Co., 1939, pp. 70, 71).

53. *Supra*, pp. 174, 175, and 190.

54. M. J. Lagrange, *Le Judaïsme avant Jésus-Christ* (Paris, 1931), p. 272; quoted in Guignebert, *op. cit.*, p. 164.

55. In only one instance, that of his teaching on divorce, does Jesus seem to imply any criticism of the Torah (Mark 10:2-12). Then he quotes from one section of the Torah (Genesis 1:27) which he regards as more important than the rule on divorce (Deuteronomy 24:1).

56. As, e.g., their wearing conspicuous tassels and phylacteries (Matthew 23:5), ritual washing of cups and dishes (Matthew 23:25; Mark 7:4; Luke 11:39), fasting (Matthew 9:14), long prayers (Mark 12:40; Luke 20:47), etc. There were 39 kinds of work prohibited on the Sabbath day (see Mark 2:23-28; Matthew 12:1-8; Luke 14:1-6).

57. Such as Nicodemus (John 3:1-15). Gamaliel (Acts 5:33-40) advocated that the Sanhedrin take a tolerant attitude toward the Christian religion. Paul was a Pharisee; later he referred to Pharisaism as "the strictest sect of our religion." (Acts 26:5).

58. The Pharisees earned for themselves the epithet "parushim" ("the separated ones"). Modern counterparts of this epithet would be words like "puritan" and "sabbatarian." The common people were called "am-haares" (literally, "people of the land"); they heard Jesus gladly (Mark 12:37).

59. Acts 22:3.

60. Judah Goldin, "The Period of the Talmud," in L. Finkelstein, ed., *The Jews: Their History, Culture, and Religion*, pp. 131, 132.

61. Canon Box thinks that Jesus' invective against the Pharisees in the gospels may have been primarily directed against this group (*op. cit.*, p. 841).

62. *Supra*, pp. 174, 175.

63. Though the origin of the word "Sadducee" is obscure, it may have been derived from Zadok, a priest under Solomon (I Kings 4:4).

64. Acts 23:8.

65. Mark 11:15-18; Matthew 21:12-16; Luke 19:45-48. As a result of this episode "the high priests and the scribes and the leading men of the people were trying to destroy him" (Luke 19:47), an unbreakable combination.

66. Famous Jewish historian who was born in 37 A.D. and died in 100. His books, *The Antiquities of the Jews* and *On the Jewish War* are sources of valuable information as to Jewish history and culture.

67. *Supra*, p. 212.

68. Called Judas of Galilee in Acts 5:37.

69. Simon the Zealot, or Cananean (Mark 3:19; Luke 6:15; Acts 1:13).

70. *Supra,* p. 213.

71. The discovery of other documents similar to the ones found in Cairo, in a cave on the shores of the Dead Sea in the spring of 1947, has served to highlight interest once again in the Covenanters of Damascus. Among the finds discovered in the cave were two copies of the Book of Isaiah, a commentary on Habakkuk, the *Rule* of the New Covenant, a copy of a book entitled *Psalms of Thanksgiving,* and a pamphlet called *Rule of Battle for the Sons of Light.* A. Dupont-Sommer, in his *The Dead Sea Scrolls* (N.Y.: Macmillan, 1952), believes that the sect of the New Covenant was a branch of the Essenes, but this has yet to be accepted by the majority of scholars.

72. *Supra,* p. 446, footnote 41.

73. *Supra,* p. 447, footnote 58.

74. Mark 2:15-17; Matthew 9:10-12; 11:19; Luke 15:2. Jesus' "heart was touched at the sight of them, because they were like sheep that have no shepherd; . . ." (Mark 6:34; cf. Matthew 9:36).

75. Mark 12:34.

76. Mould (*op. cit.,* p. 477) believes that the Magnificat (Luke 1:46-55) may have been a favorite hymn among the pietists and that Jesus may have commended them in the first beatitude of his sermon on the mount; "Blessed are those who feel their spiritual need, for the Kingdom of Heaven belongs to them!" (Matthew 5:3).

77. *Supra,* pp. 91, 92.

78. *Supra,* p. 93.

79. Quoted in S. J. Case, *op cit.,* page 80.

80. "Full proselytes were those who accepted the three essential obligations of Judaism, *viz.,* (a) circumcision, (b) the ritual bath, and (c) sacrifice at the temple . . . Proselytes of this type conformed to all the requirements of the Law . . .

. . . The half-proselytes . . . recoiled from circumcision and from the exigencies of strict conformity to the Law . . ." (C Guignebert, *op. cit.,* pp. 233-234).

81. Greek proselytes in Antioch became Christians in great numbers (Acts 11:19-26). Paul met proselytes in Antioch in Pisidia (Acts 13:43). Thessalonica (Acts 17:12), and Athens (Acts 17:34).

82. The process of canonization really began with the Deuteronomic Reform, with its code of laws and the literature produced under its impetus (*supra,* pp. 126, 127). The second step was the completion of the Pentateuch, or Torah, some time shortly before 400 B.C. (*supra,* pp. 167, 168).

83. The author, Ben Sirach, composed Ecclesiasticus *ca.* 180 B.C.

84. The threefold division of the later Hebrew Bible. The grandson believes that Ecclesiasticus ought to be added to the religious literature of his people.

85. e.g., Malachi 4:4, Ecclesiasticus 24:23-29; I Maccabees 1:56, 57.

86. Nehemiah 13:28. The Samaritan schism was complete shortly before 332 B.C.

87. As is indicated in Luke 2:41-52, and in Jesus' frequent references to the Torah in his teachings.

88. *Ca.* 165 B.C. *Supra,* pp. 189-193.

89. Daniel 9:2.

90. Ecclesiasticus 46:1-6, 11, 12; 46:13—47:11; 47:12—49:3, 6-10.

91. As in Acts 13:15; 28:23.

92. Luke 24:44, the only verse in the New Testament where a book of the Writings is mentioned along with the Torah and the Prophets.

93. A late and artificial designation given to them because they alone of this group were employed in the worship of the synagogue.

94. *Supra*, pp. 189, 190; I Maccabees 1:56, 57.

95. S. R. Driver, "The Formation of the Old Testament," *The Abingdon Bible Commentary*, p. 97.

96. Probably Psalms, Song of Songs, Proverbs, and Ecclesiastes. The other books of the Hagiographa are classified by Josephus among the Prophets.

97. *Supra*, pp. 174 and 202.

98. *Supra*, pp. 169, 170.

99. Compare James 1:19 with Ecclesiasticus 5:11; Hebrews 11:35, 36 are reminiscent of II Maccabees 6, 7. The Wisdom of Solomon is reflected in Romans 1:20-32; 9:21; II Corinthians 5:4; Ephesians 6:14; Hebrews 1:3; and Matthew 27:43.

100. Some pulpit Bibles in Protestant churches include the apocryphal books, as do some family Bibles and *The Complete Bible* of Smith and Goodspeed.

101. Who wrote Ecclesiasticus (50:27).

102. I Esdras 3:1—5:6. This book was written in Alexandria some time between 200 and 100 B.C.

103. *Supra*, pp. 91, 92.

104. *Supra*, pp. 169, 170.

105. Judith 12-15. This is also reminiscent of Jael (Judges 5). The book ends with a poem in praise of Judith (chapter 16).

106. II Chronicles 33:12, 13. The more historically reliable account of Manasseh in II Kings 21:1-18 makes no mention of such a captivity.

107. *Supra*, pp. 92, 116, 122.

108. Ecclesiasticus 1:1-20; 24:1-22 (cf. Proverbs 8:22-31).

109. *Supra*, pp. 176-178.

110. This is somewhat the pattern of all apocalyptic writers (*supra*, pp. 188, 189).

111. This word means literally writings attributed to fictitious authors, and in this sense would apply to some books in the Old Testament and in the Apocrypha, as, for instance, all the books attributed to Solomon. But in a technical sense it applies to Jewish writings of the period from 200 B.C. to 200 A.D.

112. R. H. Charles (*The Apocrypha and Pseudepigrapha in English*, Oxford: Clarendon Press, 1913, volume II) has added to the standard list some writings entirely unknown to the ancient Christians. At least one pseudepigraphical writing was found in the 'Ain-Feshka cave near the shores of the Dead Sea in the spring or summer of 1947 (see A. Dupont-Sommer, *The Dead Sea Scrolls*, N.Y.: Macmillan, 1952, pp. 45-52).

113. See M. R. James, *The Lost Apocrypha of the Old Testament: Their Titles and Fragments* (N.Y.: Macmillan, 1920).

114. Jesus came into conflict with the authorities of Judaism over this subject (Mark 2:23-28; Luke 6:1-5; 13:10-16).

115. As in the book of Daniel (*supra*, p. 193). Paul's name for the evil one in II Corinthians 6:15, Belial, may have been derived from the "Beliar" of Jubilees 1:20. Following the last judgment, says the book of Jubilees, men will live for a thousand years (23:27-30; 50:5; cf. Revelation 20:2, 3).

116. A sibyl was a woman in a cave who uttered prophetic words by divine inspiration. The original sybil was said to have lived in Erythrae, near Smyrna. She and the other sybils were very popular in the Hellenistic world.

117. The Son of Man in I Enoch is similar in character to the "one like a man" in Daniel 7:9-14 (*supra*, pp. 192, 193).

118. I Enoch 46:1, as translated by R. H. Pfeiffer in "The Literature and Religion of the Pseudepigrapha," in G. A. Buttrick, ed., *The Interpreter's Bible*, I, p. 430. The expression "Son of Man" is used in the New Testament in Mark 13:26; 14:61, 62; Matthew 24:30; 26:63, 64; Luke 22:67, 68; Acts 7:56; Revelation 1:13.

119. I Enoch 45:4, 5; 91:16, 17.

120. I Enoch 6-36. But in 87-90 the resurrection is for all of the righteous and none of the wicked.

121. I Enoch 90:28-36. I Enoch 91-104 regards the messianic kingdom as of temporary duration, concluding with the judgment. There is thus no uniform teaching in I Enoch about the events at the end of this age and in the future world.

122. The highest heaven is reserved for the archangels, forces, dominions, orders and governments, cherubim and seraphim, thrones, and many-eyed ones, where the Lord is enthroned in the distance (20, 21). The paradise prepared for the righteous is on the third level (chapter 9), as is also the terrible place of torture for the unrighteous (in the northern part of the same third heaven—chapter 10). That makes it easier to understand how Dives and Lazarus are within sight and sound of each other but in a far different climate (Luke 16:19-31.) Paul locates paradise in the third heaven (II Corinthians 12:2-4).

123. The Testament of Gad 3-6, *passim*. The translation is by R. H. Charles as quoted in Mould, *op. cit.*, p. 461. See also R. H. Charles' *Religious Development between the Old and New Testaments* (N.Y.: Henry Holt, 1914), p. 156.

124. See Hebrews 11:37.

125. *Supra*, pp. 182-186.

126. Perhaps because of I Kings 4:32, where Solomon's songs were said to number five thousand.

127. Translation by R. H. Charles, quoted in Mould, *op. cit.*, p. 458. This shows that a half century before the time of Jesus many Jews were looking forward to a messiah of peace, one who would win his conquests through the inner compulsion of truth and reason rather than through physical force.

128. The Mishna originally was a body of oral tradition which grew up as an enlargement and an interpretation of the Torah (*supra*, pp. 214-216). It was put into written form *ca.* 200 A.D. Traditions arising subsequent to this were added to the Mishna to comprise the Talmud, which was compiled in the sixth century A.D.

129. *Supra*, pp. 327, 328, and 448, footnote 71.

130. The Old Testament tradition has the Messiah as a descendant of David from the tribe of Judah.

CHAPTER TWENTY-ONE

1. Acts 18:2. Claudius banished the Jews from Rome, probably in 49 A.D. This is mentioned by the Latin author Suetonius (77-114 A.D.) in his *Life of Claudius* (25. 4); he says the Jews were in constant turmoil because of Christ (see J. A. Scott, *We Would Know Jesus*, N.Y.: The Abingdon Press, 1936, p. 20).

2. Paul tried to preach in Bithynia (Acts 16:7), but for some unknown reason was prevented from doing so. Later, Christians became very numerous in that province.

3. Pliny's letters and Trajan's replies are extant. See translation in W. D. Schermerhorn's *Beginnings of the Christian Church* (N.Y. and Nashville: Abingdon-Cokesbury, 1929), pp. 67-69.

NOTES 451

4. *Ibid.*, pp. 69, 70. Tacitus' evidence is all the more reliable because he mentions Jesus quite incidentally. His facts are remarkably parallel to those in the gospels (cf., e.g., Luke 3:1).

5. *Supra,* p. 450, footnote 128.

6. As quoted in C. T. Craig, *The Beginning of Christianity* (N.Y. and Nashville: Abingdon-Cokesbury, 1943), p. 57.

7. *Supra,* p. 447, footnote 66.

8. Quoted in Scott, *op. cit.,* p. 17.

9. Jesus himself seems to have indicated that there would be such a return (Matthew 16:28) and two men in white at the ascension expressed belief in it (Acts 1:11). Paul in his earlier writings was dominated by this idea (see I Thessalonians 4:16, 17). Later he evidently had to give up this belief.

10. The author of Luke-Acts (Luke 1:1-4) mentions the testimony of "eyewitnesses" who handed down the teachings to the gospel writers.

11. I Corinthians 11:23, 24.

12. I Corinthians 15:3, 4. Cf. Acts 10:36-42. The only reference in the book of Acts to any of the words of Jesus on the part of the apostle Paul is in Acts 20:35: "It makes one happier to give than to be given to."

13. Two of the most prominent are Martin Dibelius of Heidelberg, who set forth the principles of this technique in 1919 in a volume translated into English in 1935 (*From Tradition to Gospel,* N.Y.: Scribner's; cf. also his *The Message of Jesus Christ,* N.Y.: Scribner's, 1939), and Rudolf Bultmann of Marburg, who wrote, in 1921, a volume translated into English in 1934 (*Form Criticism: a New Method of New Testament Research,* Chicago: Willett, Clark, and Co.).

14. Jesus himself had been vague about the time of his return (see Matthew 25:13). Paul had spoken of the "Day of the Lord" as coming "like a thief in the night" (I Thessalonians 5:2; cf. also II Peter 3:8-10). By the time II Peter was written (*ca.* 150 A.D.) so many Christians were questioning the doctrine of the second coming of Christ that the author expresses his strong conviction that there is no hope for those who won't believe in it (II Peter 3:1-7).

15. An expression used by some of the Old Testament prophets, such as Amos (*supra,* pp. 103, 104), Isaiah (*supra,* pp. 117, 118), and Zephaniah (*supra,* pp. 131, 132).

16. Though there is difference of opinion among scholars as to which one of Paul's letters was written first, most agree that he began his letter-writing activity during the winter of 49-50 A.D. in the city of Corinth (Acts 18:1-22). Thus his earliest letters are contemporary with Q.

17. So called because it is the first letter of the German word "quelle," meaning "source." As we shall see later, Q is a hypothetical document which seems to be the best answer to the problem of the source of the non-Marcan materials common to the gospels of Matthew and Luke.

18. As reported in the *Church History* of Eusebius (written in 325 A.D.). The "Matthew" who arranged these words of Jesus may have been the Matthew of the gospels (called Levi in Mark 2:14 and Luke 5:27, but Matthew elsewhere).

19. *The New Testament: Its Making and Meaning* (N.Y.: Abingdon-Cokesbury Press, 1946), pp. 106-108.

20. Reconstructions of Q by A. Harnack, O. Holtzmann, J. Wellhausen, H. H. Wendt, J. C. Hawkins, B. Weiss, J. Weiss, and other New Testament scholars may be read in J B. Moffatt, *An Introduction to the Literature of the New Testament* (N.Y.: Scribner's, 1929), pp. 197-202. The student may also refer to the exhaustive and definitive study of the literary sources of the gospels by

B. H. Streeter, *The Four Gospels* (N.Y.: Macmillan, 1925); his reconstruction of Q is on pp. 273-292.

21. E. F. Scott, *The Literature of the New Testament* (N.Y.: Columbia University Press, 1945), p. 40.

22. Matthew, Mark, and Luke are called the "synoptic gospels," because they give a basically identical portrait of Jesus, agree in what little chronology they have for the events of his life, and exhibit such unusual similarities in phraseology and content that scholars are convinced that there is some close literary connection among them. The relationship among these three synoptic gospels constitutes the "synoptic problem." The fact that Mark is the earliest of the three synoptic gospels and the source of the other two has been determined by inductive study of the gospels themselves—a close comparison of the content, order, and wording of the three gospels. E.g., in the arrangement of their material, the authors of Matthew and Luke both follow Mark's outline; also, in narrative material, where Matthew and Luke agree they tend to agree with Mark. The Gospel of John is so different in form and content and so much later than the synoptic gospels that it must be studied separately.

23. Acts 13:5, 13; 15:37-39; Colossians 4:10; II Timothy 4:11; Philemon 24. John Mark was admirably equipped to record some of the events in the gospel narrative; his home in Jerusalem may have been the place where Jesus and his disciples met for their Last Supper together (Mark 14:12-26; Matthew 26:17-30; Luke 22:7-20; John 13:1—17:26), and the early Christian community must often have gathered there for prayer and fellowship (Acts 12:12). Mark was the nephew or cousin (Colossians 4:10) of Barnabas. Mark's autograph has been seen by some in the person of the scared young man who ran away from the Garden of Gethsemane at the time of Jesus' betrayal and arrest (Mark 14:51, 52), but this is not certain.

24. Cf. *supra* p. 236.

25. III. 39. 15, as translated in F. C. Grant, "Introduction to the Gospel According to St Mark," *The Interpreter's Bible,* VII, p. 630. The presbyter's statement is probably limited to the opening sentences; the rest is Papias' comment.

26. *Against Heresies,* III. 1. 1; cf. Eusebius' *Church History* V. 8. 3. In citing this, F. C. Grant, (*loc. cit.*) indicates that Irenaeus' statement may be only an echo of Papias' some forty years earlier. F. C. Grant's *The Earliest Gospel,* (N.Y.: Abingdon-Cokesbury Press, 1943, pp. 52-57) points out the difficulties of being entirely certain that the Mark to whom the early tradition attributed the authorship of the gospel was the John Mark who figures in the Book of Acts. He feels that Mark's gospel is a compilation of the oral tradition current in the Christian community at Rome in the sixties. Some of the materials may have been in written form before 60 A.D. (see Branscomb, B. H., *The Gospel of Mark,* N.Y.: Harper's, 1937, pp. xxiii-xxv).

27. In Mark 7:3, 4, the author explains the Jewish custom of hand-washing, indicating he has in mind non-Jewish readers of his gospel. In Mark 15:34, the author feels it necessary to translate the Aramaic expression "Eloi, Eloi, lama sabachthani?"

28. Such as the word translated "one of his guard" (Mark 6:27).

29. Romans 16:13.

30. I Peter 5:13 links Mark to the church "in Babylon (Rome)." Babylon is often used in Christian literature instead of Rome (cf. Revelation 16:19).

31. *Supra,* p. 213. The key verse is Mark 13:14: "But as soon as you see the dreadful desecration standing where he has no right to stand" (the reader

NOTES 453

must take note of this), "then those who are in Judea must fly to the hills." The indefinite phrase "where he has no right to stand" may mean that the temple had then ceased to exist.

32. One of his favorite words is "immediately" ("straightway" in the King James Version—Mark 1:30, etc.).

33. M. E. Lyman, *The Christian Epic* (N.Y.: Scribner's, 1943), p. 91.

34. By the beginning of the second century Mark had lost its original ending. Verses 9-20 of chapter sixteen are found in none of the early manuscripts, and even in later documents they appear in several diverse forms. Mark 16:7 refers to a possible appearance of Jesus in Galilee, but nothing in the spurious endings suggests such an appearance.

35. Probably the document Q (see *supra*, p. 451, footnote 18).

36. The words in Matthew 24:2 may refer to the actual destruction of the temple.

37. See *supra*, pp. 236-238.

38. *Op. cit.*, pp. 230-261.

39. Acts 15; Galatians 2:1-14.

40. "Introduction to the Gospel According to St. Matthew," *The Interpreter's Bible*, VII, pp. 238, 239. M was composed *ca.* 65 B.C. and was brought to Antioch by Christians who fled from Jerusalem because of the outbreak of the Jewish wars.

41. Matthew 7:28; 11:1; 13:53; 19:1; 26:1. Matthew's fivefold division may be suggested by the Pentateuch.

42. Parallel materials are scattered in the Gospel of Luke.

43. The Gospel of Matthew is the only one which explicitly mentions the church (16:18; 18:17).

44. Luke-Acts was originally intended to be a literary unit, as is shown by the prefaces to Luke (1:1-4) and Acts (1:1, 2). Both volumes were dedicated to the same man, Theophilus, who may have been a Roman official (note the phrase "Your Excellency" in Luke 1:3). The separation of the two volumes was one of the unfortunate episodes in the development of Christian literature in the early period.

45. Colossians 4:14. Cf. Luke 8:43 with its parallel passage in Mark 5:26.

46. As indicated in Philemon 24, Colossians 4:14, II Timothy 4:11, and the so-called "we passages" of Acts (16:10-17; 20:5-15; 21:1-18; and 27:1—28:16). Objections to the Lucan authorship of this material are summarized in Barnett, *op. cit.*, pp. 167-168.

47. *Op. cit.*, pp. 531-539.

48. *Op. cit.*, p. 173.

49. Luke 1:1-4.

50. This would account for Acts' abrupt ending before any mention is made of the disposal of his case before the imperial court.

51. *Supra*, pp. 238-240.

52. *Supra*, pp. 236-238.

53. E.g., compare Matthew's "Blessed are those who are hungry and thirsty for uprightness" (5:6) with Luke's "Blessed are you who are hungry now" (6:21).

54. "Introduction to the Gospel According to St. Luke," *The Interpreter's Bible*, VIII, p. 13. See *supra*, p. 241. According to a recent reconstruction (F. C. Grant, *The Growth of the Gospels*, N. Y.: The Abingdon Press, 1933, pp. 74-81), Q contained 252 Lucan verses or parts of verses.

55. *Op. cit.*, pp. 199-222. Streeter goes ahead to suggest that Luke combined Q and L to form "Proto-Luke," on the basis of which the later complete gospel

was constructed. This was supported by Vincent Taylor in his *Behind the Third Gospel* (Oxford: Clarendon Press, 1926), but such a concept is too imaginary and hypothetical to commend itself *in toto* to modern scholars (see Gilmour, *op. cit.,* pp. 16-18).

56. Acts 24:27. It is ordinarily dated *ca.* 60 A.D.

57. For a complete list of materials possibly derived from L see Barnett, *op. cit.,* p. 109.

58. However, some scholars believe that the reign of Tiberius should be counted as beginning from his accession as coregent of Augustus, which would make his fifteenth year 26-27 A.D.

59. Though Luke's reference (3:23) to Jesus' being "about thirty years old when he began his work" seems to favor the earlier date. John's imprisonment (Mark 1:14; Matthew 4:12) cannot be dated with any degree of accuracy.

60. Josephus (*Jewish War* II. 8. 1; VII. 8. 1) says it raised a storm of protest among the Jews and led to an insurrection in Galilee. Luke himself mentions it in Acts 5:37. It is improbable that any Roman census would have required a man to travel to the home of his ancestors.

61. See I. J. Peritz, "The Chronology of the New Testament," *The Abingdon Bible Commentary,* p. 874.

62. M. E. Lyman, *op. cit.,* pp. 124-127.

63. John 20:31.

64. H. M. Battenhouse, *New Testament History and Literature* (N.Y.: The Ronald Press Co., 1937), pp. 178-179.

65. W. B. Denny, *The Career and Significance of Jesus* (N.Y.: The Ronald Press Co., 1933), p. 30.

66. Matthew 2:1.

67. Matthew 2:16.

68. Luke 2:2. Cf. *supra,* p. 245.

69. Dionysius Exiguus (d. 556 A.D.), a monk in Rome, was the first to suggest the reckoning of time as before and after the birth of Jesus. Unfortunately he made a mistake in computing the year one as 754 A.U.C. ("ab urbe condita," "from the founding of the city" of Rome, which took place *ca.* 753 B.C.). Herod died in 750 A.U.C.

70. For the cult of Mithra, see *supra,* p. 206. Also, the Christians in the fourth century believed that the universe was originally created at the time of the spring equinox (March 25 in the Julian calendar); if Jesus were with God "in the beginning" (John 1:1), as Christians then believed, his inception would have thus occurred on March 25 and his birth nine months later, at the time of the winter solstice (December 25). Actually, if shepherds "were keeping watch through the night over their flock in the open fields" (Luke 2:8), spring or autumn would be a more satisfactory time of year for the day of Jesus' birth.

71. *Supra,* p. 120.

72. Luke (1:26, 27; 2:4) says that Nazareth was the home town of Joseph and Mary before the birth and that they returned to Nazareth soon after presenting Jesus in the temple (2:22, 39), an event which would have taken place when Jesus was forty days old (Leviticus 12:1-4). Matthew knows of no previous residence in Nazareth and has them go to Nazareth quite unexpectedly after the flight into Egypt, when Jesus would have been approximately 2 years old (Matthew 2:19, 23).

73. Mark 6:1-4; Matthew 13:54.

74. Mark 10:47; 14:67; 16:6; Luke 18:37; 24:19; John 18:5, 7; Acts 2:22; 3:6; 4:10; 6:14; 10:38; 22:8; 26:9 (cf. also Matthew 2:23).

75. Romans 1:3. However, cf. Mark 12:35-40, where Jesus seems to deny that the Messiah was a "Son of David."

76. Luke 2:40-52.

77. A phrase originated by John Oxenham.

78. *Supra,* p. 447, footnote 66.

79. The extracanonical gospels are of little help (see M. R. James, ed., *The Apocryphal New Testament;* Oxford: Oxford University Press, 1950). Stories in the Gospel of Thomas (written *ca.* 150 A.D.) picture Jesus as the wonder-boy of the carpenter shop, who is able to bring life into clay sparrows, miraculously punish those who annoy him and cure those to whom he is attracted. These stories are so late and so illustrative of the tendencies to regard the childhood of Jesus as supernatural that they are usually regarded as historically unreliable.

80. Mark 6:3; Matthew 13:55, 56. The four brothers of Jesus were named James, Joseph, Judas, and Simon. The sisters are not named.

81. Such as the parable of the housebuilders (Matthew 7:24-27; Luke 6:47-49), the story of the man who built bigger barns (Luke 12:16-21), the parable of a man who started to build a tower but was not able to finish it (Luke 14:28-30), his interest in the temple buildings (Mark 13:1, 2; Matthew 24:1, 2; Luke 21:5, 6), and his parable about hiring laborers (Matthew 20:1-16).

82. Sepphoris had been completely destroyed by the Romans as a penalty for a revolt headed by Judas of Gamala shortly after the death of Herod the Great. It was rebuilt by Herod Antipas.

83. *Supra,* pp. 217, 218.

84. Deuteronomy 6:4, 5. See *supra,* p. 125.

85. Luke 2:46, 47.

86. H. M. Battenhouse, *The Bible Unlocked,* p. 320.

87. 3:1. Later Christian tradition, accepting Jesus as the Messiah, saw in John a reincarnation of Elijah (John 1:25; cf. *supra,* p. 431, footnote 19) and a fulfillment of the prediction in Deutero-Isaiah of the one shouting in the desert: "Get the Lord's way ready" (Luke 3:4-6; cf. Isaiah 40:3-5). Jesus considered John as "far more than a prophet" (Luke 7:26).

88. Luke very wisely states, following the three "temptations" in the wilderness: ". . . The devil . . . left him till another time." Probably the severest trial of all came to Jesus in the Garden of Gethsemane, but with the same victorious conclusion; here Jesus prayed: "Take this cup (of martyrdom) away from me! Yet not what I please but what you do!" (Mark 14:36).

89. Mark 1:14. John's tragic death is recorded in Mark 6:17-29.

90. Mark 1:15.

91. The contrast between Jesus and John is clear in Luke 7:33-35 (cf. Matthew 11:18, 19). John may have disapproved of Jesus' approach (Matthew 11:2-6). John's movement continued beyond his death, for Paul found followers of John in Ephesus *ca.* 55 A.D. (Acts 18:24—19:7).

92. According to John 1:35-51, Andrew and Simon had been disciples of John the Baptizer. John Zebedee, Philip, and Nathanael may also have been in John's entourage.

93. John 21:25.

94. Mark 1:16-21.

95. Mark 1:29.

96. Mark 1:21-34.

97. For further discussion of the length of Jesus' ministry see I. J. Peritz, *op. cit.,* p. 875.

98. Mark 1:45.

99. Probably today we would call them "non-churchgoers" (*supra*, p. 217).

100. Mark 3:22.

101. Mark 3:21. The "relatives" were probably Mary and Jesus' brothers, for verse 31 refers to their coming to see him.

102. Mark 12:37. For the "am-haares," see *supra*, p. 447, footnote 58, and p. 217.

103. Sometimes a son neglected the care of his parents by declaring on oath that the provision he might otherwise have made for his parents was "corban," i.e., devoted to God.

104. Mark 6:31-44; Matthew 14:13-21; Luke 9:10-17; John 6:1-14.

105. John 6:15.

106. Mark 8:27-33 (cf. also Matthew 16:13-20; Luke 9:18-22).

107. Matthew 23:37.

108. The transfiguration is recorded in Mark 9:2-13; Matthew 17:1-13; Luke 9:28-36.

109. Perhaps Luke found most of the materials in the so-called Perean ministry of Jesus in his special source L (*supra*, pp. 244, 245).

110. Luke 9:51-56.

111. Mark 10:32-40. Would James and John have replied so readily if they had realized that Jesus was talking about the baptism of martyrdom? Some have seen in this passage an intimation of the actual martyrdom of James and John (cf. Acts 12:1, 2).

112. Mark 10:2-12 (cf. *supra*, p. 447, footnote 55). Thus Jesus went beyond the censure of Herod which had been expressed by John.

113. Luke 19:1-10.

114. Six of the sixteen chapters in Mark deal with the closing scenes in the life of Jesus, eight of the twenty-eight in Matthew, five of the twenty-four in Luke, and ten of the twenty-one in John.

115. McFadyen, J. F., "The Life of Jesus Christ," *The Abingdon Bible Commentary*, pp. 899-900.

116. Matthew 21:11.

117. Mark 11:11. Each succeeding night of the last week was spent in Bethany or its neighborhood, perhaps in the home of Mary and Martha (John 11:1). There is no general agreement as to whether the triumphal entry occurred on Sunday, Nisan 9 (Battenhouse, *op. cit.*, p. 357, footnote 3), or Monday, Nisan 10 (McFadyen, *op. cit.*, p. 900).

118. This traffic in animals and birds dates from the Deuteronomic Reform (*supra*, p. 434, footnote 12).

119. Mark 11:15, 16. Many casually used the court of the Gentiles as a short cut.

120. Mark 11:17.

121. Cf. Jeremiah 7:11; Isaiah 56:7. Part of Jesus' indignation was due to the fact that prayer was impossible for the Gentiles amid the sights and sounds and smells of an animal and bird market and the yells of cheating money-lenders. This was the only part of the temple area in which the Gentiles were permitted.

122. This last question was raised by Jesus himself.

123. Matthew 26:15; 27:3. Perhaps the coin was the silver shekel, worth about sixty-seven cents.

124. *Supra*, p. 452, footnote 23.

125. Findlay, J. A., "Introduction to Luke," *The Abingdon Bible Commentary*, p. 1054. The nature of the meal is implied in Luke 22:15.

126. I Corinthians 11:23-27. Of the synoptic accounts, the closest resemblance to Paul's is found in Luke, though Luke 22:19, 20 is probably an interpolation based on I Corinthians 11:24, 25, as these words are not found in some of the early manuscripts.

127. Perhaps the second part of the Hallel Psalms (115-118) (cf. *supra*, p. 443, footnote 58).

128. Mark 14:26.

129. The word "Gethsemane" means "oil press." It was contrary to the Torah (Deuteronomy 16:1-7) to leave Jerusalem on the feast night, so Jesus and his disciples could not have gone back to Bethany. Gethsemane was one of Jesus' favorite resorts for meditation and prayer during this last week.

130. Mark 14:32-41.

131. *Supra*, pp. 250, 251.

132. H. M. Battenhouse, *op. cit.*, p. 372.

133. The fourth gospel says that a cohort of Roman soldiers was present (John 18:12).

134. Mark 14:48, 49.

135. Mark 14:50.

136. What Jesus had said was: "Do you see these great buildings? Not one stone shall be left here upon another that shalt not be torn down" (Mark 13:2). What the witnesses said was: "We ourselves heard him say, 'I will tear down this sanctuary built by men's hands, and in three days I will build another, made without hands'" (Mark 14:58). Jesus' original comment had ben perverted and misunderstood.

137. Mark 14:61, 62.

138. Mark 14:64. There is some doubt as to whether the Sanhedrin had lost the power to pass capital sentences on prisoners by this time (cf. John 18:31). In any case, the priests wanted to shift the blame for their infamous deed on Rome.

139. The "trial" before the Sanhedrin was illegal in several respects: it was held on a feast day, on the day before a Sabbath, before defense witnesses could be heard, without sufficient examination of the evidence against the defendant, without a quorum (twenty-three persons) and a written record of the vote, without the lapse of a day before passing sentence, and without due respect for the person of the defendant (H. M. Battenhouse, *op. cit.*, p. 375, footnote 2).

140. Luke 23:2. The second charge was a falsehood (cf. Mark 12:14-17). The third contained the real accusation. Translate "Messiah" as "king" and Pilate could not disregard the charge.

141. Luke 23:11.

142. Meaning "place of a skull." It was thus named either because it was a hill in the shape of a skull or because it was a place associated with death. Its exact location is not known. The traditional site is about a quarter of a mile west from the northwest corner of the temple, within the walls of the city. But the gospel narrative calls for a place outside the city (John 19:20), but near to it, and also near a highway (Mark 15:29). The place now quite commonly accepted as the site lies on the north of the city, near the Damascus gate.

143. John 19:17.

144. Mark 15:21. Simon was the father of Alexander and Rufus, the latter of whom was later prominent in the church in Rome (cf. Romans 16:13; *supra*, p. 239.

145. The Roman Catholic Church has worked out fourteen "stations of the cross" along Jesus' "via dolorosa" from Pilate's judgment hall to Golgotha. Each station is represented by fresco, picture, statue, or otherwise, arranged around the walls of the sanctuary. At each station prayers are offered up in memory of the event represented. Some of the events are taken from the canonical gospels; others from extra-canonical literature.

146. Mark 15:25.

147. Mark 15:34-37.

148. Luke 23:34, 43, 46; John 19:26, 27, 28, 30; Mark 15:34 (repeated in Matthew 27:46).

149. In the so-called "Lord's Prayer" (Matthew 6:9-15).

150. Mark 14:36 (cf. *supra*, p. 259).

151. Luke 23:34 (Revised Standard Version).

152. Luke 23:46.

153. Mark 15:34 (Matthew 27:46).

154. Luke 23:50-53. Its location is not known.

155. Mark 15:39.

156. I Corinthians 15:3-8. All of these appearances can be identified with some mentioned in the gospels, except the ones to James and Paul.

157. Acts 9:1-9.

158. Matthew 4:23.

159. Mark 4:1-9, as paraphrased in Rall, Harris Franklin, *The Teachings of Jesus* (N.Y. and Nashville: Abingdon-Cokesbury Press, 1930), p. 19.

160. Particularly in the Matthean version (chapters 5-7).

161. Several illustrations of each of these might well be cited. "You are the salt of the earth" (Matthew 5:13) is a metaphor. When Jesus says his disciples will be sent out "like sheep among wolves" (Matthew 10:16), he is making use of a simile. His words are full of paradoxical statements, such as "If anyone wishes to be first, he must be the last of all and the servant of of all" (Mark 9:35). Hyperbole, or exaggeration, is illustrated by the famous saying of Jesus: "It is easier for a camel to get through the eye of a needle than for a rich man to get into the Kingdom of God' (Mark 10:25). Instead of seeking the thought behind the vivid, picturesque language of these expressions, many Christians have mistakenly insisted on exact obedience to the letter of the commands.

162. A parable is a story taken out of life and told to illustrate a great moral or religious teaching. The most typical of Jesus' parables is the parable of the sower (Mark 4:1-25; Matthew 13:1-23; Luke 8:4-18).

163. Mark 4:10-13; Matthew 13:10-17; Luke 8:9, 10.

164. Mark 12:37. The best-known of Jesus' parables is the parable of the prodigal son, or, as it should be called, the parable of the forgiving father (Luke 15:11-32).

165. Matthew 7:24-27. The poetic form was suggested by Rall, *op. cit.*, pp. 28-29, based on the American Standard Version, copyright 1929 by the International Council of Religious Education.

166. Matthew 5:21, 22, 27, 28, 33, 34, 38, 39. In his teaching on divorce, Jesus supplants one part of the Torah with another which he regards as more authoritative (Mark 10:2-12). This is the only instance in which Jesus rejects any part of the Torah; most of his critical anti-legal comments are directed against the Mishna (cf. *supra*, p. 447, footnote 55). For a complete analysis

of Jesus' attitude toward the Old Testament laws see Branscomb, B. Harvie, *Jesus and the Law of Moses* (N.Y.: Richard R. Smith, Inc., 1930).

167. Mark 1:22.

168. The so-called "beatitudes," or "blesseds" (Matthew 5:2-12) illustrate the positive character of Jesus' teaching method.

169. Jeremiah 3:4, 5 (cf. *supra,* p. 141).

170. Matthew 5:48.

171. Mark 10:18.

172. Matthew 10:31.

173. Mark 2:27.

174. This is illustrated by Jesus' parable of the laborers in the vineyard (Matthew 20:1-16).

175. Matthew 5:44, 45.

176. God is like the father in the parable of the forgiving father (Luke 15:11-32; cf. *supra,* p. 458, footnote 164).

177. Luke 15:7.

178. Luke 18:13.

179. Luke 23:46.

180. Matthew 7:21.

181. As in the opening words of the Lord's Prayer (Matthew 6:9).

182. Matthew 6:15. The picture of the last judgment in Matthew 25:31-46 is based on ethical requirements: "In so far as you did it . . ." or "In so far as you failed to do it for one of these people who are humblest," "you did it," or "you failed to do it for me."

183. Mark 12:30.

184. Branscomb, B. Harvie, *The Message of Jesus* (N.Y. and Nashville: Abingdon-Cokesbury Press, 1926), p. 62.

185. Including the synonymous phrase "the kingdom of heaven" (used in Matthew because of the author's hesitance to give expression to the word "God"), Jesus used this phrase sixty times in the gospels.

186. Mark 1:15.

187. Matthew 26:29; Mark 14:25.

188. Craig, Clarence T., "The Proclamation of the Kingdom," in *The Interpreter's Bible,* VII, pp. 145-146.

189. Mark 9:1.

190. Mark 13:30.

191. Mark 14:25; Luke 22:16, 18. Cf. also Matthew 8:11; 25:34. Luke, the least eschatological of the Synoptic gospels, has collected a series of words of Jesus which enforce his eschatological message (6:24-26; 10:13-15; 11:39-52; 12:35-40, 49, 51-59; 13:1-9, 23-25, 34, 35; 17:26-30). Paul also understood that the kingdom was about to come (II Corinthians 15:51; I Thessalonians 4:15).

192. Extremely apocalyptic statements attributed to Jesus, such as the discourses in Mark 13, Matthew 24, and Luke 21, probably represent the early church's point of view more than they do Jesus'.

193. Luke 17:21.

194. Matthew 11:2-6 (cf. also Matthew 12:28; Mark 3:27; Luke 10:18, 23, 24).

195. Matthew 25:13 (cf. also Mathew 24:36; Mark 13:32).

196. Luke 6:20. Jesus considered wealth a definite handicap for entrance into the kingdom.

197. Mark 10:14, 15.

198. Matthew 21:31.

199. Matthew 8:11.

200. Matthew 5:10.

201. Matthew 6:33.

202. Mark 9:43-48.

203. Matthew 5:20.

204. Matthew 7:21.

205. Luke 9:62.

206. As illustrated by the parables of the hoard of money buried in a field (Matthew 13:44) and the costly pearl (Matthew 13:45).

207. Mark 4:26, 30; Matthew 13:24, 31, 33, 44, 45, 47; 18:23; 20:1; 22:2; 25:1.

208. Branscomb, op. cit., p. 86.

209. Mark 4:31, 32; Matthew 13:31, 32.

210. Mark 4:26-29.

211. Matthew 13:33; Luke 13:21.

212. Matthew 13:44.

213. Matthew 13:45, 46.

214. Matthew 13:47-49. Longer parables are as follows: the parable of the unforgiving slave (Matthew 18:23-35), the parable of the laborers in the vineyard (Matthew 20:1-16), the parable of the wedding banquet (Matthew 22:2-14; Luke 14:15-24), and the parable of the ten bridesmaids (Matthew 25:1-13).

215. Matthew 6:25.

216. Matthew 5:45.

217. Matthew 5:22, 28, 32, 37, 44.

218. Matthew 6:1-18.

219. Matthew 25:31-46. We must consider the concept of the kingdom of God as more inclusive than the church—though the church is a vital part of the kingdom — or any outward organization of any kind. Whatever groups are controlled by righteousness, love, and truth may be said to be under the reign of God.

220. For a more detailed discussion of the teachings of Jesus see Branscomb, B. Harvie, The Teachings of Jesus (N.Y. and Nashville: Abingdon-Cokesbury Press, 1931), the best in its field.

CHAPTER   TWENTY-TWO

1. Mark 4:31, 32; Matthew 13:31, 32.

2. See supra, pp. 263, 264.

3. This title does not accurately describe the contents of the book and may have been added at a later time (see Scott, op. cit., p. 80). The chief character in the book is Paul; Peter occupies a large section, but only two or three other apostles make any appearance at all.

4. Supra, pp. 243, 453, footnote 44.

5. Acts 1:1, 2. Nowhere does the author give us a clue to his conception of the nature and purpose of the second volume. Perhaps the preface to the Gospel of Luke was meant to cover the whole work (Luke 1:1-4; cf. supra, p. 243).

6. Supra, pp. 243, 453, footnotes 45 and 46.

7. Macgregor, G. C. H., "Introduction to the Book of Acts," The Interpreter's Bible, IX, pp. 3-23, argues for the Lucan authorship of Luke-Acts, reviving the conclusions of Ramsay (especially his St. Paul the Traveller and the Roman Citizen; London: Hodder and Stoughton, 1896) and Harnack (The Acts of the Apostles, translated by J. R. Wilkinson; London: Williams and Norgate,

1909, and *Luke the Physician,* translated by J. R. Wilkinson; London: Williams and Norgate, 1907). The great five-volume work edited by F. J. Foakes Jackson and Kirsopp Lake (*The Beginnings of Christianity;* London: Macmillan, 1920-33) represents the point of view of scholars opposed to the Lucan authorship (see *supra,* p. 453, footnote 46, and Barnett, *loc. cit.*).

8. *Supra,* p. 243.

9. The "we-sections" are as follows: Acts 16:10-17; 20:5-15; 21:1-18; 27:1−28:16. "The problem of the authorship of Luke-Acts is, then, the problem whether or not the person who wrote the 'we' sections was responsible for the finished work" (Barnett, *op. cit.,* p. 166).

10. E. g., Romans 15:19; II Corinthians 11:24-28.

11. Acts 1:8.

12. Acts 2:1-4.

13. Acts 1:4, Revised Standard Version, better than Goodspeed's "in foreign languages." It refers to the phenomenon of "glossalalia" which was a frequent and highly prized type of ecstatic behaviour among the early Christians. Paul found it necessary to curb it in his churches later (I Corinthians 12:6-11; 14:1-19, 23, 26).

14. Acts 2:12, 13.

15. Acts 2:14-40.

16. Acts 2:32, 33, 36.

17. Acts 2:41, 42.

18. Acts 2:46.

19. Acts 2:46, 47.

20. Because of certain abuses which crept into the church at Corinth in connection with the Agapé and the Eucharist, the former had to be separated from the latter (I Corinthians 11:17-34). By 115 A.D. the Eucharist was observed in the morning and the Agapé in the evening (Battenhouse, *op. cit.,* p. 421, footnote 1).

21. Acts 3:1-10; 5:15; 9:32-42.

22. Acts 2:44, 45.

23. Mary, the mother of Mark, evidently retained her home in Jerusalem (Acts 12:12).

24. This story is dramatically related in Acts 5:1-11. Ananias' sin was lying to the holy spirit (verse 3).

25. Acts 4:32-37. This "communistic" experiment was soon supplanted by the sending of alms to the mother church by the richer daughter churches (Acts 11:29, 30; Galatians 2:10; Romans 15:25-28; II Corinthians 8:1-7).

26. Acts 4:1-22; 5:17-42.

27. Acts 4:18 (cf. Acts 5:40).

28. *Supra,* p. 215.

29. Acts 5:35-39.

30. Acts 6:1.

31. Acts 6:3. The appointment of these seven "deacons" marks the beginning of officials in the church. Leadership was in the hands of the apostles as long as they were alive, but with the end of the apostolic age, leadership passed more and more to the deacons, elders, bishops, and other selected officials.

32. Acts 6:9. The rabbi of this synagogue may have been a young Pharisee named Saul of Tarsus.

33. Acts 7:2-53.

34. Acts 7:57, 58. This occurred *ca.* 32 A.D.

35. Acts 7:58-60. This is the first mention in the book of Acts of the man who was to become the great Christian missionary of the first period of the church's expansion.

36. Acts 8:1-40. The pioneer missionary in Samaria was Philip. The author of Acts is not clear whether he was the Philip who was one of the twelve, or the deacon mentioned in Acts 6:5, or some other Philip. Peter and John officially welcomed the new Samaritan converts (Acts 8:14-17). The Ethiopian eunuch baptized by Philip (Acts 8:27-40) may have become the founder of the Christian church in Abysinnia.

37. Acts 8:3.

38. Acts 9:1, 2. This journey took place *ca.* 32 A.D.

39. Acts 8:40. Caesarea was evidently Philip's home (Acts 21:8); it was the headquarters of the Roman procurators of Judea (*supra,* p. 211).

40. Acts 9:35; 10:1—11:18. The story of Peter's contact with Cornelius, together with his vision of the sheet let down from heaven, shows how the universalistic truths of the Christian gospel were taking root in Gentile soil.

41. Acts 11:19-26. Antioch was henceforth to be the great missionary center of Christianity.

42. *Supra,* pp. 279, 280.

43. Acts 12:1-4. This Herod was Herod Agrippa I (*supra,* p. 212), he had been ruler of Iturea and Trachonitis since 37 and Galilee and Perea since 39. In 41, the emperor Claudius made him king of all Palestine. He probably started persecuting the Christians to please the Pharisees. The disciple John may have been killed along with his brother James (cf. Mark 10:35-40). Someone set Peter free; he appeared at the home of Mark's mother, where they were praying for him, and then left Jerusalem until after Herod's death (Acts 12:5-17). Herod's death is recorded in Acts 12:23.

44. James, the eldest of the four brothers of Jesus, succeeded Peter as the head of the Jerusalem Christian community. Conservative and Judaistic, James' party often acted as a stumbling-block to Paul's Gentile mission (Acts 15:1-33; Galatians 1:18—2:14; *supra,* p. 241).

45. The chief contribution of the Palestinian church to later Christian history was the compilation and preservation for all later times of the records of the life and teaching of Jesus which were ultimately embodied in the gospels. The gospels of Mark, Matthew, Luke, and John, the document "Q", and certain other written records were all produced outside of Palestine, but they were based on reminiscences of Jesus first collected in the Palestinian church, especially during the period of oral tradition (*supra,* pp. 233-235). "The mind of this church was conservative, and by clinging to institutions which had served their day it missed its share in the great missionary enterprise. But with this reverence for the past it cherished the memory of Jesus as he had actually been. Paul refused to know Christ after the flesh, and the Gentile church, like its grand apostle, was devoted to the living Lord, risen and glorified. In Palestine the believers still looked back to the earthly Master. . . . Without these records of the life of Jesus our religion would be incalculably poorer, and they come to us out of that period when the Palestinian church appeared to be so inactive that it is hardly mentioned in history (Scott, E. F., "The Beginnings of the Church," *The Interpreter's Bible,* VII, pp. 185-186).

CHAPTER TWENTY-THREE

1. *New Testament History and Literature,* p. 279.

2. *Supra,* pp. 239, 243, and 274.

3. Acts 15:1-31.

4. *Supra,* pp. 213 and 216.

5. Acts 9:11; 22:3. Paul calls it "no insignificant city" (Acts 21:39). This is reminiscent of the comment of the geographer Strabo (64 B.C. - 19 A.D.), a native of Tarsus, who considered it the leading philosophical center of his time, ahead of Athens and Alexandria (*supra,* p. 444, footnote 6). The university at Tarsus had been founded at the time of Alexander the Great (336-323 B.C.). When Cicero was governor of Cilicia (51-50 B.C.), Tarsus was the capital of the province.

6. Knox, John, *Chapters in a Life of Paul* (N.Y. and Nashville: Abingdon-Cokesbury Press, 1950), p. 74.

7. Philippians 3:5.

8. Romans 11:1. Cf. also Galatians 1:13, 14; 2:15; II Corinthians 11:22.

9. Acts 22:28. For the privileges of Roman citizenship see *supra,* p. 209.

10. Acts 23:6. Cf. also Acts 26:5; Philippians 3:5.

11. Acts 23:16.

12. Cf. Ramsay, William M., *St. Paul the Traveller and the Roman Citizen* (N.Y.: G. P. Putnam's Sons, 1896), p. 35.

13. *Supra,* pp. 219-224.

14. In Acts 22:3 Paul speaks of being "brought up" in Jerusalem, and in Acts 26:4 he mentions having lived there "from my youth up"—both indicating he was still in his teens when he went to Jerusalem.

15. *Supra,* pp. 214, 215.

16. Acts 22:3. Gamaliel appears in the book of Acts as a man of courage and of a conciliatory spirit; in the Sanhedrin he recommended a mild policy toward the Christians (Acts 5:34-40; *supra,* pp. 215 and 279).

17. *Supra,* p. 234.

18. II Corinthians 5:16, in the King James Version, seems to indicate that Paul knew Jesus "after the flesh," but Goodspeed translates the expression "outwardly" and the Revised Standard Version "from a human point of view." What Paul is saying is that before his conversion he had a false judgment of Jesus, which he gave up later. It probably does not mean that Paul knew Jesus during the latter's lifetime. However, for a differing point of view see Ramsay, William M., "Did Paul See Jesus?" in Kepler, Thomas S., ed., *Contemporary Thinking About Paul* (N.Y. and Nashville: Abingdon-Cokesbury Press, 1950), pp. 122-127.

19. Acts 18:3; II Thessalonians 3:7-12. It was customary for rabbis to learn a trade.

20. *Supra,* p. 461, footnote 32.

21. Acts 26:11. In other words, Paul gave his moral approval to the condemnation of the Christians and became the Sanhedrin's agent in their pursuit.

22. Saul was probably his Jewish name and Paul his Roman name. The latter is used exclusively after Acts 13:9. John Mark is another example of a Jew with both a Jewish name and a Roman one.

23. Acts 7:58. See *supra,* pp. 279, 280.

24. Acts 8:1-3 (cf. Galatians 1:23; I Corinthians 15:9; Philippians 3:6).

25. Acts 9:1, 2.

26. One by Luke (Acts 9:3-19), and two purporting to be by Paul himself (Acts 22:6-16; 26:12-18).

27. 1:11-17.

28. I Corinthians 9:1, 2; 15:3-11 (cf. II Corinthians 4:6).

29. Paul's conversion is similar in many respects to the famous theophanies of Moses (*supra*, p. 55) and I Isaiah (*supra*, pp. 112, 113).

30. Acts 26:12-20.

31. Acts 9:8, 9. Paul's letters tell us nothing of this.

32. Acts 9:10-19. This was not the same Ananias as the one mentioned in Acts 5:1-5 (*supra*, p. 278). The Christians in Damascus must have received this one-time arch persecutor of their religion with mixed feelings.

33. Galatians 1:16, 17. Luke knows nothing of this.

34. Acts 9:19-25. Paul's letters substantiate Luke's account. In II Corinthians 11:32, 33, Paul mentions the governor "under King Aretas" as being a party to the plot. Aretas ruled Arabia (Nabatea) from 9 B.C. to 40 A.D. Perhaps Paul had stirred up trouble for himself in his kingdom earlier.

35. This phase of it lasted three years (Galatians 1:18).

36. II Corinthians 11:24. Luke's narrative in Acts does not mention these occasions. According to Deuteronomy 25:1-4, the guilty party could be flogged with forty lashes, but it was Jewish custom to stop at thirty-nine lest they break the law by miscounting.

37. Galatians 1:18. Perhaps Peter told Paul more of the story of Jesus' earthly life and ministry. The meeting lasted two weeks.

38. Acts 9:28, 29.

39. Acts 9:27; 13:1—14:28.

40. Galatians 1:19. For James, see *supra*, pp. 241, 462, footnote 44.

41. Acts 9:29, 30.

42. Galatians 1:21. Luke does not mention this period.

43. Acts 15:41.

44. *Supra*, p. 281.

45. Acts 11:27-30. Luke says this famine was world-wide and occurred during the reign of the emperor Claudius (41-54 A.D.). We know from Josephus (*Antiquities*, XX. 5. 2) that such a famine took place *ca.* A.D. 46, approximately fourteen years after Paul's conversion (*supra*, p 462, footnote 38).

46. *Supra*, pp. 238, 239.

47. Acts 13:1-3. The "laying on of hands" is not to be considered an ecclesiastical ordination, for the whole church at Antioch was not involved. It was simply a recognition of the fact that the holy spirit had called Barnabas and Paul for special services.

48. Acts 13:4, 5. Barnabas was a native of Cyprus, explaining why the missionaries decided to go there first. The gospel had been preached there earlier, and some of the Christians from Cyprus had begun the work among the Greeks at Antioch (Acts 11:19, 20; *supra*, pp. 280, 281).

49. Acts 13:10, 11.

50. Acts 13:13. Paul refused to take him on his next journey, causing a rift between himself and Barnabas (Acts 15:37-40), but fellowship must have been eventually restored, for Mark is with Paul in his Roman prison (Colossians 4:10; *supra*, p. 452, footnote 23).

51. Luke records this sermon in Acts 13:16-41. It is typical of Paul's message and his usual method of evangelistic approach.

52. Acts 13:42, 43. The audience was composed of Jews, whom Paul called "men of Israel," proselytes, and God-fearers (*supra*, pp. 218 and 448, footnote 80).

53. Acts 13:46, 47.

54. Acts 13:50. The pattern of events at Antioch in Pisidia was repeated many times in Paul's lifetime: preaching in the synagogue, rejection by the Jews, enthusiastic reception by non-Jews, ejection from the city by a mob.

55. Acts 13:51—14:6.

56. Acts 14:6-18. This incident provided one of the few hints as to what Paul looked like. The dignified figure of Barnabas caused him to be identified as Zeus, father of the gods in the Greek pantheon, who had a temple dedicated to his worship in Lystra. Paul was evidently younger in appearance than Barnabas, shorter of stature, more eloquent and energetic, suggesting the Greek god Hermes, or Roman Mercury, the god with the winged feet, the messenger of Zeus (Jupiter).

57. Acts 14:19, 20. Ordinarily stoning was fatal.

58. Luke gives us no other details.

59. Acts 14:21-28. The total distance traveled by the apostles was about fourteen hundred miles, half by land and half by water, and the time involved was at least two years. Churches had been established in at least four cities, perhaps in more, composed of Jewish and Gentile converts, with the latter predominating.

60. Acts 15:1, 2. According to Paul's own account (Galatians 2:1), this visit to Jerusalem took place fourteen years after his first journey to that city (Galatians 1:18; *supra,* p. 288) and hence seventeen years after his conversion (*supra,* pp. 286, 287). Therefore, if Paul was converted in 32 A.D. *supra,* p. 462, footnote 38), the Apostolic Council was held in 49. For differing views concerning Pauline chronology see Knox, *op. cit.,* pp. 74-85, and Peritz, *op. cit.,* pp. 878-879.

61. Acts 15:6-29.

62. Cf. George Holley Gilbert, *The Student's Life of Paul* (N.Y.: Macmillan, 1927), pp. 89-99.

63. *Supra,* pp. 267, 458, 459, footnote 166.

64. Peter had to have a vision before he would go to the house of the Gentile Cornelius (Acts 10:23-43). Also, those who proclaimed the gospel most zealously confined their efforts at first to the Jews (Acts 11:19).

65. Galatians 2:9. They did not even insist that Titus be circumcised (Galatians 2:3), something demanded by a group referred to by Paul as the "false brothers" (Galatians 2:4), evidently extreme Judaizers. Paul and Barnabas were allowed to work among the heathen, while James, Peter, and John would continue to work among the Jews.

66. Acts 15:7-11. Peter is thus represented as presenting Paul's essential message.

67. Acts 15:29.

68. The letter from Jerusalem was read to the Christians in Antioch (Acts 15:30-33), and the reaction was favorable. It was taken by Paul and Silas on their journey through Asia Minor to Europe (Acts 16:4), but he never refers to it in any of his letters and never requires any of his Gentile converts to observe any of the instructions in it (see I Corinthians 8). The decree evidently proved to be of no practical value and soon fell into neglect.

69. *Supra,* pp. 281, 282.

70. Galatians 2:12-14.

71. Galatians 2:11.

72. Jesus had been criticised for eating with "irreligious people and tax-collectors" (Mark 2:16; *supra,* p. 252), and Peter had been censured for eating with Cornelius (Acts 11:3).

73. Galatians 2:14-21.

74. Acts 15:36. Perhaps Paul was concerned with what the Judaizers might be doing among the Christians in Galatia.

75. *Supra*, p. 464, footnote 50.

76. Acts 15:38-41. The rupture between Paul and Barnabas was evidently not permanent, for Paul speaks of Barnabas later in a way which shows that they were not deeply alienated from each other (I Corinthians 9:6). The character of Barnabas now all but disappears from apostolic history. Silas had been a prominent member of the Jerusalem church (Acts 15:22, 27, 32; *supra*, p. 294).

77. Acts 15:41. Some of the churches in Syria and Cilicia had been founded by Paul during the "obscure period" (*supra*, p. 289).

78. Paul had lived in Tarsus for several years following his conversion (*supra*, pp. 288, 289).

79. *Supra*, pp. 290-292.

80. Acts 16:1-3. Timothy's circumcision did not show an inconsistency on Paul's part. Timothy was already half-Jewish; he had not been compelled to accept circumcision before he could become a Christian. This conciliatory gesture toward Jewish groups would help the Christian missionaries to win more adherents for the new faith.

81. Acts 16:6.

82. Christians were very numerous here in the second century, as revealed in the letters of the younger Pliny (*supra*, p. 232).

83. Acts 16:7.

84. Acts 16:9.

85. Notably William M. Ramsay, *St. Paul the Traveller and the Roman Citizen*, p. 203.

86. For the "we-sections," see *supra*, pp. 275, 461, footnote 9. Edgar J. Goodspeed (*Paul*; Philadelphia: The John C. Winston Co., 1947, p. 71) suggests that Paul may have had an attack of malaria at Troas and called in Doctor Luke to treat him.

87. Acts 16:10.

88. Acts 16:13-15. The fact that Paul's first congregation on European soil was composed entirely of women was symbolic of the part women were to play in the expanding Christian church. Lydia was evidently a devout proselyte of some means, with a house big enough to entertain the quartet of missionaries. For the first two hundred years of their history, the Christian churches met for worship in the homes of the wealthier members (see Philemon 2).

89. Acts 16:18.

90. The church at Philippi was the only one which Paul allowed to send him any gifts. They sent him money several times (Philippians 4:15-17); toward the end of his life they contributed toward his needs when he was a prisoner in Rome and even sent him a man to be his companion in prison (Philippians 4:18).

91. Acts 16:19-24. This is the first time Paul incurs opposition from a Gentile source. The imprisonment of Paul and Silas was a flagrant violation of their rights as Roman citizens (*supra*, p. 209). Paul later speaks of the "ill-treatment and insults" he endured at Philippi (I Thessalonians 2:2).

92. Acts 16:37.

93. Acts 16:38-40. Apparently Luke stays in Philippi; the pronoun in Acts shifts back from "we" to "they" until Acts 20:5, when once again Luke joins Paul's party at Philippi.

94. Acts 17:1. Important in modern times as the commercial city of Salonika, Thessalonica was already an ancient city when Paul visited it. Cicero had lived there while in exile. Like Tarsus (*supra*, pp. 283, 284), Thessalonica was a free city, with all the privileges of local self-government.

95. Acts 17:2. Paul's language in his first letter to the Thessalonians implies a more extended visit to Thessalonica than is indicated in Acts. Paul speaks of working "night and day, . . . in order not to be a burden to any of you" (I Thessalonians 2:9); he also speaks of encouraging each of his converts individually (I Thessalonians 2:10-12).

96. Philippians 4:16.

97. I Thessalonians 1:6-9.

98. Acts 17:6, 7.

99. Two Thessalonian Christians later accompanied Paul to Jerusalem with the collection: Aristarchus and Secundus (Acts 20:4). Aristarchus was with Paul on his voyage to Rome (Acts 27:2). The Judaizers who had started trouble for Paul in Thessalonica had either come across the Aegean from Galatia or were native Thessalonian Jews who had heard of Paul's earlier experiences in the Galatian synagogues (*supra*, pp. 291, 292).

100. Acts 17:11, 12.

101. *Supra*, pp. 203, 204. Though no further mention is made of Beroea in the New Testament, Paul's work there must have produced permanent results, for one of those who accompanied Paul to Jerusalem with the collection was Sopater of Beroea (Acts 20:4).

102. Acts 17:13-15.

103. Acts 17:16, 17. Athens was the most famous city in the province of Achaia and the chief literary and intellectual center of the Hellenic world. In Paul's day, the Parthenon, dominating the city from its location atop the Acropolis, was already nearly five hundred years old. Paul was not impressed by the beauty of the buildings in Athens nor the brilliance of the Stoic and Epicurean philosophers with whom he argues; his chief concern was with the polytheistic religion of the Athenians. They were so "extremely religious" and tolerant of all gods that they had included among their idols an altar dedicated "to an unknown god!" (Acts 17:22, 23).

104. "Spermologos" in the Greek, literally "seed-picker," used originally of birds and then of anyone who picks up odds and ends.

105. Acts 17:18-21.

106. The address is in Acts 17:22-31.

107. Acts 17:28. The quotation is from the *Phaenomena* of Aratus (born *ca.* 310 B.C., a native of Soli in Cilicia), a Stoic poet. A similar line is in a poem, *Hymn to Zeus*, written by an earlier Greek poet, Cleanthes. Both poems represent the growing tendency toward monotheism in the thought of many Greeks contemporary with and just prior to the beginning of Christianity.

108. Acts 17:34. There is no mention of any church having been established in Athens.

109. I Corinthians 2:1-5. King James Version.

110. Acts 18:1. According to Luke, Silas and Timothy did not see Paul until they rejoined him in Corinth (Acts 18:5). but in I Thessalonians 3:1, 2, Paul says he sent Timothy from Athens to Thessalonica; so Timothy must have reached Paul in Athens, a meeting of which Luke knows nothing.

111. I Thessalonians 3:11.

112. Acts 18:2, 3. The emperor Claudius had expelled all the Jews from Rome in 49 A.D., according to the Roman historian Suetonius, perhaps because of a dispute between Jews and Christians in Rome. Aquila and Priscilla had been a part of this exodus. Later, Paul took them with him to Ephesus (Acts 18:18; Romans 16:3).

113. Acts 18:4, 5; I Thessalonians 3:6. Because of Timothy's good news, Paul wrote I Thessalonians, perhaps the earliest of the twenty-seven books in the New Testament and contemporary with the document Q (*supra*, pp. 236-238, 451, footnote 16). A few weeks later, Paul wrote II Thessalonians. Some scholars think Paul also wrote Galatians during this same year and a half stay in Corinth.

114. Acts 16:1-8. Other prominent people who became Christian were Erastus, the city treasurer (Romans 16:23), Chloe (I Corinthians 1:11), and Stephanas (I Corinthians 1:16). Crispus and Gaius (Titus Justus) are mentioned in I Corinthians 1:14 as having been baptized by Paul.

115. The language of I Corinthians 1:26, 28, indicates that most of the Greek converts were from lower classes, "not many . . . wise, not many . . . influential, not many . . . of high birth."

116. I Corinthians 1:12.

117. I Corinthians 16:3.

118. I Corinthians 12:1-11.

119. Acts 18:13.

120. Acts 18:14, 15.

121. Acts 18:17. This action shows how the Jews were hated by the Gentiles. Sosthenes may have become a Christian after this episode, for a man of that name was with Paul in Ephesus when he wrote I Corinthians (1:1).

122. Acts 18:18, 19.

123. Acts 18:18. The requirements of the vow are given in Numbers 6:5, 13-18.

124. Acts 18:19-22. Perhaps Paul wanted to be in Jerusalem for the Passover feast. Earlier on this same journey Paul had planned to work in Ephesus, but had been unable to do it (*supra*, pp. 295, 296).

125. The journey had taken between two and a half and three years and had covered some twenty-five hundred miles.

126. Acts 18:23. Some scholars think that Paul wrote his letter to the Galatians from Antioch, during this interim (cf. Goodspeed, *op. cit.*, pp. 103-112; Battenhouse, *The Bible Unlocked*, pp. 474-475).

127. Acts 18:23. Evidently traveling alone, Paul's route would roughly correspond with the one he and Silas had followed three years earlier (*supra*, pp. 295, 296), at least as far as Antioch in Pisidia.

128. *Supra*, pp. 290-292, 295, 296. Paul probably wanted to complete the task of restoring the Galatian Christians to fellowship with him—a task he had begun in his letter to them.

129. *Supra.*

130. Acts 20:31.

131. Paul's selection of Ephesus as a place of missionary activity is in harmony with his usual strategy (*supra*, pp. 295, 296). It must have been a bitter disappointment to him when he was not allowed to work there earlier (Acts 16:6).

132. Acts 19:1-7. One of their number, Apollos, had brought enlightenment to Ephesus before Paul's arrival. He was converted to Christianity by Aquila

NOTES

and Priscilla (Acts 18:24-28). For the relationship between Jesus and John see *supra*, p. 455, footnote 91.

133. Acts 19:13-16.

134. Acts 19:19, 20.

135. According to archaeologists working in the ruins of Ephesus, the temple to Artemis was 342 feet 6½ inches long and 163 feet 9½ inches wide (Gilbert, *op. cit.,* p. 142).

136. Its chief artistic treasure was a painting of Alexander by Apelles, worth two hundred thousand dollars (*ibid.,* p. 143).

137. Acts 19:35.

138. Hill, *The Apostolic Age,* p. 177, quoted in Battenhouse, *New Testament History and Literature,* p. 315, footnote 1 (cf. *supra,* p. 417, footnote 10).

139. Acts 19:24, 25. It was Demetrius, spokesman for those who made these objects out of silver, who opposed Paul.

140. Perhaps the one mentioned in Acts 19:29.

141. Paul speaks of fighting wild beasts in Ephesus (I Corinthians 15:32), though he probably means theological opponents who fought against him with bestial ferocity.

142. Acts 19:8-10.

143. Acts 19:10. Romans 16, now regarded by most scholars as a fragment of a letter of Paul to the Ephesians, mentions a great many names of Christians who were associated with Paul in his Ephesian ministry.

144. The seven churches mentioned in Revelation 1-4 — Ephesus, Smyrna, Pergamum, Thyatira, Sardis, Philadelphia, and Laodicea—may all have been founded during Paul's Ephesian ministry. Paul wrote a letter to the church at Colossae, which he had never visited, and to Philemon, a prominent member of that church. He also speaks of a Laodicean letter (Colossians 4:16) and a Christian group at Hierapolis (Colossians 4:13).

145. I Corinthians 16:9.

146. II Corinthians 1:8.

147. Acts 19:13-20.

148. Acts 20:20, 21.

149. Acts 20:34, 35.

150. Most scholars recognize a fragment of the lost letter in II Corinthians 6:14—7:1.

151. *Supra,* pp. 297, 298.

152. Acts 19:25-27. Cf. *supra,* p. 469, footnote 139.

153. Acts 19:28, 29, 34. Paul's traveling companions, Gaius and Aristarchus, were seized. Paul wanted to speak to the crowd in his own defense, but his followers and some of the native leaders restrained him (Acts 19:30, 31).

154. Acts 19:32.

155. Acts 19:33-41.

156. Acts 20:1.

157. Acts 19:21; Romans 1:13; 15:22-24; I Corinthians 16:6. Erastus and Timothy had already been sent to Macedonia (Acts 19:22), perhaps to arrange for collections among the churches there. In Greece ((II Corinthians 9:1, 2) and Galatia (I Corinthians 16:1), provisions were already being made for it.

158. II Corinthians 2:12, 13. He had already been in Troas a few years earlier (*supra,* p. 296).

159. II Corinthians 7:5-16. Here Paul wrote II Corinthians 1-9 (*supra,* p. 304).

160. Acts 20:2.

161. II Corinthians 8:18, 22.

162. Acts 20:3.

163. Romans 16:23.

164. Romans 1:15; 15:23.

165. Romans 15:25-28. This collection was Paul's final attempt to bind together his Gentile churches with the mother church in Jerusalem (cf. Galatians 2:10).

166. Acts 20:3.

167. The committee was composed of Sopater of Beroea, Aristarchus and Secundus of Thessalonica, Gaius of Derbe, Timothy of Lystra, and Tychicus and Trophimus of Ephesus (Acts 20:4). Luke joined Paul at Philippi (Acts 20:5), and may have served as the representative of that church. The Corinthians may have considered Paul as their representative (I Corinthians 16:4).

168. Acts 20:6.

169. Acts 20:7-12.

170. Acts 20:17-38.

171. Romans 15:30, 31.

172. Acts 20:22-25. At the end of the address Paul quotes one of the words of Jesus unrecorded in the gospels: "It makes one happier to give than to be given to" (Acts 20:35; supra, p. 451, footnote 12).

173. Acts 20:36-38.

174. Acts 21:1-6.

175. Acts 21:4. In his determination to go to Jerusalem, Paul reminds us of Jesus who "set his face toward Jerusalem" (Luke 9:51; supra, pp. 253-255).

176. Acts 21:7-15.

177. Acts 21:17. No mention is made of the collection; presumably Paul delivered it into the hands of Peter and James, but that it helped cement relations between Paul's Gentile mission and the mother church is doubtful, in the light of subsequent events.

178. Acts 21:18, 19.

179. Acts 21:20-24. Paul had not encouraged Jews to forsake the law of Moses; he had taught that Jesus was the Messiah and that salvation was by grace and not by works of the law (cf. Galatians 2:15, 16).

180. Acts 21:26.

181. Acts 21:28.

182. Acts 21:29-32. The stone which was placed at the entrance of the Court of the Women is now in the museum at Istanbul. It reads: "No foreigner may enter within the railing or boundary line of the sanctuary. Whoever is caught is himself responsible for the consequences, which are death" (as quoted in Battenhouse, The Bible Unlocked, p. 493, footnote 2).

183. Acts 21:28. Four hundred Jews had been slain by the procurator Felix at the time of this rebellion, but the leader had escaped (Josephus, Antiquities, xx. 8. 6).

184. Acts 21:33-36.

185. Acts 21:37—22:21.

186. Acts 22:22.

187. Acts 22:23-29 (cf. supra, p. 209).

188. Acts 23:1.

189. Not the same Ananias as the one mentioned in Acts 5:1-5 (supra, p. 278). nor the one mentioned in Acts 9:10-19 (supra, p. 287).

190. Acts 23:3. Paul later claimed that he didn't know Ananias was the high priest (verse 5).

191. Acts 23:6-10.

192. The story of the plot is told by Luke in Acts 23:12-23. This is the only reference we have to any of Paul's family connections (*supra*, p. 284). The number of soldiers accompanying Paul is uncertain; for Luke's "two hundred men (infantry), . . . seventy mounted men and two hundred spearmen" (Acts 23:23) is confusing. Lysias sent a letter to Felix explaining the circumstances of Paul's arrest and his belief Paul was innocent (Acts 23:26-30). Felix was procurator of Judea from 52 A.D. until his replacement by Festus some time between 58 and 60 A.D.

193. Acts 24:5, 6.

194. Acts 24:10-21.

195. Acts 24:22.

196. Acts 24:23, 27. Some scholars think that some of Paul's "prison letters," especially Colossians and Philemon, were written from Caesarea during the years 56-58 A.D., but a later date for these letters is more probable. Paul doubtless had Luke, Timothy, and Tychicus as his helpers during this period; when Luke was not occupied running errands for Paul, he may have been collecting material for his gospel and the Book of Acts (*supra*, pp. 244, 245).

197. Acts 24:26. Felix should have known better than to expect a bribe from a poor, but honest, tent-maker evangelist.

198. Acts 24:24, 25. Drusilla was the youngest daughter of Herod Agrippa I (*supra*, pp. 212, 462, footnote 43) ruler of Palestine from 41 to 44 A.D., and the younger sister of Herod Agrippa II (mentioned in Acts 25:13-32), ruler of parts of Galilee and Perea, Abilene, Iturea, and Trachonitis, from his capital city of Caesarea Philippi.

199. Acts 24:27.

200. Acts 25:1-7. The charges were those mentioned earlier in Acts 24:5, 6, with possibly some others added. Paul's reply is terse: "I have committed no offense against the Jewish Law or the Temple or the emperor." (Acts 25:8).

201. Acts 25:10, 11 (cf. *supra*, p. 209). Paul made this appeal to avoid being turned over to the Jewish authorities, a course of action toward which Festus seemed to be leaning. Paul doubtless thought he would get a fairer trial in Rome than in Palestine; then, too, he would no longer be in danger from Jewish assassins. Also, the decision of the imperial tribunal would be final. Paul would welcome, as a byproduct of his appeal, the chance to get to Rome.

202. Acts 25:12. Once the fateful words, "Caesarem appello," escaped the lips of a Roman citizen, there was no retraction.

203. Acts 25:13 (*supra*, p. 471, footnote 198). Elder sister of Drusilla and Agrippa, Bernice became the mistress of the emperor Titus.

204. Acts 25:13-27.

205. *Supra*, p. 308.

206. Acts 26:1-29 (*supra*, pp. 286, 287).

207. Acts 26:32.

208. Acts 27:1—28:16. Luke was evidently on shipboard with Paul, for this is the fourth and last of the "we-sections" (*supra*, pp. 275, 461, footnote 9).

209. Acts 27:1.

210. Acts 27:2, 9. Navigation on the Mediterranean Sea was considered dangerous after the middle of September, and sea travel was usually not resumed until early in March.

211. Acts 27:2. He had been one of the collection committee (*supra*, p. 470, footnote 167).

212. Acts 27:6. Luke says there were "about seventy-six of us on board" (Acts 27:37).

213. Acts 27:7, 8.

214. Acts 27:9, 10. It is interesting that Paul, a prisoner, was allowed to express an opinion. He had had a good deal of experience as sea, having been shipwrecked three times before (II Corinthians 11:25).

215. Acts 27:11, 12.

216. Acts 27:13-17.

217. Acts 27:18-26.

218. Acts 27:27-32.

219. Acts 27:33-38.

220. Acts 27:29-44.

221. Acts 28:1-6. The attitude of the inhabitants toward Paul's encounter with the snake was fairly prevalent among Jews during the Old Testament period (*supra*, pp. 128, 129, 142, 145, and 178).

222. Acts 28:7-10.

223. Acts 28:11-15.

224. Acts 28:17-28.

225. Acts 28:30.

226. Acts 28:16, 20, 30, 31.

227. Philippians 1:1; Colossians 1:1; Philemon 1.

228. Philemon 24; Colossians 4:10, 14.

229. Philemon 23; Colossians 1:7. The Colossian church had been taught the gospel by Epaphras, who had probably been one of Paul's assistants while he was at Ephesus (*supra*, p. 469, footnote 144).

230. He delivered the letter to the Colossians (4:7).

231. Philemon 10; Colossians 4:9.

232. Philippians 2:25-30; 4:18. He had been sent by the Philippian church to be Paul's companion in Rome, but had become ill (*supra*, p. 466, footnote 90).

233. Philippians 1:12-18. Paul had converted some of the members of the emperor's own household (Philippians 4:22).

234. Philippians 1:19-30.

235. "There is some evidence that if the prosecution failed to put in an appearance within two years, they lost their case by default (see discussion by Lake, *Beginnings of Christianity*, V, 330-31)" (Macgregor, *op. cit.*, p. 349). Automatic release at the end of two years may be inferred from Luke's "two full years" in Acts 28:30 (*supra*, p. 313).

236. "The Life of Paul," *The Interpreter's Bible*, VII, p. 199. Hatch admits in the same article (*loc. cit.*) that he is on very uncertain ground when he affirms that Paul was released without a trial.

237. *Op. cit.*, pp. 222-224. He gives little evidence that there really was a trial. He believes Paul's case was brought before a representative of the emperor rather than the emperor himself. Battenhouse (*The Bible Unlocked*, p. 508; *New Testament History and Literature*, p. 330) also assumes that the pastoral letters are genuinely Pauline, at least in historical nucleus and evangelistic spirit.

238. As he had long hoped to do (Romans 15:24). Late in the first century, Clement of Rome, in a letter to the Corinthians (I Clement 5:5-7), wrote of Paul, as having "gone to the extreme limit (i.e., the farthest bounds) of the West." "The Muratorian Canon, a second century document composed of

New Testament books positively accepts Paul's journey to Spain as a historical fact" (Battenhouse, *The Bible Unlocked*, pp. 507-508, footnote 3).

239. II Timothy 4:6-8.

240. A sharp contrast from his earlier attitude toward Mark (*supra*, pp. 290, 295).

241. II Timothy 4:9-21.

242. Gilbert, *op. cit.*, pp. 231, 232.

243. Acts 20:37, 38 (*supra*, pp. 306, 307).

244. *Supra*, pp. 243, 244.

245. *Op. cit.*, p. 350. This is also the position of Goodspeed (*op. cit.*, p. 211) and Craig (*The Beginning of Christianity*, pp. 264-265).

246. *Supra*, p. 451, footnote 18; p. 239.

247. Gaius refers to Paul's being beheaded on the Via Ostiensis, just outside of Rome.

248. Romans 8:35-39.

249. *Supra*, pp. 300, 301, 468, footnote 113.

250. Such as the correspondence between Trajan and Pliny (*supra*, p. 232) and imperial rescripts which carried the empire's official business between the capital city and the provinces.

251. Philemon 1.

252. Romans 1:1, 7.

253. I Corinthians 1:1, 2.

254. Sosthenes joins Paul in greeting the church at Corinth (I Corinthians 1:1). Others involved in greetings are Timothy (II Corinthians 1:1; Philippians 1:1; Colossians 1:1; Philemon 1; I Thessalonians 1:1; II Thessalonians 1:1) and Silas (I Thessalonians 1:1; II Thessalonians 1:1).

255. Romans 1:1-7. John Knox, "Introduction to Romans," *The Interpreter's Bible*, IX, p. 379, points out that Romans was written to a church with which Paul was not intimately acquainted, and which he may have felt had erroneous ideas of his position and some doubts as to his apostolic authority. He sought to correct this attitude in the first sentence of his letter and thus to gain the sympathy and support of his readers right at the start.

256. I Thessalonians 1:2, 3.

257. Philemon 4-7.

258. As in Philemon 8-20.

259. This section takes up the greatest part of Paul's doctrinal masterpiece: Romans (1:16—11:36). In I Thessalonians it occupies the second and third chapters.

260. Such as I Thessalonians 4:1—5:22; Romans 12:1—15:13.

261. As Philemon 23, 24; Colossians 4:10-17; Philippians 4:21, 22.

262. As Philemon 25; I Thessalonians 5:28; Philippians 4:23.

263. I Corinthians 16:21; Galatians 6:11; Colossians 4:18; II Thessalonians 3:17; Philemon 19. The amanuensis who wrote Romans 16, actually a letter to the Ephesians, was named Tertius (Romans 16:22).

264. Martin Dibelius, *A Fresh Approach to the New Testament and Early Christian Literature* (N.Y.: Scribner's, 1936), p. 145. That Paul's letters were intended to be spoken is further indicated by the fact that Paul directed that some of his letters should be circulated among several churches. In Colossians 4:16 he directed that neighboring churches should exchange the letters he had sent them.

265. As early as the opening years of the third century, Origen of Alexandria was driven to the conclusion that "the author is known to God alone" (Scott, *The Literature of the New Testament*, p. 198).

266. *Supra,* pp. 314-317.

267. For further discussion of this problem see Quimby, Chester W., *Paul for Everyone* (N.Y.: Macmillan, 1944), p. 60; Barnett, *op. cit.,* pp. 183-185; Riddle, Donald W., and Hutson, Harold H., *New Testament Life and Literature* (Chicago: University of Chicago Press, 1946), pp. 175-177; Scott, *op. cit.,* pp. 179-180; Goodspeed, *op. cit.,* p. 216; Goodspeed, *The Meaning of Ephesians* (Chicago: University of Chicago Press, 1933); and Beare, Francis W., "Introduction to Ephesians," *The Interpreter's Bible,* X, pp. 597-605.

268. I Corinthians 5:9; II Corinthians 2:4; 7:8; Colossians 4:16.

269. II Corinthians 6:14—7:1; Romans 16; II Corinthians 10—13; and the Pauline fragments in the pastoral letters.

270. *Supra,* p. 468, footnote 113.

271. Acts 17:1-10; *supra,* pp. 298, 299.

272. I Thessalonians 3:1-3; *supra,* p. 467, footnote 110.

273. I Thessalonians 3:6-8.

274. I Thessalonians 5:14.

275. I Thessalonians 4:3-8.

276. I Thessalonians 4:13-18. Paul continues the discussion, saying that no one could say when the Lord would come, but it would be soon and sudden, "like a thief in the night" (I Thessalonians 5:2). So, people must be ready at any and all times.

277. I Thessalonians 4:11, 12. Paul deals with this problem more at length in II Thessalonians.

278. I Thessalonians 2:13-16.

279. I Thessalonians 3:7, 8.

280. I Thessalonians 5:12-22.

281. II Thessalonians 2:2.

282. II Thessalonians 2:1-12.

283. II Thessalonians 3:6-13. Paul signed this letter at the end, so they would know what his signature looked like (II Thessalonians 3:17).

284. *Supra,* p. 468, footnote 113. Raymond T. Stamm, "Introduction to Galatians," *The Interpreter's Bible,* X, pp. 438-441, makes out a good case for Ephesus as the place where Paul wrote Galatians, some time between 53 and 55 A.D., during the short interval between his writing II Corinthians 10-13 and II Corinthians 1-9. Barnett, *op. cit.,* pp. 25-30, favors Antioch as the place and the year 49 as the date for Galatians, just before the visit of Paul to Jerusalem recorded in Acts 15:2-21. Goodspeed, *Paul,* pp. 103-112, selects Antioch as the place and 52 the year for Galatians, just after Paul's return from his first trip to Europe. John Dow (*The Abingdon Bible Commentary,* p. 208) and Mould (*op. cit.,* p. 574) select Corinth near the close of Paul's eighteen months' visit there.

285. Acts 13:14—14:21; 16:1-6 (*supra,* pp. 290-292, 295). According to the "North Galatian Theory," Paul was writing to churches in the northern part of that province, in north central Asia Minor, with its principal cities of Pessinus, Tavium, and Ancyra (modern Ankara), which he presumbably visited in Acts 16:6 and revisited in Acts 18:23. In favor of this view are Gilbert (*op. cit.,* pp. 260-272) and Moffatt (*op. cit.,* pp. 90-101). For able discussions of the problem see Stamm, *op. cit.,* pp. 435-437, and George S. Duncan, "Critical Problems Related to Galatians," in Kepler, *op. cit.,* pp. 219-221.

286. Galatians 2:11-14; 4:10; 5:2-6. The controversy over whether to admit Gentiles to Christianity or not had apparently not been ended by the decision reached at the apostolic council in Jerusalem (Acts 15:1-35; *supra,* pp. 292-295).

287. Galatians 2:18-20; 5:11, 14, 22-24.

288. Stamm, *op. cit.*, p. 429. The paragraph of thanksgiving, customary in Paul's letters, is missing from this one (*supra*, pp. 318, 319).

289. Galatians 1:1-5.

290. Here Paul is quoting from the Septuagint version of Deuteronomy 27:26.

291. Habakkuk 2:4 (cf. Romans 1:17; Hebrews 10:39; *supra*, p. 435, footnote 15).

292. Deuteronomy 21:23.

293. Galatians 3:10-14. In studying Paul's letters to the Galatians and the Romans, Martin Luther found some of the assurance that he had been vainly looking for in the mediaeval church. The doctrine of justification by faith became one of the cornerstones of the Protestant Reformation.

294. Galatians 2:16, 17.

295. Galatians 3:24, 25.

296. Galatians 3:2; 4:3-6.

297. Or, "let him be anathema," as close as Paul ever comes to swearing.

298. Galatians 1:6-9.

299. Galatians 1:11, 12.

300. Galatians 1:13—2:14; *supra*, pp. 292-295.

301. Galatians 5:6; 6:15.

302. Galatians 6:17.

303. Galatians 4:31; 5:1.

304. Galatians 2:17.

305. Galatians 5:22, 23.

306. Galatians 2:20.

307. Galatians 5:24.

308. Galatians 5:13, 16-18.

309. Galatians 5:15.

310. Galatians 6:12, 13.

311. Galatians 3:26-29.

312. Galatians 6:11.

313. Galatians 6:18. Whether the letter was successful or not we have no way of knowing, but the fact that Galatians was preserved indicates that it may have helped the early church considerably in its battle for Christian liberty.

314. *Supra*, p. 304. For the founding of the church at Corinth see Acts 18:1-21 (*supra*, pp. 300-302).

315. Edgar J. Goodspeed, *An Introduction to the New Testament* (Chicago: The University of Chicago Press, 1937), p. 39.

316. I Corinthians 5:9. This first letter of Paul to the Corinthians is the famous "lost letter," a fragment of which may be preserved in II Corinthians 6:14—7:1. This passage deals with the same subject with which the missing letter was evidently concerned; it obviously does not belong with the material in II Corinthians before and after it. The omission of 6:14—7:1 would cause no break in thought sequence between 6:13 and 7:2.

317. I Corinthians 1:11; perhaps they were runaway slaves.

318. There were at least four of them (I Corinthians 1:12).

319. I Corinthians 6:1-6.

320. I Corinthians 11:17-34.

321. I Corinthians 5:1-5.

322. I Corinthians 7:1. The coming of the three men is mentioned in I Corinthians 16:15-18. Paul must have received many such letters, but this is the only one specifically mentioned in the New Testament.

323. I Corinthians 7:1-40.

324. I Corinthians 8:1-13.

325. I Corinthians 11:2-16; 12:1-30.

326. I Corinthians 16:1-4.

327. I Corinthians 15:1-58.

328. I Corinthians 16:8, 9.

329. I Corinthians 1:10-13. Like Christians of a later day, the Corinthians were divided according to their personal preferences. Some liked Apollos' finished phrases; some clung loyally to Paul as the church's founder; others preferred the rugged style of Peter, one of the original disciples. A fourth group refused any minor allegiance, declaring they were the only ones in Corinth who really followed Christ.

330. I Corinthians 3:3-9.

331. I Corinthians 3:11.

332. I Corinthians 3:18—4:1.

333. I Corinthians 5:2-5. Whether the punishment Paul recommends for the offender is excommunication or physical death is not certain. His ultimate objective is to save the man's soul.

334. I Corinthians 6:1-8.

335. I Corinthians 6:9, 10, 18-20.

336. Was Paul ever married? This is a question about which there is no certain answer. Members of the Sanhedrin married, but, in spite of Acts 26:10, there is no evidence that Paul belonged to that august body. The implication of this verse is that Paul certainly had no living wife when he wrote I Corinthians. From the entire chapter it seems highly unlikely that Paul ever had been married.

337. I Corinthians 7:1, 2, 7-11 (cf. verses 25-40).

338. I Corinthians 7:20 (cf. verses 21 and 24).

339. I Corinthians 10:14-22.

340. I Corinthians 10:25-28.

341. I Corinthians 8:8-13.

342. Genesis 2:18, 21-23 (cf. I Timothy 2:13). For Paul, the divine order of creation ought to be expressed in social custom.

343. I Corinthians 11:3-10 (cf. also I Corinthians 14:34, 35).

344. I Corinthians 11:17-22. Such carousing was not so strange in a Greek environment; some of the Corinthians may have belonged to the cult of Dionysus (*supra*, p. 207). Ultimately, these disorders probably led to the separation of the liturgical act, or Eucharist, from the common meal (*supra*, p. 461, footnote 20).

345. I Corinthians 11:23-27. Paul's version is the earliest account of the institution of the rite of the Lord's Supper in the New Testament (*supra*, pp. 258, 259, 457, footnote 126). He probably got it from the oral tradition, in which some materials later incorporated into the gospels were preserved (*supra*, p. 234).

346. I Corinthians 11:27, 28.

347. For "glossalalia" see *supra*, p. 461, footnote 13 "Moffatt in his *N. T. Commentary on I Cor.*, p. 208, describes them as 'Broken murmers, incoherent chants, low mutterings, *staccato* sobs, screams, and sighs, dropped from the speakers' lips in hurried, huddled utterances'" (Quimby, *op. cit.*, p. 84, footnote 1).

348. I Corinthians 12:4-6.

349. I Corinthians 12:12, 27, 28, 31.

350. Nowhere does Paul show more clearly how entirely his thought is ruled by the spirit of Jesus than in I Corinthians 13. Wilbert F. Howard ("First and Second Corinthians," *The Abingdon Bible Commentary*, p. 1187) calls it a "lyrical interpretation of the Sermon on the Mount—the Beatitudes set to music." Every Christian should know it from memory and follow its teaching implicitly. A vast literature has grown up around this chapter; one of the most classic is Henry Drummond's *The Greatest Thing in the World*, which has been printed in many editions.

351. I Corinthians 14:5.

352. I Corinthians 14:18, 19.

353. I Corinthians 14:26-28.

354. I Corinthians 15:3-9 (*supra,* pp. 264, 265).

355. Philippians 3:21.

356. Acts, 9:4 (*supra,* pp. 286, 287).

357. Perhaps from oral tradition (*supra,* p. 234).

358. I Corinthians 15:3-5, 8.

359. I Corinthians 15:14, 15, 17.

360. I Corinthians 15:20.

361. I Corinthians 15:42-44, 52, 53, 57.

362. I Corinthians 16:1-4. At the Jerusalem Council Paul had promised to "remember the poor" (Galatians 2:10). The collection of a great offering for the church at Jerusalem occupied much of Paul's time and attention while he was at Ephesus and upon his return trip from there to Palestine via Macedonia and Greece.

363. I Corinthians 16:5-9 (cf. Acts 19:21; 20:1, 2).

364. I Corinthians 16:21-24.

365. I Corinthians 4:17; 16:10.

366. II Corinthians 3:1; 11:5, 22.

367. II Corinthians 2:5; 7:12.

368. II Corinthians 2:1; 12:14; 13:1, 2.

369. II Corinthians 2:4. This letter is also mentioned in verse 3.

370. II Corinthians 2:9 (cf. 7:8).

371. II Corinthians 2:12, 13; 12:17, 18. Titus had possibly visited Corinth earlier to encourage the Christians there to give liberally to the collection for the Jerusalem saints (II Corinthians 8:6).

372. II Corinthians 7:5-16 (*supra,* p. 305).

373. II Corinthians 10:1-6.

374. II Corinthians 10:7-11.

375. II Corinthians 10:14-16.

376. II Corinthians 11:1, 2, 4-6.

377. II Corinthians 11:12, 13.

378. II Corinthians 11:16-23. Then there follows Paul's famous catalogue of the things he has done and endured on behalf of the gospel (II Corinthians 11:23-27; *supra,* p. 289).

379. II Corinthians 12:9-12.

380. II Corinthians 11:7, 8.

381. II Corinthians 11:9.

382. II Corinthians 12:14-17.

383. II Corinthians 12:20, 21; 13:2, 3, 9-11.

384. II Corinthians 7:5-7.

385. With the exception of II Corinthians 6:14—7:1 (*supra,* p. 475, footnote 316).

386. II Corinthians 1:3, 4.

387. II Corinthians 2:6-10.
388. II Corinthians 2:15—3:3.
389. II Corinthians 4:1, 2, 5, 6.
390. II Corinthians 4:7-10.
391. II Corinthians 4:16—5:1.
392. II Corinthians 5:14.
393. II Corinthians 5:17-21.
394. *Supra,* pp. 289 and 477, footnote 378.
395. II Corinthians 6:11-13; 7:2-4.
396. II Corinthians 7:5-16.
397. *Supra,* p. 477, footnote 362.
398. II Corinthians 8:7-11.
399. II Corinthians 9:6, 7, 13, 15.
400. Acts 20:3; *supra,* p. 305.
401. Romans 15:19, 23-25, 28, 29 (cf. Romans 1:10-15). For the collection, see *supra,* p. 470, footnote 165, and p. 477, footnote 362, and p. 342.
402. Romans 1:11-13.
403. *Supra,* p. 195.
404. Acts 2:10.
405. Jewish Christians like Aquila and Priscilla (Acts 18:2) may have been among these (*supra,* pp. 301, 468, footnote 112).
406. *Supra,* p. 317.
407. Acts 15:1-29; Galatians 2:1-10 (*supra,* pp. 292-294). Aquila and Priscilla had been ejected from Rome in 49. Paul says he has wanted to come to Rome "for many years" (Romans 15:23).
408. *Works* III. 373, quoted in Knox, "Introduction to Romans," *The Interpreter's Bible,* IX, p. 362.
409. For evidence for this see Knox, *ibid.,* pp. 362, 363.
410. 3:9.
411. 4:1.
412. 9:10.
413. Romans 1:1-7.
414. Romans 1:16, 17. Again Paul quotes Habakkuk 2:4 (cf. Galatians 3:11; Hebrews 10:39; *supra,* p. 435, footnote 15).
415. Romans 1:18—3:20.
416. Romans 3:20-24. Paul adds illustrations from the life of Abraham (3:25—4:20; cf. Hebrews 11:8-12).
417. Romans 5:1-5.
418. Romans 5:6-11. Paul continues by drawing a contrast between the ruin caused by Adam and the restoration achieved through Christ (5:12-21).
419. Romans 6:8-11.
420. Romans 6:15, 22, 23.
421. Romans 7:7, 14-17, 21-25.
422. This chapter belongs among the mountain-peak chapters of the Bible, along with I Corinthians 13 and 15 (*supra,* pp. 330, 334, 335, 477, footnote 350) and Hebrews 11.
423. Romans 8:1-4, 6, 10, 11, 14, 16-18, 28-35, 37-39.
424. Romans 12:1, 2.
425. Romans 12:3-5, 9-13.
426. Deuteronomy 32:35, 36. Paul also probably had Leviticus 19:18 in mind.
427. Proverbs 25:21, 22.
428. Romans 12:14-21.

429. Romans 13:1-7. This is another section of Paul's writings about which there has been much disagreement. Sometimes Christians have interpreted this to mean that any ruler should command absolute obedience, as in the period when "the divine right of Kings" prevailed. At other times, Christians have rejected Paul's teachings completely and have left no place in their thought for the necessary functions of the state.

430. Romans 13:8-10.

431. Romans 13:11-14.

432. Romans 14:1, 3, 7, 8, 14, 15-17, 20, 21 (cf. I Corinthians 8-10; *supra*, p. 332).

433. Romans 15:1, 2, 7-9.

434. Romans 16:1.

435. Romans 16:3-16.

436. Romans 16:17-20.

437. Romans 16:21-27.

438. Priscilla and Aquila (Romans 16:3) were in Ephesus when Paul wrote I Corinthians 16:19. Epaenetus is referred to as "the first man in Asia to turn to Christ" (Romans 16:5). Goodspeed, *op. cit.*, pp. 85-86, thinks that Romans 16 was added to Romans when the Pauline letters were brought together at Ephesus *ca.* 90 A.D. This would insure the preservation and circulation of the brief Phoebe letter.

439. Knox, *op. cit.*, pp. 367-368.

440. *Supra*, p. 314. A few scholars assign the prison letters to the period when Paul was in difficulties in Ephesus (*supra*, p. 304; see the discussion in Scott, *op. cit.*, pp. 189-190, as it applies particularly to Philippians).

441. The story of Paul's first visit to Philippi is given in Acts 16:10-40 (*supra*, pp. 296-298).

442. Philippians 4:15-18.

443. Philippians 2:25-30.

444. Philippians 1:1-11.

445. Philippians 1:12-26.

446. Philippians 1:27.

447. Philippians 2:5-11, 14-16.

448. See Goodspeed, *op. cit.*, pp. 90-96; Barnett, *op. cit.*, pp. 69-78; Quimby, *op. cit.*, pp. 89-91. Scott, *op. cit.*, pp. 186-190, thinks the letter is a unity as we have it.

449. *Supra*, pp. 323-328.

450. Philippians 3:2-4, 7-11.

451. Philippians 3:12-15.

452. Philippians 3:17—4:1.

453. Philippians 4:8, 9.

454. Philippians 4:11-13. The letter to the Philippians tells us a great deal concerning the closing years of Paul's life (*supra*, pp. 313, 314).

455. Colossians 1:7, 8; 4:12.

456. Colossians 4:9.

457. Acts 19:10 (*supra*, p. 469, footnote 144).

458. Colossians 1:13-20. We see in this passage a new element in the theology of Paul: the doctrine of the divine Logos, pre-existent with God in creation and revelation (see John 1:1-18).

459. Colossians 2:2-4, 6-10.

460. Colossians 2:23.

461. Colossians 3:1-5, 8-17.

462. Colossians 3:18—4:1 (cf. Ephesians 5:22—6:9; I Peter 2:18; 3:1-7).

463. Colossians 4:7-9.

464. Colossians 4:15, 16 (cf. also verse 13). Paul's letter to the Laodiceans has almost certainly been lost (*supra*, p. 320 and p. 475, footnote 316), though Goodspeed (*op. cit.*, pp. 109-124) identifies it with Philemon.

465. Colossians 4:18.

466. The church at Colossae met in Philemon's house (Philemon 2).

467. Philemon 4, 5, 8-19, 21, 22.

468. Cf. Colossians 3:22—4:1.

469. Ernest F. Scott (*op. cit.*, pp. 179-185) numbers Ephesians among the genuine letters of Paul, as do also C. H. Dodd, "Introduction to Ephesians," *The Abingdon Bible Commentary*, pp. 1222-1225) and Roy Battenhouse (*New Testament History and Literature*, pp. 350-352, and *The Bible Unlocked*, pp. 505-506, especially footnote 4). The most complete statement of the position against the Pauline authorship is given in Goodspeed, *The Meaning of Ephesians* (Chicago: University of Chicago Press, 1933). Along with that, see also Goodspeed, *An Introduction to the New Testament*, pp. 222-239, Barnett, *op. cit.*, pp. 181-191, Moffatt, *op. cit.*, pp. 373-395, and Francis W. Beare, "An Introduction to Ephesians," *The Interpreter's Bible*, X, pp. 597-610.

470. Ephesians 3:4.

471. Ephesians 2:20.

472. Ephesians 2:2, 3, 11.

473. Ephesians 1:15; 3:2, 3; 4:21; 6:18-20.

474. *Supra*, pp. 302-305.

475. Ephesians 4:14.

476. Ephesians 4:17, 22-27, 31; 5:3, 6-13.

477. *Op. cit.*, p. 600.

478. The words "at Ephesus" in Ephesians 1:1 are omitted in the best manuscripts (Papyrus 46, our only second century manuscript, and the fourth century codices Sinaiticus and Vaticanus). They evidently are a gloss derived from the title ("to the Ephesians") which was put at the head of this letter by the second century editors of the letters of Paul. All the other letters are addressed directly to "the devoted adherents. . . in Philippi" (Philippians 1:1), to "the church of God that is at Corinth" (II Corinthians 1:1), etc.; but this one is addressed in the most general way possible "to God's people who are steadfast in Christ Jesus" (Ephesians 1:1).

479. Some time between 90 and 95 A.D. (*supra*, pp. 243 and 274).

480. *Op. cit.*, pp. 603-604.

481. *Supra*, p. 355

482. Ephesians 1:3-10.

483. Ephesians 1:17-23.

484. Ephesians 2:13-19.

485. Ephesians 3:14-21.

486. Ephesians 4:3-6, 11-13, 15.

487. Ephesians 5:22-33.

488. Ephesians 6:1-9.

489. Ephesians 6:10-17.

490. Although Barnett (*op. cit.*, pp. 282-284) believes that they should be dated from the last half of the second century; as such, they would be chronologically the latest books of the New Testament.

491. Those who regard the pastoral letters as genuinely Pauline have a means of reconstructing the closing years of his life (*supra*, pp. 314-317, 320).

492. I Timothy 1:18, 19 (cf. 3:9; 4:6; 5:8; 6:10, 21).

493. I Timothy 4:1-3. Thus does the author graphically denounce the heretics of his day.

494. I Timothy 3:15 (cf. 4:3; 6:5; II Timothy 2:15, 18; 3:8; 4:4; Titus 1:14).

495. I Timothy 4:13, 16 (cf. 6:1; II Timothy 3:10; Titus 2:10).

496. I Timothy 6:20, 21.

497. II Timothy 1:12-14 (cf. I Timothy 1:10; 6:3; II Timothy 4:3; Titus 1:9; 2:1).

498. Compare I Timothy 6:15 and II Timothy 1:12, 18; 3:1; and 4:1, 2 with I Thessalonians 4:13—5:3, II Thessalonians 2:1-12, I Corinthians 7:26-32; 15:23-28, 52; 16:22, II Corinthians 5:1-5, Romans 8:23, Philippians 3:20, 21, and Colossians 3:4 (*supra*, pp. 321-323).

499. See Moffatt, *op. cit.*, pp. 406-408.

500. I Timothy 3:1-7 (cf. Titus 1:7-9).

501. Titus 1:5, 6 (cf. I Timothy 5:17-19).

502. I Timothy 3:8-10, 12, 13.

503. I Timothy 3:11.

504. I Timothy 5:9, 10. The author explains why he doesn't want widows under sixty to be included among the church officials; they either want to marry or become idle gossips and busybodies (I Timothy 5:11-16).

505. I Timothy 6:2, 3 (cf. II Timothy 1:13; 4:3-5; Titus 1:9; 2:1-10).

506. I Timothy 1:3-6, 9, 10.

507. I Timothy 4:7.

508. I Timothy 4:12-14, 16.

509. II Timothy 2:14-17, 22-26.

510. II Timothy 3:6-8 (cf. II Timothy 4:3, 4; Titus 1:10-16; 3:9-11).

511. II Timothy 3:14-17. The "books" and "parchments" mentioned in II Timothy 4:13 probably refer to Christian scriptural writings. In I Timothy 5:18, Luke 10:7 is quoted on a par with Deuteronomy 25:4. Here for the first time we have a word of Jesus designated as "scripture."

512. II Timothy 2:2, 3, 5.

513. I Timothy 5:22 (cf. I Timothy 5:1-8, 19, 20; 6:3-10; Titus 1:10-16).

514. I Timothy 6:11-14.

515. II Timothy 4:6-8.

CHAPTER TWENTY-FOUR

1. *Supra*, pp. 252-263.

2. *Supra*, pp. 279-281, 291, 292, 297-299, 301-317.

3. *Supra*, pp. 232, 238.

4. For emperor worship, see *supra*, pp. 208, 209.

5. Perhaps under the Neronian persecution.

6. Hebrews 10:32-36.

7. Hebrews 12:3, 4, 7, 11, 12.

8. See *supra*, pp. 320, 473, footnote 265.

9. Hebrews 2:3. Paul claimed his "good news" came directly "through a revelation of Jesus Christ" (Galatians 1:10-12).

10. Various interesting suggestions have been made as to the identity of its author. Tertullian and Origen thought that it was Barnabas. Luther selected Apollos. Others have selected, at various times, Luke, Clement of Rome, Silas, Philip, and even Aquila and Priscilla.

11. Hebrews 1:1-4. A letter usually began with a salutation, giving the name of the writer and a greeting to the recipients.

12. Hebrews 13:22.

13. Chapters 3 and 4 constitute a digression which is a good specimen of an early Christian sermon.

14. Hebrews 2:5.

15. Hebrews 6:9.

16. Hebrews 8:1.

17. Hebrews 11:32.

18. Hebrews 1:3.

19. Hebrews 8:5.

20. Hebrews 2:8-10 (cf. Hebrews 1:1-4; John 1:1-18; Colossians 1:13-20; *supra*, pp. 355, 356).

21. Hebrews 7:1-10.

22. *Op cit.*, p. 196.

23. Hebrews 13:24, 25.

24. Hebrews 6:4-6.

25. Hebrews 10:26, 27.

26. H. T. Andrews, "Introduction to Hebrews," *The Abingdon Bible Commentary*, p. 1296.

27. Hebrews 1:1—3:6.

28. Hebrews 5:1-10. Melchizedek was priest-king of Salem, a friend of Abraham (Psalm 110:4; Genesis 14:17-20).

29. Hebrews 7:20, 22, 23-28; 8:1, 2, 6; 9:11, 12; 10:9-14.

30. Along with I Corinthians 13 and 15 and Romans 8 (*supra*, pp. 330, 477, footnote 350, 334, 335, and 347).

31. Hebrews 11:1, 2. This author's understanding of faith is quite different from Paul's; for the latter, it is the trust and self-surrender by which we open our hearts to God; in Hebrews, faith is the power in us to understand what is beyond the senses. The author illustrates this from many examples in Old Testament history (Hebrews 11:3-31).

32. Hebrews 11:32-40.

33. Hebrews 12:1, 2.

34. Hebrews 13:1-5, 7-9, 16.

35. *Supra*, pp. 373 and 374.

36. Revelation 2:13.

37. Revelation 13:12, 15.

38. For apocalypticism in Judaism and the book of Daniel, see *supra*, pp. 188-193.

39. A "slave" of Jesus Christ (Revelation 1:1), "brother and companion in the distress" (Revelation 1:9; cf. also Revelation 1:4 and 22:8).

40. Revelation 18:20; 21:14.

41. As reported in Eusebius, *Church History*, VII. 25.

42. The communities John addresses in Revelation 1-3 were in the vicinity of Ephesus. The author shows acquaintance with Paul's collected letters, which were published at Ephesus (*supra*, p. 361).

43. Revelation 1:9.

44. Revelation 1:4.

45. Revelation 1:11.

46. Revelation 1:3; 22:18.

47. *Supra*, pp. 302-305.

48. Revelation 2:3-6. The Nicolaitans were idolaters and fornicators, similar to the immoral people in the church at Corinth (I Corinthians 5).

49. Revelation 2:10. Polycarp, bishop of Smyrna, suffered martyrdom there in 156 A.D.

50. Revelation 2:12-17.

51. Revelation 2:20.

52. Revelation 3:1-3, 5.

53. Revelation 3:7-13.

54. Revelation 3:15-21.

55. Revelation 5:1.

56. Revelation 5:12.

57. Revelation 5:13.

58. Revelation 6:2. Interpretations of the various symbolic representations in the Apocalypse of John differ from one another. Certainly his readers would have known his exact meaning, for his so-called "visions" relate to events contemporary with him and his readers and not to events in any century since his time. The white horse may refer to victorious war or to Christ coming forth to conquer (cf. Revelation 19:11).

59. Revelation 6:4.

60. Revelation 6:6.

61. Revelation 6:8. Probably pestilence is meant. The phenomena associated with the breaking of the first four seals are some times referred to as "the four horsemen of the Apocalypse."

62. Revelation 6:9-11.

63. Revelation 6:12-17 (cf. Joel 2:30, 31; Isaiah 50:3; 34:4; 2:19; Hosea 10:8; Ezekiel 32:7; Luke 23:30; *supra*, pp. 103, 104, 117, 131, 132, 168, 169, and 188).

64. Revelation 7:16, 17.

65. The sanctity and mystical quality of the number seven (the days of the week) is of great antiquity. It was a sacred number to other ancient people as well as the Hebrews (see Jesus' use of "seven" and "seventy-seven" in Matthew 18:21, 22).

66. Revelation 8:1-13.

67. I.e., those who were not among the 144,000 men who were "marked with the seal" of God (Revelation 7:4, 5).

68. Revelation 9:4-10.

69. Revelation 9:16. Both the locusts and the demon horsemen reveal the ancient belief that the very air was filled with spiritual powers of darkness continually at war with God and his people.

70. Revelation 9:20, 21.

71. Revelation 10:1—11:14.

72. Revelation 12:1, 2. The woman, in the author's imagination, may have stood for the true Israel; the child is Christ.

73. Revelation 12:3, 4. The dragon is similar to the chaos monster of Babylonian mythology. In Jewish mythology, the figure of the serpent is used; it is also called Satan (Revelation 12:9), who was hurled out of heaven. Therefore, the first of the last great struggles between good and evil had already taken place in heaven, and evil has been defeated.

74. Revelation 12:17.

75. Revelation 13:1, 2. The "animal," or Anti-Christ, in the book of Revelation has been variously interpreted by premillenialists all through history; some of the figures identified with it have been Mohammed, Napoleon, Kaiser Wilhelm II, Hitler, Stalin, and the pope. Actually the author had in mind

the Roman Empire as personified in Nero and Domitian. The reference in Revelation 13:3 to the animal's having been healed of a mortal wound may refer to a popular belief that Nero was not dead but had fled to Parthia, whence he would return with an avenging army.

76. Revelation 13:8.

77. Called "the false prophet" in Revelation 16:13; 19:20; 20:10.

78. The second animal may refer to the imperial priesthood and Roman officials who compelled all men to worship the emperor and put to death those who refused (supra p. 373).

79. Revelation 13:11, 12, 14-17. The number of the animal was 666. The meaning of this mystical number is not known. Some have suggested that the numerical values of the Hebrew letters of "Neron Caesar" total 666 (see F. B. Clogg, "Revelation," in The Abingdon Bible Commentary p. 1388).

80. The word "Babylon" in Revelation 14:8 means Rome. In the Old Testament Babylon would have been typical of the enemies of Israel; Rome, the new Babylon, is the foe of the Christian church, the true Israel.

81. Revelation 14:13.

82. Revelation 14:9-11.

83. Revelation 14:19, 20. It is difficult to reconcile this picture of a punishing deity with the conception of God in the teachings of Jesus (supra, pp. 267-269).

84. Revelation 15:3, 4.

85. Revelation 16:1-21. These predictions have never been exactly fulfilled in history. The author believed that the calamities would be coming soon; he had no idea that the earth would last as long as it has.

86. Revelation 17:1—18:24. The "eighth king" of 17:11 was probably Domitian.

87. This final battle between good and evil is called Armageddon (Revelation 16:16), literally the "mountain of Megiddo." Megiddo was the famous battlefield of Israel (Judges 5:19; II Kings 23:29). Solomon had extensive stables there (supra, p. 427, footnote 48).

88. Revelation 19:11, 12, 14; 19:16—20:3. The "thousand years" referred to is the millennium, during which the martyrs will be restored to life and reign with Jesus. This is the "first resurrection" (Revelation 20:5).

89. Revelation 20:10.

90. Revelation 20:15. Various attempts have been made, so far unsuccessfully, to date the end of the world and the various other events predicted in the book of Revelation. Such attempts betray complete misunderstanding of the visionary nature of the Apocalypse of John and of the author's belief that what he saw would take place soon. The prophecies in Revelation were never intended to be taken literally.

91. Revelation 21:1-4. The description of the holy city in Revelation 21:9—22:5 has influenced subsequent Christian thought concerning heaven. Poets, painters, and musicians have been inspired by Revelation's imaginative power: Dante, Milton, Michelangelo, Tintoretto, Handel, Dürer, Blake, etc.

CHAPTER TWENTY-FIVE

1. Supra, pp. 236-246.

2. As quoted by Eusebius, Church History, VI. 14. 7, and printed in Barnett, op. cit., p. 226.

3. See Luke 1:1-4.

4. John 20:30, 31.

5. John 6:35.

6. John 11:25, 26.

7. John 13:23; 19:26; 21:7, 20. He is called the "other disciple" in John 18:15, 16; 20:2.

8. John 21:20, 24.

9. Paul refers to John as one of the "pillars" of Judaistic Christianity (Galatians 2:9).

10. James and John had a material conception of Jesus' Messiahship (Mark 10:35-45); they wanted to call down fire upon an inhospitable Samaritan town (Luke 9:51-55); Jesus' special nickname for them was "sons of thunder" (Mark 3:17).

11. We know from Acts 12:2 that James was beheaded by Herod Agrippa I (*supra*, p. 462, footnote 43). Jesus had predicted that both James and John would suffer martyrdom (Mark 10:39).

12. Acts 19:8-10 (*supra*, pp. 303 and 304).

13. Acts 19:1-7. In the fourth gospel, the author lays repeated stress on the subordination of John the Baptizer to Jesus (as in John 1:6-8, 19-36).

14. See II John I; III John 1.

15. As quoted in Moffatt, *op. cit.*, p. 598. Papias thus distinguishes John the Elder from John the Apostle.

16. John 1:1-18.

17. Philo made use of the word "Logos" more than thirteen hundred times in his writings (*supra*, p. 204).

18. *Supra*, pp. 355, 356, 375, 376.

19. The only mention in the fourth gospel of the birth of Jesus.

20. John 1:1-5, 14, 16-18.

21. John 3:16.

22. John 1:47, 48.

23. John 4:16-19.

24. John 13:19, 21, 26.

25. John 18:4.

26. John 1:14-17.

27. John 2:11 (cf. 4:39, 53).

28. John 5:36; 10:38.

29. John 10:17, 18.

30. John 17:1.

31. John 19:17; cf. Mark 15:21.

32. As in Mark 1:35.

33. John 11:41, 42.

34. One of the purposes of the fourth gospel may have been to combat a form of heresy later known as Gnosticism, particularly in that type of Gnosticism called Docetism. Believing that matter and flesh were inherently evil, the Docetists denied the reality of Jesus' incarnation. This point of view was roundly condemned in I John (especially 4:2, 3). The church at Colossae had been infected with an early form of this heresy (*supra*, pp. 355 and 356); the heresy had evidently grown until it had become a serious threat to the churches around Ephesus by the time the fourth gospel was written.

35. As in John 4:1-4.

36. John 4:6-8; 19:28.

37. John 7:1; 8:59; 10:39, 40; 11:54.

38. John 11:33-36.

39. John 18:20, 22.

40. John 12:32.
41. John 14:6, 7.
42. John 5:19-23.
43. John 6:35, 37, 40, 48-51.
44. John 8:12 (cf. also 1:4; 9:5; 12:46).
45. John 10:7-11, 14-16.
46. John 11:25, 26.
47. John 17:1-3.
48. John 15:1, 2, 4-7, 10.
49. John 17:21-23.
50. John 3:3.
51. John 3:31-36.
52. See *supra*, pp. 321-323.
53. Such as the author of II Peter.
54. John 14:1-3, 15-20. Sometimes it sounds as if the author is speaking of Jesus himself as returning, sometimes as if Jesus is going to send a "Helper" to take his place. Actually, the two concepts are the same; the Helper is Christ's spirit, Christ himself in a new and higher manifestation.
55. John 14:25-28.
56. John 16:7, 8, 12, 13, 15, 16. John 14-17 constitute Jesus' farewell discourse delivered to his disciples at the last supper in the upper room.
57. *Supra*, pp. 387 and 388.
58. John 3:17-19.
59. John 5:24, 25.
60. John 10:30, 38.
61. John 14:9.
62. Dionysius of Alexandria (*supra*, pp. 380, 381) maintained that the gospel of John and I John were both written by the same author.
63. I John 1:4; 2:1, 7, 8, 12-14, 26; 5:13.
64. I John 2:3-6.
65. I John 4:2, 3. For the term "Antichrist" see *supra*, pp. 483, 484, footnote 75. Perhaps the author was acquainted with the Apocalypse of John.
66. I John 4:7-12, 16, 18-21.
67. I John 2:22, 23; 4:2, 3; 5:5, 6.
68. I John 1:1-4. Docetism had also been condemned in the fourth gospel (*supra*, p. 485, footnote 34). Tradition says that John's chief antagonist was the heretic Cerinthus, who was active in Ephesus *ca.* 95 A.D.
69. I John 1:8-10.
70. I John 3:4-6.
71. I John 1:6, 7.
72. "The chosen lady and her children" (II John 1).
73. II John 7, 10, 11. Probably these heretics were the Docetists of I John (*supra*, p. 486, footnote 68) and the fourth gospel (*supra*, p. 485, footnote 34).
74. II John 4.
75. II John 12.
76. II John 5, 6.
77. III John 9.
78. III John 10.
79. III John 10, 13, 14.

CHAPTER TWENTY-SIX

1. Sometimes the Johannine letters are included among the General letters.
2. As Hebrews (*supra,* pp. 373, 374) and Revelation (*supra,* pp. 380, 381).
3. I Peter 4:12; 5:9.
4. I Peter 4:13-16 (cf. *supra,* pp. 232, 238, 373, 374, 380, 381).
5. The "Babylon" of I Peter 5:13 (cf. Revelation 14:8; 16:19; 17:5; 18:2, 10, 21; *supra,* p. 484, footnote 80).
6. I Peter 1:1, 2.
7. I Peter 2:13-17. This is similar to Paul's point of view in Romans 13:1-7 (*supra* pp. 349 and 350). For an opposite attitude toward the state see Revelation 13:1—14:20 (*supra,* pp. 385-387).
8. I Peter 1:3-7.
9. I Peter 2:4, 5, 9.
10. I Peter 4:1, 2.
11. I Peter 2:21-25.
12. I Peter 5:4.
13. I Peter 3:18-20; 4:6. This may help to explain the origin of one of the phrases in the Apostles' Creed: "He descended into hell."
14. I Peter 4:7 (cf. 5:10).
15. I Peter 4:7-9.
16. I Peter 5:1-3, 5.
17. Ministers who preach against elaborate women's clothing and fancy jewelry find one text in I Peter 3:3, 4. Women are called "the weaker sex" in I Peter 3:7.
18. I Peter 3:8, 9.
19. James 1:1. At first thought, the ones addressed seem to be Jews, but the "twelve tribes" symbolically refer to all Christians, as in Revelation 7:4-8 (*supra,* p. 383).
20. Acts 12:2 (*supra,* p. 281).
21. Matthew 13:55; Mark 6:3; I Corinthians 9:5; 15:7; Acts 1:14; 12:17; 15:12-21; Galatians 1:19; 2:9; *supra,* pp. 241, 292-295.
22. As quoted in Scott, *op. cit.,* p. 215.
23. James 2:14-18, 26.
24. James 2:1-7.
25. James 5:1-6.
26. James 3:1, 2. 5-8 (cf. 1:26).
27. James 1:27 (cf. *supra,* p. 415, footnote 5).
28. James 1:2-4.
29. James 1:12, 17.
30. James 1:19, 20.
31. James 3:16-18.
32. James 4:1, 7-11, 17.
33. James 5:9.
34. James 5:13-16.
35. Jude 17 and 18.
36. Jude 1. Tradition says that the author was Jude, the brother of Jesus (Matthew 13:55; Mark 6:3), and thus the brother of James (*supra,* p. 408).
37. Jude 1.
38. *Supra,* pp. 355, 356, and 485, footnote 34.
39. Jude 3, 4, 8, 10, 12, 13, 16, 19, 22, 23.

40. Jude 24, 25.

41. II Peter 1:1, 14, 17, 18; 3:1, 15.

42. In fact, II Peter 2:1—3:3 is almost word for word the same as Jude 4-18.

43. II Peter 3:16. The heretics had been using his letters. "There are some things in them hard to understand, which ignorant, unsteadfast people twist to their own ruin, just as they do the rest of the Scriptures" (*ibid.*).

44. II Peter 3:4.

45. II Peter 1:16-18.

46. II Peter 3:8, 10.

47. Jude 22 and 23.

48. II Peter 1:4-8.

49. II Peter 3:14, 15, 17, 18

BIBLIOGRAPHY

General Reference Works

BUTTRICK, GEORGE ARTHUR, ed., *The Interpreter's Bible*. Twelve volumes. New York and Nashville; Abingdon-Cokesbury Press, 1951-1957.

EISELEN, FREDERICK CARL, LEWIS, EDWIN, and DOWNEY, DAVID G., *The Abingdon Bible Commentary*. New York: The Abingdon Press, 1929.

FERM, VERGILIUS, ed., *An Encylopedia of Religion*. New York: Philosophical Library, Inc., 1945.

FRAZER, JAMES G., *The Golden Bough*. Twelve volumes. New York: Macmillan, 1923.

GEHMAN, HENRY SNYDER, ed., *The Westminster Dictionary of the Bible*. Philadelphia: The Westminster Press, 1944.

HASTINGS, JAMES, ed., *A Dictionary of Christ and the Gospels*. Two volumes. New York: Scribner's, 1908-1909.

HASTINGS, JAMES, ed., *A Dictionary of the Bible*. New York: Scribner's, 1921.

HASTINGS, JAMES, ed., *A Dictionary of the Bible*. Five volumes. New York: Scribner's, 1911.

HASTINGS, JAMES, ed., *Encyclopaedia of Religion and Ethics*. Thirteen volumes. New York: Scribner's, 1910-1927.

JACKSON, SAMUEL MACAULEY, ed., *The New Schaff-Herzog Encyclopedia of Religious Knowledge*. New York and London: Funk and Wagnalls Co., 1908-1912.

MILLER, J. LANE, and MILLER, MADELEINE S., eds., *Encyclopedia of Bible Life*. N.Y.: Harper and Bros., 1944.

MILLER, J. LANE, and MILLER, MADELEINE S., eds., *Harper's Bible Dictionary*. N.Y.: Harper and Bros., 1952.

SMITH, GEORGE ADAM, *The Historical Geography of the Holy Land*. Twenty-fifth edition, revised. New York: Ray Long and R. R. Smith, 1932.

TREVER, JOHN C., *Cradle of Our Faith: The Holy Land*. United

States Junior Chamber of Commerce. Wichita, Kansas: Historic Counselors, Inc., 1954.

WRIGHT, GEORGE ERNEST, and FILSON, FLOYD VIVIAN, *The Westminster Historical Atlas to the Bible.* Philadelphia: The Westminster Press, 1945.

Books on Religion

AMES, EDWARD SCRIBNER, *The Psychology of Religious Experience.* Boston: Houghton Mifflin Co., 1910.

BRADEN, CHARLES S., *The World's Religions.* Revised edition. New York and Nashville: Abingdon-Cokesbury, 1954.

BRIGHTMAN, EDGAR SHEFFIELD, *A Philosophy of Religion.* New York: Prentice-Hall, 1947.

BRONSTEIN, DANIEL J., and SCHULWEIS, HAROLD J., eds., *The Philosophy of Religion.* New York: Prentice-Hall, Inc., 1954.

CRANSTON, RUTH, *World Faith.* New York: Harper and Bros., 1949.

DURKHEIM, EMILE, *Elementary Forms of the Religious Life.* J. W. Swaim, translator. New York: Macmillan, 1926.

FERM, VERGILIUS, *First Chapters in Religious Philosophy.* New York: Round Table Press, 1937.

FERM, VERGILIUS, ed., *Forgotten Religions.* New York: Philosophical Library, Inc., 1949.

FERM, VERGILIUS, ed., *Religion in the Twentieth Century.* New York: Philosophical Library, Inc., 1948.

FINEGAN, JACK, *The Archaeology of World Religions.* Princeton, N.J.: Princeton University Press, 1952.

FINEGAN, JACK, *Youth Asks About Religion.* New York: Association Press, 1949.

FOSDICK, HARRY EMERSON, *As I See Religion.* N.Y.: Macmillan, 1932.

HARKNESS, GEORGIA, *Conflicts in Religious Thought.* New York: Harper and Bros., 1949.

HARTSHORNE, CHARLES, and REESE, WILLIAM L., eds., *Philosophers Speak of God.* Chicago: The University of Chicago Press, 1953.

HOUF, HORACE T., *What Religion Is and Does.* Revised edition. New York: Harper and Bros., 1945.

HUTCHINSON, JOHN A., and MARTIN, JAMES ALFRED, JR., *Ways of Faith.* New York: The Ronald Press, 1953.

JAMES, WILLIAM, *The Varieties of Religious Experience.* New York: Longmans, Green and Co., 1902.

KING, WINSTON L., *Introduction to Religion.* New York: Harper and Bros., 1954.

LONG, EDWARD LEROY, JR., *Science and Christian Faith*. New York: Association Press, 1950.

MOORE, GEORGE FOOTE, *The Birth and Growth of Religion*. New York: Charles Scribner's Sons, 1923.

NIEBUHR, H. RICHARD, *The Social Sources of Denominationalism*. New York: Henry Holt and Co., 1929.

NOSS, J. B., *Man's Religions*. New York: Macmillan, 1949.

POTTER, CHARLES FRANCIS, *The Story of Religion*. Garden City, N.Y.: Garden City Publishing Co., Inc., 1929.

SCHOEN, MAX, *Thinking About Religion*. New York: Philosophical Library, 1946.

SMITH, W. ROBERTSON, *The Religion of the Semites*. London: A. and C. Black, Ltd., 1923.

SOPER, EDMUND DAVISON, *The Religions of Mankind*. Third edition, revised. New York and Nashville: Abingdon-Cokesbury, 1951.

WACH, JOACHIM, *The Sociology of Religion*. Chicago: University of Chicago Press, 1944.

WIDGERY, ALBAN G., *What Is Religion?* New York: Harper and Bros., 1953.

WIEMAN, HENRY NELSON, and HORTON, WALTER MARSHALL, *The Growth of Religion*. Chicago and New York: Willett, Clark, and Co., 1938.

WILLIAMS, J. PAUL, *What Americans Believe and How They Worship*. New York: Harper and Bros., 1952.

WRIGHT, WILLIAM K., *A Student's Philosophy of Religion*. New York: Macmillan, 1935.

YERKES, R. K., *Sacrifice in Greek and Roman Religions and Early Judaism*. New York: Charles Scribner's Sons, 1952.

Books on the Bible as a Whole

ALBRIGHT, WILLIAM FOXWELL, *From the Stone Age to Christianity*. Baltimore: Johns Hopkins Press, 1940.

ANDERSON, BERNHARD W., *Rediscovering The Bible*. New York: Association Press, 1951.

BAILEY, ALBERT E., *Daily Life in Bible Times*. New York: Charles Scribner's Sons, 1943.

BARTON, GEORGE A., *Archaeology and the Bible*. Philadelphia: American Sunday School Union, 1937.

BATTENHOUSE, HENRY M., *The Bible Unlocked*. New York: D. Appleton-Century Co., 1940.

BLAIR, EDWARD, P., *The Bible and You*. New York: Abingdon-Cokesbury Press, 1953.

BOWER, WILLIAM C., *The Living Bible*. New York: Harper and Bros., 1936.

BOWIE, WALTER RUSSELL, *The Bible*. New York: Association Press, 1945.

BREASTED, JAMES HENRY, *Ancient Times*. Boston and New York: Ginn and Co., 1916.

DODD, C. H., *According to the Scriptures*. New York: Charles Scribner's Sons, 1953.

DODD, C. H., *The Bible Today*. Cambridge: Cambridge University Press, 1951.

FINEGAN, JACK, *Light from the Ancient Past*. Princeton: Princeton University Press, 1946.

FOSDICK, HARRY EMERSON, *A Guide to Understanding the Bible*. New York: Harper and Bros., 1938.

FOSDICK, HARRY EMERSON, *The Modern Use of the Bible*. New York: Macmillan, 1925.

GOODSPEED, EDGAR J., *How Came the Bible?* New York and Nashville: Abingdon-Cokesbury, 1940.

GOODSPEED, EDGAR J., *The Story of the Bible*. Chicago: University of Chicago Press, 1936.

HARKNESS, GEORGIA, *Toward Understanding the Bible*. New York: Charles Scribner's Sons, 1954.

LYNIP, RYLLIS GOSLIN, *Great Ideas of the Bible*. Two volumes. New York: Harper and Bros., 1954, 1955.

MOULD, ELMER W. K., *Essentials of Bible History*. New York: The Ronald Press. Revised edition. 1951.

STREIBERT, MURIEL, *Youth and the Bible*. New York: Macmillan, 1930.

SWAIM, J. CARTER, *Do You Understand the Bible?* Philadelphia: The Westminster Press, 1954.

SWAIM, J. CARTER, *Right and Wrong Ways to Use the Bible*. Philadelphia: The Westminster Press, 1953.

Books on the Old Testament

ANDERSON, BERNHARD W., *Understanding The Old Testament*. New York: Prentice-Hall, Inc., 1957.

BAAB, OTTO J., *The Theology of the Old Testament*. New York and Nashville: Abingdon-Cokesbury Press, 1949.

BAILEY, ALBERT E., and KENT, CHARLES FOSTER, *History of the Hebrew Commonwealth*. New York: Charles Scribner's Sons, 1935.

BEWER, JULIUS A., *The Literature of the Old Testament.* New York: Columbia University Press, 1933.

FINKELSTEIN, LOUIS, ed., *The Jews: Their History, Culture, and Religion.* New York: Harper and Bros., 1949.

FLIGHT, JOHN W., and FAHS, SOPHIA, *The Drama of Ancient Israel.* Boston: Beacon Press, 1949.

FOWLER, H. T., *The Origin and Growth of the Hebrew Religion.* Chicago: University of Chicago Press, 1916.

GUIGNEBERT, CHARLES, *The Jewish World in the Time of Jesus.* S. H. Hooke, translator. New York: E. P. Dutton and Co., 1939.

HYATT, J. PHILIP, *Prophetic Religion.* New York and Nashville: Abingdon-Cokesbury, 1947.

IRWIN, WILLIAM A., *The Old Testament: Keystone of Human Culture.* New York: Henry Schuman, 1952.

JAMES, FLEMING, *Personalities of the Old Testament.* New York: Charles Scribner's Sons, 1947.

KING, ALBION ROY, *The Problem of Evil.* Christian Concepts and the Book of Job. New York: The Ronald Press, 1953.

KNOPF, C. J., *The Old Testament Speaks.* New York: Thomas Nelson and Sons, 1933.

LESLIE, ELMER A., *Jeremiah.* New York: The Abingdon Press, 1954.

LESLIE, ELMER A., *The Prophets Tell Their Own Story.* New York and Nashville: Abingdon-Cokesbury, 1939.

LESLIE, ELMER A., *The Psalms.* New York and Nashville: Abingdon-Cokesbury Press, 1949.

LONGACRE, LINDSAY B., *The Old Testament: Its Form and Purpose.* New York: Abingdon-Cokesbury Press, 1945.

MATTHEWS, I. G., *The Religious Pilgrimage of Israel.* New York: Harper and Bros., 1947.

MOORE, GEORGE FOOTE, *Judaism.* Three volumes. Cambridge: Harvard University Press, 1927-1930.

OSTERLEY, W. O. E., and ROBINSON, T. H., *Hebrew Religion, Its Origin and Development.* New York: Macmillan, 1930.

PATERSON, JOHN, *The Goodly Fellowship of the Prophets.* N. Y.: Charles Scribner's Sons, 1948.

PATERSON, JOHN, *The Book That Is Alive.* N.Y.: Charles Scribner's Sons, 1954.

PFEIFFER, ROBERT H., *Introduction to the Old Testament.* New York: Harper and Bros., 1941.

ROBINSON, H. WHEELER, *The Old Testament: Its Making and Meaning.* New York and Nashville: Abingdon-Cokesbury, 1937.

SCHURER, EMIL, *A History of the Jewish People in the Time of Jesus Christ.* John Macpherson, Sophia Taylor, and Peter Christie, translators. Edinburgh: T. and T. Clark, 1901-1911. Third and fourth editions.

SMITH, J. M. POWIS, *The Prophets and Their Times*. Second edition revised by William A. Irwin. Chicago: University of Chicago Press, 1942.

SNELL, HEBER CYRUS, *Ancient Israel: Its Story and Meaning*. Salt Lake City, Utah: Stevens and Wallis, 1948.

TORREY, C. C., *Ezra Studies*. Chicago: University of Chicago Press, 1910.

WALLIS, LOUIS, *Young People's Hebrew History*. New York: Philosophical Library, Inc., 1953.

Books on the Apocrypha

CHARLES, R. H., ed., *The Apocrypha and Pseudepigrapha of the Old Testament*. Two volumes. Oxford: Oxford University Press, 1913.

GOODSPEED, EDGAR J., *The Story of the Apocrypha*. Chicago: University of Chicago Press, 1939.

PFEIFFER, ROBERT H., *History of New Testament Times*. With an introduction to the Apocrypha. New York: Harper and Bros., 1949.

PFEIFFER, ROBERT H., ed., *The Apocrypha*. King James Version. New York: Harper and Bros., 1953.

Books on the New Testament

ALLEN, CADY H., *The Message of the Book of Revelation*. New York and Nashville: Abingdon-Cokesbury, 1939.

ANGUS, S., *The Environment of Early Christianity*. New York: Charles Scribner's Sons, 1922.

ANGUS, S., *The Mystery-Religions and Christianity*. New York: Charles Scribner's Sons, 1925.

ANGUS, S., *The Religious Quests of the Graeco-Roman World*. London: J. Murray, 1920.

BARNETT, ALBERT E., *The New Testament: Its Making and Meaning*. New York and Nashville: Abingdon-Cokesbury, 1946.

BATTENHOUSE, HENRY M., *New Testament History and Literature*. New York: The Ronald Press Co., 1937.

BECK, DWIGHT M., *Through the Gospels to Jesus*. New York: Harper and Bros., 1954.

BEILER, IRWIN ROSS, *Studies in the Life of Jesus*. New York and Nashville: Abingdon-Cokesbury, 1936.

Bouquet, A. C., *Everyday Life in New Testament Times*. New York: Charles Scribner's Sons, 1954.

Branscomb, B. Harvie, *Jesus and the Law of Moses*. New York: Richard R. Smith, Inc., 1930.

Branscomb, B. Harvie, *The Message of Jesus*. New York and Nashville: Abingdon-Cokesbury, 1926.

Branscomb, B. Harvie, *The Teachings of Jesus*. New York and Nashville: Abingdon-Cokesbury, 1931.

Bright, John, *The Kingdom of God*. New York: The Abingdon Press, 1953.

Bundy, Walter E., *Jesus and the First Three Gospels*. Cambridge: Harvard University Press, 1955.

Buttrick, George Arthur, *The Parables of Jesus*. New York: Harper and Bros., 1928.

Case, Shirley Jackson, *Jesus: A New Biography*. Chicago: University of Chicago Press, 1927.

Case, Shirley Jackson, *The Evolution of Early Christianity*. Fourth impression. Chicago: University of Chicago Press, 1923.

Case, Shirley Jackson, *The Historicity of Jesus*. Second edition. Chicago: University of Chicago Press, 1928.

Colwell, Ernest C., *An Approach to the Teaching of Jesus*. New York and Nashville: Abingdon-Cokesbury, 1947.

Colwell, Ernest C., and Titus, Eric L., *The Gospel of the Spirit*. New York: Harper and Bros., 1953.

Craig, Clarence Tucker, *The Beginning of Christianity*. New York and Nashville: Abingdon-Cokesbury, 1943.

Craig, Clarence Tucker, *The Study of the New Testament*. New York and Nashville: Abingdon-Cokesbury, 1939.

Denny, Walter Bell, *The Career and Significance of Jesus*. New York: The Ronald Press, 1933.

Dibelius, Martin, *A Fresh Approach to the New Testament and Early Christian Literature*. New York: Charles Scribner's Sons, 1936.

Dodd, C. H., *New Testament Studies*. New York: Charles Scribner's Sons, 1954.

Enslin, Morton S., *Christian Beginnings*. New York: Harper and Bros., 1939.

Filson, Floyd V., *Opening the New Testament*. Philadelphia: The Westminster Press, 1952.

Finegan, Jack, *Rediscovering Jesus*. New York: Association Press, 1952.

Foakes Jackson, F. J., and Lake, Kirsopp, eds., *The Beginnings of Christianity*. Five Volumes. London: Macmillan, 1920-1933.

FOSDICK, HARRY EMERSON, *The Man from Nazareth.* New York: Harper and Bros., 1949.

GILBERT, GEORGE HOLLEY, *The Student's Life of Jesus.* New York: Macmillan, 1929.

GILBERT, GEORGE HOLLEY, *The Student's Life of Paul.* New York: Macmillan, 1899.

GLOVER, TERRIOTT R., *The World of the New Testament.* Cambridge: The University Press, 1931.

GOODSPEED, EDGAR J., *An Introduction to the New Testament.* Chicago: University of Chicago Press, 1937.

GOODSPEED, EDGAR J., *Paul.* Philadelphia and Toronto: The John C. Winston Co., 1947.

GOODSPEED, EDGAR J., *The Meaning of Ephesians.* Chicago: University of Chicago Press, 1933.

GRANT, FREDERICK C., *An Introduction to New Testament Thought.* New York: Abingdon-Cokesbury Press, 1950.

GRANT, FREDERICK C., *The Earliest Gospel.* New York and Nashville: Abingdon-Cokesbury, 1943.

JAMES, M. R., ed., *The Apocryphal New Testament.* Oxford: Oxford University Press, 1950.

KEE, HOWARD CLARK, and YOUNG, FRANKLIN W., *Understanding the New Testament.* New York; Prentice-Hall, Inc., 1957.

KEPLER, THOMAS S., ed., *Contemporary Thinking about Jesus.* New York and Nashville: Abingdon-Cokesbury, 1944.

KEPLER, THOMAS S., ed., *Contemporary Thinking about Paul.* New York and Nashville: Abingdon-Cokesbury, 1950.

KLAUSNER, JOSEPH, *From Jesus to Paul.* William F. Stinespring, translator. New York: Macmillan, 1943.

KNOX, JOHN, *Chapters in a Life of Paul.* New York and Nashville: Abingdon-Cokesbury, 1950.

LAYMON, CHARLES M., *The Life and Teachings of Jesus.* New York: The Abingdon Press, 1955.

LYMAN, MARY ELY, *Jesus.* New York: Association Press, 1937.

LYMAN, MARY ELY, *The Christian Epic.* New York: Charles Scribner's Sons, 1936.

MCNEILE, A. H., *An Introduction to the Study of the New Testament.* Second edition revised by C. S. C. Williams. Oxford: at the Clarendon Press, 1953.

MOFFATT, JAMES, *An Introduction to the Literature of the New Testament.* New York: Charles Scribner's Sons, 1929.

QUIMBY, CHESTER WARREN, *Paul for Everyone.* New York: Macmillan, 1944.

QUIMBY, CHESTER WARREN, *The Great Redemption*. New York: Macmillan, 1950.

RALL, HARRIS FRANKLIN, *Christianity*. New York: Charles Scribner's Sons, 1940.

RALL, HARRIS FRANKLIN, *New Testament History*. New York and Nashville: Abingdon-Cokesbury, 1914.

RALL, HARRIS FRANKLIN, *The Life of Jesus*. New York and Nashville: Abingdon-Cokesbury, 1917.

RALL, HARRIS FRANKLIN, *The Teachings of Jesus*. New York and Nashville: Abingdon-Cokesbury, 1930.

RIDDLE, D. W., and HUTSON, H. H., *New Testament Life and Literature*. Chicago: University of Chicago Press, 1946.

SCOTT, ERNEST F., *The Fourth Gospel, Its Purpose and Theology*. New York: Charles Scribner's Sons, 1907.

SCOTT, ERNEST F., *The Literature of the New Testament*. New York: Columbia University Press, 1936.

SCOTT, JOHN A., *We Would Know Jesus*. New York: The Abingdon Press, 1936.

STREETER, BURNETT HILLMAN, *The Four Gospels*. New York: Macmillan, 1925.

UHLHORN, GERHARD, *The Conflict of Christianity with Heathenism*. Egbert C. Smyth and C. J. H. Ropes, translators. Revised edition. New York: Charles Scribner's Sons, 1906.

INDEX

Israel 46, 55-60, 62, 66, 67, 69, 73-76, 78, 80-82, 88, 90-92, 95-108, 110-113, 119, 122, 125, 127, 129, 138, 140, 141, 143-145, 147, 154-156, 161, 163-165, 168, 171, 180, 181, 188, 189, 196, 213, 228, 233, 238, 277, 279, 284, 308, 348, 376, 383, 419-421, 423, 430, 440, 464, 483, 484

Israel, Book of the Chronicles of the Kings of, 428

Israelite (s) 46, 55, 57, 60-63, 65-68, 70, 72-75, 77, 84, 85, 88, 92, 96, 100, 103, 107, 122, 128, 170, 193, 284, 338, 393, 421, 428, 429, 431, 437

Issus 295

Istanbul 470

Italian 313

Italy 311, 376, 446

Iturea 212, 462, 471

"J" document 83, 111, 421

Jabesh-gilead 74

Jachin 429

Jacob 46, 49, 52, 53, 55, 60, 82, 104, 118, 119, 155, 226, 270, 418

Jael 449

Jaffa (Joppa) 221, 280

Jahweh 22, 52, 55-63, 65, 69-71, 73, 84-86, 90, 95-97, 99-104, 106-113, 115, 117, 118, 122-124, 127, 128, 131-135, 137-144, 147-150, 152-158, 161, 167, 168, 170, 171, 180, 181, 249, 419, 421, 423, 425, 429, 431, 437

Jahwism 31, 55, 57, 60, 63, 69, 73, 84, 93, 95, 99, 125, 422, 426, 429, 431, 434

James, brother of Jesus, 241, 264, 288, 293, 294, 302, 307, 408, 455, 462, 464, 470, 487

James, Fleming, 56, 105, 422, 425, 437, 442

James, M. R., 449, 455

James, son of Zebedee, 251, 252, 254, 255, 259, 281, 391, 408, 456, 485

James, William, 17

James, the Book of, 405, 408-410

Jamnia 220

Jashar, Book of, 71, 427

Jason 299

Jebusites 76, 165, 418

Jehoahaz 436

Jehoiachin 160, 430, 436

Jehoiakim 93, 136, 137, 436

Jehoram 91, 431

Jehoshaphat (recorder) 82

Jehoshaphat, king of Judah, 91, 97, 169, 181

Jehovah 421

Jehu, king of Israel, 91, 100, 106, 429

Jehu, son of Hanani, 97

Jephthah 70, 375, 378

Jeremiah 75, 93, 95, 111, 128, 131, 135-143, 219, 226, 227, 268, 433, 437, 438, 442

Jeremiah, the Book of, 135, 219

Jericho 43, 58, 66, 111, 173, 194, 254, 255, 432

Jeroboam I 80, 88-90, 97, 181, 434, 442

Jeroboam II 91, 101, 105, 106, 111, 171, 427, 431

Jerome 221

Jerusalem 45, 50, 52, 61, 74, 76-79, 81-83, 85, 86, 89, 90, 93, 101, 102, 111, 112, 115, 118-120, 122, 124, 125, 129, 131, 135-139, 141-144, 147-149, 152, 153, 155, 160-162, 164, 165, 169, 174, 181, 184, 190, 194, 195, 211, 213, 216, 217, 219, 222, 224, 226, 227, 236, 240-242, 248, 252-256, 258, 264, 275, 276, 278-281, 284-289, 292-294, 301, 302, 305-307, 309, 310, 315, 325, 329, 336, 342-344, 387, 389, 408, 428, 433, 435-441, 443, 445, 452, 457, 466, 467, 474, 477

Jesse 88

Jesus 110, 111, 118, 128, 142, 156, 157, 170, 172, 193, 201, 208, 211, 212, 214, 216, 217, 219, 221, 224-227, 231-238, 240, 241, 243-272, 274-281, 283, 285-288, 291, 293, 295, 296, 299, 300, 306, 308, 317, 318-320, 322-327, 330, 335, 338, 340-342, 345-347, 353-359, 361-363, 365, 367, 369, 373-380, 382, 385, 389-397, 399-402, 406-409, 412, 413, 434, 436-438, 441, 443, 445-460, 462, 464, 465, 469, 470, 480, 482-486

Jethro 55, 57, 58, 422

Jew (s) 55, 56, 93, 137, 143, 147-152, 154, 159-168, 170, 171, 173-175, 185, 186, 188-190, 193, 194, 201, 202, 208, 211-223, 225, 226, 228, 231, 233, 240, 243, 251, 261, 267, 269, 270, 274, 277,

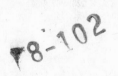